Contract law

DIRECTIONS

Contract Law

DIRECTIONS

10th Edition

RICHARD TAYLOR

DAMIAN TAYLOR

OXFORD
UNIVERSITY PRESS

OXFORD
UNIVERSITY PRESS

Great Clarendon Street, Oxford, OX2 6DP,
United Kingdom

Oxford University Press is a department of the University of Oxford.
It furthers the University's objective of excellence in research, scholarship,
and education by publishing worldwide. Oxford is a registered trade mark of
Oxford University Press in the UK and in certain other countries.

Seventh Edition 2019
Eighth Edition 2021
Ninth Edition 2023

Published in the United States of America by Oxford University Press
198 Madison Avenue, New York, NY 10016, United States of America

British Library Cataloguing in Publication Data
Data available

Library of Congress Control Number: 2026935459

ISBN 9780198978367

Printed in the UK by Bell & Bain Ltd., Glasgow

The manufacturer's authorized representative in the EU for product safety is
Oxford University Press España S.A. of Parque Empresarial San Fernando de Henares,
Avenida de Castilla, 2 – 28830 Madrid (www.oup.es/en or product.safety@oup.com).
OUP España S.A. also acts as importer into Spain of products made by the manufacturer.

MIX
Paper | Supporting
responsible forestry
FSC® C007785
FSC
www.fsc.org

This edition of the book is dedicated to Ivy, whose arrival since the previous edition has brought so much joy and happiness.

Guide to using the book

Contract Law Directions is enriched with a range of features designed to help support and reinforce your learning. This guided tour shows you how to fully utilize your textbook and get the most out of your study.

Learning objectives

Each chapter begins with a bulleted outline of the main concepts and ideas you will encounter. These serve as a helpful signpost to what you can expect to learn by reading the chapter.

> **LEARNING OBJECTIVES**
>
> **This chapter will help you to:**
>
> - recognize a contract as an agreement between two parties;
> - understand the difference between an objective and subjective point of view;
> - distinguish between an offer and an invitation to treat;

Examples

Every day we enter into a contract of some kind, whether it be buying a new phone or getting on a bus. In each chapter you will find everyday scenarios illustrating how contract law applies within the context of real-life situations.

> **EXAMPLE**
>
> **Subjective and objective points of view**
>
> I am a former professional footballer with a collection of football memorabilia including international caps, football programmes, etc. which I keep in a glass display cabinet at home. I also have the ball from the 1995 FA Cup Final with which I scored a hat-trick and which is normally kept separately on display at my former club.

Figures and flowcharts

Numerous figures and flowcharts illustrate this book providing a colourful representation of concepts, processes, and cases. Use these in conjunction with the text to gain a clear understanding of even the most complex concepts.

Figure 2.2 Butler Machine Tool Co. Ltd *v* Ex-Cell-O Corporation (England) Ltd (1979)

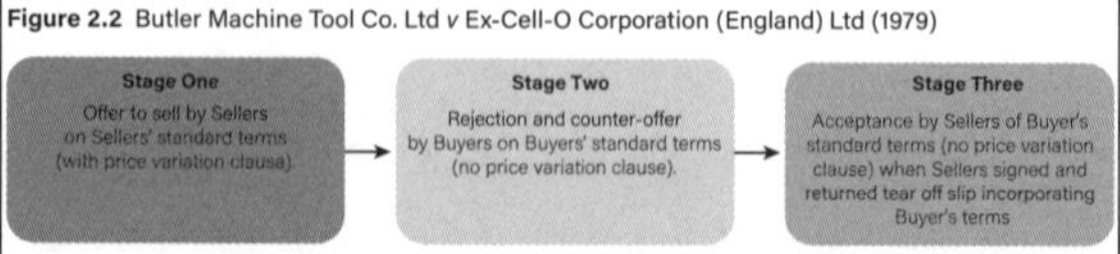

Linking boxes

There are a myriad of connections linking the topics within contract law. Linking boxes will help you to appreciate the threads that run through the subject and understand how contract law relates to other areas of law.

> **LINK TO . . .**
>
> **Mistake (Chapter 8) and Misrepresentation (Chapter 7)**
>
> A party is mistaken when that party's subjective view of the agreement does not match the objective approach favoured by the courts. Objectively, you agreed to sell me an ice lolly in the earlier example, but you believed, mistakenly, that you had agreed to sell me an ice cream. Check out Chapter 8 for a discussion of when the courts override the

Definition boxes

Key terms are highlighted when they first appear and are clearly, concisely explained in definition boxes. These terms are collected in a glossary which can be found on the online resources that accompany this book.

> **estoppel:**
> Estoppel is designed to prevent unconscionable conduct and usually stops a person denying what that person has said or done. Its potential scope can be very wide and vague, and we will encounter promissory estoppel in Chapter 4 when we deal with consideration. Estoppel used in this sense means that the court is effectively gagging the offeror; it knows that the acceptance was not actually received but an invisible hand is placed over the offeror's mouth preventing the offeror from saying so.

Case close-ups

Summaries of key cases are boxed throughout so you can easily pick out the significant facts and details.

> **CASE CLOSE-UP**
>
> ***Carlill* v *Carbolic Smoke Ball Co.* (1893)**
>
> The Smoke Ball Co. promised £100 to anyone who bought and used its Carbolic Smoke Ball three times daily for two weeks according to the printed directions supplied with each ball, but who nonetheless caught flu. Mrs Carlill bought the smoke ball and used it as instructed but caught flu. Clearly, the company had made an offer to Mrs Carlill (and

Thinking points

Why was a particular decision reached in a certain case? Is the law on this point rational and coherent? Is contract law fit for purpose? Thinking points draw out these issues and provide valuable practice in critical thinking.

THINKING POINT

Think of all the times you have made a contract in recent months. On how many occasions did someone make an identifiable offer to you which you thought about and then accepted? Do you think the law's use of the offer and acceptance model reflects today's business practices?

Chapter summaries

The central points and concepts covered in each chapter are distilled into summaries at the ends of chapters. These provide a mechanism for you to reinforce your understanding and can be used as a revision tool.

Summary

A contract requires that the parties reach an agreement which normally consists of ing offer and acceptance.

1. Objective approach

The courts generally look at what A appeared to mean based on what A said and d

Digging deeper

Deepen your legal understanding with extended and interesting content.

Digging deeper

One of the more difficult issues in this chapter has been the question of wheth what extent the postal rule applies to modern methods of communication which precisely instantaneous (in the way that telex or, arguably, fax machines were) bu the delay is much less than the delay between posting a letter and its receipt (suc relatively short delays normally involved in email communication). The tendency h

End-of-chapter questions

Questions at the end of each chapter will help you develop analysis and problem-solving skills.

Questions

1. 'The Offer and Acceptance model is flawed—only an agreement is necessary.'
2. 'Contractual obligations are not based upon the consent of the parties bec courts look at what they said and did and not what they actually meant.' Disc
3. How can a seller ensure that he or she only makes an invitation to treat an

Further reading

Selected further reading is included at the end of each chapter to provide a springboard for further study. This will help you to take your learning further and guide you to the key academic literature in the field.

Further reading

Books

Chen-Wishart, M, *Contract Law*, 7th edn (Oxford University Press, 2022) ch 2 (not 2.6 and 2.7).

McKendrick, E, *Contract Law: Text, Cases, and Materials*, 11th edn (Oxford Universi 2024) ch 3.

New to this edition

This edition has been fully revised and incorporates a number of new cases mostly at Supreme Court level, including the following:

Guest v Guest (Supreme Court) (estoppel)

Barton v Morris (Supreme Court) (implied terms)

Tesco v USDAW (Supreme Court) (implied terms, specific performance)

Patarkatsishvili v Woodward-Fisher (HC) (misrepresentation)

Law Debenture Trust v Ukraine (Supreme Court) (duress)

Nature Resorts v First Citizens Bank (Privy Council) (undue influence)

Waller-Edwards v One Savings Bank (Supreme Court) (undue influence)

SSHD v Public and Commercial Services Union (Supreme Court) (privity)

Aficionados of car parking regulations continue to be catered for, in the exclusion clauses chapter, by reference to the progress, or lack of it, of the draft codes issued under the Parking (Code of Practice) Act 2019.

Preface

Although a completely new work, this book has its roots in a book on contract written (by the first named author) for Blackstone Press in the 1980s which proved to be very popular with students and which went to six editions and numerous reprints. In the Preface to that book, the (obviously very young) author flippantly ascribed responsibility for errors and omissions to his two young children, Deborah and Damian, then aged about seven and three respectively. Deborah had a sense of social responsibility and so, naturally, went into a career other than law but Damian chose for some strange reason to follow (very loosely) in the general direction of his father. As a result, we found ourselves in 2006 writing the first edition of the present book together, since when Damian can truly be regarded as at least jointly responsible for any errors or omissions. He now also fully justifies the prediction made in the 1989 Preface to the third edition, where the author noted that 'my children quickly grow older and shrewder and will no doubt soon be demanding a share of the royalties' which, by the fourth edition it was noted, 'they spend in advance.' Damian is now getting a taste of his own medicine as his three young children draw down their own advance royalties against their own learned contributions, which we look forward to receiving and incorporating in due course!

One of the stated aims of that earlier book for Blackstone was to put a *slightly* older and wiser head on the younger or less experienced shoulders of the reader. This book goes one step beyond that by combining a still older and wiser head with a somewhat younger and more recently educated (and, allegedly, more attractive) head so as to give you, the reader, the benefit of both; that is, the benefit of someone with substantial experience of teaching and examining law combined with the insights of someone who relatively rather more recently had to grapple with the pleasures and pains of having to study it (and who has now also had very considerable experience of applying it in commercial practice and litigation). It was naturally a great privilege and pleasure for us to write this book together and it is truly a work of joint authorship, with each paragraph and sentence having a little of each of us in it. We hope that the end product will provide you with the directions and signposts to enable you to understand and find your way around the fascinating subject that is the law of contract. It is designed to enable you not only to feel at home with the central principles but also to appreciate the more difficult and complex issues. We are both very grateful to those at universities up and down the country who provided so many constructive comments following the publication of the first nine editions and we have thoroughly revised and updated this tenth edition to take account of such comments and recent case law.

We would also like to record our special thanks to Grace Howard at OUP who has once again been so supportive, helpful and encouraging in enabling us to produce this new edition.

Richard Taylor
Damian Taylor
November 2025

Outline contents

Detailed contents

Table of Cases

United Kingdom

European Union

Other Jurisdictions

Australia

Canada

New Zealand

Singapore

United States

Table of legislation

UK legislation

Statutes

Statutory instruments

European legislation

Directives

Other jurisdictions

Germany

New Zealand

United States

1 Introduction

LEARNING OBJECTIVES

This chapter will help you to:

- understand the aim of this book;
- explore the law in general;
- identify contractual obligations as voluntarily chosen obligations;
- recognize different responses available under the law;
- realize that contracts can arise in a variety of formal and informal situations; and
- view contract law in its social and political context.

Introduction

This book is primarily intended for students who are studying the law of contract for the first time. If you are such a student, then you are also quite likely to be at the beginning of your study of law in general. Think of yourself as an explorer; your immediate task is to explore the law of contract. You wouldn't set off to explore Thailand without any idea of its geography or of where it is in relation to other countries, and if you did, you would not get very far and would very easily become lost. In the same way, if you are to study the law of contract, you will need a map, and this Introduction aims to provide one.

This book is part of the 'Directions' series and therefore one of our aims is to provide you with a map and directions so that you can navigate your way through the contract jungle. Like any other explorer, you cannot rely solely on your map and must use other aids to help you on your journey, and we're not talking about a compass or the stars, but rather about the need to pick up the law reports and journals and, dare we say it, on occasion other textbooks. You will quickly find that studying law is all about reading lots of different materials and forming your own opinions. This textbook aims to make the first part easier for you (the reading bit) because it tries to give you a clear framework which will help you to make much more sense of your other reading and studying. You are of necessity much more on your own when it comes to forming an opinion, as this is something only you can do (but we'll give you plenty of ideas and help). The main point is that we have tried to be honest and, in addition to making clear the more straightforward aspects of the subject, have also spent a little bit more time and effort explaining the more difficult bits of the law, rather than missing them out or misleadingly oversimplifying them (as in chemistry GCSE where they tell you that electrons spin around a nucleus in a particular pattern and then at A level change their story and say 'It's a little bit more complicated than that'). Of course, this book will not give you an answer to every contract law issue (even a comprehensive practitioner work cannot do that) but we believe that it addresses all the issues you are likely to come across in your first exposure to contract law.

1.1 Exploring law

The problem with the law, but also part of its fascination, is that it is always changing, always evolving into something new and (hopefully) something better. Like an archaeologist, we must scrape away present-day distractions so that we can see how our law has grown and taken the form we see today. To understand properly what contract law *is*, it would help if we could see what contract law *was*. We must avoid the temptation to dive straight into the ever-increasing mass of law building up every day and instead try to see what is distinctive about contract law as compared with other branches of law and why it operates in the way that it does.

Today's English Law can trace *some* of its roots as far back as the law of the Roman Empire, but, just as the great Colosseum and aqueducts of Rome have fallen into disrepair, so has its law. The modern law in England retains few of the traits of its highly logical and structured predecessor and by comparison it might be thought at first sight to be rather disordered. The result is that not only law students, but also experienced academics, solicitors, barristers and judges, are often bewildered by the apparently unstructured mass of law that confronts them. This lack of obvious structure can lead us into errors such as if we fail to recognize and treat as alike cases which, as a matter of principle, are alike or if we fail to differentiate and distinguish between cases which are in principle dissimilar.

Part of the solution lies in taxonomy. Taxonomy is the science of categorization, something you might have come across if you studied biology, where you split the animal world into vertebrates and invertebrates, and so on. Taxonomy tells us how to recognize a whale as a mammal and not as a fish. Whether a creature is a 'mammal' rather than a 'fish' does not depend on whether the subject swims or lives in the sea but rather on whether it produces milk for its young and (less reliably in fact) on whether it reproduces by live birth. If we are not aware of this distinction then we may be misled into thinking that the white liquid we see issuing from a female fish is milk when it is in fact a stream of eggs, or that a whale is a fish and searching in vain for a place where the whale lays its eggs. The taxonomy based on reproductive characteristics has been found to be useful and meaningful, which is why it is quite well known. Even so, it can be misunderstood partly because not all mammals reproduce by live birth—just one or two lay eggs, such as the platypus, but these do produce milk for their young, so it is the production of milk for the young which is the surest and most significant indicator.

In this book our subject is contract law. We must decide where our subject fits within the overall scheme of our law and what is a useful taxonomy or scheme of classification. We must identify what contract law has in common with other areas of law and what makes it unique. We must ask why it has a special category reserved for it. We must try to avoid mistaken classifications which exclude cases that ought to be included, rather like the platypus that is really a mammal even though it lays eggs, and we must not include cases that ought to be excluded. The late Professor Peter Birks, one of the leading academic lawyers of recent times, worked hard to create a secure and useful taxonomy for English law and what follows reflects in part (but rather dimly) some of his ideas—see 'Three Maps', Chapter 2 of *Unjust Enrichment*, 2nd edn (Oxford University Press, 2005) by Peter Birks to read his views first-hand.

1.2 The categories of English law

1.2.1 **Public and private**

We can immediately separate public and private law. Public law governs the relationship between citizens and the State (i.e. the UK as a State and all the government bodies, local authorities and the myriad other bodies that play a role in running the countries that form the UK). It explains how we are governed and by whom. It sets out the basic rules of our society and explains what will happen if they are broken. When the criminal law, which is just one of the areas of public law, is broken, it is the State, in the name of the Crown—*Rex* (the King), no longer *Regina* (the Queen)—that prosecutes the criminal offender. Hence criminal law cases are named *R* v *[Defendant]*. In contrast, private law is primarily concerned with disputes between private bodies, such as individuals or business entities. It provides an answer when a careless driver runs into the back of me or when a builder agrees to improve my home but leaves me with a shell. My dispute here is with the careless driver or with the builder, and the State takes a back seat. The State still provides the courts, the judges and the legal framework for settling the dispute but the litigants are two private parties (so cases are named *[Claimant]* v *[Defendant]*). Sometimes the distinction becomes blurred. A public body, such as a local authority, might borrow money from a bank or agree to sell me a house or engage in some other task which is commonly performed by private bodies or persons. In these circumstances private law principles may apply to the public body even though the dispute is between a citizen and the State in the form of the public body. However, the private law principles may be modified or influenced so as to reflect the public element of such a dispute.

1.2.2 **Private law subdivision: property and obligations**

Contract law is part of private law. Private law distinguishes between *property* rights on the one hand and personal obligations on the other (sometimes referred to respectively as rights *in rem* and rights *in personam*). The Latin names are arguably useful because they convey the distinction more clearly and accurately. In this context, '*rem*' means 'thing' and property rights (rights *in rem*) connect a person to a thing. You have property rights in this book, in the simplest case, because you bought it and now own it. Think of the property right as an imaginary string connecting you to your book (with acknowledgements to Peter Birks for this rather useful form of 'string theory'). The string represents your rights over the book (see Figure 1.1). *Anyone* who, for example, takes the book without your permission risks breaking the string and interfering with your rights over the book, and therefore potentially commits a wrong against you by interfering with your property right. Your right is not simply a personal right against any particular named individual not to interfere with your book, but it is a right to the book which is in principle good against anyone who interferes with it.

Figure 1.1 My rights over an object (property rights (or rights *in rem*))

In contrast, personal obligations (rights *in personam*) connect one person to another person, not to a thing. If you promise to take me to London in your car and I promise to pay you £50 in return, then the law recognizes the personal obligations created between us. The imaginary string is in my hand with the other end tied around your neck (or around your chest or waist if you feel more comfortable that way). I can pull the string and demand my transport, the performance of your promise (see Figure 1.2). You too have a string around my neck and can pull it to demand your £50 fee. If either of us refuses to perform then the string will snap (fortunately it is normally designed so that it is the string that snaps and not your neck!) but one of us will, quite literally, have broken our obligation and may have to provide a remedy, *usually* compensation (the law of contract does not normally think it wise to drag people kicking and screaming from the court and force them to perform their obligations—that is why the string normally snaps and damages are paid instead). The important point is that we are connected person to person rather than person to thing. Contracts connect people in this person-to-person way and thus give rise to personal rights and obligations rather than property rights, or, expressing exactly the same thing in other more ancient words, they give rise to rights *in personam* rather than rights *in rem*. (Hopefully, you can see that Latin expressions are not something to be afraid of, nor, on the other hand, do they have any special powers, except perhaps succinctness.)

There may of course be a 'thing' or 'property' which is involved in the obligations which we have undertaken and created—for example, if you promise to pay me £50 for the book which I promise to sell to you when I have finished with it. But the obligation here is still a personal one between the two of us and not in the thing itself. If I give or sell the book to B rather than carry out my personal obligation to you to deliver it to you, your remedy is a personal one against me (again usually only compensation) and you cannot normally go and demand the book from B—the reason being that you only had a personal right against me and not a property right in the book. The property right has been given to or acquired by B and B can rely on B's property right against you (as indeed against the whole world). On the other hand, if I have not given or sold the book to B and still own it but am simply refusing to hand it over, it may be that, in some circumstances (e.g. if the book is unique or rare), the remedy for breach of my personal obligation to deliver the book may be an order that I specifically perform my obligation and deliver the book to you rather than just compensate you. The fact remains that the obligation is a personal one between the two of us and does not in itself automatically protect your claim to the book against the whole world or against persons generally. Contract is thus part of the law of obligations rather than the law of property rights. Of course, if my contract is to sell, for example, a house, and I carry out my obligation by transferring the ownership of the house to

Figure 1.2 Rights between persons (obligations/rights *in personam*)

Figure 1.3 How personal and property rights can be affected in the same transaction

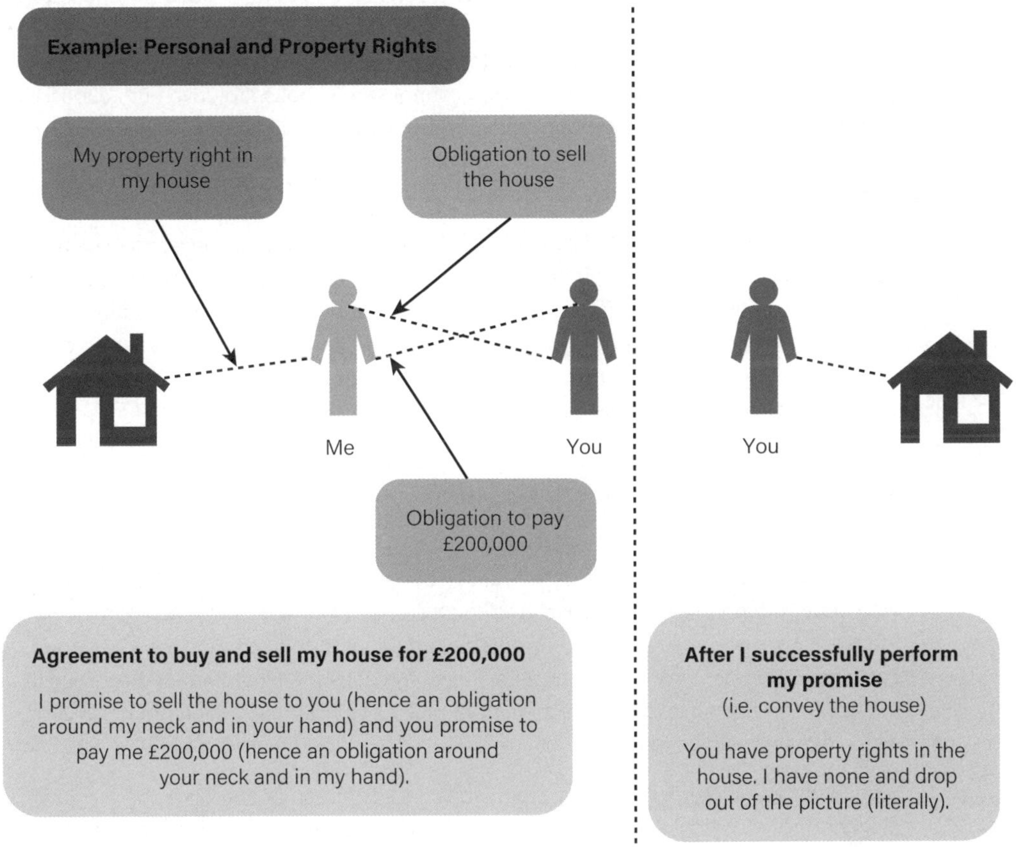

you in a conveyance then property rights are affected and are transferred from me to you. But the contract itself only creates a personal obligation to transfer and it is the actual transfer or conveyance, done in pursuit of the contract, which affects the property right (see Figure 1.3).

1.2.3 **Obligations subdivision: contract, wrongs, unjust enrichment, and others**

Contract and wrongs

The law of obligations itself can be, and traditionally has been, divided into smaller categories (although there can be controversy about whether this further subdivision is always helpful). Obligations are generally categorized by reference to how they are created (a bit like mammals being classified by reproductive factors). In the previous example of a promise to convey my house in return for payment, your obligation to pay me and my obligation to convey the house arose because of our *consent* or *choice* to perform for each other and *voluntarily* create obligations between us. The obligations can be seen to be *voluntarily* chosen and created rather than being involuntarily *imposed* on us by law. This is the central case of a contractual obligation—one voluntarily created, chosen and consented to in exchange for something in return.

In contrast, some obligations are not chosen voluntarily in this sense. Take the example of a careless driver (you!) running into the back of me. The law imposes a primary obligation to take care with your driving so as not to cause harm or injury to me as a road user in your vicinity. The obligation here is not based on choice and is not voluntarily chosen. You have chosen to drive, yes, but the obligation to drive *carefully* is imposed on you by the law, whether you like it or not (and if you break this primary obligation, a secondary obligation to pay compensation will also be imposed). You cannot say, 'I choose to drive but I choose not to have the obligation to take care.' You have broken the primary obligation to take care, *which was imposed upon you*, as opposed to an obligation which you *voluntarily took on yourself or chose to assume* as in the case of a contractual obligation.

These imposed duties are created by the law of 'wrongs.' This does not *necessarily* mean that you have done something wrong (bad) if you break them (some wrongs impose strict liability (no-fault) obligations) but, having said that, breach of a duty, that is, committing a wrong, does usually involve some sort of misconduct (such as crashing your car into me). Wrongs include both *equitable* and *common law* wrongs, the latter being known as 'torts' and being the wrongs that you are most likely to meet alongside the law of contract.

Equity and the common law

'Equity' describes the second jurisdiction which existed alongside the common law in England up until 1873. The head of this jurisdiction was the Chancellor of the Exchequer who preferred more 'equitable' solutions than the strict rule-based approach of the common law. So, if you received an unfavourable judgment in the common law courts, you could seek judgment from the Chancellor who might look more carefully at the justice of the case. The two jurisdictions were merged in 1873 to create one supreme jurisdiction which remains with us today.

A second meaning of 'common law' encompasses both equity and common law jurisdictions and refers to judge-made law as opposed to statutory law which is made by the legislature. 'Common law' countries are those that follow the English tradition of building up a body of law through the courts (such as the USA, Australia, Canada and most Commonwealth States) rather than laying it down at the outset in a code (as in France and many other European countries).

This is the crucial distinction in classical theory between voluntarily assumed contractual obligations, which are the focus of this book, and obligations imposed by the law to prevent wrongs. Contractual obligations in principle arise voluntarily and are freely chosen, which is why we talk about 'freedom of contract.' Dodgy drivers do not enjoy such a freedom; they must take reasonable care regardless of their views on the matter.

Muddying the waters

It would be nice and neat if things could be kept as (relatively) simple as that. Unfortunately, choice and voluntariness are to some extent matters of degree and it is not always easy to draw a sharp line between obligations imposed by the law and those freely chosen. If I agree to sell you a car, it seems obvious that I voluntarily promise not only to hand over the physical thing, the car, but that I also implicitly promise you that the car is mine to sell and has not been stolen by me from someone else (the true owner). The law implies an obligation whereby I guarantee that I am the owner and there is relatively little strain saying that it is an obligation which I create voluntarily. But the law actually goes further than that obvious implication and also implies, in sales in the course of a business, an obligation that the car is of satisfactory quality. This may seem fair enough in most circumstances, but it may not exactly be the obligation that I would have assumed voluntarily if left to my own devices. In principle I may be able to limit or exclude the implied term about quality but if I am selling to a 'consumer' I am not allowed even to do this and thus the law in effect imposes certain obligations in a contract irrespective of what the parties, or at least one of them, might want. Thus, it begins to look much more like a tortious, imposed obligation rather than a contractual one. If I choose to sell goods, especially if I do it in the course of a business to a consumer, certain obligations are imposed on me just as if I choose to drive a car, certain obligations are imposed upon me. Freedom of contract is limited in order to protect the consumer, who in truth may be a less well-informed party than the seller and/or who may not have much choice about the terms under which the car is purchased if all dealers use the same terms. The freedom to contract and to choose the obligations agreed to in the case of a consumer purchaser may be illusory and so the law modifies the classical central case of contract as a freely chosen obligation and protects the weaker party by dictating certain aspects of the obligations which are created. Thus, the boundaries between contract and tort are not always clear cut and in practice, as we will see throughout the book, in many contexts the law of contract has to be considered alongside the law of tort. Still, it is generally regarded as useful to have a distinction between the central case or 'paradigm' contract as involving a voluntarily created obligation, as opposed to the central case of a tortious obligation which is one imposed by the law. Contract and tort can perhaps be seen as two ends of a spectrum but with many situations where obligations arise at some point part way between the two ends of the spectrum, for example the potential for selling a sub-standard car (see Figure 1.4).

Figure 1.4 The contract and tort spectrum

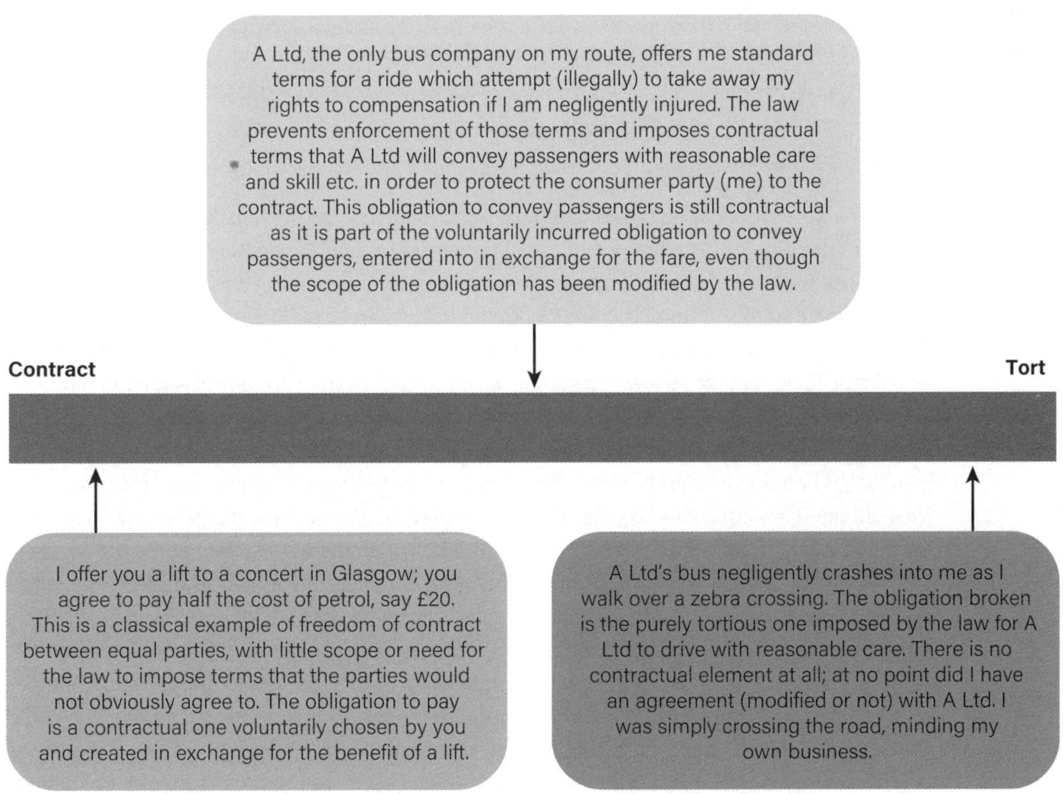

A third source of obligations—unjust enrichment

Just to make matters even more interesting, a third type or manner of creating obligations is now widely recognized. (If you are reading this book for the first time you could quite sensibly skip this section for the moment, go straight to *1.4 Formal and informal contracts* and come back to this section at a later date.) Although this third category is commonly referred to interchangeably as 'restitution' and 'unjust enrichment', Professor Birks (again) persuasively argued that it is best regarded and described as that class of cases where an obligation is imposed in response to *unjust enrichment* (and that 'restitution', like 'compensation', describes a response to, rather than the source of, an obligation). The obligations in these cases do not arise from a voluntary act of creation nor are they imposed to prevent a wrong, but instead they are imposed for *another* reason: to prevent or remedy unjust enrichment. Such an obligation arises:

(1) if a defendant is enriched;

(2) at the expense of the claimant;

(3) unjustly; and

(4) in the absence of a legally recognized defence.

An example may help. Unknown to me, my employers mistakenly pay an extra £1,000 into my bank account. A month later they realize their mistake and ask for the return of the money. Do I have an obligation to repay? I did not ask them to overpay me and I have not consented to or chosen voluntarily to incur any obligation to pay them back. Neither have I breached a duty since I have not behaved carelessly or deceived them or failed to tell them anything that I should have done. Therefore, the law of tort does not impose any obligation on me to repay. But there is a law which says I do have an obligation and it is best explained (it is thought) by saying it is because:

(1) I am enriched (by £1,000);

(2) It is at the expense of my employers (they have lost £1,000);

(3) My enrichment is unjust (it was paid by mistake, not as a gift or as part of my salary); and

(4) I do not have a defence (for example, I have not changed my position in reasonable reliance on the payment (i.e. spent it as money I genuinely thought I was entitled to)).

This third type of obligation based on unjust enrichment can be very useful in situations where there is nearly a contract but not quite. For example, A and B negotiate about B building a new house for A and when virtually all the terms are agreed, B starts work draining the land in anticipation that the contract is going to be signed as soon as planning permission is received. A allows B access to A's land to start the drainage work. Planning permission is then refused and A's building cannot be erected so A now does not sign the contract. Is A under an obligation to pay for B's work? It may be difficult to make A do so as A never expressly or voluntarily agreed to pay for this preliminary work which B chose to start (perhaps B started the work because B had no other work at the time, and B wanted to save time in case some other work was obtained later on). On the other hand, A allowed B to start the work by letting B on to the land and freely accepted the benefit of the land being drained. A is enriched by the increase in value of the land, it is at the expense of B (in the sense that B has expended time, effort and resources) and in the circumstances, especially given A's free acceptance of B choosing to start and allowing B on to the land, that enrichment is unjust because it was done on the (failed) assumption that a contract would materialize (and there would appear to be no relevant defence). At one time the law might only have allowed B to claim something if B could show there was or should be a sort of implied contract or a promise to pay *as if* there was a contract—a so-called *quasi (as if)* contract—because it was assumed that all obligations arose either in contract or tort. Now it is much more likely that any recovery would be based on the unjust enrichment of A, and the notion of *quasi* contract is regarded as best avoided.

A complete categorization

Any classification must not be so watertight that it is closed to future discoveries. When we classify living things into mammals, fish, and so on we must be careful to leave room for new life forms that *might* be discovered in the future, no matter how implausible they are now; aliens from Mars, for example. We also need to tidy away all the odd creatures that don't quite fit into any of the established categories, and so we should therefore add an *others* category to the end of our list. If we really did discover Martians and we could find common features in our extra-terrestrial friends then we might slot them into our existing categories; for instance, if they closely resembled fish, or ourselves. On the other hand, they might be unique so that they merit a wholly new category to themselves. This is in effect what Professor Birks and many others have done with the category 'unjust enrichment' which is regarded as so distinct a source of obligations from consent or wrongs that it deserves a place as an individual third category. However, there are also a number of other odd obligations that arise, for example when one person intervenes in another's affairs when that other person cannot help themself (known as *negotiorum gestio*). Such obligations are clearly not based on consent as the obligation is premised on the fact that the intervention is uninvited, nor are they based on a breach of duty or (arguably) on unjust enrichment, with the result that they fall into the residual 'other' category. See Figure 1.5 for an overall classification which accommodates such a category.

Figure 1.5 The location of contract law in the general scheme of the law

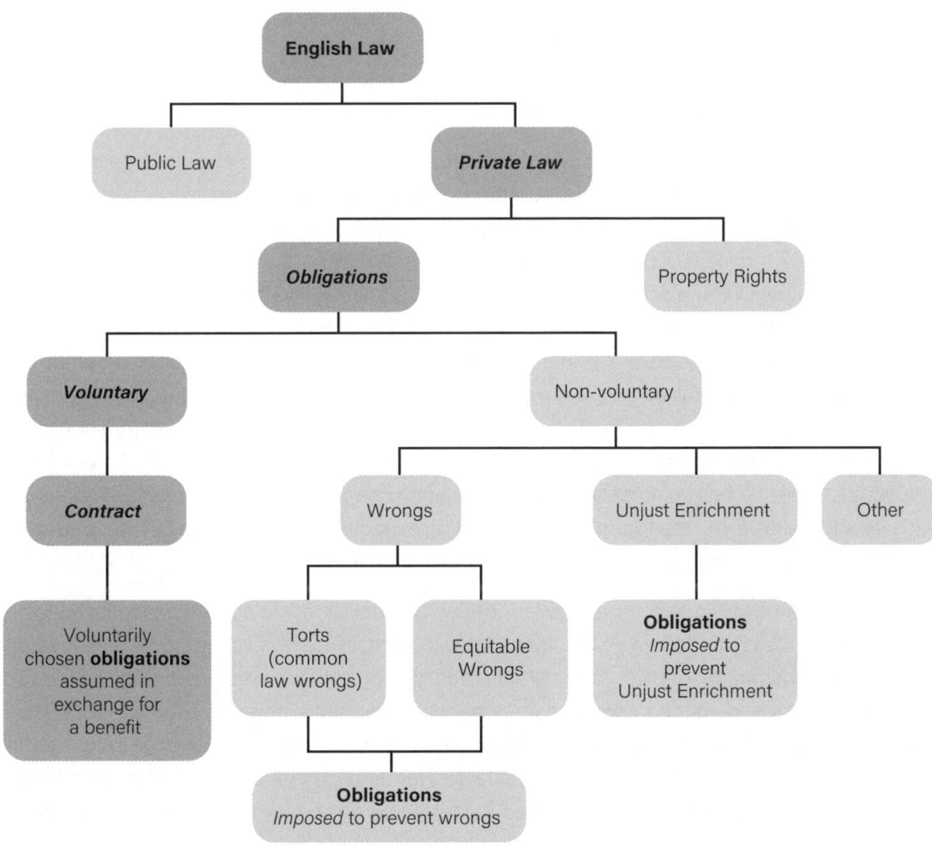

1.3 Responses

The previous subdivision of obligations focused on the source of the obligation: consent, law of wrongs, unjust enrichment, and so on. Obligations can also be divided according to response. Compensation and restitution are the main responses you will come across in this book.

Restitution means 'giving back' the benefit received, so if you are mistakenly paid £1,000 the law will respond to your unjust enrichment by placing you under an obligation to make restitution; an obligation to pay back the £1,000. Restitution may also, according to some, include 'gain-based' damages. In Chapter 11, you will see the argument that sometimes damages for breach of contract can, very exceptionally, be measured according to how much the contract breaker gained from his breach. This party is not 'giving back' money to the claimant (there may never have been any money received from the claimant) but is rather 'giving up' the profits made from the breach. These profits could have come from a wide variety of people independent of the claimant and so it would be odd to say that the money is being given back to the claimant. This 'giving up' (of profits) meaning of restitution is sometimes called disgorgement to distinguish it from the 'giving back' sense of restitution. Restitution can also be a response for a tortious breach of duty. When a notorious spy breached his duty of confidentiality to the UK government by publishing a book based on his experiences, the House of Lords ordered him to give up the profits from the book (i.e., ordered restitution (disgorgement) of the profits).

Whilst restitution focuses on the defendant's *gain*, compensation focuses on the claimant's *loss*. If you knock me down in breach of your duty to drive carefully then you will have to compensate me for my loss. If I have lost an arm, then the court will try to put a value on how much my arm was worth to me. Losses in contract and tort tend to be different because contracts are generally forward looking and promise a benefit in the future, whereas torts generally try to maintain your current position and impose a duty not to cause certain types of harm.

Breach of contract normally results in compensation for the loss of the expectations generated by the contract. When you enter into a contract you expect the other side to perform and so, if there is a failure to perform, you are awarded compensation aimed at putting you in the position as though the promise had been performed—you get the value of what had been promised to you. For example, if you paid £400 and were promised a week in a five-star hotel (a good bargain, you might think) you can expect substantial compensation if you only get a three-star hotel and experience—perhaps several hundred pounds to compensate you for not getting what you expected and were promised. If you have made a good bargain by agreeing to pay a competitive price for something which is promised to be very good (i.e. a five-star hotel for £400), you will normally be better off if you can sue for breach of contract because the compensation will reflect the other party's voluntarily chosen obligation or promise to provide something of high quality and will give you the (good) bargain that you expected. It is for this reason that damages in contract are thus often called 'loss of bargain' or 'expectation' damages.

In contrast, damages in tort, for example for misrepresentation, are sometimes referred to, in this context at least, as 'reliance' damages and will normally be less advantageous as they do not give you the benefit of your good bargain but try to put you back in the position as though you had never *relied* on the misleading statement and had not entered into the contract. They compensate you for how much worse off you actually are, rather than for how much better off you could have been. So, if you have paid £400 for a holiday because of a tortious misrepresentation that the hotel is five-star when in fact it is a three-star hotel which is only worth

£300 your damages would only be £100 because this is the extent to which you are worse off due to the tort, that is, due to relying on the misrepresentation. In contrast, if there was a contractual promise that it was five-star and such a holiday would be worth £800, you would get £500 damages in contract, based on the value of what you were promised and expected (£800) minus what you actually received (£300).

1.4 Formal and informal contracts

We have focused up to now on how contractual obligations are created and how their breach is remedied rather than on what contracts look like. Try to forget any preconceptions you might already have about contracts being embodied in lengthy documents with lots of small print. Certainly, there are many contracts that do fit that stereotype, and these may be very important as examples of extremely valuable contracts. There are also quite a number of contracts where consumers, for example, have to be provided with written details in order for the contract to be valid. However, in terms of numbers of contracts made, the vast majority are made quite informally with little or no written or other record. Jumping on a bus leads to the creation of a contract whereby you agree to pay and the bus operator agrees to transport you safely. Picking up your paper or magazine in the newsagents and handing over your coins or tapping out your payment is another contractual transaction, as is your visit to the cinema or your download of the latest music track on to your computer or smartphone, etc. More obviously, signing up for a new credit card or for a new mobile phone involves entering a contract, as does purchasing more minutes or data. So does entering a promotional competition run by a newspaper or broadcaster or offering a reward if your lost dog is found. You also have a contractual relationship with your university or college, your landlord or your employer (or perhaps your personal trainer, if you have one). Some of these contracts are one-offs with someone you might never see again (think about a meal in a local restaurant on a foreign holiday); others are part of a longer-term relationship, for example with your university or college (which may influence the extent to which you will want to resort to legal remedies if something goes wrong). Some contracts are performed more or less as soon as they are created (think about buying from a vending machine) whilst others provide for things to be done a long time in the future (think about life assurance contracts or a construction contract to build the Olympic Stadium). Some are governed by detailed and specific rules laid down by statute (e.g. contracts of employment and credit card agreements); others are totally unregulated (e.g. selling last year's law books to unsuspecting first year students). The detailed rules and factors applicable to any one particular contract may have some peculiarities or special features not applicable to contracts generally. However, they all share the fact that they are, by and large, the consequence of a voluntary choice to enter into them (even though life might be rather difficult if you tried to avoid entering any contracts at all) and there are some basic principles which are generally applicable to virtually all contracts even though these principles may sometimes be modified in particular cases. These principles are the subject matter of this book and tell us how contracts are created, whom they affect, what they contain, how they may be flawed and vulnerable to challenge, how they may be modified or come to an end and what remedies are available when they are broken. You will see from the table of contents that these questions are addressed in the four parts of the book under the four headings of Creation, Contents, Defects and Finish.

1.5 The role and context of contract

There is a huge amount of literature about the role that contract law plays in modern democracies and the economic, political and social contexts in which it operates, and which influence its structure and development. The bargain or exchange model of contract (see especially Chapter 4 on Consideration) is most closely associated with overtly capitalist, laissez-faire, individualistic/free market-oriented philosophies (i.e. every man for himself, with the State very much taking a back seat) which some critics say unduly influenced it in the critical stages of its development in the eighteenth and nineteenth centuries. The emergence of mixed economies, greater state intervention, social welfare and communitarian philosophies in the twentieth century undoubtedly tempered the 'pure,' classical, voluntary exchange model (which may in truth have always been something of a myth) and has made the law much more ambiguous and complex. The enforcement of promises which have been reasonably relied upon rather than those which have been given in exchange for a benefit has become an alternative or additional theme underlying the law, and the protection of reasonable reliance rather than expectations has been urged as a more appropriate imperative (see again Chapter 4). Freedom of contract has also been increasingly subjected to restraints to protect weaker parties such as consumers and the less economically powerful (see Chapter 6 for an example in the context of exclusion clauses).

Ironically, just as Atiyah was publishing his brilliant analysis of 'The Rise and Fall of Freedom of Contract' under that title in the late 1970s, a number of economies in the common law world were entering a phase in which free market principles were about to be reasserted in the name of economic efficiency and greater overall wealth creation, for example in the UK under Prime Minister Margaret Thatcher and in the USA under President Ronald Reagan. An effectively enforced and relatively unhindered law of contract is now seen by some to be one of the key building blocks (along with democracy) for a successful and viable economy, society or State. The demise of the Socialist command and control economies as compared with the apparent success (at least in economic terms) of 'Western Capitalism' gave a fresh boost to the individualistic/free market aspects of contract theory, although virtually everyone agrees that some controls on freedom of contract are appropriate and necessary. Since writing that last sentence for the first edition we have experienced the 'credit crunch' and the banking bailouts of 2008 and the subsequent growing popular distrust of 'globalization,' which may indicate that the pendulum is about to swing back more strongly in terms of controls and regulation and that the free market may be less trusted to reach optimal or acceptable results. More recently, the Covid-19 pandemic has shaken conventional thinking on many aspects of society in ways which are likely to affect the context and future development of the law of contract.

The belief in the power of the market and the support that contract law provides for the operation of markets has led to contractual approaches being introduced into areas of activity which were traditionally seen as beyond its reach. Thus, the provision of public services was increasingly made subject to market disciplines and to the law of contract through privatization (e.g. of utilities and railways), compulsory competitive tendering (e.g. in prisons) and 'best value' initiatives (e.g. in local authorities). Huge internal markets were created (e.g. within the BBC and within the National Health Service) and contractual regimes imported into previously bureaucratic and regulatory activities such as the provision of publicly funded legal services. The hope was that contractual discipline would secure more efficient, responsive and high-quality outcomes such as one might see in a free market because suppliers are closer to and more dependent on the consumers of the service and more aware of the need to generate business and the income that comes with it. The extent to which contract law can be usefully or beneficially transposed into an artificial or controlled environment is a controversial question (and some of the above trends already seem to have been largely reversed, e.g. in relation to railways) but there can be little doubt that the law of contract is of increasing interest, importance and complexity in modern democracies and that its principles operate, or are borrowed, in subtly different ways in a wide variety of contexts.

The importation of contract law principles into public-sector activities (or its retreat) is not the direct concern of this book, however. The aim of this book is to explain and illuminate the core rules and principles that underpin the law of contract in the central context in which contract law operates: that is, in its operation as between relatively autonomous individuals, companies or bodies, exchanging goods and services and creating personal obligations with one another, in pursuit of economic and/or personal fulfilment rather than in pursuit of public-sector goals or functions. That will be a difficult enough task on its own, but it is as well to be aware that there is the wider context of the society, and indeed the world, in which contract law operates and which influences its rules and how they develop and change and how they are utilized and enforced. If nothing else, this should underline the fact that the nature, role and content of contract law is a dynamic and contentious matter about which reasonable people may disagree even though, paradoxically, contract law itself is primarily concerned with the consequences of the opposite phenomenon: when reasonable people do agree.

? Questions

1. Think how many contracts you have entered into in the last week, the last month and the last year.
2. How many of them are over and done with and how many are ongoing?
3. How much choice did you have about what your obligations were under the contract? (Don't forget that the price you pay is one of the key obligations.)
4. How much choice did the other side have about the terms of the contract (i.e. the obligations they incurred as well as the obligations imposed on you)? (Think about whether they were more concerned about competitors you might go to instead, or about government regulation or about getting you to come back again—what other factors do you think they might have to take account of?)
5. What do you do (or should you do) with the paperwork when you buy a new mobile phone or go on to a new tariff? When does it become important?
6. What happens when you are not satisfied with what you get or don't get under a contract? Who do you turn to and what do you expect to happen? Are your legal rights the most important thing, are they irrelevant and if not, what is their importance?
7. If you buy a set of headphones via the Internet from a supplier in California, should English law or Californian law govern your purchase? Should you be able to sue the Californian company in the English courts or should you have to travel to California to have your case heard? If you can sue in England could the English courts apply Californian law?

PART I

CREATION OF OBLIGATIONS

The three chapters in this Part of the book explain how two parties can go from owing each other no contractual obligations to having a fully formed contract. As explained in Chapter 1, creating a contract is, in principle, a matter of choice. Contractual obligations are not imposed on us by the law as in the law of torts but are voluntarily assumed. The power to create a contract is a power given to everybody; all you have to do is follow a deceptively simple formula or 'recipe', and there you have it, your own fully formed contract!

The formula or recipe is as follows: once you have identified who you are willing to contract with:

(1) create an agreement with them (Chapter 2);

(2) check that your agreement is sufficiently certain (Chapter 3);

(3) make sure you both intend a legal relationship (Chapter 3); and

(4) remember to provide some consideration (Chapter 4).

You will not create a contract if any of these listed ingredients are missing. You might create some other sort of legal relationship if, for instance, ingredient 4 (consideration) is missing, but it will not be a contract (see Chapter 4). Ingredient 2 is not frequently a problem and ingredient 3 can often be presumed, but both can cause problems from time to time. The list in Figure 2.0 can act as a checklist to ensure that a contract has been formed (especially useful in answering problem questions; check each factor is present before concluding that a contract has been formed).

Figure 2.0 Creation of a contract

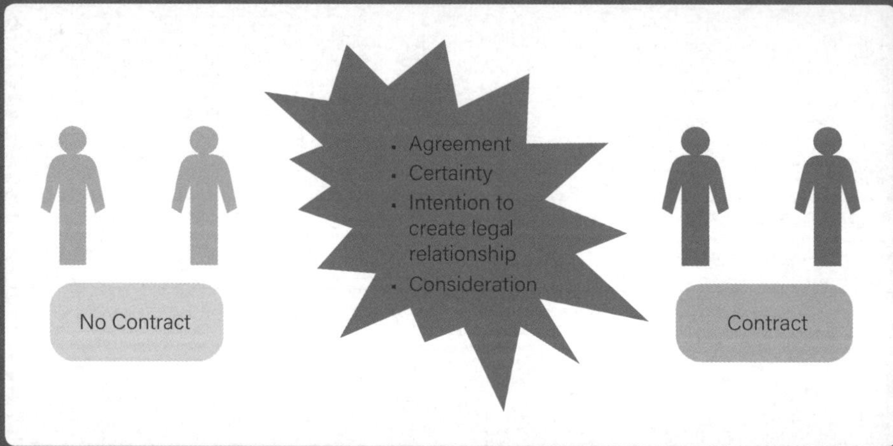

2 Agreement

LEARNING OBJECTIVES

This chapter will help you to:

- recognize a contract as an agreement between two parties;
- understand the difference between an objective and subjective point of view;
- distinguish between an offer and an invitation to treat;
- understand how an offer can be accepted and revoked; and
- understand the difference between unilateral and bilateral contracts.

Introduction

We established earlier that this book's main concern is with obligations. In particular, it is concerned with those obligations which are 'contractual.' When two parties create contractual obligations between themselves we can say that a contract has been formed. Chapter 1 explained that a contractual obligation is special because it arises from a party's voluntary choice or consent to create the obligation in return for something from the other party. Because we do not create contractual obligations every time we choose to do something for somebody else, we must look at which particular choices give rise to contractual obligations and contracts.

All contracts are agreements (even though not all agreements are contracts). Agreements are consensual events of a particular type, requiring that the minds of the two parties meet on matters which are the subject of the agreement. The classic bilateral contractual agreement involves A agreeing to be bound to do X in return for B promising to do Y, and B agreeing to be bound to do Y in return for A promising to do X (see Figure 2.1).

This meeting of minds is sometimes described as *consensus ad idem*, that is, agreement on the same thing (in the earlier example, agreement about exchanging X for Y), and it is the principle at the heart of contract law.

Figure 2.1 Classical bilateral agreement—A is obliged to do X and B is obliged to do Y

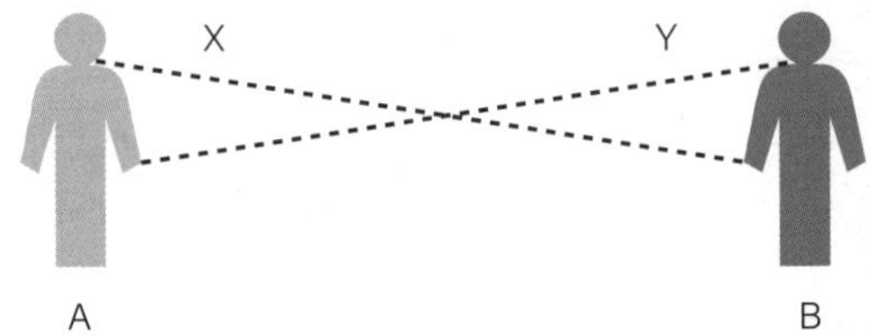

It may help at this point to point out that discussions often centre on the individual promises each side agrees to be bound by (simply another way of describing the obligations they are bound by). In the example given earlier of A contracting to do X in return for B contracting to do Y, A is promising to do X and is the promis*or* in relation to this part (X) of the contract and A's promise is given to B who is thus the promis*ee*. B however is also a promisor (unless it is a unilateral contract where B has already performed B's part (see section 2.9)); B is promising to do Y and in relation to this part of the contract (Y) A is the promis*ee*.

Usually when we talk about promisor and promisee we are focusing on just one promise/obligation, on just one side of the contract; for example if we are talking about the obligation to do X, A will be the promisor and B the promisee.

2.1 The objective test of agreement

You might think that it should be easy to establish whether there has been a 'meeting of minds.' Unfortunately, the cases show that there is often confusion between what a party *meant* and what was actually *said*. If you meant to sell me an ice cream (X) but I heard you say that you were selling ice lollies (Z) then there is clearly no meeting of our minds—one of us is thinking X (ice cream) but the other is thinking Z (ice lollies).

2.1.1 **The courts' approach**

To combat this problem the courts have generally adopted an *objective* approach, one which attaches significance to external appearances rather than to what was subjectively or internally intended. Of course, in many instances the parties will be subjectively in agreement with each other *and* there will be the outward, objective indications of that agreement. Such cases, however common, are unlikely to lead to litigation because it is clear from all points of view that an agreement has been reached.

In *The Hannah Blumenthal* (1983), a term in a contract for the sale of a ship provided that all disputes should be settled by an arbitrator. The seller claimed that the buyer had agreed to abandon this contract and the House of Lords considered what was necessary to create such an agreement to abandon the original contract, including the method of dispute resolution. None of the Law Lords condoned a purely subjective approach and Lord Brightman thought that it was necessary for 'the Buyers to so conduct themselves as to entitle the Sellers to assume . . . that the contract was to be abandoned.'

We can therefore say that the court stands in the seller's shoes and asks what the reasonable person would have concluded from the events. The sellers would be entitled to assume that the contract was abandoned if that reasonable person would think it abandoned. This approach is objective but from the viewpoint of the sellers, that is, a reasonable person looking at the buyer's conduct through the seller's eyes. One difficulty with this approach is in deciding how many of the party's actual characteristics the reasonable person should adopt when stepping into their shoes. If the party is blind, then will the reasonable person also be blind? If the party has a lot of background knowledge about the circumstances, then will the reasonable person also assume this knowledge and interpret the events in light of that knowledge? If the reasonable person takes on none of the characteristics or knowledge of the party then the view will be that of a detached reasonable person, a fly-on-the-wall perspective. If the reasonable person takes on too many of the party's characteristics and thoughts, then the view will hardly be objective at all but will instead become virtually subjective; the reasonable person will be in danger of becoming the actual party.

Subjective and objective points of view

- A *subjective* point of view looks into the mind of a party. It aims to discover what that party actually intended and understood.
- An *objective* view looks at external factors and describes how the *reasonable person* would have understood what was said and done.

Who is the 'reasonable person'? The reasonable person is an imaginary person created by judges who you might think of as your 'Average Joe' type of character.

There are two types of objective points of view (see Howarth (1984) and Vorster (1987)):

(1) Promisee or promisor objectivity. The reasonable person stands in the shoes of either the promisee or the promisor and views the events from that perspective.

(2) Detached objectivity. The reasonable person stands in no one's shoes, but observes the events as though a fly on the wall.

Another example of the courts preferring an objective approach can be found in *Upton-on-Severn Rural District Council* v *Powell* (1942). Mr Powell called out the Fire Brigade to put out a fire on his property. He thought that the services were free, as did the Council which ran the Fire Brigade. Later, the Council realized that Mr Powell lived outside their 'catchment area' and should have been charged for the services. The court found that there was a contract to pay for the fire services even though at the time of contracting there was a clear subjective agreement that the services were to be provided free of charge. The result can be explained on the basis that a fly on the wall, knowing that the services were only free if Mr Powell resided in the catchment area, would have thought that the agreement involved a promise to pay for the services. Had the court looked from the perspective of a reasonable person in Mr Powell's shoes then the result may well have been different; such a person might quite reasonably expect to receive fire services for free (even in the 1940s).

The judgment of the Court of Appeal in *Powell* is short and reveals little of the court's reasoning. An alternative explanation of the result is that there was in truth no objective agreement to pay for the service and so no real *contractual* obligation to pay the Council. Instead, the obligation to pay arose from a non-contractual event, namely unjust enrichment.

The court mistakenly labelled the obligation as contractual due to the pressures to force non-contractual liability into a contractual framework at a time when the law of restitution and unjust enrichment was under-developed. The important point on this alternative view is that any obligation to pay the Council was *not* based on Mr Powell's consent to be bound but on some other principle of law.

LINK TO . . .

Mistake (Chapter 8) and Misrepresentation (Chapter 7)

A party is mistaken when that party's subjective view of the agreement does not match the objective approach favoured by the courts. Objectively, you agreed to sell me an ice lolly in the earlier example, but you believed, mistakenly, that you had agreed to sell me an ice cream. Check out Chapter 8 for a discussion of when the courts override the objective agreement because of one party's mistake. Chapter 7 deals with some other cases where one party's mistake was induced by something the other party said or did (misrepresentations). Why do you think that the parties' internal (subjective) beliefs sometimes override the objective approach to agreement?

2.1.2 The rationale for the courts' approach

It is not immediately obvious *why* the external, objective appearance of each party's intentions should prevail over their internal, subjective intentions. If contractual obligations really are supposed to be based upon the voluntary consent and the meeting of the minds of each party then a subjective approach, one that reveals what the parties actually consented to in their own minds, should dominate. There must be a good reason for the courts to sideline subjective intentions in favour of objective ones.

One danger with the subjective approach is that individuals often forget, whether it be innocently or conveniently, what their intentions were and may present a version which is favourable to them, and difficult to prove wrong, when a dispute arises. It is easier to adopt an objective approach and judge them on what they said and did at the time of contracting, given that 'even the devil does not know what the thought of man is.'

This 'impossible to know' explanation cannot totally justify the strength with which the objective approach is applied since cases like *Upton-on-Severn Rural District Council* v *Powell* show that the objective approach may still prevail even when it is quite clear to the court what the actual intentions of each party are. Also, the courts are quite used to dealing with difficult issues of fact in their everyday business and there is no reason for them to shy away in this situation.

The real reason for the objective approach, it is suggested, is not that the *courts* might have difficulty in determining the parties' true intentions after the event but that at the time of the alleged contract the *parties themselves* cannot know one another's true intentions. Obligations arise out of agreements that a person has *appeared* to have made, since to do otherwise would mean that another party could never safely rely on any agreement as it would always be possible that the first party meant something different from what was actually said. In short, the objective approach enhances certainty and encourages reliance. The price of these benefits is that the actual intentions of a party are sidelined, damaging the claim that contracts are based upon the parties' consent.

EXAMPLE

Subjective and objective points of view

I am a former professional footballer with a collection of football memorabilia including international caps, football programmes, etc. which I keep in a glass display cabinet at home. I also have the ball from the 1995 FA Cup Final with which I scored a hat-trick and which is normally kept separately on display at my former club.

If I offer to sell my football memorabilia collection to you for £20,000 and you accept, there are five possible viewpoints of our agreement. The first two describe our conflicting subjective understandings of the agreement:

(i) You believe that I intend to include the 1995 FA Cup Final ball in the sale.

(ii) I do not intend to include it, as I regard it as quite separate from the other memorabilia.

We are subjectively in disagreement and there is no *consensus ad idem*.

The third and fourth possible viewpoints are objective views of what was said and done. The concern is not with how we actually understood the events but how reasonable people in our positions would have understood these events.

(iii) Would a reasonable person in my position have thought that my offer included the FA Cup Final ball? Probably not, given my knowledge that it is displayed separately at a different location.

(iv) What would a reasonable person in your position have thought? If you knew from newspaper reports that I had a large collection of memorabilia and that I had been given the 1995 ball at the end of the match you might reasonably think that it was included.

Clearly these two approaches are not purely objective because the reasonable person is placed in our shoes and so some of our actual knowledge and characteristics are relevant.

The final viewpoint (v) is that of a detached observer, a reasonable person standing in neither of our positions. This is the view which a 'fly on the wall' would get of the agreement. This is a 'purer' objective viewpoint as it is untainted by the personal knowledge and characteristics of each party. Evidence about the market prices for the items in question might be one factor here. If the price of £20,000 is quite common for this sort of collection of memorabilia and an FA Cup Final ball might in itself commonly fetch a higher price, then the detached observer might well conclude that the ball was not included, and the court may well adopt this viewpoint.

2.2 Identifying an offer and acceptance

2.2.1 The dual requirements of offer and acceptance

Contractual obligations arise out of (voluntary) agreements. Given that the courts adopt an objective test and look for external evidence of agreements, what counts as such evidence?

The courts could adopt a liberal approach in which they simply look at all the circumstances and see if the parties appear, objectively, to have reached agreement. The trouble with this approach is that it easily descends into an assessment of what each party actually subjectively intended. More importantly, it can openly reveal the extent to which the law is unpredictable. The law avoids this—at least in theory—by means of the dual requirements of offer and acceptance. In order to establish an agreement, one party must make an offer which must then be accepted by the other party. This formula breaks down the inquiry into manageable chunks and the courts can determine whether there has been an agreement by going through the criteria necessary to identify first an offer and then an acceptance.

Not everyone has always approved of this technical, formulaic approach. A more liberal approach was suggested by Lord Denning MR in *Butler Machine Tool Co. Ltd* v *Ex-Cell-O Corporation (England) Ltd* (1979) and again in *Gibson* v *Manchester City Council* (1979). In the first case the majority of the Court of Appeal, in resolving a problem involving the so-called battle of the forms, based their decision on the more traditional offer and acceptance analysis (and indeed this formed an alternative ground for Lord Denning). In the *Gibson* case, the House of Lords actually reversed the Court of Appeal's decision that, looking at the evidence as a whole, there was a concluded agreement, and instead held that there had been no matching offer and acceptance. Lord Diplock recognized that 'there may be certain types of exceptional contracts which do not fit neatly into the normal analysis of offer and acceptance but that the exchange of correspondence was not one of them.' The traditional approach (subject to exceptions) was affirmed by the Court Appeal in *Tekdata Interconnections Ltd* v *Amphenol Ltd* (2009). The Court accepted that a course of dealing between the parties might display an intention not to be bound by the terms dictated by the traditional offer and acceptance model, but this was not such a case.

Clark v *Earl of Dunraven* (1897) is a good example of the sort of exceptional case that Lord Diplock probably had in mind: all the competitors in a race unambiguously agreed to be bound to one another by the rules of the competition but the large number of competitors and the different times at which they entered made it artificial and virtually impossible to identify individual offers and acceptances between each and every competitor.

It is worth contrasting Lord Diplock's view that it is only exceptional cases 'which do not fit easily into the normal analysis of offer and acceptance' with Lord Wilberforce's view in *New Zealand Shipping Co. Ltd* v *A. M. Satterthwaite & Co. Ltd* (1975) that the traditional approach is 'often at the cost of forcing the facts to fit uneasily into the marked slots of offer, acceptance and consideration.' The benefits of precedents and ease of application under the more methodical traditional approach must be weighed against the uncertainty and artificiality necessary in practice to force the facts into the necessary categories of offer and acceptance. The difficulties with the traditional approach have led to accusations that the courts sometimes 'reason backwards,' that is, decide first whether there should be a contract and then work out how to fulfil the offer and acceptance criteria. In effect this is the liberal approach dressed up as the offer and acceptance formula.

The traditional approach may be open to criticism, but in practice it constitutes the key requirements normally required to establish an agreement. In the absence of an offer and acceptance, it will be very difficult to argue that there is a contract and thus the remainder of this chapter will examine the so-called rules of offer and acceptance.

THINKING POINT

Think of all the times you have made a contract in recent months. On how many occasions did someone make an identifiable offer to you which you thought about and then accepted? Do you think the law's use of the offer and acceptance model reflects today's business practices?

2.3 The offer

One party must intend, or appear to intend, in accordance with the objective approach, to make an offer capable of being accepted by another. It is sometimes difficult to decide whether A actually intends to make an offer or whether A is merely inviting B to make an offer. The distinction is crucial because it affects B's ability to create a binding agreement. If a genuine offer is made, then B can bind the maker by simply accepting the offer. If only an invitation is made, then there is nothing for B to accept. B can make an offer in response which A may then choose to accept or reject, but A will have the final say on whether there is an agreement.

The courts look carefully at the facts of each case in order to distinguish between offers and what they call **invitations to treat**. An example may clarify the situation.

invitations to treat
An invitation to treat falls short of being an offer capable of binding acceptance; instead it is an invitation for the other party to make an offer, which the former party is free to accept or reject.

EXAMPLE

Offer or invitation to treat?

If A says to B 'I am selling my pen for £2,' A's communication could be interpreted as either:

- A is offering the pen for sale to B and B need only accept the offer to create a binding agreement; or
- A is inviting B to offer to buy the pen, should B wish to do so. A may then accept B's offer and create a binding agreement. Alternatively, A may reject B's offer and choose to sell to someone else or not at all.

There are therefore two possible routes to an agreement:

(1) Offer + Acceptance = Agreement

(2) Invitation + Offer + Acceptance = Agreement

plus alternatives which result in no agreement, that is:

(3) Offer + Rejection = No Agreement

(4) Invitation + Offer + Rejection = No Agreement

If the facts were changed so that A said 'I'm offering you this particular pen for £2, you have half an hour to accept' or 'This pen is yours for £2 if you want it' then the analysis would be much easier. A has almost certainly made an offer to B rather than an invitation to treat. Unfortunately, people often do not express themselves as clearly as this in everyday life.

CASE CLOSE-UP

***Gibson* v *Manchester CC* (1979)**

Mr Gibson argued that there was a contractual obligation between himself and Manchester City Council. He demanded that the Council perform its obligation to sell him his council house, but the Council denied that any obligation had ever arisen on the basis that it had never made an offer to Mr Gibson. There were four important events on which the case turned. Firstly, Mr Gibson had asked the Council to inform him of the price of buying his council house and the details of a possible mortgage. Secondly, the Council wrote back to Mr Gibson, stating that it might be prepared to sell him the house for £2,180 but the maximum mortgage it could provide was £2,177, and the letter invited Mr Gibson to make a formal application to buy his council house by completing the enclosed application form. Thirdly, Mr Gibson returned the application form and, once his request to lower the price had been refused, he wrote again asking the Council to proceed with his application form and the house was removed from the Council's maintenance list and on to its house purchase list. Fourthly, the Labour Party won control of the Council and decided to stop the sale of council houses unless there was already a binding contract of sale. In the Court of Appeal, Lord Denning thought that there was an agreement, there being 'no need to look for a strict offer and acceptance.' When the Council appealed to the House of Lords Lord Diplock criticized Lord Denning's approach and was unable to find any matching offer and acceptance. He emphasized the fact that the Council's letter stated that it '*may* be prepared to sell' and invited Mr Gibson to 'make a formal application to buy.' The Council did not intend the letter to allow Mr Gibson to create a binding agreement between them, and simply meant to inform him that it may be willing to sell to him if *he* made an offer. It therefore only made an invitation to treat. Mr Gibson's reply amounted to an offer (step 3) but this was not accepted by the Council and so it was not under an obligation to sell.

Sellers will often not have given any thought to whether they are making an offer or an invitation to treat and there will be no clear intention. People often have more pressing matters than deciding whether a potential purchaser could create a binding agreement with them. In their minds, it often seems unimportant or does not occur to them to question whether there is an offer followed by an acceptance or an invitation to treat followed by an offer followed by an acceptance. They become interested only when things go wrong and the agreement is questioned, as in *Gibson* v *Manchester CC* where the political changes brought the question of whether there was a binding contract to the fore.

There are many common everyday situations where it is difficult to be confident about actual intentions. For example, when an item is displayed in a shop or advertised in the media it is often difficult to be sure whether the vendor is making an offer or merely inviting offers. Consider the following scenario: if you advertise your bike in the student newspaper are you offering your bike for sale or inviting other students to make an offer? Initially you might think you are offering the bike for sale—after all, that is your *purpose*—but would you really want to be bound to sell your bike to every reader who replied to you? In the interests of certainty, it is sometimes necessary for the courts to fall back on to a presumption. A presumption is not the same as a guess because it applies consistently in all similar cases. Vendors can therefore assess in advance of any legal proceedings whether the display of goods or an advertisement will constitute an offer or an invitation to treat. The presumption must not only be consistent but also render the most practical result. In general, vendors want to reserve their position and not open themselves up to being bound by every reply. Trade would obviously be hampered if the slightest hint of an offer to sell resulted in sellers being bound to sell to anyone who accepted. It is therefore commonly presumed that a vendor only intended to make an invitation to treat. When you read about presumptions it is essential to bear in mind that the primary aim is to ascertain, objectively, the vendor's intention. It is only when this intention is unclear that a presumption is necessary. You should therefore first look for any evidence of the offeror's intention.

2.3.1 **Using presumptions to clarify intention**

Advertisements

In *Partridge* v *Crittenden* (1968), the aptly named Mr Partridge placed an advertisement in the classified section of the 'Cage and Aviary Birds' periodical. It included the words 'Quality British ABCR . . . Bramblefinch cocks, Bramblefinch hens 25s each.' A magistrates' court found that the advertisement was an offer for the sale of a wild bird and so contravened s.6 of the Protection of Birds Act 1954. On appeal to the High Court, the advertisement was held to be an invitation to treat and so it did not constitute an offer or an offence under the statute.

The fact that Mr Partridge had not used the words 'offer for sale' did not mean that the advertisement could not be an offer but, in Ashworth J's words: 'at least it strengthens the case for the appellant [Mr Partridge] that there is no such expression on the page.'

Ashworth J made it clear that he was not applying a fixed rule of law but instead interpreting the actual advertisement: 'the insertion of an advertisement *in the form adopted here* under the title "Classified Advertisements" is simply an invitation to treat' (emphasis added). It is clear that the judge was not saying that all advertisements will be invitations to treat and, because the form of words adopted was ambiguous, we can say that the Court of Appeal presumed that the advertisement was an invitation to treat. They presumed in favour of an invitation to treat because it made practical sense and because Mr Partridge had not indicated to the contrary. Mr Partridge, who, despite his name, presumably only had a limited stock of birds, would be in a sticky situation if the advertisement counted as an offer and he was bound to provide everyone who accepted with a Bramblefinch cock or hen. The most important point to remember is that the court first looked carefully at the words used and the surrounding circumstances and could have reached a contrary conclusion had they been different.

A contrasting example is the United States case of *Lefkowitz* v *Great Minneapolis Surplus Store* (1957). An advertisement for three fur coats for $1 each, first come, first served, was held to be an offer. Whilst US law is obviously not binding in England and Wales, it is often used as an example of how a case *might* be decided in England and Wales. It is important to note that the advertisement was limited to the first three customers. In this context it was reasonable to reject the usual presumption of an invitation to treat and conclude that the shopkeeper intended to make an offer to the first three customers. Had the advertisement not been limited to the first three customers then it would have been contrary to the likely intentions of the shopkeeper and commercially unreasonable to require the shop to supply the whole of Minnesota with fur coats for $1 if they came into the shop and accepted the offer. Alternatively, if it was clear that there would be no problem in supplying all those who accepted—if the shopkeeper had a fur coat for everyone in Minnesota—then the usual presumption could be displaced, and the advertisement could still be held to be an offer.

We can therefore conclude that many advertisements will be mere invitations to treat, like the one in *Partridge* v *Crittenden.* However, if the advertiser makes it clear that an offer is intended, or includes features in the advertisement which displace the presumption in favour of an invitation to treat, then the advertisement will be an offer. If the shopkeeper limits the number of people who can accept the offer, as in *Lefkowitz*, or demonstrates that there are no problems with meeting a large number of acceptances, this may dislodge the presumption.

Displays

The display of goods is almost always ambiguous. Unlike advertisements, which by their very nature contain some form of written expression, a vendor need only place the goods in a window in order to display them. The vendor may add an expression of intention next to the display, but this is commonly omitted.

In *Pharmaceutical Society of Great Britain* v *Boots Cash Chemists (Southern) Ltd* (1953) the Pharmaceutical Society brought an action against Boots for selling poisons contrary to s.18 of the Pharmacy and Poisons Act 1933. The Act made it an offence to sell certain poisons without the supervision of a registered pharmacist. The Society argued that Boots had sold such poisons without the necessary supervision when two customers had picked up drugs from the self-service shelves and put them into their basket. Boots argued that the sale did not take place until the goods were presented at a till, where there was the necessary supervision. The case therefore rested on where and when the agreement to sell took place—by the shelves or at the till. The Court of Appeal agreed with Lord Goddard CJ's decision at first instance that the display of a product on a shelf was not an offer which could be accepted by the customer placing it in their basket. The sale could not have therefore taken place by the shelves. Instead, the display was an invitation to treat and the customer offered to buy the product by taking it to the till (where it would normally be accepted). Similarly to *Partridge*, the case follows the general presumption that sellers will want to reserve their position and make only an invitation to treat.

Somerville LJ, like Lord Goddard CJ, felt that the decision was justified because 'one of the most formidable difficulties' with the Society's argument was that a customer would be bound to pay for an item once placed in the basket and would not have the option of later substituting it with a different item. According to this line of reasoning, the display had to be an invitation to treat so that the customer was not bound until the offer to purchase the items was accepted at the till. However, this is not a watertight explanation of why a display of goods should not be treated as an offer. You could argue that the display is an offer which is only accepted by a customer when *presenting* the goods at the till (especially given that later we shall see that an acceptance must normally be communicated to the offeror). Up until presentation of the goods, a customer would be free to swap the item or put it back as many times as he or she liked. Boots would still have won under this alternative analysis because there would have been supervision at the point of acceptance, but treating a display as an offer could be important in different circumstances.

The distinction between an offer and an invitation to treat mattered in *Fisher* v *Bell* (1961). The defendant, Mr Bell, displayed a flick-knife in his shop window when it was a criminal offence to offer flick-knives for sale. A police constable thought that he was making an offer to sell the knife, not an unreasonable assumption given that Mr Bell's reported response to the allegation was: 'Fair enough!' However, the court held that no offence had been committed and the case is often cited as an authority for the proposition that a display of goods is an invitation to treat. Actually, the point was not argued; both counsel agreed that the display was, under contractual principles, not an offer but an invitation to treat. The real argument was whether the statutory wording of the offence adopted the normal contractual meaning of 'offer' or whether the words could be read more widely so as to make Mr Bell criminally responsible even if it was not an 'offer' for the purposes of the law of contract. An examination of the wording clearly revealed that it could not be read as widely as the prosecution desired and so Mr Bell had committed no offence.

Rather than accepting the Court of Appeal's reasoning in *Boots*, a better justification for treating a display as an invitation to treat is that otherwise a shop with limited stock may find itself unable to supply everybody with whom it has a contract. As with advertisements, if it is made clear that any display is limited to a certain number of customers, as in the advertisement in *Lefkowitz*, or that there is sufficient quantity of stock to meet all acceptances, then the display may be interpreted to be an offer.

The results in *Boots* and *Fisher* v *Bell* reinforce the point that, generally speaking, a display of goods will be presumed to be an invitation to treat. Only if special circumstances are present will the display be an offer. Special circumstances may consist of a clear intention to be bound by all acceptances or evidence that there would be no problem supplying all those entitled to accept the offer.

Auctions

Auction sales can appear complicated because there are three people involved: the seller, the auctioneer and the bidding public. It is difficult to determine who makes an offer to whom. The difficulties are compounded because the auctioneer acts both in a personal capacity and also as the seller's agent; think of the auctioneer as having a split personality. Acting as an agent simply means that everybody pretends that the auctioneer is the seller and so an offer or acceptance by the auctioneer acting as agent counts as an offer or acceptance by the seller.

Auctions are generally governed by the same rules as a display of goods in a shop window. The difference is that the display is made in the auction room, or, with more difficulties, on an Internet site, such as eBay. An auctioneer displaying goods, on behalf of the seller and acting as the seller's agent, only makes an invitation to treat and it is the bidders who make offers to buy, the highest of which is accepted in the customary fashion by the fall of the auctioneer's hammer (s.57(2) Sale of Goods Act 1979). The auctioneer can withdraw the goods from the auction at any time before a bid is accepted. In *British Car Auctions* v *Wright* (1972) an auctioneer was convicted of making 'an offer to sell' an unroadworthy car contrary to the Road Traffic Act 1960. His appeal was allowed on the same grounds as *Partridge* v *Crittenden* and *Fisher* v *Bell*. The court held that the advertisement and display of the car was only an invitation to treat and that the words of the statute ('offer to sell') must bear their technical contractual meaning.

Auctions with and without reserve

Many auctions are held 'with reserve.' This means that there is a minimum price which must be met before the goods can be sold; a priceless work of art will not be knocked down to 50 pence even if that is the highest bid. In such a case the seller will stipulate in advance that the auctioneer must not sell for less than a certain price. On other occasions an auction will be 'without reserve' where the item being auctioned will be knocked down to the highest price, even if this is only 50 pence and a fraction of the item's usual value. When the auction is 'without reserve' it is important to distinguish between what the auctioneer does on behalf of the seller (as agent) and what is done in the auctioneer's own personal capacity. The courts will still presume that the auctioneer is making only an invitation to treat on behalf of the seller but they will presume that the auctioneer in a personal capacity is making an *offer* to sell to the highest bidder (there is only one person who can meet this condition, so only one person can accept and there is no danger of being bound to an unlimited number of bidders). *This* offer is accepted by making the highest bid of the auction, the same conduct which also constitutes an offer by the bidder to enter into the main contract of sale. The seller will still be able to withdraw the item from auction if the offer, from the highest bidder so far to enter into the main contract of sale, has not been accepted by the auctioneer as agent for the seller. However, the auctioneer will personally be in breach of an obligation to sell to the person who had made the highest bid up to that point. The contract between the auctioneer and the highest bidder is called a collateral (or side) contract to signify that the auctioneer, in his personal capacity, is making a collateral (or side) promise to perform his role of agent and create the main contract of sale between the seller and the highest bidder.

In *Warlow* v *Harrison* (1859) a horse was offered at auction without reserve. The claimant bid £60 and this was followed by a bid of £61 from the owner, to which the auctioneer knocked down (i.e. accepted). Once the claimant realized that the owner had outbid him, he tendered his money to the auctioneer and demanded the horse on the grounds that he was the highest legitimate bidder (owners cannot make legitimate bids in auctions without reserve—otherwise they could easily push the price up to a satisfactory level). The Court of Exchequer Chamber rejected the claimant's plea that the auctioneer was the claimant's agent (as well as the seller's) in order to complete the contract of sale but they held *obiter dicta* (by the way—a phrase which signifies that the judge's comment was not necessary to decide the case before him (and so it does not bind lower or equivalent courts)) that the claimant could succeed if he changed his plea to allege a breach of contract by the auctioneer (the collateral contract described earlier). This means that they thought the claimant had a good case on the facts but had pleaded his case incorrectly. Martin B said that in an auction without reserve the auctioneer *personally* promises that the item will be sold to the highest *bona fide* bidder and this was clearly not done on the facts as the item was knocked down to the owner who was not a *bona fide* bidder. The contract between the auctioneer and bidder had been breached. This approach was approved in the Court of Appeal decision *Barry* v *Davies (trading as Heathcote & Co.)* (2001). In that case, two engine analysers valued at £14,000 each were offered for sale in an auction without reserve. The highest bidder, who had bid only £200 for each item, sued for breach of contract after the auctioneer withdrew the goods from the auction. The Court of Appeal found that there was a contract between the auctioneer and the highest bidder for the auctioneer to sell without reserve to the highest bidder. This was breached when the goods were withdrawn. Note in these cases that because it is the auctioneer who has broken the contract but is not the owner of the goods, the remedy will normally be a damages claim against the auctioneer rather than an action against the seller in relation to the specific goods under a contract for sale.

Scott (2001) has argued that it would be inconsistent if no contract arose between the auctioneer and the highest bidder in an auction *with* reserve once the reserve price has been exceeded. This can be justified on the basis that in an auction with reserve the auctioneer offers to sell to the highest bidder on the condition that the bid exceeds the reserve.

Tenders

A seller who has (or who wishes to attract) a number of potential purchasers may invite these potential purchasers to submit a tender. This is like an auction by correspondence where each person is asked to make just one bid. The request for tenders will normally amount to an invitation to treat, whilst the tenders will constitute offers to buy the goods at the tendered price. This of course reflects the normal intention of the seller who wants to encourage as many offers as possible in order to be able to accept the most attractive one.

Sometimes, rather as in the case of auctions, the actions of the seller are interpreted as an offer to accept the highest tender and not as an invitation to treat. In *Harvela Investments* v *Royal Trust of Canada* (1986) the seller of a number of shares invited the claimant and the second defendant to make confidential bids for the shares by 3 p.m. the following day. The seller offered to sell to the highest bidder who complied with the set conditions, thus displacing the usual presumption that a seller usually invites the buyers to make an offer. The issue in the House of Lords really centred on the construction of 'the highest bidder.' The claimant had bid C$2,175,000 (a fixed bid) and the second defendant 'C$2,100,000 or C$101,000 in excess of any other bid' (a referential bid). The House of Lords held that the offer to accept the highest bid was limited to fixed bids because the intention of the seller was to devise a process which would ensure a sale of the shares, giving each party an equal chance to purchase them and ensuring that each bid contained the maximum each party was willing to pay. If referential bids were permitted, then a sale might never happen if both parties made referential bids. Moreover, a party which made a fixed bid would never be able to win and the bids would not indicate the absolute maximum each party would be prepared to pay. (Of course, a party is free to stipulate that referential bids will be accepted, although thought then needs to be given as to how to break the deadlock if all parties make a referential bid.) The sellers therefore breached their obligation owed to the claimant when they accepted the second defendant's referential bid over the claimant's fixed bid.

In *Blackpool & Fylde Aero Club* v *Blackpool Borough Council* (1990) the Council invited tenders to be placed in its letterbox before a set deadline. The claimants placed their tender in the box before the deadline, but it was not collected by the Council. The general presumption applied so that the Council made only an invitation to treat and the flight club made an offer which was not accepted. However, the Council was held to have made an offer to *consider* all tenders which were posted before the deadline. The claimants accepted this offer by posting their tender before the deadline. The Council breached this collateral agreement because it did not even consider the Club's tender.

SUMMARY POINTS

(1) Whether an offer or an invitation to treat is made depends upon the apparent intentions of A, objectively ascertained.

(2) If A's intentions are unclear then the court will generally presume that only an invitation to treat was intended.

This is because:

- *A will generally want to reserve his or her position and have the option of rejecting any offers received in response to the invitation to treat; and*
- *it would often be commercially unreasonable to place A under an obligation to supply all those people who reply.*

The courts are more likely to find an offer existed if:

- *it is limited to a certain number of acceptances* (Lefkowitz *v* Great Minneapolis Surplus Store);
- *it is possible to meet a large number of orders;*
- *it is of a limited nature, for example to consider a reply* (Blackpool & Fylde Aero Club *v* Blackpool Borough Council)*; or*
- *there are other practical reasons for finding an offer.*

2.4 Rejection, counter-offers and inquiries

We saw earlier that parties do not always clearly label their words as 'offer' or 'invitation to treat.' The same is true in relation to the responses to offers, even once it has been clarified that it is an offer that one is dealing with. In this respect we need to distinguish between rejections, counter-offers and inquiries. Rejections are the simplest, whereby an offeree effectively says 'thanks, but no thanks.' The original offer is rejected and no longer exists: that is, it can no longer be accepted if the offeree changes his or her mind. A counter-offer, by contrast, is made when the offeree changes the terms of the offer and bounces it back for the offeror to accept.

EXAMPLE

Counter-offer

Alan: 'I offer to sell my car for £500.' (Offer)

Bert: 'I'll buy it for £400.' (Counter-offer)

The important point here is that if Alan chooses not to accept Bert's new offer, Bert cannot simply revert to the original offer to sell for £500 and accept that original offer because his counter-offer is normally regarded as having destroyed or terminated the original offer, just as a rejection would have done. He can of course make a fresh offer to buy for £500 but it would then be up to Alan whether he wishes to accept.

An inquiry is different again because the inquirer does not intend to bounce back an offer capable of acceptance but instead only intends to find out more about the offer. For example, the inquiry 'Are you including the in-car hi-fi?' does not reject the original offer and so even if the answer comes back 'No, the hi-fi is not included,' the offeree can still accept the original offer.

The classic case on counter-offers is *Hyde* v *Wrench* (1840) where a typical haggling scenario took place. Wrench offered to sell his farm to Hyde for £1,000. Hyde responded by offering £950. Wrench rejected this offer and Hyde tried to accept Wrench's original offer of £1,000. The case rested on whether Hyde's counter-offer to buy for £950 also constituted a rejection of Wrench's original offer. If it did then Hyde could not later accept the offer he had previously rejected. If it did not then Hyde was entitled to accept the offer and Wrench could be ordered to hand over the farm. Lord Langdale MR thought that once Hyde made an offer of his own, 'he thereby rejected the previous offer made by the defendant [Wrench]'. Hyde could not therefore later on accept Wrench's offer. This appears to merge a counter-offer and rejection into one so that all counter-offers must necessarily entail a rejection of the original offer. However, it is not difficult to imagine that some counter-offers are intended to be exactly that, that is, offers and nothing more. Offerees attempting to do this are trying to have their cake and eat it; they would like to introduce new terms in the form of a counter-offer, but they also want to reserve their ability to accept the original offer. *Hyde* suggests that the courts will prevent this by interpreting most counter-offers as also constituting rejections, but it remains to be seen whether a counter-offer can be made whilst expressly preserving the original offer.

Inquiries are one way in which a party can introduce potential new terms to the other party without making a counter-offer that is also likely to count as a rejection of the original offer. The inquirer is effectively testing the water, reserving the ability to accept the offer but also assessing the offeror's inclination to negotiate. Again, there are grey areas where it is difficult to tell whether an inquiry is in reality a counter-offer/rejection.

In *Stevenson, Jacques and Co.* v *McLean* (1880) the defendant offered to sell some **delivery warrants** for 40s. The claimants sent a telegram to the defendants asking: 'Please wire whether you would accept forty for delivery over two months, or, if not, the longest limit you would give.' This was because the claimants wanted to find out how flexible the warrants would be, that is, over what period the iron could be delivered, before they accepted the offer to buy them. Lush J rejected the defendant's argument that the case was the same as *Hyde* v *Wrench* in that the claimants had rejected the defendant's offer and made a counter-offer. He held that the form of the telegram was one of inquiry and not a counter-offer or rejection. It did not offer 'forty for delivery over two months' but instead asked what time limit the defendants would accept. Drawing the line between an inquiry which implies a counter-offer and one which does not is a difficult job.

delivery warrants
Pieces of paper which give the person holding them the right to demand delivery of the goods represented, iron in this case.

In the contractual sphere the crucial point is to determine whether an offer is still open for acceptance. At present, *Hyde* v *Wrench* ensures that offers have a short lifespan; counter-offers generally kill them off immediately. The severity of this approach depends on how the courts distinguish counter-offers and inquiries. If the courts find counter-offers very easily then offers will be a more endangered species. Alternatively, if the courts favour inquiries, then offers will stand for longer without rejection. You might want to consider whether in some cases it would be a better policy to place the onus of revoking an offer on the offeror, rather than implying a rejection from a counter-offer as in *Hyde* v *Wrench*.

2.5 Acceptance

2.5.1 **Acceptance or counter-offer?**

Acceptance by the offeree brings the offer to an end and creates an agreement between the parties. Acceptance can be as simple as 'I agree', although unfortunately, as in the case of offers, life is rarely that simple.

Just as we distinguished an offer from an invitation to treat, we must also distinguish an acceptance from a counter-offer. We saw earlier that counter-offers usually prevent the original offer from being accepted because they are often interpreted as rejections.

Counter-offers can also look like acceptances. In general an acceptance must be the 'mirror image' of an offer whilst counter-offers are obviously offers on different terms. The counter-offer in *Hyde* v *Wrench* was quite clearly not an acceptance of the original offer because Hyde proposed a different price. Difficulties arise when the response to an offer is *almost* a mirror image of the offer, but not quite. Businessmen simply do not conduct their negotiations in terms which mirror each other and to strictly enforce the 'mirror rule' would severely hamper business.

EXAMPLE

Acceptance or Counter-offer

A offers to sell A's red car for £500 with a one-year guarantee. If B responds by saying that he will buy it for £400 then we saw from *Hyde* that this will be a counter-offer by B and a rejection of A's offer. The same would be true if B responded that B would buy A's blue car for £500; the response would again not match the offer. When the price or the subject matter in the response does not mirror the offer, it is easy to see why there is no agreement. However, if B's response mirrored A's price and referred to the same (red) car but said 'with the usual 18 months' guarantee' do you think that this would be a sufficient breach of the 'mirror image rule' to mean that the response did not constitute an acceptance?

The problem of one side introducing a different term is exacerbated when it is recognized that many businesses have their own set of pre-printed standard terms on which they want to contract. A and B may quite quickly agree on what they are buying and selling and for what price but they will often keep on swapping their standard terms in what is known as a 'battle of the forms.' The original offer will refer to A's standard terms and B's response will refer to B's standard terms. A may then respond to B using A's standard terms and so on and so on. Each party throws a fat bundle of its standard terms at the other until one party eventually gives in and accepts the other's terms. In other words, the battle will be won by the party which fires the last shot. This means that if B responds by offering to contract on B's standard terms and A accepts this offer without trying to incorporate A's own terms, then the contract will be on B's terms as these were the 'last shot.' It is not always clear however, even on this analysis, who has fired the effective last shot.

In *Butler Machine Tool Co. Ltd* v *Ex-Cell-O Corporation (England) Ltd* (1979) the sellers offered to sell a machine tool for £75,535 on their standard terms which included a price variation clause. The buyers responded by ordering the machines on their own standard terms which did not contain a price variation clause. The sellers signed and returned a tear-off slip from the buyer's order which stated 'we [the sellers] accept your order on the Terms and Conditions stated thereon' but also included a letter stating that the order was entered into in accordance with the seller's earlier offer (see Figure 2.2).

The Court of Appeal held that the sellers made the first offer, which was rejected by the buyers when they made a counter-offer on different terms, following *Hyde* v *Wrench*.

Figure 2.2 Butler Machine Tool Co. Ltd *v* Ex-Cell-O Corporation (England) Ltd (1979)

Stage One
Offer to sell by Sellers on Sellers' standard terms (with price variation clause).

→

Stage Two
Rejection and counter-offer by Buyers on Buyers' standard terms (no price variation clause).

→

Stage Three
Acceptance by Sellers of Buyer's standard terms (no price variation clause) when Sellers signed and returned tear off slip incorporating Buyer's terms

This counter-offer was then accepted by the sellers when they returned the tear-off slip and their letter referring to their original offer amounted only to a reference to the price and machine agreed to, not to the terms. The sellers' letter was thus not an effective last shot as it did not incorporate their terms. The effective last shot was therefore the buyer's counter-offer which was accepted by the sellers signing and returning the tear-off slip. If the Court of Appeal had interpreted the sellers' letter as incorporating their original terms, including the price variation clause, it seems that there would have been no contract as the letter would have been a further counter-offer which the buyers never accepted. As it was, however, the contract was concluded on the buyers' terms so they did not have to pay the increase in the price which would have been payable under the price variation clause.

TRW v *Panasonic AS Europe Gmbh* (2021) is a case which can be contrasted with *Butler* in that the sellers, Panasonic, had fired a very effective *first* shot in requiring the buyer, TRW, to sign a 'customer file' in 2011 which incorporated Panasonic's general conditions subjecting any contract between them to German law. The conditions applied exclusively to the entire business relation between the parties, unless the defendant agreed otherwise in writing, and any conditions of the buyer that diverged from the GCs would be invalid. In 2015 and 2016 TRW ordered parts from Panasonic 'in accordance with' TRW's own terms and conditions which provided that commencement of work or delivery of the order would constitute acceptance of these terms. There was no requirement to communicate acceptance of these terms or to acknowledge TRW's terms in writing. The Court of Appeal had no hesitation in upholding the trial judge's view that the original signed customer file was the effective document on the overall facts of this case and explicitly prevented TRW's attempt to incorporate their own terms from being an effective last shot. The contract was thus governed by German law and any legal action about the quality of the parts supplied had to be pursued in the German courts.

Finding an agreement on the terms of one side or the other, as in the above cases, is not the only way in which the courts can defuse a 'battle of the forms.' In *British Steel Corp.* v *Cleveland Bridge and Engineering Co. Ltd* (1984) British Steel had supplied all but one of the steel nodes requested by Cleveland but the parties did not conclude their negotiations over the exact terms of the contract. Robert Goff J held that the parties' negotiations did not form a contract, but British Steel could recover the value of their performance (the steel nodes) under a restitutionary obligation. Neither side won the 'battle' because there was no contract. However, the unjust enrichment of Cleveland was avoided by imposing a restitutionary obligation for them to pay British Steel a reasonable price for the nodes.

However, in two subsequent cases, the Court of Appeal and the Supreme Court have been reluctant to allow a contract to fail where a matter has not been finalized in negotiations. In *Trentham Ltd* v *Archital Luxfer* (1993) Steyn LJ emphasized that where a transaction has been performed on both sides it will often be easier to treat any missing element as inessential.

The idea behind this is that if the parties have turned their 'battle of the forms' (their mix of offers, counter-offers and rejections) into a workable business relationship capable of performance by both sides, then any missing elements which technically prevent the acceptance from being a mirror image of the offer can be ignored. If the battling parties can make peace, then the cracks in the mirror can be smoothed away. In *RTS Flexible Systems Ltd* v *Molkerei Alois Müller GmbH & Co. KG* (2010) the Supreme Court distinguished *British Steel* and *Trentham* on their individual facts. In *RTS*, the parties had agreed terms 'subject to contract' and begun work before the terms were put into a final contract. The Supreme Court overturned the Court of Appeal's decision that there was no contract but emphasized that the fact that the parties had commenced performance did not necessarily mean that there must be a binding contract; in certain cases, there will not be a contract despite performance by the parties (as in *British Steel*).

2.6 Communication of acceptance

Once we have ruled out the possibility that a purported acceptance is in fact a counter-offer, we must then ask whether it conforms to the general rule that an acceptance must be communicated to the offeror (the person who made the offer), normally in the sense that it must come to his attention. In *Carlill* v *Carbolic Smoke Ball Co.* (1893) Lindley LJ observed that, 'as a general proposition, when an offer is made, it is necessary in order to make a binding contract, not only that it should be accepted, but that acceptance should be notified.'

In *Brogden* v *Metropolitan Rly* (1877), the Railway Company sent Brogden, their regular coal supplier, a draft contract to fix the price of coal at 20s. per ton from 1 January 1872. Brogden filled in the name of an arbitrator in a blank space left in the draft and returned it marked 'approved.' The alteration meant that this constituted a fresh offer by Brogden which required an acceptance from the Railway Company. The Railway Company simply put the contract in a drawer and forgot about it. Lord Blackburn thought that this 'merely private act' could not constitute acceptance. Lord Blackburn's comments are *obiter dicta* (which simply means that they are not binding as a matter of precedent, not that they are insignificant, especially when a judge as distinguished as Lord Blackburn is cited) because the case was decided on the basis that the parties' conduct in carrying out the purported agreement constituted an offer and acceptance. Another, not unrelated situation where communication of acceptance is often not required is in unilateral contracts, of which the *Carlill* case mentioned earlier is the classic example.

CROSS REFERENCE

See Acceptance by conduct, in section 2.7.1 and Offer and acceptance in unilateral contracts, in section 2.9.1.

More generally, even where communication is in principle required, the courts have manipulated the concept of 'communication' and developed technical rules to determine whether a particular acceptance has been successfully communicated. In some circumstances the courts have in effect discarded the rule and allowed an acceptance to be binding where it has been sent to, but not actually received by, the offeror.

An acceptance sent by instantaneous communication is generally binding when it is *received* (whereas one sent by non-instantaneous means is generally effective when sent—the so-called postal rule dealt with later). Even with instantaneous communications, the courts have flexibly interpreted the meaning of 'received' in order to reach their preferred conclusion.

2.6.1 Instantaneous communication

When the parties communicate face to face (a form of instantaneous communication) it is fairly obvious whether the offeror has received the acceptance, but unusual circumstances may cause problems. In *Entores* v *Miles* (1955) Denning LJ thought that if a person's words were drowned out by an aircraft passing overhead then they would have to be repeated for there to be effective receipt and communication. However, if the offeree (the person speaking) reasonably believed that the words were heard and it was the offeror's fault that they were not, the offeror would not be allowed to argue that the necessary communication was not received. So, if you tell me that you accept my offer, but I do not hear you because I was not listening or not concentrating, then you will be deemed to have successfully communicated your acceptance. You, along with the rest of the population, need to be able to rely on a reasonable belief that the acceptance was communicated.

When electronic means of communication are preferred to more traditional face-to-face exchanges there are inevitably more things to go wrong; the telephone line may go dead, an email might be garbled on receipt or the paper may run out on the fax machine. Moreover, it is difficult to classify some modern modes of communication as either instantaneous or non-instantaneous because they work on a completely different basis to the old-fashioned methods of face-to-face communication or post. Email or text messages are instantaneous in comparison to the post but there is a good argument that they only arrive when you choose to access them from a central server, perhaps several days after they were sent. On the other hand, a crucial difference between email and the post is that an email is generally *available* from the instant it is sent—all you have to do is access your account. By contrast, there is an inevitable delay with the post which is out of the control of both parties.

Denning LJ in *Entores* had to deal with a case involving cutting edge technology of the 1950s known as the telex machine:

> Communications by Telex are comparatively new. Each company has a teleprinter machine in its office; and each has a Telex number like a telephone number. When one company wishes to send a message to the other, it gets the Post Office to connect up the machines. Then a clerk at one end taps the message on to his machine just as if it were a typewriter, and it is instantaneously passed to the machine at the other end, which automatically types the message on to paper at that end.

Denning LJ said that if the line went dead when the purported acceptance was sent there would be no contract because the sender would know that the communication had not been successful and should repeat the message when the line re-connected. However, if the offeree reasonably believed that the acceptance had been received by the offeror, but in fact it had not, then the legal effect of the communication would depend upon the fault of the offeror. If it was the offeror's fault that the acceptance did not get through—perhaps due to lack of ink or because of poor maintenance of the machine—then the offeror would be **estopped** (barred) from denying that the acceptance was received.

> **estoppel** Estoppel is designed to prevent unconscionable conduct and usually stops a person denying what that person has said or done. Its potential scope can be very wide and vague, and we will encounter promissory estoppel in Chapter 4 when we deal with consideration. Estoppel used in this sense means that the court is effectively gagging the offeror; it knows that the acceptance was not actually received but an invisible hand is placed over the offeror's mouth preventing the offeror from saying so.

In *The Brimnes* (1975) the evidence at trial established that a notice withdrawing a vessel in response to the late payment of the hire was printed out on the defendants' telex machine at 5.45 p.m. The defendants claimed that they did not receive the telex until the next morning when it was read by their staff. The Court of Appeal held that the notice was received not when it was read by the defendants' staff, but at 5.45 p.m. the previous evening, because it was the defendants' fault that their staff had gone home early or not checked the telex machine properly. Again, the concept of fault was used to determine whether an acceptance was received.

The artificial approach demonstrates the courts' backwards reasoning in relation to offer and acceptance. They claim to look first at whether there is an offer and second at whether there is an acceptance communicated to the offeror, but in reality they ask 'should there be a contract in these circumstances?' and then determine according to the merits whether there has been a successful communication of acceptance.

On the actual facts of *Entores* there was no mechanical or technical problem with the exchange of telex communications. However, it was important to determine *where* the contract had been made, that is, where acceptance took place, in order to find out in which jurisdiction the defendant could be sued. A Dutch company in Amsterdam made an offer to an English company which then responded with a counter-offer of its own. The Dutch company accepted this counter-offer by a telex which the English company received in London. The Court of Appeal held that the contract was concluded in London because in these circumstances the instantaneous communication was only complete when it was received, thus the contract was only complete when the telex was received in London. The basic rules about communication can be represented as in Figure 2.3.

Figure 2.3 Summary of communication of acceptance

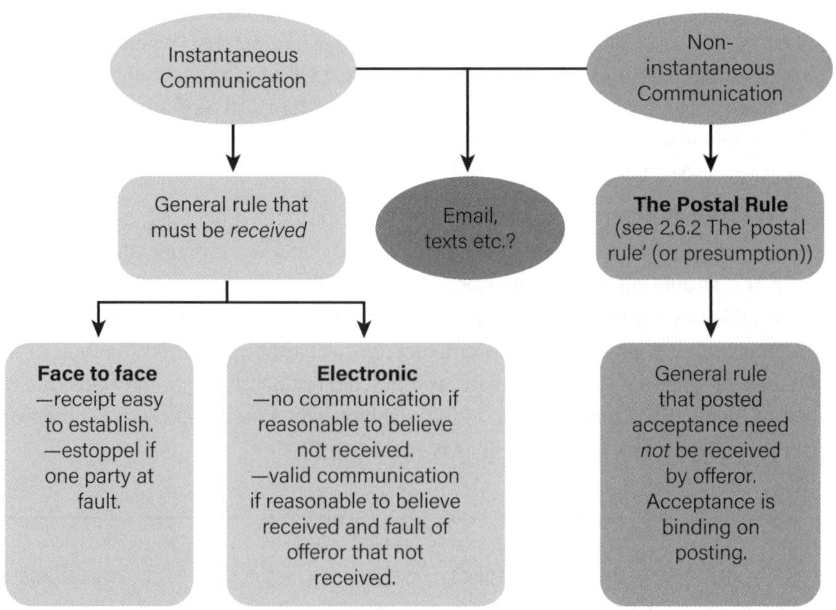

2.6.2 **The 'postal rule' (or presumption)**

Whilst the cases discussed earlier are consistent with the rule that an acceptance must be communicated to an offeror, the cases dealing with posted acceptances depart from the rule completely. The 'postal rule' decrees that a posted acceptance is binding from the moment of posting without any communication to the offeror.

The central problem is that when communications are sent over a distance and there is a time difference between dispatch and receipt it is impossible for both parties to know simultaneously that they have become bound to one another. The choice made by the postal rule places any uncertainty on the offeror because the offeree may knowingly accept at any time after the offer has been made by posting the acceptance but the offeror will not know that the offer has been accepted until actual receipt (as will be seen later, offerors can protect themselves by specifying that they will only be bound if and when the acceptance is received, but in the absence of such a restriction, the law favours offerees who do not have this option available).

In *Adams* v *Lindsell* (1818) D posted a letter on Tuesday offering to sell wool at a certain price to C, indicating that C should accept in due course of post. C only received the letter on Friday evening because D had incorrectly addressed the letter. C sent his acceptance by post that evening. By Sunday, D thought that he would have received a letter by due course of post if C wanted to accept and so he sold the wool the next day to somebody else. He then received C's acceptance. The Court of Appeal held that there was a contract between C and D because D could not say that C's acceptance had arrived too late (i.e. later than due course of post) as it was his fault that the offer letter did not get to C in good time. The court also thought, and the case has stood as an authority for this proposition, that it was not necessary for the letter to have been received by D for it to constitute a binding acceptance of the offer. They reasoned that if the law demanded that D should have receipt of C's acceptance before he became bound then it would only be fair to allow C to have notice of D's receipt of his acceptance before he became bound and so on and so on. The best result was simply to say that actual communication to the other party was not necessary when an acceptance was posted (see Figure 2.4).

Most students gleefully scribble down the postal rule safe in the knowledge that, as it is a rule, they cannot get the wrong answer. You should not make this mistake. The postal rule is deceptive, and it is important to pay attention to its limits. The postal rule has only been

Figure 2.4 Adams v Lindsell (1818)

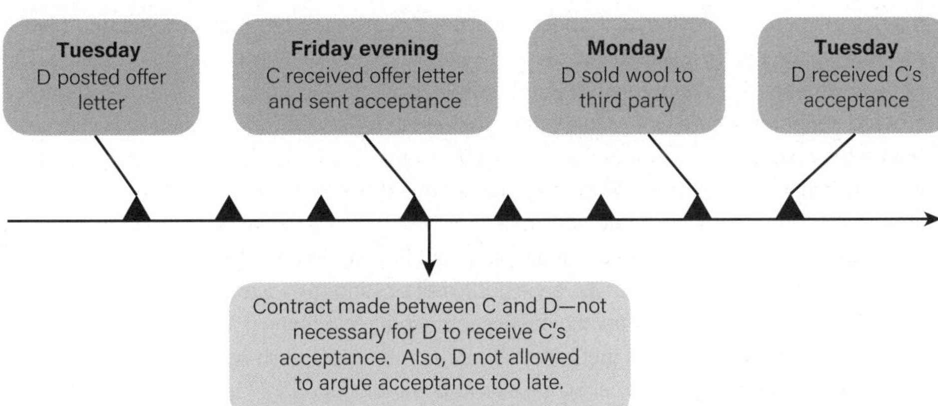

applied in a limited number of circumstances and is subject to contrary intention, so it is really no more than a presumption. You cannot assume that it will automatically apply whenever the post is used or that it is extended into new areas:

- The postal rule will not apply if it would lead to manifest inconvenience and absurdity (*Holwell Securities* v *Hughes* (1974)). A specific example of this wide principle can be seen when the wording of the offer is inconsistent with the application of the postal rule. If I offer to sell you my iPod for £50 but state that your acceptance must be *received* by next Wednesday, then your acceptance will only bind me when I receive it and not when you post it. In *Holwell Securities* v *Hughes* an option was granted (i.e. an offer was made) to P and said to be exercisable 'by notice in writing to D within six months'. One week before the deadline a properly addressed letter containing the notice was posted by P but never received by D. The Court of Appeal agreed with the trial judge that the offer did not rule out the possibility of P giving notice by post, but the offer required 'notice . . . *to* D' and so D had displaced the postal rule and the acceptance would only be binding when it was actually received by D.
- The postal rule does not apply to revocations of offers. In *Henthorn* v *Fraser* (1892) the offeror tried to revoke his offer by post. A dilemma arises in this situation: should the revocation be effective upon posting, just as an acceptance is; or should an offeree be able to post an acceptance safe in the knowledge that there is a concluded agreement, regardless of any posted but not yet received revocation? The conflict was resolved in favour of the offeree (again) and the postal rule was said not to apply to revocations of offers or modifications. As a result of this, a posted acceptance will be binding at the moment of posting so long as a revocation has not already been received by the offeree. To apply a postal rule to revocations would deprive offerees of much of the benefit of the postal rule since they could not rely on a posted acceptance in case the offeror had in the meantime posted a revocation.
- If the postal rule applies, the fact that the acceptance never arrives will not normally matter. If it can be shown that the acceptance was posted correctly but it is proved that it was not received by the defendant then there is still a binding agreement made at the time of posting. In *Household Fire and Carriage Accident Insurance* v *Grant* (1878) Thesiger J recognized that this could lead to injustice and inconvenience but saw no other way of fairly allocating the consequences of the Post Office's error. In cases where the letter is actually received, such as *Adams* v *Lindsell*, the issue is *when* the agreement was made, not whether it was made at all.

The courts have not made a ruling on all the possible circumstances in which the postal rule may be involved. For instance, if I post my acceptance to you but then call you and revoke my acceptance before it is received then it is unclear whether my acceptance is binding. The issue is whether the postal rule will apply as it usually does to bring the time of acceptance forward so that it occurs before the letter is received by you, and most crucially in this case, before the revocation is communicated to you. On the one hand, you cannot be prejudiced if the revocation is effective and no contract is upheld because you will not know about my acceptance until it is delivered to you. In fact, the contract may have been a bad one for you and allowing the overtaking revocation would benefit you. On the other hand, I am given the opportunity to speculate at your expense and, after posting my acceptance and binding you, I could watch the market and revoke my acceptance by telephone if it is moving against me. There is no clear authority on the matter. There is the old Scottish case of *Dunmore* v *Alexander* (1830) which appears to allow a second communication to overtake the first, but the majority seemed to treat the case as revocation of an offer, not revocation of an acceptance, and there is normally no problem in revoking an offer before acceptance. The dissenting judge did treat it as an attempt to revoke an acceptance but held it was ineffective once the other party was bound, as would be the case under the postal rule once the acceptance is posted. There is in truth no obvious solution to the problem, but a good starting point might be that an acceptance effective on posting ought to be capable of withdrawal by an overtaking revocation (since that is what the offeror will generally rely upon) but the courts should be able to reach the contrary conclusion having regard to the actual facts and surrounding policy concerns in an individual case (e.g. where the revoking acceptor is clearly unfairly speculating).

This section has split communications into two types based on whether they are instantaneous or not. The courts are increasingly going to have to deal with more modern forms of communication and decide how to apply the existing law. The courts may stick with the present divide and weigh up whether the new method is more like the telex or more like the post. A fax is clearly very similar to a telex and has correspondingly been treated as an instantaneous form of communication—see *JSC Zestafoni* v *Ronly* (2004) at para. 75 which meant that the contract in that case was made in England where the fax was received. However, many new and emerging technologies are often difficult to compare to more traditional ones; an email is in some ways similar to a letter, in some ways similar to a telex and in other ways something unique—there is generally a delay or gap between sending and receipt, but in most cases the gap is very short.

Lord Wilberforce may have foreseen such problems when he remarked in *Brinkibon Ltd* v *Stahag Stahl und Stahlwarenhandel GmbH* (1983) that:

> Since 1955 the use of telex communications has been greatly expanded, and there are many variants on it . . . No universal rule can cover all such cases: they must be resolved by reference to the intentions of the parties, by sound business practice and in some cases by a judgment where the risks should lie.

The tendency increasingly seems to be to opt in most cases to treat modern methods of communication as instantaneous and therefore, in the general run of cases, as effective when received—see for example *Thomas* v *BPE Solicitors (a firm)* (2010) for the (*obiter*) adoption of this rule in relation to contracts created via email. The email was received in the inbox at approximately 6 p.m. but that still leaves the question of whether having been received, it should be treated as communicated, given that on the facts of this case, it was a Friday evening. In the context in which the email was sent, it was held that this was still within working hours (even though in fact the recipient had gone home) so the email was effectively communicated (but it was not an acceptance for other unrelated reasons). On the other hand, an email received at 2 a.m. would not normally be regarded as communicated until the start of business the next working day. Equally, there may be cases where an email is sent (but not received) well within working hours and which the sender might reasonably expect to be both received and accessed that day and it may be harsh to say that the sender cannot rely on the acceptance which the sender reasonably thought had been transmitted because for some reason the electronic receipt of the email was (unknown to the sender) substantially delayed until the following day. In such a case, notwithstanding the normal approach that an email should be subject to the instantaneous communication or 'receipt' rule, the court would perhaps still have to look at the overall context and the conduct and expectations of the parties in order to assess on whom the 'risks should lie.' See the 'Digging deeper' section at the end of the chapter for further detail.

2.7 Mode of acceptance

2.7.1 **Prescribed mode of acceptance**

An offeror has the right and ability to be picky. The person making the offer is able to introduce more or less any term that he or she likes. It follows that the offeror can dictate how an acceptance should be made in order to constitute a valid acceptance of the offer. An eccentric offeror might perhaps require any potential offeree to run to the top of a mountain and shout out the acceptance into the valley below; that is the offeror's prerogative (but may result in few takers). In general, offerors are more practical than that, but they may have very good reasons for prescribing certain modes of acceptance. We saw that in relation to the postal rule offerors can require that acceptance is *actually* communicated to them and not just placed in the post. Offerors can go further and state that acceptance by post would not be acceptable and that they must instead be contacted by text or instant message.

In practice, the courts will interpret offers prescribing certain modes of acceptance strictly and an offeror should make it very clear that acceptance will *only* be valid by the stipulated mode, if that is what the offeror intends. In other words, the offeror should indicate whether the chosen method of acceptance is *obligatory* or *permissive*. In *Manchester DCE* v *Commercial and General Investments* (1970) the claimant invited tenders including the condition that '[t]he person whose tender is accepted . . . shall be informed of the acceptance of his tender by letter sent to him by post addressed to the address given in the tender.' The claimant preferred the defendant's tender and sent a letter to the defendant's surveyor purporting to accept the tender. Because the defendant's surveyor was not the address given on the tender a question arose whether there was a valid contract. Buckley J held that the letter did constitute a valid acceptance because the conditions did not stipulate that posting a letter to the address given in the tender was the *only* means of accepting the tender, it was simply one possible way. The acceptance would be valid so long as it was by a mode that was not any more disadvantageous to the defendant than the prescribed mode. Moreover, the mode of acceptance had originally been proposed by the offeree, the claimant, and presumably for his benefit. It was therefore possible for him to waive strict compliance with it so long as he did not adversely affect the defendant. This latter reasoning is weak because there is a certain inconsistency in saying that it was the defendant who made the offer (in response to the claimant's invitation to treat) and to then also say that it was the claimant and not the defendant who should be treated as introducing the prescribed modes of acceptance despite it appearing as a term of the offer made by the defendant. Parties often negotiate at length before an offer and acceptance can be identified and, if the law is committed to an offer and acceptance approach to agreement, the important point should not be who suggested a certain term but who actually made the offer with that term in it. Moreover, a party may propose a term that will operate against the proposer, as a concession to make the contract more attractive to the other side, not necessarily because the proposer wants that actual term in the contract.

The distinction between obligatory and permissive modes of acceptance was reinforced by Lord Denning MR (using the terms 'mandatory' and 'directory') and Scarman LJ in *Yates Building Co. Ltd* v *J. R. Pulleyn & Sons (York) Ltd* (1975). The offeror had stipulated that acceptances should be made by registered post but, despite being sent by unregistered post, the offeree's acceptance was held to bind the offeror. The purpose of prescribing registered post was to protect the offeree, and seeing that the offeror had actually received the letter without delay, no one, and certainly not the offeror, was prejudiced by the use of unregistered post. The case of *Greenclose* v *National Westminster Bank* (2014), discussed in the 'Digging deeper' section at the end of this chapter, provides a contrasting illustration where a standard form contract provided that notice 'may be given in any manner set forth' in a list which did not include email. The use of one of the modes of communication specified in the list was held to be mandatory and therefore notification by email could not be effective.

Acceptance by conduct

It is obvious throughout this chapter that written and spoken words can be ambiguous, but more obscure still is the situation where the parties use no written or spoken words, but instead make their agreement by conduct. In *Brogden* v *Metropolitan Rly* (1877) we have already seen that the 'mere private act' of the Railway Company in putting the contract in its drawer could not constitute an acceptance because it was not communicated to the coal suppliers. However, a contract was eventually found by relying on the conduct of the parties in ordering coal according to the terms of the agreement and treating it as binding.

Such an approach is necessary because speech, writing and conduct are all examples of human modes of communication. To disallow acceptance by conduct would be tantamount to saying that body language is not a form of communication. The difficulty with conduct is that it is often even more difficult to interpret than written words or speech—is a person splashing around in the water waving or drowning? Consequentially this is an area in which the courts are creative and look at the conduct as a whole in order to decide whether there has been a contract. They open themselves up to the allegation of 'backwards reasoning' because, in reality, the courts are asking whether there should be a contract in these circumstances, rather than strictly following the rules of offer and acceptance. In fairness, it is difficult enough to identify an agreement from conduct never mind an individual offer and acceptance.

In *Brogden* the parties were sloppy and did not take the relatively simple steps to conclude a contract. It is not unreasonable to say that on balance their conduct did not amount to a contract. However, the contract had been entered into to avoid the recent wild fluctuations in the price of coal and both parties had relied upon the negotiated price in their latest deals. Perhaps the court felt that Brogden was simply trying to escape from what had become a bad deal for them. It wanted to prevent them from one minute relying upon the contract and then, another minute, when it suited Brogden, denying its existence and taking advantage of their own sloppiness. However, whilst a party's conduct might not always be sufficient to give rise to a contract, it might amount to a *representation* that there was a contract. The courts could then directly protect the reliance of each party through estoppel rather than having to resort to raising contractual obligations between the parties (see section 4.5).

CROSS REFERENCE
This idea of protecting reliance through estoppel is examined in Chapter 4.

Acceptance by silence

The law often makes a distinction between positive conduct and omissions—in criminal law it is an offence to push a person off a cliff but not normally an offence to omit to call a warning before someone steps off the edge. The same is true in contract law. Whilst conduct may amount to an acceptance, doing nothing, that is, silence, will rarely count. The reasoning is the same as in other areas of law; a person must not be put under a duty to act without good reason. If silence were readily accepted as a mode of acceptance in contract law, then I could go around telling everybody in sight that I would assume they had accepted my offer to buy all their property for 10 pence if I did not hear from them within one hour. This would place a duty on everybody I met to reject my offer within one hour if they did not want to be bound—clearly a ridiculous situation. Therefore, the general rule established in *Felthouse* v *Bindley* (1862) is that silence cannot constitute an acceptance. In that case a nephew and his uncle had negotiated the sale of the nephew's horse. They misunderstood each other and became confused about the agreed price. In a letter, the uncle suggested that they split the difference and that if he heard no more about it he would consider the sale done for this middle price. The nephew said nothing more to the uncle but clearly accepted the new price because he told his auctioneer to withdraw the horse from auction in which it was to be sold as he had already sold it to his uncle. The auctioneer nevertheless sold the horse in the auction by mistake and the uncle sued him for interfering with his property rights over the horse (known as the tort of conversion). It was held that the uncle had not become the owner of the horse, and therefore had no title to sue, because the contract of sale between the uncle and nephew lacked an acceptance and so never existed. You should note that it was the uncle (the offeror) who claimed there was a contract, and it was he who had introduced the idea that acceptance could be by silence—if instead it had been the nephew who sought to enforce the contract, a different result might have been appropriate.

In *Re Selectmove* (1995) a company offered to pay its tax bill in monthly instalments. The tax collector suggested that the company (offeror) could assume that he had accepted if they heard nothing more. On the facts, the tax collector (offeree) had no authority to accept the company's offer to pay in monthly instalments and so his suggestion to introduce silence as a mode of acceptance did not bind the Inland Revenue. Putting that issue on one side, the Court of Appeal saw no problem in principle with an *offeree* binding himself to speak within an ascertainable period of time if he did not want to be bound. As discussed earlier, the situation is different when an *offeror* tries to impose silence as a mode of acceptance. In reality, where the offeree says 'consider your offer accepted if you hear no more within *x* days', this can be regarded as an express but conditional acceptance which only takes effect on the expiry of a given period without an express rejection.

The courts have in any event not always refused to acknowledge acceptance simply by silence. In *Vitol* v *Norelf* (1996) Lord Steyn noted that silence could constitute acceptance in exceptional circumstances. He cited the Court of Appeal in *Rust* v *Abbey Life* (1979) where a woman's inaction over seven months was thought to be sufficient to establish her acceptance of an investment policy taken out on her behalf.

A further related situation is where the offeree takes the benefit of offered services when there had been a reasonable opportunity to reject them and reasons to know that they were offered with the expectation of compensation (a situation where silence can constitute acceptance under the US Restatement of Contracts 2d. s.69). If I watch a window cleaner clean my windows, knowing that the window cleaner expects to be paid for the work, then it is arguable that I have accepted an offer to clean my windows in return for a fee.

US Restatement of Contracts

The American Law Institute, a private institution made up of distinguished lawyers, has brought together in its (second) Restatement of Contracts the common principles of the law of contract drawn from decisions across the various States. It does not count as legislation by the government nor is it binding on the courts, but it gives us, as academics, a good idea of what other common law lawyers are thinking and how English law might choose to deal with a particular issue.

The principle that I should pay the window cleaner is clearly sound but it is far from clear that the solution lies in contract. Arguably, there is no real agreement for me to pay for the services, only an expectation on the part of the window cleaner and my awareness of that expectation. Perhaps the obligation for me to pay should arise from unjust enrichment—I have been enriched (benefited) at the window cleaner's expense (by his efforts) and the remaining question is whether it was 'unjust.' Consider whether it should matter if the window cleaner is simply 'chancing it' (like a busker who plays on the off chance that you may pay) and cleans all the windows on the street in the hope that some people will pay him, or if the cleaner regularly cleans your windows and you simply haven't got around to making an agreement.

2.8 The death of an offer

2.8.1 **Revocation of an offer**

So far we have addressed a sequence of events starting with an invitation to treat followed by an offer and ending with an acceptance. This section addresses the possibility (already mentioned in passing) of squeezing a revocation of an offer in between the offer being made and an acceptance.

The first point to note is that a revocation cannot take place after an acceptance; it is too late as an agreement has already been formed (see Figure 2.5).

We saw earlier that a revocation will not benefit from the postal rule (*Henthorn* v *Fraser* (1892)) and that it must actually be communicated to the offeree before taking effect. This communication does not necessarily have to come directly from the offeror. In *Dickinson* v *Dodds* (1876) Dodds made an offer to Dickinson that remained open until 12 June. Dodds sold the property he had offered for sale before any acceptance by Dickinson and Dickinson heard about this from a third party. Despite this knowledge, Dickinson tried to accept the offer; Dodds refused to transfer the property and Dickinson sued to enforce the contract. It was held that there was no contract between Dodds and Dickinson. The Court of Appeal thought that the communication by the third party to Dickinson was tantamount to Dodds telling him 'I withdraw the offer.' It therefore appears that anybody can communicate a revocation, although it remains to be seen how the courts would deal with facts in

Figure 2.5 Timing of a revocation

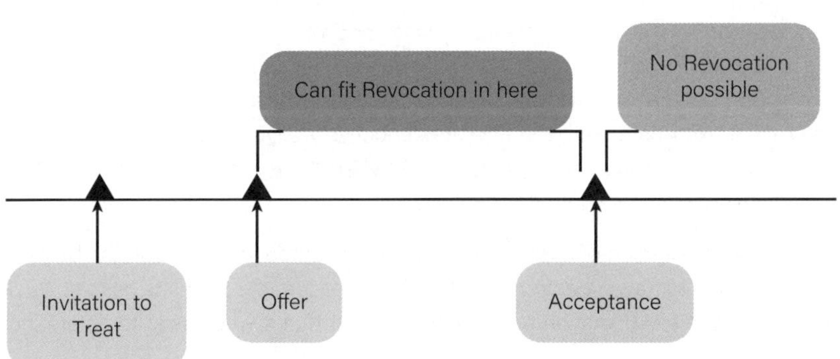

which a busybody interfered in the parties' business. Should an offeree have to take seriously every person who communicated a revocation or only those whom it is reasonable to believe?

The other issue thrown up by *Dickinson* v *Dodds* is the fact that even though the offer is stated to be open until a particular time, it can be revoked before that time—there is no enforceable promise to keep it open because there is nothing—no consideration—given in return for any such promise. Of course if the offeree pays for, or gives something in return for, the promise to keep the offer open—as in an option agreement—the promise to keep it open is then binding.

CROSS REFERENCE
See Chapter 4 for more on consideration.

Where an offer is made to the whole world or to an indeterminate number of persons at large (commonly but not exclusively in unilateral contract situations) it may be impractical or impossible to communicate the rejection to them all. In this case it is generally accepted in line with the American case of *Shuey* v *US* (1875) (promise of reward revoked seven months later) that it is enough if the offeror takes reasonable steps to publicize the revocation—which will generally involve giving the same amount of publicity to the revocation as to the original offer. It is arguably implicit in such an offer that it may be withdrawn by similar methods to its initial publication or, as Strong J said in the (US) Supreme Court, the offeree 'should have known that it could be revoked in the manner in which it was made.'

2.8.2 **Lapse of an offer**

Although an offeror is not generally bound by his statement that the offer will be open until a certain time in the sense that there is still freedom to revoke it before then, the offeror can, by such a statement, place a time limit on the offer and prevent the offeree from accepting after that time. Think of this as like a timer switch on an explosive device; once the timer hits zero, the offer self-destructs. In *Dickinson* v *Dodds* (discussed earlier) the offer was open until 'Friday 9 o'clock, A.M.' Had the offer not been revoked and had Dickinson not tried to accept it, then the offer would have been extinguished as the clock chimed 9 a.m.

Not all offers have a specific expiry date and the courts will sometimes have to decide whether a reasonable time has elapsed to avoid offers being accepted years after they were made. In *Ramsgate Victoria Hotel Co.* v *Montefiore* (1866) an offer was made in early June to purchase shares in the Hotel Company. Montefiore heard nothing until late November when he was informed that he had been allotted shares in the Hotel Company. He refused to accept them, and the court agreed that the Hotel Company's acceptance had come too late because the offer had already expired by lapse of time.

The theoretical underpinning of preventing an offer being accepted after a reasonable time is unclear (see Buckley LJ *obiter dicta* in *Manchester Diocesan Council for Education* v *Commercial and General Investments Ltd* (1969)). The lapse of an offer can be seen as an operation of the principle that an offeror may stipulate the mode of acceptance (see section 2.7.1). When there is a fixed time limit, the offeror is effectively saying that in order to accept, the offeree must do X within a particular time frame. When there is no fixed time limit the courts will imply a reasonable time limit into all offers.

Alternatively, the implication of a reasonable time limit can be explained on the basis that the offeree is presumed to have rejected the offer after a reasonable time has passed. Buckley LJ strongly preferred this explanation because he thought that it was easier to determine when an offeree should be taken to have rejected an offer than to determine the length of time for which an offeror intends to keep the offer open. He thought it was more difficult to imply a reasonable time limit on behalf of the offeror because this involved assessing what might happen in the future once the offer had been made.

2.8.3 **Rejection of an offer**

We mentioned earlier in relation to counter-offers that an offer comes to an end when it is rejected by the offeree. Common sense dictates that an offeree should be free to reject an offer for any reason whatsoever and, once rejected, the offer terminates.

2.9 Unilateral contracts

The term 'unilateral contract' is freely bandied about by writers and students alike but often not explained or understood. It should be contrasted with bilateral contracts, which are two-sided, so, you might conclude, unilateral contracts must be only one-sided! Of course, this is wrong because, like the tango and many other pleasures, it takes two to contract. What is one-sided, however, in a unilateral contract is the obligation. Only *one* party assumes an obligation, that is, promises to perform a certain act, whereas in a bilateral contract *both* parties assume obligations and make promises to perform (see Figure 2.6).

The well-known case *Carlill* v *Carbolic Smoke Ball Co.* (1893) illustrates the point well.

The contract in *Carlill* was unilateral because only one party, the company, was under any obligation when the contract was formed. By way of contrast, the typical contract for the sale of land is a classic example of a bilateral contract. Both parties commit themselves in advance: the seller promises to deliver a good title and the purchaser promises to buy the land and pay the price. Both parties assume obligations at the time of entering the contract.

Figure 2.6 The difference between bilateral and unilateral contracts

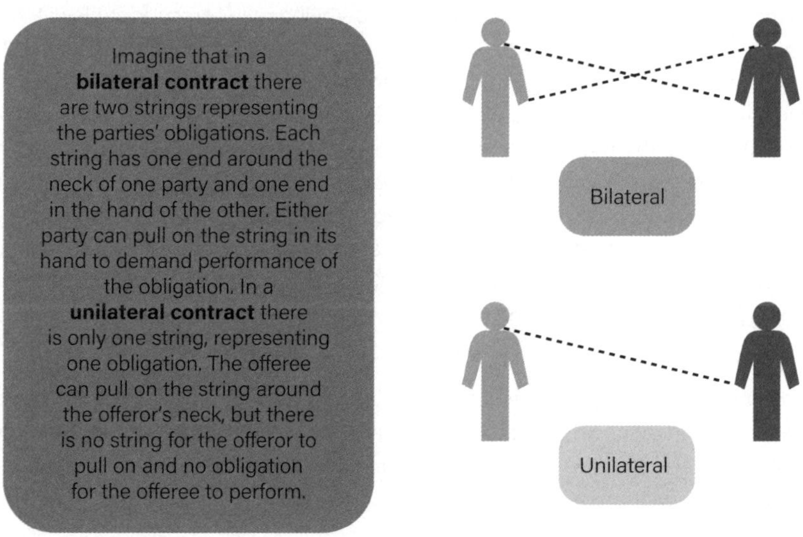

CASE CLOSE-UP

***Carlill* v *Carbolic Smoke Ball Co.* (1893)**

The Smoke Ball Co. promised £100 to anyone who bought and used its Carbolic Smoke Ball three times daily for two weeks according to the printed directions supplied with each ball, but who nonetheless caught flu. Mrs Carlill bought the smoke ball and used it as instructed but caught flu. Clearly, the company had made an offer to Mrs Carlill (and the rest of the world) and the Court of Appeal enforced its promise to pay Mrs Carlill when she caught flu. Lindley LJ dismissed the argument that the advertisement was merely a 'puff' (i.e. 'marketing-speak' and not meant to be taken seriously) on the ground that the advert expressly stated '1000l. is deposited with the Alliance Bank, Regent Street, shewing our sincerity in the matter.'

Note that Mrs Carlill, however, made no promises; she merely bought and used the smoke ball and caught flu. She was under no obligation to catch flu or to use the product and she could have stopped at any time without incurring any *liability* to anyone, although of course she had to comply with all the company's conditions before she became *entitled* to anything.

2.9.1 Offer and acceptance in unilateral contracts

You might be wondering why a promisor would ever enter a unilateral contract under which the promisor is the only party obliged to perform—what benefit is the promisor getting from the other party? However, as exemplified by the *Carlill* case discussed earlier, the promisor (the Carbolic Smoke Ball Co. in that case) receives all its benefit up front; its promise to pay £100 was premised on the condition that Mrs Carlill bought its product (and subsequently caught flu). The offer made by the Company was therefore accepted by Mrs Carlill as soon as she performed the specified condition (buying the Smoke Ball); this simultaneously placed the Company under an obligation to pay her money if she caught flu and constituted a benefit to the Company (in terms of increased revenue). This key feature of unilateral contracts means that they usually stick out like a sore thumb—being readily recognizable in the form, 'If you fulfil the following conditions' (e.g. find my lost dog, purchase my product, etc.), 'I promise to do X in return' (usually pay you a sum of money). Lord Diplock has referred to them as 'if contracts' (*Harvela Investments* v *Royal Trust Co. of Canada* (1985)). The essential point though is that 'you', the promisee, must not yourself be *promising* to perform the condition, for example promising to find the lost dog, because, if you are, the contract will be bilateral. Instead, you are simply being given the choice to perform an act which will amount to acceptance of the offer and activate the offeror's obligation 'to do X in return.' It will be quite clear in most cases that no promise is being made in return—it would be fairly rash for anyone actually to promise to find a lost item and the objective approach will normally ensure that no such promise is being given or is to be implied.

You may well be admiring the logic of this distinction between unilateral and bilateral contracts and yet wondering why, apart from for semantic reasons, the distinction needs to be made. The answer is that the normal rules for offer and acceptance are often not applicable, or only applicable with modification, to unilateral contracts.

Advertisements

The normal rules applicable to offers were modified in the *Carlill* case where, remember, an advertisement was treated as an offer even though advertisements are usually presumed to be invitations to treat. It would have been absurd to have held that Mrs Carlill only made an offer in response to the Smoke Ball Co.'s invitation to treat. The Company would be free to reject this 'offer' with impunity, having already had the benefit of seeing the conditions fulfilled (in the form of Mrs Carlill's purchase, not to mention other increases in sales from the promotion). Thus, the court in *Carlill* paid regard to the advertiser's intention and the practical commercial concerns pointing towards an offer rather than an invitation to treat.

CROSS REFERENCE
See *Partridge* v *Crittenden* at section 2.3.1.

Communication of acceptance

Similarly, the requirement of communication of acceptance, except in the sense of communication of the fact that the condition has been fulfilled, is not normally required in unilateral contracts. In the *Carlill* case, it was thus not necessary for Mrs Carlill to communicate to the Smoke Ball Co. that she had accepted the offer before using the Smoke Ball and catching flu. Bowen LJ said that an offeror may 'in his offer impliedly indicate that he does not require notification of the acceptance.' Part of the underlying rationale was that 'as notification of acceptance is required for the benefit of the person who makes the offer, the person who makes the offer may dispense with notice to himself.' This latter statement was quoted by Elias LJ in the Court of Appeal in *Attril* v *Dresdner Kleinwort Ltd* (2013) where there was an offer to bankers to set up a lucrative guaranteed bonus pool (of 400 million euros) and it was plain that the employer had 'dispensed with the need for any response to the offer at all.' This case in some ways goes even beyond waiving the need to *communicate* the acceptance and effectively says on the facts there was no need to *do anything* by way of acceptance (contrast *Carlill* where the Smoke Ball had to be used and flu to be caught) since Elias LJ went on to say of the promise in *Attril*:

> This was a promise without any disadvantage, actual or potential, of any kind to the employees. Nobody hearing the promise made in this announcement would for one moment expect the employee to be able to benefit from it only if he or she positively accepted the offer. It would be a wholly formal and unnecessary exercise; the only sensible implication is that all employees who might potentially benefit from the promise would be deemed to have accepted it.

You may be thinking that an offer of a share in a multi-million-euro bonus pool was an offer that could not be refused but legally it seems to have been an offer that did not even need to be accepted (or at least one where acceptance is deemed to have taken place)!

Returning to the more typical sort of unilateral contract, if A, the acceptor, did in fact communicate in advance an acceptance of this type of offer, for example an offer of a reward for finding lost property, A would be in danger of creating a bilateral contract whereby A agrees or promises to find the property, or at least to spend a reasonable amount of time and effort searching for it, whereas the essence of a unilateral contract is that the acceptor (the offeree) makes no promises to do anything.

This feature of unilateral contracts, distinguishing them from bilateral contracts, was crucial in *Rollerteam* v *Riley* (2017) where the question in the Court of Appeal was whether a settlement agreement to the value of several million pounds was enforceable even though it did not comply with s.2(1) of the Law of Property (Miscellaneous Provisions) Act 1989 which requires contracts for the sale or other disposition of an interest in land to be made in writing incorporating all the terms. The Act only applies to executory contracts for the future sale or disposition of land and not to a contract which immediately puts such a sale or disposition into effect. The contract was found to be a unilateral one whereby Ms Riley, the transferor, accepted the unilateral offer, which she was under no contractual obligation to do, by executing the trust declarations which transferred the land immediately. The requirement of writing for executory contracts did not therefore apply and the contract, which only came into existence once executed, was enforceable and the balance of £1.7 million was recoverable by Ms Riley and her sister.

Revocation

Furthermore, the rules for revocation are arguably different for unilateral contracts (or more accurately, for offers which have the potential to be converted into unilateral contracts by acceptance; Lord Diplock appears to have overlooked this point in *Harvela Investments* v *Royal Trust Co. of Canada* (1985) where he seems to envisage the creation of a unilateral contract before the offeree has done anything that could constitute acceptance). We say 'arguably' because this issue has not been settled definitively by the courts (and so constitutes good exam material).

The normal rule is of course that an offeror can revoke (i.e. withdraw) the offer at any time before acceptance, but this can appear to operate harshly where a person has started to perform the conditions required to complete a unilateral contract but has not yet completed them. The usual, faintly absurd, example is of A promising B £50 if B walks from London to York, or, if it is an American discussion, if B walks across the Brooklyn Bridge (which might be more realistic, the £50 perhaps being regarded as danger money!). It would certainly look unfair, when B has walked nine-tenths of the way to York (or nine-tenths of the way across the bridge), if A could suddenly appear and say 'I revoke my offer.' Thus, there are suggestions that a unilateral offer cannot be withdrawn once the other party has started to perform. This was certainly the effect of Denning LJ's approach in *Errington* v *Errington* (1952) and also Goff LJ (*obiter dicta*) sitting in the Court of Appeal in *Daulia Ltd* v *Four Millbank Nominees Ltd* (1978), although the judges reached this result by different routes. In the latter case, although Goff LJ accepted that the offeror is not bound until the conditions are performed in full, an implied obligation not to prevent the condition becoming satisfied arises as soon as the offeree starts to perform. This implied obligation must also be a unilateral promise because the offeror is effectively saying, 'If you commence performance, I will not revoke the main unilateral promise or prevent you from completing the conditions in any other way.' You should contrast this implied promise approach with that of Denning LJ in *Errington* v *Errington* where a father had bought his son and daughter-in-law a house (a generous and admirable gesture demonstrating that the current difficulties faced by first-time buyers are not new) and said (rather less generously) that it would be theirs if they paid off the mortgage. The couple were under no obligation to pay off the mortgage and so this translates into a unilateral contract of 'if you pay off the mortgage in full, I will transfer full title in the land to you.' The father died and his widow sought possession of the house, but Denning LJ held that the promise 'could not be revoked by him [the father, or his estate] once the couple entered on performance of the act.' This appears to lay down a strict rule of law that unilateral offers cannot be revoked once the offeree has commenced performance. However, on the facts of the case Denning LJ actually went on to say there was an implied promise by the father 'that so long as they paid the instalments to the building society they should be allowed to remain in possession.'

LINK TO . . .

Express and implied promise (5.3.1 Terms implied in law and in fact)

Implied promises or implied contracts are best compared to an express promise or contract. An express promise is one which is actually spoken or written down by one party, that is, expressed by him. An implied promise is not actually expressed by the party making it but the courts can attribute such a promise to that party when it is reasonable and necessary to do so; they assume that the party intended to make such a promise and would have expressed it themself had they thought about doing so.

One can distinguish promises implied in fact (as previously) from promises implied in law. This latter type of promise is not based on a party's intention at all. The courts recognize that there was no intention to make such a promise but deem there is one anyway. This 'legal fiction' is sometimes used to arrive at a conclusion that the court thinks is appropriate.

If one wishes to be creative in this area (if not, you can skip this paragraph) you could point out that there is a difference between saying that there is a strict rule of law that unilateral offers cannot be revoked after a certain stage and saying that withdrawing the offer will constitute breach of a secondary implied unilateral contract. Under the latter approach, the offer may be withdrawn in fact and in law (but in breach of the secondary promise not to revoke the offer) and an obligation to pay damages for breach of the secondary promise will arise. It is not necessarily the case that the damages for breach of that implied promise will be as high (given the duty to mitigate, see Chapter 11) as would be the case under the rule of law approach where the offer cannot be withdrawn and an offeree who had started performance when the offer was revoked would have to complete performance and sue the offeror for breach of contract (arguing that the revocation was ineffective). This is, arguably, an inefficient solution as the offeree must perform a task which the offeror no longer wants before the offeree is entitled to compensation.

The implied promise approach is more flexible and may, according to the facts of the case, not apply where the reward far outweighs the effort required for performance as it may not be reasonable in such circumstances to imply a promise not to revoke the offer midway through performance. *Luxor* v *Cooper* (1941) is an example where an estate agent was to be paid £10,000 (a very large sum back then) if a property was sold to purchasers introduced by him. The estate agent introduced a willing and able purchaser, but the defendant chose not to sell to him. The House of Lords refused to imply a term that would have the effect of binding the defendant 'not to refuse to complete the sale to a client whom the agent has introduced.' This court clearly took the view that the case was a commercial one where the agent had taken the risk, in return for a large fee for relatively little work, that he might put in effort that the defendant might ultimately render useless.

By contrast to an implied promise basis, a rule-based explanation of the restriction on revocation may appear to be less flexible and there may be a danger that it will be applied in all situations, whether or not it is reasonable to prevent the revocation of the promise midway through performance. But a rule can be expressed flexibly, that is, the rule could be that the offeror cannot revoke if the offeree has started to perform unless it is clear that the risk of revocation was one taken on by the offeree. This may be the sort of rule that the law in effect applies (or implies into the contract as a matter of law), whether or not the parties have thought about it or could be said to have impliedly agreed to it. Of course, the offeror can expressly provide for something different or more subtle (e.g. that the offer cannot be revoked after a *particular* stage of performance has been reached). An offeror however will generally be reluctant to spell out a power to revoke as it would discourage others from acting on the offer, which is why a starting rule which protects offerees is a good idea because it puts the onus on offerors expressly to exclude it. It might be argued that *Luxor* v *Cooper* is a different sort of case and is not really about the ability to revoke: the offer was never revoked; it was simply never accepted because the acceptance plainly depended on an act of the offeror (selling his house to the person introduced). The offeree knew that from the start and took the risk in light of the handsome fee.

Questions of implication in a unilateral contract involving an estate agent also arose in *Wells* v *Devani* (2019) where the claimant, the estate agent, told the seller of flats over the phone that he would act for him for 2 per cent plus VAT commission. Shortly thereafter the agent managed to find a buyer for the flats who subsequently completed the sale. The seller refused to pay the commission and the question was whether there was a contract between them as the oral conversation did not specify the event on which the commission was to be paid. This could have been any one of a number of events, including finding a buyer who contracts to buy or alternatively finding a buyer who actually completes the purchase. The Supreme Court held that the terms were objectively clear and that the seller had agreed to pay the commission to the agent on completion of the transaction by the purchaser. Alternatively, a term could be implied to that effect to give the agreement business efficacy. Thus, the estate agent was ultimately more successful in this case than in *Luxor* v *Cooper* as not only was the unilateral offer never revoked but also the offeree was allowed to complete the requested act entitling him to payment.

Another interesting unilateral contract case dealing with similar issues came before the Supreme Court in *Barton* v *Morris (in place of Gwyn-Jones)* (2023) where the defendant orally agreed to pay an unusually large sum of £1.2 million if the claimant introduced a purchaser who bought the property for more than £6.5 million. The claimant did successfully introduce a purchaser, who, however, only paid £6 million. Clearly the claimant was not entitled to the special fee of £1.2 million and the defendant argued he was entitled to nothing as the oral contract, properly interpreted, provided for a fee if, and only if, a purchase price of £6.5 million or more was obtained. The Court of Appeal disagreed with this interpretation and took the view that, the contract being silent as to whether any sort of fee would be payable if a lesser price was secured, there was room for recovery of a reasonable fee for services rendered. The reasonable fee was based on the value of the services as evidenced by other contracts which the defendant had entered into with other agents. This produced a figure of £435,000 (not bad work if you can get it, but much less than the £1.2 million fee for a sale at £6.5 million). However, on appeal to the Supreme Court, by a three to two majority, the decision of the Court of Appeal was reversed and the claimant was held to be entitled to nothing. The majority considered that the agreement only provided for a fee if there was a sale for at least £6.5 million and there were no grounds for implying a term that reasonable remuneration would be paid if there was a sale below that figure. In contrast, Lords Leggatt and Burrows in the minority thought that such a term could and should be implied. Lord Burrows also considered that even if one could not imply such a term, the law of unjust enrichment would lead to the same result so as to prevent the defendant from unjustly benefiting from the work done by the claimant, who only did that work on the basis that he would be remunerated. The latter approach would be controversial with those who consider that the law of unjust enrichment should not contradict or undermine the rights of the parties as determined by the contract, but the alternative view, shared by both minority judges, that a right to be remunerated should be implied into the contract itself is quite persuasive (and this was also the view of Davis LJ in the Court of Appeal). The case is arguably more like *Wells* v *Devani* (where a sale was completed and there was remuneration for performance of the requested act) rather than *Luxor* v *Cooper* (where no sale took place, so no actual performance and therefore no fee payable). The decision of the majority in the Supreme Court in *Barton* v *Morris (in place of Gwyn-Jones)* however is effectively that the *only* requested performance under the unilateral contract was a sale above £6.5 million and a sale below that figure did not count.

Returning to the issue of revocation of offers in unilateral contracts, you should note that losses caused by revocation are not only a phenomenon in unilateral contracts: an offeree in a bilateral contract can easily incur substantial expenses before finding out that the offer has been withdrawn or not made at all. A crucial difference is that expenses or reliance incurred in the run-up to a bilateral contract have often not been requested by the offeror in the same way as they have been in the unilateral contract. In some cases the law of unjust enrichment may again come to the rescue and create an obligation to pay the value of the work done (see *William Lacey (Hounslow) Ltd* v *Davis* (1957) where a builder did more than the usual preparatory work when he was told that he would be awarded a development contract). In bilateral contract cases involving *requested* preliminary acts, the courts appear increasingly to be prepared to find a preliminary unilateral contract which effectively binds an offeror who has requested the offeree to act in a particular way to enter into a subsequent bilateral contract with him. *Harvela Investments* v *Royal Trust Co. of Canada* (1985) is a simple example of this (unilateral contract to accept the highest bid, i.e. to enter into a bilateral contract with the highest bidder). The case of *Moran* v *University of Salford (No.* 2) (1993) is less obvious but perhaps a more interesting one. In that case there was a unilateral contract to accept a student's offer to join a course if he refrained from going to another institution and sought to enrol at Salford at the start of the term. In each case the completed unilateral contract leads to a subsequent bilateral contract and B's requested reliance is protected by restricting A's freedom to avoid the creation of the subsequent bilateral contract. *Blackpool & Fylde Aero Club* v *Blackpool Borough Council* (1990) is a similar sort of case where the unilateral contract did not go so far as involving an obligation to *accept* B's tender or offer but merely to *consider* it. If the courts are prepared to imply a promise to enter into a bilateral contract when a party has relied upon the other's request, then the idea of implying a promise not to revoke a unilateral promise which has been relied on (or of imposing a rule to a similar effect) seems unexceptional.

Digging deeper

One of the more difficult issues in this chapter has been the question of whether or to what extent the postal rule applies to modern methods of communication which are not precisely instantaneous (in the way that telex or, arguably, fax machines were) but where the delay is much less than the delay between posting a letter and its receipt (such as the relatively short delays normally involved in email communication). The tendency has been generally to move away from the postal rule and to say that the communication, for example the email, is only effective when received.

Would you expect your own email acceptance to be binding immediately after you have sent it? More significantly perhaps, would you expect to be bound by an email which had been sent to you but which had never arrived?

There does seem to have been a more general move away from the postal rule as the default rule since its heyday in the mid-nineteenth century (see Gardner, 'Trashing with Trollope' (1992) 12 OJLS 170). In relation to emails, this has been further discussed in Nolan,

'Offer and Acceptance in the Electronic Age' in Burrows and Peel (OUP, 2010) etc. and in the Singapore case of *Chwee Kin Keong* (2004) 2 SLR R 594 as well as in the UK in *Thomas* v *BPE Solicitors* discussed in section 2.6.2. The use of the post for making contracts is decreasing rapidly, as it is for many other purposes (when did you last write a letter as opposed to sending a text or email?) The significance of the postal rule in practical terms is therefore much reduced. Indeed, one might argue that the most relevant question today is not whether the postal rule applies—it rarely does—but whether under the 'receipt' rule there has indeed been effective or sufficient communication. This can be seen not only in the cases such as *The Brimnes* in section 2.6.1 (telex effective when received even though not actually communicated), and *Thomas* v *BPE* but also in the interesting case of *Greenclose* v *National Westminster Bank* [2014] EWHC 1156 (Ch).

In *Greenclose* the bank had the right to extend an agreement 'by giving notice to' Greenclose by 11.00 a.m. on 30 December. The agreement mentioned a number of methods of communication including fax but not email. The bank sent its notice by email, which arrived at 9.45 a.m. but was not read until after 11.00 a.m. The High Court held that email was not a permissible means of communication under the contract (the use of one of the prescribed methods was thus mandatory—compare the cases in section 2.7.1 and also the subsequent case of *Lehman Brothers* v *Exxonmobil Financial Services* (2016) where *Greenclose* was distinguished on this point at para. 126). Even if email had been permissible, the words 'by giving notice to' (see the similar approach to these words in *Holwell* v *Hughes* in section 2.6.2) would have required actual communication and not simply delivery of the email. It was accepted by the judge, in line with the cases mentioned earlier, that the postal rule has no application to emails, that an email (even where permitted as a mode of acceptance) is only effective on receipt and that the significant issue is what counts as effective receipt for the purposes of acceptance.

The question of when something is effectively received and communicated in relation to postal deliveries (e.g. the question of whether it is when put through your letterbox or whether it is only when you have actually opened and read it) rarely arose in the past because the default rule was that the letter was already effective when posted. Therefore, what counts as receipt did not usually come into it. However, with the significant reduction in the use of the postal rule, the meaning of receipt now becomes crucial. In particular, it will often be crucial to decide whether receipt is satisfied merely by delivery or whether there must be actual communication (see now the *Lehman Brothers* case at paras 138–156). Just as with the choice under the postal rule between sending and receipt, the choice between delivery and actual communication as to what counts as effective acceptance will vary according to the objectively reasonable expectations of the parties on the particular facts and a judgement of where the risks should lie (as per Lord Wilberforce in *Brinkibon* in section 2.6.2).

What does this reference to 'where the risks should lie' mean? Suppose you have sent out offers by email to be accepted by Sunday and I accept your offer by means of an email that is delivered into your inbox on Sunday morning. If you don't read the email until Monday morning, because you have not recovered from your Saturday night partying until then, that is a risk that you took and therefore the risk should lie with you. The acceptance should clearly be valid due to the time of its delivery on Sunday, within the deadline, when you really ought to have read it. However, if I do not send my email of acceptance until two minutes to midnight on Sunday and it arrives in your inbox one minute before midnight (by which time you will obviously be tucked up in bed), it is much less clear that I have validly accepted. I have arguably taken the risk that you will not now see any emails until Monday morning and that risk should now lie with me. Therefore, my email would on this basis be too late since, although it was delivered on Sunday (just about), it was not effectively communicated until it was (quite reasonably) read by you on Monday morning.

Summary

A contract requires that the parties reach an agreement which normally consists of a matching offer and acceptance.

1. Objective approach

The courts generally look at what A appeared to mean based on what A said and did rather than what A might have meant in A's own mind.

2. Agreement as offer and acceptance

The courts normally insist on identifying an offer followed by a matching acceptance.

Offers are distinguished from invitations to treat by looking at the objective intentions of the parties. If these are unclear, certain presumptions can be used.

3. Acceptance

An acceptance must mirror the offer made or it may be held to be a counter-offer and rejection, putting an end to the offer.

Acceptance must generally be communicated to the party who made the offer but a posted/dispatched acceptance is normally effective once posted/dispatched (the 'postal rule') without any actual communication to or receipt by the party who made the offer.

Parties may accept an offer by their conduct but usually not by silence.

4. Death of an offer

An offer can be revoked at any time by the party who made the offer, even via a third party (in appropriate circumstances) but the revocation must be communicated to the other side before acceptance, and the postal rule does not apply.

An offer may expire by elapse of time, either expressly or by implication. A party is free to reject an offer for any reason.

5. Unilateral contracts

This 'if you do X, I'll do Y' type of promise/contract is unilateral or one-sided in that only the person making the offer promises/undertakes a contractual obligation—the recipient of the offer may choose to perform the requested 'X' but never promises to do so and thus there is an obligation on one side only (the offeror).

An offer/promise may be more readily found to have been made if it requests such a unilateral act rather than inviting a counter-promise.

Acceptance is made by actually doing 'X' as requested by the offeror, thereby completely performing one side of the contract. Revocation is unlikely to be permitted once the recipient of the offer has commenced performance of the requested 'X', although the theoretical basis for this—a strict rule of law or an implied secondary unilateral promise—is uncertain.

Questions

1. 'The Offer and Acceptance model is flawed—only an agreement is necessary.' Discuss.
2. 'Contractual obligations are not based upon the consent of the parties because the courts look at what they said and did and not what they actually meant.' Discuss.
3. How can a seller ensure that he or she only makes an invitation to treat and not an offer? How do the presumptions for advertisements, displays, auctions and tenders affect the seller's position?
4. When should an acceptance sent by email be binding? Justify your answer.
5. 'A party who starts to perform a unilateral contract does so at their own risk.' Discuss.

Further reading

Books

Chen-Wishart, M, *Contract Law*, 7th edn (Oxford University Press, 2022) ch 2 (not sections 2.6 and 2.7).

McKendrick, E, *Contract Law: Text, Cases, and Materials*, 11th edn (Oxford University Press, 2024) ch 3.

O'Sullivan, J, and Hilliard, J, *The Law of Contract*, 11th edn (Oxford University Press, 2024) ch 2.

Articles

Ball, S, 'Work carried out in pursuance of letters of intent: Contract or restitution' (1983) 99 LQR 572.

Gardner, S, 'Trashing with Trollope: A deconstruction of the postal rules in contract' (1992) 12 OJLS 170.

Howarth, W, 'The meaning of objectivity in contract' (1984) 100 LQR 265.

Nolan, D, 'Offer and acceptance in the electronic age' in *Contract Formation and Parties* (Burrows and Peel eds, Oxford University Press, 2010) 61.

Rawlings, R, 'The battle of the forms' (1979) 42 MLR 715.

Scott, KN, 'The auction house: With or without reserve' [2001] LMCLQ 334.

Vorster, JP, 'A comment on the meaning of objectivity in contract' (1987) 103 LQR 274.

3 Certainty and the intention to create legal relations

LEARNING OBJECTIVES

This chapter will help you to:

- realize that vague or incomplete agreements cannot normally form the basis of a contract;
- recognize that the parties to an agreement must intend to create a legal relationship in order to form a contract;
- apply a presumption of intention in domestic and commercial agreements;
- distinguish between executory and executed agreements; and
- understand that vague or incomplete agreements are more likely to be interpreted as sufficiently certain when they have been performed (executed).

Introduction

Most undergraduate courses start by teaching that an agreement is necessary to form a contract, then move on to analyse the dual requirements of offer and acceptance in depth, followed by consideration. Two further requirements, certainty and the intention to create legal relations, often take a back seat and are tagged on to the end of a reading list. This chapter will be short, but its importance should not be underestimated: in practice, large sums of money can hinge on whether an agreement is uncertain and void, and on whether there was an intention to create a legal relationship.

The initial section on certainty could form part of Chapter 2 on the formation of an agreement as—even if the requirements of offer and acceptance are met—an uncertain agreement is no agreement at all. The requirement that the parties intend to create a legal relationship is a safety catch which prevents people from stumbling unwittingly into a contractual situation.

Agreements and contracts

'Agreements' and 'contracts' are often used interchangeably in the law. Reference is sometimes made to a 'contract' but later it is revealed that in fact the contract is void and never existed (e.g. due to lack of intention to create legal relations). It is more accurate to say that only an agreement existed (i.e. that there was offer and acceptance) which did not give rise to contractual obligations or a contract. Rather than writing about 'void contracts' (which have never existed as contracts and so are 'non-contracts') we will refer in this Part of the book to agreements which may or may not give rise to contracts. If the agreement lacks one of the necessary ingredients for creating a contract (e.g. it is not intended to create legal relations or lacks consideration) then it will never form a contract and its description simply as an agreement will be appropriate. If all of the creation requirements are met then the agreement may form a contract and it will be appropriate to then describe it as such. Later on in this book you will come across voidable, rescinded and terminated contracts. Unlike 'void contracts', these actually are (or were originally) valid contracts, but the courts have decided to unravel or cancel them for some reason. The important difference is that a contract has been formed in these cases, whereas a 'void contract' never even gets beyond being, at most, an agreement and is possibly not even that if it turns out that the 'agreement' lacked certainty, which is the first issue we will look at.

3.1 Certainty

This section first deals with cases where the parties have used ambiguous or unclear language and then looks at cases where the parties have deliberately left terms to be agreed at a later date. In the former cases, the agreement is often described as 'vague' whilst in the latter cases it is described as 'incomplete'. You should not worry unduly about separating these two types in your mind because the cases on vagueness always shade into incompleteness. By way of example, if an agreement is vague about the price to be paid then it is in reality incomplete as it lacks a term specifying the price. By contrast, an agreement can be incomplete without being vague if the parties agree to come to an agreement at a later date. Such a contract is clear on the face of it as to how the price should be determined (by agreement of the parties) but, as we will see later, the courts are reluctant to enforce such an agreement unless there is a mechanism included for completing the agreement in the event that the parties fail to agree on the price.

One danger in this area is to think of an agreement as a thing that must be certain from the outset. In reality, the focus is on whether any obligations allegedly created by the agreement are workable, in the sense that they can be enforced by the courts. You will therefore come across some agreements where the terms are initially uncertain but are allowed to stand on the basis that the court feels that it would be able to enforce the obligations created in the event of a breach.

3.1.1 **Vague agreements**

In *Scammell* v *Ouston* (1941) the buyer purchased a lorry with the price to be paid 'on hire purchase terms' over two years. The problem centred on the meaning of 'hire purchase terms.' The House of Lords held that the agreement was uncertain and therefore the contract argued for was void (i.e. did not exist). Viscount Maugham conceded that in some cases it was possible to imply terms that would explain what 'hire purchase terms' meant, but it was impossible to do so in this case. He thought that the words had such a wide range of possible meanings that it was impossible to arrive at a single one.

It is useful to compare *Scammell* v *Ouston* with *Hillas & Co. Ltd* v *Arcos Ltd* (1932) where an agreement to buy and sell timber contained two important terms. The first was that the buyer would buy 22,000 standards of 'fair specification.' The second was that the buyer was granted an **option** to buy '100,000 standards.'

option
An irrevocable promise by one party to another, who may call for performance of the promise at any time up to a specified date.

When the buyers tried to exercise their option (i.e. called on the sellers to perform) the sellers did not have any timber to sell to them and so the buyers sued for breach of the option. Much of the debate centred on the meaning of '100,000 standards' in the option. The phrase was undeniably vague, but would the court imply terms explaining what '100,000 standards' meant?

The House of Lords accepted that the agreement was complete and binding. Lord Tomlin thought that the option implicitly referred to 100,000 standards of fair specification, like the first term for the sale of 22,000 standards of fair specification, even though it did not expressly say so. He also thought that the meaning of 'fair specification' was itself vague, although it was again possible to imply a meaning to make it sufficiently certain on the basis that the parties must have attributed some meaning to 'fair specification' because they had performed the first term relating to the sale and purchase of 22,000 standards of fair specification. In other words, by accepting the first batch of timber, the buyers must have accepted that it was of 'fair specification' and therefore attributed a meaning to 'fair specification.' Lord Tomlin also looked at evidence of how the timber trade was conducted so that he could imply a specific meaning into the phrase 'fair specification.' He came to the conclusion that 'fair specification' meant:

> that the 22,000 standards are to be satisfied in goods distributed over kinds, qualities, and sizes in the fair proportions having regard to the output of the season 1930, and the classifications of that output in respect of kinds, qualities, and sizes. That is something which if the parties fail to agree can be ascertained just as much as the fair value of a property . . . Thus there is a description of the goods which if not immediately yet ultimately is capable of being rendered certain.

LINK TO . . .

Incompleteness (Chapter 3, section 3.1.2)

Why do you think it was important that the standard of the timber could be ascertained even if the parties failed to agree (see the last line of Lord Tomlin's conclusion quoted earlier)? Refer to section 3.1.2 on incomplete agreements where we look at cases where the parties agree to come to an agreement without providing any other mechanism for completing their agreement if they fail to agree.

LINK TO . . .

Executory and executed agreements (Chapter 3, section 3.3)

Why was so much weight placed on the fact that the parties in *Hillas* had already performed the part of the agreement requiring the sale of 22,000 standards of fair specification? Note that Lord Tomlin recognized that if 'fair specification' could not be made certain then both the agreement to sell 22,000 standards of fair specification and the option to buy 100,000 standards could not give rise to contractual obligations. What kind of problems would there be if the sale of 22,000 standards of fair specification (which had already taken place) was held not to be a binding obligation?

The low cost flights industry provides two more recent examples of apparently vague terms being treated as sufficiently certain in the Court of Appeal. Firstly, in *Durham Tees Valley Airport* v *bmibaby* (2010), the court found in favour of the airport that a promise by the airline to establish a '2 based aircraft operation' for ten years at the airport was not void for uncertainty even though this did not impose a liability to operate a specific number of flights. The second example is *Jet2.com* v *Blackpool Airport* (2012), where it was the airline that won. The Court of Appeal found that a promise by the airport to 'use their best endeavours to promote Jet2.com's low cost services . . . and use all reasonable endeavours to provide a cost base that will facilitate Jet2.com's low cost pricing' was binding. This meant that after four years of allowing Jet2 to operate some flights outside normal opening hours, it was a breach of the best endeavours clause for the airport to suddenly say it was no longer allowed. As is often the case (see section 3.3 on executed agreements), the fact that the term had been given meaning to in a contract that had actually been operating for four years already was an important consideration. As Longmore LJ put it:

> The 'out of normal hours' use of the airport caused no problems for four years; reasonable endeavours had been used to promote Jet2's low cost services. [The airport's] sudden change of stance needed a justifiable explanation. The judge did not think there was one and neither do I.

THINKING POINT

It is interesting to note that the losers in both of these cases have each since gone out of business (bmibaby Limited in September 2012 and Blackpool Airport in October 2014). That this happened (in each case two years after the relevant decision) may or may not be coincidental. Do you think it tells us anything about what drives commercial parties to litigation in the first place and/or what may be the effects of losing a case thought worth litigating up to Court of Appeal level? Read Lewison J's dissenting judgment in the *Blackpool Airport* case where he starts almost prophetically by noting that it would be possible, but unusual, for a commercial organization to promise to run a loss-making business for a period as long as fifteen years.

In *Walford* v *Miles* (1992) the House of Lords had to decide whether an agreement to negotiate and an agreement not to negotiate could be enforceable. The seller agreed in principle to sell its business to the buyer. Whilst they negotiated the exact terms of the sale the parties agreed to a 'lock out' agreement that prevented the seller from negotiating with any other party, therefore giving the buyer exclusive access to the seller. The seller subsequently changed its mind about selling to the buyer and sold to a third party instead, prompting the buyer to bring an action for breach of the 'lock out' agreement. The buyer also argued that there was an implied term in the 'lock out' agreement that the seller would negotiate in good faith with the buyer. The buyer therefore argued that the seller had made two separate promises giving rise to the following obligations: (1) an express obligation not to negotiate with any other party; and (2) an implied obligation to negotiate with the buyer in good faith (see Figure 3.1).

Lord Ackner thought that the implied 'agreement to negotiate in good faith' was unenforceable for uncertainty. Negotiating in good faith is intrinsically vague because a crucial part of any negotiation is the ability to leave for any reason whatsoever. If there are no proper or improper reasons for leaving the negotiating table then it is not possible to judge whether a party has negotiated in good faith once negotiations have broken down. Of course, you may like to point out that, whilst the propriety of some negotiating positions might be borderline and uncertain, there are plenty of examples of outright bad faith which can be identified (e.g. if a party simply does not turn up to negotiate).

Figure 3.1 *Walford* v *Miles* (1992)

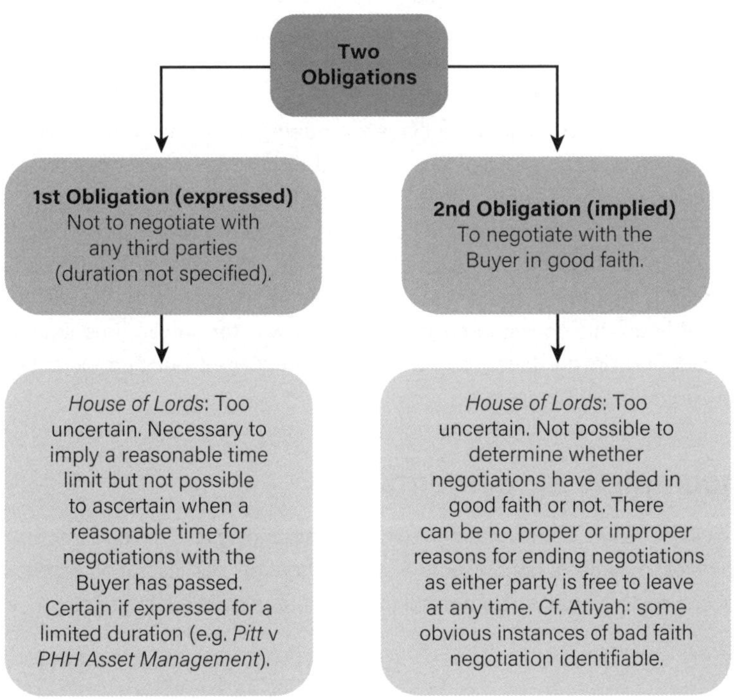

THINKING POINT

Imagine an agreement in which the parties laid down the minimum standard required from each party in a negotiation. Would a breach of one of these minimum standards—say, an obligation to be present to negotiate at 9 a.m. on a particular date—be enforceable? When the parties simply agree to negotiate in good faith without expressly laying out the standards for the negotiation is it fair to imply that they are asking the courts to apply minimum standards to their negotiations, even if the court cannot define with precision exactly what good faith negotiation requires of the parties (if anything)? See now the discussion by Teare J in the *Emirates Trading* case later in the chapter.

Lord Ackner then addressed the validity of the 'lock out' agreement itself. He thought that negative agreements not to negotiate with a third party were enforceable if they were for a definite duration. The reason for this is linked to the earlier discussion relating to when it is proper for a party to walk away from negotiations. An indefinite 'lock out' agreement would—by implication—last for a 'reasonable time' and a 'reasonable time' can only be determined by looking at when good faith negotiations could properly come to an end. In other words, a reasonable time for the seller to refrain from negotiating with other parties rested on what was a reasonable time for the seller to negotiate in good faith with the buyer. As discussed earlier, the duty to negotiate in good faith is vague because there are no proper reasons for ending negotiations and, as a consequence, an indefinite agreement not to negotiate is also vague. The 'lock out' in *Walford* v *Miles* was void for uncertainty as it was not for a fixed period, but a 'lock out' agreement for a fixed two-week period was upheld in *Pitt* v *PHH Asset Management Ltd* (1993). Furthermore, *Walford* v *Miles* was distinguished in *Emirates Trading Agency LLC* v *Prime Mineral Exports Private Ltd* (2014) where a dispute resolution clause, requiring the parties first to 'seek to resolve the dispute or claim by friendly discussion' and only to refer the dispute to arbitration after four weeks, was held enforceable. It was not uncertain in that it had 'an identifiable standard of fair, honest and genuine discussions aimed at resolving the dispute' and the objective was 'to avoid what might otherwise be an expensive and time consuming arbitration'. Again it should be noted that the obligation, effectively to discuss in good faith, was enforceable on this occasion partly because it was for a fixed time, four weeks, and, as the court found on the facts, had actually been carried out and executed (thus the arbitration could legally begin).

3.1.2 Incomplete agreements

The courts will not enforce an agreement which is missing essential elements. *May & Butcher* v *The King* (1929) provides a good example of this where the parties put off agreeing a price at the time of contracting but instead agreed to agree the price at a later date.

CASE CLOSE-UP

***May & Butcher* v *The King* (1929)**

May & Butcher agreed to buy surplus tentage from the Disposals Board (a representative of the Crown charged with selling off surplus equipment produced for the First World War). The agreement provided that the price and the dates for payment were to be agreed from time to time between the Board and the buyer.

The House of Lords held that the agreement was incomplete at the time of its creation as it lacked a price and payment schedule. The argument ran that if you had asked the buyer and the Board how much they would pay and receive and when, they would not have been able to tell you. Viscount Dunedin accepted that an agreement may leave something to be determined in the future—for instance, by a third party—and still be certain but it must not rely upon the parties coming to an agreement in the future. On the facts, the incomplete agreement could not be made to work because it contained an agreement for the parties to agree the price at a later date—an agreement to agree.

The principle in *May & Butcher*—that an agreement to agree is unenforceable—was reaffirmed by Lord Denning MR in *Courtney and Fairbairn Ltd* v *Tolaini Brothers (Hotels) Ltd* (1975) where the parties agreed to negotiate fair and reasonable contract sums to pay for the construction work to be done. The construction contract was incomplete and void for uncertainty because the price was to be agreed between the parties at a later date.

The second important point to come out of *May & Butcher* relates to the interpretation of s.8 of the Sale of Goods Act ('SoGA') 1979. SoGA 1979 regulates the sale of goods (i.e. 'things', such as televisions, cars and other physical objects).

STATUTE

SoGA 1979 s.8

1) The price in a contract of sale may be fixed by the contract, or may be left to be fixed in a manner agreed by the contract, or may be determined by the course of dealing between the parties.
2) Where the price is not determined as mentioned in point (1) the buyer must pay a reasonable price.
3) What is a reasonable price is a question of fact dependent on the circumstances of each particular case.

Viscount Dunedin (applying SoGA 1893, a predecessor of SoGA 1979) thought that s.8(2) only applied to cases where the contract was silent on the price, i.e. where it was not fixed, left to be fixed in the future or to be determined by course of dealing, as permitted by s.8(1). On the facts of *May & Butcher* the agreement was not silent on the price as it provided that the price was to be agreed from time to time and so s.8(2) could not apply. We saw earlier that this agreement to agree left the contract incomplete and uncertain.

LINK TO . . .

Vagueness (Chapter 3, section 3.1.1)

Is it necessary for the courts to say that an agreement with a term left to be agreed in the future does not form a contract (i.e. any purported contract is void) or could the courts imply an agreement for a reasonable price in the event of no agreement?

The case of *Hillas* discussed in section 3.1.1 Vague agreements was very similar to *May & Butcher* in the sense that a 'fair specification' was implicitly something which the parties would have to agree at a later date. The court in *Hillas* was prepared to imply a meaning into the phrase 'fair specification' but the court in *May & Butcher* would not imply a price.

One distinction worth making is that the parties in *May & Butcher* expressly left the price to be agreed between themselves. The courts could be accused of rewriting the parties' contract and overriding their freedom of contract if they implied an agreement for a reasonable price because this is clearly not something agreed by the parties. Less damage is done to the parties' freedom of contract in a case such as *Hillas* where there was never actually an express agreement between the parties to agree in the future the meaning of 'fair specification.'

The courts will accept an agreement to agree as workable when the parties provide a mechanism for completion in the event of their not being able to agree. Such an agreement is therefore incomplete from the outset (because the price has not yet been decided) but the courts are happy to enforce obligations arising from the agreement because they are capable of being ascertained. In *Foley v Classique Coaches Ltd* (1934) the buyer agreed to buy all its petrol from the seller 'at a price to be agreed by the parties in writing and from time to time.' At this stage the agreement looked suspiciously like the one in *May & Butcher*, but a later term provided that 'if any dispute or difference shall arise on the subject matter or construction of this agreement the same shall be submitted to arbitration.' The Court of Appeal was happy to enforce the obligations under the agreement because the parties had provided a mechanism (i.e. referral to arbitration) for completing their agreement if they were unable to agree. Their obligation to pay could be ascertained even if the parties failed to agree because an arbitrator would set the price. Interestingly, the agreement in *May & Butcher* contained a similar arbitration clause which read: 'It is understood that all disputes with reference to or arising out of this agreement will be submitted to arbitration.' Viscount Dunedin thought that this clause did not provide a completion mechanism in the event of there being no agreement over the price and payment schedule because it referred only to 'disputes.' In his own words, the problem in the case was 'a failure to agree, which is a very different thing from a dispute.' The slightly wider

Figure 3.2 Summary of courts' approach to incomplete prices

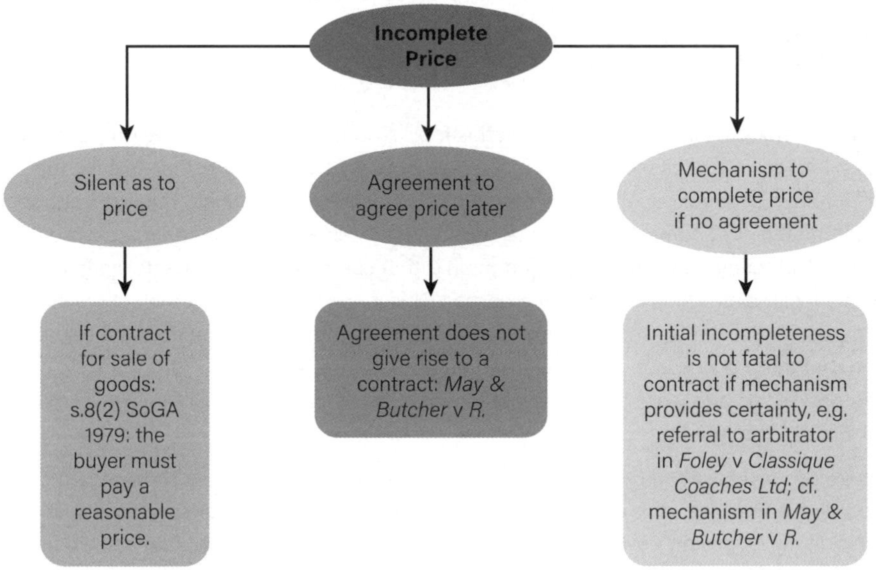

wording in *Foley* to include disputes or differences arising on the subject matter or construction of the agreement can perhaps justify the different conclusions (as summarized in Figure 3.2), but section 3.3.2 discusses a more secretive motive.

A final point to note is that SoGA 1979 provides a solution if the mechanism for ascertaining the price fails in a contract for the sale of goods.

STATUTE

SoGA 1979 s.9

1) Where there is an agreement to sell goods on the terms that the price is to be fixed by the valuation of a third party, and he cannot or does not make the valuation, the agreement is avoided; but if the goods or any part of them have been delivered to and appropriated by the buyer he must pay a reasonable price for them.
2) Where the third party is prevented from making the valuation by the fault of the seller or buyer, the party not at fault may maintain an action for damages against the party at fault.

We can see that if an arbitrator appointed by the parties fails to ascertain a price there will be no contract. This is common sense; Parliament does not want the courts to have to enforce obligations to pay a price when that price has not been ascertained and is therefore incomplete. However, if the agreement has been partly performed (i.e. the goods delivered) then Parliament has quite sensibly refused to scrap the agreement but instead has provided that a reasonable price is payable.

3.2 An intention to create a legal relationship

If you are a student looking for rules, then this topic contains two, but they are only prima facie or 'first impression' rules which can be reversed in appropriate circumstances. Like the rules of offer and acceptance, such rules are called (rebuttable) presumptions. The first (rebuttable) presumption is that domestic and social agreements lack an intention to create a legal relationship. The second (rebuttable) presumption is that commercial agreements are intended to create a legal relationship between the parties. This means that in a commercial relationship, the burden is on the person claiming that there is no intention to create legal relations to prove that there is no such intention. In *Attrill* v *Dresdner Kleinwort Ltd* (2013) the employers could not do this and were therefore liable to provide the promised multi-million-euro bonus pool. Elias LJ thought that:

> there was a very strong presumption that a promise of this nature would be intended to be legally enforceable . . . this was a promise made in the context of a pre-existing legal relationship. In my judgment, viewed objectively, the natural inference would be that any promises made to staff relating to the terms of their employment would take effect in the same way as other contractual terms.

This quotation reminds us that, in line with the general approach to contractual formation, the court will ascertain the parties' intentions objectively and not by reference to the actual state of each party's mind; see Longmore LJ in *Maple Leaf Macro Volatility Master Fund & Anor* v *Rouvroy* (2009), para. [17]. In that case, the Court of Appeal upheld the first instance judge's finding that there was a binding contract despite the fact that the judge had found that one of the parties did not subjectively intend to be bound when it signed the contract. In contrast to the *Dresdner Kleinwort* case, in *Blue* v *Ashley* (2017), a promise by Mike Ashley (the owner of Sports Direct) to Jeffrey Blue, a consultant employed by him, that he would pay him £15 million if Mr Blue could get the share price of Sports Direct to double in price was held not to be binding. Although the parties were in a commercial relationship with one another, the promise was made in a public house when several pints of beer had been consumed and was in the course of a jocular conversation with others. As Leggatt J put it, 'no reasonable person present in the Horse and Groom . . . would have thought that the offer to pay Mr Blue £15 million was serious and was intended to create a contract.' (It also failed for uncertainty since there was no period specified within which the share price had to double, the trial judge having rejected Mr Blue's evidence that the period was specified as within three years. In the event, the share price doubled in just twelve months, leaving the claimant ultimately feeling rather blue!)

3.2.1 **Domestic agreements**

In *Balfour* v *Balfour* (1919) Mr Balfour promised to pay his wife, Mrs Balfour, £30 per month whilst his government post abroad kept them apart. Mrs Balfour sued Mr Balfour for her monthly allowance after they had made their separation permanent. Two of the three Lords Justices in the Court of Appeal thought that there was no contract on the basis that Mrs Balfour had not provided consideration for the promise of Mr Balfour, but the third, Atkin LJ, expressly based his refusal to enforce the agreement on the lack of an intention to create a legal relationship: 'I think it is plainly established that the promise here was not intended by either party to be attended by legal consequences.'

CROSS REFERENCE

See Chapter 4 for a discussion of Consideration.

Neither Mr Balfour nor Mrs Balfour had expressly said that they did not intend to create a legal relationship and so we can say that Atkin LJ presumed this to be the case. In arriving at this presumption, his Lordship was plainly influenced by the fact that the two parties were married: '[It] is quite common, and the natural and inevitable result of the relationship of husband and wife, that the two spouses should make agreements between themselves . . . To my mind these agreements, or many of them, do not result in contracts at all.'

This emphasizes the point that married couples make agreements in order to get on with their everyday lives rather than to create legal relationships. Further, his Lordship thought that if all such agreements gave rise to legal obligations, 'then the small courts of this country would have to be multiplied one hundredfold.' This type of argument is commonly known as the 'floodgates argument' and is put to work across all areas of law. The fear is that too many cases would be brought before the courts if domestic agreements were legally binding; the 'floodgates' would burst open under the weight of proceedings. The floodgates argument rarely amounts to anything more than scaremongering unless it is backed up with reliable evidence: do you really think that there would be a huge influx of cases where husbands sued their wives and friends argued their disputes across a courtroom? Atkin LJ also made it very clear that the law had no business interfering with family affairs. He said: 'The parties themselves are advocates, judges, courts, sheriff's officer and reporter. In respect of these promises each house is a domain into which the king's writ does not seek to run, and to which his officers do not seek to be admitted.'

The presumption is therefore based partly on the likely intentions of the parties and partly on the court's reluctance to adjudicate on domestic matters. This policy of non-interference in the domestic sphere is independent from the parties' intention and, if the presumption is based on this ground, you might argue that it is more accurate to say that the intention to create legal relations is deemed rather than presumed.

The presumption is weaker when the parties are splitting up their property after the end of their relationship. In such a situation their agreements are not as commonly 'the natural and inevitable result of the relationship' but instead are made in order to create specific rights between the parties. This is illustrated by the Court of Appeal's decision in *Merritt* v *Merritt* (1970).

CASE CLOSE-UP

***Merritt* v *Merritt* (1970)**

Mr Merritt left Mrs Merritt for another woman and moved out of the matrimonial home. They met subsequently to sort out their financial affairs. Mr Merritt promised to pay Mrs Merritt £40 per month and to transfer his share in the house once she had paid off the mortgage. With typical clarity, Lord Denning MR distinguished the facts from *Balfour* v *Balfour*, stating that in this case 'it may be safely presumed that they intend to create legal relations.' He pointed out that in *Balfour* v *Balfour* the parties were living happily together at the time of the promise, whereas Mr and Mrs Merritt's agreement arose after a breakdown in their marriage. His Lordship noted that '[t]hey then bargain keenly.'

The position of separated couples is more akin to businessmen approaching the negotiating table than partners sorting out their domestic affairs. The presumption is accordingly rebutted; or (which amounts to the same result) there is no overriding policy reason to deem that there is no intention to create legal relations.

The presumption is not limited to married couples. Any domestic or social arrangement will attract the presumption to various degrees. In *Balfour* v *Balfour* Atkin LJ spoke about agreements to take a walk together or of hospitality. Cohabiting couples also make everyday agreements which are more attributable to their relationship than their desire to create binding obligations. The key point in these situations is that the agreement is underpinned by the obligations of trust inherent in the relationship between the parties; they do not intend and do not need to create any legal obligations.

It is important to remember that, as in *Merritt* v *Merritt*, the presumption against an intention to create a legal relationship can be rebutted; it is only an initial guess as to what the parties intended and, if the circumstances suggest that two domestic or social parties did in fact intend to create legal relations, the presumption will be reversed. We will see in section 3.3.2 that detrimental reliance by one party was a sufficient reason to rebut the presumption in *Parker* v *Clark* (1960). Furthermore, in *Radmacher* v *Granatino* (2010) a majority of the Supreme Court considered that the parties to increasingly common 'ante-nuptial' agreements can be thought to intend that they should be of legal effect.

3.2.2 **Commercial agreements**

As noted earlier, there is an opposite presumption that commercial agreements are intended to create legal relationships. Generally speaking, commercial parties expect to be able to enforce an agreement if the other side does not perform its promise and recover any losses suffered as a result of the breach. That is not to say that commercial parties will always sue on a breach—they rarely do as it is generally better for the business relationship (and cheaper) to solve the dispute amicably—but, as a last resort, they expect the protection of the law (and that is why for particularly valuable transactions they pay lawyers large sums of money to draft their contracts—which is one reason why there are so many law courses and so many lawyers!).

As was the case with the social and domestic agreements, the presumption may be displaced, for example by an express statement in the agreement that it is not to create a legal relationship. In *Rose & Frank Co.* v *J. R. Crompton Bros* (1925) the agreement was binding in honour only because the parties agreed that:

> This arrangement is not entered into, nor is this memorandum written as a formal and legal agreement, and shall not be subject to legal jurisdiction in the Law Courts of either the United States or England, but it is only a definite expression and record of the purpose and intention of the three parties concerned, to which they each honourably pledge themselves with the fullest confidence—based on past business with each other—that it will be carried through by each of the three parties with mutual loyalty and friendly co-operation.

Scrutton LJ rejected the first instance judge's reasoning that an agreement not to create legal relations was contrary to public policy for ousting the jurisdiction of the courts. He made it clear that the courts should follow the expressed intentions of the parties and only presume an intention when the parties had not made their intentions clear. This clearly shows that the will of the parties—their freedom to contract—will prevail over the desire of some judges to control all commercial agreements. You might be wondering why people in business bother to make an agreement if it has no legal effect—is it worth the paper it is written on? In banking practice 'comfort letters' are used literally; they provide comfort to lenders that they will get their money back. A borrower's parent company (i.e. its main shareholder) will usually be saying something along the lines of 'we will try to be a really good parent company and make sure that our subsidiary pays all your money back.' The bank does not expect to be able to sue on this agreement, and should insist on receiving a **guarantee** if it wants to have legally enforceable rights against the parent company.

guarantee
A binding promise made by A to B to perform C's obligations owed to B if C fails to perform (e.g. C's failure to pay a debt to B).

In *Kleinwort Benson Ltd* v *Malaysia Mining Corp.* (1989) the following wording in a comfort letter was held not to contain an intention to create legal relations: 'It is our policy to ensure that the business of [our subsidiary] is at all times in a position to meet its liabilities to you under the above arrangements.' Companies must be careful not to promise to 'guarantee' or 'undertake' to do anything as this is more likely to be interpreted as a binding agreement.

The intention behind certain commercial agreements is sometimes tricky to classify.

In *Esso Petroleum Ltd* v *Commissioners of Customs and Excise* (1976) the House of Lords had to decide whether the free World Cup coins offered to drivers who bought four gallons or more of petrol were produced for sale. If they were then Esso had to pay tax on them (hence the presence of Customs and Excise). The Law Lords considered whether there was a contract in relation to the coins (there was obviously one in relation to the petrol) between Esso and drivers who bought more than four gallons. Lord Simon, Lord Fraser and Lord Wilberforce thought that the parties intended to create legal relations because, in the words of Lord Simon, 'the whole transaction took place in a setting of business relations.' Lord Russell and Viscount Dilhorne thought that there was no intention to create legal relations because it was simply unnecessary in order for the 'free coins' scheme to work. It was in the interest of Esso to abide by its coins offer and disgruntled drivers who were denied their coins would simply refuse to buy Esso petrol in the future, rather than consider their legal rights. The majority took the view that the coins contract was collateral to the main contract for the sale of petrol and so the coins were not produced for sale but as consideration to enter into the main contract for petrol. In the final analysis, it was not fatal to Esso's case that a majority of Law Lords thought there was a contract governing the coins.

In *Baird Textile Holdings Ltd* v *Marks & Spencer plc* (2002) M&S terminated a thirty-year-old relationship with their main clothes supplier. The supplier claimed that this relationship gave rise to an agreement under which M&S had promised not to terminate the relationship except on reasonable notice of three years. The House of Lords rejected the claim on the basis that M&S had deliberately avoided entering into formal long-term contracts with the supplier and consequentially it did not intend to create legal relations between it and the supplier.

Where there is not an express agreement, but an alleged agreement based on conduct over a period of time, the presumption does not apply and the onus is on the party claiming that a binding agreement was made to prove that there was an intention to create legal relations, as is discussed at para. 106 of *Assuranceforeningen* v *IOPCF*.

The operation of the presumptions in this area is summarized in Figure 3.3.

Figure 3.3 Summary of intention to create legal relations

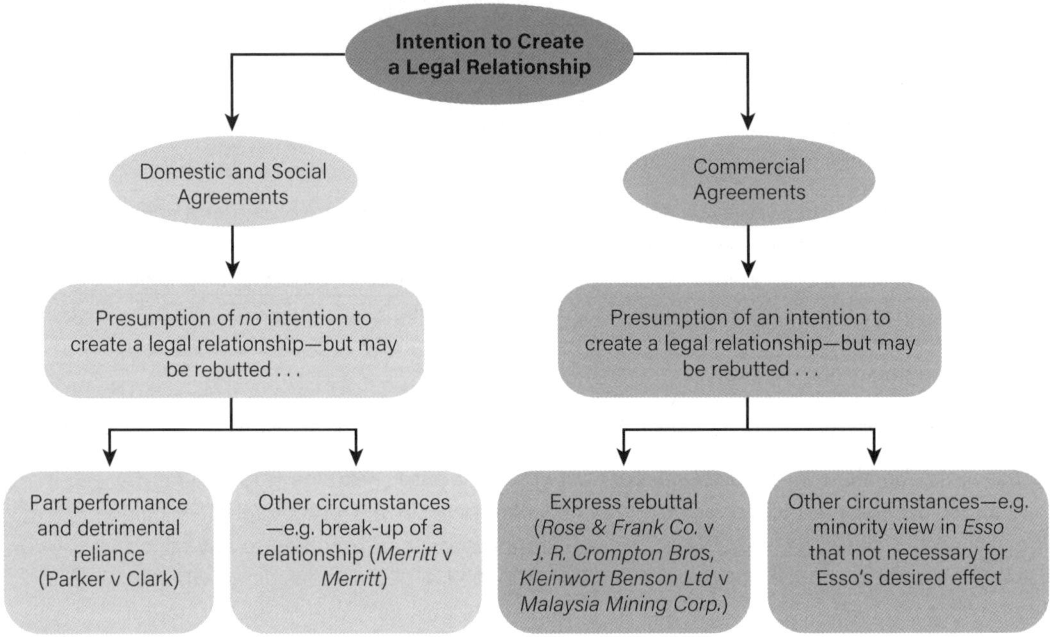

3.3 Executory and executed agreements

3.3.1 **Basis of the distinction**

Agreements are sometimes performed instantaneously but often there is a gap between completing the agreement and performance. Agreements are known as 'executory agreements' before either side has performed any part of the agreement, such as when a university promises to provide tuition for three years and a student promises to pay the appropriate fees each year. Once performance has commenced the agreement becomes executed, for example once the student attends university and eventually completes the course. There are differing degrees of executed agreements, in the same way that there are differing degrees of performance, and so an agreement may be partly or wholly executed depending upon the extent of its performance. The label 'executory' or 'executed' is therefore simply a way of stating whether there has been any performance.

The courts are reluctant to find that there is no contract once performance has begun (i.e. once the agreement is partly executed). By performing the agreement the parties have shown that the agreement is workable in practice and that it is robust enough to meet many of the objections that the agreement is too uncertain to be workable. Similarly, it can appear extremely harsh to find that there is no enforceable contract in a situation where a party has performed their part of the agreement and relied upon the agreement to their detriment.

EXAMPLE

Partly executed agreement

If, pursuant to an agreement, I spend time and money building a house for you and I get to the point where only the roof has to be added, it would seem harsh for a court to say that our partly executed agreement has not formed a contract (e.g. for uncertainty). The consequence would be that I could not claim the price from you even though I had virtually built your house. By asking for a contractual right to enforce the agreement I am asking for my bargain: the price in return for a house. If the courts leave me with an almost finished house but no money then I am denied my bargain and have wasted expenses. Consider whether the law of unjust enrichment could provide a remedy on the basis that you have been enriched (to the value of a roofless house) at my expense (in the case where the house is built on your land).

3.3.2 **Application of the distinction in the case law**

The Supreme Court decision in *Wells* v *Devani* (2019) (discussed in 2.9.1) illustrates the point well. The Court of Appeal had by a majority found that the oral agreement was incomplete as it was unclear in their view whether the claimant was entitled to be paid his commission on finding a purchaser who contracted to buy or on finding a purchaser who actually went on to complete the purchase. The Supreme Court however found that the agreement was sufficiently certain. The normal understanding was that estate agents are paid on the completion of the sale and the agreement was clearly made on this basis. The claimant had done everything required under the contract by finding a purchaser who had completed and was therefore entitled to his commission. Alternatively, even if the express agreement could not be said to be clear about the triggering event for payment, that uncertainty could be resolved by *implying* a term that the agent was entitled to be paid once a purchaser had completed. The Court thus demonstrated a determination on the facts to ensure that the executed agreement be seen as sufficiently certain (so as to remunerate the claimant for the work done), if necessary by resorting to the implication of a term into an agreement which, without it, would not be complete.

We also saw at the end of section 3.1.2 that s.9 SoGA 1979 distinguishes between executed and executory contracts, implying a reasonable price in the case of executed agreements. The case law on uncertainty and intention to create legal relations also demonstrates such a distinction, although it is not as openly expressed. In relation to incomplete agreements, the agreement to buy and sell petrol in *Foley* had been performed for three years (i.e. it was executed) whereas the agreement in *May & Butcher* was executory—neither side had yet performed. The court interpreted the *Foley* agreement in such a way that an arbitrator could ascertain the price in the event of the parties failing to agree, but in *May & Butcher* it placed a stricter interpretation on the clause referring disputes to an arbitrator, holding that a failure to agree did not amount to a dispute. The different results could be due to an underlying policy of the courts to enforce obligations when the agreement is executed (such as the agreement in *Foley*). The cases on vague agreements also display the same trend to favour executed agreements. In *Hillas*, the court was comfortable implying a meaning to '100,000 standards' and 'fair specification' in the partly executed agreement. By contrast, in *Scammell* v *Ouston* a meaning could not be implied into 'hire purchase terms' in the executory contract.

Denning J recognized this broad principle in favour of enforcing executed agreements at first instance (and he was supported by the Court of Appeal) in *British Bank for Foreign Trade Ltd* v *Novinex Ltd* (1941). Denning J said:

> [I]f there is an arrangement to supply goods at a price 'to be agreed', or to perform services on terms 'to be agreed' then, although, while the matter is still executory there may be no binding contract, nevertheless, if it is executed on one side, that is, if the one does his part without having come to an agreement as to the price or the terms, then the law will say that there is necessarily implied from the conduct of the parties a contract that, in default of agreement, a reasonable sum is to be paid.

The distinction between executed and executory contracts is also utilized in the context of an intention to create a legal relationship. Just as the court will strain to enforce a vague or incomplete executed agreement, it will also strain to find an intention to create legal relations in an executed agreement. In *Parker* v *Clark* (1960) a couple sold their house and loaned the proceeds to their daughter to help her buy a flat in reliance on an agreement that they live with an elderly couple and receive a share of the elderly man's will. Devlin J held that their agreement was enforceable as it was inconceivable that the elderly couple could break off the agreement at any time and leave the younger couple with nowhere to live. In rebutting the presumption of no intention to create legal relations, it appears that he was influenced by the substantial detrimental reliance of the younger couple who had partly performed the agreement by moving out of their old home and loaning the proceeds.

LINK TO . . .

Introduction (Chapter 1)

The policy of enforcing executed agreements relates to the theoretical basis for contract law.

If the courts favour executed agreements they are ostensibly protecting reliance placed on the agreement. The traditional approach to contract law is that the parties are free to contract and their expectations and bargains will be protected. Protecting reliance through contractual obligations shifts the emphasis away from the parties' intentions and towards their actions, leading the courts to rewrite the parties' agreement for them. This latter approach is known as 'paternalistic', as opposed to the 'individualist' approach that protects the parties' freedom of contract.

Digging deeper

The question is often asked as to whether there should be a separate doctrine of intention to create legal relations or whether it should really be seen as an aspect of the rules on offer and acceptance, especially given that the essence of an offer is that it is made with an intention that it become binding upon acceptance by the other party. *Blue* v *Ashley*, discussed at section 3.2, is an interesting example where the offer to pay £15 million was not regarded as an offer made with intention to be bound (not even morally, according to the judge) and separately there was no intention to create legal relations. McKendrick is of the view that on balance it is better to have the separate doctrine and that it is likely to be of increasing importance if the doctrine of consideration (for which, see Chapter 4) loses its force as the distinguishing feature of enforceable agreements. O'Sullivan and Hilliard on the other hand think it is better regarded as part of the rules on offer and acceptance rather than as a separate doctrine. This may seem a rather semantic question except that there are cases where it is clear that there is agreement but not (yet) an intention to create legal relations. Thus in sales of land (and houses built on that land) the parties will normally have reached agreement on the price but their agreement is almost invariably made expressly 'subject to contract' and thus is not intended to be legally binding until contracts are formally 'exchanged' once the purchaser has the mortgage or other finance in place and is ready to commit contractually to the agreement. The Court of Appeal in *Joanne Properties* v *Moneything Capital* (2020) held (para. [33]) that the trial judge had 'seriously undervalued the force of the "subject to contract" label' which had been the heading on all the relevant communications between solicitors. The Court emphasized (para. [34]) that 'where negotiations are carried out "subject to contract", the mere fact that the parties are of one mind is not enough', thus illustrating again, quite nicely, the distinction between agreement and intention to create legal relations.

A related and interesting point is made in *A Restatement of the English Law of Contract*, now in its 2nd edition (Burrows, OUP, 2020). This modern and concise *English Restatement*, written by Professor Burrows (now Lord Burrows JSC) in collaboration with an advisory group of leading judges, academics and practitioners, is well worth consulting on a wide range of issues. Paragraph 10(5) of the text of the *Restatement* says: 'It is commonplace in a written contract for there to be no intention to create legal relations until all the parties have signed the document.' The commentary explains that this has been included 'because it is often not appreciated that many commercial agreements are not binding unless and until there has been signature by all the parties.' One might therefore say that the presumption of intention to create legal relations in such commercial cases is modified so as to be an intention to create legal relations once all parties have signed. Such examples tend to suggest that the intention to create legal relations is indeed best seen as a separate requirement to those of offer and acceptance.

Summary

1. Certainty

An agreement must be capable of being enforced by the courts in order to form a contract. The courts will not enforce an uncertain (vague or incomplete) agreement.

An initially vague agreement may be made certain by implying a meaning into the vague terms. An agreement to negotiate in good faith (but not an agreement not to negotiate with anyone else for a fixed period) is vague and incapable of being made certain.

An agreement is initially incomplete if some of its terms are not yet decided. The terms can be completed through a mechanism provided for in the agreement or by statutory implication. They cannot be left to be agreed by the parties at a later date; such an agreement cannot be enforced and cannot form a contract.

2. Intention to create legal relations

Both parties must intend to enter into a legal relationship in order to form a contract.

There is a presumption that domestic and social agreements are entered into without the intention to enter into legal relations but this does not apply to express commercial agreements, where the necessary intention can almost always be presumed unless expressly excluded.

The particular circumstances of each case and part performance or detrimental reliance by one party may influence the court's decision to depart from the presumptions.

3. Executory and executed agreements

Partly or fully performed agreements are known as 'executed' whilst wholly unperformed agreements are 'executory.'

The courts appear to be more willing to find an enforceable agreement where there is an executed agreement—despite a degree of vagueness or incompleteness—particularly where one party has relied on the agreement to his detriment.

? Questions

1. In August 2006, Wembledon tennis club agreed a seven-year supply contract with Loadsofballs Ltd. Loadsofballs must supply 'International Tennis Federation approved tennis balls' for the next seven of Wembledon's annual June tournaments with the price to be agreed six months before the start of each tournament. It is September 2006 when Loadsofballs' chief executive rings you (his lawyer) in a panic because he has heard that all the top tennis players are pulling out of Wembledon and he wants reassurance that he has a valid contract for the supply of balls. How would you respond? Would your answer be any different if the call came in January 2010 and there had been no problems between the parties at past tournaments?
2. Is it necessary to have presumptions in respect of the intention to create legal relations? What purposes do they serve?
3. 'The protectionist policy of enforcing executed but not executory agreements is an affront to the parties' individual freedom to choose how and when they contract.' Discuss.

Further reading

Books

Chen-Wishart, M, *Contract Law*, 7th edn (Oxford University Press, 2022) sections 2.6 and 2.7.

McKendrick, E, *Contract Law: Text, Cases, and Materials*, 11th edn (Oxford University Press, 2024) chs 4 and 7.

O'Sullivan, J, and Hilliard, J, *The Law of Contract*, 11th edn (Oxford University Press, 2024) paras 3.1–3.19 and ch 4.

Articles

Hedley, S, 'Keeping contract in its place: Balfour v Balfour and the enforceability of informal agreements' (1985) 5 OJLS 391.

Hoskins, H, 'Contractual obligations to negotiate in good faith: Faithfulness to the agreed common purpose' (2014) 130 LQR 131.

4 Consideration and estoppel

LEARNING OBJECTIVES

This chapter will help you to:

- explore beyond the simple legal definition of 'consideration' as a benefit to one party and a burden to the other;
- understand when a promise to do something one party is already obliged to do can constitute good consideration;
- distinguish between bargain and non-bargain promises; and
- understand when, and to what extent, the courts will give effect to non-bargain promises.

Introduction

This chapter deals with one of the most controversial aspects of English contract law and forces us to ask the all-important question: 'What is special about contracts?' It is not immediately obvious why, if two parties come to an agreement which is certain and they intend to create legal relations, the law should refuse to enforce it as a contract unless it is supported by consideration. Why do the courts insist on there being 'consideration'? What is so important about this requirement? Before tackling these underlying questions, we will ask a simpler question: 'What do the courts mean when they talk about "consideration"?'

4.1 Definition of consideration

Many sound essays on consideration start with Lush J's definition in *Currie* v *Misa* (1875):

> [A] valuable consideration, in the sense of the law, may consist either in some right, interest, profit or benefit accruing to the one party or some forbearance, detriment, loss or responsibility, given, suffered or undertaken by the other.

This definition can act as a solid starting point, but you should recognize that it omits some important details.

4.1.1 **The two sides of a contract**

Firstly, the definition looks at consideration from two angles (as a benefit to one party or a detriment to the other) but it does not look at both sides of the contract. By 'both sides of the contract' we refer to the fact that, in a bilateral contract, each party makes a promise to the other and so there are promises on each side of the contract.

EXAMPLE

Bilateral contract

I promise to drive you to Oxford and you promise to pay me £50. Each promise can be looked at independently and so the contract has these two sides. Your promise to pay me £50 involves both a benefit to me and a detriment to you (the two angles on consideration) and is given in return for your promise to pay me on the other side of the contract (the two sides of a contract). Conversely, my promise to drive you is both a benefit to you and a detriment to me and is given in return for your promise to pay me.

In this example, if I drive you to Oxford and you refuse to pay me, *I will sue you* and the court will focus on your obligation to pay me and not on the other side of our contract (my promise to drive you to Oxford). The explanation for this is simple: I am asking the court to enforce only one side of the contract, your obligation to pay me—the court has not been asked to enforce my promise to drive you and so it is unconcerned whether that promise is supported by consideration. However, my promise to you is not entirely irrelevant: when the court looks for consideration in relation to your promise to pay me, I will point to what *I* have promised in return, that is, in promising to drive you to Oxford (which promise, as it happens, I have already carried out, although this is not actually crucial).

Our case could equally focus on the other side of our contract. If you pay me in advance and I refuse to drive you, *you will sue me*, and the court will this time focus on my obligation to drive you and not on the other side of our contract (your promise to pay me). When the court looks for consideration in relation to this side of the contract, you will point to what *you* have promised in return, that is, your promise to pay me (again, you have actually performed your promise, but this is not actually crucial).

The important point to take away from all this is that there will normally be separate considerations on each side of the contract but what counts as consideration in any given contractual dispute will depend on which obligation on which side of the contract the court is asked to enforce, and this will obviously depend on who is suing whom. If this is all a bit confusing, see Figure 4.1, in which the strings representing each obligation (side) of the contract may remind you that each string has to be supported by consideration and a dispute will only normally focus on one string.

4.1.2 **Sufficient and adequate consideration**

Secondly, the benefit or detriment (remember, Lush J described consideration in terms of benefits accruing to one party and detriment by the other) must be a *legally sufficient* benefit or detriment as opposed to simply a *factual* benefit or detriment. This simply means that 'benefit' and 'detriment' have special definitions in the law and something you would normally

Figure 4.1 Bilateral contract

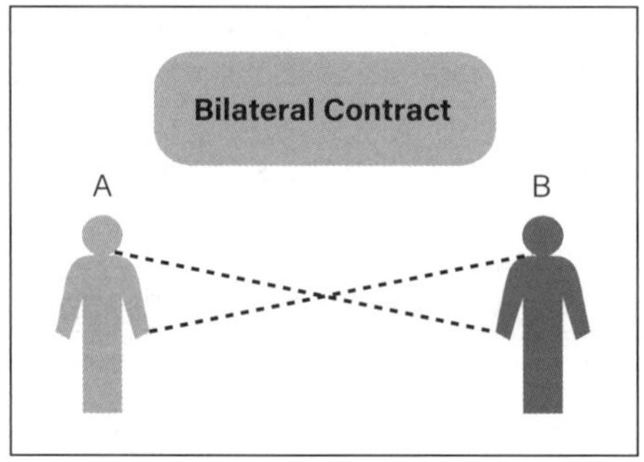

A's Executory Promise to pay (benefit to B and burden to A) is Consid. for B's promise to deliver →

← B's Executory Promise to deliver (benefit to A and burden to B) is Consid. for A's promise to pay

Double, or two-way BARGAIN or exchange

consider to be a benefit might not be a *legally sufficient* benefit, and therefore not consideration, in the eyes of the law.

'Sufficient' does not mean that consideration needs to be adequate; in other words, the benefit or detriment need not be equivalent in value to that which is received in return. In the earlier example, it is not necessary that your benefit (the drive to Oxford) is worth about £50; you could promise me £1 or 1 pence or, as you will sometimes read, a peppercorn, if I agree to that in return. The point is that the benefit or detriment must be 'legally sufficient' in the sense that the law recognizes that benefit or detriment as constituting consideration, but its value is irrelevant. In *Chappell* v *Nestlé* (1960), Nestlé promised to send a record to anyone who sent in a postal order for 1s. 6d. and three Nestlé chocolate wrappers. It did not matter that the wrappers in themselves were worth very little and did not equal the market value of the record, even when added to the 1s. 6d. (7½ pence); Nestlé were free to request whatever they wanted (they obviously hoped to benefit economically from the arrangement out of increased sales of chocolate). The wrappers were part of the consideration and there is no doubt that in an appropriate case they could be the whole of the consideration. This reflects the general theme throughout the law of contract that the parties are generally free to make their own agreements and apply their own valuations, and so the courts will not interfere if a promisor thinks that it is worth providing a benefit in return for something which, on the face of it, is of little value, such as wrappers.

Legally sufficient consideration

So, now that we have established that value is irrelevant so long as the benefit or burden is legally sufficient, we must examine what benefits and burdens will count as legally sufficient.

In *White* v *Bluett* (1852), a son was upset by his father's distribution of property amongst his children and complained to his father. The father said that he would forgive a debt owed to him by the son if he stopped complaining. The court held that ceasing to complain could not be good consideration for the promise to forgive the debt because the son did not have a right to complain. Thus, it appears that giving up rights can be legally sufficient benefit but giving up something you had no right to do in the first place cannot. However, it now seems strange to say that a person has no right to complain (free speech has come a long way since 1852) and perhaps it would be more appropriate today to say that the son did give up a right or freedom to complain and suffered a detriment in return for the promise. By way of contrast, in the US case of *Hamer* v *Sidway* (1891) the consideration for an uncle's promise to pay $5,000 was his nephew's abstinence from tobacco, liquor and gambling. The New York Court of Appeals thought that the nephew had a right to these things and his decision to forgo these things constituted consideration for the promise. One way to reconcile *White* v *Bluett* with the more liberal approach to rights in *Hamer* v *Sidway* is to reclassify *White* as a case which would today be decided on the basis of there being no intention to create a legal relationship (or, less likely in this case, duress). We shall see throughout this chapter that the doctrine of consideration has often been used as a reason (or a consideration) against (or in favour of) the enforcement of a promise, only to be later superseded by a more specific doctrine (such as intention or economic duress).

Giving up a legal right to sue a promisor (known as compromise of a claim) is certainly a legally sufficient benefit or burden, even if the claim is speculative (see *Pitt* v *PHH Asset Management Ltd* (1993)), and this is something which the courts actively encourage in order to avoid unnecessary and expensive litigation.

Figure 4.1 shows the typical executory (yet to be performed) bilateral (obligations on both sides) contract and illustrates a clear bargain or requested exchange. Remember that the dotted lines represent obligations between the parties and each party can pull on the string (tied to the other's neck) to call for the performance of the other side's obligation. In an executory bilateral contract these obligations also form the benefit/burden which make up the consideration for the other's obligation. Each party incurs an obligation and by so doing provides consideration for the promise or obligation of the other party. Because each side incurs an obligation, it is a double or two-way bargain. Which of the two promises we investigate to see if there is consideration depends on which promise we are looking to enforce.

At first sight, the unilateral contract in Figure 4.2 does not look like a bargain because only one party, A, is under an obligation and B does not undertake an obligation in return. However,

Figure 4.2 Unilateral contract

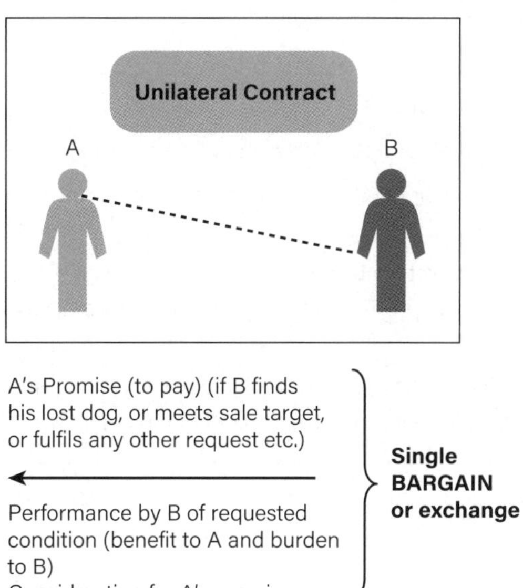

A promises to pay B *if* B performs the requested condition. B provides consideration for this promise by performing the condition, not by promising to do so.

Although B is never under an obligation to do this, once B has done it the contract is formed. It is a one-sided contract in the sense that only A is obliged to do anything. Only A's promise can be enforced and so we are only looking for consideration from B. In contrast to bilateral agreements, there is a single bargain—A has bargained for (requested) B's performance and has got it in return (exchange) for his promise.

4.1.3 **Bargains and consideration as the price of promise**

The third and most important omission from the *Currie* v *Misa* definition is the rule that the courts will only enforce *bargains*. The crucial finding of fact in *Nestlé* was that Nestlé had *requested* the wrappers as the consideration for their promise. This request provides the reason *why* a benefit was conferred on Nestlé and it is what makes the promise a bargain: I will give you a record if you give me three wrappers (plus a postal order) in return.

Think of a bargain as a deal or an exchange where both parties come away with something they have requested from the other. Forget about the type of 'bargain' you hear of on the High Street which means a 'good deal' or a 'special offer'; we are not concerned with whether the bargain is good or bad for either party, provided that there has been an exchange (which in a free market tends to move goods and services to where they are most highly valued).

In *Combe* v *Combe* (1951) Mr Combe promised his ex-wife £100 per annum. There was no consideration for the promise despite the fact that Mrs Combe had conferred a benefit and incurred a detriment through not applying to the courts for maintenance. The decisive factor was that there was no evidence that the husband requested his wife not to apply for maintenance; there was therefore no bargain because the wife abstained from applying to the court of her own accord—this detriment was not strictly given in return for her husband's promise. Sometimes consideration is referred to as the 'price paid for the promise' to emphasize this bargain element. Lord Dunedin in *Dunlop Pneumatic Tyre Co. Ltd* v *Selfridges & Co. Ltd* (1915) said that consideration is 'the price for which the promise of the other is bought.' The courts look for a request because this shows that the promisor intended to get something in return for the promise and intended to create a bargain.

2nd Restatement of Contracts

The American Law Institute's 2nd Restatement of Contracts expressly requires a bargain:

s.71 1) To constitute consideration, a performance or return promise must be bargained for.

2) A performance or return promise is bargained for if it is sought by the promisor in exchange for his promise and is given by the promisee in exchange for that promise.

As demonstrated by the facts of *Shadwell* v *Shadwell* (1860), parties often do not make their requests explicit and the courts are left to fill in the gaps.

CASE CLOSE-UP

***Shadwell* v *Shadwell* (1860)**

An uncle heard that his nephew intended to get married and promised him a yearly income on 'starting' until his own income reached a certain level. The marriage was alleged to be the consideration (Byles J, although dissenting, somewhat controversially acknowledged that marriage may be a detriment and even more controversially seemed to go on to compare it to breaking a leg!) but the case hinged on whether the uncle *requested* the marriage consideration or whether it was merely the *condition* for an unenforceable gift.

It was not at all clear that the uncle was referring to the beginning of the claimant's marriage (as opposed to his career) by the use of the word 'starting' but the majority of the court held (in a judgment by Erle CJ) not only that he was referring to the marriage but that he impliedly requested it since the promise was an inducement for the nephew to marry; it was something the uncle wanted and was prepared to pay for. Byles J thought that there was no consideration on the basis that, even though the marriage could be a detriment, it was already arranged, and it was not expressly or impliedly requested by the uncle. *Shadwell* v *Shadwell* also supports the proposition that doing something one is already obliged to do can constitute good consideration; on the facts the nephew was already contractually obliged to marry his fiancée (although that would not now be the case under the current law) and yet doing this very thing was consideration for his uncle's promise.

The tricky subject of existing duty is examined in further detail in section 4.3.

EXAMPLE

Requests and conditions

Whilst a unilateral contract (as in *Shadwell*: 'if you marry X, I will pay you an income') is a form of bargain, it is often difficult to distinguish between an (enforceable) unilateral contract and an (unenforceable) gratuitous promise subject to a condition. The key distinction is that a unilateral contract contains a requested benefit or burden (as found by Erle CJ) but the condition to which a gratuitous promise is subject is not requested by the promisor (the view of the facts taken by Byles J in *Shadwell*). An example may help to clarify this.

A father promises his son a round-the-world ticket if he passes his university final exams. On the one hand, this could be interpreted as a unilateral ('if') contract because the father requests that his son passes in return for the promise of a round-the-world ticket. On the other hand, it could be interpreted as a gratuitous (i.e. free) promise to buy a round-the-world ticket subject to a condition, that is, if the son passes. The first interpretation seems to be the most natural because the father has an interest in his son's success and it would be odd if he intended to give his son the option of passing or failing; rather, he is requesting good results and he is willing to bargain and pay for them. Compare to the position if the father promises to buy his son a round-the-world ticket if he fails his exams. Again, this could be construed as a unilateral 'if' contract ('if you fail, I promise to buy you a round-the-world ticket') or as a gratuitous promise to buy a round-the-world ticket conditional on a fail. The more natural interpretation in this situation would be the latter as the father does not want his son to fail (the round-the-world ticket is perhaps a consolation prize); there is no bargain and no unilateral contract. An important factor is therefore whether the father is benefited by the request/condition.

So, no right to a round-the-world ticket if the promise is gratuitous. This may look unfair, not because the ticket was bargained for (it was not) but because the son may have relied on the gratuitous promise in deciding to take the exam in the first place. However, pure reliance is not consideration and the son must show that he suffered a detriment (perhaps if he had deferred a while, he would have had a better chance of getting a better mark). Taking this line of thought further, if the son may or may not take the exam, it could be that you can imply a request from the father, not that the son should fail, but that he should take the exam: 'In return for taking the exam (as requested) I promise you a ticket should you fail.' This would be an enforceable unilateral contract—compare with *Carlill Carbolic Smoke Ball Co.* in Chapter 2 (in return for you buying my product as requested, I promise you £100 if you use it as directed and still catch flu), where the promise was supported by consideration, not because the company requested that its customers catch flu (that would be ridiculous), but because the company requested its customers to buy the product (the consideration) and promised to pay them if they caught flu.

4.2 Past consideration

It is not difficult to remember the rule that past consideration is not good consideration from cases such as *Re McArdle* (1951) but it is equally important to remember what past consideration means and why it is not good consideration.

Past consideration refers to a time before the *making* of a promise. In *Re McArdle*, the claimant had voluntarily carried out the improvements to the property two years before the unenforceable (and effectively gratuitous) promise to pay her for doing so. The fact that the promise said 'in consideration of' your carrying out the improvements did not turn the improvements into good consideration as the improvements had already been made (and were thus 'past') by the time the promise was made.

However, as mentioned at the start of this chapter, the fact that the consideration is already past when a party seeks to *enforce* the promise is not a problem: for example, if the defendants had promised to pay for the improvements in return for her promising to do them in the future, and she had then subsequently made the repairs and sued on the promise to pay her. This would simply be *executed* consideration: consideration performed *after* the promise and in return for it. Even though it is past in relation to the dispute or time of enforcement, it would not be past in relation to the time the promise was made, and thus it would be good consideration. Valid consideration is often *executed* in the sense that it has already been performed (even if it started out in life as an executory promise)

Figure 4.3 Executed and past consideration

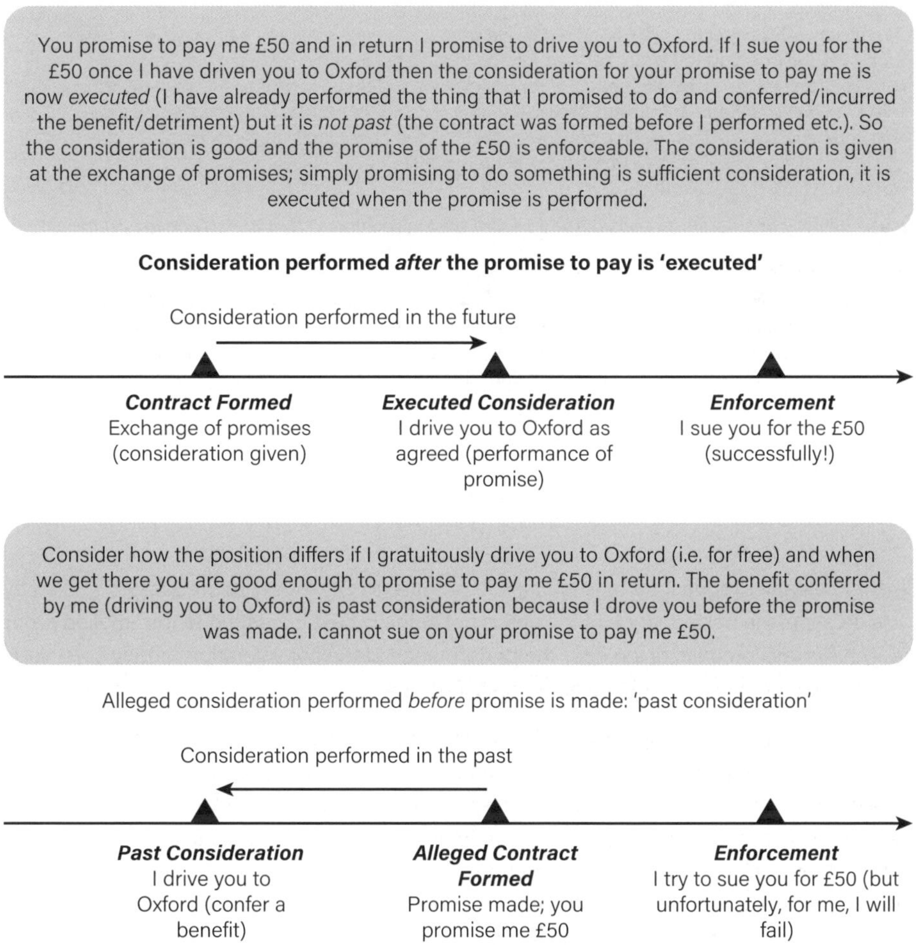

by the time one party seeks to enforce the other party's promise (otherwise you could never safely perform your side of the contract until you were sure that the other side had performed or would do so). In summary, consideration only amounts to *past* consideration if it was performed before the return promise was made, that is, before the contract was formed (see Figure 4.3).

The past consideration rule is best explained as a consequence of the rule that contracts must be bargains, that is, that consideration must be requested by the promisor as the price of the promise. You can see that if the consideration (the benefit or burden) has been incurred before the promise then it is hardly possible that the promisor could have requested it as the price of the promise (the request must obviously come before performance of the thing requested). There is a so-called exception to allow for what might look like a past act, performed before any express agreement to pay for it, to be treated as consideration on the basis that there was an earlier implied request and an understanding from the beginning that the act would be paid for. The Privy Council in *Pao On* v *Lau Yiu Long* (1980), following older cases such as *Re Casey's Patents* (1892), recognized that such apparently past consideration would actually be good consideration for a contract. The reasoning behind this is that at the

Figure 4.4 The so-called exception to past consideration—earlier implied promise

As in the example just given, I drive you to Oxford and when we get there you promise to pay me £50 in return. The benefit conferred by me (driving you to Oxford) appears to be past consideration because I drove you before the promise was made so, as previously explained, I normally cannot sue on your promise to pay me £50. However, if before I drive you there is an implied promise to pay (e.g. my car is black and has a taxi sign on it!—or perhaps you have always paid me for previous lifts) then the consideration is no longer past in relation to this new implied promise.

Implied promise made before consideration, consideration is *not past* in relation to that *earlier implied promise*

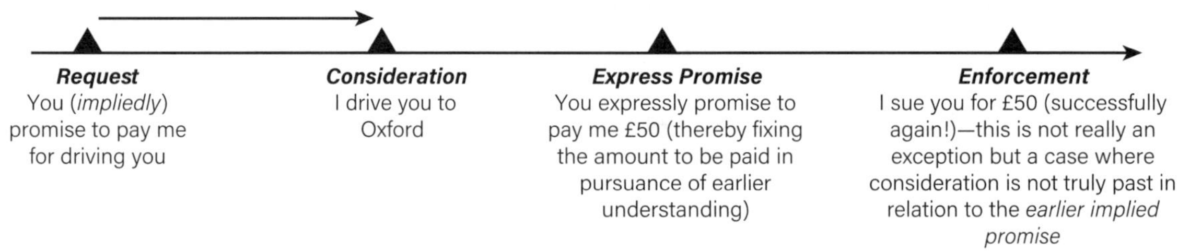

time of the earlier request there is an *implied* promise to pay for the act requested and so the consideration, the performance of the act, is not actually past in relation to this implied promise. The express promise given after the performance of the consideration merely crystallizes or quantifies the earlier implied promise (see Figure 4.4).

It is of course easier to imply an earlier promise to pay (and a request) where the person performing the requested act is acting in the course of a business or profession (as in *Re Casey's Patents*) rather than in a social or domestic context (as in *Re McArdle*), on the basis that people in business rarely perform acts gratuitously in the hope that someone will want to pay them—but compare to the situation where someone washes your car windscreen whilst you are stationary at a traffic light without giving you the opportunity to accept or reject the service. They obviously do this in the hope that you will pay them, but should you be contractually obliged (on the basis of an implied request) to pay them the value of the service received?

4.3 Performance of a pre-existing obligation

So far in this chapter we have introduced two basic definitions of consideration (consideration as a legal benefit or burden and consideration as the price of a promise) and discussed the past consideration rule. This next section tackles the thorny question of whether the performance of an existing duty can count as a legal benefit or burden in order to form consideration for a promise (an exam favourite). The simple issue at the heart of this question is whether doing something you are already obliged to do can *legally* count as a benefit or detriment. We will look at three situations: existing non-contractual obligations (public duties), existing contractual obligations (or duties) owed to a third party and existing contractual obligations (or duties) owed to the promisor.

4.3.1 **Performance of a non-contractual obligation (public duty cases)**

Performance of an existing non-contractual duty generally cannot in itself form good consideration. In *Collins* v *Godefroy* (1831) the promise to pay a witness who was already under a public duty to give evidence lacked consideration. The witness did nothing above what he was already obliged to do and therefore he did not receive or incur a legal benefit or detriment in return for the promised payment. By contrast, in *Glasbrook Brothers Ltd* v *Glamorgan CC* (1925) the owner of a colliery promised to pay the police if they provided security during a miners' strike. Again, it was accepted that the mere performance of the existing general public duty of the police to protect the colliery could not form good consideration, but on the facts it was held that the police had gone beyond this duty by providing more protection than they were obliged to do. By *exceeding* their public duty, the police did something they were not obliged to do and so provided a benefit and incurred a detriment which amounted to good consideration. The principle now applies to modern policing by virtue of s.25 of the Police Act 1996, as applied in *Harris* v *Sheffield United FC* (1987) (request for special police services at a football stadium implied from conduct of organizing an event that could not otherwise be held safely). *Glasbrook* and *Harris* were applied in *Leeds United* v *Chief Constable West Yorkshire Police* (2013) where it was held that, in contrast to the policing inside the ground (as in *Harris*) and in the land immediately outside it owned and controlled by Leeds United, policing in the wider area around the club not owned and controlled by them (but less than 200 yards away) could not be charged for as these duties were merely performed in discharge of their public duty to maintain law and order. This case was followed and applied in *Ipswich Town FC* v *Chief Constable of Suffolk Constabulary* (2017) where the question of whether the land was publicly or privately owned was emphasized and the club were found (on appeal) not to be liable for policing costs in relation to roads where the club had a traffic control order and stewards but which were nevertheless on public land on which the police were performing their public duty to maintain law and order.

Good consideration but subject to a public policy exception?

Despite the traditional requirement, exemplified earlier, to exceed a non-contractual duty before it can constitute good consideration, Denning LJ suggested in *Ward* v *Byham* (1956) that the mere performance of a public duty may sometimes constitute consideration. In that case, a mother promised to look after her child in return for a promised income. Denning LJ thought that there was consideration for the promise of the income despite the fact that the mother was already under a statutory duty to look after her child. However, the other two members of the Court of Appeal found that the mother provided consideration by promising to keep the child *well* looked after and *happy* (rightly or wrongly the law does not require children to be happy), and so this promise exceeded her statutory duty and amounted to consideration even on the traditional view.

One way to reconcile Denning LJ's approach with the cases discussed earlier is to say that a promise simply to perform an existing public duty *is* sufficient consideration so long as enforcement of the promise is not contrary to public policy (see Denning LJ in *Williams* v *Williams* (1957)). Such an approach can be justified on the basis that even if the public duty is not exceeded, the promisor directly and personally receives a promise that the public duty will be performed. The other party now owes two obligations: a non-contractual obligation (as before) and also a contractual obligation to the promisor (thus there is a legal benefit and detriment). One criticism often levelled at this type of argument is that it is circular. The promisor

(P) only gets a right to sue (to compel the other person to perform the public duty) if P's own promise is binding as consideration in return for the promise to perform the public duty, but the question of whether P's own promise is binding is the very thing we are trying to establish. This is not a valid criticism because the whole of consideration is steeped in this circularity: in the classic executory bilateral contract, a wholly executory promise to perform is good consideration for another party's wholly executory promise to perform and so the validity of one promise is dependent on the validity of the other.

A more significant argument against is that in very many cases of performing an existing public duty, a personal contractual right to performance of the public duty is not conferred because the promise is to pay *if* the public duty is performed—that is, it is a unilateral promise or agreement—and the promisee is never obliged (contractually at least) to perform the public duty. Thus, it may be easier to argue that performance of a public duty should at least be good consideration if there is a promise to perform it rather than merely the fact of performance (and also provided that there is no public policy reason against enforcement).

THINKING POINT

Why do you think that there must be a public policy exception if the performance of a public duty can constitute good consideration?

A relevant factor is that individuals, especially those in public office such as the police, should not be able to extract extra payment for doing (or agreeing to do) something they are already obliged to do as a matter of public duty. Clearly, there is a danger of corruption or extortion and that they may perform in a manner which is more to the benefit of their private paymaster than for the public benefit; cases such as *Collins* v *Godefroy* can be explained as examples of transactions potentially against public policy. The promise to pay the witness was clearly close to the line separating an honest payment and a bribe (although it is worth noting that modern practice involves compensating witnesses for expenses/loss of earnings and experts are paid a fee).

4.3.2 **Performance of a contractual obligation owed to a third party**

This section deals with a relatively confusing issue which becomes much clearer once you understand what is meant by: (i) a third party; and (ii) a contractual duty owed to a third party. The concept of the third party is used (somewhat confusingly, you may think) to refer to a 'party' who is *not* one of the contracting parties. The actual parties to the contract (who promise to perform and to whom the promises are made) are thus the first and second parties—even if there are in fact, as there may well be, three, four, five or more *actual* parties to the contract. Any other individual (i.e. not a contracting party) who becomes involved in the facts or is affected by the contract, although known as a 'third party', is in fact an 'outsider' who is *not* a party to the contract. As Groucho Marx might have said (he actually said it about marriage), 'I wouldn't want to be a party to any contract where the parties would be prepared to have me as a party'—but he could still be the third party! Relatively recently things have got rather better for third parties because the Contracts (Rights of Third Parties) Act 1999 gives them wider rights to take benefits from certain contracts, as we shall see in Chapter 13 on

Figure 4.5 Third parties

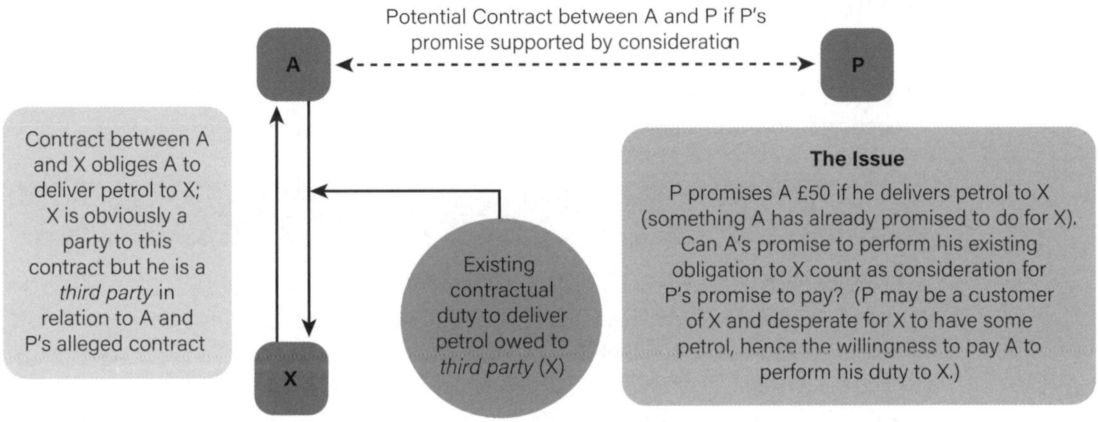

'Privity,' but the crucial distinction between a third party and an actual party to the contract remains in that only the latter can be under a contractual obligation or duty.

In Figure 4.5, when the expression 'contractual duty owed to a third party' (let's call the third party X) is used, it refers to a contractual duty owed by one party (A) to X, who therefore actually *is* a party to some *other* contract (a contract between A and X), but it is important to distinguish this *other* contract from the one immediately at hand between A and the promisor (P). Under *this* contract (between A and P), A is putting forward the existing contractual duty, say to deliver petrol, which A already owes to X (under the *other*, A to X, contract) as consideration for P's promise to pay for the petrol. X is thus a third party as far as the A-to-P contract is concerned, with which we are primarily concerned, but X is obviously very much a party to the *other* contract (the A-to-X contract). You might say that it is all relative really—X is a third party (i.e. not a party) relative to *this* contract (the A-to-P contract) but obviously is a party in relation to the *other*, A-to-X contract (and P is a third party in relation to the A-to-X contract).

The performance of a contractual duty owed to a third party can form good consideration for a promise, and so the answer to the final question in the final box in Figure 4.5 is 'yes.' Wilde B made this clear in *Scotson* v *Pegg* (1861) when he said: '[T]here is no authority for the proposition that where there has been a promise to one person to do a certain thing, it is not possible to make a valid promise to another to do the same thing.' We also saw earlier at section 4.1.3 that the facts, if not the reasoning, in *Shadwell* v *Shadwell* support the proposition. The clear rule that this type of existing duty is good consideration has since been approved by the Privy Council in *New Zealand Shipping Co. Ltd* v *A. M. Satterthwaite & Co. Ltd* (1975) (*actual performance* of an existing contractual duty to unload the ship) and *Pao On* v *Lau Yiu Long* (1980) (*a promise to perform* an existing contractual duty not to sell shares for twelve months). In the latter case, an allegation of duress was rejected on the facts. If the promise to reward someone for carrying out their contractual duty (even though owed to another) is obtained through economic duress (see Chapter 9), the promise may not be enforceable on that ground. This is regarded as a better approach than saying that the performance of the existing obligation is not consideration in the first place and is arguably an approach which should or can be applied to existing public or non-contractual duties, as discussed in the previous section, and which, as will be seen, is increasingly influential in the third category, to be discussed next.

4.3.3 Performance of a contractual obligation already owed to the promisor

The issue at stake in relation to performance of a contractual obligation already owed to the promisor is deceptively simple: can a second promise by P to do something P is already obliged to do for A constitute good consideration for a second promise by A to P?

EXAMPLE

Existing duty to promisor

I promise to paint your wall and you promise to pay me £20 in return. There is obvious benefit and burden for each of our promises and there is a clear exchange. Imagine that I find the work much harder than I originally thought and I promise to finish painting your wall (which I am already contractually obliged to you to do) if you make a fresh promise to pay me an extra £10. Could I enforce your promise for the extra £10? What have I given you in return for that promise?

The traditional rule derived from *Stilk* v *Myrick* (1809) is that a promise to perform a contractual obligation already owed to the other party will not constitute good consideration.

CASE CLOSE-UP

***Stilk* v *Myrick* (1809)**

Two sailors deserted ship. The captain of the ship promised the remaining sailors that he would divide the wages of the deserters between the remaining sailors (i.e. pay them extra) if they got the ship home. When the ship returned to London, the captain refused to honour his promise and one of the sailors sued for the extra amount. According to Campbell's report, Lord Ellenborough decided that there was no consideration for the captain's promise: the sailor had already promised to sail the ship for its entire voyage and so he could not rely on a promise to do the same thing again as consideration for the extra sum promised by his captain. Although the captain obtained a *practical* benefit (in dissuading any further desertion and getting his ship home), he did not gain any *legal benefit* over and above what he was already entitled to under the existing contract with the claimant (who also did not incur a legal detriment in excess of what he was already legally obliged to do).

In *Williams* v *Roffey Bros & Nicholls (Contractors)* (1990) the Court of Appeal took a different approach. Whilst being at pains to stress that *Stilk* v *Myrick* was not being overruled, they nevertheless enforced Roffey Bros' promise to pay an extra £10,300 if Williams finished the flats on time (see Figure 4.6). Despite Williams promising only to do what he was already obliged to do, Roffey Bros, it was said, obtained a *practical* benefit because they would avoid a penalty clause in their own contract with the Housing Association and a more favourable payment scheme was put in place so that Williams was only paid per completed flat. Glidewell LJ thought that a practical benefit was sufficient (i.e. 'legal') consideration for a promise to pay extra so long as there was no economic duress or fraud. So, the result in *Williams* v *Roffey*

Figure 4.6 *Williams* v *Roffey Bros & Nicholls (Contractors)* (1990)

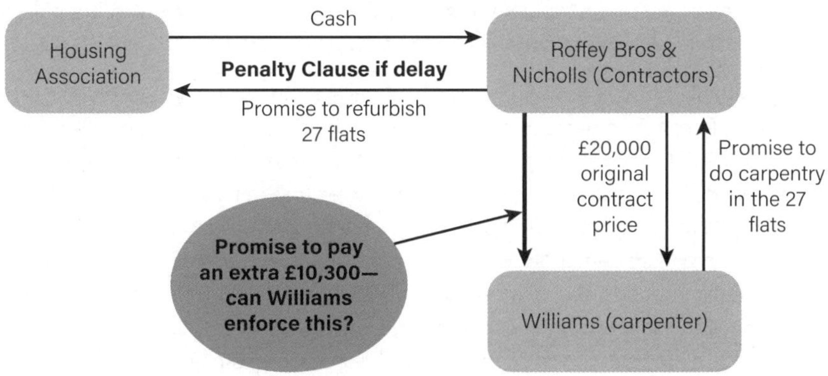

Some time after the original contract . . .

- Williams had been paid £16,200 but only completed nine out of 27 flats.
- Roffey Bros agreed that original price (£20,000) was too low and promised to pay an extra £10,300 (note that the suggestion came from them; so no threat from Williams, making duress unlikely).
- The extra was to be paid at the rate of £575 per flat completed.
- Williams completed eight more flats but was only paid an extra £1,500. He stopped work and sued Roffey Bros for the extra promised.

appears to depend on two key factors, one positive, the practical benefit to the promisor, and the second negative, the absence of duress. This absence of duress was thought to be reasonably clear on the facts since it was not Williams who took the initiative to ask for the extra payment (nor was there any express threat not to complete) but rather it was Roffey Bros who suggested the extra payment in recognition of the contract being initially underpriced.

Glidewell LJ referred to *Stilk* v *Myrick* as a decision 'enunciated in relation to the rigours of seafaring life during the Napoleonic wars . . . subjected . . . to a process of refinement and limitation in its application in the present day.' It is worth noting that according to a report of *Stilk* v *Myrick* by Espinasse, Lord Ellenborough did not decide the case on a lack of consideration but instead he approved of the policy in the similar case of *Harris* v *Watson* (1791). In that case, Lord Kenyon refused to uphold a promise to pay sailors extra because sailors would then hold their captains to ransom and 'it would materially affect the navigation of this kingdom.' History has not treated Espinasse very kindly, and, despite his appearing in the case as counsel, his version is not regarded as reliable. One judge reportedly went as far as to say, 'I do not want to hear from Espinasse or any other ass!' and another asserted that he was deaf and 'heard one half of the case and reported the other!'

LINK TO . . .

Duress (Chapter 9)

In fairness to Espinasse, he was, in a way, ahead of his time in suggesting that the promise in *Stilk* v *Myrick* was not enforced because it would have been against public policy to do so. Enforcing the promise would encourage sailors everywhere to put pressure on their captains to pay them more for doing the same work, safe in the knowledge that the courts would enforce the promise in the event of a dispute.

Since the days of *Stilk* v *Myrick*, the courts have developed a specific doctrine to deal with cases where one party has put too much pressure on another party in the build-up to a contract. This is known as economic duress and is discussed in Chapter 9.

How do you think that this development affects the doctrine of consideration? Now that actual cases of economic duress can be dealt with independently, should *Stilk* v *Myrick* be discarded as old law? Or is it still a valid point to say that a promise to perform a contract with the other party is not a legal benefit to that other party? The reality is that it is usually possible to find a way round *Stilk* v *Myrick* if thought desirable—either by finding that there is a practical benefit to the promisor, as in *Williams* v *Roffey*, or by finding on somewhat flimsy grounds, as in *North Ocean Shipping* v *Hyundai* (1979), that the existing duty has been exceeded, in that case by the shipbuilders providing correspondingly increased security in return for a promise by the purchasers to pay an extra 10 per cent for the ship.

The view is increasingly being taken that *Williams* v *Roffey* has for most practical purposes overturned the rule in *Stilk* v *Myrick* and that provided a practical benefit can be identified (as it normally can be or otherwise why would the promisor have made the fresh promise to pay more), the promise to perform, or the performance of, an existing duty can be good consideration for the fresh promise, *provided that there is no duress*. In *Adam Opel GmbH* v *Mitras Automotive (UK) Ltd Costs* (2007) it was the presence of duress that was the problem rather than the absence of consideration. The claimant van manufacturer notified its supplier (the defendant) that it was redesigning its van and would terminate the defendant's contract for the supply of bumpers; the defendant's response was to demand increased payments or it would cease supplying bumpers immediately. The claimant paid the extra sums as it could not afford to have its immediate supplies disrupted but later claimed the sums back on the grounds that the agreement to pay extra was vitiated by duress; alternatively, it lacked consideration. Deputy Judge David Donaldson QC found that the agreement was supported by consideration, but it was voidable for duress; at paras [41] and [42] he admitted that he was puzzled by the Court of Appeal decision in *Roffey* but he was bound to follow it and find that the agreement was supported by consideration. He said of the relationship between the doctrines of consideration and duress: 'The law of consideration is no longer to be used to protect a participant in such a variation (e.g. to the original payment terms in the supply contract). That role has passed to the law of economic duress, which provides a more refined control mechanism, and renders the contract voidable rather than void.' Similar comments were made by Leggatt J at para. [59] in *Blue v Ashley* (2017) where he said of the existing duty rule that 'it may sometimes have helped to protect contracting parties against exploitation through the other party refusing to do what it had contracted to do unless some extra payment or benefit was provided. But it is now recognised that this mischief is better addressed by other doctrines such as economic duress and public policy. The decision . . . in *Williams v Roffey* . . . effectively rendered the rule obsolete.'

Another way in which it has always in theory been possible to get round the *Stilk* v *Myrick* problem has been to find that the original contract has been rescinded, that is, set aside by agreement between the parties, and therefore there is no longer an existing duty to worry about. There is a case to this effect from America, *Watkins* v *Carrig* (1941), which the English courts have been reluctant to expressly rely on (Purchas LJ for example resisted the attractive invitation to do so in *Williams* v *Roffey*), but there are earlier English authorities to the same effect such as *Raggow* v *Scougall* (1915), where an agreement to accept lower wages during the war in return for continued employment was upheld even though the employers were already obliged to provide continued employment under the existing contract which 'had been torn up by mutual consent.' The original contract can only be rescinded by mutual agreement if both parties still have obligations to perform under it, otherwise there will be no consideration on one side of the agreement to rescind the contract. But if, as is normally the case, there are still things to be done on both sides (as indeed there were in *Williams* v *Roffey*), this is a perfectly credible or at least workable explanation of how the new promise can be binding. The original contract is freely set aside by each party giving up its rights under it and then a new promise is made for fresh consideration which is not the subject any longer of a previously existing duty. In *Compagnie Noga* v *Abacha (No 4)* (2003) Tuckey LJ approved of this analysis at para. 57 of his judgment and even dismissed the idea that there had to be some interval between the rescission of the old contract and the fresh promise supported by consideration which was previously due under the old contract—the two could be simultaneous and even contained in the same document.

In the light of all this, it is not perhaps surprising that para. 8(5) of *A Restatement of the English Law of Contract* (2016) suggests that existing duties, including those owed to the promisor, are good consideration in the absence of duress (or other public policy reasons). The rather more recent Court of Appeal decision in *MWB* v *Rock Advertising* (2016) provided further evidence of this trend towards enforceability but before considering this important case, which we will see subsequently stalled somewhat when it reached the Supreme Court in 2018, the related problem of part payment of a debt needs first to be examined.

4.3.4 **Part payment of a debt**

The traditional principle that the performance of a contractual duty owed to the promisor is not good consideration has also governed agreements to discharge a debt. When a loan agreement is made, the **debtor** makes a promise to pay back all of the debt (and usually some interest). A promise to accept part payment in discharge of the whole debt is not good consideration for the debtor's promise to pay such a sum as the debtor is already obliged to pay that part of the debt (and the remaining debt). The result is that a promise by a **creditor** to accept a smaller amount in discharge of a larger amount is not binding and the creditor can normally still sue for the full amount of the debt. However, the promise may be binding if the debtor goes beyond the existing obligation *at the creditor's request*, for example by paying in kind or in a different manner, etc.

Debtor and creditor A debtor is a person who owes money to a creditor. In a loan contract the borrower is the debtor and the lender is the creditor. The terms have wider meaning and are not restricted to loan agreements; for example, a supplier who provides goods 'on credit' (i.e. with payment to be made in the future) to a business is a creditor and the business is a debtor as the business owes the supplier the value of the goods.

A very old case known as *Pinnel's Case* (1602) first laid down the part payment of a debt rule (including the exception) and the rule was later approved in the House of Lords in *Foakes* v *Beer* (1884). Mrs Beer had previously brought an action against Dr Foakes and had been awarded £2,090. Mrs Beer promised that if Dr Foakes paid £500 immediately and the balance in instalments, she would not take further proceedings against Dr Foakes. It is important to remember that Mrs Beer was entitled to the full sum on the day of judgment and interest on the sum for each day it remained unpaid. By allowing Dr Foakes more time to pay without charging any interest she effectively accepted a smaller sum in place of a larger sum. Mrs Beer then failed to honour her promise and sued Dr Foakes for interest on the sums paid by instalments (i.e. for the full sum owed). Mrs Beer's promise not to sue for the full amount was held to be unenforceable for lack of consideration and so she was entitled to recover the interest. Lord Blackburn was clearly uncomfortable with the judgment because he could see that timely payment of part of a debt could often be of real practical benefit to a businessman (the proverb 'a bird in the hand is worth two in the bush' springs to mind here). However, he felt unable to persuade the other judges of this and concurred with the judgment.

The conundrum which this gives rise to is why a practical benefit can amount to consideration for a promise to pay extra (as in *Roffey Bros*) but not for a promise to accept less (*Foakes* v *Beer*). In *Re Selectmove* (1995) the Court of Appeal felt unable to apply the *Williams* v *Roffey Bros* practical benefit approach to a promise to receive less because that would effectively overrule the House of Lords in *Foakes* v *Beer* (something the Court of Appeal cannot do). The inconsistency has therefore been at least partly due to the doctrine of precedent (the rule that courts must follow the decisions of equivalent and higher courts). Whilst the Court of Appeal in *Williams* v *Roffey Bros* could sideline *Stilk* v *Myrick*, a decision of the King's Bench, it could not do the same in *Re Selectmove* to *Foakes* v *Beer*, a House of Lords decision which it felt was directly in point.

EXAMPLE

Contrasting promise to pay more with promise to accept less

Richard contracts with Dodgy Builders Ltd to build his conservatory. He promises to pay them £8,000 when the conservatory is finished. After the frame has been built, Dodgy Builders realize that they underestimated the cost of putting on a roof and they ask for some more money so that they can complete the job without making a loss on it. Richard promises to pay Dodgy an extra £1,500 because he cannot face having half a conservatory in his garden for much longer and he is planning a garden party for his grandson's birthday party and will need to hire a marquee for £3,000 if the conservatory is not ready on time. If Richard only pays the original contract price of £8,000 on completion can Dodgy Builders sue for the extra £1,500 promised? *Stilk* v *Myrick* suggests that the promise to pay the extra £1,500 is unenforceable because Dodgy Builders are already under an obligation to complete the conservatory and so they neither confer a legal benefit on Richard nor incur a legal detriment themselves. However, *Williams* v *Roffey Bros* would find consideration if Richard received a practical benefit from having the work completed—for example, completion in time for his grandson's birthday and avoiding the cost of the marquee (but compare to *Roffey* where the sub-contractors were *contractually* obliged to pay the penalty clauses if construction was delayed; in this case it would be Richard's choice to hire a substitute marquee)—and there was no duress or fraud.

Imagine now that Richard is a rich man and in a bid to get richer, he decides to lend £100,000 to Dodgy Builders Ltd for a year at 10 per cent interest. Twelve months later, Dodgy Builders inform Richard that they will struggle to pay back his £100,000 plus the interest because an economic slowdown has meant that there is very little work for builders (especially dodgy ones). Richard decides to cut his losses and he promises to accept the original £100,000 in discharge of the total debt (which, now that a year has gone by, is £110,000). Because Richard has accepted a lesser sum in discharge of a larger sum his promise lacks consideration (*Foakes* v *Beer*). It is not possible to argue that the practical benefit of receiving most of his money now (rather than risking actually getting much less of it or none later) is consideration for Richard's promise because *Re Selectmove* pointed out that this would effectively overrule the House of Lords' decision in *Foakes* v *Beer*. Richard can therefore sue for the interest on the loan even though he promised to discharge the full debt. The law of contract appears therefore to have adopted an inconsistent position; Richard's promise to pay extra may be enforceable under *Williams* v *Roffey* but his promise to receive less is unenforceable. However, we will see later that there may be a way for Dodgy Builders to stop Richard going back on his promise to discharge the debt (if in doing so he would be acting inequitably—which he may not be on these facts) by using a rather different doctrine than consideration—see promissory estoppel in section 4.5.1. Furthermore, *Re Selectmove* looked at one point as though it had to be read in the light of *MWB* v *Rock Advertising* although on the facts of the example just given, the outcome would not necessarily be different unless, as we will see, one can identify some practical benefit over and above simply getting one's hands on the money now and avoiding the risk of greater default later.

The decision of the Court of Appeal in *MWB* v *Rock Advertising* (2016) was potentially the most significant decision in this area since *Williams* v *Roffey* and in effect, before the Supreme Court disposed of the case on other grounds in 2018, appeared to collapse the distinction between promises to pay more and promises to accept less. Rock occupied offices in London, paying a monthly licence fee to MWB for several years. In August 2011 it decided to expand and agreed to pay MWB a higher fee for the larger offices for twelve months starting 1 November 2011: £3,500 for the first three months and then £4,443.34 from February 2012. Things did not go well for Rock and they were £12,000 in arrears by late February 2012. At the end of March, MWB locked out Rock and gave notice terminating the agreement and subsequently sued for arrears and damages under the agreement. Rock counterclaimed, alleging that there had been an oral agreement at the end of February whereby Rock could pay less than the contractual amount (of £4,443.34) for a few months but pay more later in the year so that the arrears would be paid off by the end of the year. The oral agreement was denied by MWB on a number of grounds, but the judge found that it had been made and the Court of Appeal accepted both the fact of the agreement and also that it was not ineffective despite a clause in the written agreement requiring any variations to be in writing (the anti-oral variation clause—it was on this point that the Supreme Court subsequently diverged from the Court of Appeal and held that the oral variation was ineffective). The key question for the purposes of consideration was whether the oral promise to accept a lesser payment for the earlier parts of the year was binding even though it was less (taking account of the time value of money) than the existing duty (rather like *Foakes* v *Beer* being a part payment because of the interest).

The trial judge said there was consideration for this oral promise because there was potential commercial benefit to MWB 'in retaining an existing tenant, even if a questionable payer, in the hope of recovering its arrears rather than . . . allowing the property to stand empty for some time at further loss to themselves.' Kitchin LJ in the Court of Appeal agreed with the judge on this point and distinguished *Foakes* v *Beer* and *Re Selectmove* since the benefit to the creditor, MWB, was not simply recovering some of the arrears immediately but also that 'Rock would remain a licensee and continue to occupy the property with the result that it would not be left standing empty for some time at further loss to MWB.' His Lordship also went on to note there had been no suggestion of any duress and so, like *Williams* v *Roffey*, there was a practical benefit which amounted to good consideration. The oral variation (on the erroneous assumption that it was not invalidated by the anti-oral variation clause) was therefore binding and would remain so for so long as Rock continued to make the revised payments (an important limitation which should be borne in mind).

Arden LJ agreed with Kitchin LJ and added her own reasoning where she made it clear that she did not consider there could be any distinction between agreements to pay more, as in *Roffey*, or agreements to pay less, as in this case. Nor should there be any distinction between agreements to pay debts and agreements to do work. The application of the *Roffey* principle to part payment of a debt would not conflict with *Foakes* v *Beer* or *Pinnel's case* because the practical benefit identified was akin to the 'Hawk, horse or robe' exception to *Pinnel's case* whereby payment in kind, which may be more beneficial to the creditor than money, can be consideration if freely accepted instead. The law as stated by Arden LJ involved recognizing consideration 'in the form of a practical benefit which he sought and which is an identifiable benefit over and above the mere fact of accommodating the debtor and not having to enforce the debt' (para. 87).

The implication of the Court of Appeal decision in *MWB* v *Rock* would not have been that *Foakes* v *Beer* should necessarily be overruled or that part payment of a debt would automatically be able to discharge the debt. It would depend on all the facts of the case and on whether there is a genuine accord (and an absence of duress or undue pressure) and also whether one can identify a real, even if marginal as in *MWB*, practical benefit over and above the simple benefit—that is, the bird in the hand—always inherent in actually being paid something. The extra benefit need not be great, consistently with the rule that consideration must be sufficient but need not be adequate, that is, not equal in value to that of the promise. However, in the Supreme Court the view was taken that issues of consideration did not actually arise as the oral variation was ineffective in the light of the anti-oral variation clause. Lord Sumption said at para. [18]: 'that makes it unnecessary to deal with consideration. It is also, I think, undesirable to do so. The issue is a difficult one . . . any decision on this point is likely to involve a re-examination of the decision in *Foakes* v *Beer*. It is probably ripe for re-examination. But if it is to be overruled or its effect substantially modified, it should be before an enlarged panel of the court and in a case where the decision would be more than *obiter dictum*.'

Whilst it is disappointing that the consideration issues were ultimately not ruled upon in the Supreme Court, the Court of Appeal decision in *MWB* provides fertile material for speculation as to how the law might ultimately develop. One further point to note from the Court of Appeal decision is that Arden LJ (as she then was) thought that the oral promise supported by consideration in the form of a practical benefit gave rise to a collateral unilateral contract and so was only enforceable if the debtor actually completed performance although it could not be withdrawn (see section 2.9.1) once the debtor had started to perform, that is, by making the first payment required under the rescheduled debt. Her Ladyship acknowledged two articles by M. Chen-Wishart on this point which are listed in the further reading at the end of this chapter. Kitchin LJ preferred to express no opinion on this way of describing the oral contract although his statement that the oral promise was only binding as long as Rock continued to make the payments amounts to something very similar. The collateral unilateral contract approach arguably has a number of advantages in that it explicitly requires performance (which is more clearly a practical benefit) and not just a promise to perform and it leaves the original promise intact, which may be important if the debtor/performer fails to complete under the new contract and the promisor wishes to revert to that contract to sue for damages based on the costs involved in that first contract.

Another interesting point arising from *MWB* is that it clearly envisages that the practical benefit has to be something over and above the benefit inherent in actual performance (in order to distinguish the situation from *Foakes* v *Beer*) and if that is translated back to the *Williams* v *Roffey* type of case it would mean that one cannot simply assume practical benefit from actual performance just because the promisor has made a fresh promise in order to obtain it and thus that *Williams* v *Roffey* cannot be assumed to displace *Stilk* v *Myrick* in every case.

The Court of Appeal decision in *MWB* also considered the impact of estoppel, which will be covered within the section on enforcing non-bargain promises, after the last topic of consideration has been examined which relates to consideration moving from the promisee.

4.4 Consideration must move from the promisee

Before we move on to estoppel, this last section on consideration looks at the rule that the 'consideration must move from the promisee.' This simply means that the benefit must be conferred (or the detriment incurred) by the promisee (if the promisee wants to sue on the promise) and not by someone else. Thus in *Tweddle* v *Atkinson* (1861), the fathers of a soon-to-be-married couple promised to pay the soon-to-be husband a sum of money upon the marriage. The consideration for each promise was the promise of the other (i.e. the bargain was, 'I'll give him some money if you do too'). After the wedding, the bride's father neglected to pay the money but the court held that the husband could not sue for the promised money because the consideration was provided by his own father (by promising to do the same thing) and was not provided by the son who was trying to enforce the promise (his father—the 'promisee'—could of course have sued). The case is closely linked to the doctrine of privity which is considered in Chapter 13. Note also that although consideration must move from the promisee the consideration need not move to the promisor so that if the promisor requests that the promisee should benefit someone else (not the promisor) this will be good consideration (if the promisor has requested it, the promisor must be taken to regard it as a benefit).

4.5 Enforcing non-bargain promises

The traditional approach to consideration outlined earlier illustrates that the courts only enforce bargains. The promise in *Combe* v *Combe* was not enforced precisely because the husband had *not* made a bargain that in return for his promise to pay his ex-wife, she would refrain from applying to the courts for maintenance. She did that of her own volition and so this detriment—this mere reliance on the promise—could not amount to consideration for her husband's promise.

CROSS REFERENCE
See the 'Digging deeper' section at the end of this chapter.

There is a wealth of opinion on whether such non-bargain promises should be enforceable, but there are essentially two broad trains of thought: the first is to accept the traditional narrow view of consideration in which only bargains form contracts but to supplement it with a non-contractual regime in which non-bargain promises are given effect to through estoppel; the second is to widen the definition of consideration beyond bargained-for promises so that non-bargain promises are enforceable as contracts.

Enforcing non-bargain promises in other jurisdictions

You might find this section easier to understand if you read the following outline of the nature of the problem we are dealing with and how other jurisdictions have dealt with it.

We are dealing with non-bargain promises, that is, promises where the promisor does not request anything in return; the promise is given for free, for nothing, gratis (hence the promise is gratuitous). For example, because I think my niece is a splendid person, I promise to pay her £100 tomorrow. She does not have to do anything in return and I have not asked her to do anything. Should she be able to enforce my promise against me?

Some people have a fundamental problem with enforcing a promise which is given for free; perhaps the promisee should be grateful for the promise and simply call it 'tough luck' if the promisor fails to perform. Whether or not you think such a promise should be enforceable, the case for enforcement is a lot stronger if the promisee relies on the promise to their detriment. In the earlier example, this would be the case if my niece took a friend out for an expensive meal in reliance on my promise to pay her tomorrow. Arguably, she should be entitled to sue me for at least the money she has spent on the meal (say £60)—her reliance interest—if not for the full £100—her expectation interest—which is the normal full contractual measure for breach of a contract (see Chapter 11 for a full explanation of contractual damages).

Australian law, like English law, does not recognize a non-bargain promise as a contract on the grounds that it lacks consideration. However, in *Walton Stores (Interstate) Ltd* v *Maher* (1988) the High Court of Australia (the country's top court) positively enforced a non-bargain promise under the doctrine of estoppel where it would be 'unconscionable' to do otherwise (see the later section entitled 'A wider role for promissory estoppel').

In contrast, the US Restatement of Contracts (2d) s.90 states that non-bargain promises are enforceable as contracts when the promisee has foreseeably relied on the promise and justice requires the promise to be enforced. However, the successful claimant does not necessarily receive the normal contractual measure of damages as these are 'limited as justice requires'; this might (but often does not) mean limiting the damages to the 'reliance interest' or some part thereof.

4.5.1 Estoppel

Despite its application in a huge number of cases, the word 'estoppel' is surprisingly difficult to define. You are unlikely to have heard of it before your legal studies began and it has no everyday equivalent, but it is one of the most fundamental principles running throughout the law.

In essence, estoppel is a principle which prevents a person who, by his words or conduct, leads another to believe in a certain state of affairs from going back on such words or conduct when it would be unjust or inequitable to do so. So, if you lease a flat to a tenant at a particular rent and then agree to accept half the rent for a certain period of time, you cannot subsequently claim the difference between the lower rent and the full rent due under the lease. It would be unfair for you to blow hot and cold—to say one minute that the rent is half price and then go back on your promise and seek the additional amount on top of the rent paid. The key point to remember is that estoppel is not a contractual doctrine in the strict sense (e.g. it is not concerned with enforcing agreements that are supported by consideration (bargains)). In the earlier example, your promise to accept half the rent (without at least something more as per *MWB* v *Rock*) is gratuitous and unsupported by consideration and yet the law of estoppel might still hold you bound where it would be unjust not to do so (even if there is no practical benefit to the creditor as would be required under *MWB* and thus no consideration even under that case, and certainly not under the *Foakes* v *Beer* line of cases where a gratuitous promise to accept less is unenforceable *as a contractual promise*).

There are a large number of different types of estoppel (effectively variations on the common principle applied in different contexts) but we are concerned with the following two: estoppel by representation and promissory estoppel.

Estoppel by representation

As its name suggests, estoppel by representation is not concerned with promises but instead can arise when one party makes a false representation *of fact* upon which the other party acts. Where justice demands (and this flexibility is the key feature of all estoppels), the first party is estopped (i.e. barred) from denying the truth of their representation (they have to argue their case as though the facts were as they had represented them). In *Jorden* v *Money* (1854) Mrs Jorden had said time and time again that she would not enforce a bond (a type of debt) against Mr Money. Mr Money then married, relying on his belief that the bond (debt) would not be enforced and that his financial position was secure. In order to make his position crystal clear, Mr Money sought a declaration from the court that he had been validly released from the bond and he also sought an injunction to prevent it being enforced. Mr Money could not argue that he had been released from the debt under a contract because at the time the Statute of Frauds required such contracts to be in writing and signed. He therefore had to argue his case in estoppel. The House of Lords decided that Mrs Jorden had *promised* not to enforce the bond in the future, but she had not made a statement *of fact* that the bond had been discharged. Accordingly, she was not estopped from denying that the bond was discharged because estoppel only applied to statements of fact and not to promises. For a promise to be enforced, it had to comply with the statutory rules on contracts, which this promise did not.

Promissory estoppel

At this point, you might well think that any attempt to enforce a promise (as opposed to a representation) by estoppel is doomed to fail because the House of Lords in *Jorden* v *Money* clearly ruled that estoppel only applied to statements of fact and not promises as to the future.

However, in *Hughes* v *Metropolitan Railway Company* (1877), the House of Lords gave effect to conduct which amounted to a promise as to future conduct. The landowner Hughes served notice on the Railway Company to perform repairs on the property it leased from him within six months, on pain of forfeiture of the lease. The Railway Company said that it would carry out the repairs but, before it did this, it wished to hear from Hughes on its proposal for

Hughes to buy the Railway Company's leasehold interest in the property. The parties entered into negotiations but they did not arrive at an agreement and Hughes sought to eject the Railway Company from the property six months after it had been served the notice of repair (the Railway Company performed the repairs two months later). The House of Lords held that Hughes' conduct had led the Railway Company to believe that Hughes would suspend his strict rights under the lease during the period of negotiation and it would be inequitable to allow Hughes to later enforce those strict rights; in essence, Hughes was held to have promised that he would not treat the two months of negotiations as counting towards the six months in which the Railway Company had to repair the property, with the consequence that the Railway Company had completed the repairs in time.

The decision in *Hughes* was largely ignored until Denning J brought it into the limelight in *Central London Property Trust Ltd* v *High Trees House Ltd* (1947) where he said: 'The law has not been standing still since *Jorden* v *Money*' before identifying a broad principle—now known as promissory estoppel—'a promise intended to be binding, was intended to be acted upon and in fact acted upon is binding so far as its terms properly apply.' In the case itself, the landlord had leased out some flats in London for £2,500 per year but the Second World War intervened and, unsurprisingly, it was difficult for the tenant to sublet the flats as he had originally intended. The landlord said that he would accept £1,250 per year in discharge of the tenant's obligation to pay £2,500 per year. Denning J thought that the promise to accept less was enforceable only so long as the wartime conditions existed. As soon as the war ended and the flats could be sublet again the landlord could claim the full contractual rate of £2,500 without acting inconsistently with his promise. This was sufficient to dispose of the case because the landlord only claimed the full rent from the end of the war. However, Denning J's principle would have estopped the landlord from claiming the extra rent (the difference between £2,500 and £1,250), if he had claimed it during the war years, because the promise to accept less was intended to be binding, was intended to be acted upon and was acted upon. Whilst it was accepted that the relied-on promise did not create 'a cause of action in damages,' the landlord could not have acted inconsistently with his promise and claimed the original contract price of £2,500 per year for the war years. The landlord's legal right to the full rent during the war had therefore been extinguished.

It is worth noting that Denning J navigated his way around the House of Lords' decision in *Jorden* v *Money* (which laid down the rule that estoppel only operates on statements of fact and not on promises of future conduct) by sidelining the case as one in which Mrs Jorden did not intend to be legally bound—you might like to read the judgment in both cases and make your own mind up on what was the ratio of *Jorden* v *Money.*

The *High Trees* principle represents an innovative and creative use of estoppel, but its limitations as compared with contract are well illustrated by *Combe* v *Combe*, decided just four years later in 1951. We saw in section 4.1.3 that the promise in *Combe* v *Combe* lacked consideration because there was no request from Mr Combe that his wife should abstain from applying for maintenance and thus no bargain. However, the first instance judge had based his award to Mrs Combe of £600 arrears (for the past six years) on promissory estoppel. This was reversed by Denning LJ (now in the Court of Appeal) where he said:

> Much as I am inclined to favour the principle of the *High Trees* case, it is important that it should not be stretched too far lest it should be endangered. It does not create causes of action where none existed before. It only prevents a party from insisting on his strict legal rights when it would be unjust to allow him to do so, having regard to the dealings which have taken place between the parties.

He explained that the principle did not overthrow the doctrine of consideration, which was 'too firmly fixed to be overthrown by a side wind', and also that the existing contractual obligation, which often provides the setting for promissory estoppel, must still be supported by consideration. A key limit on the scope of promissory estoppel is therefore that it only works *in the context* of a bargain, even though it results in the enforcement of a non-bargain promise to modify or discharge that bargain. In this way promissory estoppel is parasitic on bargains because it cannot operate without a pre-existing obligation, which, if it is contractual in nature, must of course be supported by consideration and hence be a bargain. In *High Trees* the original lease contract was supported by consideration; the principle enunciated by Denning LJ simply prevented the landlord from saying 'Let's reduce the rent; you can have it for £1,250' and then saying 'I've changed my mind, pay me the contract figure of £2,500.' Normal contractual principles (i.e. the requirement of consideration) state that the non-bargain promise to reduce the rent is unenforceable. Counsel in *Combe* v *Combe* was credited by Birkett LJ with inventing the phrase 'promissory estoppel can be used as a shield but not as a sword' and, whilst many students remember this catchy little metaphor, it does not in itself explain the scope of promissory estoppel. You need to ensure that you understand that promissory estoppel is a 'shield' because it can block actions on *pre-existing obligations* where there has been a fresh promise unsupported by consideration (i.e. a non-bargain promise) *to modify or discharge the pre-existing obligation*; in this way, the landowner Hughes was not allowed to rely on his strict legal rights under the lease because these had been modified when he indicated that time would stop running against the Railway Company during the negotiations. Similarly, the tenant in *High Trees* sought to use estoppel defensively against the claim by the landlord based on his strict legal rights under the lease (the difference being that the landlord's claim for the full rent after the war succeeded in this case because the estoppel only extinguished his strict rights for the duration of the war).

Promissory estoppel cannot be used aggressively as a 'sword' in the sense that it cannot be used to enforce a standalone non-bargain promise to pay £100. The promisee must therefore wait to be sued on a pre-existing obligation and then use promissory estoppel as a defence, that is, as a shield. Under English law, promissory estoppel mitigates the harshness of the rule that a promise to modify or discharge a contract must be supported by consideration, but it goes no further than this as things stand at the moment.

EXAMPLE

The scope of promissory estoppel

Facts

I lend you £100. You are under a contractual obligation to pay me £100. Later on, you explain how it's tough being a student and I agree, in order to help you continue your studies, that I will accept £75 in discharge of the debt. You pay me £75 and go and buy a new textbook that you could not afford before. Later, I rethink my generosity and sue you for the extra £25; do I have a case?

Analysis

Foakes v *Beer* and *Re Selectmove* make it clear that there is no consideration for my promise to discharge the debt and so there is no contract for the partial discharge of the debt (this would still be the case even under the Court of Appeal's approach in *MWB* unless there is some identifiable benefit to me, which there does not appear to be unless perhaps I am your close relation with an interest in your continuation of your studies); the contractual obligation to pay the balance stands and you still owe me £25. However, my promise to discharge the debt on receipt of £75 was intended to be binding and intended to be acted on by you. You acted on it (by paying me £75 and also by buying the textbook) and so, following Denning J in *High Trees*, I will not be allowed to enforce my strict legal rights under the original loan agreement if to do so would inequitably allow me to act inconsistently with my promise. Whether you can resist my claim to the £25 indefinitely is another question. It may be that the estoppel only suspends rather than extinguishes your obligation to pay and it might be that it can be revived after you have been given reasonable notice—after all, you can to some extent resume your original position by selling the book or possibly even getting a refund, or I could wait until you graduate and become a rich and successful lawyer and then sue you (all within the six-year limitation period of course)!

Alternative facts

Imagine now that there was no prior loan agreement. You are therefore under no pre-existing obligation to me. You explain how it's tough being a poor student and I promise to pay you £25 to help you along. You again buy that long sought-after textbook (this one, of course!).

Analysis

There is obviously no consideration for my promise because you have given me nothing in return and so there is no contractual obligation for me to pay you. My promise was intended to be binding and intended to be acted upon, and you did act upon it, but the courts will still not enforce my promise. This is because the law of estoppel can only prevent me from acting inconsistently with a promise to modify or discharge a pre-existing contractual obligation; it cannot make me honour all of my promises by positively enforcing them as though they were contracts. The key point is not that all relied-upon promises are enforceable, but that I cannot blow hot and cold, as in the first version of the facts, telling you one minute that the debt is discharged and the next minute that you owe me £100. Sorry, but in the second version, I don't have to pay you £25!

In *MWB* the Court of Appeal considered whether the landlords were bound by the principle of promissory estoppel and concluded on the facts that they were not. This did not matter too much because the court had already decided that they were bound anyway on the basis that the promise was supported by consideration because there was a practical benefit to the promisor. Part of the reason why promissory estoppel did not apply was that although Rock had paid out £3,500 in accordance with the new agreement, it did not suffer any detriment thereby (it owed much more than that) and thus it was not inequitable for MWB to enforce the original agreement by giving notice as it did. The decision in the Court of Appeal thus brings out the difference between the basis of consideration in this type of case—(impliedly) requested benefit, which was found to exist—and promissory estoppel—detrimental reliance rendering it inequitable to go back on the promise, which was lacking. What seems a little odd on the other hand, you may think, is that the Court of Appeal effectively concluded that the landlords got something (not very much, admittedly) of practical benefit which they had bargained for but that on the other hand it would not have been inequitable for them to go back on their word!

A wider role for promissory estoppel?

Other jurisdictions are not satisfied with English law's defensive approach to promissory estoppel. In Australia, a non-bargain promise can be positively enforced even if it does not seek to modify or discharge a pre-existing contract. In *Walton Stores (Interstate) Ltd* v *Maher* (1988) Walton Stores had led the Mahers to believe that they would enter into a contract for the lease of Maher's land. This amounted to an implied promise to complete a contract, a promise that was unsupported by consideration because Walton Stores had not requested anything in return; there was therefore no bargain. Walton Stores was estopped from reneging on this implied promise because, on the facts of the case, it would have been unconscionable to do so. Unconscionability is a very difficult concept to describe, but it is best to think of it as a judge's perception of what is so unjust or unfair that the court should not be prepared to allow it to happen. The conduct of Walton Stores was unconscionable because they knew that Maher had begun demolition and building work and had incurred expenses in reliance on the expected contract. It was therefore unfair to watch Maher spend all that money and effort and then back out of the contract.

In the High Court of Australia, Brennan J reasoned that if promises to modify or discharge an obligation could be enforced then promises to create new obligations should also be capable of enforcement. Surely allowing either type of promise to be breached is capable of being unjust in the right circumstances? The argument is that if the doctrine of consideration is drawn so narrowly that only bargain promises are enforceable then promissory estoppel should expand to cover both promises to discharge an obligation and promises to create a new obligation.

The US Restatement of Contracts (2d) s.90 states that:

> A promise which the promisor should reasonably expect to induce action or forbearance on the part of the promisee . . . and which does induce such action or forbearance is binding if injustice can be avoided only by enforcement of the promise. The remedy granted for breach may be limited as justice requires.

Remembering that the US Restatement of Contracts (2d) s.71 laid down that only bargains could constitute good consideration, we can see that s.90 is intended to catch non-bargain promises *where the promisee has foreseeably relied on the promise* and justice requires the promise to be enforced (even though the reliance was not requested). This liability does not *necessarily* entail the full normal contractual measure of damages and it may be limited to reliance damages because it rests upon reliance and what justice requires, rather like the Australian doctrine of promissory estoppel.

Other aspects of promissory estoppel

Returning to English law, even if a non-bargain promise fits within the limits placed on promissory estoppel in *Combe* v *Combe*, it is not exactly clear what are the precise requirements for, and effects of, promissory estoppel. In *High Trees* Denning J mentioned four requirements relating to the promise:

(1) The promisor must intend it to be binding;

(2) He must intend it to be acted upon;

(3) It must be acted upon; and

(4) The promisor must attempt to act inconsistently with his promise.

Later cases have shown that more is necessary. Firstly, it must be *inequitable* (unfair) for the promisor to insist upon his strict legal right after he has promised that he would not. This requirement was introduced by Lord Denning MR in *D. & C. Builders Ltd* v *Rees* (1966) where a firm of builders accepted a lesser sum in discharge of a larger sum. Lord Denning MR thought that, despite their promise to accept less, it was not inequitable for the builders to insist on full payment of the existing debt because Rees had exploited the builders' desperate need to be paid some money in order to avoid insolvency. This case was decided before the doctrine of economic duress was introduced, but it was obvious that promissory estoppel, being an equitable doctrine, would not tolerate any undue pressure being placed on the promisor. (The result would be no different now even under the *MWB* Court of Appeal approach as there would still be no consideration as there is no evidence of additional practical benefit and even if there were, there was hardly an absence of duress.)

➤ CROSS REFERENCE

See Chapter 9, section 9.1.4 for economic duress.

In *Collier* v *P & M J Wright (Holdings) Ltd* (2007) Arden LJ relied upon Denning LJ's judgment in *Rees* to propose a radical restatement of promissory estoppel according to which inequity would be established if a debtor offered to pay part of the debt, the creditor freely accepted that offer and the debtor then paid part of the debt in reliance on the creditor's acceptance that such payment would discharge the debt in full. At para. [42] she said:

> The facts of this case demonstrate that, if (1) a debtor offers to pay part only of the amount he owes; (2) the creditor voluntarily accepts that offer, and (3) in reliance on the creditor's acceptance the debtor pays that part of the amount he owes in full, the creditor will, by virtue of the doctrine of promissory estoppel, be bound to accept that sum in full and final satisfaction of the whole debt. For him to resile will of itself be inequitable. In addition, in these circumstances, the promissory estoppel has the effect of extinguishing the creditor's right to the balance of the debt.

However, this restatement risks depriving the equitable doctrine of its distinguishing characteristic: namely, that equity provides relief where justice requires it to do so. This requires there to be an independent assessment of whether it would be inequitable for the creditor to resile from the promise and Kitchin LJ in the Court of Appeal in *MWB* made this very point at the end of para. 61 of the judgment saying that 'all will depend upon the circumstances.' Arden LJ herself defended what she had said in *Collier* v *Wright* by pointing out that the issue in *Collier* had been whether there should be a full trial and it would be at the trial that the question would be examined of whether it was inequitable to go back on the promise. In effect, her Ladyship is agreeing that the ingredients of promissory estoppel leave a discretionary evaluative question for the court to determine whether, and to what extent, the promisor should be estopped from going back on his word. There would in any event be no need to push promissory estoppel too hard as a way round *Foakes* v *Beer* if the practical benefit argument could lead to the debt being discharged via consideration.

A second, related issue with promissory estoppel is that it is unclear whether the promisee must rely on the promise *to his detriment*. In *High Trees* it is difficult to see how the tenant acted to his detriment by simply paying less money per year and in *The Post Chaser* (1982) Robert Goff J thought that detrimental reliance was not necessary for promissory estoppel. However, it is easier to show that it would be inequitable to allow the promisor to deviate from the promise when there has been detrimental reliance (i.e. detrimental reliance is helpful in proving inequity). On the facts, the promisee's position had not been prejudiced by his reliance on the promise and Robert Goff J held that it was not inequitable to allow the promisor to rely upon his strict legal rights under a pre-existing obligation. The approach of making detriment a factor in assessing whether it is inequitable to resile on the promise also seems to be inherent in the judgment of Kitchin LJ in *MWB*.

Thirdly, the promise must be clear and unequivocal. In *Woodhouse AC Israel Cocoa Ltd SA v Nigerian Produce Marketing Co. Ltd* (1972) the promise was too ambiguous to support a contractual agreement to vary an existing contract and it followed that it must also be too ambiguous to support promissory estoppel. After all, the effect of promissory estoppel would be to vary the contract also. You should have noticed by now that most cases involving promissory estoppel fail on the facts (i.e. the courts are unwilling to deviate too far from enforcing promises supported by consideration).

The final point to note about promissory estoppel relates to its effect and the question of the extent to which, or the duration for which, it will prevent someone going back on a pre-existing promise. We know that the promisor is estopped from asserting his strict contractual rights when he has promised not to do so, but is the effect of this estoppel temporary or permanent? The question generally arises when there is a contract with recurrent or continuing obligations. Some cases suggest that promissory estoppel extinguishes the promisor's rights forever, but others suggest that the original contract can be resurrected by giving notice. In this latter case the promissory estoppel is suspensory only. In *Tool Metal Manufacturing Co. Ltd* v *Tungsten Electric Co. Ltd* (1955) the owner of a patent promised not to enforce the strict rights he had under a contract. He did this because the Second World War interrupted the contract (as in *High Trees*) and the Court of Appeal held that the promise could be revoked by giving reasonable notice; in other words, the promissory estoppel only operated to suspend the strict rights under the contract and not to extinguish them entirely. In *High Trees* Denning J appeared to say that the right to collect full rent for the war years had been extinguished but this did not apply to the years after the war because the promise was only meant to apply to the war years. This might appear to be a different route to the same solution if it makes little difference whether the estoppel is said to be suspensory in effect or whether the promise is held to relate to a specific or limited time. But in *High Trees*, the obligation to pay the full rent during the war years was not suspended; those particular obligations were extinguished forever, even if the obligations to pay the full rent in the years after the war were unaffected and thus revived. In reality, the exact effect of promissory estoppel in a particular case will depend on the precise nature of the promise made and to what extent it would be inequitable to allow the promisor to go back on it, but there seems little doubt that in an appropriate case, particular legal rights can in effect be extinguished.

This approach can also be seen in comments in the Court of Appeal in the *MWB* case, where Kitchin LJ said at para. 61: 'It may be the case that it would be inequitable to allow the promisor to go back upon his promise without giving reasonable notice, as in the *Tool Metal* case; or it may be that it would be inequitable to allow the promisor to go back on his promise at all with the result that the right is extinguished. All will depend on the circumstances.'

CROSS REFERENCE

See Chapter 11, section 11.2.1 for discussion of expectation and reliance.

Digging deeper

We have seen earlier that, in certain circumstances, non-bargain promises can be enforced through promissory estoppel. Professor Atiyah has suggested that instead of accepting the narrow model of consideration and supplementing it with a doctrine of estoppel, the law should widen the scope of consideration so that it includes some non-bargain promises. In this way, non-bargain promises can form contracts.

'Consideration: A Restatement' in *Essays on Contract* (1986) sets out a revised version of his view, first expressed in 1971, that consideration simply means that there is a good reason to enforce a promise. He argues that, historically, judges had to decide out of all the promises that came before them which they would enforce and which they would not. When they found a good reason to enforce a particular promise they said it was supported by consideration. A promise without a good reason for enforcement lacked consideration. Since then the meaning of consideration has narrowed into the doctrine outlined earlier in this chapter, leading to the exclusion of gratuitous non-bargain promises from the law of contract. Atiyah argued that if we remember the true meaning of consideration then many non-bargain promises will not necessarily lack consideration and may possess a good reason to enforce them.

As a consequence, the law of contract should not simply look for bargains. These are not the sole 'good reasons' justifying enforcement, and reliance on the promise by the promisee may also be a good reason (i.e. relied-upon promises would be enforceable). The similarity to the estoppel cases is striking but the important point is that Atiyah believed that relied-upon promises would form *contracts* and not merely estoppels. Atiyah used *Jorden* v *Money* as evidence that the doctrine of promissory estoppel is unnecessary. He thought that the promise not to enforce the bond was supported by consideration despite the fact that there was no bargain. Mr Money's reliance on the promise provided a good reason to enforce it and the only reason why the case had to be pleaded on the basis of estoppel by representation was that the Statute of Frauds had not been complied with. Quite rightly, the House of Lords would not allow the Statute of Frauds to be avoided by pleading an estoppel as opposed to a contract. A case not regulated by the Statute of Frauds would be decided on the basis of a clear contract supported by consideration, with no need for Denning J in *High Trees* to enunciate a doctrine of promissory estoppel. Having put forward his case for restating consideration, Atiyah proposed a more fundamental change to the law of contract. He suggested that contracts should focus on protecting reliance rather than expectation. In order to understand this next step we need to fast-forward to the subject matter of the latter part of this book: damages for breach of contract—although the issue has also been touched upon in Chapter 1.

The usual response to a breach of contract is to fulfil the expectations of the non-breaching party. This means that he is put in the position he would have been in had the breach not happened. The 'expectation interest' is protected. So, if I promise you a car if you win a competition, then you will expect a car. To protect your expectation interest the courts must order me to buy you a car (or at least give you the value of a car). You would not be happy with compensation for the time and money you spent on entering the competition as that would be much less and you made a bargain and won. An alternative approach, not usually used as a response to the breach of a bargained-for promise, is to compensate the non-breaching party for any loss caused through relying on the promise (protecting his 'reliance interest'). Again, if I promise gratuitously to give you £50 you will expect £50 but your reliance loss will be nothing. If, in reliance on my promise, you give £20 to a charity, then your reliance loss is £20.

Atiyah argues that this latter response should be used more often once we accept his restatement of consideration. This is probably the most crucial part of Atiyah's essay and the link between his criticism of the current narrowness of the doctrine of consideration and his view on a more appropriately flexible response to the breach of a promise is important. The present system, where only bargains are supported by consideration, protects the expectation interest of a promisee. This can be justified on the basis that the promisee has 'paid for' or 'bought' his expectation by giving something in return to the promisor. A system based on Atiyah's 'good reason' view of consideration will enforce some non-bargain promises, perhaps for the reason that the promisee relied on the promise. In relation to these promises, the promisee has not given anything in return for the promise. The promisee has not 'paid' for the full expectation interest to be protected and so the remedy may be limited to the loss incurred in reliance. You could think of this as a type of insurance: if you pay an extra premium (consideration) you get increased cover instead of the standard cover. So, if you pay for a promise you may be better protected if the promise is broken; you will get what you expected instead of simply compensation for your reliance loss.

We have explained that there are many opinions on how non-bargain promises should be treated, but that you should focus on two main approaches. The first retains the narrow view of consideration but supplements it with the doctrine of promissory estoppel which enforces non-bargain promises which seek to vary or discharge bargained-for promises. The US Restatement of Contracts (2d) and the High Court of Australia will, in certain circumstances, enforce non-bargain promises but there is some debate over what the appropriate remedy is. If the remedy is to meet the promisee's expectation interest, then promissory estoppel will take over from contract and it would be pointless to distinguish between bargain and non-bargain promises. However, the remedy in the US Restatement may be limited as justice requires, which suggests that only the reliance interest may be protected in certain cases (although it seems in practice this limitation is widely ignored). In the related area of proprietary estoppel, the Supreme Court in *Guest v Guest* (2022) (a classic proprietary estoppel case involving non-contractual assurances by parents that they would leave a share of their farm to a son if he continued to work for them on the farm) wrestled at length with the complexities of the alternative bases of recovery for this type of estoppel. The majority favoured the view that expectation should be at least the starting point for compensation in this case when the parents fell out with the son and cut him out of their will. Thus the son should get the value of his promised share of the farm, about £1.3 million, subject to deductions for getting it early, that is, before his parents died. Lord Leggatt on the other hand considered that compensation for detrimental reliance (working for 32 years on the farm for little pay) would be sufficient in this case (amounting to £610,000 which he could have earned by working elsewhere if he had not relied on his parents' promise).

The second approach to the treatment of non-bargain promises is to argue that the modern-day doctrine of consideration is too narrow and that non-bargain promises should be capable of forming contracts. The problem with this approach is that the normal contractual measure of protection may be too strong for non-bargain promises which are only enforceable because they have been relied upon. Atiyah has suggested that automatic protection of the expectation interest is inappropriate anyway and in many cases it will be better to protect only the reliance interest, but how do we decide which measure to apply and when? If a distinction is made between bargain and non-bargain promises, then is the situation really any different from the current position? The answer to this latter question is still 'yes' as far as English law is concerned because of the current limitation on estoppel—that it does not create a cause of action but only stops someone going back on a promise not to enforce existing legal rights.

The result is that English law is left with a mixed bag of doctrines and must muddle through as best it can; we are therefore likely to continue to see more cases like *Williams* v *Roffey Bros* where the courts are forced to stretch the limits of consideration (to such a degree that it is subject to the criticism that it 'invents' consideration where it feels that a party should be given a contractual remedy) and more cases like *Combe* v *Combe* and *Collier* v *P & M J Wright (Holdings) Ltd* where, having failed to establish consideration, the parties will try their hand at promissory estoppel. In addition, we shall see in Chapter 9 how the doctrine of duress has developed to take over ground which was once ruled by the doctrine of consideration.

Summary

1. Definition of consideration

Consideration is a benefit or burden provided or incurred by the promisee in return for the promise and is an essential ingredient of the contract.

Each promise in a contract must be supported by 'sufficient' (i.e. valid) consideration but the value or amount of the consideration does not have to be equal to what is given in return.

2. Consideration as the price of promise

The benefit or burden must be requested by the promisor as the price for the promise because the courts will normally only enforce bargains/exchanges.

A request is more likely to be implied when the act done in return for a promise clearly benefits the promisor.

3. Past consideration not sufficient

The benefit or burden must be conferred or incurred at or after the time of the promise—otherwise it is regarded as past and insufficient. This is really a consequence of the rule that consideration must be requested as the price for a promise.

4. Performance of a pre-existing obligation

Performance of pre-existing obligations raises problems because it may appear that there is no legal burden shouldered by the promisee above what the promisor is already legally obliged to do and no legal benefit to the promisor above what the promisor is legally already clearly entitled to expect.

There is no problem if the requested performance can be characterized as one which goes beyond any pre-existing duty since the extra requested benefit and burden is clear.

Performance of a pre-existing non-contractual obligation (public duty) can or arguably should constitute a legal benefit or burden so long as the enforcement of the promise is not contrary to the public interest.

Performance of a pre-existing contractual obligation owed to a third party definitely is a legal benefit/burden.

Performance of a pre-existing contractual obligation owed to the promisor is not in itself regarded as a legal benefit or burden but, if the promisor receives a practical benefit from the performance and there is no duress or fraud, then there may be a legally recognized benefit for a promise to pay extra and thus consideration.

Part payment of a debt cannot of itself be a sufficient consideration for a promise to discharge the debt (even though the Court of Appeal in *MWB* v *Rock* appeared to recognize that an identifiable practical benefit to the creditor over and above simply the actual receipt of the money could be regarded as consideration, this cannot yet be regarded as the law since the Supreme Court reversed the decision on a totally different ground and declined to decide the issues relating to consideration which would only have been *obiter*).

5. Consideration must move from the promisee

The benefit or burden must be conferred or incurred by the promisee, although the benefit need not be conferred directly on the promisor provided it is conferred in accordance with the promisor's request.

6. Non-bargained-for (but relied-on) promises

A promise to discharge or vary a pre-existing contractual obligation may, if relied on by the debtor, prevent a creditor from enforcing that pre-existing obligation (via promissory estoppel) when it would be inequitable to allow the promisor to do so, although such a promise may in some circumstances only appear to suspend rights rather than extinguish them.

Promissory estoppel may be used as a shield but not a sword (i.e. to prevent a promisor from acting inconsistently in relation to a gratuitous promise to discharge or modify a pre-existing obligation, but not to enforce a gratuitous promise on its own). Atiyah has argued that consideration really means 'a good reason to enforce a promise' and that all foreseeably relied-upon promises should be enforced. Other jurisdictions such as the USA and Australia also sometimes directly enforce relied-upon promises but not necessarily as contracts.

One difficult question raised in all these instances where there is no bargain is whether to fully protect the promisee's expectations or just the promisee's reliance.

? Questions

1. Multi-Build plc has agreed with Blueburn Rovers, the Premier League Champions, to refurbish their sports stadium at a cost of £10 million, the work to be completed by 1 July. The stadium is to be used by the Football Association (FA) for the World Cup finals taking place in early August. In March, Multi-Build informs Rovers that, due to bad weather conditions and worker strikes, the stadium is unlikely to be ready until the end of August. Hearing of this on the national news, the FA contacts Multi-Build and offers it £1 million out of the profits of the World Cup if the work is completed on schedule. Rovers are also distraught that they may lose out on the prestige and commercial opportunities which come with hosting the World Cup finals and so they offer Multi-Build an extra £500,000 if the work is completed on schedule and a further £500,000 if Multi-Build incorporate an extra ten snack bars into the design.

Multi-Build completes the stadium (including the additional snack bars) in June. The World Cup finals, however, fail to make as much profit as anticipated and in September the FA tells Multi-Build that as a result it can only pay £600,000. Multi-Build accepts this 'as total discharge, in consideration of the complimentary tickets and facilities provided by the FA for the directors of Multi-Build at the finals.' In October, the FA signs a lucrative sponsorship deal and Multi-Build, hearing of this, thinks that it should be paid the outstanding £400,000.

The World Cup has been a disaster for Rovers; their star player has broken his leg and they sold far fewer hot dogs and pies than they expected. They tell Multi-Build that they can only have the original £10 million and that they should count themselves lucky to get that.

Advise Multi-Build.

2. 'The law of contract is based upon bargain yet the rules of consideration fail to recognize economic reality.' Discuss.
3. 'The doctrine of consideration is too firmly fixed to be overthrown by a side wind' Denning LJ, *Combe* v *Combe* (1951). Discuss.
4. You are a computer expert and find compromising pictures of a well-known Home Office politician newly posted on the Internet. You offer to find and delete all references and links to the pictures if he processes your fiancée's visa application. He agrees. Is your agreement enforceable? If not, *precisely* why not? What if, before he had agreed to your offer, you told him that it would be very easy for you to email all of the pictures to the tabloid press?
5. If Bert voluntarily starts work on a building site before a contract has been signed with Build'em High, should he receive any money for the work done if Build'em High later decides not to complete the contract? What if Build'em High knows that Bert is spending a lot of time and money on preparing the building site and keeps on telling him how lucrative the contract will be once it is signed and how he will appreciate all the work he has done up front?

Further reading

Books

Chen-Wishart, M, *Contract Law*, 7th edn (Oxford University Press, 2022) ch 3.

McKendrick, E, *Contract Law: Text, Cases, and Materials*, 11th edn (Oxford University Press, 2024) ch 5.

O'Sullivan, J, and Hilliard, J, *The Law of Contract*, 11th edn (Oxford University Press, 2024) ch 5.

Articles

Atiyah, PS, 'When is an enforceable agreement not a contract? Answer: when it is an equity' (1976) 92 LQR 174.

Chen-Wishart, M, 'A bird in the hand: Consideration and contract modifications' in Burrows and Peel eds, *Contract Formations and Parties* (Oxford University Press, 2010).

Chen-Wishart, M, 'Reforming consideration—no greener pastures' in Degeling, Edelman and Goudkamp eds, *Contract in Commercial Law* (Thomson, 2016).

Cooke, E, 'Estoppel and the protection of expectations' (1997) 17 LS 258.

Halson, R, 'The offensive limits of promissory estoppel' [1999] LMCLQ 256.

O'Sullivan, J, 'In defence of Foakes *v* Beer' (1996) 55 CLJ 219.

Treitel, GH, 'Consideration: A critical analysis of Professor Atiyah's fundamental restatement' (1976) 50 ALJ 239.

Case notes

(1988) 104 LQR 362 (*Walton Stores (Interstate)* Ltd v *Maher*).

PART II

CONTENTS AND BORDERS

Part I introduced the essential ingredients common to all contracts. We saw that contractual obligations cannot be formed unless there is an agreement, certainty, an intention to create legal relations and consideration. This next Part delves deeper into the contract itself and looks at the nature or type of contractual obligations formed. Think of a contract as a cake. All cakes have the same essential ingredients: eggs, flour, sugar and fat. It is possible to put in other items, such as chocolate chips or a cream filling (a tasty prospect), but it is fair to say that you cannot make a cake without the essentials. Once we know that we have created a cake as opposed to, say, a biscuit, we can look one level deeper and ask what kind of cake we have created and what does it contain: a jam and cream sponge or a cherry madeira cake? In the same way, once we have identified that we have a contract on our hands, as opposed to say a tort (not a torte!), we must look carefully at the contract to find out what types of contractual obligations have been formed and what are their contents and their limits.

We will look at these in turn:

(1) Chapter 5 is concerned with the positive aspects of the contract—its positive terms.

(2) In Chapter 6, we look at the negative or limiting aspects, as indicated by exclusion clauses—which can be thought of as negative terms.

(3) Chapter 7 is concerned with the territory just beyond the borders of the contract, where we find the representations which are not part of the contract but which influenced its creation and which, if false, are remedied by the law on misrepresentation.

5 Positive terms

LEARNING OBJECTIVES

This chapter will help you to:

- distinguish between a term of the contract and a representation;
- understand what a collateral contract is;
- understand when a term will be implied in fact into a contract to give effect to the parties' intentions and when a term will be implied in law as a matter of policy; and
- distinguish between conditions, warranties and innominate terms and understand the different consequences flowing from the breach of each type of term.

Introduction

The terms of the contract give substance to the parties' obligations. They lay down what each party is expected to do in performance of its obligations, and so it is crucial in any dispute to first establish the terms of the contract before looking to see whether one party has failed to perform its obligations.

There are three key questions you should ask yourself when looking at the terms of a contract:

(1) Is a statement a term of the contract or merely a representation?
(2) Can any other terms be implied into the contract?
(3) If a statement is a term of the contract, is it a condition, a warranty or an innominate term?

5.1 Terms and representations

5.1.1 The distinction between terms and representations

Terms are part of the contract but representations are not; they float around the edge of the contractual relationship but are outside its borders and do not form part of it. We describe representations as 'floating' because they are made around about the time of contracting and they can give rise to damages and affect the validity of the contract, but they do not actually constitute the terms of the contract.

The distinction between terms and representations is made mainly in order to decide what remedy is available if a particular statement is unfulfilled. If the statement forms a term of the contract then there is an *automatic* right to damages for its breach, but there is no *automatic* right to damages if the words are a representation that turns out to be untrue. We shall see in Chapter 7 that a false representation *may* entitle the innocent party to damages (if there is fault) but the usual remedy is to unravel the contract (known as rescission, see Chapter 7, section 7.1) and even this remedy can be lost if, for example, a third party's rights would be affected. Whilst the protection against false representations increased considerably during the last third of the twentieth century, the point remains that the remedies for breach of a term and those for a false representation are *different*.

5.1.2 How to distinguish a term from a representation

warranty (first sense)
A warranty is a term of the contract, as opposed to a representation which is not part of the contract. A warranty constitutes a promise or guarantee which, if broken, automatically entitles the other party to damages to make good the promise.

The test used to distinguish a term from a representation is based on the parties' objective intentions. As the parties are not normally conscious of the distinction when they make their contracts it is unlikely that a particular statement will be labelled as 'term' or 'representation'. You should bear this in mind when tackling a problem question in an examination and realize that you cannot recognize a term from a representation merely by looking at the words used. It is necessary to look at the circumstances and ask what a reasonable person would think of a particular statement in its overall context. In *Oscar Chess Ltd* v *Williams* (1957), Mr Williams sold a car to the dealers, Oscar Chess Ltd. Mr Williams said that the car was a 1948 model because this is what the registration book stated. The car was in fact a 1939 model (worth much less). The dealers were obviously aggrieved because they had bought a 'lemon' and they claimed the difference in value between a 1948 model and a 1939 model as damages for breach of contract. Denning LJ explained very clearly the different ways in which the word **warranty** is used (you should read his judgment; as usual he explains complex issues in a simple, easy-to-read manner).

The key point about warranties is that their breach gives rise *simply* to a right to damages for breach of contract, unlike representations, where there is no right to contractual damages. The case of *Oscar Chess* rested on whether Mr Williams' statement that the car was a 1948 model was a warranty—a term of the contract—or a representation, as the former would result in an award of damages for breach of contract, but the latter would not. In applying an objective test of intention, Denning LJ recognized that he must look not at the thoughts of the parties but at their words and behaviour. He thought that it was easier to infer a warranty when the person making the statement knew or should have known the facts; a reasonable person would infer that such a speaker would intend those words to be part of the contract.

This is because a warranty, as a term of the contract, is a *promise* that the facts are true. If the facts are not true, then the promisor has broken his promise and breached his contract. It is therefore more reasonable to interpret a statement of fact as a promise of the truthfulness of those facts when the person making the statement is in a position to know the truth or otherwise of the facts. In the event, Denning LJ thought that Mr Williams was not in a position where he should have known the true facts: he relied on the misleading registration book as much as the dealer, and so the statement was a representation and not a warranty. Lord Denning also noted that if an agreement is later written down it is likely that any oral statements repeated in the written contract are intended to be warranties and conversely that any omitted are likely to be representations. This is common sense because the parties are likely to record only those statements which they intend to form terms of the contract and not those statements which they do not intend to form terms of the contract. However, this is not an absolute rule and omitted oral statements can still form warranties if there is an appropriate objective intention; it is not necessarily the case that the parties intended all non-written terms to be excluded from the contract. See the box on the parol evidence rule for further details.

The parol evidence rule and signatures

Denning LJ's observation on the effect of writing down an agreement raises the issue of the 'parol evidence rule.' This rule states that a written contract cannot be supplemented by oral terms; the written document is final. The Law Commission (Report No.154, Cmnd. 9700 1986) concluded that this rule was in fact circular and said no more than that oral statements were inadmissible when a contract was wholly recorded in writing, but admissible when the contract was part written or wholly unwritten. Obviously, a wholly written contract cannot have any additional oral terms and so there is no need to admit evidence of them. The admissibility of oral statements really rests on whether a written document was intended to form all the terms of the contract (in which case the oral statements are irrelevant) or whether the written contract formed only part of the contract (in which case the oral statements may form terms of the contract if they were intended to do so). As usual, the parties' intention must be established objectively. 'Entire agreement clauses' are often used to make it clear that the written contract is intended to contain all the terms and that oral statements are not to be given effect to. These clauses are generally effective to exclude oral statements from the contract, although there are, as always, ways round this, such as in *J N Hipwell & Son* v *Szurek* (2018), discussed in section 5.3.3, which illustrates that extra terms (largely reflecting the intentions behind the oral statements) can still be *implied* into an otherwise entirely written agreement if they are necessary to give the contract business efficacy. A related point concerns oral variations *after* the contract has come into force. It is quite common for a written contract to include a NOM clause, a No Oral Modification clause, which says that any variations also have to be in writing and signed. Can an oral agreement to vary the terms nevertheless be effective? The Court of Appeal in *MWB* v *Rock Advertising* (2016) (discussed in Chapter 4, section 4.3.4) had thought yes but the Supreme Court (2018) took the opposite view and reversed the decision and held that NOM clauses (rather like entire agreement clauses) do prevent subsequent oral agreements from varying the contract.

Of course, the parties can get rid of a NOM clause by agreeing to do so in writing as required by the NOM clause itself and then other oral variations would be effective. Failing such agreement in writing however, the main protection for a party who mistakenly thought the oral agreement had successfully varied the contract and adversely changed their position in reliance on it would be via doctrines such as estoppel if applicable (in *MWB* the Court of Appeal had already found estoppel did not apply) but not through the contract itself.

It is clear from *L'Estrange* v *Graucob Ltd* (1934) that the terms in a written document will be terms of a contract (warranties) if the document is signed by the party accepting them. This will be the case even if the party did not read the terms, or was not even expected to read them, although fraud or misrepresentation may prevent the terms from binding. A party's signature is therefore virtually conclusive proof that they intend to contract on those terms.

It is commonplace but nonetheless useful to compare the facts of the *Oscar Chess* case with *Dick Bentley Productions Ltd* v *Harold Smith (Motors) Ltd* (1965).

CASE CLOSE-UP

***Bentley Productions Ltd* v *Harold Smith (Motors) Ltd* (1965)**

The dealers, Harold Smith (Motors), sold a car to Dick Bentley Productions Ltd stating that it had done 20,000 miles, as shown on the odometer (the mileage recorder, to the non-technically minded). The odometer was incorrect and so the question arose: was the statement that the car had done 20,000 miles a warranty or a representation?

Lord Denning MR thought that on these facts the dealer was in a position to know or at least find out the true mileage and so he concluded that the term was intended to be a warranty and not a representation, as the statement about the age of the car had been in *Oscar Chess*. Note that in *Oscar Chess* the roles were reversed and the sale was to, not by, a dealer. This may explain why the non-expert seller was not expected to know the age of the car.

Aside from the knowledge of the speaker and the effect of writing, there are other ways in which the courts have sought to discover the objective intentions of the parties. In *Routledge* v *McKay* (1954) a long interval between making the statement and finalizing the agreement indicated that the statement was a representation and not a warranty. In *Bannerman* v *White* (1861) a statement that the hops had not been treated with sulphur was intended to be a term of the contract because of the importance to the buyer of having sulphur-free hops. You might like to think about whether it matters that the seller knows (or ought to know) of the importance of this to the buyer.

The constant appeal to the intentions of the parties may seem to you to be wearing a bit thin now; judges say that they are following the parties' intentions, but they appear to make the distinction on the basis of what is the most reasonable outcome. Do you think the relative fault of the speaker in *Oscar Chess* and *Dick Bentley* was really an important indicator of the parties' intention regarding the terms of the contract? It often seems that where the

Figure 5.1 Distinction between warranties and representations

Not Terms of the Contract	Terms of the Contract
Representations	*Warranties*
No automatic right to damages. Primary remedy is rescission but this may sometimes be barred (see Chapter 7).	Automatic right to damages if the warranty is broken.

Distinguishing a Representation from a Warranty

Two Approaches:

1) Look at the parties' objective intentions:

(a) Should the speaker have known of the truth of the statement (Oscar Chess/Dick Bentley)?
(b) Was the statement later written down (Denning LJ obiter in Oscar Chess)?
(c) How long elapsed between the making of the statement and the conclusion of the agreement (*Routledge* v *McKay*)?
(d) How important was the statement (*Bannerman* v *White*)?

2) Forget about the objective intentions, if the parties' intentions are unclear then ask what is the appropriate remedy? (Is this the approach the courts really take?)

(a) If damages are more appropriate (enforcing the bargain) then find a warranty.
(b) If rescission is more appropriate (undoing the bargain) then find a representation.

parties' intentions are unclear the courts will look at what is the most suitable remedy and then decide whether the statement is a warranty or a representation in order to achieve the most appropriate result. In other words, the court thought that the dealer should not have an automatic right to get damages for breach of contract from Mr Williams in *Oscar Chess*, but it thought that one dealer should have an automatic right to damages against the other dealer in *Dick Bentley*. The distinction between representations and warranties and the approaches to making the distinction are summarized in Figure 5.1.

5.2 Collateral warranties

We established earlier that terms of the contract, warranties, are distinguished from non-terms, representations, by the objective intentions of the parties. However, even if a statement cannot for some reason constitute a term of the contract, the courts may think that the remedy for breach of contract is justified and hold that the statement is a term, a warranty, in a collateral contract, a contract on the side. For instance, the parol ('parol' meaning oral, nothing to do with 'parole' or early release) evidence rule (see earlier box) has the effect that oral statements cannot be warranties in a wholly written contract, but to get around this the court in *De Lassalle* v *Guildford* (1901) held that a landlord's oral statement that the drains worked was a collateral warranty to the written lease. Because the lease was in writing and supposed to constitute the whole contract, the court used the idea of a collateral warranty to give a remedy in damages for breach of the collateral warranty, without interfering with the main written contract. This is a fudge, and you should not be afraid of saying so. In effect the courts are saying 'we can't allow the statement to form a term of the contract, but we'll make up another (collateral) contract so it can be a term of that contract; problem solved.' This 'escape route' was also used in *Shanklin Pier Ltd* v *Detel Products Ltd* (1951) to evade the privity rule. The Shanklin Pier owners employed a firm of decorators to paint their pier. The decorators contracted to buy paint from Detel, a manufacturer of paint (the main contract). The pier owners had previously asked Detel whether their paint was suitable for piers (waterproofing is obviously a must) and Detel stated that it was. Detel's statement obviously could not form a warranty under the main contract for the sale of the paint to the decorators because the pier owners were not a party to it and so could not sue under it. However, the court thought that the pier owners deserved a remedy directly against Detel for the consequences of Detel's false statement and so it held that the statement was a collateral warranty in a separate side contract between Shanklin Pier and Detel on which the former could sue the latter for breach of warranty (consideration being provided for this collateral contract by Shanklin specifying Detel's paint to the decorators, see Figure 5.2).

CROSS REFERENCE
See Chapter 13 for details of this rule.

Collateral warranties are not always used to evade inconvenient rules of law but can instead form a term relating to a party's conduct in the run-up to the contract. It is not strictly necessary to add the prefix 'collateral' to this type of warranty because there is no reason why the statement cannot be a warranty in the main contract, unlike in the earlier examples. In *Esso* v *Mardon* (1976) Esso had told the prospective tenant of their petrol station that the station would sell 200,000 gallons after three years. Esso had forgotten that the design of the petrol station had been altered so that it no longer faced the main road and the station consequentially sold only about 60,000 gallons. The Court of Appeal refused to find a warranty in the lease contract that the station would sell 200,000 gallons, but instead found a collateral warranty that the statement referring to 200,000 gallons had been prepared with reasonable care and skill. Lord Denning MR said that Esso possessed expertise and knowledge in this area and their stated estimate could be interpreted as a warranty that they had made it with reasonable care and skill. They broke this warranty when they forgot to take account of the change in design and so they were liable in damages to the tenant. An important point to

Figure 5.2 *Shanklin Pier Ltd* v *Detel Products Ltd* (1951)

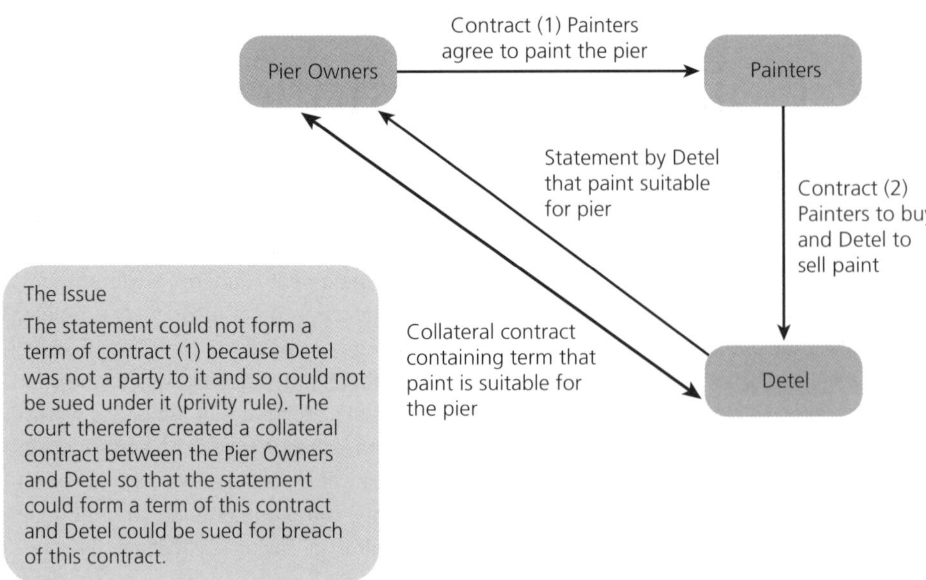

bear in mind is that Lord Denning did not think that it was a term of the contract that the station would sell 200,000 gallons; Esso did not promise or guarantee this figure on pain of damages. Instead, Esso promised, as a term of the contract, that the estimate of 200,000 gallons had been made with reasonable care and skill. The warranty therefore related to their behaviour prior to the contract, not to events after the contract. The claimant therefore could not claim damages based on the erroneous 200,000 estimate but only based on what his position would have been if a more careful (lower) estimate had been given—in which case he would not have entered the contract at all and wasted all that he did on it. There is little difference in this type of case between a warranty as to due care and skill and liability based on negligent misrepresentation, which was indeed another ground of the decision. In the more common type of case where the warranty is a promise or guarantee of a result or an outcome, the difference between contractual damages compensating for loss of that result or outcome and damages in tort is much more significant (see Chapter 1).

5.3 Implied terms

5.3.1 Terms implied in law and in fact

So far in this chapter we have dealt only with statements actually spoken or written by the parties, ignoring all the extra nuances that inevitably surround every communication. It is not always easy to express precisely everything that you intend to communicate, and it is a valuable skill to be able to communicate clearly and concisely using a minimum number of words.

EXAMPLE

Implied communication

You call to your fellow student, 'Bar at eight?' From the tone of your voice she knows that you are asking a question, and from the overall context, including previous similar arrangements, she knows that you are suggesting meeting her in the Student Union at 8 p.m. (rather than inquiring about her high jump performance!). All this information is implied from the surrounding circumstances in order to make sense of the expressed statement; you are aware of this and so you can comfortably use abbreviated sentences safe in the knowledge that your friend will know what you mean.

This example illustrates how words can be implied in order to clarify one party's *intention*, but the law sometimes implies terms on the quite different basis that in certain circumstances it is considered to be a 'good thing' that certain terms are implied. For instance, whenever goods are being sold the law implies certain promises relating to title and quality (see the Sale of Goods Act 1979 and specialist works on this area of law for more details—it should be noted that terms of this nature were first implied by statute in the Sale of Goods Act of 1893 which itself was largely codifying implied terms already recognized by the common law). There is no pretence that both parties actually intend there to be a promise that the goods are of satisfactory quality, but the law thinks that it is a good thing that there should be such a promise and so one is implied. Thus, there is a distinction between terms implied *in fact* (terms actually intended but not expressed) and terms implied *in law* (implied not because they are intended by the parties but inserted by the courts or legislature because they think it is a good idea).

Lord Denning distinguished these two types of implied terms (in reverse order) in *Shell UK Ltd* v *Lostock Garage Ltd* (1977), referring to terms implied in law as 'the first category' and terms implied in fact as 'the second category.' You could read his judgment in the case report (extracts given later), as it provides a very clear framework for a messy area of law in which alternative classifications such as terms implied by custom, statute and common law, by emphasizing the source of the implication, only obscure the rationale and criteria for it:

> The first category comprehends all those relationships which are of common occurrence, such as the relationship of seller and buyer, owner and hirer, master and servant, landlord and tenant . . . In all those relationships the courts have imposed obligations on one party or the other, saying they are implied terms. These obligations are not based on the intentions of the parties, actual or presumed, but on more general considerations . . . In these relationships the parties can exclude or modify the obligation by express words, but unless they do so, the obligation is a legal incident of the relationship which is attached by the law itself . . .
>
> . . .
>
> The second category comprehends those cases which are not in the first category. These are cases, not of common occurrence, in which from the particular circumstances a term is to be implied. In these cases the implication is based on an intention imputed to the parties from their actual circumstances . . . Such an imputation is only to be made when it is necessary to imply a term to give efficacy to the contract and make it a workable agreement in such a manner as the parties would clearly have done if they had applied their mind to the contingency which has arisen.

These two different types of implied term will now be considered in the order set out by Lord Denning.

5.3.2 **Terms implied in law**

The facts in *Liverpool City Council* v *Irwin* (1976) would probably these days be the subject of one of those 'Neighbours from Hell'-type programmes. The tenants of a block of council flats had refused to pay their rent because the flats were constantly vandalized to the extent that the lifts, stair lighting and rubbish chute rarely worked. The council asked the court to throw the tenants out and the tenants responded that the council was in breach of implied contractual terms. The tenants had to imply terms into the contract because their tenancy agreement only listed the obligations of the tenants and was silent on the obligations of the council. In other words, the written tenancy agreement said to the tenants, 'You must do this, must not do that, but the council is not obliged to do anything.' Quite clearly, it is inconceivable that the council as landlord could be under no obligations at all. At the very least the landlord was obliged to grant exclusive possession of the flats with a covenant for quiet enjoyment: that is the whole point of a tenancy (see Lord Wilberforce's speech). The key question was whether the council was obliged to maintain the lifts, stairs and rubbish chutes, because, if it was, the tenants could claim damages for breach of those terms. Lord Wilberforce thought that the answer rested on a test of necessity: was it necessary to imply such terms where there was a relationship of landlord and tenant for the lease of high-rise blocks? The case therefore rested on terms implied by *law* and not by *fact* because the rationale for implying the terms was based on the *parties' relationship* and not their unexpressed *intentions*. On the facts, Lord Wilberforce thought that it was necessary to imply an obligation for the council to take reasonable care to keep the blocks in reasonable repair and usability, but the evidence did not reveal a breach of this term. Note that the use of the word 'reasonable' appears here not as the test for implying the term but as part of the description of the scope of the term implied. Lord Wilberforce deliberately used a test of *necessity* to distinguish his test from the more liberal test of *reasonableness* used by Lord Denning when the case was in the Court of Appeal (Lord Denning thought that a term should be implied when it is *reasonable* to do so, as opposed to when it is *necessary* to do so). However, as Lord Denning pointed out subsequently in *Shell UK* v *Lostock Garage*, the Court of Appeal in *Liverpool CC* v *Irwin* was asked to imply a term *in fact* whereas the House of Lords was asked to imply a term *in law*. Whilst Lord Denning's reasonable test may have been inappropriate for implying terms in fact (as he had tried to do in the Court of Appeal in *Irwin*), a test of reasonableness was adopted by Lord Cross in the House of Lords in *Liverpool CC* v *Irwin* in relation to implying a term in law.

If we accept Lord Cross's analysis, then we must conclude that Lord Wilberforce overreacted in his desire to dispel Lord Denning's idea that terms could be implied in fact if it was reasonable to do so; Lord Wilberforce did not have to go the whole way and use a test of necessity for terms implied by law as well as those implied in fact. The different tests fit in well with the courts' reluctance to fetter the parties' freedom of contract because the higher test of necessity for terms implied in fact means that less damage is done to the parties' intention. If a term really is necessary then it is likely that the parties would have intended it to be part of the contract, more likely than that they would have such an intention in relation to a term that is simply reasonable. On the other hand, a test based on reasonableness is acceptable when terms are implied in law because the aim is not to establish what the parties intended, merely to place reasonable terms in common types of contracts, and the decision to imply a term or not is in effect a policy decision. The courts effectively have to ask themselves what *should* be the obligations between a landlord and tenant, a seller and buyer, or any other common relationship which comes before the courts. This point was recognized even by Lord Wilberforce in *Liverpool* v *Irwin* when he accepted that the search for terms implied in law was based on 'wider considerations.'

In *Scally* v *Southern Health and Social Services Board* (1991) Lord Bridge appears to have sided with Lord Wilberforce when he held that the test for implying a term into a doctor's contract of employment (an implication of law) was one of necessity. Despite this, he still managed to imply a term that the Health Board was obliged to draw to the doctor's attention his rights to buy extra years under his pension plan, a conclusion which suggests that in reality a test of reasonableness was applied. How could the notification of pension rights be *necessary* to such a contract? It was only 'necessary' because the contractual relationship was very precisely defined as including a requirement based on reasonableness, that is, 'the employee cannot in all the circumstances reasonably be expected to be aware [of the potential benefit available to him].' In contracts of employment more generally the House of Lords in *Mahmud* v *BCCI* (1998) confirmed the existence of an implied term (in law) of mutual trust and confidence between employer and employee. However, in *Crossley* v *Faithful and Gould Holdings* (2004) the Court of Appeal rejected the argument that a term should be implied in law that an employer should take care for an employee's well-being since such a term was neither necessary nor reasonable as it would impose an unfair and unreasonable burden on employers. Dyson LJ noted that it may be better to focus on 'questions of reasonableness, fairness and the balancing of competing policy considerations' rather than 'on the elusive concept of necessity.' *Barton* v *Morris* (2023), already discussed in section 2.9.1, is another example where the majority of the Supreme Court found there were no grounds for implying a term in law to give the claimant a fee if the property sold for under £6.5 million and the claimant could not be regarded as an estate agent acting for a seller so as to benefit from the terms normally implied into contracts made in the course of relationships of that nature.

5.3.3 **Terms implied in fact**

A term is implied in fact on the basis that the parties intended it to be a term of the contract but simply did not express it as a term—rather as in the example discussed earlier, you intended to meet your friend outside the Student Union bar, but you felt that it was not necessary to express this in so many words. This is sometimes referred to as the 'officious bystander' test whereby 'something is so obvious that it goes without saying so that if, while the parties were making their bargain, an officious bystander were to suggest some express provision for it in their agreement they would testily suppress him with a common, "Oh, of course!"' (MacKinnon LJ in *Shirlaw* v *Southern Foundries* (1939)). The test is one of strict necessity and is not easily satisfied but the leading case of *The Moorcock* (1889) shows how it can be.

CASE CLOSE-UP

***The Moorcock* (1889)**

The defendants owned a jetty which extended into the River Thames. In order to unload at the jetty at low tide, it was necessary to ground the vessel being unloaded on the river bed. The defendants had taken no steps to ascertain whether it was or was not a safe place for the vessel to ground. Whilst unloading, *The Moorcock* grounded on the bed of the Thames and sustained damage.

The Court of Appeal held the defendant to be under an implied obligation to take reasonable care that the wharf was safe. Bowen J made it clear that the implication was founded on the presumed intentions of the parties and that it was *necessary* to give 'business efficacy' to the transaction. The business of the wharf owners could not be carried on if incoming ships did not believe that the wharf was reasonably safe to dock in. The owners were the only party who could know whether the wharf was safe and so it was necessary to imply an obligation to take care that it was safe. It is worth noting that, as in *Liverpool* v *Irwin*, an absolute obligation was not implied (i.e. to ensure that the wharf was safe) but only an obligation to take reasonable care that the wharf was safe.

Construction of the contract and implication of terms in fact

The Privy Council considered the different formations of the tests used to imply terms in fact in *Attorney-General of Belize* v *Belize Telecom* (2009). Lord Hoffmann (delivering the judgment of the Board) confirmed that the courts could not simply incorporate terms which would make the contract fair or reasonable. He considered the key question to be: 'is that what the instrument, read as a whole against the relevant background, would reasonably be understood to mean?' It is important to recognize that Lord Hoffmann did not through the use of the word 'reasonable' intend to downgrade the strict requirement that it must be *necessary* to imply the term in question (see *Mediterranean Salvage & Towage Ltd* v *Semar Trading & Commerce Inc. (The Reborn)* (2009)). Instead, he intended to emphasize that the process of implying a term into a contract was part and parcel of the court's task of contractual construction.

Lord Hoffmann set out how the courts should construe written contracts in *Investors Compensation Scheme Ltd* v *West Bromwich Building Society* (1998) and *Chartbrook Ltd* v *Persimmon*

Homes Ltd (2009) and these two House of Lords decisions have subsequently been followed by the Supreme Court decision in *Rainy Sky* v *Kookmin Bank* (2011). Whilst there is not the scope in this book to go into detail on what is a very important matter in practice, the key point from these cases is that the courts will construe contracts according to an objective test by looking at how the document would have been understood by a reasonable person having all the background knowledge which would reasonably have been available to the parties at the time of the contract, preferring, as in the *Rainy Sky* case, where there are two possible meanings, the one which was most consistent with business common sense. This meant that in the latter case, a guarantee bond issued by a bank guaranteeing the repayment of multi-million dollar instalments paid by purchasers to a ship builder was interpreted as applying not just to cases where the builder was in breach of contract but also to cases where the builder became insolvent, since insolvency of the builder was the main situation where the protection provided by the bonds was needed by the purchasers and so this interpretation was the one consistent with the commercial purpose of the contract. However, it should be noted that in the later Supreme Court case of *Arnold* v *Britton* (2015) the importance of the words used was re-emphasized and where these words were clear, even if, as on the facts, they lead to a harsh or imprudent result, the commercial purpose of the contract cannot be used to alter the natural and ordinary meaning of the words used. However, this is not to say that the Supreme Court in *Arnold v Britton* was 'rowing back' from a more contextual approach in *Rainy Sky* to a more literal approach, as the Supreme Court itself was subsequently keen to deny in *Wood v Capita Insurance* (2017) para. [14]. Lord Hodge said at para. [13]: 'Textualism and contextualism are not conflicting paradigms in a battle for exclusive occupation of the field of contractual interpretation. Rather, the lawyer and the judge, when interpreting any contract, can use them as tools to ascertain the objective meaning of the language which the parties have chosen to express their agreement' and at para. [14] that 'Rainy Sky and Arnold were saying the same thing.'

Returning to Lord Hoffmann's approach in *Belize Telecom*, his view was that the process of construing the words on the page and implying words which the parties did not write on the page is the same and comes down to how a reasonable person would construe the written agreement. The test of necessity is, on this view, just the same as saying that, although there is an obvious term missing which is necessary to make the contract work, the reasonable person would understand the agreement to include such a term. The key point however is that this remains a test of necessity and also remains very different from saying that a term will be implied if it is reasonable to do so.

The Supreme Court subsequently confirmed and made clear in *M&S* v *BNP Paribas* (2015) that Lord Hoffmann was not seeking in *Belize Telecom* to change or dilute the nature of the test for implying a term in fact, contrary to how some commentators had read his words. The business efficacy and officious bystander tests still remain relevant and the test remains one of necessity (not absolute necessity but necessity to give the contract business efficacy, which does involve a value judgement). In relation to the view of Lord Hoffmann that implication of a term was part of the process of construction, Lord Neuberger, giving the majority judgment, was much less keen because it was capable of being misunderstood and somewhat sidelined it by describing it as 'a characteristically inspired discussion rather than authoritative guidance on the law of implied terms.' This might sound a little bit like damning with faint praise. Lady Hale followed up on Lord Neuberger's comments in *Byron* v *Eastern Caribbean Amalgamated Bank* (2019) in the

Privy Council where she disarmingly explained the difference between construction of the contract and implication of terms as follows:

> ... construing the words of the contract involves deciding what the parties meant by what they did say. Implying terms into the contract involves deciding whether they would have said something that they did not in fact say had the matter occurred to them. And until one has decided what the parties meant by what they did say, it will be difficult to set about deciding what they would have said.

Returning to *M&S*, Lord Carnwath gave a separate judgment which was more supportive of Lord Hoffmann's approach in *Belize* which he described as 'a valuable and illuminating synthesis of the factors which should guide the court.' Lord Clarke also gave a separate judgment and managed to agree with both Lord Neuberger and Lord Carnwath, and reiterated the most important point that 'although Lord Hoffmann emphasized that the process of implication was part of the process of construction of the contract, he was not resiling from the often stated proposition that it must be necessary to imply the term and that it is not sufficient that it would be reasonable to do so.'

Application of the necessity test for terms implied in fact

The facts of the *M&S* case provide a good example of the difference between the test of necessity (the applicable test) and a test of reasonableness (which is insufficient). M&S leased premises in London from Paribas; the rent was over £1 million per year and the lease was to run until 2018. However, there was a break clause in the lease allowing M&S to terminate the lease as from 24 January 2012 provided they gave six months' notice, were not in arrears of rent on 24 January and also paid a premium of £919,000 plus VAT. M&S did all this, paying not only the premium but also the three months' advance rent payable on 25 December 2011 amounting to £309,000 plus VAT (which they had to do so as not to be in arrears on the break date of 24 January 2012). They thus validly terminated the lease but then claimed (not unreasonably, you may think) the part of the advance rent attributable to the period of two months after the lease terminated on 24 January 2012. The lease said nothing about any portion of the rent payable in advance being recoverable so M&S had to argue that there was an implied term that the apportioned part of the rent could be recovered for the two-month period during which they were no longer tenants (the small matter of over £200,000). The Supreme Court unanimously held that such a term, reasonable whilst it might seem, did not satisfy the necessity test, especially given that the lease was a long commercial document on which both parties would have had legal advice, and which could have expressly dealt with the matter. It could not be said that *both* parties would have agreed with such a clause if asked about it and the apparent unfairness of the landlords being able to keep the two months' rent did not look so contrary to the parties' apparent intentions when one remembered that the lease also provided for a premium of over £900,000 to be paid if the break clause was exercised—keeping a further £200,000 was not out of line with this approach to financial recompense to the landlords for early termination.

The approach in *M&S* to terms implied in fact was applied and, in contrast, found to be satisfied in *J N Hipwell & Son* v *Szurek* (2018) due to an obvious gap in the written contract (a lease) concerning who was responsible for maintaining the safety of electrical services to the building. The gap was to be 'plugged' (appropriately enough, you may think) as a matter of business necessity by implying an obligation on the landlord to ensure that the electrical installation was safe (this gave the contract business efficacy since the lease expressly gave the landlord a right of entry for this and related purposes).

Finally it should be noted that a decision about an implied term in fact in one particular contract does not mean the same decision will be made in a dispute arising from what might look like a similar contract (contrast the position for terms implied in law). This can be seen by comparing two cases on implying a term about selling development assets within a reasonable time. In *Yoo Design Services* v *Iliv Realty* (2021) the Court of Appeal held that it was not necessary on the facts to imply a term that flats should be sold within a reasonable time (which was unsuccessfully alleged to be necessary so that the claimants could receive their relatively small commission due on the sales). In contrast, in *Sparks* v *Biden* (2017) the High Court had held that there was a term implied in fact that a developer had to sell, within a reasonable time, dwellings constructed on what had previously been the claimant's land (in order that the claimant could receive his substantial 'overage' payments due on the sales, which payments were a significant part of the overall deal and were intended to fund the claimant's pension). As Carr LJ put it at para. [79] of *Yoo Design*, 'The court's task is to assess each contract individually in light of its own peculiar terms and relevant factual context. Comparison with findings as to the existence (or non-existence) of implied terms in other bespoke contracts is unlikely to assist.'

Tesco v *USDAW* (2024) provides a good example of a term being implied in fact under the strict necessity/business efficacy/obviousness test. A number of employees were promised 'retained pay,' that is, pay increased by around a third, on a permanent basis, in 2007 in return for agreeing to relocation. In 2021 Tesco sought to dismiss them and then rehire them on a contract without the enhanced pay. It was held by the Supreme Court that there was an implied term that prevented Tesco from doing so. The promise of permanent enhanced pay did not make business sense if Tesco could at any time dismiss the employee in order to remove the enhanced pay, so the implied term was necessary to give business efficacy to the contract and was also 'so obvious that it goes without saying.'

As Lord Burrows and Lady Simler put it at [48]:

> . . . the proposed implied term is capable of clear expression and goes no further than is necessary in this case. . . . Tesco's contractual right to terminate the contract on notice cannot be exercised for the purpose of removing or diminishing the right of that employee to receive retained pay. It operates to qualify (rather than contradict) the express contractual right to terminate on notice. It does not mean that Tesco cannot dismiss for any other unrelated reason (including lack of capability, misconduct, or redundancy). The stringent tests applicable to the implication of a term by fact are satisfied.

The difference between terms implied in law and those implied in fact is summarized in Figure 5.3.

The implication of terms in fact can have far-reaching consequences, as with the House of Lords' decision in *Equitable Life* v *Hyman* (2000) where the term implied, that the directors would not use their discretion so as to override or undermine the rights of those with guaranteed annual rate policies, effectively cost a once powerful Life Assurance Society £1.5 billion and led to its virtual collapse, rocking the whole life assurance industry in the process.

5.3.4 **Implied term that the parties will perform the contract in good faith**

This is a fast-developing aspect of the law relating to implied terms. A general duty of good faith is a common feature of the law of contract in many legal jurisdictions (including, but not limited to, those in continental Europe). It has traditionally not been recognized as a general

Figure 5.3 Summary of the distinction between terms implied in law and in fact

	Terms Implied in Law	**Terms Implied in Fact**
Application	To contracts where there is a common relationship, such as landlord and tenant (*Liverpool* v *Irwin*) or buyer and seller (Sale of Goods Act 1979).	To rare cases where the particular circumstances make it necessary to imply a term.
Rationale	Not based on the parties' intention (but can be expressly excluded). Based on 'wider considerations' (i.e. policy decisions).	Based on what the parties must have intended but did not express.
Test	What terms are reasonable to imply (Lord Cross in *Liverpool* v *Irwin* and Lord Denning MR in *Shell* v *Lostock*). Compare to test of necessity favoured by Lord Wilberforce in *Irwin* and Lord Bridge in *Scally*.	What terms are necessary to make the contract work (give it business efficacy, e.g. *The Moorcock*). What they would have said 'of course' to, if asked by an officious bystander.
Example	In the House of Lords in *Liverpool* v *Irwin* the contract concerned the relationship between a landlord and tenant of high-rise flats. An obligation to take reasonable care to keep in reasonable repair and usability was implied using the test of necessity (Lord Wilberforce) and the test of reasonableness (Lord Cross).	In *The Moorcock* an obligation to take reasonable care that the wharf was safe was implied in the particular circumstances. This was necessary to give the contract business efficacy and to reflect the parties' presumed intentions. In contrast in *M&S* v *BNP Paribas* it may have been reasonable but it was not necessary to imply a term allowing the apportioned rent to be repaid for the period after the lease ended.

principle in English Law which, it is said, deals with issues of good faith by means of other doctrines (for example via the rules relating to exemption clauses and penalties as well as by recognizing good faith in specific circumstances such as insurance contracts). Indeed traditionally, the case of *Walford* v *Miles* (1992) has been cited as showing an antipathy to notions of good faith since in that case (see section 3.1.1) the House of Lords rejected the implication of a duty to negotiate in good faith which it regarded as too vague and uncertain. But that was a case about good faith in negotiations for a contract not yet formed rather than good faith in the performance of an existing contract. In the years since *Walford* v *Miles*, good faith had increasingly been a feature of various developments in the law of implied terms, in particular in contracts of employment and in contracts where one party has a discretion which the courts have held has to be exercised reasonably and in good faith. The most significant development however came in *Yam Seng* v *ITC* (2013), which concerned an agreement whereby Yam Seng distributed 'Manchester United' fragrances (which, unsurprisingly perhaps, turned out not to have the sweet smell of success) in certain overseas markets. This included duty-free sales in Singapore where, crucially, ITC gave false information about the price to be charged by non-duty-free competitors who effectively undercut Yam Seng's prices. Leggatt J, as he then was, held that the contract was not a simple one-off exchange but a 'relational contract' involving a 'longer term relationship between the parties to which they make a substantial commitment.' In this contract, which required a high degree of communication and co-operation, it was necessary, in order to give the contract business efficacy, to imply a term that the contract would be performed in good faith. By knowingly giving false information, ITC were clearly in breach of this duty to perform in good faith and the breach in all the circumstances was sufficient to entitle Yam Seng to terminate a contract which had already turned sour in a number of other respects.

The good faith term implied in *Yam Seng* was put on the basis of a term implied in fact (necessary to give business efficacy) and the same justification was put forward by Leggatt LJ (as he had now become) in *Sheik Tahnoon* v *Kent* (2018) in the Court of Appeal to imply a term of good faith in a joint-venture hotel and travel business. However, his lordship also said that the term could alternatively be justified as one implied in law as being required by the nature of the contract as relational and therefore implicitly requiring (in the absence of agreement to the contrary) good faith in its performance. This was perhaps a move by Leggatt LJ designed to gain wider acceptance of the good faith implied term, as may be beginning to happen, as is illustrated by the decision in *Bates* v *Post Office (No 3)* (2019). Fraser J, in this mammoth piece of litigation concerning the contractual relationship between sub-postmasters and the Post Office, decided that it was a relational contract and that a duty to act in good faith was implied as a matter of law. This duty meant that the parties (para. 911) 'must refrain from conduct which in the relevant context would be regarded as commercially unacceptable by reasonable and honest people.' It was made clear that this goes beyond simply acting honestly. As to what is meant by a relational contract, a number of factors which would point in that direction are given at para. 725 of the judgment, not all of which are necessary or exhaustive. However, it is essential that the first indicator in the list is satisfied, that is, that there must be 'no specific express terms in the contract that prevent a duty of good faith being implied into the contract.' In other words, the parties can expressly exclude the duty of good faith and if they do it is not a relational contract. If they do not expressly exclude it, the duty to act in good faith is implied as a matter of law in relational contracts (but not in commercial contracts generally).

The issue of the implied term to act in good faith is clearly going to be the subject of further case law which will clarify, modify, expand or restrict its operation (and will probably end up coming before the Supreme Court of which Lord Leggatt is now a member!). In the meantime, it reveals a process whereby the same term might be initially argued to be implied in fact as being necessary to give business efficacy to a particular contract with certain characteristics (*Yam Seng*) but then subsequently argued (*Bates* v *Post Office*) to be implied in law in all contracts of a certain type (unless the particular contract excludes it).

5.4 Conditions, warranties and innominate terms

5.4.1 **The basic distinction**

In section 5.1 we separated terms of the contract from non-terms. We followed Denning LJ in *Oscar Chess* in calling the former 'warranties' and the latter 'representations.' Denning LJ also referred to a second usage of the expression **warranty** as opposed to **condition** which is

warranty (second sense)

The word warranty is also used to describe a term of a contract that is not a condition and gives the right to damages but not termination upon breach of the warranty.

condition

Conditions are terms of the contract that give the right to terminate AND claim damages upon breach of the condition.

used to distinguish between non-vital and vital terms, and this distinction between conditions and warranties forms the subject matter of this next section. One way to reconcile the two usages of 'warranty' is to say that if something is a term of the contract it is at the very least a warranty giving a right to damages but if it is a vital term of the contract it will count as a condition rather than simply as a warranty and will give the right to terminate for breach as well as a right to damages. This classification of terms as conditions or warranties cuts across the separation between express and implied terms addressed in section 5.3, with the result that implied terms just as much as express terms may be classified as either conditions or warranties. Thus, many of the terms implied by ss.12–15 of the Sale of Goods Act 1979, such as to title or quality, are conditions whereas some of them, such as those relating to freedom from encumbrances and quiet enjoyment, are merely warranties. The distinction between conditions and warranties, just like that between warranties and representations, is very much a reflection of the remedy considered to be appropriate in the circumstances. Whilst the right to damages is a very useful and powerful remedy in many situations, the right to terminate the contract and no longer to be required to perform your own part or accept performance from the other side can often be equally as important, or more so, as will be seen.

Take any contract and it will soon become obvious that some terms are more important than others. If I agree to service your car, a term that I will service it by Friday (because you need it to drive to the airport to catch a flight for your holiday) is clearly more important to you than a term that I will ensure that the courtesy light turns on when the door is opened. If I fail to service the car by Friday you could rightly expect more stringent protection than if I failed to fix the light. The most important terms in a contract are known as conditions and the breach of a condition allows the innocent party to effectively tear up the contract so that both parties are released from further performance and the innocent party can recover damages: a fairly comprehensive combination of remedies. Until relatively recently, the general assumption was that all other terms were classified as warranties, the breach of which did not give the innocent party the option of tearing up the contract, and both parties, including the innocent one, continued to be bound by their obligations, but the innocent party could sue for damages flowing from the breach. Today the courts overtly recognize a third type of term, the **innominate term**, which is innominate (nameless) because it cannot accurately be described as a condition or a warranty—it falls in the no-man's-land halfway between a condition and a warranty (hence sometimes also referred to as an intermediate term) because sometimes its breach allows the innocent party to tear up the contract and sometimes it does not, in which case the innocent party has to be content only with damages. The remedies which are available following the breach of an innominate term depend upon the facts and on the seriousness of the breach and its consequences.

> **innominate terms**
> An innominate term is a third type of term, neither a condition nor a warranty—it is a kind of intermediate or hybrid term because sometimes its breach gives a right to termination and sometimes it only gives a right to damages, depending on how serious the consequences of the breach are.

One more crucial definition to introduce you to before we delve into the niceties in this area is 'termination', which is the more correct expression for what we have previously described as the innocent party being able to 'tear up' the contract.

> **Termination**
> Termination refers to the situation where the innocent party chooses to bring the contract to an end either for breach of condition or for serious breach of an innominate term. This means that the innocent party can refuse to accept any further

performance from the party in breach and, often even more crucially, can refuse to continue to perform its own side of the bargain (including refusing to pay the price, which is particularly useful if it has agreed too high a price or made a 'bad bargain'). The innocent party can also additionally sue for damages caused by the breach (see Chapter 11).

Note that sometimes instead of 'termination', the rather confusing expression 'rescission for breach' is used. Be aware that this is quite different from rescission for misrepresentation (see further Chapter 7) so it is far preferable to speak of 'termination' rather than 'rescission for breach.'

Returning to the earlier example, if I fail to service your car by Friday, and you are entitled to and do terminate the contract, you are now free to have the car serviced by someone else (and do not have to pay whatever price, high or low, you agreed with me) and I may also have to pay you damages in addition. You will be entitled to terminate if the term about servicing by Friday is a condition (the right to terminate here is automatic) or alternatively if it is an innominate term *and* the breach is sufficiently serious to justify that remedy. The differences between the different types of terms and their remedial consequences are illustrated in Figure 5.4.

Figure 5.4 How warranties and conditions fit into the terms/non-terms distinction

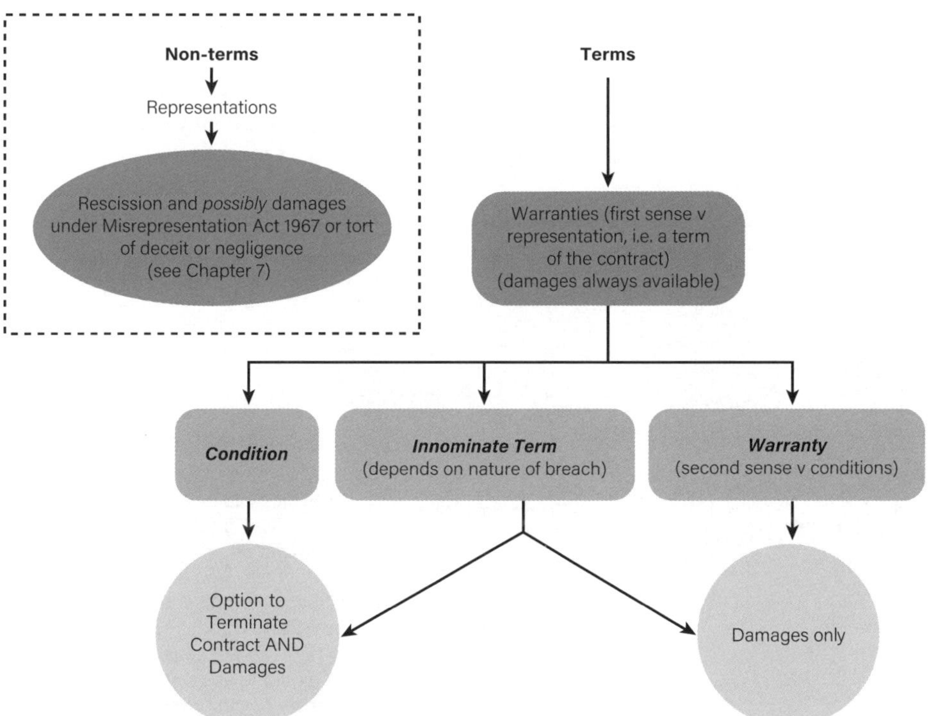

5.4.2 The general test for conditions, innominate terms and warranties

Although we introduced this section with a discussion of Denning LJ's distinction between vital and non-vital terms, it is not strictly true that conditions, warranties and innominate terms are classified according to their importance in the contract. The more fundamental truth, you will not be surprised to learn, is that the distinction is based on the parties' intentions: they are free to designate any term as a condition if they wish to do so (even the term that I should fix your courtesy light) but, given the more serious consequences which attach to breach of a condition, conditions tend to be the more important terms.

In *Lombard North Central plc* v *Butterworth* (1987) clause 2(a) of a contract for the lease of a computer provided that punctual payment of the rental sums 'shall be of the essence of this lease.' The Court of Appeal held that the parties intended clause 2(a) to be a condition of the contract. This was because time was said to be 'of the essence', indicating that *any* breach of the clause would go to the root of the contract and would entitle the other party to terminate—it was thus a condition. The Court of Appeal was troubled by this result because the clause effectively meant that a minor breach consisting of, say, payment being one day late gave the lessor the option to terminate the agreement and claim damages for his full loss of the whole bargain (see Figure 5.5). The lessor can effectively tell the lessee, 'Don't bother performing any more, just pay me the value of our bargain.' This extreme remedy may be justified when the breach is a serious one which destroys the core of the bargain, but it seems a little harsh when the breach is a minor one which would be peripheral to the main benefit of the contract. On the other hand, you may feel that a party who signs up to a clause clearly signalled to be a condition should be held to these extreme consequences. By giving the parties the power to freely choose which terms are conditions the courts have given the parties the power to elevate their losses to the value of the whole bargain even when the direct losses from the breach are minor. The downside of all this can be that one party may be encouraged to terminate the contract and claim damages rather than negotiating with the other party to remedy the breach and save the contract. You might want to think about which approach is the fairest and most economical in which situations.

Figure 5.5 Different consequences of holding term in *Lombard* as a warranty or as a condition

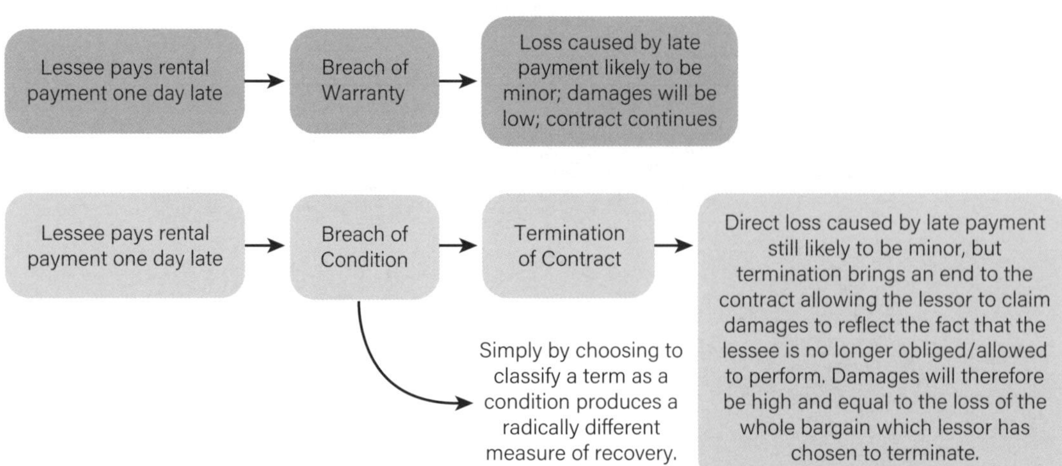

LINK TO . . .

Penalty clauses (Chapter 11)

We shall see in Chapter 11 that clauses which oblige a breaching party to pay a sum in excess of a genuine pre-estimate of loss may be void as a penalty clause (unless there is a legitimate interest and the payment is not unconscionable or extravagant in relation to that interest). In *Lombard*, another clause in the contract, clause 6, obliged the lessee to pay all past and future rentals if he breached his obligation to pay punctually and the lessor claimed possession of the computer. Clause 6 was void as a penalty clause.

Clause 2(a) had more or less the same effect as the penalty clause but Mustill LJ thought that it could not be set aside because this 'would be to reverse the current of more than 100 years' doctrine, which permits the parties to treat as a condition something which would not otherwise be so.' So even though a minor breach of Clause 2(a) would give the lessor his whole bargain in damages, the court felt unable to interfere with the parties' intention to make this a condition of the contract, but at the same time they felt obliged to strike out a penalty clause which attempted to do more or less the same thing.

The courts will not always accept the parties' wording so readily. In *L. Schuler* v *Wickman Machine Tools* (1973) clause 7(b) of a distribution agreement provided that 'it shall be a condition of this agreement' that Wickman shall send a representative to solicit orders from major car manufacturers at least once a week. Wickman failed to make the weekly visit on a couple of occasions and Schuler terminated the agreement, relying on the breach of the condition in clause 7(b). Despite expressly referring to clause 7(b) as a condition, the House of Lords thought that the parties did not mean this in its technical legal sense and held that the term was not a condition. Schuler was therefore not entitled to terminate the contract. Lord Reid thought that the consequences of clause 7(b) being a condition were 'so unreasonable that it must make me search for some other possible meaning of the contract.' He could not believe that the parties intended one missed visit to give Schuler the right to terminate the whole contract (but compare to *Lombard* where it was reluctantly accepted that a minor delay in payment gave the lessor the right to terminate the lease). Lord Reid used clause 11 of the contract to support his conclusion that clause 7(b) was not a condition. Clause 11 provided that the contract may be terminated if there had been a material breach and *a failure to remedy that breach within sixty days of being asked to do so*. Obviously, if clause 11 governed *when* a right to terminate arose after a breach of clause 7(b) then clause 7(b) could not be a condition with the immediate right to terminate upon breach. By reading the contract as a whole, Lord Reid concluded that clause 7(b) was not intended to be a condition and Schuler had no right to terminate the contract (contrast Lord Wilberforce's dissenting view and refusal to assume 'that both parties to this contract adopted a standard of easy going tolerance rather than one of aggressive, insistent punctuality and efficiency').

5.4.3 **Time clauses**

The courts are clearly often uncomfortable with the all-or-nothing consequences of the twofold distinction between conditions and warranties; either *all* breaches of a particular term give rise to a right to terminate or *no* breaches give such a right. When a term has been designated a condition there is no room for saying, 'that breach wasn't so bad, the innocent party should not be allowed to terminate.' Where the contract is badly or unclearly drafted, as in *Schuler*, they can avoid conferring an inappropriate automatic right to terminate by saying that there was no clear intention that the clause should be a condition. Certain *types* of clause have however clearly been recognized as conditions. In *Bunge Corporation* v *Tradex SA* (1981) the House of Lords had to decide whether a term requiring 'at least 15 consecutive days' notice' was a condition. Time stipulations in mercantile contracts for the sale of goods were generally thought to be intended to be conditions because such contracts often form only one part of a 'string' of contracts (like a chain of contracts for the sale of a house) and timely performance in one part of the string is essential. It was also important in the interest of certainty that the term should be a condition so that the parties would know that *any* breach of the time stipulation would give a right to terminate. There would be no need to look at the consequences of the breach and ask 'was that serious enough to give rise to a right to terminate?', only a need to look at a calendar and calculate fifteen days. Moreover, the contract in the case was a standard international contract for the sale and shipping of goods and it was important for future certainty that merchants everywhere knew what the term meant and how it would be interpreted by the courts.

Similarly, in *Samarenko* v *Dawn Hill House* (2011) the Court of Appeal held that failure of the purchaser to pay a deposit of £450,000 on a specified date, as required by the contract of sale for the land for a sum of £4.5 million which had previously been entered into, was a breach of condition, permitting the seller to terminate the contract immediately. Time was of the essence as far as the term requiring payment of the deposit was concerned (and even though the sellers unnecessarily gave a further five days for payment, this was still not complied with so they were still entitled to terminate after those further five days had elapsed).

5.4.4 **Statutory terms**

The correct classification, as already noted, may also be set by statute. The Sale of Goods Act 1979, s.10 provides that time is not of the essence in a contract of sale (i.e. not a condition) unless a different intention appears. In other cases, the Act implies certain terms which are expressly stated to be conditions or warranties irrespective of the intentions of the parties (see Sale of Goods Act 1979, ss.12(5A), 13(1A), 14(6) and 15(3)). The designation as a condition of the term that 'the goods will correspond with the description' in s.13, and the consequent automatic availability of the remedy of termination, has given rise to some cases that appear to result in an injustice, as in *Arcos* v *Ronaasen* (1933) where a quantity of wooden staves described as ½ inch thick exceeded that description by up to about 1/16 of an inch. The House of Lords confirmed that the buyers could reject the goods for breach of condition even though they were still perfectly usable for the intended purpose of making wooden barrels and the main reason for rejecting them was that the market price had fallen since the contract. A similar result was thought to be quite obvious by the Court of Appeal in the earlier case of *Re Moore & Landauer* (1921) where the discrepancy related simply to the fact that tins of fruit were packed twenty-four to the case rather than thirty to the case (the total quantity of tins nevertheless being correct). More flexibility in such a situation would now be available as a result of the insertion of s.15A into the Sale of Goods Act 1979 (by the Sale and Supply of Goods Act 1994). Section 15A(1) provides that where in a contract of sale:

> (a) the buyer would, apart from this subsection, have the right to reject goods by reason of a breach . . . of a term implied by section 13, 14 or 15 above, but
>
> (b) the breach is so slight that it would be unreasonable for him to reject them,
>
> then, if the buyer does not deal as a consumer, the breach is not to be treated as a breach of condition but may be treated as a breach of warranty.

Whether this provision would actually rescue the seller in a case like *Arcos* would depend on whether a variation of 1/16 of an inch would be regarded as 'so slight that it would be unreasonable for the buyer to reject' and also on whether the operation of s.15A is excluded under subsection (2) on the grounds that 'a contrary intention appears in, or is to be implied from, the contract.' The general verdict on s.15A appears to be that in seeking increased flexibility it creates too much uncertainty in commercial agreements where predictability is important. It can be seen however as part of the wider movement to seek greater flexibility where appropriate by means of the innominate term, to which we now turn.

5.4.5 **Innominate terms**

The innominate term is an attempt to avoid, in appropriate situations, the rigidity of the two-fold distinction between conditions and warranties. The downside with the innominate term approach is that the advantages of certainty referred to by the House of Lords in *Bunge* are lost because the parties do not know whether they can terminate until *after* the breach and its consequences are revealed and analysed. In *Hong Kong Fir Shipping Co Ltd* v *Kawasaki Kisen Kaisha Ltd* (1962), a clause in a contract for the hire of a ship (a charterparty) provided: 'she being in every way fitted for ordinary cargo service.' This 'seaworthiness clause' was breached and the charterer (hirer) of the ship sought to terminate the charterparty. The Court of Appeal thought that it was contrary to common sense to conclude that the parties intended *any* breach of this clause to give rise to a right of termination. Upjohn LJ gave the example that there could be a breach if a nail was missing from one of the timbers; surely this could not be intended to allow termination? He emphasized that it was open to the parties to expressly or by implication make such a clause a condition (as in *Lombard* and *Bunge*), but in the absence of such an intention it was not necessary for the court to conclude that the term must be a warranty and limit the innocent party to damages only. In his view, there was an intermediate type of term where the court must ask whether the breach goes so much to the root of the contract that it makes further commercial performance of the contract impossible. If it is, then the innocent party may terminate; if not, he is limited to damages only. On the facts of the case, the seaworthiness clause was breached largely because the crew were incompetent, which led to breakdowns and delay. Upjohn LJ thought that the effects of this breach were not serious enough to allow termination because the contract would be able to continue with a different crew with seventeen months still remaining out of the twenty-four-month contract period; the breach did not go to the root of the contract or, as Diplock LJ put it, deprive the innocent party of 'substantially the whole benefit' to be obtained from their own performance.

Diplock LJ's speech in *Hong Kong Fir* is worth reading in detail because it gives some insight into the basis of how terms are classified. He posed the question: in what events will a party be relieved of his obligations to perform (i.e. when can a contract be terminated)? He thought that some of these events could be specified in advance by the parties (such as by express condition or a cancellation clause) and some by statute, but not all events could be predicted. The courts must sometimes decide whether a particular event should give rise to a right to terminate a contract using the test of whether the event deprives the innocent party of '*substantially the whole benefit*' of the contract. *The Hansa Nord* (1976) is a good example of a case where it did not and the Court of Appeal interpreted an express term, even in a Sale of Goods contract, as an innominate term rather than as a condition to give itself the flexibility to prevent termination where the goods could still be used for their original purpose. The buyers only wanted to get out of the contract because the market price had fallen and they could repurchase the rejected goods much more cheaply from a third party on the open market.

It is worth stressing that if a party is deprived of substantially the whole benefit of the contract due to the other party's breach (or equally if the term broken is a condition), it is for the innocent party to *choose* whether to terminate, so that there is no danger of one party profiting from their own wrong (i.e. if termination was automatic on the occurrence of such a breach then it may suit the breaching party in some instances for the contract to be at an end, e.g. if a seller is in breach but the market price has risen).

The choice as to whether or not to terminate is often referred to as the innocent party's right 'to elect' whether to accept the 'repudiatory' (or 'fundamental') breach as putting an end to the contract or whether instead to affirm the contract and allow it to continue. Until recently it was possible that there was an exception to the right to elect in respect of repudiatory breaches of employment contracts but the Supreme Court in *Geys* v *Société Générale* (2012) has now clarified that the elective theory applies here too (but see *MSC Mediterranean Shipping* v *Cottonex* (2016) in the Court of Appeal, discussed in Chapter 12, section 12.1.5, for the controversial suggestion that there are situations where termination is automatic). Keeping the contract alive, even for a short period, can *sometimes* be highly beneficial as compared with accepting the repudiatory breach as terminating it. In *Geys* it meant that the employer's attempted summary, but technically unlawful, dismissal of the appellant was not accepted in November/December by the appellant as terminating his employment contract, which therefore continued until the employer adopted a lawful manner of summarily dismissing him in January. The fact that the employment contract was kept alive and only terminated in the new year made a difference of millions of euros to the compensation payable to the appellant under the contract as it meant the bonuses earned in a different and more lucrative year became the basis for the calculation. As Lord Sumption said in his dissent, the appellant was 'a lucky man.'

In contrast to the benefits of keeping the contract alive in the case just discussed, delay before choosing to exercise the right to terminate can sometimes cause problems for the innocent party. Firstly, delay can be treated as evidence of an intention to affirm the contract so that the right to terminate is thereby lost. The innocent party is nevertheless allowed a reasonable time to consider its position, as is illustrated by the case of *Force India Formula One Team* v *Etihad Airways* (2010) (several months in the context of the complex facts of that case, which would nevertheless be a fascinating read to fans of F1). Secondly, even if the delay is not treated as evidence of affirmation, events during the delay may mean that there is no right to terminate in response to the breach by the time the election to terminate is sought to be exercised.

This issue arose in *Ampurius Nu Homes* v *Telford Homes* (2013) where Telford were the developers of four inter-related blocks of commercial units (A, B, C and D), to be leased to Ampurius for a 999-year term. The developers had to stop work, temporarily at least, in June 2009 on blocks A and B due to lack of funding but continued to work on blocks C and D. Whilst the cessation of work for an indeterminate period and the consequent uncertainty at *that* time of whether blocks A and B would ever be completed was capable of being a breach, which might possibly have justified termination at the time of the breach, by the time that Ampurius sought to exercise the right to terminate in October 2010 work on blocks A and B had already resumed (albeit only a few weeks earlier). The resumption of work in effect had, at least partly, remedied the breach in that the cessation of work had now ended and *the question of whether the effects of the breach were serious enough had, crucially, to be judged at the time of the purported termination not the earlier date of the breach.* The uncertainty consequent on the breach as to whether all four units would ultimately be completed had now ended and the delay in their completion of up to a year or so (which could be compensated by an award of damages) was not so significant in terms of the ultimate benefit to be obtained by Ampurius under the contract which envisaged leases for a period of 999 years. It did not deprive them of substantially the whole benefit of the contract (nor did it even deprive them of the benefit of a substantial part of the contract, a somewhat less demanding test that was mentioned as an alternative, but which is probably best avoided as not setting the bar high enough to justify termination).

To conclude in relation to the right to terminate for breach, breach of a condition will always give the other party the right to terminate (save for where s.15A of the Sale of Goods Act 1979 applies). The breach of a warranty will never do so. The breach of innominate terms (which are neither conditions nor warranties) may or may not, depending on the facts, deprive the innocent party of substantially the whole benefit of the contract and thus may or may not give the innocent party the right to terminate. This is all supposedly in accordance with the intentions of the parties who can make a term a condition or a warranty (or indeed an innominate term) by expressly saying so or by giving other indications of what the effects of a breach should be. The default position however currently seems to be moving in favour of innominate terms, as can be seen from *Ark Shipping* v *Silverburn Shipping* (2019), where (at para. 46) Gross LJ said of the classification of terms that:

(i) it is a matter of the intention of the parties on the true construction of the contract;

(ii) where, upon the true construction of the contract, the parties have not made the term a condition, it will be innominate if a breach may result in trivial, minor or very grave consequences;

(iii) unless it is clear that a term is intended to be a condition or (only) a warranty, it will be innominate.

The distinctions between conditions, innominate terms and warranties are summarized in Figure 5.6.

Figure 5.6 Summary of the distinction between conditions, innominate terms and warranties

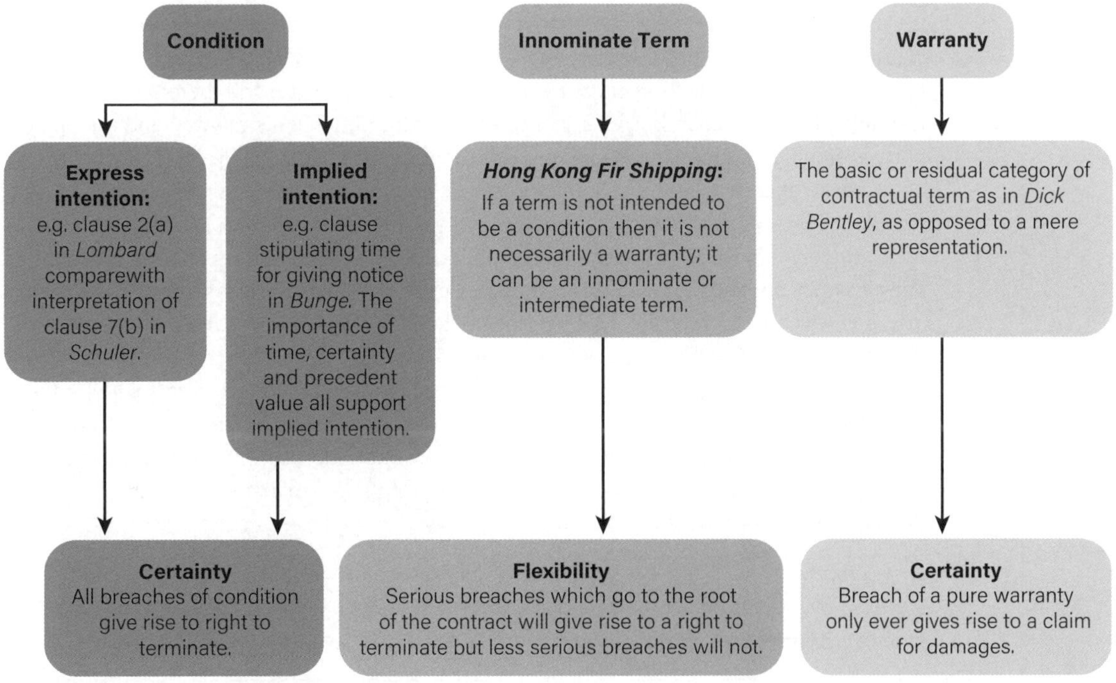

THINKING POINT

Note that an innominate term remains an innominate term irrespective of what remedy is given on the facts—the fact that only damages are given as in *Hong Kong Fir* does not convert it into a warranty; it remains an innominate term so that if the same term is breached in the future with effects that do deprive the innocent party of substantially the whole benefit, the remedy then would be termination—and still the term would only be innominate because it may in yet other cases be broken in a less serious manner where only damages would be appropriate.

Digging deeper

It has been suggested (Reynolds, 1981) that the threefold distinction between conditions, innominate terms and warranties could be trimmed down to just two—a distinction between conditions and non-conditions. The breach of the former would always give a right to terminate whereas the breach of the latter may or may not, depending on the seriousness of the breach. In effect, this twofold distinction would treat warranties in the same way as innominate terms so that it would not be possible to have a term which can only ever give rise to damages. The question you might ask is whether the law should deprive the parties of this possibility of designating a term as a pure warranty in the sense that its breach will never give the innocent party the right to terminate. The issue is further discussed in Treitel at para. 18-051 where judicial *dicta* to the effect that there may only be two categories of term are considered before concluding that the weight of authority supports threefold division and that this is preferable. Interestingly though, the very next paragraph of Treitel notes that 'judicial classification of a term as a warranty is rare.' The important issue in practice is usually whether a term is a condition or innominate and the issue of whether it is a pure warranty does not arise. Most of the cases are, as in *Schuler* v *Wickman* and *Hong Kong Fir* itself, cases where the effects of the breach are not significant and therefore one party is arguing for a condition because that gives the right to terminate anyway and the other party is arguing that the term is innominate so that termination is not available on the facts because the effects of the breach are not serious enough. Whether all warranties are in effect innominate terms which could give rise to the right to terminate would only really be an issue where you have the opposite (and probably quite rare) factual situation of an apparently insignificant term of the contract (perhaps expressly labelled as a warranty) breached in a way which exceptionally gives rise to very serious consequences. It could be argued that the benefits of certainty involved in saying a warranty can never give rise to the right to terminate are largely illusory since if the consequences of breach were very serious, the court may well find that the parties did not mean to use the word warranty in this pure or restricted sense, just as happened in relation to the word 'condition' in *Schuler* v *Wickman*. If the parties really want to preclude the possibility of a right to terminate for breach of a given term, it might be easiest simply to say so expressly.

What problems might occur if Reynolds' twofold distinction were adopted? How could the parties provide that breach of a particular term will never give the other party the right to terminate? Is there any reason why the law should deprive them of making this choice?

Summary

1. Warranties and representations

Warranties are terms of the contract and their breach automatically gives a right to damages for breach of contract. Representations are not terms of the contract. The consequences of a false representation are dealt with in Chapter 7, but damages are not automatically available and in any event are calculated differently from those for breach of contract.

The courts use an objective test of intention to determine whether a particular statement is a warranty or a representation.

Certain factors, such as whether the party making the statement knows or ought to know its truth, whether it is included in a written document, the interval between the statement and the formation of the contract and the evident importance attached to it by the parties are significant in determining the objective intention behind the statement.

2. Collateral warranties

Collateral warranties are terms created in secondary contracts when it is not possible or appropriate to insert the term into the main contract (for example, because of the parole evidence rule or the privity rule).

The term 'collateral warranty' is also used to refer to a term which relates to how a particular pre-contractual statement has been prepared (i.e. that a statement was prepared with reasonable care).

3. Implied terms

The courts will imply terms into a contract to reflect the unexpressed intentions of the parties (terms implied in fact) and to reflect policy decisions (terms implied in law). Terms will only be implied in fact when it is necessary to do so in order to make business sense of the contract. There is some debate over whether terms will be implied in law merely when it is reasonable to do so or only when it is necessary. There is increasing momentum towards recognizing an implied term to perform in good faith, especially in relational contracts.

4. Conditions, warranties and innominate terms

Terms are divided into conditions, warranties and innominate terms for the purpose of resolving whether their breach gives rise simply to a right to damages or whether in addition the innocent party has the option to terminate the contract.

A breach of condition gives the innocent party the right to terminate the contract—a remedy that brings the contract and all future obligations to an end as well as allowing the innocent party to sue for damages.

A breach of warranty only gives rise to an action for damages whereas a breach of an innominate term may, depending upon the seriousness of the breach, give rise to an option to terminate if it deprives the other party of substantially the whole benefit of the contract or, if it does not do so, it will simply provide an action for damages.

Where the parties have not made it absolutely clear that a term is intended to be a condition or it would be unreasonable to assume the parties intended it as such, the tendency is to interpret it as an innominate term rather than a condition so as to avoid giving an inappropriate automatic right to terminate for a relatively trivial breach and to promote and preserve a flexible response to breach of contract.

The need for predictability in commercial contracts—for example in relation to time clauses—means that some terms will be recognized as conditions even though the actual consequences of the breach may not initially be very serious.

? Questions

1. Tennis star Tim Lobem agreed to act as coach to Buster Slasher, the Managing Director of Slasher Rackets Ltd. The terms of the contract stated:

   'Lobem will not play in any doubles tournament except as Slasher's partner. Lobem will use only equipment manufactured by Slasher Rackets Ltd.'

   Lobem and Slasher entered the Kinky Cola International Tournament but on the day of the first round of doubles, Slasher was taken ill and unable to play. Lobem accepted an invitation to play with his good friend Si Borg and, by mistake, played with a racket manufactured by SuperServe Ltd. Slasher has told Lobem that he is terminating the contract. Advise Lobem.

2. 'The law not only identifies, but also classifies, the content of a contract in an arbitrary and imprecise manner.' Discuss.

3. 'The law of contract is based on the intentions of the parties so there is no justification for the courts implying terms in fact or in law.' Discuss.

Further reading

Books

Chen-Wishart, M, *Contract Law*, 7th edn (Oxford University Press, 2022) ch 10.1–10.4 and 10.6 and chapter 12.2.

McKendrick, E, *Contract Law: Text, Cases and Materials*, 11th edn (Oxford University Press, 2024) chs 8 and 10 and ch 22.3.1–22.3.4.

O'Sullivan, J, and Hilliard, J, *The Law of Contract*, 11th edn (Oxford University Press, 2024) ch 7 and paras 15.15–15.37.

Articles

Peden, E, 'Policy concerns behind implications of terms in law' (2001) 117 LQR 459.

Phang, A, 'Implied terms in English Law—some recent developments' [1993] JBL 242.

Reynolds, F, 'Discharge of contract by breach' (1981) 97 LQR 541.

Spencer, JR, 'Signature, consent and the rule in *L'Estrange v Graucob*' (1973) 32 CLJ 104.

Staughton, C, 'How do the courts interpret commercial contracts?' (1999) 58 CLJ 303.

6 Exemption clauses

LEARNING OBJECTIVES

This chapter will help you to:

- understand what exemption clauses are and how they can be used to allocate risks;
- examine the courts' approach to incorporation, interpretation and invalidity of exemption clauses in an attempt to control their abuse; and
- understand the statutory controls still contained in the Unfair Contract Terms Act 1977 plus those formerly contained in that Act in relation to consumers together with the Unfair Terms in Consumer Contracts Regulations 1999, now replaced by the statutory regime for consumers enacted in the Consumer Rights Act 2015.

Introduction

Exemption clauses provide that one party will not be liable in certain situations; they defeat or limit liability. Exemption clauses have traditionally had a bad press because they have been misused, often to the detriment of consumers (i.e. you and I and the general public who buy goods and services), and the courts have responded to this by repeatedly looking for ways to cut them down. Nevertheless, you should keep in mind that they are not irredeemably evil or objectionable. Exemption clauses can be used perfectly sensibly by the parties to allocate risk between them. Sometimes it is more efficient for one party to take on a certain risk, perhaps because that party has insured against that risk or wants the contract to be priced as low as possible, and an exemption clause can allocate the risk in this particular way. To take a simple example, if you have already purchased annual travel insurance, you may not want to pay the full price for a holiday which includes a money-back guarantee if you are too ill to travel or if there are any other disruptions to travel arrangements, and so you may prefer to pay a lower price and agree that the holiday company can exclude any responsibility it might have in these eventualities. Freedom of contract theory insists that the choice is the parties' and not that of the courts. Parties can bargain with or without exemption clauses but they must live with the consequences of their bargain.

6.1 The control of exemption clauses

So why are the courts traditionally so set against exemption clauses, apparently in defiance of the parties' freedom of contract? The answer is that the courts do not object to exemption clauses in themselves, but they object to the *abuse* of exemption clauses. The whole ideology of freedom of contract is based on the assumption that the parties have a free choice and, in an ideal world, a consumer will always have a choice between companies that use exemption clauses and those that do not. In practice, you often find that many if not all the companies offering a particular type of service use standard forms which contain exemption clauses and so there is no real choice. Furthermore, these exemption clauses are often in such small print and so long and boring that no one (not even the conscientious law student) ever reads them. In these circumstances, choice is just an illusion; if you want the goods or service on offer then you have to accept the exemption clause whether you are conscious of it or not. Even if there is some difference between the terms on offer from different suppliers, the chances are that you will not have enough time or patience to discover which provider offers the best terms. Parties who use exemption clauses are often in strong bargaining positions and can use standard-form contracts to surreptitiously impose extremely wide and unreasonable exclusions of liability, safe in the knowledge that the other party will not even read these clauses, let alone object to them. It is this type of behaviour, this abuse of the parties' freedom to contract, that the courts, and increasingly legislators, are concerned to prevent.

EXAMPLE

The use and abuse of exclusion clauses

Imagine that you buy a computer direct from the manufacturer, Compubuild.com. Naturally, you expect that the manufacturer will replace the computer if it is faulty because you bargained for a working computer, not a dud one. Compubuild will need to factor into its prices the cost of replacing broken computers so that it still makes a profit. If it costs £500 to replace a computer and the manufacturer expects to supply ten defective computers out of a year's supply of 1,000, then it needs to bring in extra turnover of £5,000, £5 per computer, to cover the cost of replacing computers. However, if a different manufacturer, Cheepcomputers.com, is allowed to exclude its liability for defective computers it can simply leave you with a defective computer and not bother charging the extra £5 per computer (which superficially makes its computers appear initially to be a more attractive buy than Compubuild's). To avoid the risk of being left with a defective computer you could buy insurance against defects. If you can buy insurance for less than £5 then Cheepcomputers offers the best deal; you pay a lower price (even with the added cost of independent insurance) than if you bought from Compubuild.com, whilst still being covered against the risk of defects. If you cannot or do not want to buy such insurance, you may well feel you are better off paying £5 more to Compubuild rather than allowing Cheepcomputers, by means of an exemption clause, to transfer to you the risk of the computer supplied by them being defective. The courts will be particularly reluctant to enforce such a clause transferring the risk to you if you were unaware of it because it was expressed in obscure language and buried in the small print which you had no real awareness or choice about.

The most obvious defence against such abuse would be to declare unreasonable exemption clauses invalid. The Court of Appeal tried to do this on a number of occasions in the mid-twentieth century by means of the 'fundamental breach' doctrine (see section 6.3.3) but the House of Lords put it firmly in its place when it emphatically confirmed in *Photo Production* v *Securicor* (1980) that the courts had no common law power to strike down unreasonable exemption clauses. Such a common law power was no longer necessary by then anyway because Parliament had stepped into the fray with the Unfair Contract Terms Act 1977 (UCTA), which provided a statutory basis for invalidating unreasonable exemption clauses. The European Union subsequently introduced in 1993 a Directive on Unfair Terms in Consumer Contracts requiring all Member States to legislate against such terms, resulting in another layer of legislative control, the Unfair Terms in Consumer Contracts Regulations (UTCCR), which first came into force in 1995 and which were revised in 1999. Both these legislative layers of control have now been reorganized in the Consumer Rights Act 2015 (CRA), which replaces and repeals the parts of UCTA relating to consumers plus the UTCCR themselves (which only ever dealt with consumers) with a new unified statutory scheme for business to consumer contracts. It also amends UCTA so as to leave it operational as the statutory framework of control for contracts other than those caught by the consumer scheme. These legislative developments will be discussed later after we have considered the courts' approach at common law, which is still of some significance. Although the primary weapon of declaring unreasonable exemption clauses invalid was unavailable at common law, the courts have used two other hurdles, *incorporation* and *interpretation*, which they developed in order to bring down objectionable attempts to exclude liability. If the courts can rule that an exemption clause has not been *incorporated* into a contract, or *interpret* it in such a way that it does not cover the liability in dispute, this can be almost as good as finding the clause to be invalid. The major problems with these two common law controls are the danger that the courts will distort the normal rules of incorporation and interpretation in order to indirectly control unreasonable exemption clauses and the converse problem that sometimes these devices are simply ineffective to counter a very obvious and clearly worded but unreasonable clause. Given the statutory powers now available to strike down unreasonable or unfair clauses, neither of these problems is quite so acute as once was the case and the rules of incorporation and interpretation can be applied today in a somewhat less pressurized environment. The main mechanisms for control of exemption clauses are illustrated in Figure 6.1.

6.2 Incorporation

6.2.1 **Signature**

An exemption clause, like any other term, will be incorporated into a contract if it is contained in a signed contractual document, as in *L'Estrange* v *Graucob* (1934) where the purchaser of a vending machine was bound by a very wide exemption clause contained in the small print on the order form which she had signed. Scrutton LJ said: 'When a document containing contractual terms is signed, then, in the absence of fraud, or, I will add, misrepresentation, the party signing it is bound, and it is wholly immaterial whether he has read the document or not.'

The basis for this rule lies in the objective approach to intention. If C has signed a document then it is reasonable to conclude that C agrees to all the terms in that document. C may not have even read the terms but the important point is that C's signature makes it *appear* as though C has. As we shall see in Chapter 8, the objective approach will not apply when one

Figure 6.1 Control of exemption clauses

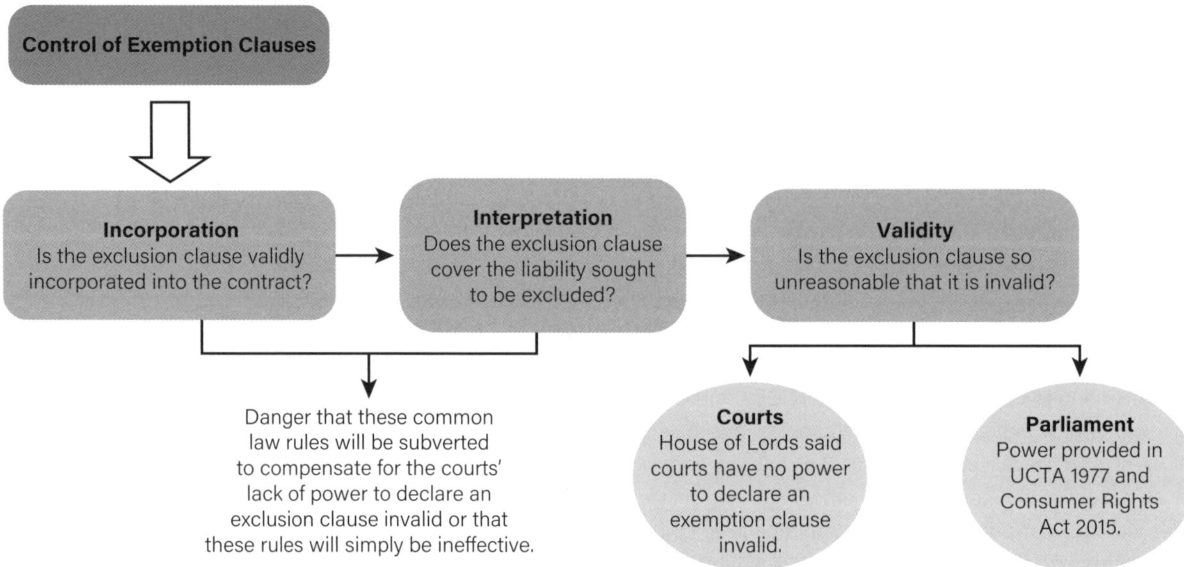

party negligently causes the other party to have a different subjective intention (see *Scriven Bros* v *Hindley* (1913)). The rule in *L'Estrange* does not therefore apply, as was signalled by Scrutton LJ, when the signature is obtained by misrepresentation (i.e. when one party causes the other to think that the document being signed contains terms different from those it contains in reality). This is nicely illustrated by *Curtis* v *Chemical Cleaning Co.* (1951) where a woman took a wedding dress to the Chemical Cleaning Co. to be dry-cleaned. When she asked why she had to sign a receipt which in fact contained a clause excluding liability 'for any damage howsoever caused' she was told unwittingly by the assistant that it was because the cleaning company did not accept liability for any damage to the beads or sequins on her dress. This was quite untrue and a misrepresentation (albeit one made innocently) because the clause clearly excluded liability for *all* damage. The cleaning company stained the wedding dress but was prevented from relying on the exemption clause to exclude its liability since, in the words of Denning LJ, 'a false impression was created.' You might want to consider what the position would have been had the beads or sequins been damaged rather than the dress: would the clause, as represented, covering beads and sequins, have been incorporated into the contract?

LINK TO . . .

Mistake (Chapter 8)

Chapter 8 explains that the objective approach will not apply when one party makes a mistake and the other party knows that the mistake has been made (see *Smith* v *Hughes* (1871)). Spencer (1973) has argued that a mistake known to the other party, even if there has not been a misrepresentation, should also act as an exception to the rule in *L'Estrange*, so that if a party knows that the other party has not read the exclusion clause, it should not form part of the contract. On this analysis, even though C's signature to the clause makes it appear as though C intended to include it as a term of the contract, the other party cannot rely on this objective approach to intention if they knew that the C did not subjectively intend this. However, so far the courts have only very rarely allowed a mistake to override C's signature when it is so severe that the document is of a totally different character to the one C thought C was signing and the mistaken party can say it 'is not my deed' (the doctrine is known as *non est factum*, see *Gallie* v *Lee* (1971)).

6.2.2 **Notice**

It is obvious that not every contractual document will be signed and the law recognizes this by allowing terms to be incorporated by notice. This might be as simple as showing the other party a written set of terms but not requiring the document to be signed, although the following cases show that the facts can become much more complicated. In *Parker* v *South East Railway Co.* (1877) Mr Parker paid to leave his bag in the Railway Company's cloakroom, but unfortunately it was lost or stolen. Mellish LJ was faced with the question of whether the printed terms on the back of a ticket given to Mr Parker, one of which excluded liability for packages exceeding £10, had been incorporated into the contract between Mr Parker and the Railway Company. He thought that first of all Mr Parker had to see or know that there was writing on the ticket and if he knew there was writing and knew or believed that the writing contained conditions (terms), then he was bound by them. Provided he knew there was writing on the ticket, even if he did not know or believe that the writing contained conditions, he would still be bound 'if the delivering of the ticket to him in such a manner that he could see [there] was writing upon it, was, in the opinion of the jury, reasonable notice that the writing contained conditions.' The case is the foundation of the courts' general approach to the issue of incorporation by notice, that is, that what matters is not whether the claimant has become aware of the detail of the exemption clause (although of course if there is full awareness the clause will be incorporated) but whether the person seeking to rely on the clause has taken reasonable steps to bring it to their attention. What is reasonable notice will obviously change from case to case depending upon the actual circumstances, but some general points can be made.

Timing of notice

Firstly, and rather obviously, notice of terms must be given before or at the time the contract is made. In *Olley* v *Marlborough Court Ltd* (1949) a contract was formed at the hotel reception desk and the hotel owner could not rely on an exemption clause that was only notified to the guest when she entered the bedroom and saw a notice on the wall.

When faced with a question of notification of terms the most important step is to establish when the contract was formed. The courts do not seem to worry about split seconds so that where an exemption clause is notified on the back of a ticket, the notice will be sufficiently contemporaneous with the contract even though technically the contract (the offer and acceptance) will have taken place a split second before the ticket was handed over. Where the contract is formed at a staffed ticket booth it is conceivable that a passenger who objects to the terms notified on the back of his rail ticket can return the ticket and demand their money back on the basis that no agreement has been reached. Automatic ticket machines present a different problem and cannot be dealt with in this way. In *Thornton* v *Shoe Lane Parking* (1971), in order to get into the defendant's multi-storey car park a driver had to drive up a ramp, insert payment and take a ticket from a machine. Lord Denning MR said that the contract was concluded at this point and any notice of terms on the ticket came too late. The reason behind this strict approach to timing is that, unlike the situation where one is dealing with another person rather than a machine, the driver 'may protest to the machine, even swear at it; but it will remain unmoved. He is committed beyond recall.'

Contractual documents

Secondly, the notice must be made on a 'contractual' document. In a sense this is a circular statement: if the notice forms part of the contract then of course the document is a contractual one, and if the notice is not part of the contract then the document has no contractual significance. The important point to remember is that the document must be one on which the reasonable person would expect to find contractual terms. It is 'contractual' in the sense that it looks as if it might contain contractual terms. No reasonable person would search through an in-flight magazine for the terms of a contract, but a reasonable person might check the back of an airline ticket for such terms (although we have never been tempted to do so). In *Chapelton* v *Barry UDC* (1940), an exemption clause written on the back of a ticket for the hire of a deckchair was not incorporated into the contract. The Court of Appeal held that the ticket was a 'mere receipt,' given out so that a deckchair users could prove that they had paid for their chairs. It was not reasonable to expect deckchair users to check this receipt for notification of terms, in part because it was usual practice that people would sit on the deckchairs for some time before payment was collected and a receipt given out. Be aware that not all receipts will fail to incorporate terms into the contract; everything depends on the facts and whether it is reasonable to find terms of the contract on a receipt of that kind.

Notice of existence not contents

Thirdly, only reasonable notice of the existence of terms is normally required, not their detailed contents. A good illustration of how harshly this rule has at times operated in the past can be seen in *Thompson* v *London, Midland & Scottish Railway Co.* (1930) where a clause excluding liability for negligently causing personal injury was incorporated into a contract with an illiterate passenger by notice on the face of the ticket saying 'Excursion. For conditions see back' and on the back of the ticket it was stated in small print that the conditions could be found in the company's timetables (in fact on page 552 of a timetable costing 20 per cent of the price of the ticket).

THINKING POINT

Do you think that many passengers of the previously discussed railway company were ever subjectively aware of the term excluding liability? Even out of those passengers who had bought a timetable, do you think many would have understood and actively accepted the term? Does the passenger have an opportunity to reject the offer of travel if he does not want to accept the term excluding liability?

What is the downside of requiring a company to give notice of the exact contents of terms to its passengers? How big would a railway ticket have to be if it included all terms governing the relationship between company and passenger? Should it matter whether the passenger is a regular traveller with that railway company?

Higher degree of notice for onerous or unusual terms

Fourthly, and by way of qualification to the previous point, a higher degree of notice is required when the term is onerous or unusual. Lord Denning said in *J Spurling Ltd* v *Bradshaw* (1956) (and quoted himself on this point in *Thornton*—you know you've made it when you can quote your own previous judgment in the Court of Appeal) that some exemption clauses 'would need to be printed in red ink on the face of the document with a red hand pointing to it.' Therefore, reasonable notice means different things depending on how unusual or onerous an exemption clause is. Clarke (1976) objected that the courts turned to declaring a clause unincorporated because they had denied themselves the power of declaring it void for being unreasonable: 'a discredited rule of public policy has been reinstated as a rule based on an inference from the intentions of the parties; the plaintiff is only deemed to know of and assent to terms that are usual.' On the other hand, the rule can be seen as a legitimate application of the objective approach to intention in that an unusual term is more likely to take a reasonable person by surprise and not be implicitly assented to, rendering explicit notice of that term necessary.

It is important to ask when a clause will count as unusual or onerous. If it is unusual because it is unreasonable (as suggested by Lord Denning MR in *Thornton*) the rule does seem to be a subversive way of striking out at the validity of exemption clauses (as argued by Clarke). In *Interfoto Picture Library Ltd* v *Stiletto Visual Programmes Ltd* (1988) a term of the contract imposed a fine for any hired transparencies that were returned late (it does not matter that the clause was not an exemption clause, the rules of incorporation apply to all terms). The Court of Appeal thought that the plaintiffs had not done what was necessary to draw this unreasonable and extortionate clause fairly to the attention of the defendants. In *AEG (UK) Ltd* v *Logic Resource Ltd* (1996), in respect of a clause which made the business purchasers of defective electrical equipment responsible for the (£4,000) cost of transporting them back to the manufacturer for repairs, the only remedy afforded to them by the contract, Hobhouse LJ (although he was in the minority in deciding that the clause was incorporated) made some interesting comments on *Thornton* and *Interfoto*:

> In my judgment, and this is where I part company from my Lords, it is necessary before excluding the incorporation of a clause . . . to consider the type of clause it is. Is it a clause of the type which you would expect to find in the printed conditions? If it is, then it is only in the most exceptional circumstances that a party will be able to say that it was not adequately brought to his notice by standard words of incorporation. If a party wishes to find out precisely how a clause of a normal sort has been worded, he should ask for the actual text of the clause. This case is not analogous to either of the two cases upon which the appellant founds. The Interfoto case involved an extortionate clause which did not relate directly to the expected rights and obligations of the parties. In the Shoe Lane Parking case, it related to personal injuries and the state of the premises and not to the subject matter of the car parking contract, which would, in the view of the Court of Appeal, have been concerned with damage to property.

The earlier cases, on this view, are based on the terms being of a *type* which one would not expect to find in the particular contract, rather than them simply being harsh or unreasonable. The latter problem, Hobhouse LJ not unpersuasively argues, is better addressed directly through the Unfair Contract Terms Act 1977 (see section 6.5.1) under which all three judges in the *AEG* case agreed the clause was unreasonable and unenforceable. The manner in which the tests for incorporation can be used as mechanisms of control is illustrated in Figure 6.2.

Figure 6.2 Incorporation of exclusion clauses by signature and notice as a control mechanism

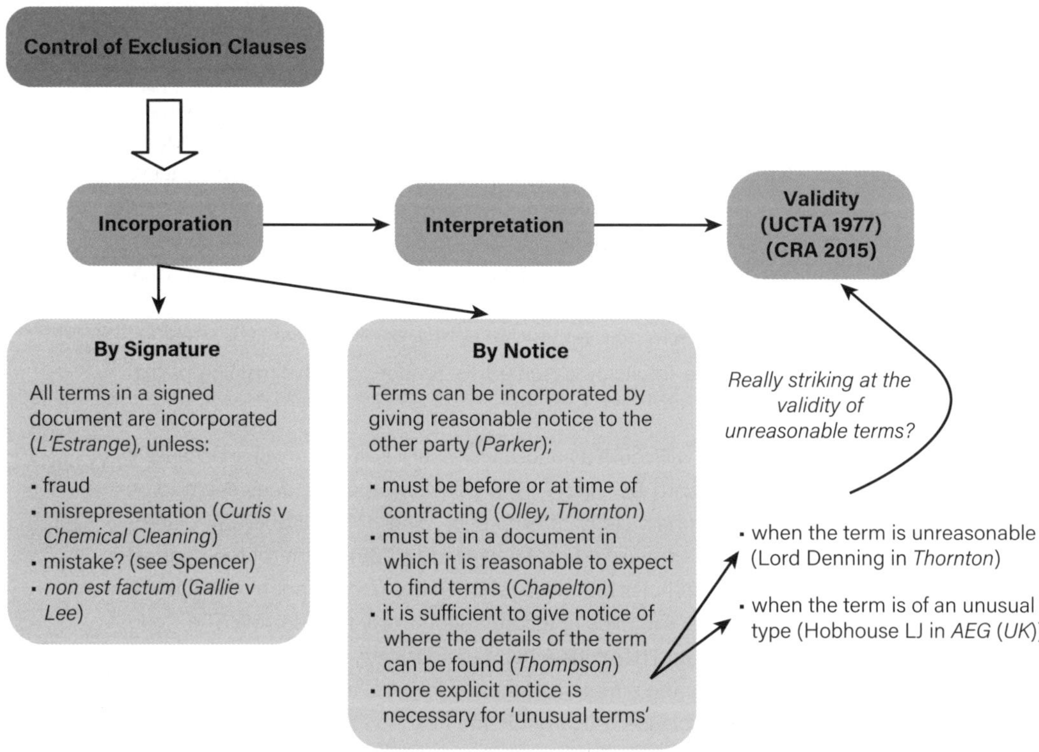

CASE CLOSE-UP

***O'Brien* v *MGN Ltd* (2001)**

The case of *O'Brien* v *MGN Ltd* (2001) shows that the question of whether reasonable notice has been given can be a finely balanced issue on the facts. Hale LJ thought it 'would make an excellent question in an undergraduate contract law seminar or examination. Like all good questions, it is easy to ask and difficult to answer.'

The claimant appeared to have won a £50,000 prize in a newspaper scratch-card competition. Unfortunately, due to a mistake, 1,472 other individuals had received cards indicating such a prize on the day in question and the newspaper refused to pay, referring to its Rules which provided (by Rule 5) for a draw to select one winner from the 1,472 in this situation. The Rules had been printed in the newspaper on some days but not on the day in question, although there was a statement that '[n]ormal Mirror Group rules apply,' of which statement the claimant was aware. The trial judge found that reasonable notice of Rule 5 had been given and the majority of the Court of Appeal (Hale and Potter LJJ) agreed with him and did not consider Rule 5 to be 'onerous or unusual.' Part of the reason was that, despite the sympathy felt for the claimant's disappointment and the corresponding lack of sympathy for the newspaper, the rule 'merely deprived the claimant of a windfall for which he has done very little in return,' unlike the more onerous and unusual clauses in *Interfoto* v *Stilletto* and *Thornton* v *Shoe Lane Parking*.

Hale LJ said that 'in any event, the words "onerous or unusual" are not terms of art. They are simply one way of putting the general proposition that reasonable steps must be taken to draw the particular term in question to the notice of those who are to be bound by it and that more is required in relation to certain terms than to others depending on their effect.' Her Ladyship went on to find that 'just enough' had been done in this case.

Sir Antony Evans however only agreed with the result because he was reluctant to interfere with the trial judge's finding of fact unless it was clearly wrong, which he could not say given that two judges in the Court of Appeal were of the same opinion. For his own part, however, he considered that 'a Rule which gave the "winner" no more than a further chance to obtain the prize was sufficiently onerous, if not unusual, to require greater prominence than was given to this one.' Clearly more than one answer is possible to the question posed by this case, which may perhaps be said to be an illustration of the saying, 'you pays your money and you takes your choice.'

The test of onerous or unusual continues to be discussed in the case law but, as Figure 6.2 implies, it is merely one of the control mechanisms for exclusion clauses and it is specifically those terms which are arguably onerous or unusual that are much more likely to be found unreasonable anyway under UCTA or the CRA. For example, *Goodlife Foods* v *Hall Fire Protection* (2018) concerned a fairly wide exclusion clause, excluding liability for fire damage in a contract which was specifically for the installation of fire suppression equipment. The clause was held by the Court of Appeal not to be onerous or unusual given the relatively low contract price and the possibility and indeed advisability of the claimant being able to purchase its own insurance cover (and indeed the dispute was really between two insurance companies rather than the contracting parties). Even if the clause could be regarded as onerous or unusual, the court found that in a contract between two equally sized businesses, it had been fairly brought to the attention of the other party, as the opening paragraph of the conditions of the contract made it clear there would be no liability for damages. Furthermore, the clause was regarded as reasonable under UCTA. In contrast in *Bates* v *Post Office (No 3)* (2019), Fraser J found that a number of the Post Office's terms *were* onerous or unusual and insufficient notice had been given of them but the terms were incorporated on the separate ground of being in a signed document. However, the onerous or unusual terms incorporated due to signature were still of no avail to the Post Office as they were found to be unreasonable under UCTA.

More recently, in *MS Amlin Marine NV v King Trader Ltd* (2025) the Court of Appeal has reviewed the existing authorities and labelled them as dealing with the 'onerous clause doctrine' which was held not to apply or to prevent the incorporation of a 'pay first' clause in a complex marine insurance policy (which significantly limited, and on the facts excluded, the insurer's obligation). It was noted that, in this particular commercial context, a professional broker would have scrutinized the documents on behalf of the insured and could be expected to draw the insured's attention to any unduly onerous clause so that it could be negotiated away (at a price) if necessary or desirable.

6.2.3 **Course of dealing**

Even if there are no signed terms and no reasonable notice it is still possible to incorporate terms into a contract if there has been an established course of dealing between the parties. In other words, if the parties have usually contracted on certain terms in the past, it will not matter that on one particular occasion they did not incorporate those terms into the contract in the usual way. In *Hardwick Game Farm* v *Suffolk AA* (1969) the parties had contracted three or four times a month over a period of three years on terms that excluded the seller's liability for latent defects in pheasant food. On one particular occasion the pheasant food contained poison and the sellers sought to rely on the exemption clause. It was held that the terms could not be regarded as incorporated by notice because, on this particular occasion, they had been notified to the buyer after the contract had been formed (see *Olley* v *Marlborough Court Ltd* in section 6.2.2) but the terms were incorporated by reason of the long course of dealing. It was reasonable to assume that both parties thought they were contracting on the same terms they had always contracted on. By contrast, in *Hollier* v *Rambler Motors (AMC) Ltd* (1972) Mr Hollier signed a document containing terms for his car's service on each of the previous three or four times he visited Rambler Motors over a five-year period, but, on one occasion when he was not asked to sign the terms, they were not incorporated into the contract by their previous course of dealing. It seems that the course of dealing must be longer and more consistent than three or four times over five years.

Businesses and consumers

Hardwick Game Farm and *Hollier* raise an interesting distinction between businesses and consumers which runs throughout the law's approach to exemption clauses and which, as we will see, is now fundamental in terms of statutory controls but which is also often at work in the application of the common law rules currently under discussion. In *Hardwick Game Farm* both parties were businesses whereas Mr Hollier was a consumer, a normal individual like you or me, who bought goods and services for his own personal use. The law tries to protect consumers because they often have less knowledge, fewer resources and a weaker bargaining position than businesses and are therefore more susceptible to having unreasonable or unfair clauses imposed upon them. You could therefore argue that an additional reason why an exclusion clause was not incorporated in *Hollier*, but was in *Hardwick Game Farm*, was because the courts wanted to protect Mr Hollier, a consumer, from Rambler Motors, a business, that tried to exclude its liability.

6.2.4 **Trade custom**

Even if there has been no signature, no reasonable notice and no sufficient past course of dealing it is still possible to incorporate a term on the ground that it is so common in the parties' area of business that they must have intended it to be a term of the contract. In *British Crane Hire Corporation* v *Ipswich Plant Hire Ltd* (1974) both parties rented out heavy plant equipment in the course of their business. Ipswich Plant Hire desperately needed a crane at short notice and so they quickly agreed a price for hire from British Crane Hire but the normal contractual terms were not signed. They had dealt with each other on just two previous occasions in the previous year, which in itself was not considered on the facts to be a sufficient course of dealing. Nevertheless, Lord Denning MR thought that the objective intentions of each party were that the usual trade terms of British Crane Hire were incorporated into the contract. He emphasized the fact that both parties operated in the same trade and knew the type of conditions usually incorporated in a contract for the hire of a crane. They were in an equal bargaining position and in those circumstances it was reasonable to conclude that the terms formed part of the contract.

6.3 Interpretation

If an exemption clause has been incorporated into the contract the courts' next line of defence is through interpretation. The courts have to work out what the parties intended their words to mean, always bearing in mind that the objective approach focuses on what the parties *appear* to have intended rather than what they actually (subjectively) intended. Even when the parties' subjective intentions are removed from the picture, there is plenty of scope for ambiguity and argument over the meaning of the terms. In short, even the reasonable person encounters difficulties interpreting the terms of the contract.

Lord Hoffmann summarized the principles judges should follow when interpreting terms (not just exemption clauses) in *ICS* v *West Bromwich Building Society* (1998). He emphasized that judges should take a 'purposive' approach that looks for the parties' objective intentions rather than a 'literal' approach that looks for a dictionary definition for the words used.

6.3.1 Contra proferentem

The person responsible for including the clause in the contract has the opportunity to make the wording clear and so should be the one to lose out if there is any ambiguity. For example, a term of an insurance contract in *Houghton* v *Trafalgar Insurance Co. Ltd* (1954) excluded liability if the car was carrying an excess 'load' but this was interpreted as not applying to the situation where the car was carrying too many passengers; 'load' was interpreted as restricted to baggage and not passengers. In *Andrews Bros (Bournemouth) Ltd* v *Singer & Co.* (1934) the contract for the sale of cars provided that 'all conditions, warranties and liabilities implied by statute, common law or otherwise are excluded' but this was ineffective to exclude liability for breach of an *express* term.

Lord Diplock warned against taking the **contra proferentem** approach too far in *Photo Production* v *Securicor* (1980): 'in commercial contracts negotiated between businessmen capable of looking after their own interests . . . it is, in my view, wrong to place a strained construction on words in an exemption clause which are clear and fairly susceptible of one meaning only.' Nevertheless the Court of Appeal felt constrained, even in a commercial case, to follow a previous line of authority of strict construction in the case of *The Mercini Lady* (2010). This concerned a widely drafted exemption clause which stated there are 'no guarantees, warranties or representations, express or implied' relating to 'merchantability, fitness or suitability of the oil for any particular purpose.' However, it did not expressly refer to conditions and so was not effective to exclude liability for breach of condition under the Sale of Goods Act 1979. In contrast, this case was distinguished in *Air Transworld* v *Bombardier* (2012), which concerned the purchase of a private jet (so take care next time you are buying one). Cooke J considered that the words 'all other . . . obligations . . . or liabilities express or implied arising by law' were sufficiently clear to exclude the statutorily implied conditions since the language was in his judgment 'fairly susceptible of only one meaning (to employ the expression used by Lord Diplock in *Photo Production*).' This may well be indicative of a less restrictive approach to the interpretation of exclusion clauses in commercial agreements as is also illustrated by *Transocean Drilling UK* v *Providence Resources* (2016). In this case a clause indemnifying each party for liability for the other's consequential loss was held to be effective in the Court of Appeal and it was not appropriate to restrictively interpret the clause as had been done by the trial judge. Moore-Bick LJ said at para. [20] that *contra proferentem*

contra proferentem
A term meaning 'against the person proffering it, or putting it forward,' and the exemption clause will be interpreted against the person seeking to rely on it so as to exclude their liability.

'has no part to play . . . when the meaning of the words is clear, as I think they are in this case; nor does it have a role to play in relation to a clause which favours both parties equally, especially when they are of equal bargaining power.' *Transocean* was applied in *Persimmon Homes* v *Ove Arup* (2017), another situation involving two commercial parties of equal bargaining power, where it was held that a clause excluding 'any claim for asbestos' was clear and the *contra proferentem* rule was not relevant. Even in a commercial case, however, if the words are not clear, the clause will not be effective—see *Soteria Insurance* v *IBM* (2022) where a clause excluding liability for 'loss of profit, revenue [or] savings' did not cover on its natural and ordinary meaning 'wasted expenditure' which was a different type of loss for these purposes (notwithstanding the Court of Appeal also subscribing to the conventional view that reliance damages for wasted expenditure are really a part of the expectancy—see Chapter 11, section 11.2.1).

A further example of the courts finding the narrow principles of construction inappropriate can be found in the Supreme Court case of *Impact Funding Solutions* v *Barrington Support Services* (2016) where the clause in a commercial contract was regarded not so much as one excluding a liability which would otherwise arise by operation of law but rather as one defining the scope of the obligation undertaken (see also the discussion in section 6.5.3 of the 'relevant obligation or duty'). The *contra proferentem* approach will no doubt continue to be important however in the context of consumers. Even when the contract involves a consumer, though, it is obvious that a very clearly worded exemption clause will stand up to the courts' strict approach—see the exemption clause in *L'Estrange* v *Graucob* for an unambiguous example which went one step further than that in *Andrews* v *Singer* by referring to 'any *express or implied* condition, statement or warranty, statutory or otherwise' (emphasis added). Such a clause would however now be likely to be ineffective anyway under the CRA.

6.3.2 Excluding liability for negligence and fraud

Negligence

A particularly strong line has traditionally been taken against clauses which seek to exclude liability for **negligence**. The rationale behind this is that the parties generally want and expect each other to take reasonable care and so very clear wording is necessary to exclude liability for negligence. It is one thing to exclude my **strict liability** under the contract which would otherwise be imposed whether or not I was at fault, but quite another to deny my liability to compensate you even if I have been negligent. The Privy Council provided some guidance in *Canada Steamship Lines* v *The King* (1952), the effect of which can be summarized as follows:

negligence A person is negligent who breaches a duty to take reasonable care; a claimant must therefore prove fault (in the sense that the defendant did not take reasonable care). The duty can be imposed by law (e.g. the tort of negligence) or by contract (where the parties agree to take reasonable care in performing their promises).

strict liability Strict liability describes a no-fault obligation: e.g. the obligation on the seller of goods to provide goods which are of satisfactory quality which does not depend on whether the seller is at fault and which is broken even if the reason for the defect is the fault of the manufacturer. The promise to provide satisfactory goods is strict and is not simply a promise to take reasonable care.

(1) does the clause expressly exempt from negligence, in which case it is effective? or

(2) are the words wide enough in their ordinary meaning to cover negligence, in which case the clause may still be effective? unless

(3) there is some head of damages other than negligence (not fanciful or remote) which the words could be construed as applying to rather than to negligence.

In other words, according to these guidelines (which, as will be seen, are now in the process of being diluted) a very clearly worded clause which expressly excludes liability for negligence by using that very word or a synonym (such as neglect or default—see *Monarch Airlines* v *Luton Airport* (1998)) will be effective, and even an exemption clause which is less explicit may be treated as wide enough to cover negligence, but not if effect can be given to it by saying it covers some other potential liability but not negligence. A good (though somewhat painful) example of the latter process can be found in *White* v *John Warwick* (1953) where a clause purporting to exclude liability 'for any personal injuries' to the rider of a tricycle whose saddle tipped up was given effect to by saying it covered the defendant's strict liability under the contract to supply a safe tricycle but was then effectively exhausted and did not cover the liability for negligence in tort (it should be noted that this liability, for negligently caused *personal injury*, in any event could not possibly be excluded today in the light of the statutory control since introduced in s.2 of UCTA). In contrast, in *Alderslade* v *Hendon Laundry* (1945) the only responsibility of the laundry in relation to lost items was to take reasonable care, that is, not to be negligent (there was no strict liability under the contract, unlike *John Warwick*), and so the clause, even though it did not mention negligence or a synonym, did cover negligence—otherwise it would be of no effect at all (it may be noted that such a clause covering negligence could still be effective today even after UCTA, provided it was shown to be reasonable, since it did not relate to *personal injury* but to *property*).

Two other cases can be contrasted. The exemption clause in *The Raphael* (1980) provided that the defendants were 'not liable for . . . any act or omission' and, despite not expressly mentioning negligence, it was wide enough to cover negligence but not so wide as to cover any other liability. On the other hand, the clause in *EE Caledonia* v *Orbit Valve* (1994) was wide enough to cover negligence but it could also realistically cover liability for a breach of statutory duty, and so it was ineffective to exclude liability for negligence.

You should remember that the *Canada Steamship* guidelines are exactly that; they are guidelines and not rules to be applied automatically. Even if an exemption clause falls within the guidelines, the courts may still interpret it in such a way that liability for negligence is not excluded. In *Hollier* v *Rambler Motors* (section 6.2.3) the exemption clause normally signed by Mr Hollier stated that 'the company is not responsible for damage caused by fire to customers' cars on the premises.' Whilst this did not expressly cover negligence it was clearly capable in principle of doing so and, rather like the situation in *Alderslade*, the only legal liability on the garage that it could refer to was in relation to negligently caused fires—garages are not generally liable for fires on their premises unless they have been negligent. However, the Court of Appeal in this case was not prepared to allow the garage to exclude its liability in negligence and construed it as simply a warning to the customer that the garage was not liable for fires unless there was negligence. Salmon LJ said of the ordinary man (rather optimistically, you may think) that he would say to himself, 'Well, what they are telling me is that if there is a fire due to any cause other than their own negligence they are not responsible for it.' His Lordship concluded that 'if the defendants were seeking to exclude their responsibility for a fire caused by their own negligence they ought to have done so in far plainer language than the language here used.' This extremely strict interpretation, which robs the clause of any real legal effect, can be explained, firstly, on the ground that Mr Hollier was a consumer and, secondly, because Parliament had not yet given the courts power to strike down unreasonable exemption clauses under UCTA 1977.

As with the *contra proferentem* rule, the *Canada Steamship* approach is increasingly becoming less strictly applied, especially where there are two equal commercial parties, as can be seen in *Persimmon Homes* v *Ove Arup* (2017) where the words in an exclusion clause 'any claim in relation to asbestos' were held to exclude liability for negligence. Jackson LJ at para. [59] said: 'In my view, the canons of construction elucidated in the *Canada Steamship* line of cases are of very little assistance in the present case.' Having said that, his Lordship then went on to find that even if one did apply the *Canada Steamship* principles, the clause would still be effective since the words of the exclusion clause overall were 'in their ordinary meaning wide enough to cover negligence' and it was 'not possible to think of any non-negligent claim relating to asbestos which the parties might have had in mind.' The trend to a less literal approach based on more general principles of interpretation was however reinforced in the Supreme Court in *Triple Point Technology* v *PTT* (2021), where Lord Leggatt said at para. [111]:

> To the extent that the process has not been completed already, old and outmoded formulas such as the three-limb test in Canada Steamship Lines Ltd v The King [1952] AC 192, 208, and the 'contra proferentem' rule are steadily losing their last vestiges of independent authority and being subsumed within the wider . . . principle [of interpretation] . . .

Fraud and deliberate wrongdoing

It should be obvious that if the courts are so reluctant to allow the exclusion of liability for negligence, they are not going to allow parties to exclude liability for their *own* fraudulent conduct. By definition, fraud involves dishonesty and it would be intolerable if an *individual* were able to act in such a manner with impunity and there is a rule of public policy prohibiting this—see *S Pearson & Son Ltd* v *Dublin Corp.* (1907) dealing with exclusion of responsibility for fraudulent misrepresentation. Nevertheless, Lord Loreburn recognized that, at least where a company is acting through its agents, different considerations might apply and it might then be a matter of construction: 'I will not say that a man himself innocent may not under any circumstances, however peculiar, guard himself by apt and express clauses from liability for the fraud of his own agents. It suffices to say that in my opinion the clauses before us do not admit of such a construction.'

The point is that a principal is liable for its agent's fraud even if the principal did not itself act fraudulently; in this peculiar 'inherited' fraud situation there are fewer policy objections against allowing a party to exclude its liability for (its agent's) fraud. If exclusion of such responsibility is in theory possible, Lord Bingham in *HIH Casualty and General Insurance Ltd* v *Chase Manhattan Bank* (2003) at para. [16] emphasized that such intention must be expressed in very clear and unmistakable terms on the face of the contract. Although concerned with a somewhat different situation, *Photo Production* v *Securicor* (1980), discussed in section 6.3.3, is in fact a good example of a company successfully seeking to shift the risk of one of its own employees acting criminally, rather than fraudulently, on to the other party to the contract. To fully understand the House of Lords' decision in this case, one has to say something of the now defunct doctrine of fundamental breach.

6.3.3 **Fundamental breach**

Some terms are so fundamental to the purpose of the contract that it is almost inconceivable that the parties could have agreed to exclude liability for their breach. Lord Roskill in *The TFL Prosperity* (1984) confirmed that the courts will rarely conclude that the parties intended to exclude liability for a fundamental breach. He said that the charter in that case 'virtually ceases to be a contract for the letting of the vessel' if the exclusion clause is interpreted so that fundamental terms could be breached without financial redress.

EXAMPLE

Fundamental breach

If I agree to provide you with a taxi ride to the airport and I turn up with a tandem cycle instead of a taxi (or provide a drunken driver rather than a sober one) it would be very strange if I could claim that I should be able to rely on an exemption clause to avoid any liability under the contract. The whole point of your promise to pay me for the taxi was that you would get a promise in return and the option to sue me if I fail to perform my promise, i.e. provide a taxi (or a sober driver). An exclusion clause would degrade my promise to provide a taxi (with a sober driver) into a mere statement of intention (to provide a taxi if I felt like it), something you could have got for free.

In the mid-twentieth century, the Court of Appeal, led by Lord Denning MR, attempted to introduce a stronger rule that completely outlawed the exclusion of liability for fundamental breach. The proposed rule was one of law, which meant that it would apply regardless of the parties' intentions, whereas under a rule of interpretation the parties could make it explicitly clear that they intended to exclude liability for fundamental breach and the courts could do very little about it.

Fundamental breach as a rule of law

In *Karsales* v *Wallis* (1956) Denning LJ said (in a case where a consumer bought a car that was incapable of self-propulsion) that 'the general principle [is] that a breach which goes to the root of the contract disentitles the party from relying on the exemption clause.' The House of Lords in *Suisse Atlantique* (1967) took the opportunity to reject this rule of law when Lord Reid said *obiter dicta* that the validity of an exemption clause could not depend on whether there has been a fundamental breach. He thought that the rule was too indiscriminate because it treated business and consumer contracts alike, but the solution should be left to Parliament, a more appropriate forum for making such policy decisions (Parliament enacted the Unfair Contract Terms Act 1977 a decade later). Lord Denning, however, did not give up and managed to conclude in *Harbutts Plasticine Ltd* v *Wayne Tank & Pump Co. Ltd* (1970) that the House of Lords had affirmed rather than rejected the doctrine of fundamental breach so that when a contract is terminated for breach of a fundamental term, the contract *and any exemption clause in it* come to an end (rather like the claimant's factory which the defendant's breach had caused to burn down). *Harbutts* was itself firmly overruled by the House of Lords in *Photo Production* v *Securicor* (1980), where it was pointed out that termination does not bring a contract to an end, it simply cancels any future obligations with the result that the contract and any exemption clauses still stand—a proposition which was also enshrined, unnecessarily it now seems, in UCTA 1977, s.9(1), a section which in fact is now repealed by

Figure 6.3 Fundamental breach in the Court of Appeal and the House of Lords

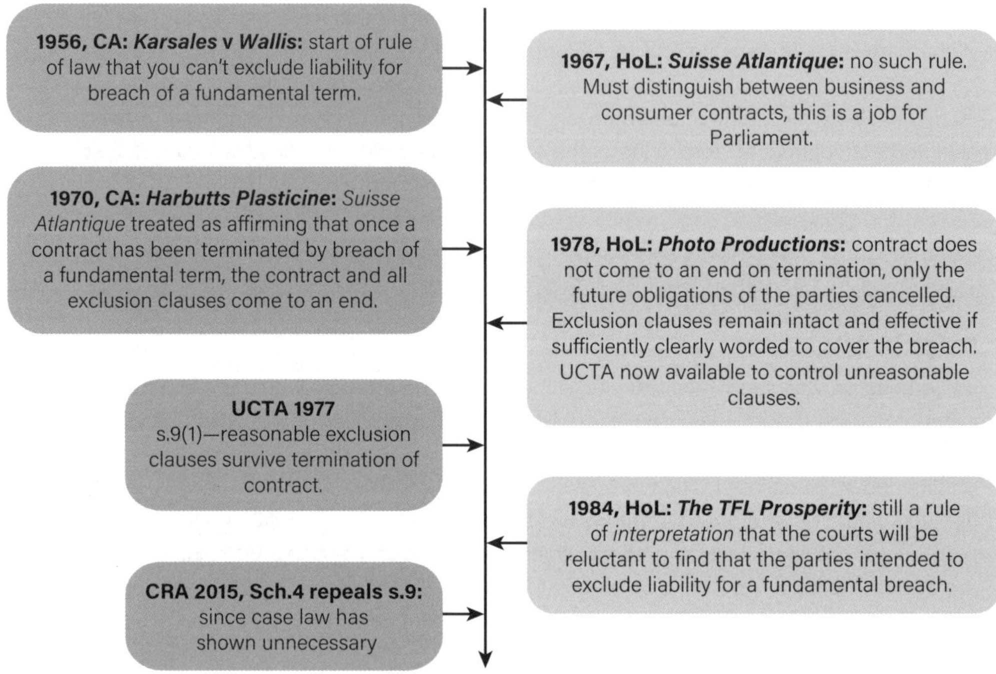

Sch.4 of the CRA. The actual decision in *Photo Production* meant that Securicor were able to exclude their responsibility for their employee deliberately starting a fire which ultimately burned down the factory which he was supposed to be guarding. There are a number of key features of the case that should be borne in mind in trying to understand why the House of Lords was prepared to interpret the clause as covering this disastrous breach:

- **(a)** the parties were assumed (perhaps too readily) to be of equal bargaining power;
- **(b)** Securicor were (relative to the value of the factory) not paid very much for the security they provided; and
- **(c)** the clause qualified the exemption it conferred by the words 'unless such act or default could have been foreseen and avoided by the exercise of due diligence by the company as his employer'.

The clause therefore transferred the risk, of a properly vetted and trained employee unforeseeably doing something crazy, to the factory owners who could cover themselves by insurance. The rise and fall of fundamental breach is illustrated in Figure 6.3.

6.4 Limitation clauses

A limitation clause does not completely absolve a party from liability but instead places a limit, a ceiling, on the maximum liability. For example, in *Ailsa Craig Fishing* v *Malvern Fishing* (1983) (another spectacular *Securicor* case), a limitation clause limited liability to £1,000, so that the damages could be less than but not more than £1,000 (even though the actual loss caused was assessed at £55,000).

LINK TO . . .

Damages (Chapter 11)

Liquidated damages: It is worth comparing a limitation clause to a liquidated damages clause (see Chapter 11) which acts as a pre-estimate of damages. If a liquidated damages clause provides for damages of £1,000 that is what the innocent party will receive regardless of their actual loss (if the actual loss is less than the pre-estimate then liability will actually have been extended). By contrast, a limitation clause simply places a maximum limit on the damages that can be recovered and the party's actual loss will determine the precise value of damages (up to this maximum limit).

In holding that the limitation clause was effective to limit Securicor's liability to £1,000, Lord Wilberforce said:

> Clauses of limitation are not regarded by the courts with the same hostility as clauses of exclusion; this is because they must be related to other contractual terms, in particular to the risks to which the defending party may be exposed, the remuneration which he receives and possibly also the opportunity of the other party to insure.

With respect, the same considerations may be applicable to exclusion clauses, as we saw in the discussion of *Photo Production*, and the distinction is often only a matter of degree when one considers how close to zero in percentage terms the limitation of liability can become. Liability was limited to 1.8 per cent of the actual loss in *Ailsa Craig* and 0.33 per cent in *George Mitchell* v *Finney Lock Seeds* (1983). Nevertheless, the less strict approach to the interpretation of limitation clauses was approved by the House of Lords in the latter case so it is a distinction you should be aware of and should be prepared to comment on. A subsequent House of Lords decision, *Bovis* v *Whatlings Construction* (1995), shows that even limitation clauses can still be construed with a degree of strictness, even if not to the same extent as exclusion clauses. Thus the clause limiting damages for delay to £100,000 did not cover delay which amounted to a repudiatory breach leading to complete non-performance.

6.5 Statutory control (other than in relation to consumer contracts)

6.5.1 **The Unfair Contract Terms Act 1977 (UCTA)**

Background to UCTA

Under the common law, the courts can only attack an exemption clause by refusing to incorporate it into the contract or by interpreting it in such a way that it does not exclude the liability incurred. They cannot simply declare a clause invalid. We saw earlier that Lord Denning took objection to this limitation on the court's power at common law and in *Thornton* he tried to distort the rules of incorporation by notice to such a degree that it would be virtually impossible to incorporate an unreasonable exemption clause. In a series of Court of Appeal decisions he heralded the introduction of a rule of law prohibiting the exclusion of liability for a fundamental breach. The traditional attitude of the majority of the judges meant that the courts took the limitation on their power seriously and they largely rejected Lord Denning's attempts to strike, directly or indirectly, at the validity of unreasonable exemption clauses.

They were ultimately happy to do so because Parliament provided redress against unreasonable exemption clauses in many situations when it enacted UCTA. It handed the courts the weapon that Lord Denning had fought for: the power to declare certain terms invalid. Of course, the courts still had to decide whether a term had been validly incorporated and interpret that clause, but there was no longer the same pressure to distort these processes.

In the Law Commission Report number 69 (1975) on which the Act was based, the Law Commission recognized that all exemption clauses are not of the same type, the situations in which they occur vary significantly and the need for control is more pressing in some situations than in others. This is the key to understanding the Act because the Act is based on a number of significant distinctions and definitions which form the basis of the Act's control of exemption clauses. Identifying these distinctions and definitions and understanding their rationale will enable you to remember the important provisions of the Act and to apply them in a sensible manner.

This may be the first time in your course that you have had to look in detail at an Act of Parliament as opposed to case law. To deal successfully with a major Act like this you need first of all to understand what prompted the Act and what its principal aims were, as just discussed. You then need to develop a picture of the overall structure of the Act, how it fits together and which are the important sections, before going on to consider the meaning of the important sections in more detail and looking at the interpretation they have received. However, the scope of UCTA has changed radically as a result of the CRA, which repeals some significant parts of it, essentially those dealing specifically with business to consumer contracts. It nevertheless remains of major, and indeed critical, importance for contracts between businesses.

Scope of UCTA

UCTA is divided into three Parts, with Part I providing most of the law relevant to England and Wales (the subject matter of this book). Part II deals with Scottish law and Part III deals with miscellaneous provisions relevant to the whole UK, such as s.27, which deals with evasion of the Act by choice of foreign law, which need not concern us too greatly at this stage. Section 1 sets out some of the boundaries of the Act by defining key terms such as 'negligence' and 'liability' and referring to excluded contracts in Sch.1. Later sections (ss.13 and 14) also provide definitions of other key terms such as 'exemption clause' and provide general interpretation guidelines. Sandwiched in between those definitions are the key operative sections that distinguish between different types of contractual terms and how they fall to be examined under the Act (s.2 to s.7). The main provisions we shall look at are: s.2 (terms excluding liability for negligence); s.3 (terms excluding liability for breach of contract generally); and s.6 (terms excluding liability for breach of terms implied by the Sale of Goods Act 1979). The application of these central sections can produce one of two possible outcomes. It may provide outright that the exemption clause is ineffective, or, in other cases, it may make the effectiveness of the clause subject to the test of reasonableness, which is outlined in s.11 and Sch.2.

All that may seem like a lot to take in at this stage, but remember that you are only aiming for an overview of the Act before you begin to tackle the most important details. Figure 6.4 might help.

Figure 6.4 Scope of the Unfair Contract Terms Act 1977

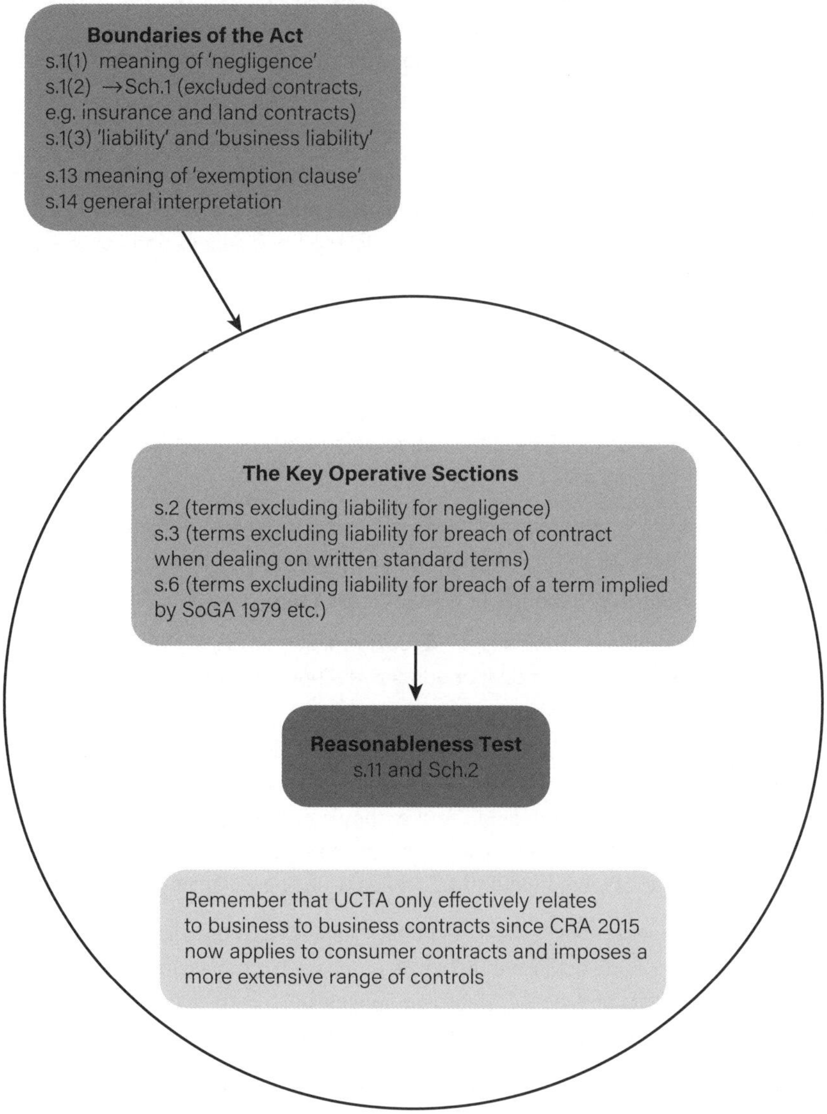

6.5.2 **Boundaries of operation of UCTA**

Business liability

One of the first things to note about the operation of the Act comes appropriately enough in s.1(3), which provides that the main provisions of the Act (ss.2–7) only apply to business liability and therefore not, in the main, to any exclusions of liability made by a private individual not acting in the course of a business. The main reasons for this are that such exclusions are comparatively rare and even where they occur there is unlikely to be any opportunity to impose unfair terms on the weaker party. However, the restriction to business liability does not apply to s.6 (see s.6(4)), which controls clauses excluding liability for breach of the terms implied by statute into contracts for the sale or hire purchase of goods (although this exception is more apparent than real since many of these terms can only arise in sales in the course of the business). The restriction to business liability also does not apply to s.8 dealing with the exclusion of liability for misrepresentation. It is not easy to say precisely why these sections are not restricted to business liability except to say that they are largely re-enactments, with minor modifications, of provisions initially founded in earlier statutes—namely the Supply of Goods (Implied Terms) Act 1973 and the Misrepresentation Act 1967.

The general restriction to business liability means that the Act will normally steer clear of contracts between two private individuals and instead focus on the cases where a business is seeking to exclude or restrict its liability (now only to another business and not to a consumer since the latter is dealt within the CRA). Where neither party is in business, they are assumed to be on roughly an equal footing and UCTA will not rush to their assistance if one party seeks to exclude its non-business liability to the other. Conversely, even where both parties are in business, as in the cases with which the Act is now primarily concerned, some businesses are much more powerful than others and their exercise of this power needs to be scrutinized under the Act, which looks carefully at their attempts to exclude 'business liability' because of the inherent risk of abuse.

Under s.1(3) the liability sought to be excluded is 'business liability' (and so subject to regulation under the Act) if it arises from the breach of an obligation arising:

(i) from things done or to be done 'in the course of a business'; or

(ii) from the occupation of premises used for business purposes of the occupier (but not if access is given for recreational or educational purposes and those purposes are not the business purposes of the occupier).

So, for example, a farmer's liability to hikers who cross his land is not a business liability because their access is for the purpose of recreation and recreation is not the nature of the farmer's business (farmers plough fields so that they can grow crops, not so that hikers can walk across them safely). In contrast, a sports centre also allows people access for recreation but it is in the business of recreation and so it owes a 'business liability' to those people.

The Act fails to give much further guidance on the meaning of 'in the course of a business' and in ss.1(3)(a) and 14(1) simply advises that 'business' *includes* a profession and the activities of government departments and local or public authorities, but this does not provide firm limits to the meaning of 'business', demonstrating only that businesses need not be run for profit.

Totally ineffective clauses and those subject to reasonableness

The second thing to notice about the Act is that, as has already been mentioned, some exclusions of liability are rendered completely ineffective, whereas others are only effective 'insofar as they satisfy the test of reasonableness'. Generally speaking, those singled out for total ineffectiveness are those which are the most objectionable or which are most likely to result from inequality of bargaining power. Following enactment of the CRA the main examples of sections rendering clauses totally ineffective are s.2(1) dealing with exclusion of liability for *death or personal injury* caused by *negligence* (the rationale for singling these out is self-evident) and s.6(1) dealing with the implied terms as to title in contracts of sale and hire purchase of goods. The latter are singled out because the exclusion is of a liability which is implied in law, that is, one which the law ordains ought to be imposed as a matter of policy, and it is also one which is fundamental to the purpose of a contract to pass title in goods.

Most of the other exclusions of liability which the Act affects are not made totally ineffective but are merely subjected to a reasonableness test. However, even these are selected on various criteria because the Act does not apply to all exemption clauses and only imposes the reasonableness test in those situations where control is likely to be necessary. Again, understanding why the Act selects certain criteria will help you to remember the criteria themselves. Thus s.2(2) subjects clauses excluding liability for *negligently* caused loss or damage *other than death or personal injury* to the reasonableness test, reflecting the well-established concern at common law about clauses excluding liability for negligence. Similarly, s.3 imposes a reasonableness test on some clauses excluding contractual liability—not all contractual liability because there are often good reasons for excluding such liability, especially where it is strict—but now only where the party affected by the clause is dealing 'on the other's written standard terms of business' (where the probability that there has been little choice about accepting them is obvious—see *African Export-Import Bank* v *Shebah* (2018) for the question of when an industry standard model set of terms can become 'the other's' written standard terms within the Act—the answer being when they are habitually used by the other, but even then, there would not be a dealing on written standard terms where there have been substantial variations negotiated).

Similarly, what is now s.6(1A) of the Act (formerly this was effected by s.6(3)) subjects clauses excluding liability for breach of the implied terms as to description and quality and so on in the Sale of Goods Act 1979 to the reasonableness test (in business to business contracts) since there is again an obvious potential issue about the fairness of excluding obligations implied by statute.

Thus far the provisions of the Act identifying the main types of terms and situations to which the Act is applicable have been considered and that has involved looking at ss.1, 2, 3 and 6. The main effects of these sections and the split between terms rendered ineffective and those subjected to a test of reasonableness are illustrated by Figure 6.5. The main issue that remains is the application of the reasonableness test, but before we deal with that issue it is worth saying something about the meaning of the concept of an exemption clause under the Act.

6.5.3 **The nature of exemption clauses under the Act**

The operative sections which we have looked at, ss.2, 3 and 6, each control terms which 'exclude or restrict' liability. This reflects the normal view of an exclusion or limitation clause; such clauses either totally exclude or limit a liability which has previously arisen. The sequence of events might go as follows: formation of a contract—breach of contract—formation of a secondary obligation to pay damages (i.e. a liability)—exclusion or limitation of this latter liability by an exemption clause.

Duty-defining clauses

However, the Act does not simply apply only to these run-of-the-mill types of exemption clause. There are much more subtle ways of excluding liability without actually stating it in so many words. The logic behind this more secretive method of evading liability is that if an obligation is defined in such a loose way that it will be difficult to breach, no liability will arise to start with, making it unnecessary to include or rely on a term excluding liability. Looking at the sequence in Figure 6.6, we see that if the obligation is so defined that it will hardly ever be breached, the case will never even reach stage 2 and so there can be no liability (stage 3) or any need for an exclusion of liability (stage 4). In practice, what is the difference between excluding a liability once it has arisen and framing an obligation so that the liability never arises? The main point is that strangling a liability at birth is as potentially abusive as excluding the liability later in its life.

Figure 6.5 Split between clauses which are ineffective and those subject to reasonableness test

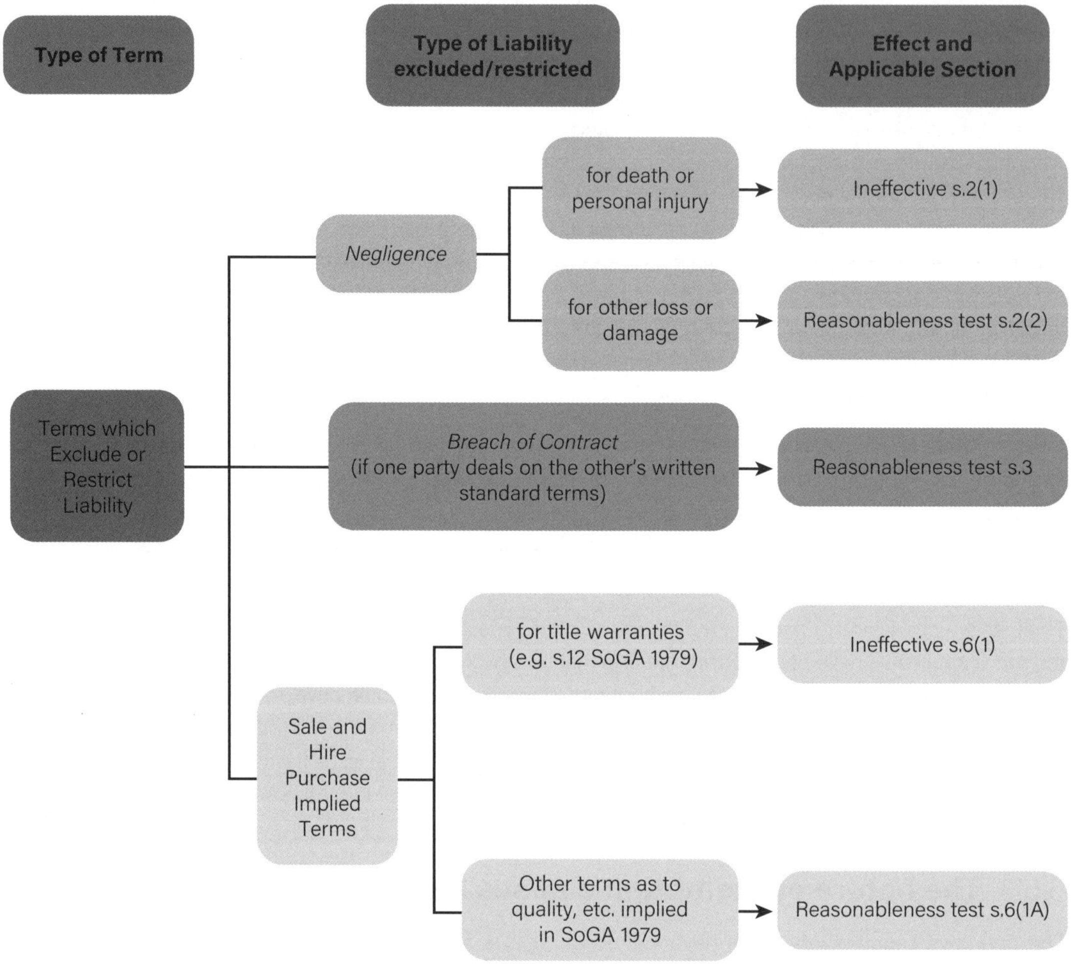

B Coote (*Exception Clauses*, Sweet & Maxwell, 1964) in particular argued that any apparent difference between the two practices is illusory. All exemption clauses are actually **duty-defining terms** (obligation) defining clauses. This is because it is nonsense to say that an obligation exists when the liability for its breach has been excluded. In other words, stages 2, 3 and 4 in Figure 6.6 are false because there cannot be a breach if liability has effectively been excluded. Exclusion clauses therefore amend the obligations of the parties, striking out of the contract those obligations for which there can be no liability. On this view, there is no such thing as a term that excludes a liability once it has arisen because an effective exclusion clause prevents it arising in the first place.

duty-defining terms Exclusion clauses traditionally wait for a liability to arise and then act to exclude this liability (see Figure 6.6). Duty-defining terms act by defining the parties' obligations in such a way that the liability never arises. In both cases one party will succeed in avoiding liability, either by exclusion or by definition.

Figure 6.6 The orthodox view of an exemption clause

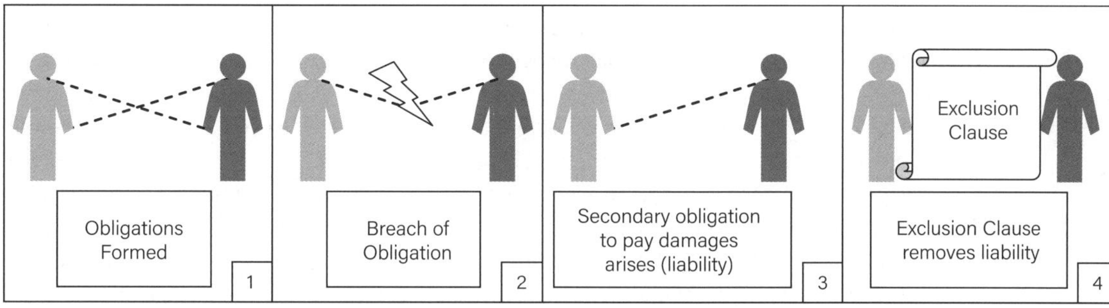

EXAMPLE

Excluding liability v preventing it arising

I sell you a 'sound' bike and you ride it off-road and the chassis snaps in two. You sue me for breach of contract (claiming that the bike was not sound) and I point to an exclusion clause in the contract that excludes any liability for damage caused by taking the bike off-road. We can say that I am originally liable for the damage to the bike but this liability is excluded as soon as it arises.

Compare the scenario where I sell you a bike 'sound except for off-road riding.' There is no obligation for me to provide a bike suitable for off-road riding and so there can be no liability when you ride it off-road and break the chassis. There is no exclusion clause but the result is the same as if there had been one. I have excluded any liability for off-road damage by definition, rather than by outright exclusion.

In order to catch these duty-defining clauses, the last sentence of s.13(1) extends the scope of the Act so that s.2 and s.6 (the relevant sections for our purposes) will 'prevent excluding or restricting liability by reference to terms and notices which exclude or restrict the relevant obligation or duty.' The main point to understand about this difficult section is that it is unclear. Any attempt to provide a watertight explanation of exactly which clauses s.13 intends to cover will send your head spinning and is doomed to fail. The test could potentially apply to all terms of the contract because by defining the obligations in one particular way, the parties have necessarily rejected other possible obligations. Think of the parties as starting with a blank sheet of paper. As they begin to write down their obligations they necessarily favour some obligations over others; the ones they write down provide not only a record of their obligations under the contract, but also a negative of the obligations they have excluded from (i.e. not included in) the contract. In this way all terms of the contract are exemption clauses.

However, it would be an intolerable intrusion into the parties' freedom of contract if all terms became subject to review under the Act. Careful attention must be paid to the reference in s.13(1) to excluding or restricting the '*relevant* obligation or duty.' This means that not all of the obligations excluded by definition (i.e. those omitted from the parties' sheet of paper) need to count as 'excluded or restricted' under the Act. But how are the courts to decide when a 'relevant' obligation has been excluded by definition? One way is to imagine that there are certain obligations which *should* be in a contract and any term which excludes or restricts such obligations falls within s.13(1). This provides a defined core of 'relevant' obligations against which the parties' chosen obligations can be measured. For instance, we might say that there should be a term that a driver of a mechanical digger will take reasonable care. If the contract defines the driver's obligations differently then this will amount to an exclusion of the driver's duty of care (an exclusion of negligence which will fall within s.2). A term that defines other obligations of the driver (such as wearing a certain uniform) will necessarily exclude alternative obligations (such as the alternative obligation of the driver wearing his own clothes) but this will not be considered to be an exclusion of liability because the driver's appearance is not considered important enough to be part of the obligations which *should* be in the contract. By having a core set of obligations to measure the parties' obligations against, it is possible to make sense of the s.13(1) phrase 'exclude or restrict the relevant obligation or duty.'

Transferring or excluding liability

Two cases, *Phillips Products Ltd* v *Hyland* (1987) and *Thompson* v *T Lohan (Plant Hire) Ltd* (1987), dealt with condition 8 in the standard form contract drafted by the Construction Plant-hire Association. Both cases involved a hirer who hired a digger (plant) from the owner who also supplied a driver for the digger. It is important to realize that normally the owner would be vicariously liable for the driver as an employee, but condition 8 stated that 'the hirer shall be responsible for all claims arising in connection with the operation of such plant by the said drivers or operators.'

In *Phillips* the driver negligently damaged the hirer's property whilst operating the digger and, when the hirer claimed damages from the driver and the owner, they pointed to the clause arguing that it *transferred* all liability to the hirer and so it did not fall within s.2(2) UCTA which only applied to *exclusions* of liability. Slade LJ was in no mood to argue over these linguistic technicalities. He said: 'There is no mystique about "exclusion" or "restriction" clauses. To decide whether a person "excludes" liability by reference to a contract term, you look at the effect of the term. You look at its substance.' He concluded that the clause did exclude the liability of the owner, under both the normal meaning of exclusion and its extended meaning under s.13(1): 'On the facts of this particular case, the effect of condition 8, if valid, is to negate a common law liability in tort which would otherwise admittedly fall on the plant-owner.' This 'but for' test requires the court to ask: 'Would the party seeking to avoid liability be liable if this clause did not exist?'

As noted earlier, this could potentially be applied to all of the terms of a contract because they all exclude other alternative obligations. The real question should not be 'what would the position be without this term?' (because all terms exclude some other obligation) but 'does this term exclude an obligation that should be in the contract (i.e. a "relevant" obligation)?' The problem then encountered is that the courts will look as though they are implying terms into the contract: also, what should be the test for deciding which obligations should be in a contract; only reasonable obligations? In *Thompson*, the driver negligently killed a third party, Mr Thompson, and so the analysis was different from *Phillips* because the person claiming damages (Mr Thompson's widow) was not subject to condition 8. It was clear that she should have damages; the outstanding question was whether the owner or the hirer paid them. The court held that on this occasion condition 8 did not fall within s.2(2) because it transferred liability for negligence from the owner to the hirer. The widow was not left without somebody to sue (as was the case in *Phillips*). Such a transfer of liability is known as an indemnity, and such clauses were subject to the reasonableness test under s.4 UCTA only if the contract was with a consumer (as was clearly not the case in the two cases earlier).

The whole area of duty-defining clauses is not at all easy to understand. If the previous discussion has seemed a little impenetrable then the following summary may help to make things clearer.

The whole purpose of the Act is to stop certain parties from unfairly avoiding liability for their acts. The most obvious example of this is when a party uses an exemption clause to exclude his liability for something he is obliged to do. However, the Act also aims to catch instances where one party *should* be under an obligation to do a certain act (e.g. to take reasonable care) but the parties have framed their obligations in such a way that that party is not under such an obligation. This 'duty defining clause' is as much an exclusion of liability as is a traditional exemption clause. The difficulty is deciding which obligations a party *should* be under; s.13(1) attempts to do this by referring to such obligations as 'relevant obligations' but this simply begs the questions rather than providing guidance.

Other terms having the effect of an exemption clause

Section 13(1) also extends s.2 and s.6 to cover terms which make it excessively difficult or prejudicial to enforce a liability and terms that try to introduce restrictive rules of evidence. As with duty-defining clauses, these can have the same effect as excluding liability outright.

The last sentence of s.13(1) (referring to terms which exclude the relevant obligation or duty) does not apply to those terms governed by s.3 (terms excluding liability for breach of contract in certain situations other than sales of goods, etc.). However, for these breach of contract cases (dealing on the other's written standard terms), s.3(2)(b) catches terms which purport to allow a party to render no performance or a substantially different performance from that which was reasonably expected—which is analogous to a term which restrictively defines the duty.

➡ **EXAMPLE**

Substantially different performance

Contract A is an agreement to deliver a rental car at 9 a.m. tomorrow subject to a clause stating that the rental company will not be liable for any loss suffered where the car is delivered up to three hours late.

Contract B is an agreement to deliver a rental car at 9 a.m. tomorrow morning, 'delivery time guaranteed to within three hours.'

The two contracts are essentially to the same effect but the first obviously involves an exemption clause whilst the second may appear not to do so and thus appears to be outside the controls imposed by the Act. However, assuming that the party receiving delivery of the car was dealing on the other's written standard terms, s.3(2)(b) prevents a party by reference to any contract term claiming to be entitled to render a performance substantially different from that reasonably expected of him.

Suppose that the car is not delivered until 11.59 a.m. Under contract A, there is clearly a breach but one which is on the face of it covered by an exemption clause and the question will be whether the clause was reasonable. Under contract B, there does not appear to be an exemption clause but the question is whether performance has been rendered which is substantially different from that reasonably expected. The answer might turn on factors such as how clearly communicated the reference to three hours was, how much was being paid and how long the rental was for—if it was only for the rest of the day then the section is perhaps more likely to apply than if the rental was to last for another week, because in the latter case the loss of the morning is proportionately less significant. Even if the Act does apply (i.e. if the performance was substantially different from what was reasonably expected) that is not the end of the matter—one then has to ask whether the term providing for the three-hour window was itself reasonable, a concept we will consider in the next section after you have studied Figure 6.7.

Figure 6.7 How s.13 and s.3(2) prevent evasion of the Act and 'feed into' the operative sections

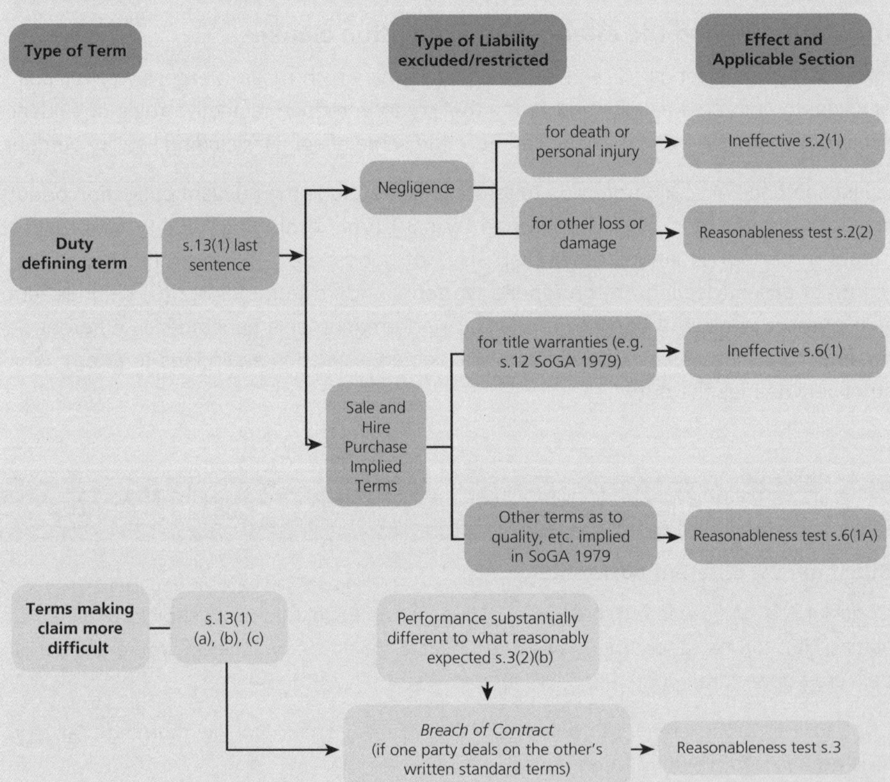

6.5.4 **The reasonableness test**

The stock criticism of tests of reasonableness in any branch of the law is the uncertainty and unpredictability that they can introduce. It is therefore important to know how far the Act provides guidance as to the application of the reasonableness test (always remembering that it is not all terms to which the test is applicable). The principal section providing such guidance is s.11, which itself also refers to specific criteria in Sch.2 (the latter are strictly speaking only applicable to exclusions of implied terms in contracts under which goods pass but there is no doubt that they constitute useful pointers in relation to other types of contracts).

The first point to note about s.11 is its last subsection, subs.(5), which puts the burden of proving reasonableness on the person relying on the clause, which is a crucial point when there are factors pointing either way, as in *St Albans City and District Council* v *International Computers Ltd* (1996). This represented an important change from the original provision in a precursor of the Act, the Supply of Goods (Implied Terms) Act 1973.

The test of whether the term was a fair and reasonable one to include

Section 11(1) marks another potentially significant change from the position under the earlier statute which controlled exemption clauses in sale of goods contracts. The question under the 1977 Act is whether the clause was a fair and reasonable one to have included *at the time of entering the contract*, rather than whether it is fair and reasonable to allow reliance on it now. This shifts the emphasis from the particular damage actually suffered, and from the circumstances of the breach, and clearly emphasizes instead the fairness of the bargain when it was struck, and this can have quite significant effects on whether the clause is likely to be upheld. For example, it might be fair and reasonable to allow reliance on a clause given the actual damage suffered and the liability actually excluded on the particular facts but the clause may not have been a fair and reasonable one to include in the contract because of its potential width and its potential to be relied on in other fact situations which could not be regarded as fair. Conversely, if the clause was fair and reasonable having regard to what the parties knew or ought reasonably to have contemplated at the time of the contract, the fact that it is later found to operate harshly should in principle be irrelevant.

That this is the correct approach under the Act was confirmed in *Stewart Gill Ltd* v *Horatio Myer & Co.* (1992), where Lord Donaldson stated: 'The issue is whether "the term [the whole term and nothing but the term] shall have been a fair and reasonable one to be included". This has to be determined as at the time when the contract is made and without regard to what particular use one party may subsequently wish to make of it.'

The clause in question was sought to be used to prevent the purchasers setting off (see s.13(1)(b) UCTA) their claim for damages against their liability to pay the balance of the price. This particular aspect and use of the clause by the sellers was regarded as reasonable but the clause could not be relied upon because it also prohibited the setting off of any credits or payments against the purchase price—which was clearly a much wider and a totally unreasonable prohibition. (It should be noted however that a no-set-off clause is not always regarded as unreasonable on the facts—see for example *FG Wilson (Engineering)* v *John Holt & Co* (2012).) The potential use to which the clause might be put on the facts of the *Stewart Gill* case however made it unreasonable even though the use to which it was actually being put was not unreasonable. The term as a whole had to be evaluated, and not just the part being relied upon in this instance, since the reasonableness test looks at whether *the term* was reasonable to include at the time of the contract. Nor should the unreasonable parts be severed from the reasonable and only the latter upheld because questions such as whether a customer ought reasonably to have known about the extent of a term (see UCTA Sch.2 para.(c)) do not make much sense if the customer could not know in advance to what extent the clause might be relied upon.

The not unattractive result is that anyone drafting an exemption clause has to ensure that it is sufficiently widely worded to cover the damage to be excluded in accordance with the common law test and yet at the same time has to take care not to make the clause any wider than is necessary since that will only increase the risk of it being judged unreasonable whereas a narrower clause might have been reasonable and still sufficient to protect the defendant. The wise drafter will also break down the various exemptions into separate clauses and subclauses so that the unreasonableness of one particular clause will only affect that one and will not infect the other separate clauses which may still remain valid if reasonable.

A further point to note about the test of reasonableness is that the question is merely whether the particular term was a reasonable one to include in this contract, not whether the term would be reasonable in any other circumstances. Coupled with the observations of Lord Bridge in *George Mitchell* v *Finney Lock Seeds* to the effect that the appellate courts will be reluctant to interfere with the findings of trial judges as to whether a clause is reasonable, this means that decided cases are going to be of relatively little help in predicting how the same clause might fare in a different set of circumstances before a different trial judge. This can clearly be illustrated if one looks at *Waldron-Kelly* v *BRB* (1981) and compares it with *Wight* v *BRB* (1983). In the former case a clause limiting liability for lost luggage by reference to its weight rather than its value was held to be unreasonable but in the latter case the same clause was held to be reasonable on the particular facts in a different county court.

That is not to say that the appellate courts will always feel bound to agree with the trial judge's assessment of reasonableness as is illustrated by *Watford Electronics* v *Sanderson* (2001) where the Court of Appeal reversed the trial judge and found the exclusion clauses to be reasonable. Chadwick LJ noted that the agreement had been negotiated by 'experienced businessmen representing substantial companies of equal bargaining power' and thought that in this situation the court should not interfere unless 'satisfied that one party has, in effect, taken unfair advantage of the other—or that a term is so unreasonable that it cannot properly have been understood or considered.' The decision can be contrasted with the *St Albans* case where the decision of Scott Baker J that the exclusion clause was unreasonable was upheld by the Court of Appeal in a contract between a business and a local authority where Scott Baker J noted that the exclusion clause would have put the loss on to the shoulders ultimately of the local population rather than the business, which was well able to insure (and which was in fact insured).

The Schedule 2 criteria

More specific criteria are provided by Sch.2 for clauses excluding liability for the terms implied in contracts involving the supply of goods caught by ss.6 and 7 of the Act and it is generally agreed that these can also be relevant to other situations (and indeed they were so considered in the *St Albans* case discussed earlier in relation to terms caught by s.3). It is therefore worthwhile being able to summarize them and understand them. Again, the criteria have been selected for good reasons and understanding their rationale makes it easier to remember them.

Paragraph (a), in referring to relative strength of bargaining power, is a fairly obvious consideration and 'alternative means by which the customer's requirements could have been met' is geared to the question of how far the supplier is a monopolist (although there has been a fair amount of scepticism about how well equipped the courts are to recognize inequality of bargaining power—see e.g. Nicol and Rawlings (1980) 43 MLR 567).

Paragraph (b) covers inducements to agree to the term. If you are charged a lower price in return for the exclusion, that is likely to make the clause reasonable—see *Green* v *Cade Brothers* (1978) where a limitation clause in relation to uncertified seed potatoes was upheld because the purchaser could have bought certified seed for a higher price. This paragraph also talks about the 'opportunity for entering a similar contract with other persons, but without having to accept a similar turn'; that is, was it effectively a 'take it or leave it' situation or did the customer have a choice?

Paragraph (c) refers to whether the customer ought to have known about the existence and extent of the term. This may sound like the common law incorporation test coming back in again and most clauses which are actually incorporated will probably be reasonable under this criterion, but it may bite where the incorporation test operates harshly, for example in cases of signed documents like *L'Estrange* v *Graucob*. We saw earlier that the incorporation test is principally or normally concerned with whether reasonable notice of the existence of the term has been given rather than with whether the customer ought to have been aware of its extent but paragraph (c) makes this latter consideration directly relevant to whether a clause is reasonable under the Act (see also the discussion of the views of Hobhouse LJ in the *AEG* case discussed earlier).

Paragraph (d) is fairly self-explanatory and refers to situations where liability is conditional on compliance with a condition; for example a clause whereby liabilities are excluded unless a complaint is made in writing within a short period such as seven days. Such a clause was held to be unreasonable in *Green* v *Cade Brothers* since a defect in seeds was not capable of being easily detected until much later.

Paragraph (e) reflects the fact that where the supplier is complying with a special order it may be perfectly reasonable to exclude all obligations save conformity with the specification. The purchaser can hardly complain that a product is not fit for its purpose if it complies with the specifications laid down by the purchaser.

Limitation clauses

Section 11(4) specifies two factors which are particularly relevant to limitation as opposed to exemption clauses:

(1) the resources available to the party excluding the liability—obviously, the smaller those resources, the more understandable is a limitation of liability; and

(2) the availability of insurance—again, the less the opportunity to insure against a liability, the more understandable is the attempt to limit the liability.

In *Singer* v *Tees & Hartlepool Port Authority* (1988) it was argued that the fact that the defendants had ample resources and were in a position to insure should be 'virtually decisive' in showing that a limitation clause was unreasonable. Steyn J disagreed. All relevant factors had to be looked at. The points mentioned in s.11(4) were outweighed by a number of others, including the fact that there was an option to contract at a higher price without the limitation clause.

CASE CLOSE-UP

***Regus* v *Epcot* (2008)**

Regus v *Epcot* shows the interaction of issues such as (common law) interpretation and the various factors affecting reasonableness under UCTA.

Regus, a very large company, provided office services to Epcot, a much smaller IT training company. Due to the negligence of Regus, the air conditioning was unsatisfactory.

Ultimately, Epcot started withholding fees and relocated to another provider. In response to Regus claiming the fees owing, Epcot counter-claimed for damages. Clause 23 of Regus's standard terms (which therefore had to be shown to be reasonable as a result of UCTA s.3) had four unnumbered sub-paragraphs to which numbers were allocated by the court for convenience. Clause 23(1) and (2) referred to Regus not being liable unless it acted deliberately or negligently (which was not a problem since it was found to be negligent). However, clause 23(3) stated:

> We will not in any circumstances have any liability for loss of business, loss of profits, loss of anticipated savings, loss of or damage to data, third party claims or any consequential loss. We strongly advise you to insure against all such potential loss, damage, expense or liability.

Clause 23(4) said:

> We will be liable:
>
> - without limit for personal injury or death;
> - up to a maximum of £1 million (for any one event or series of connected events) for damage to your personal property;
> - up to a maximum equal to 125 per cent of the total fees paid under your agreement up to the date on which the claim in question arises or £50,000 (whichever is the higher), in respect of all other losses, damages, expenses or claims.

The trial judge in effect interpreted clause 23(3) so broadly that it excluded all forms of financial loss so that the limitation in the final bullet point of clause 23(4) had no financial liability which it could restrict. (The first two bullet points of clause 23(4) were not relevant since they only dealt with physical loss or harm rather than financial loss.) Whilst at common law this interpretation of clause 23(3) would have been all to the good for Regus since it would totally exclude its liability, the draconian width of the exclusion, depriving Epcot of any real remedy for the inadequate air conditioning over a lengthy period, made the clause in its totality unreasonable (see the *Stewart Gill* case discussed earlier where the potential width of the clause made it unreasonable and it was not possible to sever or rewrite it so as to make it reasonable).

The Court of Appeal however took a different approach—clause 23(3) did not exclude all types of loss but essentially it excluded losses (mainly consequential ones) which were Epcot's 'own affair' and against which it could be expected to insure. However, it did not exclude the primary loss caused by the defective air conditioning—the diminution in value of the office accommodation being supplied—and it left liability for that untouched. Given this narrower construction, clause 23(3) could be shown to be reasonable for a number of reasons (made relevant by Sch.2 to the Act), including the fact that Epcot was aware of it and had used similar terms itself in contracts with its own customers and had not sought to have the clause removed from the contract even though it had been quick to argue about other terms. Furthermore, there was not inequality of bargaining power in that Epcot had felt able to threaten to move to other suppliers of office accommodation and had ultimately done so.

The limitation in clause 23(4) to £50,000 was also quite reasonable (the monthly rental having only been £1,500) and damages were to be assessed within that limit (Epcot had at one time claimed £620 million but it was now conceded that there was no basis for that figure!). Even if clause 23(3) had been unreasonable (as the trial judge had found) it was possible and appropriate in this case to sever it, leaving the perfectly reasonable limitation clause in clause 23(4) to operate, rather than leaving the recoverable damages at large with no limitation as the trial judge's decision had effectively done. This was so even though the sub-paragraphs were not separately numbered as set out in the contract—they could clearly be distinguished from one another and the third could, if necessary, be struck out without affecting the validity of the others which did not need to be rewritten—which is something a court will not do and can be regarded as a distinction between this case and the *Stewart Gill* case.

6.6 Unfair terms in consumer contracts

6.6.1 **Background**

The Unfair Contract Terms Act 1977 represented the domestic response to the well-recognized problem of the abuse of exemption clauses by those in a superior bargaining position and until the CRA 2015 provided protection where appropriate both for consumers and non-consumers. At a wider level, the European Community adopted a Directive on Unfair Terms in Consumer Contracts in 1993 which was first implemented in the UK by the 1994 Regulations which came into force in 1995 and which were subsequently replaced by the Unfair Terms in Consumer Contracts Regulations 1999. Both the Directive and the Regulations, which fairly literally reproduced it, were based on the somewhat wider legislative controls on unfair contract terms first introduced in Germany in 1977 (the *Allgemeinen Geschäfts Bedingungen*, if you are interested in these things)—notably in the very same year that our own Unfair Contract Terms Act was enacted and in response no doubt to the same pressures and concerns. Unlike our own somewhat misleadingly entitled Unfair Contract Terms Act, the Directive and the Regulations applied to a wide range of unfair contract terms and not just to exemption clauses (however widely defined). There was, however, clearly a large degree of overlap in relation to consumer contracts between UCTA and the UTCCR which is one reason why the CRA has now attempted to weld together the two mechanisms of statutory control in relation to contracts involving consumers. It has done this by amending UCTA so that its main provisions only apply to contracts between businesses and to provide in the CRA itself for a more comprehensive scheme purely for consumers, based largely on the UTCCR, but with improvements, and also incorporating the protections applicable to consumers previously to be found in UCTA.

6.6.2 **Case law under the UTCCR**

In order to understand the CRA provisions it is necessary to consider first the case law under the UTCCR which were in force for two decades starting in 1995. The UTCCR, as their name suggests, only ever applied to 'consumer contracts' and a consumer was defined in reg.3 as a natural person (contrast the peculiar position under UCTA following *R & B Customs Brokers* v *United Dominions Trust* (1988) whereby a company could in some circumstances be 'dealing as a consumer'). Furthermore, the Regulations only applied to terms which had not been 'individually negotiated' (reg.5(1)) which, whilst being a rather similar concept to 'written standard terms' in s.3 UCTA, performed a much broader function in the Regulations since it was a precondition for their operation rather than being one of the criteria for the operation of a particular section (this precondition no longer applies under the CRA). Where the Regulations did apply, they did not automatically invalidate any particular type of term and, rather than imposing a test of 'reasonableness', they asked whether the term was 'unfair'. A term was 'unfair' under reg.5 if 'contrary to the requirements of good faith, it causes a significant imbalance in the party's rights and obligations arising under the contract, to the detriment of the consumer' (this remains the test under s.62(4) CRA).

The concept of 'good faith' is an important and reasonably well-understood notion in German law and in some other Continental legal systems but there is no Europe-wide consensus about its meaning and it is a somewhat alien transplant into the common law. The House of Lords in *Director General of Fair Trading* v *First National Bank* (2002) nevertheless felt able to interpret and apply the meaning of unfairness to the facts of the application before them without seeking a ruling from the European Court of Justice and found that the particular term was not unfair. Further guidance was indeed given as to the assessment of unfairness in reg.6 which provided (as s.62(5) CRA 2015 now does in slightly different language) that it should be done 'taking into account the nature of the goods or services for which the contract was concluded and *by referring, at the time of conclusion of the contract, to all the circumstances attending the conclusion of the contract* and to all the other terms of the contract' (emphasis added). The emphasized words meant that the approach in this respect was not dissimilar to the assessment of reasonableness under s.11 UCTA under which, as we have seen, the emphasis is on whether it was fair and reasonable to include the term in the contract rather than whether the reliance placed upon it now is fair and reasonable. The parallels with UCTA continued in so far as further guidance as to the concept of unfairness was provided in Sch.2 to the Regulations. This Schedule provided an 'indicative and non-exhaustive list of terms which may be regarded as unfair', which in effect probably meant that terms of the type listed in this so-called grey list would be presumed to be unfair unless the person seeking to rely on them could show particular reasons why the term was a fair one to be included in this particular contract (see now the slightly expanded list in Sch.2 CRA).

A potentially significant limitation on the assessment of fairness was provided in reg.6(2), which provided that:

> it shall not relate—
>
> **(a)** to the definition of the main subject matter of the contract, or
>
> **(b)** to the adequacy of the price or remuneration, as against the goods or services supplied in exchange.

This was generally known as the exclusion of 'core terms' from the controls imposed by the Regulations which were not designed to, or apt to, interfere with the essential judgement and decision of the consumer to enter into a particular bargain at a particular price (as opposed to regulating the detailed terms, incidental to that essential bargain, which details may have been unfairly included in it and which may unfairly undermine it). This 'core terms' exclusion was interpreted narrowly in the *First National Bank* case by the House of Lords, which was generally regarded as a good thing in that it means a wider range of terms would remain susceptible to control under the Regulations, as is illustrated in *Bairstow Eves* v *Smith* (2004).

CASE CLOSE-UP

***Bairstow Eves* v *Smith* (2004)**

A term providing for a payment of commission to an estate agent at an 'early payment discounted commission rate of 1.5 per cent' was regarded as the core term. Thus a term providing for payment at a rate of 3 per cent, if payment was not made within ten days of completion, even though described as the 'standard commission rate', was not part of the core terms and was thus subject to review and held to be unfair. The bargain between the parties was essentially one whereby both parties expected that the consumer would normally in practice pay 1.5 per cent (and the Regulations did not purport to interfere with this 'core term' or essential bargain or to evaluate the adequacy of this price) but the provision for doubling this commission rate in certain eventualities was not a core term, was therefore not excluded under reg.6(2) and was therefore subject to review and found to be unfair. In fairness to estate agents, who often get a bad press, the dispute in this case was actually precipitated by the consumer's solicitors, who lamentably failed to pass on to the estate agent within the ten-day period the full 1.5 per cent commission which they had already received from the consumer.

Another important point to note about the Regulations is that they, unlike UCTA, did not depend for their enforcement on the accidents of litigation between contracting parties. Regulations 10–15 provided for the Office of Fair Trading (OFT) (whose functions in this respect were in April 2014 taken over by the Competition and Markets Authority (CMA)) and other qualifying bodies to consider complaints about unfair terms and to apply for injunctions prohibiting the use or recommendation of unfair terms (the *First National Bank* case discussed earlier was an example of such an application which eventually went to the House of Lords). The relatively low number of cases in the courts initially was due to the fact that most cases under the 1994 Regulations were dealt with by the OFT by negotiation, with applications for injunctions being seen as a last resort. The widening of the enforcement provisions and the inclusion of the licensed bodies in the 1999 Regulations brought with it an increase in the number of cases coming to court (see Bright, 2000).

The Regulations were at the heart of a major stream of litigation, in which billions of pounds in bank charges were potentially at stake, involving the major banks and the OFT and which culminated in the Supreme Court's decision in *Office of Fair Trading* v *Abbey National plc and others* (2009). The Supreme Court reversed the decision of the Court of Appeal which had held that the OFT was entitled to assess the fairness of certain current account bank charges (typically around £30) under the Regulations. The case arose as a result of the UK's 'free in credit' banking system whereby customers could operate a current account for free if they remained in credit but incurred significant charges for services if they became overdrawn without prior authorization. The key issue on appeal was whether such charges constituted 'the price or remuneration, as against the services supplied in exchange' within the meaning of reg.6(2)(b) (based closely on Article 4(2) of European Council Directive 93/13/EEC). If the bank charges could be considered to be part of the 'price or remuneration', then the OFT was prohibited by reg.6(2)(b) from reviewing the terms imposing the charges for unfairness on the basis of price against quality. The Supreme Court held that the charges were excluded from review as being part of the 'price or remuneration' and that the Court of Appeal had departed from the natural meaning of the text in formulating a test that the exclusion in reg.6(2)(b) applied only to 'the core bargain or the core price but not ancillary or incidental provisions.' Even if such a test was correct, it erred in deciding that the bank charges were not part of the core bargain. The Supreme Court gave reg.6(2)(b) a much wider meaning and held that the bank charges fell within reg.6(2)(b) because they were part of a package of considerations paid by customers to the banks in return for the package of services that made up the provision of a current account. To put the decision into context, ask yourself if you get hit with a bank charge whether you feel that the charge is: (a) part of the price you pay for having an account with that bank; or (b) a penalty for going overdrawn, unconnected to the normal operation of the account. The truth of the matter is that most people will identify with (b) and consider that it is straining the words of the regulation to breaking point to suggest that the charges are paid in return for the complete package of services involved in supplying a current account. This judicial creativity might perhaps (if one were of a sceptical disposition) be attributed to the desperate state of the UK banking sector in 2008 and 2009 and the perceived need to ensure that the OFT was not given the opportunity to deprive the banks—some of them government owned—and building societies of a very substantial source of income.

The Supreme Court did not overrule the House of Lords' decision in *First National Bank*, although it is difficult to explain why the interest payments due from customers in default to First National Bank were not part of the package of considerations paid for the services supplied but the bank charges for going overdrawn paid to Abbey National and others were part of such a package.

Subsequent to the *Abbey National* case, the OFT took rather more successful action in respect of the terms typically found in gym membership contracts, such as those relating to minimum periods of membership and restricting the right to terminate, in *OFT* v *Ashbourne Management Services* (2011). However, the decision revealed once more the complexities involved in interpreting the Regulations which were agreed to be in need of clarification.

6.6.3 **The path to the reforms in the CRA 2015**

The Law Commission published a report on unfair terms in contracts (Law Com No.292) in February 2005 and noted at para. 1.4 that the existence of UCTA alongside the UTCCR means 'that the nature and scope of the combined protection afforded to consumers by these laws are wholly obscure to the inexpert reader.'

The Law Commission regarded it as 'its first task is to consider how to replace these two pieces of legislation with a single unified Act that will set out the law on unfair contract terms in a clear and accessible way.' To this end, it produced a draft new Unfair Contract Terms Bill, the main provisions and purpose of which were helpfully summarized as follows (see Appendix A to the report):

> For consumer contracts, the purpose of the Draft Bill is 'to create a unified regime reproducing the combined effect of UCTA and the UTCCR' with only minor changes of substance, while implementing the Directive in full. The substantive changes that do occur are, primarily, that (1) (as with those terms of consumer contracts that fall within UCTA) any unfair term will be invalid whether or not it was 'individually negotiated,' unless it is a 'core' term such as the

main definition of the subject matter; and (2) (again as under UCTA) the burden of proving that a term is fair will be on the business.

For business contracts in general, the purpose of the Draft Bill is to retain the effect of UCTA, which regulates various kinds of contract term excluding or restricting liability, but in a form that is consistent with the unified regime for consumer contracts. It disposes of some provisions that are unnecessary.

The proposals were generally welcomed as a sensible rationalization and simplification of the current position with the removal of some anomalies but the retention of the key mechanisms which have been successful to date in dealing with unfair exemption clauses generally and with other unfair terms in consumer contracts. However, no action was taken for a number of years pending the finalization of a new European Directive, which came in the form of the Consumer Rights Directive 2011 which created the need for a wide-ranging overhaul of consumer law, not simply in relation to exemption clauses. The Law Commission then published an Issues Paper, *Unfair Terms in Consumer Contracts: a new approach?* in July 2012, reviewing its earlier proposals in the light of the government's proposed Consumer Bill of Rights (as it was then known) and in the light of the *Abbey National* litigation. Its Advice Paper of March 2013 recommended that the exemption for main subject matter and price set out in reg.6(2) UTCCR should be reformed. In particular it should be made clear that it should apply only to terms which are transparent and prominent. To be 'transparent' a term would have to be in plain, intelligible language, readily available to the consumer and, if in writing, legible. To be 'prominent' a term would have to be presented in such a way that the average consumer would be aware of the term. The more unusual or onerous the term, the more prominent it would have to be. Other recommendations included that terms in consumer contracts should be liable to be assessed as to their fairness whether or not they had been individually negotiated.

The CRA by and large follows the Law Commission's advice. The 2015 Act replaces the UTCCR with provisions which continue to reflect the 1993 Directive with the improvements, clarifications and additions discussed by the Law Commission so as to produce a complete code for the regulation of unfair terms and notices in consumer contracts. 'Consumer' is now given a clearer definition in s.2(3) whereby he or she is an *individual* acting for purposes that are 'wholly or mainly outside that individual's trade, business, craft or profession.' As has already been seen, consumer contracts are taken out of UCTA (which is amended by Sch.4 CRA) but some of the key provisions in UCTA, in so far as they affect consumers, are included in Pt.2 of the CRA. Thus s.65 provides that a 'trader cannot by a term of a consumer contract or by a consumer notice exclude or restrict liability for death or personal injury resulting from negligence,' thereby replicating the protection found in s.2(1) UCTA (which continues to be the applicable provision in business to business contracts). Other aspects of the protection of consumers formerly found in UCTA are reflected in Pt.1 of the CRA, in particular in the sections which make it impossible to contract out of the implied terms now provided for in the same part of the Act in relation to consumer contracts for the supply of goods. Thus s.31, headed 'Liability that cannot be excluded or restricted,' lists the implied terms such as satisfactory quality and so on which cannot be excluded, effectively replacing s.6(2) UCTA in so far as it applied to consumer contracts and rendered such clauses ineffective (as opposed to subjecting them to a test of reasonableness as s.6(3) did (now s.6(1A) for business-to-business contracts)).

6.7 Control of exemption clauses and unfair terms in the Consumer Rights Act 2015

6.7.1 **Introduction**

As with the UTCCR, the CRA controls not only exemption clauses but a wide variety of other unfair terms and it now also applies to consumer notices. Our focus in this chapter is however on unfair exemption and limitation clauses. The CRA is also a very broad provision establishing in Pt.1 of the Act a comprehensive scheme for the implied terms and remedies applicable to contracts 'between a trader and a consumer for the trader to supply goods, digital content or services' (s.1(1)). Again, it is not the purpose here to describe in detail or analyse these provisions which effectively replace for consumer contracts a wide range of statutes including the Sale of Goods Act 1979 and the Supply of Goods and Services Act 1982. Rather it is to explain the nature of the controls introduced by the Act over clauses which seek to exclude or restrict the new range of rights and remedies in Pt.1 as well as the controls to be found in Pt.2 which apply to a wider range of unfair terms.

6.7.2 **The scope and organization of the CRA 2015**

Ambit of Part 1

Part 1 is divided into five chapters and Chapters 2, 3 and 4 set out the rights and remedies applicable to three types of contracts to supply—that is, contracts to supply goods, digital content and services respectively. In each of these three chapters there is a section dealing with (and by and large preventing completely) the exclusion and limitation of liability under those chapters, these sections beings ss.31, 47 and 57 respectively. These sections, which might usefully be called specific supply contract controls, have their roots in what was formerly s.6(1) and (2) of UCTA which prevented the exclusion of liability under, inter alia, the implied terms in the Sale of Goods Act 1979 (and also in relation to hire purchase). This approach is now also applied to the implied terms under the whole range of supply contracts (including not only goods but also digital content and services) in Pt.1 of the CRA. We will look at these controls in a moment but it is first important to explain the nature of the other controls on exemption clauses more broadly, which are to be found in Pt.2 of the CRA.

Ambit of Part 2

Part 2 deals with unfair terms generally, not just exemption clauses and applies as a result of s.61 to 'consumer contracts,' which means any contract 'between a trader and a consumer' (except employment or apprentice contracts) rather than just to the supply contracts covered in Pt.1. It also applies to 'consumer notices,' that is, notices which relate to 'rights or obligations as between a trader and a consumer,' or which purport 'to exclude or restrict a trader's liability to a consumer.' Part 2 is the part of the Act which directly replaces the UTCCR, but with amendments and improvements which we will come to, and it also provides, in s.65(1), an almost direct copy of s.2(1) UCTA, to apply to consumer contracts, under which it remains impossible 'to exclude or restrict liability for death or personal injury resulting from negligence.'

Part 1 further details

Returning to Pt.1 and the control of exemption from the implied terms in the various contracts of supply, s.31 is the provision relating to supply of goods and is the direct, though somewhat wider, replacement for s.6(1) and (2) of UCTA. It prevents the exclusion or restriction of a long list of liabilities by means of s.31(1) which provides:

> A term of a contract to supply goods is not binding on the consumer to the extent that it would exclude or restrict the trader's liability arising under any of these provisions—

The relevant provisions are ss.9–17 (quality, fitness for purpose, description, information, sample, right to supply, etc.) and ss.28–29 (delivery and risk).

Section 31(2) and (3) echo very closely s.13 UCTA in including within the prohibition the exclusion or restriction of a right or remedy, or making its enforcement subject to a restrictive or onerous condition and so on, and subs. (3) in particular prohibits a term from preventing an obligation or duty arising in the first place (see the discussion at section 6.5.3).

Section 47 is of very similar effect as regards the rather shorter list of implied terms (five) relating to quality and so on in contracts to supply digital content. Section 57 performs the same role in relation to contracts for services but draws a distinction between exclusion and limitation. Section 57(1) prevents a clause from *excluding* the liability implied under s.49 that the service be 'performed with reasonable care and skill' and s.57(2) denies effect to clauses seeking to *exclude* the liability under s.50 whereby information provided about the service or trader is binding. Section 57(3) is rather complex but essentially provides that a clause *limiting* the above two liabilities under ss.49 and 50 or under ss.51 and 52, concerning completion for a reasonable price or in a reasonable time, cannot prevent the consumer from recovering, in an appropriate case, the price paid or the value of any other consideration provided. Even if a clause does not limit the liability below this figure, it may still be assessed under Pt.2 of the Act as to whether it is an unfair term. So in this context, limitation clauses as opposed to exclusion clauses are not robbed of all effect but cannot go lower than the contract price and, in any event, are subject to the Pt.2 test of fairness.

Part 2 further details

As has been noted already, Pt.2 is to a large extent simply a modified replacement for the UTCCR plus it also replicates (in s.65(1)) the UCTA ban on excluding liability for death or personal injury resulting from negligence. In relation to the UTCCR, the main differences are (i) that there is no longer any mention or requirement of a term not to have been individually negotiated before it is subject to the test of unfairness (this was considered in the light of experience to be an unnecessary hurdle potentially complicating matters for consumers for little real benefit); and (ii) that the exclusion of core terms (main subject matter and price) from the assessment is now only applicable if the term is 'transparent and prominent' (see s.64(2)).

Transparent means that it 'is expressed in plain and intelligible language and (in the case of a written term) is legible' (s.64(3)).

Prominent means 'is brought to the consumer's attention in such a way that an average consumer would be aware of the term' (s.64(4))—and an average consumer is 'a consumer who is reasonably well-informed, observant and circumspect' (the typical student, I hear you say!).

In addition to the specific requirements of transparency and prominence, the actual definition of a 'core term' has been changed in an attempt to clarify some of the ambiguities which were discussed in the *Abbey National* litigation, so that it now reads as follows:

A term of a consumer contract may not be assessed for fairness under section 62 to the extent that—

(a) it specifies the main subject matter of the contract, or

(b) the assessment is of the appropriateness of the price payable under the contract by comparison with the goods, digital content or services supplied under it.

The new test is designed to make it clear that the specification of the subject matter should not be open to review in any respect but that in respect of price, whilst the *amount* agreed should not be open to review, other aspects of a term relating to price, such as at what point it should become due, can still be assessed for fairness.

The meaning of unfairness

Part 2 is in other respects very similar to the UTCCR which it replaces. The relevant time to consider fairness is still by reference to when the term was agreed (s.62(5)); the rest of the contract continues to be applicable, 'so far as practicable' apart from the unfair term (s.67), and the *contra proferentem* rule of interpretation is in effect applied (s.69(1)). The basic test of unfairness, derived from the Directive, is unchanged (and is now to be found in s.62(4))—that is, a term 'is unfair if, *contrary to the requirement of good faith, it causes a significant imbalance in the parties' rights and obligations under the contract to the detriment of the consumer*.'

The precise meaning of the italicized test of unfairness set out previously has been the subject of considerable debate and speculation. The 'requirement of good faith' is very much a concept of Continental civil law rather than common law although there has been much debate about how it might be, or whether it ought to be, incorporated into the common law, for example through the mechanism of implying a term into the contract to perform in good faith—see *Yam Seng* v *ITC* (2013) (which concerned a distribution agreement for 'Manchester United' fragrances and toiletries, so good taste and good faith, you may think, are clearly different concepts). See Chapter 5, section 5.3.4 for the later developments in relation to the implied term to perform in good faith. Good faith however is clearly and expressly imported into the statutory test of unfairness in consumer contracts; but not only is there the problem of knowing just what 'good faith' means in the common law context, there is the question of what is meant by a 'significant imbalance.'

There has been speculation that significant imbalance possibly refers to 'substantive unfairness' (actually getting a bad deal) whereas good faith might refer to 'procedural unfairness' (e.g. being misled or treated unfairly in entering the deal) or that both these comments are relevant to each part of the definition of the test of unfairness. The meaning of unfairness now has to be looked at in the light of the Supreme Court decision in *ParkingEye* v *Beavis* (2015) and the leading ECJ case of *Aziz* v *Caixa d'Estalvis* (2013) which was extensively referred to by the Supreme Court. Mr Beavis overstayed by just under an hour on a retail car park operated by ParkingEye which had clear notices allowing two hours' free parking but imposing a charge of £85 for anyone who overstayed. The case turned partly on whether the charge was unenforceable as a penalty (see Chapter 11, section 11.8) and it was decided that under the proper test for a penalty it was not (because ParkingEye had a legitimate interest in making the charge in order to make the scheme of two hours' free parking effective and the charge for those overstaying was not unconscionable or extravagant). However, the separate point arose under the UTCCR 1999 (the facts arose before the Regulations were replaced by the CRA 2015) as to whether the term of the contract providing for the charge was unfair (the corresponding provisions of the CRA 2015 are identical as far as is relevant to this case). The majority, having found that the charge was not a penalty at common law, also concluded that it was not unfair under the Regulations. Lord Toulson dissented on this point and thought that it was unfair, notwithstanding that he too sought to underpin his reasoning by reference to the *Aziz* case in the ECJ.

Lord Neuberger's (majority) judgment quoted extensively from *Aziz* which he regarded as being authority for a number of propositions including that:

- a '*significant imbalance in the parties' rights*' depends mainly on 'whether the consumer is being deprived of an advantage which he would enjoy under national law in the absence of the contractual provision';
- '*contrary to the requirements of good faith*' will depend on 'whether the seller or supplier, dealing fairly and equitably with the consumer, could reasonably assume that the consumer would have agreed to such a term in individual contract negotiations';
- 'The national court is required by Art 4 of the Directive (reg.6(1) of the 1999 Regulations) to take account of, among other things, the nature of the goods or services supplied under the contract' [see now CRA s.62(5)(a) which refers to 'the nature of the subject matter of the contract']. 'This includes the significance, purpose and practical effect of the term in question, and whether it is "appropriate for securing the attainment of the objectives pursued by it in the member state concerned and does not go beyond what is necessary to achieve them".'

The first bullet point seems to mean that significant imbalance is largely a matter of substantive unfairness, the second point suggests that 'contrary to good faith' is more a question of procedural unfairness (would a consumer, treated fairly, have entered into this agreement?) and the third bullet point appears to be concerned with matters of justification and legitimate interest.

The majority took the view that the parking scheme was overall not unfair, essentially because even though the charge was more than the compensation that the law would normally or otherwise impose for marginally overstaying a licence to park for two hours (thus some imbalance), the terms were clearly notified and motorists were clearly aware of them and freely agreed to them by parking in the car park (thus procedurally fair and in accordance with good faith). Moreover, the level of the charge did not go beyond what was necessary for the attainment of the objectives of providing a workable car parking scheme, including free parking for the majority and a reasonable rotation of users to free up spaces for other shoppers (justification and legitimate interest).

Lord Toulson dissented because he considered that it was not reasonable to assume that a consumer advised by a competent lawyer would have agreed to the charge and he considered that the majority had 'substituted their judgment of reasonableness of the clause for the question whether the supplier could reasonably have assumed that the customer would have agreed with the term.' He also considered that the approach of the majority 'waters down the test' adopted by the ECJ. Just as with the test of reasonableness under UCTA, it would seem that the test of unfairness, under what is now the CRA 2015, even when unpacked by reference to the ECJ case of *Aziz*, is a question of judgement in its application to specific facts about which reasonable judges may disagree. Indeed the very first point which Lord Neuberger quoted from the *Aziz* case was that 'the test of "significant imbalance" and "good faith" . . . merely defines in a general way the factors that render unfair a contractual term' as to which he commented himself that 'a significant element of judgment is left to the national court, to exercise in the light of the circumstances of each case.' As with UCTA, appellate courts will not be quick to interfere with the assessment of the trial judge if the right criteria have been taken into account and this too is reflected in the decision of the majority which upheld the original decision of the judge that the term was not unfair.

The grey list

Schedule 2, Pt.1, providing the 'grey list' of terms regarded as prima facie unfair, is very similar to Sch.2 UTCCR but with the addition of three new terms as recommended by the Law Commission (one of which, for example, is 'giving the trader discretion to decide the amount of the price after the consumer has become bound by the contract'). There are now a total of twenty terms listed in Pt.1 of Sch.2 as terms which may be regarded as unfair, not all of which are exemption clauses. By way of example of one that clearly is, the first term listed remains a term which tries to exclude liability for death or personal injury (not necessarily due to negligence, which is outlawed anyway under s.65) but due to any form of breach of duty (e.g. strict rather than for negligence), which exemption will still not be binding unless found to have been fair by reference to the circumstances at the time that the term was agreed. Another example is term number 13 in the Schedule, which is an instance of an exemption clause which operates by restrictively defining the obligation, in that it would (if not controlled) enable the trader 'to alter unilaterally without a valid reason any characteristics of the goods etc. . . . to be provided.'

This sort of term is interesting for another reason. It might be thought to be one that could be said to 'specify the main subject matter' and thus to be exempt from control under s.64(1)(a) (provided it is prominent and transparent). Under the UTCCR, it was not clear whether a term listed in Sch.2 could be assessed for fairness even where it might come within the definition of core terms exempt from such assessment. The Law Commission recommended that it be made clear that Sch.2 terms could always be assessed for fairness, that is, that Sch.2 takes precedence, and s.64(6) puts this into effect.

An interesting aspect of *ParkingEye* is that the term was regarded as potentially being within the grey list, being a term 'which has the object or effect of requiring a consumer who fails to fulfil his obligations under the contract to pay a disproportionately high sum in compensation' (CRA 2015, Sch.2 Pt.1 No.6, previously Sch.2 para.1e of the Regulations). Ultimately however the sum payable was not regarded as disproportionately high so it was not unfair. The odd thing is that once evaluated as not disproportionate and therefore not unfair, it ceases to be a term within the Sch.2 grey list. In other words, one only knows whether it falls within the grey list once one has evaluated whether it is disproportionate.

However, this does not seem to matter much because even if a term is *not* to be found in Pt.1 of Sch.2, it may still be assessed for unfairness (provided of course not excluded by s.64), but in this case it may be less easy to persuade a court that a term is unfair than it would be in the case of the grey list terms.

Under s.71, where there are 'proceedings before a court which relate to a term of a consumer contract' (e.g. where a trader is seeking to enforce or rely on a term such as an exclusion clause against a consumer), the court 'must consider whether the term is fair even if none of the parties to the proceedings has raised that issue or indicated that it intends to raise it.' This is a new provision which is potentially important given that very often consumers will not be legally represented in these situations. The Act still does not expressly say anything about burden of proof in relation to the question of fairness (unlike s.11(5) UCTA) as the Law Commission thought this was unnecessary and inappropriate. Enforcement of Pt.2 of the CRA by the CMA and certain other regulators continues to be provided for in Sch.3, which provides for consideration of complaints about prohibited or unfair terms (and notices) and for the obtaining of injunctions in relation to such terms (and notices).

The overall structure of the controls over unfair (exemption) clauses in the CRA is illustrated in Figure 6.8.

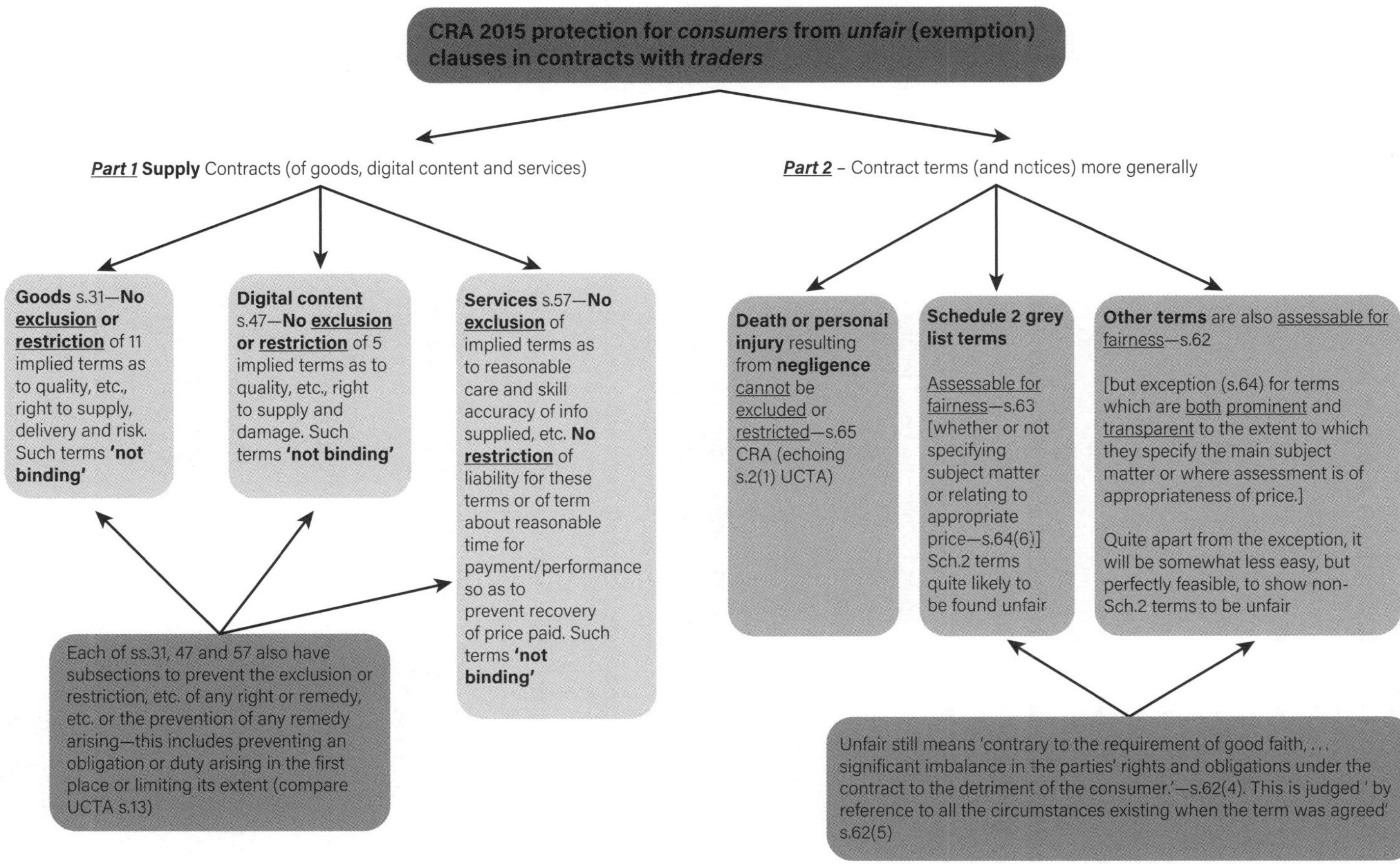

Figure 6.8 Overview of CRA 2015 controls

6.7.3 The logical approach as to the impact of statutory controls on an exemption clause following the CRA 2015

Whether the reforms to the control of unfair terms and exclusion clauses contained in the various parts of the CRA will actually simplify the understanding and operation of the law still remains to be seen. The following is offered as a logical route through the thicket of provisions and attempts to provide intelligible guidance in terms of the key questions one has to ask.

The first question is whether the party adversely affected by a clause is a consumer within the definition in s.2(3) CRA (an individual acting for purposes that are wholly or mainly outside that individual's trade, business, craft or profession). Note that, by s.2(4), a 'trader claiming that an individual was not acting for purposes wholly or mainly outside the individual's trade, business, craft or profession must prove it' so the burden is not on an individual to prove he is a consumer but it is for the trader to prove he is not.

The party adversely affected is *not* a consumer

If *not* a consumer, then there is no need to consider the CRA further, so go to UCTA (as amended). Under UCTA now, the next thing to ask is whether the clause is one excluding business liability (s.1(3) UCTA).

If so consider the following questions:

(a) Does it purport to exclude or restrict liability for negligence, in which case it is ineffective in so far as it relates to death or personal injury (s.2(1)) or alternatively, it is subjected by s.2(2) to the reasonableness test (in s.11) if it relates to other loss or damage?

(b) Does it relate to contractual liability where the party affected by it is dealing on the other's written standard terms (s.3), in which case it is subject to the reasonableness test?

(c) Does it relate to the implied undertaking as to title in a sale of goods or hire purchase contract (s.6(1) UCTA), in which case it is ineffective?

(d) Does it relate to the implied undertakings as to quality, fitness or conformity, and so on, in sale of goods or hire purchase contracts, in which case it is subject to the reasonableness test?

If it does not come within any of these four alternatives it is not one controlled by the Act and the only question is whether it is effective under the common law tests of incorporation and interpretation.

The party adversely affected *is* a consumer

If the party adversely affected is a consumer then consider whether the other party (relying on the clause) is a trader, that is, '*a person acting for purposes relating to that person's trade, business, craft or profession*, whether acting personally or through another person acting in the trader's name or on the trader's behalf' (s.2(2) CRA) (emphasis added).

If the person relying on the clause *is* a trader, consider whether the contract is one to supply goods, digital content or services (or a combination of these) within Pt.1 CRA. If so, consider whether the clause is ineffective under ss.31, 47 or 57 (in the latter case also whether it restricts liability to less than the contract price—see s.57(3)).

If the clause does not relate to one of the above contracts of supply (or if it does but is not invalidated by ss.31, 47 or 57), consider whether the clause is unfair or otherwise invalidated under Pt.2 of the CRA.

Does it purport to exclude liability for death or personal injury as a result of negligence? If so, it is ineffective under s.65(1).

Is it one of the terms mentioned in the first part of Sch.2 (the grey list)? If so, one would normally expect a court to find it to be unfair in the absence of any strong evidence justifying it as being fair. (Lord Toulson's dissent in *ParkingEye* was partly based on his view that ParkingEye had not provided any evidence supporting their claim that the consumer would have agreed to the term or that a parking scheme was only workable with a deterrent charge to overstayers. But then again, the term was only within the grey list if it was disproportionate.)

If it is not one of the clauses listed in Sch.2, it may still be assessed for unfairness but more evidence or argument will normally have to be produced to result in a finding of unfairness.

Furthermore, in the case of terms not listed in Sch.2, one also has to ask whether it is excluded from assessment under either of the limbs of s.64(1), that is, does the clause specify the main subject matter or would the assessment of its fairness concern the appropriateness of the price under the contract? (Note the precise wording of s.64(1) and see also *Office of Fair Trading* v *Abbey National* (2009) concerning this provision's slightly differently worded predecessor.) If it does fall under this prima facie exclusion for 'core terms', is it also transparent and prominent under s.64(3)–(5) as it is now also required to be? If it is both transparent and prominent, it cannot be assessed for fairness and will be valid but if it is not transparent *or* not prominent, it is now still subject to assessment for fairness under s.62 even though it is concerned with the core bargain. So to return to the *Abbey National* case, if bank charges today are not made prominent and transparent then they would be susceptible to assessment for fairness even if they could still be said to be part of the core terms.

The scheme or pathway described here covers only the main contours and there are further nuances and points of detail to be found in the actual provisions themselves in the CRA and UCTA (as amended).

Digging deeper

The CRA controls on unfair terms, you will have noticed, take us well beyond simply the control of exemption clauses and into the control of unfair terms more generally in consumer contracts. The leading cases of *Abbey National* and *ParkingEye* are themselves not cases about exclusion clauses (however widely defined) but about terms providing for payments where someone does not observe the main terms of the contract and is subject to what are alleged to be excessive charges—whether for going overdrawn on a bank account or for overstaying in a car park. The consumer lost on both occasions, for different reasons, but that should not blind us to the full potential of the controls available, including the enforcement powers passed on from the OFT to the CMA and also to other regulators such as Trading Standards, the FCA, Ofwat, Ofcom and others. The CMA provided quite detailed guidance on the unfair terms provisions of the CRA in *Unfair Contract Terms Guidance* CMA 37, 31 July 2015, and there are many other documents of interest being produced all the time on the CMA website. Even in terms of the privately litigated disputes in cases such as *ParkingEye* v *Beavis* it should not be assumed that car park operators will always now succeed in enforcing provisions for payment of significant sums as payment for overstayers. Much will depend on the scale of the charges (over £100 will be very difficult to justify), the clarity and reasonableness (or otherwise) of the signs visible to motorists and all the other circumstances. There was an interesting case decided in Wrexham County Court on 5 December 2014, *ParkingEye* v *Cargius*, which distinguished *Beavis* (before the latter had reached the Supreme Court, but that is not an issue given that the Supreme Court endorsed the approach of the trial judge by and large). The distinction from *Beavis* was on the basis that in *Cargius*, the car park was not free at any stage (and indeed the charges per hour, if paid, went down the longer one stayed). Thus the argument which was influential in *Beavis*, that without the high charge for overstayers, the operators could not generate a reasonable return to cover their costs and so on, did not apply. As a county court case, *Cargius* has very little weight as a precedent but it does show that the outcome in *Beavis* is by no means inevitable where the facts are clearly distinguishable and the justifications accepted by the majority in that case do not apply. That the decision of the majority of the Supreme Court in *Beavis* is by no means the last word, or the best way of adjudicating, on the complex problem of car parking charges is demonstrated by the enactment of the Parking (Code of Practice) Act 2019 which provides for the creation by the Secretary of State of a code of practice for the operation and management of private parking facilities including in relation to appeals against parking charges. A draft code was eventually published by the government in February 2022 which included limits on charges but the Code was legally challenged by the parking operators and was withdrawn in June 2022 pending further consultation, which ultimately took place from 11 August 2025 to 25 September 2025. One is tempted to say watch this space (but don't park in it or hold your breath!).

Summary

1. Exemption clauses

Exemption clauses are used to allocate risks between the parties to a contract. The courts can control the abuse of exemption clauses by means of the devices of incorporation and interpretation (or construction) of the terms of the contract but they cannot, at common law, declare exemption clauses invalid.

Parliament has given them that power by means of the statutory controls to be found in UCTA and now in the CRA.

2. Incorporation

Exemption clauses, like all other terms of a contract, can be incorporated by signature, reasonable notice, course of dealing or trade custom.

A greater degree of notice must be given in order to incorporate unusual or onerous terms.

3. Interpretation

Any ambiguity will be construed against a party attempting to rely on an exemption clause (the *contra proferentem* rule) and there are special rules of construction applicable when a party attempts to exclude liability for negligence or fraud. These rules are increasingly being applied less strictly to terms in commercial contracts between equal parties.

There is no rule of law that a party cannot exclude liability for a fundamental breach of a contract, although the courts will strictly construe any attempt to do so.

Limitation clauses place a maximum limit on damages and tend to be construed less strictly by the courts, although the reasons for doing this have been questioned where the limitation is severe.

4. Statutory control

(a) UCTA

UCTA controls the exclusion of 'business liability' but only against *other businesses* (where appropriate) and no longer against consumers, whose protection is exclusively now dealt with in the CRA. There are complex provisions in UCTA to discourage evasion by dressing up an exemption of liability as a denial of duty or obligation in the first place.

The most objectionable exemption clauses, for example exclusions of liability for negligently caused death or personal injury, are rendered ineffective. Other less objectionable terms where scrutiny may nevertheless be required, such as exclusions of other losses caused by negligence and exclusion clauses in written standard terms, are subjected by UCTA to a reasonableness test as are exclusions of the implied terms as to quality and so on in the Sale of Goods Act.

The test of reasonableness is applied by examining whether the clause was reasonable to include in the contract, not whether it is reasonable to rely on it now. The burden of proof is on the person seeking to rely on the clause and Sch.2 UCTA provides further guidance on reasonableness as does case law to some extent.

(b) CRA 2015

The CRA includes a comprehensive code for the control of unfair exclusion clauses and other unfair terms in *consumer* contracts. It replaces the controls formerly found in UCTA protecting persons 'dealing as a consumer' as well as the controls on unfair terms in the UTCCR and seeks to combine the best effects of both these formerly overlapping sources of protection for the consumer. Part 1 is concerned with the terms now implied under the Act in relation to contracts to supply goods, digital content and services and, in a manner analogous to the old s.6(2) UCTA, renders most attempts to exclude any such terms ineffective although in relation to services, some liabilities can be restricted to the contract price but not less. Part 2 of the CRA is very similar, and indeed identical in some respects, to the UTCCR, although there are some significant modifications and improvements and Pt.2 also includes, in relation to consumers, the prohibition on the exclusion of liability for death and personal injury which is still to be found (for businesses) in s.2(1) UCTA.

The actual test of unfairness ('contrary to the requirements of good faith' etc.) has not changed and is still also judged by reference to when the term was included in the contract and further guidance is provided in a slightly expanded Sch.2 of terms which may be regarded as unfair. Subject to the rule about Sch.2 terms, which can always be assessed, the assessment of unfairness does not extend to a term in so far as it specifies the subject matter of the contract nor does it extend to the assessment of the appropriateness of the price, but this exclusion now only applies if the term is both 'prominent' and 'transparent' as defined in s.64 of the Act.

The Regulations do not depend purely on litigation between contracting parties but are also enforced by the CMA who took over such functions from the OFT in April 2014 (independently of, and before, the CRA changes) and there are also still a number of other qualifying bodies and regulators who may be involved in enforcement.

? Questions

1. Bob regularly hires a rubbish skip from Tidy Skips. On each of the last five occasions, the invoice, received afterwards, has had the following printed on the reverse: 'Tidy Skips shall not be liable for any loss or damage howsoever caused to the customer's premises and if, notwithstanding the foregoing, any liability for damage to customer's property should arise, that liability shall be limited to a total of £100.'

   Bob telephones Tidy Skips and orders a skip to be delivered on the following day. Syd, an employee of Tidy Skips, negligently drives the delivery vehicle into Bob's wall, causing it to collapse onto Bob's new vehicle. The wall costs £500 to rebuild and the repairs to the car cost £800.

   Advise Bob, (a) where he is a joiner hiring skips for his commercial premises, (b) where he is a DIY enthusiast hiring skips at his domestic premises.
2. Does the control of exemption clauses offend against the ideal of freedom of contract? When have the courts deferred to the parties' freedom?
3. Does UCTA only apply to clauses which exclude or limit liability?
4. What is the difference between the test of reasonableness under UCTA and the test of unfairness under the CRA? Is a distinction justified?
5. Why do consumers deserve special protection from exemption clauses? Are there any other groups or bodies who deserve special protection?

Further reading

Books

Chen-Wishart, M, *Contract Law*, 7th edn (Oxford University Press, 2022) ch 10.5 and ch 11.

McKendrick, E, *Contract Law: Text, Cases and Materials*, 11th edn (Oxford University Press, 2024) chs 9, 13 and 14.

O'Sullivan, J, and Hilliard, J, *The Law of Contract*, 11th edn (Oxford University Press, 2024) ch 8.

Articles

Adams, J, and Brownsword, R, 'The Unfair Contract Terms Act: A decade of discretion' (1988) 104 LQR 94.

Bright, S, 'Winning the battle against unfair contract terms' (2000) 20 LS 331.

Clarke, M, 'Notice of contractual terms' (1976) 35 CLJ 51.

Collins, H, 'Good faith in European contract law' (1994) 14 OJLS 229.

MacDonald, E, 'Unifying unfair terms legislation' (2004) 67 MLR 69.

Nicol, A, and Rawlings, R, 'Note on *Photo Production* v *Securicor*' (1980) 43 MLR 567.

Spencer, JR, 'Signature, consent and the rule in *L'Estrange* v *Graucob*' (1973) 32 CLJ 104.

7 Misrepresentation

LEARNING OBJECTIVES

This chapter will help you to:

- appreciate when a misrepresentation makes the contract voidable so that the parties can rescind and when the parties may recover damages for misrepresentation;
- understand the essentials of a misrepresentation as a false statement of fact by one party to the other which induces a contract;
- differentiate between innocent, negligent and fraudulent misrepresentations and the advantages and disadvantages of the relevant damages claims flowing from each; and
- understand the ways in which attempts to exclude liability for misrepresentation may be controlled.

Introduction

Have you ever been had? Or to put it less colloquially, have you ever been misled? Being misled into a contract by the other party, that is being induced to enter into a contract by a misrepresentation, is the subject matter of this chapter.

Misrepresentation can be thought of as occupying a borderland at the edge of the contractual agreement. A misrepresentation is not of itself a term of the contract but it is merely something (a statement of fact rather than a contractual promise) which induced the contract.

CROSS REFERENCE

Think back to cases like *Oscar Chess* in Chapter 5 which were concerned with how to distinguish a term from a representation.

7.1 Locating misrepresentation in the law of obligations

Being just outside or beyond the borders of the contract, misrepresentation falls more naturally into the territory regulated by the law of tort. Thus, questions which arise more naturally in the law of torts, such as whether the **misrepresentation** was made **fraudulently** or was **negligent**, are important in deciding whether there should be compensation for such misrepresentations, in contrast to breach of a contractual term where fault does not normally come into it.

misrepresentation
A false statement of fact made by one party to the other which induces that other party to enter into the contract.

fraudulent misrepresentation This is established when a person makes a false statement which he knows is not true and has no belief in its truth, or which he makes recklessly, not caring whether it is true or not (***Derry*** v ***Peek*** (1889)).

negligent misrepresentation A negligent misrepresentation is established when a person makes a false statement which he may honestly believe to be true but without reasonable grounds for believing it to be true. See s.2(1) Misrepresentation Act 1967.

And yet, even though misrepresentation is partly a matter of the law of tort, its effects on the contract are also an important part of the law of contract, precisely because the misrepresentation induced the contract even though it is not part of it. As a result, the law of contract provides that the contract itself is normally **voidable** for misrepresentation, that is, liable to be **rescinded** or set aside, if induced by a misrepresentation, even a wholly innocent one. Thus whilst the law on misrepresentation goes beyond the borders of contract and into the realms of tort law in so far as obtaining compensation is concerned, it is also a vital aspect of the law of contract in relation to questions of whether the contract can be set aside or undone. Misrepresentation thus straddles the boundaries of contract and tort and is especially important because of the remedies of rescission and **damages** which it can provide and which, as we will see, can even in some instances be more favourable, attractive or powerful than those for breach of contract.

voidable contracts These are best thought of as valid but damaged contracts; the courts have decided that there is a defect in the contract (i.e. in the case of misrepresentation, that the claimant was induced to enter into the contract by a false statement) and so the claimant is given the option to rescind the contract or affirm it and carry on as normal.

rescission A remedy that allows the parties to unwind the contract. Benefits transferred between the parties are returned to the original party. The aim is to put the parties in the position they were in before the contract. Sometimes a rescinded contract is referred to as set aside.

damages The obligation to pay damages is a secondary obligation to pay a sum of money which arises in response to breach of a primary obligation (e.g. a contractual obligation or duty of care in tort). Damages for breach of contract are aimed at putting the claimant in the position as though the contract had been performed (see **Chapter 11** on Damages). In contrast, tortious damages are aimed at putting the claimant in the position as though the tort had not been committed.

EXAMPLE

Misrepresentation and its effects

Suppose your fellow student, Jules, persuades you to accompany him to a music festival in Cornwall which is to take place at the end of the month. He does this by telling you that Blurred, your favourite band, are on the bill. You pay him £50 for one of the tickets he has bought and agree to drive him in your car if he pays two-thirds of the petrol. Subsequently you also buy a £250 satellite navigation system to help you to find the remote farm at which the festival is to be held, and you remember to turn down an earlier offer from your local pub to do some paid casual work during the weekend of the festival.

A few days before the festival you discover that Blurred are not, and never were, on the bill. Let us be charitable (or naive) and suppose that Jules genuinely believed what he said to you about Blurred at the time and had relied on inaccurate information on Blurred's website (but not reflected on the festival website). The fact remains you have been misled by what Jules told you and have as a result bought the ticket from him, entered into an agreement to drive him there and invested £250 in a satellite navigation system for your car.

Your relationship with Jules may be such that legal remedies are not in practice relevant but, if a legal analysis is appropriate, and putting aside issues of intention to create legal relations, it is the law of misrepresentation which would govern the resolution of the issues. This is because the statement about Blurred is hardly likely to be a term of any contract—it would not be reasonable in all the circumstances to interpret it as a promise by Jules that Blurred will appear, not least because it is something over which he clearly has no control—and it would be treated as a false representation of fact rather than a promise about the future. It is a representation by Jules that, at the time he spoke to you, Blurred were on the bill; this was untrue, and so amounts to a misrepresentation. You were induced into buying the ticket (an executed contract) and agreeing to transport him (an executory contract). Since no term in either of these contracts has been broken you cannot, even in theory, sue him for breach of contract but you may be able to:

1) rescind the executed contract under which you purchased his ticket (i.e. return the ticket and get your £50 back); and
2) **avoid** (set aside) the executory contract to transport him so that you will no longer be bound to do it.

avoid Executory contracts (contracts where neither party has performed) may be avoided for misrepresentation. It is less appropriate (although not incorrect) to talk of rescission here because there are no benefits to be returned. Avoiding a contract for misrepresentation is a slightly different situation to a contract which is void ***ab initio*** (void from the start) e.g. because of a mistake in communication (see **Chapter 8**).

You may also want to make Jules compensate you for the fact that you have turned down the pub work or for the fact that you have bought a satellite navigation system which, even if you might eventually have bought one anyway, has already fallen in price in the shops and is now selling for only £150. As we have seen, you cannot sue for damages for breach of a term of a contract with Jules, since there is no such term that has been broken. Your only hope is damages for misrepresentation, which will depend on Jules being at fault in some way (which

Figure 7.1 Misrepresentation in the borderland—its impact on the contract and its actionability in tort

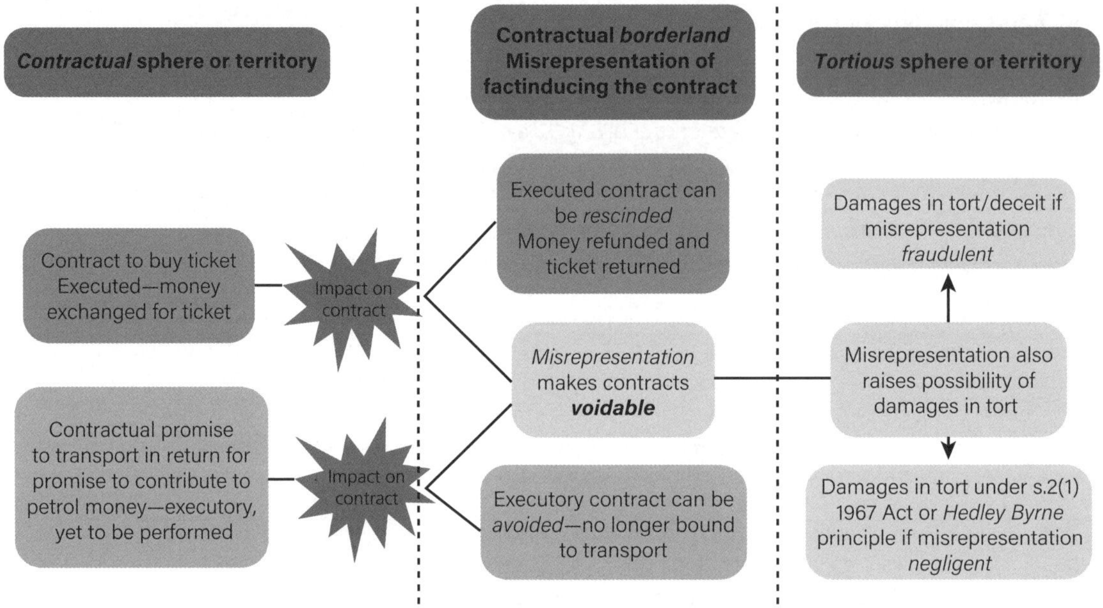

we will see, as a result of s.2(1) of the Misrepresentation Act 1967, may not be impossible even if Jules himself was misled by the band's website). The role and effects of misrepresentation are summarized in Figure 7.1.

Although the previous example may (or may not) seem relatively trivial to you and legal remedies unlikely to be pursued, exactly the same issues can arise where, instead of a student being misled about the identity of the line-up at a £50 rock concert, you are an investor misled by the seller of shares about the identity of the directors of a company the shares of which you are buying for millions of pounds—most of which money you subsequently lose. In this situation, the issues are not trivial on any view and you would be likely to take a very keen interest in the law of misrepresentation which it is the purpose of this chapter to explain.

7.1.1 **The expansion of misrepresentation**

To gain a full understanding, it is important to see the law of misrepresentation in its historical perspective because there were some dramatic changes in the 1960s (starting with *Hedley Byrne v Heller* (1964)) and some of the leading (older) cases would be themselves misleading if you forgot that they were decided in a quite different context from that which is applicable now. In particular, until the 1960s there were only two main categories of misrepresentation, fraudulent and innocent, and the concept of negligent misrepresentation was not separately recognized in English law. As a result, in relation to any older authorities about innocent misrepresentation, you need to ask yourself whether the same rule would apply today to a negligent misrepresentation or only to a wholly innocent misrepresentation. The evolution of misrepresentation and the essential difference between the pre-1964 and post-1964 situation is represented in Figure 7.2.

Furthermore, one needs to bear in mind that statements which might formerly have been classified as contractual terms might now be treated as negligent misrepresentations, given the

Figure 7.2 Evolution of misrepresentation

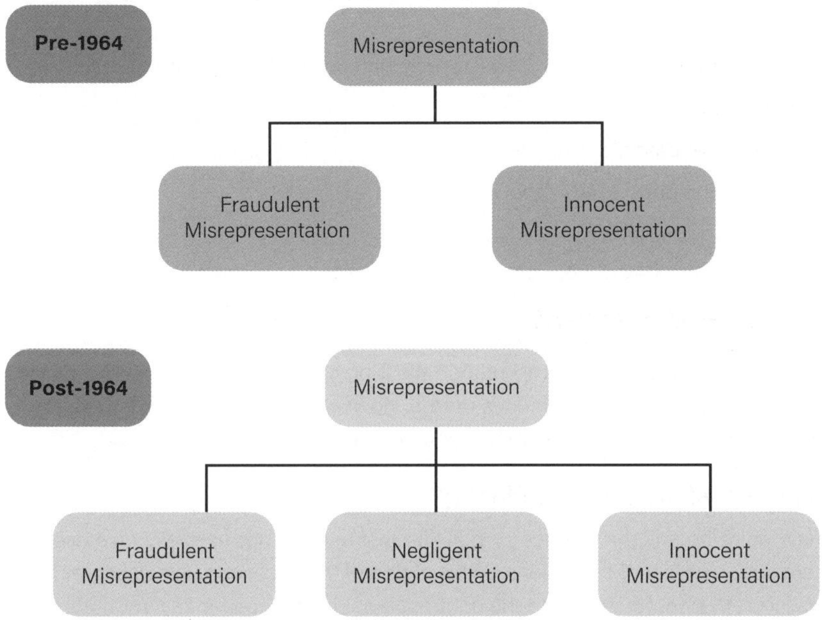

availability of damages as a remedy for these since the 1960s. A consequence of this has been an expansion of the importance of the law on misrepresentation as opposed to breach of contractual terms and this underlines the pivotal place occupied by misrepresentation in the study and understanding of the law of contract (and the whole of the law of obligations). A further complication is that in respect of contracts between 'consumers' and 'traders' there is now a separate regime for 'prohibited practices' which covers most instances of misrepresentations to 'consumers' currently actionable in damages. This is as a result of the Consumer Protection (Amendment) Regulations 2014 which amended the Consumer Protection from Unfair Trading Regulations 2008 so as to provide civil as opposed to simply criminal remedies under the Regulations. These civil remedies include 'the right to unwind' the contract (broadly similar to rescission), the 'right to a discount' (not dissimilar to damages in lieu of rescission under s.2(2) of the Misrepresentation Act 1967) and the 'right to damages' (broadly similar in effect to s.2(1) of the 1967 Act except that the test of remoteness for the new right is clearly limited to foreseeability). The details of these provisions applying to consumers contracting with a trader are complex and are outside the scope of this chapter. The Regulations (due to be replaced by new regulations to be made under s.233 of the Digital Markets, Competition and Consumers Act 2024) do not apply to contracts between two individuals *not* acting in the course of a business (so they would not apply in the Jules example earlier), nor, more significantly, do they apply to the vast majority of cases discussed in this chapter which relate to contracts between two businesses. These continue to be governed by the general law on misrepresentation, which continues to be very important within the overall law of contract and which is complex enough without the additional technicalities thrown up by the consumer regulations.

We will examine the current general law on misrepresentation by looking first at the basic essentials of misrepresentation and its effects on the contract and then at the different remedies available for the various types of misrepresentation.

7.2 Basic requirements

The key elements of the definition of misrepresentation can be highlighted as follows:

(a) a false statement

(b) of existing or past fact

(c) made by one party to the other

(d) that induces contract.

7.2.1 **A false statement**

The general rule is that a misrepresentation must be a false statement, that is, the misrepresentation must say something which is untrue. However, a party may sometimes be under a duty to speak and may also make implied statements.

A duty to speak up (disclose facts)?

The main point here is that silence or non-disclosure does not normally give rise to liability but there are a number of exceptions to this. Some of these concern special types of contract such as insurance contracts where the contract is said to be *uberrimae fidei*, that is, to require the 'utmost good faith,' and therefore there is a duty to disclose material facts. In an insurance contract, for example, the insured (i.e. you or I) possess all the material facts (i.e. how much our possessions are worth, where they are kept, etc.) and so we are under an exceptional duty to disclose these facts to the insurance company.

Outside these special categories, an exception of more general significance is that exemplified in *With* v *O'Flanagan* (1936) of a statement, in that case about the profits of a medical practice, true when made but false by the time of entering the contract for the sale of the practice. The statement, though true when made, is regarded as a continuing one which becomes false with the change of circumstances; this in effect imposes a duty to disclose the changed facts. However, it is unlikely that anyone would be bound by such a duty if they expressly state that they were not prepared to do so. In *IFE Fund SA* v *Goldman Sachs International* (2009), Goldman Sachs produced an information memorandum containing financial details of the company for which it sought investment. The Court of Appeal rejected the argument that Goldman Sachs had represented that the information published in the memorandum remained accurate as at the date the IFE Fund made their investment because the memorandum expressly made clear that Goldman Sachs did not undertake to advise IFE of any information coming to its attention after the date of the memorandum. Issues arising from cases where there is a duty to disclose changes include the question of whether the failure to disclose counts as a fraudulent misrepresentation. The question is probably largely academic because, as the Court of Appeal in *IFE Fund SA* v *Goldman Sachs International* recognized, s.2(1) of the Misrepresentation Act 1967 applies, and this gives a right to damages irrespective of fraud unless the representor 'did believe up to the time the contract was made that the facts represented were true,' so the maker of a statement in a case like *With* v *O'Flanagan* would be liable for damages under s.2(1) anyway.

Implied representations

Statements can of course be implied by conduct; for example a person who purchases goods by cheque impliedly represents (even if nothing is said) that the cheque is a valid order for the amount stated on it, which is not true and thus a misrepresentation if the representor knows, for example, that the cheque is going to bounce. Furthermore, one express statement may imply another. In particular, it may imply that there are no other facts known to the speaker which make the statement misleading. This is probably the best way of looking at so-called partial non-disclosure or 'half-truths,' as in *Dimmock* v *Hallet* (1866) where a vendor of land said that all the farms on the land were fully let. The vendor falsely impliedly represented that he knew of no other facts which made that statement misleading (he actually knew that the tenants had given notice to quit—hence the half-truth; the farms were currently fully let, and so he had not lied, but the tenants would soon be moving). The change of circumstances rule from *With* v *O'Flanagan* and the *Dimmock* v *Hallet* rule about partial disclosure/half-truths were both brought very much up to date in the Court of Appeal case of *Spice Girls Ltd* v *Aprilia World Service* (2002).

CASE CLOSE-UP

***Spice Girls Ltd* v *Aprilia World Service* (2002)**

Spice Girls Limited ('SGL') entered into a contract with Aprilia ('AWS') on 6 May 1998 whereby AWS agreed to sponsor their concert tour in return for promotional work by the Spice Girls to publicize Aprilia motorcycles and scooters. The court implied a representation from the conduct of the negotiations from 4 March onwards that 'SGL did not know and had no reasonable grounds to believe at or before the time of entry to the agreement that any of the Spice Girls had an existing declared intention to leave the group within the minimum period of the agreement [at least until March 1999].' This was true on 4 March 1998 but became false on 9 March 1998 when Geri Halliwell ('Ginger Spice') told the other members of the group that she was going to leave the group in September 1998. She confirmed this to the group and to their legal advisers on 25 April 1998 and certainly by this time the duty to disclose the changed circumstances within *With* v *O'Flanagan* was unarguable. Furthermore, the fact that the agreement referred to the individuals 'currently comprising' the five Spice Girls did not help SGL but in fact indicated that this was a misleading statement or partial non-disclosure (half-truth) in keeping back the fact that one of the Spice Girls had already indicated an intention to leave (rather like the fact that the tenants had given notice to quit in *Dimmock* v *Hallet*). SGL as a result were liable (for damages under s.2(1) of the 1967 Act) for misrepresentation.

7.2.2 **Existing or past fact**

Statements of facts have to be distinguished from a number of other types of statements about the subject matter of the contract. Thus factual statements have to be distinguished from 'mere puffs' (essentially advertising slogans, not intended to be taken seriously or literally such as 'probably the best law book in the world!'), from statements of genuine belief or opinion, from statements as to the future including statements of intention and, traditionally at least, from statements of law. It is quite common for students to recite these propositions as though they were engraved in stone without any evidence of any understanding of why such statements do not constitute misrepresentations. This is a pity since not only does this mean they have missed the opportunity to see the real basis of liability for misrepresentation, but it also means they will also be unable to distinguish the rules in the appropriate situations.

You should understand that the basic rationale underlying the requirement of a statement of fact is that facts are either true or untrue at the time the statement is made, and that a party is only justified in relying on factual statements and should not be able to complain about misplaced reliance on honestly and reasonably held opinions and beliefs, and so on.

A statement about the future cannot be wrong at the time it is made (unless one is an out-and-out determinist); it only becomes wrong at the relevant future time: you can look back retrospectively and say that you made a mistake, but at the time you made the statement, you made a misprediction about the future. In contrast, there is a justification for imposing some liability on a person who states as a fact, as opposed to merely expressing an opinion, something which the other party then relies on when entering the contract and which is capable of being true or false at the time of the statement being made. The question of whether the statement is one on which it is reasonable to rely is a factor in deciding whether to class it as a statement of opinion or of fact.

LINK TO . . .

Mistake (Chapter 8)

I am wondering whether to take an umbrella on my journey to college. I look out of the window and it does not look as if it is going to rain and so I leave my umbrella at home. I am halfway to college and the heavens open. I get wet.

Imagine instead that I look out of the window and think that it is not raining. I leave my umbrella and step out of the door and get wet because it has actually been raining already for several minutes.

In both scenarios I get wet but in the first it is because I made a misprediction and in the second it is because I made a mistake. The distinction is that in the latter case I incorrectly processed the information available to me (I thought it was dry when it was in fact raining) but in the former case I had no conclusive data on whether it was going to rain and so I made a prediction about the future, which turned out to be a misprediction; I predicted no rain when in fact it did rain.

Misrepresentations of fact and future statements are different: the former are based on available facts and are verifiable, whereas the latter are predictions which cannot currently be proved wrong or right. From this analysis we can see that misrepresentations are merely induced mistakes—one party is induced to subjectively believe that X is true when in fact it is not. You might wonder why misrepresentations entitle a party to rescind a contract whereas a unilateral mistake makes a contract void only when the other party knows that the other party is mistaken (see Chapter 8 and *Smith* v *Hughes* (1871)). Could it be that these are simply the rules of the game—that contract law gives relief more easily when a mistake has been induced by the representation of another person (who therefore has some responsibility for it) as opposed to the situation where a party unilaterally suffers from a mistake (and the other party is not implicated or aware of the mistake)?

In *Bisset* v *Wilkinson* (1927), the statement that the land would support 2,000 sheep was merely an expression of an opinion (rather than a factual statement about the capacity of the land), partly because the seller was not in any better position than the purchaser to know its true capacity. Similarly, in *Hummingbird Motors* v *Hobbs* (1986), a statement about the mileage of a second-hand car was not treated as a statement of fact because it was qualified as being correct 'to the

Figure 7.3 Misrepresentations as statements of fact and apparent exceptions

Misrepresentations	Apparent 'exceptions' to basic rule that misrepresentation must be a false statement of fact	Not Misrepresentations
• False statement of existing *fact*	Opinion that implies false statement of fact that opinion is held on reasonable grounds (*Esso* v *Mardon*).	• Opinions (*Bisset* v *Wilkinson*)
	Intention that implies false statement of fact that intention (or opinion) is actually held (*Edgington* v *Fitzmaurice*).	• Intention
	Statement of law treated as equivalent to a statement of fact OR (better view?) statement of law may imply statement of genuine belief that this is the law or that reasonable grounds exist for opinion as to law (*Pankhania*).	• Statements of Law (traditionally)

best of my knowledge and belief' and again, the seller was in no better position to know the truth than the purchaser. In contrast, in *Esso Petroleum Co. Ltd* v *Mardon* (1976), the statement about the sales capacity of the petrol station could have been treated as one of fact (it was not found necessary to do so because liability was based upon *Hedley Byrne* and upon contractual warranty) since, given the expertise of Esso, Mr Mardon was justified in relying on it as such.

This reveals the ultimate basis of the law on misrepresentation—justified reliance on verifiable statements of the other party to the contract. In addition, this points the way to understanding the apparent exceptions (summarized in Figure 7.3) to the requirement of statements of fact:

(i) A statement of opinion may nevertheless imply that the speaker is aware of reasonable grounds for the opinion (this would be an alternative way of implying a factual statement in *Esso Petroleum Co. Ltd* v *Mardon*) and that the speaker is not aware of facts which clearly invalidate the opinion—as in *Smith* v *Land & House Property Corporation* (1884) where the opinion that the hotel was let to 'a most desirable tenant' failed to mention the fact that the tenant was being pursued for arrears.

(ii) A statement as to one's intention clearly is capable of being true or false in the sense that one either has that intention or one does not. The fact that someone acts differently in the future from their previously stated intention does not make the statement of intention a misrepresentation of fact—we can all change our minds, some more than others—but there is clearly a misrepresentation (indeed a fraudulent one) if the intention was not actually held when the statement was made—as in *Edgington* v *Fitzmaurice* (1885), where a **prospectus** declared that funds subscribed would be used for the further development of the company when in fact the intention was to use them to pay off pressing debts. A more recent example can be found in *East* v *Maurer* (1991) where the vendor of one of a pair of hairdressing salons fraudulently misrepresented that he did not intend to continue to work in the other salon retained except in emergencies.

prospectus A prospectus is an information document published by a company when it wants to raise money on the public markets (e.g. by issuing shares on the Main List and admitting them for trading on the London Stock Exchange). It tells potential buyers what the company does and explains the various risks of investing in the company.

Even more recently, in *Crystal Palace FC* v *Dowie* (2008), Iain Dowie was found to have fraudulently misrepresented that he had no present intention to join rival club Charlton Athletic, a misrepresentation of fact which induced Crystal Palace to agree to release him from his existing contract as their manager.

(iii) A wilfully false misrepresentation of law has always constituted misrepresentation since it is a misrepresentation of the fact of what is the speaker's belief as to the law. Non-fraudulent misrepresentations of law, on the other hand, have not traditionally been regarded as misrepresentations of fact. Developments in the law relating to recovery of mistaken payments, where the House of Lords in *Kleinwort Benson* v *Lincoln CC* (1999) dismantled the distinction between fact and law in relation to mistaken payments, have led commentators to suggest that the distinction between fact and law in relation to misrepresentation should also be abolished. This was the conclusion of the High Court in *Pankhania* v *Hackney LBC* (2002) but it should be noted that this was only a first instance decision and the misrepresentation in that case (that the tenant of the car park being purchased was not a protected tenant) was deliberately misleading and thus misrepresented the factual question of the misrepresentor's belief. The justification for traditionally excluding non-fraudulent misrepresentations of law in the first place is probably that such statements are really analogous to opinions—it is arguable that the law is not a fixed body of rules but always subject to different interpretations by future judges—on which the other party is not justified in placing any reliance and as to which the other party is equally capable of forming an opinion.

This is consistent with the fact that statements of private rights (of which *Pankhania* was also an example) have always been treated as statements of fact, since the speaker can be expected to know about laws particularly applicable to him. *Pankhania* may therefore not be the final word about misrepresentation of law, although perhaps the best view is that the relevant distinction is not between fact and law but between fact and opinion.

7.2.3 Made by one party to the other

This requirement is subject to the usual qualification that one has to look at the objective appearance of what one person's conduct will convey to another. So if A makes a misrepresentation to B which A knows will be (or has been) passed on to C and on the faith of which C then contracts with A, A may be liable as though A had directly misrepresented the fact to C.

EXAMPLE

Misrepresentation through a third party

We negotiate over the sale of my car to you and I tell a mutual friend (falsely) that it has never been involved in an accident, knowing that this friend will pass on the information to you. If you buy the car partly relying on this information it is just as though I have told you directly and you will be able to claim the remedies available for misrepresentation.

A variation on this sort of case was decided by the Supreme Court in *Cramaso LLP* v *Ogilvie-Grant* (2014) where there was a misrepresentation, made by the respondents to E, relating to the numbers of birds on their Scottish grouse moor of which E was contemplating taking a lease. E then decided to create a limited liability partnership (Cramaso), comprising himself and his wife, which would actually take on the lease, and he continued, now as agent of Cramaso, to conduct the negotiations with the respondents which culminated in the lease being signed. The Supreme Court pointed out that the misrepresentation was (like all actionable misrepresentations) a continuing one (cf. cases such as *With* v *O'Flanagan* in section 7.2.1), and although it was originally made to E in his personal capacity, it obviously continued to influence him in concluding the lease as agent for Cramaso. It was therefore actionable by Cramaso as the party ultimately induced to enter the contract by the misrepresentation.

Although the case is also concerned with the position in Scotland concerning the particular remedy of damages for negligent misrepresentation (s.2(1) of the Misrepresentation Act does not apply in Scotland so it depends on the common law and the *Hedley Byrne* principle), the principles discussed in relation to who can be the recipient of the misrepresentation clearly apply equally to English law. Indeed Lord Reed discussed a wide range of English authorities and relied in particular on *Briess* v *Woolley* (HL) (1954), which was the converse case where a statement was made by (rather than to) an individual in their personal capacity who subsequently entered the contract as an agent for his principal. In *Briess* the principal was *liable* for the misrepresentation made by an individual prior to him becoming its agent. The Supreme Court in *Cramaso* said that the converse rule should apply so as to enable the principal (Cramaso) to *claim* in respect of a misrepresentation made to E prior to him becoming Cramaso's agent (and prior to the principal even being in existence).

The discussion in the example shows that the law of misrepresentation is concerned with statements which can be said to be made by one party to the other and that this includes statements made by or to their agents (and even by or to persons who subsequently become their agents by the time the contract is formed). It should also be borne in mind that a statement made by someone who is definitely not a party to the contract in any sense may still be actionable under the *Hedley Byrne* principle (as in *Hedley Byrne & Co. Ltd* v *Heller & Partners Ltd* (1964) itself) or as a collateral contract (as in *Shanklin Pier Ltd* v *Detel Products Ltd* (1951) where the manufacturer's statement about their paint caused the claimants to specify the paint in a contract with the decorators). Such liabilities are, however, subject to their own appropriate rules and are properly distinguished from liability for misrepresentation.

7.2.4 **Induces the contract**

This is really another way of saying that the representee must have relied on the statement. We have already mentioned in section 7.2.2 that this reliance must be justified and that this is in effect dealt with by the way in which the courts apply the distinction between statements of fact and statements of opinion.

The point here is that the reliance must actually take place. Thus if the representee makes his own inquiries, as in *Attwood* v *Small* (1838), which shows that he does not rely on the statement, he cannot claim relief for misrepresentation but if, as in *Redgrave* v *Hurd* (1881), the representee does not take advantage of opportunities to check the truth of the statement, even if he is negligent in failing to do so, he can still obtain relief. The fact that the representee has not checked for himself reinforces the inference that he has relied on the statement rather than weakens it, and there would be little point in the parties to a contract exchanging information about the subject matter if they were each under a duty to check each other's statements.

Nevertheless, one should be wary of applying the decision in *Redgrave* v *Hurd* too mechanically and the point made at the start of this chapter about the law formerly not distinguishing between negligent and wholly innocent statements is relevant here. The representor in *Redgrave* v *Hurd* was found not to be fraudulent, but was at least negligent (but the category of negligent misrepresentation was not recognized at the time). If you are faced with a problem where the representor is wholly innocent and the representee is negligent in failing to check, it may be more just to conclude that rescission should not be available. Furthermore, if the representor is negligent and damages are being claimed, as now they could be, the negligence of the misrepresentee might be a ground for reducing them under the Law Reform (Contributory Negligence) Act 1945. This possibility has been confirmed in theory by the Court of Appeal in *Gran Gelato Ltd* v *Richcliff (Group) Ltd* (1992). However, no reduction in damages was made on the facts because, although the claimants could have made their own inquiries, they had relied, as they were intended to do, on the defendant's representations, as in *Redgrave* v *Hurd*.

It is not enough to negative reliance to show that the misrepresentation was not the sole reason for entering the contract and that the representee also relied heavily on other considerations—see *Edgington* v *Fitzmaurice* (1855), where the claimant, quite apart from the misrepresentation about what his money would be used for, also relied on his mistaken belief that the prospectus promised him a charge on the property of the company. On the other hand, according to *JEB Fasteners Ltd* v *Marks, Bloom & Co.* (1983), if it is shown that the representee placed no reliance at all on the false statement and would still have entered into the contract even if the misrepresentation had not been made, then there is no inducement and no reliance.

EXAMPLE

Inducement and reliance

The approach in *JEB Fasteners* does not sit very easily with *Barton* v *Armstrong* (1976) (which was in fact a duress case but the House of Lords accepted that the same principles would apply to misrepresentation), where the House of Lords allowed rescission even though it was admitted that Barton might well have still entered into the contract without the duress. The point is that a misrepresentation can still be an inducement even though without it there would still have been sufficient other inducements to enter the contract and rescission should still be available. Perhaps the explanation of *JEB Fasteners* is that it was a damages case where the 'but for' test of causation has to be satisfied whereas in claims for rescission, the question is the broader one of inducement rather than causation. The point is not an easy one but an illustration might help.

Suppose that in situation A, to enter a contract P requires reasons to a value of 6, that the misrepresentation by D constitutes a reason valued at 2 and that P has other reasons for entering the contract valued at 7.

Situation A

Value of reasons required————————}6

Value of actual reasons————————}7————————} +2=9

(other reasons) (Misrep)

Further suppose a situation B, exactly the same as A, except that the other reasons are only to the value of 5.

Situation B

Value of reasons required——————————}6

Value of actual reasons——————————}5——————————} +2=7

(other reasons) (Misrep)

In situation A, P would still have entered the contract if the misrepresentation had not been made, and according to *JEB Fasteners* this negatives reliance. In situation B, there clearly is reliance—without the misrepresentation P would not have entered into the contract even though equally the misrepresentation on its own would not have been a sufficient reason. The argument based on *Barton* v *Armstrong* is that there is also reliance, or at least inducement, in situation A if P takes account of the misrepresentation as an additional reason, for example if it helps P to enter the contract much more confidently. On the other hand, if P takes no account at all of the misrepresentation, for example P's reasoning is 'I have reasons 1 to 7 for entering the contract and I really don't care whether D's statement is true or false', then clearly P has not in any sense relied on the statement or been induced by it and he cannot rescind. The Court of Appeal in *JEB Fasteners* is effectively saying that the claimants in that case were simply not influenced at all by the accounts (which their own investigation had shown were suspect) and decided to purchase the company solely for other reasons (primarily in order to acquire the services of the two directors). Similar issues arose in the Supreme Court case of *Hayward* v *Zurich Insurance* (2016) where the question of reliance and inducement was confirmed to be whether the representee was influenced (at least in part) by the misrepresentation. The case was concerned with a fraudulent misrepresentation which induced the insurers to settle a personal injury claim and on the particular facts it was no bar to rescission (when the true facts were later revealed) that the insurers had never believed the representation to be true. The misrepresentation (about the extent of the insured's injuries) had influenced their decision to enter the settlement agreement because they could not at that time be sure that, if the case went to trial, a judge would share their view that the representation was false. The representation was thus a reason influencing them even though they did not believe it to be true and they were not in that sense deceived. This aspect of the case depends on the fact that the representation was fraudulent (dishonest) and that the agreement to which it led was a settlement of a claim. In most other cases, not being deceived by the representation will mean on the facts that it does not influence the claimant and that there is no reliance on it and thus no remedy for misrepresentation. More recently the rule that the misrepresentation need only be one of the reasons for entering into the contract has been confirmed in *BV Nederlandse* v *Rembrandt Enterprises* (2019). The Court of Appeal said that although even in cases of fraudulent misrepresentation there is still a burden on the representee of proving that he was induced to enter the contract, there is a rebuttable evidential presumption of fact that the representee would have been so induced by a fraudulent representation intended to cause him to do just that. This presumption will be 'very difficult' for the representor to rebut and it was not rebutted on the facts of the case so the contract could be rescinded for fraudulent misrepresentation.

7.3 Remedies for misrepresentation

So far we have been looking at the basic requirements common to all misrepresentations. To identify the remedies available in any particular case one has to distinguish between fraudulent, negligent and innocent misrepresentations. However, before examining those distinctions, it ought to be stressed that, for any misrepresentation, the remedy of rescission is in principle available, although it may in actual practice not be allowed due to the various limits on the right to rescind. The question of the type of misrepresentation is primarily important in deciding what remedies in addition to rescission are available and it can also have a bearing on whether one of the limits on rescission is applicable. It therefore makes sense to look first of all at the general remedy of rescission before examining the various different types of misrepresentation.

7.3.1 **Rescission**

Self-help remedy

The first point to note is that rescission is not necessarily a remedy that one has to obtain from the court. A purchaser can rescind a contract for the sale of goods merely by returning the goods and cancelling any payment, if in a position to do so, although of course if the purchaser rescinds when there is no right to do so, the purchaser will then be the one in breach of contract. Furthermore, if you are being sued for failing to perform a contract, you can use 'rescission' as a defence and use it as an excuse for refusing to perform so as to set aside the contract, by asserting that the contract was induced by a misrepresentation and is unenforceable against you. Where, however, you have partly or fully performed your own side of the contract, you will normally need to approach the court for an order of rescission, that is, an order which unwinds or dissolves the contract and which involves the return from each party to the other of anything which has passed under the contract. It is important to distinguish this restitutionary ('giving back') remedy of rescission clearly from so-called rescission for breach (which in this book is referred to as 'termination'), which does not retrospectively unwind the contract but merely terminates it from the date of the breach. The distinction is important because the limits on the right to rescind for misrepresentation do not necessarily apply to the right to terminate for breach and also because one can clearly both terminate and claim damages for breach of the terminated contract (which still existed at the time of the breach) but one cannot rescind and still claim damages for breach of the contract which has been retrospectively expunged (although one may be able to claim damages in tort for misrepresentation).

Indemnity for expenses incurred under an obligation

An ancillary order which can also be made along with rescission (even for innocent misrepresentation) is the award of an indemnity. This is a monetary award but should not be confused with damages as it is much more limited. It only covers expenditure which the representee was obliged to incur under the terms of the contract which is being rescinded and which has benefited the other party. It is a restitutionary, rather than compensatory, remedy and is part of the restitution to the starting position which rescission is designed to achieve. If money has been paid directly to the other party then of course it will be returned as part of the remedy of rescission itself; the indemnity is instead concerned with payments made under the contract to third parties. In *Whittington* v *Seale-Hayne* (1900) the indemnity included money paid out in rates and to do repairs which the tenant was obliged to do under the lease and which benefited the landlord directly, but it did not extend to medical expenses and loss of stock which, although foreseeable, were not incurred under an obligation contained in the lease. (These latter, and other items claimed, would only be recoverable if a right to damages could have been established, which at the time would have meant proving fraud—the increased availability of damages for misrepresentation today would mean that the limited right to an indemnity is less commonly relevant.)

The limits or bars on rescission

Despite the limited nature of the indemnity associated with it, rescission itself is still, given that it unwinds the contract back to its beginning, a fairly drastic remedy and for that reason, as well as because of its equitable origins, is subject to a number of limits or 'bars', as outlined later.

(a) Restitution Impossible

Such a limit can hardly be avoided. The courts cannot order a party to 'give back' benefits if that is not possible; if a crate of whisky falsely represented to be Scotch has already been consumed, rescission is clearly impossible; the claimant can hardly expect to get the return of purchase price if the whisky has been drunk. The problems arise where the subject matter of the contract can literally be returned but it has significantly deteriorated or improved in condition. The court may still in these circumstances order rescission and order one party to pay some allowance to the other to take account of the improvement or deterioration, as in *Erlanger* v *New Sombrero Phosphate* (1838) where the claimant had to make allowance for the phosphate already extracted from the mine. In *Salt* v *Stratstone* (2015) the Court of Appeal allowed a purchaser of a car to return it and get all his money back even though he had had the use of the car for several years. The onus it said was on the vendors (who were clearly regarded as being at fault) to provide evidence of the value of the use that the purchaser had enjoyed, or of the deterioration in the value of the car, and they had not done this so no allowance was made on the facts of the case. In *Patarkatsishvili v Woodward-Fisher* (2025) the claimants had lived in a £32 million house for some years before rescission was ordered by the High Court (for fraudulent misrepresentation about a serious moth infestation). The purchasers got an order for the £32 million purchase price to be returned to them but had to allow a £1 million deduction for each year of their occupation and use of the property (although they were also awarded additional damages for fraud amounting to several million pounds—so the fraudulent misrepresentation (and the moths) proved to be very expensive for the defendant).

(b) Third-party Rights

Rescission is a personal right against the representor and the claimant cannot claim the return of property which passed to the representor under the contract so as to defeat rights acquired by a bona fide third party from the representor. This was one reason the court did not order rescission of the release agreement in *Crystal Palace FC* v *Dowie* as Coventry City had by then acquired rights to Dowie's services. The timing of rescission is important here, since if rescission can be effected before the third party acquires any rights, it will in fact prevent any such rights being obtained—see *Car & Universal Finance Co. Ltd* v *Caldwell* (1965) where the Court of Appeal held, rather generously, that the rescission was effected by notifying the AA and police of the fraud, even though the representor could not be traced and this was held to prevent an innocent third-party purchaser getting a good title to the car from the rogue. The decision has been criticized and the validity of rescinding by notifying third parties probably only applies to cases of fraud.

LINK TO . . .

Mistake (Chapter 8)

We will see in relation to mistaken identity that a mistake can sometimes negative consent so that there is no agreement and the contract is void. However, some identity mistakes (e.g. *King's Norton Metal Co. Ltd* v *Edridge, Merrett and Co. Ltd* (1897)) do not negative consent and make the contract void and so the fraudulent misrepresentation of the rogue (who has misrepresented their identity by pretending to be someone else, usually a rich and well-respected person) comes into play. This makes the contract voidable at the option of the mistaken party (whose mistake was induced by the rogue's fraudulent misrepresentation of identity), who must rescind the contract before title passes to a bona fide third-party purchaser—usually some innocent to whom the rogue has sold the car.

(c) Affirmation

The representee cannot play fast and loose with the contract. Once he discovers the falsity of the misrepresentation he must take action to avoid (rescind) the contract or he is in danger of being regarded as affirming it, as in *Long* v *Lloyd* (1958) where a lorry was defective but the purchaser had continued to use it having discovered the defects and had indeed already accepted an offer to pay some of the costs of repair. Affirmation can only occur once the claimant has discovered the falsity of the misrepresentation, but once this occurs the court may draw the inference of affirmation very quickly, especially in contracts where the value of the subject matter fluctuates rapidly (such as share purchases), since otherwise representees could speculate at the expense of the representor with no risk to themselves.

EXAMPLE

Affirmation not speculation

I subscribe for shares in Dodgy Builders plc (they've gone public and floated on the London Stock Exchange since we met them in Chapter 4) for 156 pence each in reliance on a conversation I had with the company's chief executive who told me: 'we have just made record profits of £20 million and moved into the lucrative indoor swimming pool market.' I later find out that neither of these statements is true and so the contract to subscribe for shares is voidable and I have the option to rescind. It is 7 a.m. and the market has just opened.

I decide to take breakfast and think my options over until 8 a.m. At 8 a.m. my stockbroker tells me that Dodgy Builders' share price has rocketed up to 170 pence and I should hold on to the shares. I am happy and meet a trader friend for morning coffee. My trader friend tells me that a disgruntled corporate customer has just filed litigation against Dodgy

Builders worth hundreds of millions of pounds which they are likely to lose, but not many people know this and so I should sell my shares quickly whilst they are high. I run out of the coffee shop at 9 a.m. and ring my stockbroker with an instruction to sell my shares at 170 pence (and so make a profit on my purchase) but my stockbroker tells me that the market has just heard about the litigation and the share price has crashed to 50 pence. At 9.10 a.m. I rescind the contract.

Dodgy Builders could legitimately claim that I had affirmed the contract because, even though I only waited two hours and ten minutes, I speculated at their expense and only tried to rescind the contract when the share price had fallen below the price I paid. It would be unfair to allow me to delay, hoping that the shares might increase in price, safe in the knowledge that I could always rescind the contract and get my money back if the shares fall.

(d) Lapse of Time/Laches

The difference from affirmation has traditionally been that with lapse of time, time can start to run from the date of the contract even though the truth (i.e. the falsity of the misrepresentation) has not yet been discovered. In *Leaf* v *International Galleries* (1950) five years had elapsed since the purchase of a painting innocently misrepresented to be a Constable. Five years was much too long a period to have waited and it was up to the buyer to have the authenticity of the painting checked earlier if he wanted to verify it. However, in *Salt* v *Stratstone* (2015) *Leaf* was explained as a decision prior to the 1967 Act and to have been affected by the question of whether the right to terminate for breach of condition had been lost. Since s.1 of the 1967 Act, the remedy of rescission is unaffected by whether the misrepresentation is also a term of the contract and the Court of Appeal thought that the true question in relation to rescission was not simply one of lapse of time but whether the equitable doctrine of laches applied. This involved a consideration of whether it would be inequitable in all the circumstances to grant rescission. In *Salt*, the purchaser only discovered the ground for rescission (that the car was not 'new' when sold to him) after four years (although he had tried to return the car for other reasons much earlier) but that was not his fault on the facts, rather it was the fault of the sellers so rescission was ordered despite the considerable lapse of time. The case may be an example of the courts allowing a longer period to elapse before they will hold the right to rescind for a negligent misrepresentation to be barred than might be the case if the misrepresentation was wholly innocent but factors such as when the innocent party could have discovered the truth will also be relevant.

(e) Misrepresentation Act 1967, s.2(2)

This is not so much a bar on the right to rescind but a qualification to it. As noted earlier, the remedy of rescission is quite drastic—it is an all or nothing remedy—and in some cases, particularly where the misrepresentation is innocent and the detriment to the representee small in proportion to the value of the contract as a whole, it may be rather unfair to order rescission. Section 2(2) recognizes this by giving the court discretion to award **damages in lieu of (instead of) rescission** (cf. the rights to damages for fraud and negligence, discussed later, which are available in addition to rescission).

damages in lieu of rescission

This means that the court may award damages instead of allowing the parties to rescind the contract. Therefore the contract stands valid (it is not rewound) and the representee receives damages.

William Sindall v *Cambridgeshire County Council* (1994) is an example where the court would have restricted the claimant to damages instead of rescission had it found that there had been an actionable misrepresentation in the first place. As Hoffmann LJ put it, 'in the context of a £5 million sale of land, a misrepresentation which would have cost £18,000 to put right and was unlikely seriously to have interfered with the development or resale of the property was a matter of relatively minor importance.'

THINKING POINT

There are two key issues in relation to s.2(2) which you should be prepared to discuss:

1) Is the court's power under s.2(2) available where rescission is barred anyway; and
2) What is the measure of damages under the subsection?

Application of s.2(2) when rescission is barred

As far as (a) in the previous thinking point is concerned, it is difficult to see why, as a matter of policy, the bars on rescission ought to prevent an award of damages under s.2(2), but the subsection only applies where the representee 'would be entitled . . . to rescind.' This wording is not entirely clear and the question has arisen as to whether there is a power to award damages where rescission is otherwise barred. In *Thomas Witter* v *TBP Industries* (1996) the Court of Appeal said (*obiter*) that damages under s.2(2) did not depend on the right to rescind still being in existence but *Floods of Queensferry* v *Shand Construction* (2000) is a High Court decision (again *obiter*) going the other way and the first instance decision in *Zanzibar* v *BAE* (2001) holds that there is no longer any power to award damages under s.2(2) once the right to rescind has been lost (due to a combination of lapse of time and third parties acquiring rights). A possible middle ground would have been to say that s.2(2) should not be applicable where the right to rescind has been lost through affirmation or lapse of time (where there is perhaps less justification for giving damages to a representee who has in effect thrown away the right to rescind or allowed it to lapse) but that damages under s.2(2) can be awarded where restitution 'would be' available, but is no longer available simply because it is impossible or is barred in favour of third-party rights (which is not the fault of the innocent party).

However, in *Salt* v *Stratstone* (2015) the Court of Appeal has now made it clear that for damages to be awarded under s.2(2), as a matter of interpretation, rescission still has to be available at the trial or at least it must still have been available at the time it was claimed. Although technically this was *obiter* (because the court held that rescission could, and should, still be ordered on the facts) it will be very hard now in any situation to argue that damages are available under s.2(2) if the right to rescind is not still available. The more generous attitude taken in this case to rescission still being available, despite lapse of time and difficulties in restoring precisely what has been received under the contract, to some extent at least reduces the number of situations where damages under s.2(2) cannot be awarded due to rescission no longer being available. In other words, the less restrictive the bars on rescission, the less significant is the restriction on the availability of damages under s.2(2) to cases where rescission remains available.

Measure of damages under s.2(2)

As to (b), the measure of damages, although there were some peculiar *obiter* statements in the *William Sindall* case referring to the contractual measure, the obvious solution is to make an award which would put the representee in as good a position as if the contract had been rescinded (and any indemnity awarded).

EXAMPLE

Damages in lieu of rescission

Alex buys a car from Phillippa for £2,500, but due to a misrepresentation about the car's age, the car is only worth £2,200. If Alex rescinded, he would return to Phillippa the car worth £2,200 and get his £2,500 back from Phillippa. So he has his £2,500 back in his hands.

If the court decides to award damages in lieu of rescission under s.2(2), such damages would have to achieve the same result. Since no rescission is being ordered, Alex keeps the car worth £2,200 so he needs another £300 to bring him up to the £2,500 he could have got under rescission. What these damages should not cover, however, is any other items of loss; for example suppose Alex has purchased £100 of accessories which only fit models of the year he thought he was purchasing and which are now useless to him. Such losses would have been left equally uncompensated if rescission plus indemnity had been awarded and they can only be recovered if Alex establishes some other right to damages, for example under s.2(1), which is considered later. Similarly, if the car would have been worth £3,000 if of the age represented, there should be no question of getting an award of £800 (£3,000 less the £2,200 value of the car received) since that would be to give him his contractual loss of bargain rather than returning each party to their starting positions. To gain such loss of bargain damages, Alex would have to prove that the age of the car was a term, not just a representation, and that there was therefore a breach of contract.

Fraudulent and non-fraudulent misrepresentations

A final point to note is that s.2(2) explicitly only applies to a misrepresentation made 'otherwise than fraudulently.' If the misrepresentation is fraudulent, the court has no power to substitute damages and the victim of fraud can insist on rescission (provided none of the other bars to rescission is applicable). If the victim of fraud actually wants damages instead of (or indeed in addition to) rescission he has a right to damages anyway, independently of s.2(2), as we will explain later.

Other representees, that is, those who are not the victim of fraud, may also sometimes actually prefer damages under s.2(2) to rescission but it would be wrong, quite apart from the fact that the power under s.2(2) is discretionary, to talk about them claiming damages under s.2(2). Although most discussions assume either party can take advantage of s.2(2), the only possible way a representee can do so under the terms of the subsection is to claim that 'the contract has been or ought to be rescinded' and then, rather contrarily, to invite the court to exercise its discretion to award damages instead (or hope that it does so of its own accord).

To get damages under s.2(2) you have to be prepared to take the risk that the court will instead choose to order rescission of the contract. The point is not merely an exercise in semantics but is fundamentally one of whether s.2(2) is merely intended to provide relief to representors from the drastic effects of rescission, or whether, in addition, it is meant to give representees an extra option. That it is the former and not the latter is further underlined by *Salt* v *Stratstone* (2015), discussed earlier.

THINKING POINT

Is s.2(2) designed to benefit representors, representees or both?

7.3.2 Damages (other than in lieu of rescission under s.2(2))

Fraud

The law of torts has long recognized through the tort of deceit that damages should be available for fraudulent misrepresentations, whether or not they lead to a contract. As far as fraud leading to a contract is concerned (which is the concern of a contract course) there are two main issues to be aware of: the meaning of fraud and the assessment of damages for fraud.

Meaning of fraud

As to the meaning of fraud, *Derry* v *Peek* (1889) is the case where a clear distinction was drawn between fraud and negligence (and a right to damages for negligent misrepresentation denied) and the essence of fraud was defined as an absence of a genuine belief in the truth of one's statement. Thus if you have a belief in the truth of what you say, no matter how negligent or unreasonable you are in holding that belief, you are not fraudulent, just as the directors were found, perhaps rather charitably, not to have been fraudulent in *Derry* v *Peek*. Of course, if a belief is unreasonable, you will have difficulty in establishing that you held it, but the burden of proof is on the claimant and fraud is a serious allegation not lightly found to be proved by any court and likely to be penalized in **costs** if not made out.

costs
The court makes a costs order to determine who pays for the money spent on litigation. The court has a discretion to order costs as it sees fit but generally the losing party has to pay a large proportion of the winning party's costs (and his own costs). Costs can be used to punish a party for wasting time (i.e. for alleging fraud when there was no evidence of fraud).

CROSS REFERENCE
The reliance measure—see Chapter 11 on Damages for further discussion of the difference between the contractual expectation measure and the tortious reliance measure.

CASE CLOSE-UP

***Derry* v *Peek* (1889)**

The directors of a tramway issued a prospectus to potential investors containing a statement that the company had the right to use steam power instead of horses (a big selling point in the nineteenth century). In fact, the legislation incorporating the tramway company provided that the carriages might be moved by animal power, and, *with the consent of the Board of Trade*, by steam power. After the claimant had purchased shares in the company, the Board of Trade refused their consent to the use of steam power and the company was wound up. The claimant brought an action of deceit against the directors of the company.

The House of Lords held that the statement was untrue but the directors were not liable for deceit as they honestly believed that the statement was true. It overturned the Court of Appeal's decision which had imposed liability on the basis of negligence, that is, on the finding that the directors had no reasonable ground for the belief.

Damages for fraud

As to damages for fraud, it is now clear since *Doyle* v *Olby (Ironmongers) Ltd* (1969), despite some earlier doubts, that the measure of damages is not the contractual one of putting the claimant in the position as if the representation had been true, but the tortious one of restoring the claimant to the position he would have occupied had the misrepresentation not been made, that is, the extent to which the claimant is worse off as a result of entering the contract in reliance on the misrepresentation.

CROSS REFERENCE

The remoteness test—see Chapter 11 on Damages.

It is also now clear that, as Lord Denning MR had previously indicated in *Doyle* v *Olby (Ironmongers) Ltd*, damages for fraud are not subject to the requirement of being reasonably foreseeable. Thus in *Smith New Court* v *Scrimgeour Vickers* (1996) a very large parcel of shares in Ferranti (not Ferrari!) were purchased at 82 pence per share following a fraudulent misrepresentation from the sellers but the reasonably foreseeable loss as a result of the fraud would normally have been limited to a fall of a few pence per share at the date of their purchase. However, due to a quite unrelated fraud which had been perpetrated on Ferranti by a third party prior to the shares being purchased, the market price of the shares virtually halved in the ensuing months. The House of Lords held that the *Doyle* v *Olby* test meant that the claimants could recover over £10 million in damages as the difference between the price they had paid for the shares and the price (44 pence per share) for which they were eventually able to sell them. This was the loss directly flowing from the fraud which caused them to purchase the shares which, unknown to either party, were 'already pregnant with disaster' because of the as yet undiscovered third-party fraud. That loss was directly caused and the fact that it might not have been reasonably foreseeable did not matter. Damages for fraud are thus assessed on a highly favourable basis to the claimant, partly in order to deter the making of fraudulent statements in the first place. Ironically, as will be seen, there is often now little incentive to prove fraud since the courts appear currently to take the view that the same measure of damages will be available for 'negligent' misrepresentation under s.2(1) of the 1967 Act. Before examining how this has happened, we need to distinguish the two possible bases for awarding damages for negligent misrepresentation.

7.3.3 **Negligent misrepresentation**

The case of *Derry* v *Peek* in 1889 was as significant for its denial of a remedy for negligent misrepresentation as for its definition of fraud and it was not until the 1960s that a general right to damages for negligent misrepresentation was established. When it came there was a certain amount of irony and overkill in that both the courts and Parliament each provided an independent right at about the same time.

The common law right

The House of Lords in *Hedley Byrne & Co. Ltd* v *Heller & Partners Ltd* (1964) recognized a right to damages for negligent misstatements where there was a special relationship between the parties. It was not immediately clear whether this would be applicable to pre-contractual statements by one party to another but it became clear from *Esso Petroleum Co.* v *Mardon* that it can be so applicable. It does not follow that a negligent misrepresentation inducing a contract would always give rise to liability under *Hedley Byrne* for in each case it has to be established that there is a special relationship between the parties which gives rise to the duty of care. In *Esso* v *Mardon* this was not too difficult given the expertise of the oil company as compared with the inexperienced Mr Mardon but in *Howard Marine & Dredging Co. Ltd* v *Ogden & Sons (Excavations) Ltd* (1978) all three members of the Court of Appeal expressed different views as to whether there was a special relationship. Shaw J thought there was, Lord Denning MR thought there was not and Bridge LJ was undecided. However, as this case itself illustrates, the question is no longer likely to be a crucial one since the claimants are now much more likely to rely on the more favourable right given by the Misrepresentation Act 1967.

Section 2(1): the statutory right

The Misrepresentation Act 1967 was based on the tenth report of the Law Reform Committee (Cmnd. 1782) published in 1962, that is, before *Hedley Byrne* was decided in 1963, and so quite naturally included a provision, s.2(1), to remove the long-standing lack of a remedy for negligent misrepresentation. It is rather ironic that Parliament acted so swiftly (in the Directors Liability Act 1890) to undo the narrow effects of *Derry* v *Peek* on fraud but left its more general influence to distort the law for seven decades and only provided a more general remedy for negligence three years after the House of Lords had itself at last recognized liability for negligent statements at common law.

Whatever lessons you wish to draw from that, the fact remains that s.2(1) is the important provision today as far as damages for misrepresentation are concerned, largely because the claimant essentially has only to prove that he has entered into a contract as a result of a misrepresentation by the other party, that is, he has to prove no more than he would for even innocent misrepresentation. The burden then passes to the representor to show that he had reasonable grounds for believing and did believe up to the time the contract was made that the facts represented were true and if he fails to do so he is liable in damages 'notwithstanding that the misrepresentation was not made fraudulently' provided that he would have been liable 'had the misrepresentation been made fraudulently.'

It is unfortunate that such an important provision should be expressed in such convoluted language, even more so because it has led to some rather odd applications of the section, but one thing is clear: the section is a much easier right to rely on than either common law negligence or fraud. This is amply illustrated by *Howard Marine & Dredging* v *Ogden & Sons (Excavations)* where the representors were held not to have discharged the burden of showing that they had reasonable grounds even though they had relied on a figure in the shipping world's bible, Lloyd's Register, for the capacity of the barges. They had also seen the true figure in the original shipping documents and had not shown that they had an 'objectively reasonable ground to disregard the figure in the ship's documents and to prefer the Lloyd's Register figure' (Bridge LJ).

THINKING POINT

Think about the example at the beginning of this chapter and about whether Jules could reasonably rely on what he had read on Blurred's website or whether perhaps he should have known from the festival's own website that they were not performing.

Given the burden on the representor and the difficulty of discharging it, the only advantage that *Hedley Byrne* liability might have over s.2(1) (assuming that a contract with the representor has resulted) is that *Hedley Byrne* is not limited to statements of fact but can cover negligent advice or opinions. However, where an opinion is given negligently there is usually an implied misrepresentation of fact that the opinion is based on reasonable grounds so that is no real problem (although it might lead to the defendant trying to show under s.2(1) that he had reasonable grounds to believe that he had reasonable grounds on which to base his opinions).

7.3.4 The fiction of fraud

Students, and, as will be seen, the courts, sometimes get confused by the reference to fraud in s.2(1) and the best course initially is to read the section by excluding the references to fraud and reading the words 'so liable' as 'liable in damages.' The reference to fraud was probably originally only put in to make it clear that the basic requirements of liability for misrepresentation, which are also requirements of deceit, such as a statement of fact, reliance, and so on, have to be satisfied, although it was admittedly an obscure way of doing this and it perhaps also shows how deeply ingrained the notion that damages were only available for fraudulent misrepresentation was until the 1960s. Thus modified the subsection would read as follows:

STATUTE

Modified text of s.2(1) Misrepresentation Act 1967

Where a person has entered into a contract after a misrepresentation has been made to him by another party and as a result thereof he has suffered loss, then the person making the misrepresentation shall be liable in damages unless he proves that he had reasonable grounds to believe and did believe up to the time the contract was made that the facts represented were true.

Whilst this amended version of the subsection is still not exactly child's play, we think you will agree that it is rather easier to understand. However, the courts have not been content to ignore the fiction of fraud in this way and it has had a curious effect on the way in which damages have sometimes been measured under the subsection. It is now agreed on all sides that the section does not impose liability for damages on a contractual (expectation) basis, that is, as though the misrepresentation had been true, but on a tortious (reliance) basis, as though the misrepresentation had not been made. If it were otherwise, there would be very little, although admittedly still some, point in distinguishing terms and representations and you would be treating someone who has merely misled you on a matter of present fact as though they had actually promised you something.

LINK TO . . .

Terms of the contract (Chapter 5)

Think back to the distinction between terms and representations—what was the crucial difference? If you are struggling, think about which one gives a right to damages for breach of contract. If s.2(1) gave a right to contractual damages when a false representation had been made there would be virtually no difference between a representation and a term of the contract because both would give a right to contractual expectation damages.

That the appropriate measure is a tortious one was finally unequivocally acknowledged in *Royscot Trust Ltd* v *Rogerson* (1991). In reaching this desirable conclusion, however, the Court of Appeal, in the view of many commentators, went further than was warranted in giving effect to the fiction of fraud in s.2(1). The court in *Royscot* held that the same test of remoteness applied as was laid down in *Doyle* v *Olby* (1969) for the tort of deceit, that is, all the loss directly flowing from the fraudulent inducement with no limitation as to foreseeability. Since the Court of Appeal in *Royscot* took the view that the damages were in fact foreseeable anyway, their view about the applicability of the deceit remoteness rule could perhaps be regarded as *obiter*. Indeed, in *Smith New Court* v *Scrimgeour Vickers* (1996), the House of Lords, whilst confirming the special remoteness rule for deceit, pointedly declined to express a view on the correctness of *Royscot* in this respect. (Interestingly, the deceit remoteness rule certainly does not apply to the new 'right to damages' in consumer contracts—see the new regulation 27J(4) inserted in 2014 into the Consumer Protection from Unfair Trading Regulations 2008. It should be noted that where the newly amended Regulations apply, the rights to 'redress' given by them to consumers replace any claim to damages under s.2(1) or s.2(2) of the Misrepresentation Act 1967, as a result of the insertion of a new s.2(4) into the 1967 Act.)

The deceit rule

It is worth investigating the way the courts apply the deceit rule (whether under s.2(1) or for fraud) since there is a danger that if some of the more recent cases are misunderstood, the unjustifiable recovery of expectation losses will be reintroduced into the law of misrepresentation. The key to understanding these cases is to appreciate that damages for 'loss of profits' do not always represent loss of expectation and that they can sometimes quite properly be recovered under the tortious reliance measure.

Thus in *East* v *Maurer* (1991) the claimants recovered (in a fraud case) £10,000 lost profits that they could have earned by investing in a different hairdressing business and not the £15,000 that the trial judge had found they would have earned from this business if the defendant's representation had been true. They were entitled not to the profits that they expected under this contract but the profits from some other contract which they had lost the opportunity to enter in reliance on the defendant's representation which led them into this contract.

East v *Maurer* was quite rightly distinguished in the case of *Davis* v *Churchward* (1994) (but see the criticism in (1994) 110 LQR 35 by Chandler) where the evidence was that even if the claimant had invested in an alternative business, there would still have been no profits and so no lost profits were awarded by the Court of Appeal. With respect to the criticism by Chandler, this seems correct in principle and to hold otherwise on these facts would be to reintroduce recovery for loss of expectation for deceit, a course firmly rejected by *Doyle* v *Olby* in the first place.

Lost profits caused by reliance on a misrepresentation were however correctly awarded in *Clef Aquitaine* v *Laporte Materials (Barrow) Ltd* (2001) since they were the extra profits on the contract which would have been made if the claimant had not been induced by the fraud to enter the contract on less favourable terms.

Another pair of interesting cases relate to whether the claimant is limited to the difference in value at the date of entering the contract in reliance on the misrepresentation or whether the claimant can recover for the further significant depreciation of the property purchased due to other causes or events not themselves directly caused by the defendant's misrepresentation. In *Naughton* v *O'Callaghan* (1990), the claimant was allowed to recover (under s.2(1)) the further drop in value of a racehorse due to it being unplaced in all six races it ran in the two years after purchase. A similar result was reached ultimately by the House of Lords in *Smith New Court* v *Scrimgeour Vickers* (1996) (see section 7.3.2) where the claimants recovered (in an action for fraud) not merely the losses based on the open market value at the date of the purchase of the shares but also substantial further losses which became evident when further facts about the shares subsequently emerged which had not affected the valuation of the shares at the date of purchase. Part of the justification may lie in the fact that, as Waller J noted in the first case, '[the horse] was not a commodity . . . which it would be expected the defendants would go out and sell.' In the second case, the subject matter, shares, was such a commodity but the large number of shares purchased and the reason for purchasing them precluded early disposal without adversely affecting the price.

7.3.5 **Contractual damages where the misrepresentation is also a term**

Before concluding this survey of the different rights to damages, it should be remembered that there is one more potential right to damages which is easily overlooked—damages for breach of contract. That, of course, is not damages for misrepresentation as such, it is damages for breach of a term, but a statement can be both a representation and a term—the representor can both state something as a fact which the other party relies on (a misrepresentation) and also promise in the contract that the statement is true (a term), that is, promise to put the other party in as good a position as if it were true. In such a situation, the representee may be entitled to choose whether to claim damages for breach of contract (to which it will not normally be a defence to show that the representor had reasonable grounds for thinking the statement was true) or to claim damages for misrepresentation (where it will be a defence under s.2(1) to show the statement was based on reasonable grounds). However, see *Leofelis SA* v *Lonsdale Sports Ltd* (2009) where Lloyd LJ (at para. [141]) cast doubt on whether s.2(1) is available in circumstances where a representation has not been made in advance of the contract. He considered (*obiter dicta*) that the representee cannot say that he 'has entered into a contract *after* a misrepresentation has been made to him' (emphasis added) as required by s.2(1) if the representation is not made until the moment when the contract comes into being. Of course, the representee may be able to demonstrate that the representation was made in the course of pre-contractual negotiations and then incorporated into the contract, in which case s.2(1) may apply.

Given the possible defence under s.2(1), and the fact that contractual damages will be higher if the bargain would have been a good one had the statement been true, contractual damages will often be preferable. If, however, the bargain is a bad one (even had the misrepresentation been true) the representee would more likely want to rescind and/or claim damages for misrepresentation, especially if there are extensive consequential losses which may not have been foreseeable but which are recoverable under the fiction of fraud. (Note that a representee cannot both rescind for misrepresentation and claim damages for breach—that would be ridiculous because rescission involves unwinding the contract; there would be no terms to breach—and that if the representee both rescinds and also claims damages for misrepresentation the damages will be reduced to take account of the fact that the contract has been rescinded.)

CASE CLOSE-UP

***MDW Holdings* v *Norvill* (2022)**

In *MDW Holdings* v *Norvill* (2022), it appears that MDW had entered a marginally bad bargain in that it had paid £3.58 million for all the shares in a business that would only have been worth £3.34 million even if the warranties and representations had been true. Due to the falsified matters, the bargain was rather worse, the actual value of the business when transferred being £2.95 million. The trial judge awarded damages for breach of contract—that is, the difference between the £3.34 million if the statements had been true and the £2.95 million value actually received—just under £400,000. The Court of Appeal allowed a cross appeal to the effect that MDW could instead claim damages for fraudulent misrepresentation—that is, on a tortious rather than a contractual basis. Prima facie this would be the extent to which they were worse of as a result of the fraud—the difference between what they had paid (£3.58 million) and what they had received (shares worth only £2.95 million)—approximately £625,000. However, rather surprisingly given the limited evidence, the Court of Appeal then investigated the question of whether if the misrepresentations had not been made, MDW would still have bought the shares, but at a reduced price. The tortious damages would then also be less as they would be the difference between the purchase price actually paid and the price which they would have paid (which it was assumed would have been greater than the £2.95 million value actually received). The matter was remitted to the trial judge to decide whether MDW, if it had known the truth, would not have bought at all (still thus entitling them to £625,000) or would merely have bought at a lower price. If the lower price had been, for example, £3.08 million, the damages would then have been the lesser sum represented by the difference between the price actually paid (£3.58 million) and this lower price of £3.08 million—that is, £500,000. This enquiry does seem rather hypothetical and to be unnecessary in the absence of any strong evidence of what MDW would have done if it had known the truth. The fact is that they did in fact enter the contract and the fraudulent statements were a reason for so doing, and they paid a sum which was £625,000 more than the value received and suffered that loss as a result (compare *Clef Aquitane* v *Laporte Materials* (see section 7.3.4 above) where the transaction entered into did not itself involve a loss, which is why the claimants successfully sought in the alternative the amount that they said had paid in excess of what they would have paid had they known the truth). *MDW* illustrates nicely the basic difference between contractual damages and the prima facie measure for tortious damages for fraud but may be thought to have raised an unnecessary complication (in a case where, unlike *Clef Aquitane*, there was clearly a loss on conventional principles) by asking a hypothetical question (which might reduce the damages) about the price that might have been paid if they had still chosen to enter the contract even if the truth had been known.

7.3.6 **Exclusion of liability**

We have already seen in Chapter 6 that the courts, even at common law, would not allow a person to exclude their own individual liability for fraudulent misrepresentation (*S. Pearson & Son Ltd* v *Dublin Corp.* (1907)) and that it would take exceptionally clear words to exclude such liability for an employee or agent. The **contra proferentem** approach would also no doubt apply to a clause which excluded liability for negligent misrepresentation but well-drafted broad clauses excluding such liability could be effective at common law even if they operated unfairly.

contra proferentem
'Against the person proffering it, or putting it forward' and the exemption clause will be interpreted against the person seeking to rely on it so as to exclude their liability.

The matter was addressed in s.3 of the Misrepresentation Act 1967, as substituted by s.8 of the Unfair Contract Terms Act (UCTA) 1977.

STATUTE

Misrepresentation Act 1967, s.3

If a contract contains a term which would exclude or restrict:

- any liability to which a party to a contract may be subject by reason of any misrepresentation made by him before the contract was made; or
- any remedy available to another party to the contract by reason of such a misrepresentation,

that term shall be of no effect except in so far as it satisfies the requirement of reasonableness as stated in section 11(1) of the Unfair Contract Terms Act 1977; and it is for those claiming that the term satisfies the requirement to show that it does.

Section 3 applies the reasonableness test in UCTA 1977 to clauses excluding or restricting liabilities or remedies for misrepresentation. It was effective in *Walker* v *Boyle* (1982) to invalidate an exclusion clause relating to a contract for the sale of land where the vendor had honestly but without reasonable grounds misrepresented, in response to pre-contract inquiries, that there were no boundary disputes and had sought to rely on a standard condition purporting to prevent annulment (i.e. rescission) of the contract on the basis of such answers to inquiries. Similarly, in *Cleaver* v *Schyde Investments* (2011) the Court of Appeal held that a standard condition, endorsed by the Law Society, which would have restricted the availability of rescission for misrepresentation to cases of fraud or recklessness, could legitimately be regarded on the facts as not fair and reasonable by the trial judge, even though the Court of Appeal would not necessarily have come to the same conclusion themselves. The case underlines the limited role that appellate courts have in reviewing the decisions of trial judges as to reasonableness (see the discussion of *Waldron-Kelly* v *BRB* and related cases in Chapter 6, section 6.5.4).

The question has also arisen, just as with exclusion clauses generally, whether a clause should be invalidated simply because of its potential unreasonable width or whether one should focus on the actual impact of the clause on the facts. One would expect the former to be the correct answer in the light of *Stewart Gill* v *Horatio Myer* (1992) (see Chapter 6, section 6.5.4) and indeed this was the approach taken in *Thomas Witter* v *TPB Industries* (1996), where the term was capable on its wording of covering fraud and so would have been unreasonable had it been necessary to decide the question. However, in *Zanzibar* v *BAE* (2000) a different view was taken by the Deputy High Court judge, who thought that a clause should not be construed as potentially covering fraud since it was well established that there could be no exclusion of such liability and therefore the clause should not fail simply because it theoretically might seem to cover fraud.

Entire agreement clauses

The other question which has arisen is whether an **entire agreement clause** which includes a statement that one party places no reliance on representations of the other can prevent liability for misrepresentation arising in the first place. In *Watford Electronics* v *Sanderson* (2001) the Court of Appeal decided that it could, through the operation of an estoppel, provided that certain conditions were fulfilled, including that the person relying on the non-reliance clause actually believed that the other party was not relying on any representations. In such an exceptional case it would seem that the only thing on which reliance is placed by either party is the assertion that no reliance is placed on anything else!

CROSS REFERENCE

See Chapter 4 on Consideration for the meaning of estoppel.

entire agreement and non-reliance clauses This type of clause may appear to prevent one of the basic requirements for establishing a misrepresentation (inducement) from ever arising by stating that the parties have not relied upon any representations. More generally, the clause says that the entire agreement is contained in the written contract and all previous negotiations do not form part of the agreement (are not terms) and the 'no reliance' part is added to ensure that these non-terms cannot form misrepresentations.

If such a clause is in principle capable of preventing liability for misrepresentation arising (because the claimant is estopped from asserting that the misrepresentation has been relied on) can the clause be held to be unreasonable under s.3 Misrepresentation Act 1967? Chadwick LJ in *Watford Electronics* thought not because s.3 only refers literally to clauses excluding or restricting any liability or any remedy and not to those which prevent the liability arising in the first place. The persuasive counter-view to this is that the courts should look at the substance of the matter and treat such clauses as within s.3, which after all does not automatically invalidate the clause but simply subjects it to a test of reasonableness, and this was the pragmatic view taken by the judge in the *Zanzibar* v *BAE* case discussed earlier. This latter approach has now been confirmed in the Court of Appeal in *First Tower Trustees* v *CDS* (2018) where a written misrepresentation, in response to enquiries before contract leading to a lease, was false in that it did not disclose the asbestos contamination which had recently been discovered. The non-reliance clause purported to remove liability (£1.4 million) for misrepresentation (under s.2(1) of the 1967 Act) which would otherwise arise and was therefore subject to control under s.3 of the Act. Applying the Act, the clause was unreasonable partly because it would completely undermine the important aspect of conveyancing represented by the process of making enquiries before contract to which formal written responses are made by solicitors. By way of contrast, the Court thought that a different term, in the contract for the lease rather than in the lease itself, which only stated that no reliance was made on *oral* statements, would be effective and was reasonable partly because the limitation to oral statements left open the possibility, in relation to matters which were of real importance, of using the enquiries before contract procedure to obtain written statements which would give rise to liability which would not be excluded.

THINKING POINT

Whilst the *First Tower Trustees* case clarifies that non-reliance clauses are subject to the test of reasonableness under the Act, does the decision itself create any problems in terms of certainty or predictability as to the effect of such clauses in individual contracts (see the different conclusions as to the two clauses considered) or is that simply an inevitable result of the nature of the statutory test created?

Digging deeper

The wider rights to damages now available for misrepresentation, especially the one under s.2(1) of the 1967 Act, mean that in many cases there is no longer such a significant difference between a statement being a term of the contract with a remedy in damages for breach of contract and the statement being a misrepresentation with a remedy under s.2(1). This is most obviously true where the misrepresentor cannot show reasonable grounds for believing the statement to be true, as is illustrated by *Howard Marine* v *Ogden* (see earlier) where the claim in contract failed but the claim under s.2(1) succeeded. However, as has been stressed throughout this chapter, the measure of damages for misrepresentation is different from the measure for breach of contract and, although this may not make much difference in some cases, the difference in other cases can be considerable. So the difference between terms and representations is still significant in English law. The significance of this distinction can be seen by contrasting it with the situation that has developed in New Zealand following the Contractual Remedies Act of 1979, which effectively demolished the distinction by providing in s.6 as follows:

> If a party to a contract has been induced to enter into it by a misrepresentation, whether innocent or fraudulent, made to him by or on behalf of another party to that contract—
>
> a) he shall be entitled to damages from that other party in the same manner and to the same extent as if the representation were a term of the contract that has been broken; and
>
> b) he shall not, in the case of a fraudulent misrepresentation, or of an innocent misrepresentation made negligently, be entitled to damages from that other party for deceit or negligence in respect of that misrepresentation.

The section (which is now to be found with minor amendments in New Zealand's Contract and Commercial Law Act 2017) appears to have been literally interpreted so that not only are damages automatically available for even an innocent misrepresentation but the same measure of damages ('to the same extent') is given as if there were a breach of contract. A stark illustration of this can be seen in *Marlborough District Council* v *Antimarloch Joint Venture* [2012] NZSC 11, which concerned a misrepresentation about water rights by the sellers of a vineyard which as a result was worth $125,000 less than the purchase price (the normal reliance measure in English law for misrepresentation). The New Zealand Supreme Court however awarded not only the contractual measure (in accordance with s.6) but upheld, by a majority, not merely the typical contractual award of the difference ($400,000) between the value of the property as transferred and its value as represented (the lost bargain) but instead, the award of the 'cost of cure' of over $1 million dollars on the basis of the cost to the purchaser of building a dam to provide the shortfall of water. You may think that this was rather excessive, especially as the purchaser had admitted in evidence that if he had known about the misrepresentation he would have either not entered the contract or would have negotiated a lower price (e.g. the $125,000 by which the vineyard's value was lower than the purchase price due to the absence of water rights). The distinction between representations and terms in English law means that a very different outcome and much more limited damages ($125,000) would be awarded here (probably under s.2(1)). If it was a term of the contract, in contrast, that is if the seller had not only represented as a fact that the vineyard had water rights but had also contractually promised those rights, he would, even in English law, have had to put the purchaser in the position he would have been in if the promise had been fulfilled, that is, give him the $400,000 extra that the property would have been worth with water rights. As to whether the purchaser would be entitled to the even higher amount of the cost of cure in English law, see the discussion in Chapter 11, section 11.3.1.

Summary

Misrepresentation is a statement of fact which induces the contract and operates in the borderlands of contract and tort, allowing the contract to be rescinded and (if there has been fault) giving rise to damages under tort and statute.

1. Basic ingredients

A False Statement. Non-disclosure does not normally amount to a misrepresentation, except in contracts *uberrimae fidei* such as insurance contracts, or where a party is under a duty to inform the other party of a change in circumstances, or where a statement is misleading in the light of the information withheld.

A Statement of Fact. Statements of opinion, intention or (traditionally) law are not misrepresentations. Such statements often impliedly make false statements of fact (which do amount to misrepresentations), for example that there are reasonable grounds supporting the opinion, or that the opinion or intention is genuinely held, or that the statement about the law is genuinely believed in or is based on reasonable grounds.

Inducement. The other party must rely on the false statement communicated to them. The misrepresentation need not be the sole cause of the other party entering the contract, but it must be a cause.

2. Remedies for misrepresentation

The restitutionary remedy of rescission is in principle available for all types of misrepresentations (innocent, negligent and fraudulent) and unwinds the contract by restoring each party to the position they were in before the contract.

Rescission may be lost where one of the four bars to rescission applies:

a) where restitution is impossible;
b) where a third party has acquired rights to the property which has passed under the contract;
c) where there has been affirmation of the contract; and
d) where there has been an excessive lapse of time making it inequitable to order rescission.

The court has discretion to award damages in place of rescission under s.2(2) of the Misrepresentation 1967 Act if rescission may be too drastic a remedy (but only if the remedy of rescission has not already been lost).

3. Damages

Damages for fraudulent misrepresentation are awarded under the tort of deceit and are tortious and not contractual. All losses directly flowing from the fraud are recoverable with no remoteness limitation in terms of reasonable foreseeability.

Damages for negligent misrepresentation or advice under the *Hedley Byrne* principle may be awarded where the claimant proves a special relationship and breach of the duty of care.

Damages for negligent misrepresentation may also be awarded under s.2(1) of the 1967 Act, which is highly advantageous since the burden of proof is on the defendant to show reasonable grounds for the defendant's belief rather than on the claimant to prove negligence.

The fiction of fraud in s.2(1) has been interpreted literally so that damages are tortious rather than contractual and all loss caused by the misrepresentation (no matter how remote) is recoverable.

Contractual damages may also be awarded if there is a contractual promise that the facts represented are true.

4. Exclusion of liability for misrepresentation

The courts will not allow a person to exclude liability for their own fraud and s.3 of the 1967 Act applies the UCTA test of reasonableness to clauses purporting to exclude any liability or remedy for misrepresentation (even if only negligent or innocent).

Although an entire agreement clause containing a 'no reliance' provision may in principle prevent claimants from asserting that they relied upon the representation and thus appear to prevent any liability arising, it is now clear that such a clause is subject to control under s.3 and will not succeed if it is not reasonable.

? Questions

- 'The remedies for misrepresentation have now improved so much that the distinction between terms and representations has effectively been broken down.' Discuss.
- Does the case law culminating in *Spice Girls* v *Aprilia* show that although there is no general duty to disclose, there is a duty not to mislead?
- 'Rescission is a potentially powerful remedy but it is full of holes.' Discuss.
- Have the courts been rather too gullible in their reading of the 'fiction of fraud'?
- Ann is considering buying a burglar alarm system (for her costume jewellery business) from Bert, who tells her that it still operates even if the mains electricity supply is cut off. Bert genuinely believes this to be true and a week later Ann signs a contract for Bert's company to install the system, which makes no mention of what would happen if the electricity supply fails. During that week Bert discovers that the system will not operate during a power cut but, having forgotten that he ever discussed the matter with Ann, doesn't say anything more about it. Having paid £800 for the system, Ann's shop is burgled two weeks later during a power cut and £5,000 worth of jewellery is stolen. There are other systems on the market which are not dependent on the mains supply but all cost over £1,200. Advise Ann.

Further reading

Books

Chen-Wishart, M, *Contract Law*, 7th edn (Oxford University Press, 2022) ch 5.

McKendrick, E, *Contract Law: Text, Cases and Materials*, 1qth edn (Oxford University Press, 2024) ch 17.

O'Sullivan, J, and Hilliard, J, *The Law of Contract*, 11th edn (Oxford University Press, 2024) ch 9.

Articles

Atiyah, PS, and Treitel, GH, 'Misrepresentation Act 1967' (1967) 30 MLR 369.

Beale, H, 'Damages in lieu of rescission for misrepresentation' (1995) 111 LQR 60.

Chandler, PA, 'Fraud: Damages and opportunity costs' (1994) 110 LQR 35.

Hooley, R, 'Damages and the Misrepresentation Act 1967' (1991) 107 LQR 547.

Peel, WE, 'Reasonable exemption clauses' (2001) 117 LQR 545.

Taylor, RD, 'Expectation, reliance and misrepresentation' (1982) 45 MLR 139.

PART III

DEFECTS

The previous two parts of this book have looked at how a contract is created (Part I) and exactly *what* is created (Part II). This Part deals with any defects in the contract and how these may affect the validity of the contract.

There are essentially two types of defects: substantive defects, where one party alleges that the *resulting contract* is substantively unfair; and procedural defects, where one party alleges that the *process of contracting* was unfair. You will see that the courts rarely act (at least explicitly) on the ground that the contract is substantively unfair, but they will often find that a contract is affected by procedural defects. We saw in Chapter 7, 'Misrepresentation', that false statements made in the run-up to contracting may make that contract voidable and allow the other party to rescind the contract. In Chapter 8, we will look at when a mistake (especially one which the other party takes advantage of) will make a contract void or voidable and how the doctrine of mistake overlaps with other areas of contract law. Chapter 9 deals with two types of procedural defect: firstly, where there is too much pressure in the run-up to contracting (duress); and secondly, where there is too much influence in the run-up to contracting (undue influence). Chapter 9 also looks at when the courts will set aside a substantively unfair contract as an unconscionable bargain.

8 Mistake

> **LEARNING OBJECTIVES**
>
> **This chapter will help you to:**
>
> - distinguish between communication mistakes and common mistakes of fact;
> - understand how the courts adapt the objective approach to agreement when one party mistakenly fails to communicate their subjective intention;
> - understand how the courts apply the doctrine of mistake and misrepresentation in the most common type of identity fraud cases; and
> - recognize when a contract may be void for a shared fundamental mistake of fact.

Introduction

We would like to write that a party is not bound by their agreement if they acted under a mistake, or that there is a consistent doctrine of mistake in the law of contract, or that this is the only chapter you will ever need to read in order to answer a question on mistake. But the truth is much more complicated, and requires a reappraisal of many of the topics already covered. The advantage to you, a student preparing for exams, is that this is an area of law in which very high marks can be obtained. To get those marks you must keep an open mind and try to follow the links to previous chapters. You must focus on the facts of each case and the practical issues they raise rather than how they have been labelled.

8.1 Communication mistakes and mistakes of fact

The cases fall into two broad types: firstly, those where one or both of the parties made a mistake in communicating with each other; and secondly, those where the parties successfully communicated their intentions but did so under a common mistake of fact. An example of the first type of mistake is where communication failure meant that a buyer thought they were buying *old* (therefore better quality) oats but the seller said the contract was for *new* (less valuable) oats (*Smith* v *Hughes* (1871)). Another type of example is where the seller thought that it was selling to a knight of the realm when in fact the other party was a rogue posing as the knight (*Phillips* v *Brooks* (1919)). There was a failure of communication because the seller misunderstood to *whom* the sale was being made, rather than *what* was being sold (as in the first example). These cases are often called 'unilateral mistake' cases because A has made a mistake about the intentions or identity of B. If B is unaware of the mistake made by A, the case is sometimes described as one of 'mutual mistake' since both parties are mistaken about each other's intentions—they are at cross purposes. The old case of *Raffles* v *Wichelhaus* (1864) is the classic example, where the alleged contract related to the cargo of a ship called *Peerless* but there were two ships of that name, one sailing in October and one in December, and each party had in mind a different ship. The expression 'mutual mistake' is however probably best avoided since it is used by different writers in different ways and is sometimes applied misleadingly to the type of case discussed next.

By contrast with communication mistakes, an example of the second type of case is where one ship, *The Great Peace*, was chartered by a salvage company in order to rescue a sinking ship called *The Great Providence*, but both parties shared a common mistake about the relative positions of the two ships and thought they were much closer together than they had supposed. When the truth was learned the salvage company chartered another ship which was much closer and argued that the common mistake about the position of *The Great Peace* meant there was no contract. There was no communication error because both parties successfully conveyed their intention that *The Great Peace* should help to rescue the sinking ship with no confusion over identity—they both intended the same thing and that the same ship, *The Great Peace*, should be the subject matter of the contract. Their mistake was a shared mistake regarding a quality of the subject matter of their agreement—in this case the ship's nautical location. Both parties made exactly the same mistake, they were both of the same (mistaken) mind, not at cross purposes to one another, the same mistake was therefore common to them both and thus these cases are usually and helpfully known as 'common mistake' cases. The distinction between communication mistakes and common mistake of fact cases is illustrated in Figure 8.1.

8.1.1 **Effects of a mistake**

Now that you know broadly what types of mistake you might be looking at, we will take a brief look at the various consequences that can stem from the discovery of such a mistake. It is important to understand however that the effects of a mistake do not simply follow from whether it is classified on the one hand as a communication mistake (whether or not unilateral) or, on the other hand, as a common mistake of fact. These distinctions are merely the starting point and further analysis is necessary in each type of case to decide whether the mistake is 'operative' in the sense that it affects the validity of the contract (in many cases it will not have such an effect).

Communication mistakes

The courts could decide to do nothing about a party who fails to communicate properly with the other party; they could bind them to what they appeared to say, rather than what they meant to say. Alternatively, the courts could hold that a party should not be bound unless their intentions have been properly communicated to the other party.

Figure 8.1 Communication mistakes and (common) mistakes of fact

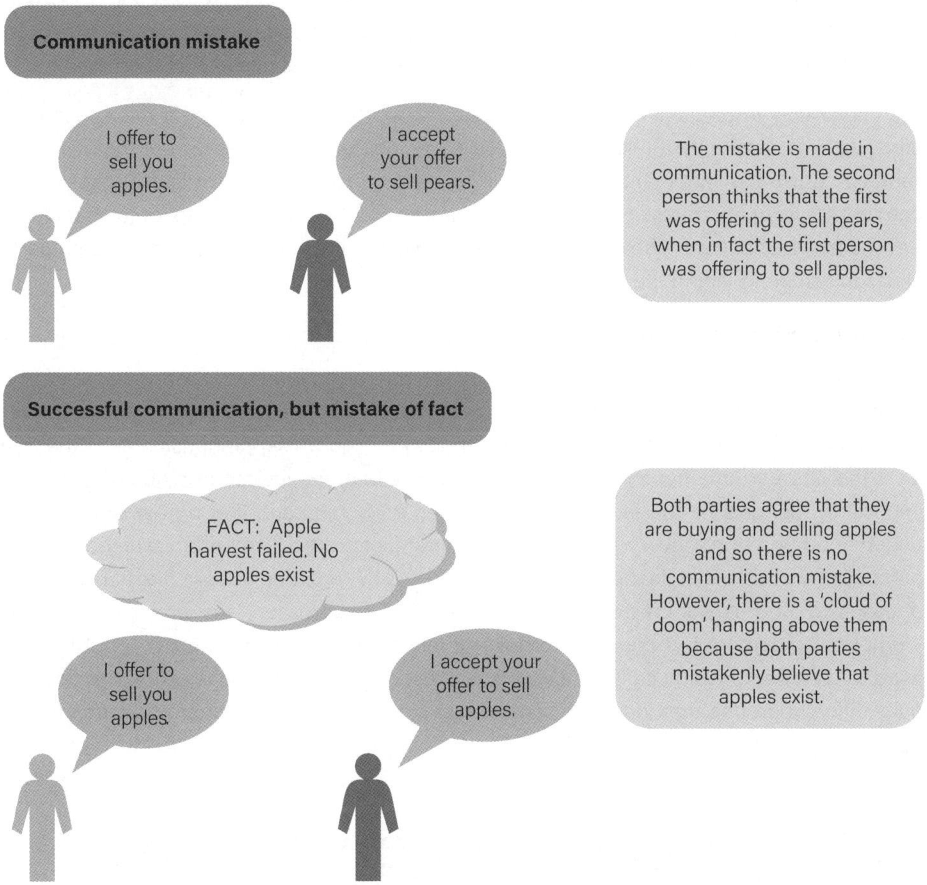

LINK TO . . .

Agreement (Chapter 2)

You may recognize the policy decision facing the courts and you should remember that the courts decided to take an objective approach to agreement and hold parties to what they appeared to say rather than what they actually meant to say; that is, the fact that A mistakenly failed to communicate A's subjective intention to the other party is irrelevant—A is bound by what A actually said.

We shall see later that there are certain (limited) circumstances where the courts will refuse to enforce the objective agreement when it diverges from a party's subjective intention and we can say that there is no agreement or (which amounts to the same thing) that the contract is **void**.

voidable contracts Voidable contracts are best thought of as valid but damaged contracts; the courts have decided that there is a defect in the contract and so the claimant is given the option to rescind the contract or alternatively to affirm it and carry on as normal.

void contracts Void contracts are not contracts at all: they have never amounted to a contract and they never will. 'Void' is a label used by the court to signify that the issue of whether there was a contract was in dispute but, on the facts, there was no contract.

If the contract is not void, it may nevertheless be voidable, that is, valid until one party avoids (nullifies) it, although this is now, after the decision in *The Great Peace* (see section 8.4.2), only going to be the case as a result of other doctrines such as misrepresentation (where the misrepresentation has caused the mistake) rather than as a result of mistake as such.

A contract may in particular be voidable when one party to the agreement has caused the other party's mistake by a misrepresentation (see Chapter 7), whether or not the misrepresentation was fraudulent (although fraud will be present in the unilateral mistake cases where one party is lying about his identity) and the innocent party is given the option of rescinding (rewinding) the contract. The contract is however valid but voidable until the innocent party elects to rescind or affirm the contract.

Common mistakes of fact

The courts could elect to enforce all contracts no matter how many misapprehensions the parties share. However, there is a good argument that in exceptional cases the parties' consent is affected when they both operate under such a major misapprehension as to the true facts that the performance of the essence of the contract as envisaged by both of them is impossible. So, despite the fact that they reached an agreement, that agreement is fatally undermined by the discovery that the fundamental facts relied upon and assumed by both parties were false so that the apparent contract should be regarded as void. The narrow range of cases where this will be the court's interpretation is discussed later under the heading 'Complete agreement but common mistake of fundamental facts' (section 8.4) but first we need to consider in which cases the courts will recognize that there is no agreement on the quite different ground that there is no agreement in the first place because of a communication mistake.

8.2 Communication mistakes

8.2.1 **Nature of a mistake**

When we talk about a person being mistaken in this context, it normally means that person is mistaken about the agreement which it otherwise appears has been made; that is, the objective agreement which that person is claiming should not be enforced because of the mistake.

In order to make sense of this discussion you must realize that 'mistake' is a relative concept. You can only be mistaken in relation to something else, usually the truth (whatever that is). Put simply, if what you believe differs from the truth then you are mistaken, but if what you believe matches up with the truth then you are not mistaken. If the terms of a contract (objectively determined) are in truth X, then you are mistaken if you think that they are Y, or Z, or indeed if you think they are anything but X. The point of all this is to show that the courts must first establish the terms of the apparent objective contract before they can decide if either party made a mistake when communicating their intentions. The courts therefore use the objective terms as a point of reference against which they can compare the subjective intentions of the parties. If you pick up only one point from this chapter, it should be that the question of whether a party has made a communication mistake is tied up in the question: 'What agreement did the parties appear to make?'

Chapter 2 explained that the courts will take an objective view of the parties' intentions in order to discover what the parties agreed. Often the parties will have *meant* to agree to exactly the same thing as they *appeared* to agree; their subjective and objective agreements will be the same. If one party was mistaken—that is, *meant* to agree to something different from the objective terms—then normally the courts will say 'tough—the objective agreement stands' because the whole point of the objective approach is to dispense with the uncertainties created by looking at a party's subjective intentions.

EXAMPLE

Objective agreements and subjective intentions

I have two bikes. One is a mountain bike and the other is a racer. I offer to sell my bike to you and you accept, but refuse to pay me when I deliver my mountain bike to your door, complaining that you intended to buy my racer.

In order to objectively determine whether there was a contract for the sale of a mountain bike (my claim) the court must look at our dealings from the viewpoint of a reasonable man standing in your shoes. Imagine that I advertised my offer in *Mountain Bike Monthly* and the court decides that there was an objective agreement for the sale of my mountain bike, therefore ignoring your subjective intention to buy my racer. In relation to our objective agreement for the sale of a mountain bike, you made a mistake. You thought that you were buying a racer but you were actually buying a mountain bike.

Imagine now that the courts decided that the objective agreement was for the sale of my racer, for example because the advert was in *Racing Bikes Weekly*. You would no longer be mistaken because you subjectively believed that we agreed to the sale of my racer. Instead, I would be the one operating under a mistake because I meant to sell my mountain bike, but objectively agreed to sell my racer, which would then be the agreement that would be enforced.

In these cases there are no grounds for treating the mistake as operative so as to affect the validity of the objective agreement which will be enforced notwithstanding the mistake made by one party.

8.2.2 Mistake known to the other party

If A *knows* that B made a mistake (i.e. that B subjectively intended something different from what B objectively appeared to intend) the courts will not allow A to rely on the objective agreement; A is prevented from 'snapping up' the mistake of the other.

CASE CLOSE-UP

***Hartog* v *Colin & Shields* (1939)**

The sellers offered to sell 30,000 hare skins for various prices per pound of weight, but they actually meant to offer the skins 'per piece' (a piece was about one-third of a pound in weight). Naturally, the buyers were more than happy to pay the asking price and receive a pound of skins instead of just one piece and so they 'snapped up' this offer. Once the sellers realized their mistake, they refused to deliver the skins and the buyer sued for damages, claiming that there was a contract for the sale of the skins at the price 'per pound.'

Singleton J rejected the buyers' claim because they knew that the sellers had made a mistake. Indeed, his judgment suggests that it would have been sufficient to show that the buyers should reasonably have known of the sellers' mistake:

> The offer was wrongly expressed and the defendants [the sellers] by their evidence, and by the correspondence, have satisfied me that the claimant [the buyers] could not reasonably have supposed that the offer contained the offerors' real intention. Indeed, I am satisfied to the contrary. That means that there must be judgment for the defendants [sellers].

When Singleton J said that 'the offer was wrongly expressed' he expressed the view that although the sellers had objectively *appeared* to offer 'per pound' they subjectively *meant* to offer 'per piece.' The objective view was 'overridden' because the buyers should have realized (and he thought that they did actually realize) that the sellers meant something different. As a result, the sellers did not have to honour the objective agreement to sell 'per pound.'

This case has considerable modern-day resonance in terms of the problems that can arise when potentially catastrophic pricing mistakes are made on websites, as is illustrated by the Singapore case of *Chwee Kin Keong* v *Digilandmall* (2004) where the price of laser printers was mistakenly changed to S$66 each from S$3,854 each. The plaintiffs purported to have bought online well over a thousand printers overnight at the lower price but the Singapore courts held both at first instance and on appeal that the streetwise purchasers clearly knew that the price was a mistake and that the defendants did not intend to sell at this ridiculously low price despite the objective intention that the price on the website might in isolation have indicated. Thus there was no contract and the apparent initial objective intention of the vendor is overridden by the subjective real intention since it was clearly known by the other party.

8.2.3 **Mistake caused by the other party**

The objective agreement can also be overridden if one party causes the other to make a mistake, as is illustrated by the following case.

CASE CLOSE-UP

***Scriven Bros & Co.* v *Hindley and Co.* (1913)**

The defendant was sold tow at an auction when he thought he was bidding for hemp ('tow' are the shorter less valuable fibres derived from hemp). The key to this case is the reason *why* the bidder made his mistake (as opposed to *Hartog* where the key was the buyers' *knowledge* of the mistake). The bidder made the wrong bid because the owner of the goods had marked both tow and hemp with the same shipping mark (in order to defraud his bank—a long story, but it was all down to insurance and misleading the insurer over the value of goods carried) and had become confused as to which lots were hemp and which were tow. After the bidder realized his mistake, he refused to pay and the owner of the tow sued for the price. Objectively, there appeared to be an agreement for the sale of tow because it was reasonable to assume that the bidder knew what he was bidding for, i.e. when the bidder made his bid it *appeared* as though he was bidding for the goods being auctioned (tow). The fact that the bidder *meant* to bid for hemp would usually be irrelevant but Lawrence J refused to enforce the objective agreement because the owner had negligently caused the bidder's mistake.

If you read the case report of *Scriven* v *Hindley* then you will notice that Lawrence J did not expressly say there was an objective agreement which was overridden because the owner negligently caused the bidder's mistake. That is not to say that the analysis earlier is not accurate; one has to bear in mind that the case was decided in 1913. Around that time it was still popular to look for matching subjective intentions in order to form an agreement. The objective approach might still prevail if one party could rely upon a 'contract of estoppel' which meant that a party could be estopped (i.e. prevented) from saying what he subjectively intended. Lawrence J therefore first said that the parties were not '*ad idem*' (i.e. their subjective intentions differed) and so there could be no contract on a subjective basis, before addressing the owner's argument that the bidder was estopped (prevented) from saying that he meant to buy hemp and that therefore there was a contract to buy tow. He decided that the bidder could not be estopped when his mistake was caused by the negligence of the owner. Thus Lawrence J started by looking for a subjective agreement (which did not exist) and refused to allow the objective agreement (what he called the contract of estoppel) to override the (lack of) subjective agreement. It is now more common for courts to start with the objective agreement and ask whether it should be overridden by the subjective intentions of a mistaken party.

It is interesting to note that the jury thought that the bidder was also partly at fault because he forgot to take his auction catalogue when he examined the hemp and so did not compare the hemp examined with the lot.

THINKING POINT

How great would the fault of the bidder have to be to prevent him from relying on this form of subjective override?

Another unanswered question revolves around the degree of fault necessary to override the objective approach. Lawrence J decided that the owner could not rely upon the objective agreement because the owner caused the mistake 'by his own negligence'—do you think that this should be the same standard of care as that required in the law of torts?

8.2.4 Mistake must be of the terms of the contract

Not all communication mistakes, even if known to or caused by the fault of the other party, will override an objective agreement. The mistake in communication must relate to a term of the contract, as opposed to just some expectation of quality.

This is a tricky distinction which boils down to whether you think the other party has promised that quality as opposed to it merely being a quality that you had assumed that the subject matter possessed. Of course you are always going to say you thought it was something that was promised as a term of the agreement rather than merely a quality that you had simply assumed to be present. The difficult thing will be persuading the court not only that you thought you had been promised that quality (even though objectively the agreement appears not to have incorporated that as a term) but that the other person knew that you had made this mistake.

EXAMPLE

Mistake as to terms v Mistake as to quality

I offer to sell you my watch and you accept. You thought my watch was a Rolex but I did not know what it was; to me it was just something that sat on my wrist and told me the time.

One scenario is that you were mistaken as to the terms of the agreement (you thought I promised a Rolex) even though objectively the agreement appeared simply to be to sell a watch. A second scenario is that you were mistaken as to the quality of the watch; you knew that I was simply promising to sell you a watch (and not promising to sell a Rolex) but one of the features that made my watch attractive to you was that you thought it was a Rolex.

In the first scenario, provided that I know that you meant to agree to different terms, I could not enforce the objective agreement on the ground that you have made a unilateral mistake as to its terms which is actually known to me (the other party).

In the second scenario, there is no mistake over the terms of the contract, and you are obliged to buy despite your unilateral mistake, even if I am aware of it (an illustration if you like of *caveat emptor*—buyer beware, since I have not misrepresented nor warranted (promised) that it is a Rolex nor is there a mistake as to the terms of the contract).

In *Smith* v *Hughes* (1871) a farmer showed a sample of oats to the agent of a racehorse trainer, who agreed to buy a much larger amount of these oats. The racehorse trainer thought that he was buying old oats (racehorses are obviously a discerning breed and prefer their oats mature) and he refused to pay the price when he received new oats. The farmer denied that any reference had been made to the quality of the oats but the trial judge ruled in favour of the purchaser. The Court of Appeal however ordered a retrial because the judge at first instance did not ensure that the jury understood the important difference between making a finding of fact that there was (a) a mistaken belief by the purchaser that the oats were old; as opposed to (b) a mistaken belief that it was a term of the contract that the oats were old. Only (b), a mistake of the terms of the contract, if known to the farmer, would prevent an agreement arising between the farmer and racehorse trainer in respect of the new oats which appeared to have been sold (and delivered). The difficulty of actually drawing this distinction is amply illustrated by the fact that the trial judge's formulation in terms of whether the defendant (the trainer) thought 'he was contracting for old oats' was held to have fudged this issue and the difficulty of showing that the mistake was actually as to the terms of the contract can also be seen from the scepticism of appellate judges, including Hannen J's observation that 'the defendant bought the oats after two days detention of the sample.'

8.2.5 **The effect of a communication mistake as to terms**

So far in this chapter we have usually concluded, where a mistake has been found to be operative, that the courts refused to enforce a particular contract. This is because in the cases discussed A has simply asked the court to enforce the objective view of the agreement and the court has sometimes overridden the objective agreement by refusing A's request because of the mistake of which A was or should have been aware (or because A was at fault in causing the mistake). In *Hartog* the buyer asked the court for damages when the seller refused to perform the alleged objective agreement to sell 'per pound' and the court answered 'No.' In *Scriven Bros* the owner asked the court for damages when the bidder refused to pay for tow in accordance with the alleged objective agreement for the sale of tow and again the court answered 'No.' In both cases it was enough for the courts to simply refuse the claimant's request to enforce the objective agreement and there was no need to decide whether there was any other valid agreement on different terms.

The situation might have been different in *Hartog* if the *seller* had asked the court to enforce an agreement on the terms that the seller subjectively intended, that is, at a price 'per piece.' Enforcing an agreement on the terms intended by the mistaken party would have to be limited to situations where the other party knew or caused the mistake (otherwise it would simply wipe out the objective approach to agreement) but it is unclear whether the courts will enforce this version of the agreement.

THINKING POINT

Should a buyer who tries to take advantage of a mistake be deemed to consent to an agreement on the terms intended by the mistaken party?

You might argue that a party who knows what the other subjectively intended but who then tries to take advantage of a different objective agreement deserves little sympathy from the law. Set against this, it is clear that the last thing on the 'knowing' party's mind is to contract on the subjective terms of the other party; by trying to snap up the objective agreement, the party implicitly rejects the subjective thoughts of the other party and there is no genuine consent.

You should form your own opinion on whether or when the subjective agreement should override completely, so that the subjective view of the mistaken party forms the basis of an enforceable agreement, or whether (or when) it should only operate defensively so as to prevent enforcement of the alleged objective agreement.

8.2.6 **An alternative approach**

The previous discussion proceeded on the basis that the courts first establish an objective agreement and then make an exception by allowing one party's subjective mistake to override this when the other party knows of the mistake. The reasons for the objective approach (certainty, reliance, etc.) disappear once the subjective intentions of a party are known and there is no need to go with what *appeared* to have been agreed. On the other hand, some commentators have argued that, rather than being subjective exceptions to the objective approach, such cases are actually examples of the objective approach in action (see Endicott, 2000). A reasonable person who knows that the other party meant to quote the price per piece would not conclude that the agreement was one for skins per pound. In other words, the reasonable person can take account of any known subjective intentions of the other party; it is as though the reasonable person is standing not only in the shoes of one party but also with that party's knowledge of the other party's intentions. The important distinction to make is that the reasonable person does NOT automatically possess knowledge of all of the other party's subjective intentions, but the reasonable person DOES possess knowledge of any intentions of the other party *which are known to the party in whose shoes the reasonable person is standing*. The problem with extending the objective approach in this manner is that it begins to look like a subjective test: the more knowledge we attribute to the reasonable person the more the question sounds like: 'What did the parties subjectively agree to?'

Whether you believe that the cases are subjective exceptions to the objective approach or examples of the objective approach itself, they are all asking the question: 'Has an agreement been formed?' This question is usually answered by an objective approach without any need to discuss the subjective intentions of the parties. However, when the subjective intentions of one party are known to the other party the courts can be said to either revert to a subjective approach or incorporate this knowledge into the objective test. The result is the same (see Figure 8.2).

8.3 Mistaken identity

8.3.1 The basic problem

This area of law can become very confusing and so it is probably best to first lay down some basics. The introduction to this chapter introduced you to the distinction between void (non-contracts) and voidable ('damaged' contracts) and understanding this section depends heavily on your ability to understand that distinction.

Cases on mistaken identity generally involve a rogue (sometimes referred to as 'crook,' 'scoundrel,' 'thief,' etc. in the cases) who pretends to be someone else (usually someone rich and respectable) in order to persuade the owner of goods to sell the goods and part with possession. The rogue then sells the goods on to a third party and disappears from sight. When the owner of the goods realizes that there has been fraud, usually when the cheque provided by the rogue bounces, the owner cannot claim from the rogue (because the rogue is broke or has disappeared or both) and so the owner looks to claim from the third party. You might be wondering 'how can the owner claim from the third party—the third party has done nothing wrong?,' but this is where the importance of void and voidable contracts comes into play.

> **title**
> Title has a complex meaning and you are likely to study it in more detail in property or land law. For present purposes, it is sufficient to imagine title as the ultimate and most powerful property rights over goods; whoever holds these property rights is the owner of the goods and can prevent anyone from interfering with his goods.

If the contract between the owner and the rogue is void (i.e. non-existent) then this means that not only did the owner not consent to an agreement with the rogue, but also the owner did not consent to transfer **title** to the goods. The rogue therefore does not acquire title to the goods and, if the rogue has no title to the goods, no title can be transferred to the third party (the rogue cannot pass on what the rogue has never received). The owner can therefore point to the goods in the third party's possession and say 'those are my goods, I am still the legal owner, give them back to me!' (or the owner may claim the value of the goods instead of the actual goods themselves). The third party is obviously upset about giving the goods back or

Figure 8.2 Two approaches to mistake as to terms

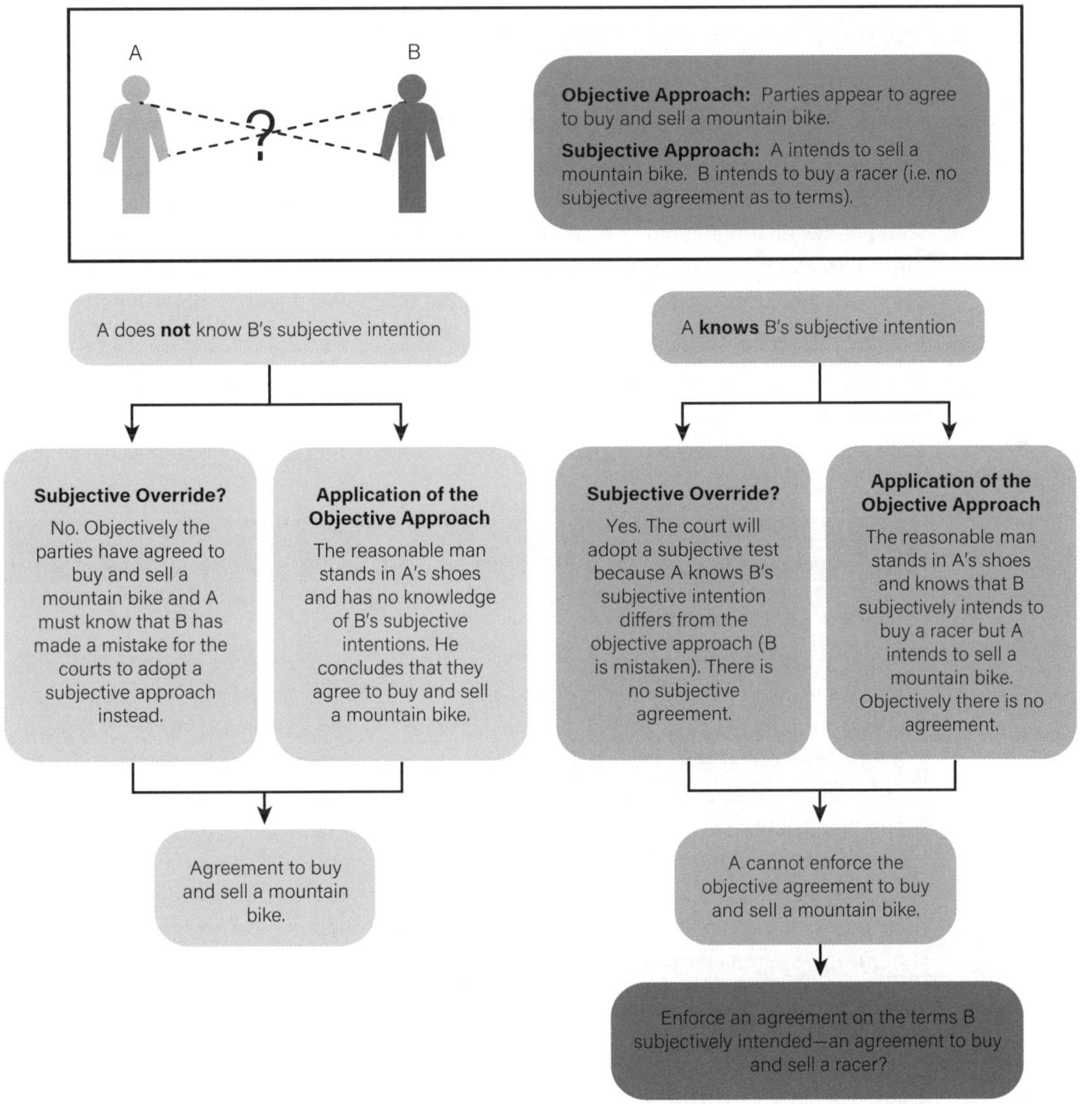

paying for their value because the third party has already paid for them once when giving money to the rogue.

CROSS REFERENCE
See Chapter 7, section 7.3.1, 'Rescission,' on the bars to rescission.

However, if the contract is voidable then the consent of the owner is still intact—damaged, yes, but still intact—and so the owner intends to pass title to the rogue and the rogue acquires title to the goods which the rogue can then pass on to the third party. The important point to remember is that at any time *before* the third party acquires title to the goods, the owner may rescind (rewind) the contract and return the money to the rogue (of course, there is none to return—the rogue has given a false cheque or not returned to pay) in return for the return of title to the goods. The situation is now the same as if the contract had been void from the outset so that the owner (with title now restored) can recover the goods or their value from the third party. The owner must however rescind the voidable contract before the third party acquires title. This point is crucial: any later and rescission will be barred because the third party will have acquired a title to the goods (assuming that the third party acted in good faith, without notice of the fraud on the original owner, and paid consideration). The result will then be that the third party has title to the goods and the original owner bears the loss of the fraud.

8.3.2 When is a contract void for mistaken identity?

The ultimate issue of 'who has title to the goods' can therefore be reduced down to the question: 'Is the contract between the owner and the rogue void for mistake?' If so, the title remains with the owner. If the contract is not void for mistake, then it will be voidable for fraudulent misrepresentation. In this case, the ultimate question is decided according to whether the owner rescinded the contract and reacquired the title before the third party purchased the goods from the rogue.

The case law has tied itself in knots over decades and the House of Lords, by three to two, neglected an opportunity to simplify this area of the law, with the consequence that it continues to be necessary to review the slight and somewhat bewildering distinctions made in the cases.

LINK TO . . .

Misrepresentation (Chapter 7)

In the typical three-party situation, the contract will always be at least voidable for fraudulent misrepresentation because the rogue fraudulently poses as someone respectable in order to induce the owner to enter into the contract. There is therefore a false statement of fact made by one party to the other which induces the other to enter into a contract (the basic definition of a misrepresentation in Chapter 7). But the fact that a contract is voidable is not enough to protect the owner if the rogue acquires the owner's title and passes it on to a third party before the contract is avoided; the contract needs to be void from the start, sometimes called 'void *ab initio*', to prevent the rogue acquiring the title and from having any opportunity to pass it on to an innocent third-party purchaser who will then have a better claim than the first owner. See also section 7.3.1 (b) 'Third-party rights'.

Face-to-face contracts

The easiest situation to deal with is when the parties deal with each other face to face. In such circumstances, the law *presumes* that the owner of the goods intends to contract with the person physically present, that is, the rogue, even though the rogue may use the name of someone else. There is therefore a valid intention to form a contract with the rogue and so the rogue acquires good title to the goods but the owner has the option to rescind the voidable contract by reason of the fraudulent misrepresentation of the rogue.

In *Phillips* v *Brooks Ltd* (1919) the rogue North entered Phillips' jewellery shop and picked out a ring. He wrote a cheque for the amount due and told the seller that he was Sir George Bullough who lived in St James's Square, a respectable part of London where you would expect a creditworthy knight of the realm to live. The shop assistant checked that Sir George's address matched the one just given to him and allowed him to take the jewellery in return for the cheque. North then pawned the ring to Brooks Ltd and the usual dispute between the owner (Phillips) and the third-party purchaser (Brooks Ltd) followed.

Pawning

For present purposes, pawning an item has the same effect as selling it. However, for other purposes, the practice is significantly different from selling an item. A pawnbroker is effectively a banker and lends people money. However, the pawnbroker wants to be sure of being repaid and so takes *security* by insisting that you deposit some valuable goods. If you fail to pay back the loan then the security interest gives the pawnbroker the right to sell your goods. This security interest in your goods is a property right and so it is valid against all the world; even if you are a rogue (surely not, we were getting on so well!) the security interest you transfer to me (the pawnbroker) is capable of defeating the original owner (assuming the contract between you, as rogue, and the owner was only voidable and that the owner has not rescinded it).

Brooks Ltd won because Horridge J decided that Phillips intended to contract with the person in front of him (North, posing as Sir George Bullough). The contract between Phillips and North was voidable due to North's fraudulent misrepresentation but Phillips lost his right to avoid the contract once Brooks Ltd acquired good title to the ring.

In *Ingram* v *Little* (1960) the two Ingram sisters sold their car to a rogue going by the name of Hutchinson. They wanted cash, he wanted to pay by (a worthless) cheque. Before accepting his cheque, they went to the local post office to check the address given by the rogue (as cautious as Mr Phillips in *Phillips* v *Brooks Ltd*) but in this case the court held that this act of caution rebutted the presumption that the sisters intended to contract with the person in front of them. The court presumed that the sisters intended to contract only with the rogue's *alter ego*, Mr Hutchinson, and so the alleged contract between the sisters and the rogue was void and they could claim the value of their car from Little, a third party who had bought the car in good faith from the rogue.

Devlin LJ dissented on the ground that the sisters were only concerned with the rogue's *creditworthiness* and not his precise identity, that is, they wanted to contract with whoever was good for his money and not simply Mr Hutchinson, and so, on his view, there were no grounds for displacing the presumption that the sisters intended to contract with the person in front of them (the rogue).

Attributes and Identity

Some commentators refer to the distinction between mistakes as to *attributes* (e.g. that the rogue is creditworthy) and mistakes as to *identity* (e.g. that the rogue is Mr Hutchinson). However, these are really just labels used to describe situations where the contract will be voidable (attribute mistakes) and those where it will be void (identity mistakes). The real issue is whether the owner *intended* to contract with the rogue (even if it was under the effect of a fraudulent misrepresentation) or not, and the courts use a presumption to establish this; if you want to dress this up as a presumption of attributes or identity then that is fine, but you should remember that deep down it is all about the owner's *intention* (or, more practically, the court's willingness to find such an intention on the facts).

In *Lewis* v *Averay* (1971) the Court of Appeal held that the contract between a rogue posing as an actor, Richard Greene (famous, ironically, for playing Robin Hood), and the owner of a car was merely voidable and not void, even though the seller had checked the rogue's identification before letting him take the car away. Again, this does not fit very easily with the decision of the majority of the Court of Appeal in *Ingram* v *Little*.

Written contracts

The courts take a different approach in relation to written contracts. In *Boulton* v *Jones* (1857) Jones posted a written order for a hosepipe to Brocklehurst (with whom he had a set-off arrangement and who would not therefore require payment), but, unknown to Jones, Brocklehurst had just transferred his business to Boulton, his former foreman. Boulton provided the hosepipe to Jones, who objected to paying for the goods, and so Boulton sued for the price. The court held that there was no contract between Boulton and Jones because Boulton must have known that Jones only wanted to contract with Brocklehurst, the person to whom he sent his order and with whom he had the **set-off** arrangement.

set-off

You have probably worked a set-off agreement hundreds of times in your life without realizing it. Very simply, if I owe you £20 and you buy goods from me for £15 then we can set off the value of the goods from the £20 I owe you so that I now only owe you £5. It's easier than me paying you £20 and then you giving me £15 back.

This case can be seen as an application of the objective approach to offer and acceptance: a reasonable person in Boulton's shoes would have realized that the offer was addressed to Brocklehurst and not to himself, and it is clear that one cannot accept an offer if it is addressed to another. This is the basis on which the case was dismissed. Pollock CB said: 'if you propose to make a contract with A, then B cannot substitute himself for A without your consent.'

THINKING POINT

The facts reveal that Jones got his hosepipe for free because he was under no obligation to pay Boulton (the contract was void between himself and Boulton), but should Jones have been under an obligation to give value for the hosepipe?

A better solution might have been to find that, because the transaction between Boulton and Jones was *executed*, the contract should have stood but it should have been *voidable* for misrepresentation or fraud by Boulton (who pretended to be Brocklehurst); Jones could therefore avoid the contract and avoid paying money to Brocklehurst, but only if it was possible to return the hosepipe to Boulton. Moreover, Jones might claim damages for misrepresentation or fraud (see Chapter 7 for more details). Alternatively, you could argue that Jones was unjustly enriched at Boulton's expense, although it is arguable that Boulton accepted the risk that Jones would not pay for the goods because he knew that Jones intended to contract with Brocklehurst (his former employer) and so he should not be entitled to restitution. Just make up your mind over whether the best solution would be to hold that the contract was void (as in the case) or voidable and whether Boulton should be entitled to a claim in unjust enrichment.

Cundy v *Lindsay* (1878) lays down the fundamental rule that a contract in writing will be presumed to be between the parties identified in the writing. Thus if A enters into correspondence with a rogue and the rogue uses the name of a different more respectable person, then any alleged contract between the rogue and A will be void because the law presumed that A intended to contract with the respectable person and not with the rogue.

On the facts of *Cundy* v *Lindsay*, Mr Blenkarn (a rogue) wrote to Lindsay ordering 250 dozen handkerchiefs. Blenkarn (being the rogue that he was) signed his letter as Blenkiron & Co., a firm well known to Lindsay, who accepted the offer by delivering the goods to the address given. Blenkarn then sold on some of the handkerchiefs to Cundy. The House of Lords favoured Lindsay and held that the contract was void and so Cundy had no title to the handkerchiefs. Lord Cairns LC reasoned that there could be no contract between Blenkarn and Lindsay because the name Blenkarn was never mentioned in any of the correspondence: 'Of him [Blenkarn] they knew nothing, and of him they never thought. With him they never intended to deal. Their minds never even for an instant of time rested on him, and as between him and them there was no consensus of mind which could lead to any agreement or any contract whatsoever.'

A similar fraud occurred in *King's Norton Metal Co. Ltd* v *Edridge, Merrett and Co. Ltd (1897)* but in this case the contract was voidable and not void. The rogue sent in an order pretending to be Hallam & Co., a fictional company. King's Norton delivered goods to the rogue under the impression that they were delivering goods to Hallam & Co., and the rogue sold them on to Edridge, Merrett and Co. King's Norton claimed that they still had title to the goods in the possession of Edridge, Merrett and Co. (just as Lindsay claimed the handkerchiefs in the possession of Cundy). However, unlike *Cundy* v *Lindsay*, the Court of Appeal found that there was a valid (though voidable) contract between King's Norton and the rogue under which title had passed to the rogue and thereafter to Edridge, Merritt and Co., who thus had good title to the goods.

The court held that King's Norton had contracted to sell the goods to the writer of the letters, and this was the rogue. AL Smith LJ considered that the case might have come within the decision in *Cundy v Lindsay* 'if it could have been shown that there was a separate entity called Hallam and Co. and another entity called Wallis [the rogue].' However, because Hallam and Co. did not exist, the only possible identity of the person signing the letters was the rogue; unlike *Cundy v Lindsay*, there was no choice between the rogue and a real-life respectable company. The distinction is perhaps less secure than you might think; in both cases the owners of the goods thought that the letter came from a respectable company when in fact it came from a fraudster.

EXAMPLE

Contract with whom?

Robin Hood is perhaps one of the most famous (but loveable) rogues of all time. If the Sheriff of Nottingham and Robin Hood made a contract by post for the Sheriff to sell bows and arrows to Robin and Robin signed his letters the Earl of Loamshire, then, following *Cundy* v *Lindsay*, you might think that the courts would refuse to recognize a contract between the Sheriff and Robin because of the presumption that a written contract is between the named parties (in this case the Sheriff and the Earl).

However, the knowledgeable reader will have noted that there is no such place as Loamshire, and thus no such person as the Earl thereof, and therefore *King's Norton* v *Edridge* would apply and, on that basis, that there would be a contract between the Sheriff and Robin which would be voidable at the Sheriff's option (once he discovered the truth, which of course would only happen once Robin was safely back in the forest with his merry men together with their bows and arrows). If Robin had meanwhile received the bows and arrows and sold them on to Friar Tuck before the Sheriff rescinded the contract then Friar Tuck would have a better title to the goods than the Sheriff and he would be entitled to keep them. Robin would no doubt have given the proceeds of sale to the poor, so everyone's happy (except the evil Sheriff, but that's OK).

Now imagine that the Sheriff and Robin contract face to face; Robin is dressed as a nobleman and claims to be the Duke of Lincoln, whom the Sheriff believes he is contracting with. The law will nevertheless presume that the Sheriff intends to contract with the rogue standing before him (Robin) even though he has deceived him by dressing as the Duke of Lincoln. This presumption will only be rebutted in rare circumstances, for instance if it is clear that the Sheriff only intends to contract with the Duke and not the person in front of him, for example if the Sheriff checks out with his vassals that the Duke of Lincoln really does exist, indicating that he is only prepared to contract with the Duke and not with the person in front of him.

The majority's opinions in *Shogun Finance Ltd* v *Hudson* (2003)

The House of Lords were recently presented with a chance to clarify the previous case law. One major problem was the artificial distinction between face-to-face contracts and contracts by correspondence: why was it that the courts presumed that the owner intended to contract with the rogue in the former case but that he intended to contract with the rogue's alter ego (if he existed) in the latter case?

Lord Phillips, delivering the main speech for the majority, stuck with the existing case law. The answer to the question 'With whom did the owner intend to contract?', according to Lord Phillips, lay in a name. Where the parties contract by correspondence, it was necessary to look at the name identified in the writing. Obviously, a name by itself cannot identify the person with whom the owner intended to contract: a name by itself is just a label and it is necessary to collect extrinsic evidence to connect the name to a person.

Boulton v *Jones*, *Cundy* v *Lindsay* and *King's Norton* were therefore correctly decided because, in the first two cases, extrinsic evidence could identify the names 'Brocklehurst' and 'Blenkiron & Co.' as the real Mr Brocklehurst and the real Blenkiron & Co. The owners, by corresponding with these names, intended to contract with the real person or company and not with the rogue and so the contracts were correctly held to be void. In *King's Norton* the rogue was the only person who used the fictitious name 'Hallam & Co.' and so the owners intended to contract with the rogue; no one else had any attachment to that name and so they could not have intended to contract with anyone else.

Lord Phillips thought that face-to-face contracts were more difficult because, unlike the correspondence cases where the owner may never even make a connection between the rogue and the name given, the owner *sees* the rogue face to face and connects the person in front of him with the name given. The law must presume that the owner intends to contract with the person in front of him, whom he believes to be the respectable person, and so the contract is not void but merely voidable (as found in *Phillips* v *Brooks Ltd* and in *Lewis* v *Averay*).

Lord Nicholls thought that the presumption should be a strong one, which suggests that *Ingram* v *Little* has been sidelined as a decision on 'very special and unusual facts' (quoting Phillimore LJ in *Lewis* v *Averay*).

THINKING POINT

Do you think that *Ingram* v *Little* was decided on 'very special and unusual facts'? (You might need to read the full facts in the case report and compare them to *Phillips* v *Brooks Ltd* and *Lewis* v *Averay* to answer this properly.)

Could it be that the Court of Appeal in *Ingram* v *Little* was just feeling particularly sympathetic to two old ladies who had been conned out of their car?

The facts of *Shogun Finance Ltd* v *Hudson*

The case involved a rogue who pretended to be Mr Patel from Leicester when he bought the claimant's (Shogun Finance's) Mitsubishi Shogun on **hire purchase** terms. Unsurprisingly, the rogue did not pay the instalments on the hire purchase and disappeared once he had sold the vehicle to Mr Hudson.

hire purchase Hire purchase is different to an outright sale of goods because the 'buyer' starts off by hiring the goods and paying an instalment fee (usually monthly) and it is only at the end of the term (say three years) that he finally purchases the goods with his final instalment. The total instalments add up to the value of the goods plus an amount for interest (usually a lot, so check this before you take out one of these 'buy now, pay later' deals) and so the effect is as though the 'buyer' had been lent the money and then used it to buy the goods. The point is that title remains with the 'seller' until the very end when the 'buyer' finally stops hiring and purchases the goods.

Shogun Finance had not transferred title to the rogue (because the rogue had only hired the vehicle and not yet purchased it) but s.27 of the Hire Purchase Act 1964 provided an exception to the rule that a person cannot give title when he himself has none, and so the case rested on whether there was a hire purchase agreement between Shogun Finance and the rogue so as to bring the case within the s.27 exception. If the case fell within s.27 then Mr Hudson would have a good title because Shogun Finance had not rescinded the contract; if it did not then the car would still belong to Shogun Finance.

The majority thought that there was no agreement because the contract was made by correspondence and the name used on the documents was Mr Patel. Shogun Finance therefore only intended to contract with Mr Patel. They checked Mr Patel's driving licence (provided fraudulently by the rogue), his address, his credit history and his (forged) signature. In the words of Lord Phillips (para. [178]):

> The particulars given in the agreement are only capable of applying to Mr Patel. It was the intention of the rogue that they should identify Mr Patel as the hirer. The hirer was so identified by Shogun. Before deciding to enter into the agreement they checked that Mr Patel existed and that he was worthy of credit. On that basis they decided to contract with him and with no-one else. Mr Patel was the hirer under the agreement. As the agreement was conducted without his authority, it was a nullity. The rogue took no title under it and was in no position to convey any title to Mr Hudson.

The hire purchase contract was therefore void and Mr Hudson could not acquire good title to the goods under the statutory exception.

The dissenting opinions in *Shogun Finance Ltd* v *Hudson*

You should also read the dissenting judgments of Lord Nicholls and Lord Millett in the House of Lords. These give a glimpse of what the law *could* be, even though they currently give an incorrect interpretation of the law.

Lord Nicholls identified *Cundy* v *Lindsay* as the problem case. Remember that in that case the House of Lords had said that the owner of the handkerchiefs had only intended to contract with the person named in the letters, 'Blenkiron & Co.' and not the rogue (Blenkarn). The contract was therefore void. Lord Nicholls thought that the contract should have been voidable because the case was indistinguishable from the face-to-face cases (*Phillips* v *Brooks Ltd* and *Lewis* v *Averay*) which were decided on a legal presumption in favour of a contract between the owner and the rogue. The contract was voidable because of the fraudulent misrepresentation. He thought that there was no reason to distinguish between correspondence and face-to-face transactions, particularly bearing in mind today's modern communication methods which blur the lines. In both cases the court should ask the question: 'Whom does the owner intend to deal with?' In both cases the answer is 'the rogue.' In the face-to-face cases it is easy to come to the conclusion that the owner intends to deal with the rogue, the person in front of him. In the correspondence cases it is less easy to establish that the owner intended to contract with the rogue because there is not the same proximity between them, but Lord Nicholls maintained that the owner still intends to deal with the rogue. That is sufficient to deal with the question of *whom* the owner intended to deal with and whether the contract is void or valid; the owner is presumed to intend to deal with the rogue, that is, the person in front of him or the person writing letters to him, and so there is no mistaken identity unless this (strong) presumption is rebutted. The question of *why* the owner intended to contract with the rogue explains how the contract is voidable; the owner was induced to contract with the rogue by the rogue's fraudulent misrepresentation, and so the owner is allowed to rescind the contract.

Lord Nicholls and Lord Millett would have therefore allowed Mr Hudson's appeal because Shogun Finance intended to contract with the rogue (the person who signed the hire purchase contract) and so there was a hire purchase contract which enabled Mr Hudson to acquire good title to the car under s.27 of the Hire Purchase Act 1964. *Cundy* v *Lindsay* would therefore have to be overruled. The differences between the majority and minority opinions are summarized in Figure 8.3.

8.4 Complete agreement but common mistake of fundamental facts

8.4.1 Common law

We can now move on to the second type of mistake discussed in the introduction to this chapter: common mistake of a fundamental fact. The typical scenario is where the parties have reached an objective agreement which would be enforceable if the facts were as they supposed them to be, but the facts turn out to be so fundamentally different that the contract is alleged to be void.

Figure 8.3 Majority and minority opinions in Shogun Finance Ltd v Hudson

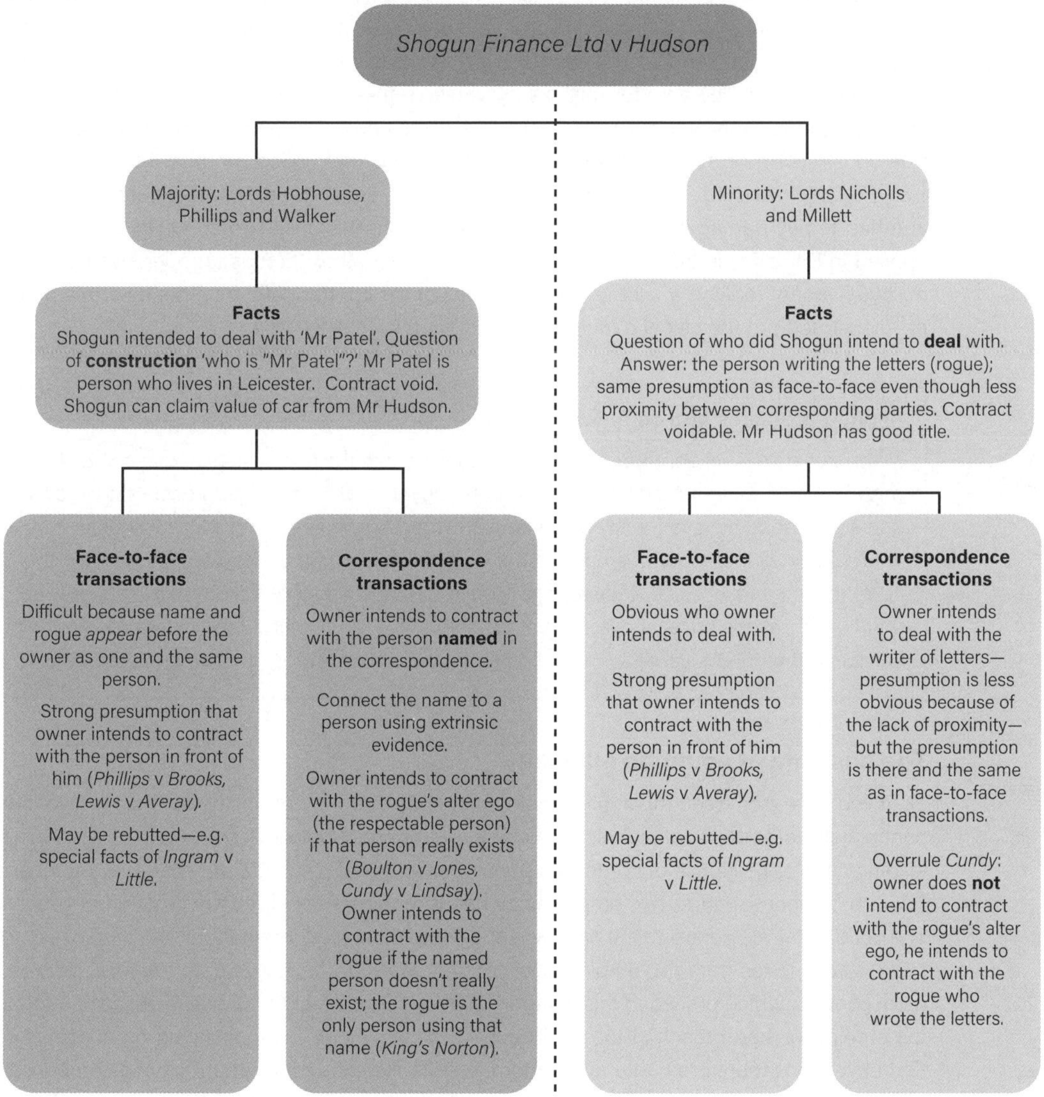

Common mistake: frustration and construction

The difference between common mistake and frustration is often merely one of timing. If the parties operate under a fundamental common mistake of what the facts are *at the time of the contract* then it is the doctrine of mistake that has to be considered, but if the parties make a fundamentally mistaken assumption at to what the facts will be *after the contract has been made* then the contract may (exceptionally) be frustrated. See for example *Amalgamated Investment & Property Co. Ltd* v *John Walker and Sons Ltd* (1976) where the building was actually listed as a protected building a short time after the formation of the contract so that the case had to be considered under the heading of frustration, whereas if the list had been signed so that the building was protected before the contract, it would have been appropriate to apply the rules relating to mistake.

The doctrine of common mistake is heavily dependent on the construction of the terms of the contract. In *McRae* v *Commonwealth Disposals Commission* (1950) the two parties agreed to buy and sell a tanker but both parties operated under the most fundamental mistake imaginable because the tanker did not exist. Such a mistake is on the face of it so fundamental that the contract should be void for mistake. However, rather than finding that the contract was void for common mistake, the High Court of Australia held that on the facts of this case the true construction of the contract meant that there was an implied promise from the sellers that the tanker existed. The tanker did not exist so the sellers were in breach of the contract and had to pay damages to the buyer. The lesson from this case (which would probably be applied in England) is that you cannot really decide whether there is an operative common mistake without looking at all the circumstances of the contract and whether its terms properly construed put the risk of a mistake on one or other of the parties.

Implied promises and common mistake

It may not always be appropriate to imply a promise that the thing exists or that some other mistake has not been made. Imagine that the buyer in *McRae* had approached the seller and said that he believed there was a tanker owned by the seller and asked the seller if he would sell it. In these circumstances it may not be appropriate to imply a promise from the seller that the tanker exists. Indeed, it may be appropriate to imply a promise from the *buyer* that he will pay the price whether or not the ship exists (particularly if the contract is speculative and the price is very low in relation to the possible rewards on finding the tanker).

The doctrine of common mistake

So, if you have dismissed the application of frustration and the possibility that the terms of the contract allocate the risk of the mistake, when will a contract be void for common mistake? The leading case is the House of Lords' decision in *Bell* v *Lever Bros* (1932), where Lever Bros paid £50,000 compensation to two employees when it terminated their contracts of employment. The contract at the centre of the case was the compensation agreement for the employees to release Lever Bros from the employment contract in return for £50,000 and *not* the employment contract which preceded this compensation agreement. Lever Bros later discovered that the employees had breached their contracts of employment (by speculating on cocoa) and that Lever Bros therefore had a right to terminate those contracts without paying compensation. Lever Bros sued for the return of the £50,000 on the basis that they paid under a mistake of fact: They would never have paid any compensation to the employees if they had known that they could terminate their employment contracts for breach. The mistake was common to both parties because the two employees also did not realize that the employment contracts could have been terminated due to breach. Even though both parties mistakenly believed at the time of the contract for the payment of £50,000 that the employment contracts could only be terminated by a compensation agreement (the mistake), the House of Lords held (by a three to two majority) that this mistake was not fundamental enough to make the compensation agreement void. The employees therefore got to keep their £50,000. The speeches of the different Law Lords did not provide any easy-to-apply test to specify precisely when a mistake would make a contract void, but they did indicate that it would do so only in the most extreme cases where it could be said that the identity of the subject matter was destroyed. In respect of mistakes as to quality, of which the mistake on the facts was an example, a mistake would only very exceptionally have this effect if it 'makes the thing without the quality essentially different from the thing as it was believed to be.' The fact that the employment contracts could have been terminated without compensation did not have this effect, thus illustrating the narrowness of the test for common mistake.

The Court of Appeal has more recently analysed the case law on common mistake in *The Great Peace* (2002), in effect confirming the narrow approach taken in *Bell* v *Lever Bros*. Lord Phillips MR identified five main elements required for common mistake to be operative (para. [76]).

Lord Phillips' five requirements

1) There must be a common assumption as to the existence of a state of affairs;
2) There must be no warranty by either party that the state of affairs exists;
3) The non-existence of the state of affairs must not be attributable to the fault of either party;
4) The non-existence of the state of affairs must render the performance of the contract impossible; and
5) The state of affairs may be the existence, or a vital attribute, of the consideration to be provided or circumstances which must subsist if performance of the contractual adventure is to be possible.

Point (1) is obvious; the doctrine of common mistake does not even come into play if the mistake is not common to both parties. If the mistake is unilateral then the rules of offer and acceptance determine what, if any, agreement has been communicated. Points (2) and (3) reflect cases such as *McRae* v *Commonwealth Disposals Commission* (discussed earlier) where the court found that, on the true construction of the contract, the Commission had promised that the tanker existed or alternatively that 'any mistake was induced by the serious fault of their own servants, who asserted the existence of a tanker recklessly and without any reasonable ground.'

Points (4) and (5) require a more detailed assessment. What precisely are the states of affairs which can render the performance of the contract impossible?

Mistake as to existence

The classic example often given of such a state of affairs is *Couturier* v *Hastie* (1856), where the corn which was the subject matter of the contract of sale no longer existed at the time the contract was made. The House of Lords held simply that on the construction of the contract, under which the parties contemplated 'that there was an existing something to be sold and bought,' the purchaser was not liable to pay the price. There was no express reference to the contract being void but in *Bell* v *Lever Bros* Lord Atkin expressly recognized that 'the agreement of A and B for the purchase of a specific article is void if in fact the article has perished before the date of sale.' The decision in *Couturier* v *Hastie* was the foundation of what is now s.6 of the Sale of Goods Act 1979 (previously s.6 of the 1893 Act). This provides that a contract for the sale of specific goods, which (without the knowledge of the seller) have perished at the time the contract is made, will be void. This provision does not apply to a situation like *McRae* since in that case the goods had not perished; they had never existed in the first place. In such a case the interpretation would normally still be that the contract is void but as we have seen from the facts of *McRae*, it is also possible that the courts may imply from the circumstances that one party has taken on the risk of the thing not existing, in which case the contract will be valid. This interpretation is not available to cases covered by s.6 (where the goods did exist but have perished at the time of the contract), which it is generally thought ought to be reformed so as to allow for a contrary intention rather than automatically providing that the contract is void in every case.

Mistakenly acquiring own title

You might think that it would be incredibly stupid to buy your own property, but it has happened and the mistake will make the contract void because, as Lord Atkin said in *Bell* v *Lever Bros*, 'such a transfer is impossible.' In *Cooper* v *Phibbs* (1867) there was agreement for the lease of a fishery. Unknown to the buyer and seller, the buyer already had a life interest in the fishery and the seller had no title and so the lease was set aside but the 'buyer' had to reimburse the 'seller' for improvements made to the fishery. Lord Atkin in *Bell* v *Lever Bros* thought that the case was correct except that the lease should have been void at common law and not merely voidable and capable of being set aside. We will see later that Denning LJ used this case to justify a doctrine of equitable mistake which has now been disapproved so it is now clear that the effect of a mistake as to title is to render the contract void. Indeed, *British Red Cross* v *Werry* (2017) provides an analogous example where H was mistakenly thought to have died without leaving a will. It was thought that D, who had lived with him for more than forty years, had not been provided for and an agreement to settle her claim against the estate gave her only a life interest in the property (plus a sum of money for repairs). Subsequently, after D's own death, a valid will leaving everything to her was found so she was effectively entitled to the property anyway at the time of the agreement, which was therefore declared void for common mistake. (She therefore inherited the property absolutely and the proceeds of its sale went to the charities in her own will.)

Mistakes as to the quality of a thing

This difficult category deals with those cases where the thing contracted for exists but is different (to varying degrees) from the thing both parties believed they were contracting for.

EXAMPLE

Mistake as to quality

Lord Atkin gave the hypothetical example of A agreeing to buy a painting from B which they both believe is by an Old Master. A has no remedy if the painting turns out to be a modern copy unless B warranted (a question of construction of the terms as in *McRae*) or represented that the picture was by the Old Master (see Chapter 7).

The belief that the painting was an Old Master can be classified as a mistake as to quality and this is not sufficient to make the contract void. However, if the mistake relates to 'an essential and integral part of the subject matter' (Lord Thankerton in *Bell* v *Lever Bros*) or to a 'vital element' (Lord Phillips in *The Great Peace*) then the contract will be void; the obvious problem is in identifying the dividing line between 'essential' and 'non-essential' attributes.

The distinction is extremely tight and it is tempting to argue, contrary to Lord Atkin's opinion, that the identity of a painter is an essential matter; no one pays millions of pounds for a copy of a Picasso by an unknown artist but they do for the original Picasso. A contract for a Picasso is, arguably, a fundamentally different kind of contract once it is discovered that the picture was painted by a copycat artist. On the other hand, if the seller has not represented or promised that it is a Picasso and you have contracted to pay the agreed high price, it is equally arguable that that is the risk that you have taken and you cannot look to the doctrine of mistake to bail you out.

Greer LJ in the Court of Appeal in *Bell* v *Lever Bros* thought that an agreement to sell a racehorse which actually turned out to be a carthorse would be void, but Lord Atkin in the House of Lords thought that an agreement to buy a horse believed to be sound would not be void if the horse turned out to be unsound. It is obviously difficult to justify why a racehorse is fundamentally different from a carthorse but a sound horse is not fundamentally different from an unsound one, but you must point out that there is a divide and, when faced with a problem question, offer reasons why the particular circumstances may or may not reveal an operative common mistake, the latter always being the more likely alternative. However, the fact that it is difficult to show an operative mistake as to quality does not mean it is impossible, as is shown by *Griffith* v *Brymer*.

LINK TO . . .

Frustration (Chapter 10)

In *Griffith* v *Brymer* (1903) the parties agreed to hire a room so that they could view the coronation procession of King Edward VII (it was not possible to watch such things on TV in those days!). The procession had already been cancelled by the time the contract was made and the court held that the contract was void (cf. the frustration cases where the procession was cancelled after the contract was made).

The result sits uneasily with other cases because it was clear that the room could still be hired (it was not as though the room had burned to the ground before the contract was made) but merely the purpose of the contract could no longer be obtained, and this mistake was found to be sufficient to make the contract fundamentally different from what the parties intended and consequently void. It should be noted, however, that the price (£100—equivalent to about £13,000 today) was *very* high if the contract was simply for the hire of a room for a day.

The actual decision in *The Great Peace* is more typical and reveals the difficulty of showing that a mistake is fundamental enough to avoid a contract. As already noted, a salvage company hired *The Great Peace* to provide rescue support for a vessel in danger of sinking. The salvage company thought that *The Great Peace* was 35 miles from the sinking vessel but in fact it was 400 miles away and the salvage company tried to avoid the contract for common mistake. The Court of Appeal held that this mistake was not fundamental enough because it was still possible for *The Great Peace* to provide rescue services, even though it would take longer to reach the sinking vessel than was originally anticipated. It was a telling factor that even once the salvage company learned the true relative positions of the vessels, they did not immediately seek to terminate the contract until they knew that they could get a nearer vessel to assist. They clearly saw there was some potential benefit to them under the contract even though it was not as great as they had originally thought.

The more recent decision in *Kyle Bay Ltd t/a Astons Nightclub* v *Underwriters Subscribing under Policy No. 019057/08/01* (2007) also demonstrates how difficult it continues to be for a claimant to win on a claim based on common mistake. The claimant nightclub was damaged by fire and claimed its loss of profits from the defendant insurers. The parties agreed to settle the insurance claim on the basis that the policy was not declaration linked (this gave the nightclub a lower amount than if they settled on the basis that the policy was declaration linked) but the judge at first instance held that the policy was a declaration-linked policy (which provides increased cover as profits rise), with the consequence that the parties' settlement agreement had been made under a common mistake. The Court of Appeal upheld the first instance judge's decision that, although the difference between the actual and assumed subject matter of the contract could be described as 'significant' (it resulted in a settlement £100,000 lower), the mistake did not render the contract void. Conceptually, the contract was not radically different to the one envisaged by the parties: the parties remained the same; the nature of the business was the same; the risks covered were the same—all that was wrongly assumed was a detail, albeit a significant detail, that the policy was not declaration linked.

8.4.2 **Equity**

The previous section illustrates that it is rare to find a mistake which makes a contract void at common law; both leading cases, *Bell* v *Lever Bros* and *The Great Peace*, ended in failure for the party seeking relief for mistake. There used to be authority for the proposition that a contract may be *voidable* in equity even if it was not void at common law. The distinction made use of the historical division between common law courts and the courts of equity where a more flexible and 'just' solution could be obtained (see Chapter 1).

The Court of Appeal rejected this distinction between mistakes in law and mistakes in equity in *The Great Peace* and stated that there is only one doctrine of common mistake—that laid down by the House of Lords in *Bell* v *Lever Bros*. The Court of Appeal's previous decision in *Solle* v *Butcher* (1950), and subsequent decisions based on it such as *Magee* v *Pennine Insurance* (1969), were therefore no longer good law.

In *Solle* v *Butcher* the parties agreed to a lease for £250 per annum, mistakenly believing that the tenancy was not subject to a statutory limit of £140. The landlord claimed that the lease was voidable and should be set aside, a contention that Denning LJ agreed with. Denning LJ's sympathies clearly lay with the landlord because he had made improvements to the building and had been advised by the tenant (who was a surveyor and the landlord's letting agent) that the statutory limit would no longer apply. It might have been more appropriate for the landlord to rely upon the innocent misrepresentation made by the tenant, rather than seek relief for equitable mistake (a view for which Denning LJ thought 'there was a good deal to be said'). Alternatively, Toulson J suggested in *The Great Peace* that relief could have been given on the basis of unconscionable conduct by the tenant; highlighting the point that even though *Solle* v *Butcher* might have been wrongly *decided*, it did not necessarily give the wrong *result*.

What you cannot now say in a case like *Solle* v *Butcher* is that such a qualitative mistake, whilst clearly not sufficient to render the contract impossible of performance or essentially or fundamentally different, and thus not sufficient to make it void for mistake at common law, somehow is still sufficiently fundamental to make the contract voidable in equity. There is no longer any such fallback doctrine of equitable mistake recognized in English law, notwithstanding any technical arguments about the rules of precedent relating to conflicting Court of Appeal decisions, since it is clear that in the House of Lords case of *Bell* v *Lever Bros* their Lordships did not consider themselves to be dealing only with the common law position. The incompatibility of *Bell* v *Lever Bros* with the now abandoned doctrine of equitable mistake is well illustrated by the facts of *Magee* v *Pennine Insurance* where a compromise agreement by the insurance company of a claim under a motor policy was sought to be avoided on the grounds that the claim could have been refused outright without any payment since unknown to both parties to the compromise, the policy was invalid. The Court of Appeal could not find the compromise agreement to be void at common law since the mistake was of such a similar nature to that held to be insufficient in *Bell* v *Lever Bros* and yet they found the agreement to be voidable in equity. Such a conclusion is no longer possible following *The Great Peace* and the overruling of *Solle* v *Butcher*, and the compromise agreement would still be valid as the mistake was not sufficiently fundamental to render the contract void.

Digging deeper

The removal in *The Great Peace* of the ability to find a contract voidable for common mistake may be thought to have left something of a gap in the law given the very narrow notion of common mistake at common law under *Bell* v *Lever Bros*. Even when overruling Lord Denning's category of mistake rendering the contract voidable in equity, Lord Phillips MR recognized that the *Bell* v *Lever Bros* approach may at times be unduly narrow when he said at para. [161]:

> We can understand why the decision in *Bell* v *Lever Brothers Ltd* did not find favour with Lord Denning. An equitable jurisdiction to grant rescission on terms where a common fundamental mistake has induced a contract gives greater flexibility than a doctrine of common law which holds the contract void in such circumstances. Just as the Law Reform (Frustrated Contracts) Act 1943 was needed to temper the effect of the common law doctrine of frustration, so there is scope for legislation to give greater flexibility to our law of mistake than the common law allows.

It may seem quite odd for the courts to remove the flexibility which was inherent in case law under Lord Denning's doctrine of equitable mistake and then to suggest that legislation could usefully provide such flexibility. However, it is quite common for the courts to say the common law is settled and that modifications and improvements are a matter for Parliament. One of the problems with the notion of equitable mistake was that no one was quite sure just exactly when it should be available (i.e. how much wider than common law mistake it was) or on what principles the discretion to set aside on terms should be (i.e. how the contract should be varied to take account of the mistake). If Parliament chose to intervene, it could perhaps lay down clear principles on these matters. The fact that it has not done so may be an indication of the difficulties involved in doing so without intervening inappropriately in the bargain actually made by the parties—see for example Article 4.105(3) of the Principles of European Contract Law (a transnational set of Principles which contracting parties may choose to adopt if they wish) which provides: 'Where both parties have made the same mistake, the court may at the request of either party bring the contract into accordance with what might reasonably have been agreed had the mistake not occurred.'

Perhaps the uncertainty involved in such an interventionist proposal may make the narrow but more predictable doctrine of common mistake under *Bell* v *Lever Bros* more palatable and more understandable. It also underlines English law's basic approach of enforcing the contract actually made by the parties rather than one which they may (or may not) have made in different circumstances if they had been better informed.

Summary

1. Communication mistakes

Communication mistakes are dealt with by the rules on offer and acceptance. A mistaken party will still be bound by the objective agreement unless the other party knew or caused his mistake as to the terms of the contract.

A mistake as to identity will normally make a contract void if the contract was made in writing, on the basis that the contract was intended to be made with the person named in the documents and who signed the contract, not with the rogue who misled the other party.

However, if the named person does not actually exist then the courts will presume that the party intended to contract with the rogue, since there cannot have been an intention to contract with a non-existent person, and the contract will therefore not be void for mistake but only voidable due to misrepresentation.

When an agreement takes place face to face a mistake as to identity will normally result in a valid contract but one which is voidable for fraudulent misrepresentation, unless the mistaken party can rebut the (strong) presumption that they intended to contract with the person in front of them, in which case exceptionally the contract may be void.

2. Common mistake of fact

If the parties have reached an agreement but a shared fundamental mistake exists at the time of the formation of the contract then the contract may exceptionally be void, although the mistake must be as to such an essential matter as to render it in essence impossible to perform. The more flexible doctrine of equitable common mistake is no longer recognized as good law.

The courts may find an express or implied term in the contract that allocates the risk of the particular mistake to one party or the other.

Questions

a) Angus lives in London and owns a large Scottish estate ideal for grouse shooting which includes Loch Tavish, the mythical home of Tav, a 60-foot-long prehistoric throw-back. Sportshoot Ltd organize shooting trips for American tourists and approach Angus for the shooting rights over his estate in July and August. Their representative tells Angus that they are the large multinational company Shootokill plc in order to impress him and secure the contract against other rival firms. On 31 July, Angus says that he is very impressed with their bid and believes that they will be a responsible company who will take care of his land, signing a contract for the lease of his estate, along with shooting rights, for £1,000.

Unknown to either party, the previous day, a BBC film crew caught a picture of Tav surfacing from the Loch and feeding on two Shetland ponies. The film is shown on the next edition of *Panorama* and Angus is interviewed on *Newsnight*, with many other networks offering him vast sums of money for exclusive filming rights over his land. Sportshoot advertises in the USA using the slogan 'Scottish Dragon Slaying' and thousands of tourists sign up to be the first to take Tav as a trophy. Angus decides that he can get far more money from leasing his land to the television companies and that he does not want Tav to get hurt so he tells Sportshoot that their contract is over. Discuss.

b) 'In the interests of certainty and security of title, the objective approach to agreement should always prevail.' Discuss.

c) 'A mistaken party should be able to enforce a contract on the terms he subjectively believed were true if the other party knew of his mistake and tried to take advantage of it.' Discuss.

d) 'There should be one presumption in relation to all types of identity mistakes and it should be that a party intends to contract with the person he actually deals with and not the person that he falsely believes he is dealing with. The law of misrepresentations takes adequate care of any outstanding problems.' Discuss.

Further reading

Books

Chen-Wishart, M, *Contract Law*, 7th edn (*Oxford University Press*, 2022) ch 6.

McKendrick, E, *Contract Law: Text, Cases and Materials*, 11th edn (*Oxford University Press*, 2024) chs 2 and 16.

O'Sullivan, J, and Hilliard, J, *The Law of Contract*, 11th edn (*Oxford University Press*, 2024) 3.20–3.59 and ch 13.

Articles

Endicott, T, 'Objectivity, subjectivity, and incomplete agreements' in J Horder (ed.) *Oxford Essays in Jurisprudence*, 4th series (Oxford University Press, 2000) ch 8.

Friedmann, D, 'The objective principle and mistake and involuntariness in contract and restitution' (2003) 119 LQR 68.

Hare, C, 'Identity mistakes: A missed opportunity' (2004) 67 MLR 993.

MacMillan, C, 'How temptation led to mistake: An explanation of *Bell* v *Lever Bros Ltd*' (2003) 119 LQR 625.

Slade, CJ, 'The myth of mistake in the English law of contract' (1954) 70 LQR 385.

Smith, JC, 'Contract: Mistake, frustration and implied terms' (1994) 110 LQR 400.

Treitel, GH, 'Mistake in contract' (1988) 104 LQR 501.

9 Duress, undue influence and unconscionable bargains

LEARNING OBJECTIVES

This chapter will help you to:

- understand when a contract will be voidable for the different types of duress, in particular if one party threatens to breach an existing contract;
- distinguish between actual and presumed undue influence and understand the elements that must be proved to show that one party exerted too much influence over the other party so as to make a contract voidable;
- understand when duress, undue influence or misrepresentation by a third party will affect a contract; and
- understand when a contract will be set aside as an unconscionable bargain where one party has taken advantage of a weakness in the other.

Introduction

This chapter deals with the principles applicable where a contract is entered into after there have been threats or improper influence brought to bear on one party or where the one-sided nature of the contract suggests that one party has been taken advantage of. The principles involved are somewhat open-ended and controversial, and are still evolving. They are discussed in turn under the traditional headings of duress, undue influence and unconscionable bargains, although it will be seen that these categories are not, at their boundaries, entirely distinct from one another.

9.1 Duress

9.1.1 Duress and pressure

Duress is a form of pressure—something which we are all under to a greater or lesser extent and is part of everyday life. *Too much* pressure (e.g. a gun to the head) can damage a person's apparent consent to a contract to such an extent that this 'consent' should not be recognized by the law and the threatened party should be able to get out of the contract. Under such circumstances the law says that the party acted under duress and the resulting contract is **voidable**. The questions you must tackle are how much pressure is needed to make a contract voidable in this way and what sorts of threats should be counted as amounting to duress.

> **voidable contract** A damaged contract. The 'innocent' party (i.e. the party subjected to duress, undue influence, etc.) has the option of unwinding the whole contract (known as rescission) or affirming it (carrying on as though nothing has happened).

Almost all of our everyday decisions are made under some sort of pressure. We go to work because we have to earn money, we buy food because we need to eat and we pay for transport because we need to be in a certain location. We do not say that those decisions are not truly voluntary just because they are made under pressure; workers do not become slaves just because they need the income generated by their work. Their actions are fully voluntary because there is a residual but substantial element of genuine choice between two or more reasonable alternative ways of achieving the same end. For example, we can, at one end of the scale, choose to eat out in expensive restaurants or we can, at the other end, choose to grow our own food, and how long and hard we need to work will be affected by our choice between these sorts of reasonable alternatives. By contrast, imagine an extreme version (no doubt being planned as we speak) of a celebrity TV show produced by a ratings-mad sadist where you are threatened with being cooked and eaten by the other half-starved contestants if you do not eat live insects in order to gain food rations for the group. A choice between eating the insects and being cooked yourself is made under the sort of pressure that it may not be reasonable to expect you to resist. You still have a choice—eat or be killed—but the latter is hardly a reasonable alternative. The pressure on your choice has reached an unbearable level so that the choice should not be recognized by the law. The pressures brought to bear on contracting parties are not usually so extreme as this but the principle is the same. Duress is therefore a synonym for *too much* pressure which denies a party the choice of a reasonable alternative.

Evaluating pressure

The previous section looked at pressure primarily from the point of view of the party to whom it is directed. We can also look at it from the perspective of the person exerting the pressure and evaluate to what extent they are acting wrongfully. In the earlier example, it would be wrong, applying our present-day standards of morality, even in the warped context of celebrity TV shows, for the rest of the group to threaten to cook you if you do not perform your task. If they threatened not to share their remaining food with you then perhaps the pressure would be more justified or reasonable. The pressures on contracting parties can therefore be evaluated in two different ways:

- **(a)** by the degree of wrongdoing involved (the legitimacy or otherwise of the pressure); and
- **(b)** by the effect it has on party autonomy (on genuine freedom of choice).

We will see that the law adopts a mixed approach and the effect of pressure on a contract will depend, to varying degrees, on both party autonomy and wrongdoing.

THINKING POINT

Should it matter whether the threat was wrongful? If a threat causes a person to enter a contract they would not otherwise have entered then why should it matter whether the threat was wrongful or 'illegitimate'?

On the other hand, do you think the law should distinguish between a person who threatens to kill the other party and a person who threatens to take their business elsewhere, even if both have an identical impact on the second party's decision to contract?

9.1.2 **Threats against the person**

Unsurprisingly, the law of contract takes a very dim view of a party who threatens to kill or injure other people since this is inevitably an illegitimate threat. In *Barton* v *Armstrong* (1976) the chairman of a company (Armstrong) threatened to kill the managing director (Barton) if he did not execute a deed in his favour. Speaking in the Privy Council, Lord Wilberforce and Lord Simon thought that Barton must show, firstly, that some illegitimate means of persuasion was used and, secondly, that there was a connection between the illegitimate means used and the action taken (i.e. that the threat caused the decision taken). Given that a threat to kill is clearly illegitimate, the case centred on the connection between the threat and the execution of the deed, that is, on the second question of whether the threat caused the other party to act. The Privy Council agreed that the threat need only be *a* reason for executing the deed rather than *the* reason or even the *predominant* reason. This should be contrasted with the approach taken by the Court of Appeal of New South Wales, which required Barton to prove that he would not have executed the deed *but for* the threat. The majority in the Privy Council (which used to be the appeal court for New South Wales, Australia) inferred from the facts found by the trial judge that the threat contributed to Barton's decision to execute the deed, even though Barton might have executed it anyway for commercial reasons. The deed was therefore voidable and could be set aside. Lord Wilberforce and Lord Simon dissented, stating that there was no reason to depart from the first instance judge's finding that Barton acted solely on commercial motives, meaning that there was no connection between the threat and the execution of the deed. Even if the dissenting judges (and the trial judge) had been correct in their interpretation of the evidence on the facts, the approach of the majority is more typical of the natural inferences to be drawn in cases of threats of violence or death. It will normally not be difficult to show that such a serious threat at least contributed to or influenced the decision to enter into the contract, even if the contract might still have been entered into without the threat. However it is important to note that in cases of economic duress, to be discussed below at section 9.1.4, a stricter test of causation is required whereby the threat must be a 'significant' cause and this involves, at the very least, showing that but for the threat, the transaction would not have been entered into.

Threats against the person as a form of duress have now been illustrated in relation to a contract between sovereign states, rather than between private individuals, in *Law Debenture Trust* v *Ukraine* (2023). Ukraine borrowed $3 billion from Russia in 2013 under various forms of pressure not to enter an Association Agreement with the EU but to borrow money from Russia instead. The Supreme Court ruled that Ukraine, when sued for repayment of the money, could put forward the defence of duress against the person since some of the alleged threats would necessarily involve the use of armed force and violence against Ukrainian military personnel and citizens. Even if the violence would be directed against individuals rather than the state of Ukraine itself, that was still capable of being duress bearing on Ukraine given the likely effect on Ukraine of the threats against its citizens. The question of whether the defence actually succeeded on the facts was to be the subject of a separate trial but you may think that the allegations about the threats appear to have been highly credible given the subsequent Russian invasion of Crimea in 2014. It should be noted that the Supreme Court hearing was concluded in November 2021 and thus did not include consideration of the subsequent wider invasion of Ukraine in February 2022. In contrast to the threats of force, threats by Russia in 2013 of economic sanctions and disruption of trade with Ukraine did not amount to illegitimate pressure in the form of economic duress (see 9.1.4 below) as they have been part of the legitimate 'armoury of states since classical times' (something you may think well illustrated in relation to the use of tariffs in 2025).

9.1.3 **Threats against goods**

Traditionally, the courts were reluctant to extend the doctrine of duress beyond threats against the person. See, for example, *Skeate* v *Beale* (1841), where the defendant *agreed to pay* an amount (just over £16), which was not actually due to his landlord, because of a threat to sell his goods which had been seized. The landlord succeeded in enforcing the agreement to pay even though the threatened sale would have been unlawful. The court thought that the defendant should have relied on his lawful remedies against wrongful seizure and sale of his goods rather than prevent the sale by entering into a contract which he did not intend to keep. However, the courts did recognize an obligation to return money *actually paid* in response to a threat against goods, even though they would not set aside an unexecuted agreement (i.e. one where no money had yet passed). In *Astley* v *Reynolds* (1731) Astley pawned his plate to Reynolds for £20 (i.e. Reynolds loaned Astley £20, taking possession of Astley's plate as **security** for the payment of the debt).

> **security** Security is used to reassure a lender that the debtor will repay the money in due course. Security rights are taken over the property of the debtor (security rights are therefore rights ***in rem***—see **Chapter 1**) and can be enforced (e.g. by selling the property) if the debtor fails to repay the loan.

Astley returned to pay the debt and Reynolds demanded £10 interest—way above the (then) legal maximum—on top of the £20 loan capital. Astley tried several times to pay a lower interest rate but eventually paid the full amount requested and then sued Reynolds for the return of the money paid in excess of the legal rate of interest. The court decided that Astley had paid under compulsion (duress) and was entitled to recover the extra money. The court was prepared to assume that Astley paid because of an immediate need to get his goods back, although they considered whether, as a reasonable alternative to paying the full amount demanded, Astley could have come to court and demanded that Reynolds return his plate, but dismissed this as a reasonable option because a man may have immediate need of his goods. The payment was therefore made under duress and could be recovered.

Skeate v *Beale* and *Astley* v *Reynolds* are generally regarded as inconsistent with one another, even though one involved an unsuccessful defence to the enforcement of an agreement to pay entered into under duress whereas the other involved a claim for the return of money already paid under duress. Although there is no case exactly on point, the modern view is that a contract may be voidable for duress of goods just as a payment actually made can be recovered if made under duress of goods. Any other rule would today be absurd given the expansion of duress to include economic duress, as outlined in the next section.

9.1.4 **Economic duress**

The modern case law is generally more concerned with economic duress than with threats to the person or to a person's goods. In particular, it has concerned itself with the economic pressure that a threat to break a contract can impose, no doubt reflecting the increased value of economic rights enshrined in contracts relative to the value of property rights in goods. Breach of contract is a civil wrong, but it is not a wrong in quite the same way that killing someone or taking someone's goods is a wrong. Take for example the one-man building contractor who quotes a low figure for building your conservatory. Halfway through the building he realizes he will go bankrupt unless you pay him some more money—should he be allowed to threaten not to complete the job and extract a binding agreement from you to pay more? His threat is not to interfere with your person or your property, but instead he is merely threatening not to carry out a legal obligation owed to you.

It is important to realize that this area of law actually focuses not on whether the builder is *allowed* to make a threat to breach his contract (he can in fact do that with impunity—it is not illegal to threaten to breach a contract, in contrast to threats to kill, which are criminal) but on whether the law will enforce any agreement that *results from* his threat to breach. Thus if the other party actually pays up because of the threatened breach, the payment is not illegal and the payer may struggle to recover the money paid if he does not act promptly (see the discussion in the example on void and voidable contracts). The main issue however is whether and in what circumstances economic duress consisting of threats to break an existing contract can be used to avoid an obligation under a new contract entered into following the duress.

The cases on economic duress

In *Occidental Worldwide Investment Corp.* v *Skibs A/S Avanti (The Siboen and The Sibotre)* (1976) the charterers of the two ships threatened that they would go bankrupt (and be unable to perform their contract to pay for the hire of the ships) if the rates of hire were not lowered (this was in fact untrue—they were perfectly capable of paying, they just did not want to). The owners knew that they would be unlikely to find new charterers in the current state of the market and so they amended the charter so that the rate of hire was less. The owners later asked the court to avoid the renegotiated charter because it had been extracted under pressure. Kerr J avoided that renegotiated charter on the ground of fraud (the charterers had lied about their financial state in order to get the new charter) but he also considered whether the charter could be avoided for duress. He concluded that it was possible for a threat to breach a contract to amount to duress but on the facts he thought that the owner's consent had not been 'overborne' by the pressure from the charterers so as to destroy his intention to contract—his consent had not been 'vitiated' (fatally flawed)—and so the charter could not be avoided on this ground (see 'The discredited "overborne will" theory' in the next subsection of this chapter for a discussion on this approach to duress).

Economic duress *was* made out (but ultimately to no avail) in *North Ocean Shipping Co. Ltd* v *Hyundai Construction Co. Ltd (The Atlantic Baron)* (1979) where the shipbuilders threatened to breach their contract to build a ship (*The Atlantic Baron*) unless the buyers paid 10 per cent more. The buyers reluctantly agreed to pay the extra, paid it, received their ship and then claimed that they were entitled to avoid the renegotiated contract. Mocatta J (having managed to find consideration for the promise to pay extra) decided that although the contract to pay the extra 10 per cent was voidable for duress, the buyers had affirmed the contract by paying the extra amount and waiting too long before claiming that the contract was avoided. *Morley* v *Royal Bank of Scotland* (2021) provides an even clearer example of affirmation where the appellant waited 5 years before seeking to avoid the contract (which in any event, it was found, was not induced by duress but freely entered into—which perhaps explains why there was such a long gap before any attempt to avoid it).

The alternatives available in the operation of economic duress, subject to this point, are illustrated in Figure 9.1.

Figure 9.1 Alternatives in the face of economic duress

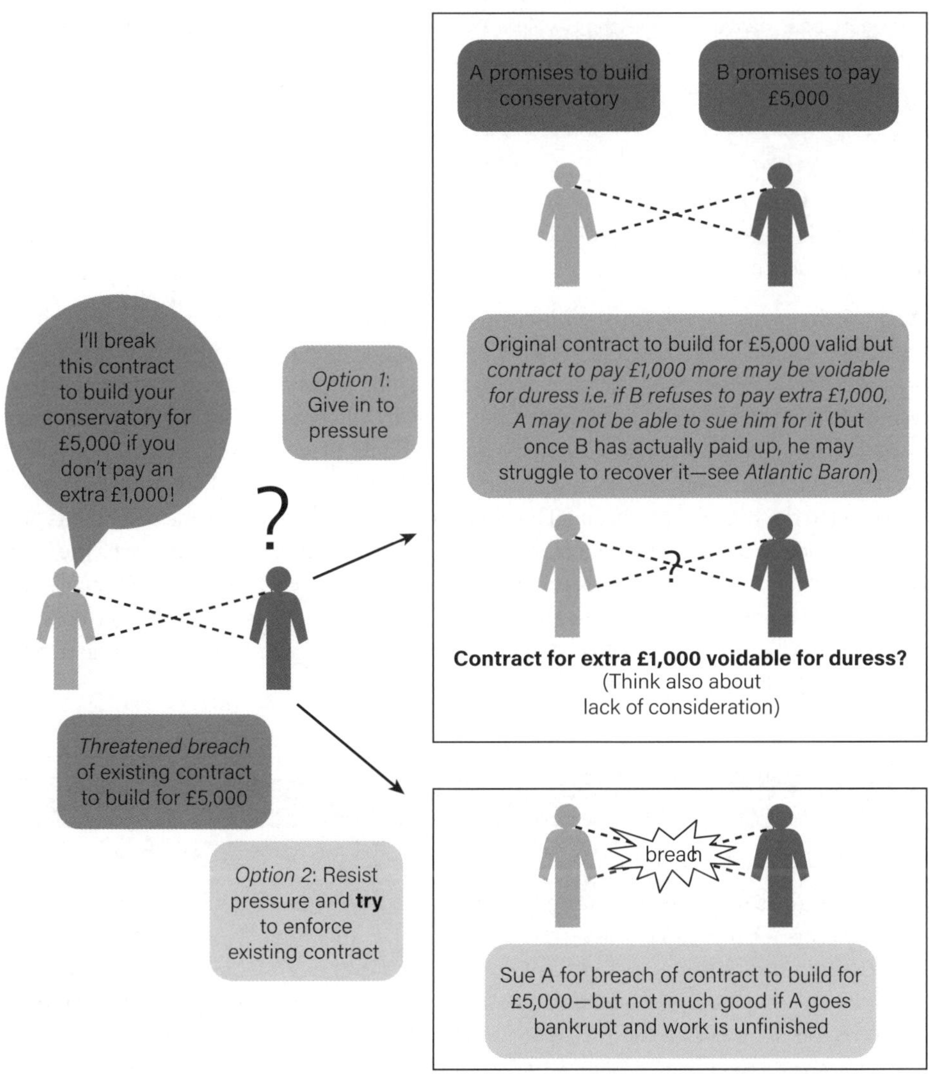

EXAMPLE

Void and voidable contracts

The Atlantic Baron highlights the importance of understanding the difference between void contracts and voidable contracts. Void contracts are contracts that have never existed: see, for example, cases of mistake where there was no matching offer and acceptance. Voidable contracts are damaged contracts: they are still valid, but they contain a defect and one party has the option of either unwinding the contract or affirming that contract (but, as *The Atlantic Baron* demonstrates, the party must not dawdle). In a sense, the 'innocent' party can choose whether to put the damaged contract out of its misery or heal it and bring it back to life. The important point to note for present purposes is that economic duress does not mean that a contract is void, merely that it is voidable and may be avoided or affirmed. In *The Atlantic Baron*, the buyers were taken to have affirmed it by paying up and then delaying their claim to recover their extra payment for eight months after delivery of the ship (which was the point at which they became free from the pressure of the threat not to deliver), but if they had acted more promptly they would have been able to avoid the new contract for economic duress.

It was thus fairly clear after these two cases in the 1970s that a contract *could* be avoided for economic duress but the right facts had not yet come before the courts for such a claim actually to succeed.

In *B. & S. Contracts* v *Victor Green Publishing* (1984) the claimants contracted to erect exhibition stands for the defendants but the work was delayed when the claimants' workmen went on strike. The defendants had hired many of the stands to exhibitors and so, because they wanted to fulfil their contractual obligations to these exhibitors, they paid in advance an extra £4,500 to the claimants so that the workmen would return to work. The Court of Appeal held that the £4,500 had been paid under economic duress; the defendants had no realistic alternative but to pay and the money could be recovered on that ground since the defendants had acted sufficiently promptly by deducting it from the balance of the contract price. The case is not quite one of avoiding a contract for duress as it was formulated as one of recovering an actual payment made (as in *Astley* v *Reynolds*, in relation to duress of goods (see earlier)). However, in *Atlas Express* v *Kafco* (1989) an unexecuted promise to pay extra was held to be unenforceable because of economic duress.

CASE CLOSE-UP

***Atlas Express* v *Kafco* (1989)**

Kafco was a small basket-weaving firm which had secured a lucrative contract with Woolworths (once a high street giant; more recently a high-profile victim of the credit crunch). Kafco contracted with Atlas Express for Atlas to deliver their baskets to Woolworths but Atlas badly overestimated how many baskets they could fit into their lorries and so the price per basket was much lower than Atlas would have normally quoted. When Atlas turned up to collect the baskets, the driver handed over a note which threatened that Atlas would drive away empty unless Kafco paid a minimum price per lorry.

Fearful of losing the lucrative Woolworths contract, Kafco agreed to the new pricing structure. Tucker J held that Atlas could not enforce the new term for a minimum price per lorry as the pressure imposed by Atlas amounted to economic duress. Tucker J also refused to enforce the contract on the alternative ground that the agreement to incorporate the new term lacked consideration as Atlas were already contractually obliged to deliver Kafco's baskets.

LINK TO . . .

Consideration (Chapter 4)

Even in the absence of duress, Atlas could not have enforced Kafco's promise to pay extra because Atlas provided no fresh consideration; they were already obliged to deliver Kafco's baskets and performing an existing obligation owed to the promisor is usually insufficient consideration.

Consideration and economic duress often seem to go together; note how in *Williams* v *Roffey* (1990) one factor in the decision to find consideration (factual benefit) was the absence of duress. By contrast, see *Adam Opel GmbH* v *Mitras Automotive (UK) Ltd Costs* (2007) (previously considered at Chapter 4, section 4.3.3), where the agreement was supported by consideration but the threat to cease supply amounted to duress and so the contract was voidable.

We have seen earlier that a threat to breach a contract will sometimes constitute economic duress but sometimes will not. It is now important to investigate the factors that determine which side of the line a particular set of facts will fall—why was the contract not voidable in *The Siboen and The Sibotre* but it was in *The Atlantic Baron* and in *Atlas* v *Kafco*?

The discredited 'overborne will' theory

The courts originally insisted that the pressure must overbear the will of the victim of duress. The idea was that contracts are formed by the free consent of the parties and so there can be no contract where that free consent has been overridden (e.g. by pressure amounting to duress). In *Pao On* v *Lau Yiu Long* (1980) the Privy Council recognized that commercial pressure may amount to economic duress but 'the basis of such recognition is that it must amount to a coercion of will, which vitiates consent. It must be shown that the payment made or the agreement entered into was not a voluntary act.' We have seen that the same approach was taken by Kerr J in *The Siboen and The Sibotre*.

The problem with this theory (see the criticism by Atiyah (1982) 98 LQR 197) is that a person under pressure still makes a very real choice in favour of the decision to pay extra or to vary the original agreement. If somebody threatens to shoot you unless you run a mile then your choice to run is very real: you want to run more than anything else in the world because you want to avoid being shot. However, the choice is not the same as if you go down to the gym and run to keep fit. In the gunman scenario your choice is compromised because the alternative is so unreasonable; if you do not run you will be shot. In the gym scenario you just risk becoming unfit if you do not run. Rather than talking about choice or consent being destroyed or the 'will overborne,' it is perhaps better to focus on the nature of the choice that is made and the extent to which it has been compromised and the reasonableness of the alternatives.

The nature and effects of the pressure

The courts have therefore moved away from a theory based on overborne will and instead consider the nature of the pressure and whether the pressurized party had a reasonable alternative open to him. Thus in assessing whether a threat to breach a contract amounts to duress, the courts look at:

(a) the legitimacy of the pressure,

(b) the causative effect of the pressure, and

(c) whether there was 'no reasonable alternative'.

(a) Legitimacy of the pressure

One view is that all threats to breach a contract are illegitimate and, as with threats against persons, the focus should be on whether the threat caused the pressurized party to enter into the contract sought to be set aside.

Alternatives to this view rely on distinguishing legitimate from illegitimate threats and this is where difficulties really surface. When can it ever be legitimate to say 'I know I promised to perform for £x, but now I will not perform unless you pay me more than £x'? Some commentators point to the facts of *Williams* v *Roffey* as an example of when a demand for more may be legitimate. The sub-contractors were on their knees but there was no duress because it was the main contractors who *offered* to pay more, rather than the sub-contractors *demanding* more (and so there was no threat). However, if the sub-contractors had demanded more then would their demand have been legitimate or implied an illegitimate threat to break the contract? They were clearly incapable of carrying on under the existing contract and history shows that more of the job was completed when they were offered more money.

However, even if the economic climate changes (as in *The Atlantic Baron* where the dollar had been devalued by 10 per cent) or one party is unable to continue then it is sometimes harsh to deny the other party their bargain; contracts should be for life, not just for as long as they suit the stronger party. We will see in Chapter 10 that sometimes the circumstances may change to such an extent that the law declares the contract at an end (frustration), but outside these cases there is a strong argument against allowing a party to *unilaterally* claim that circumstances have changed sufficiently to allow it to renegotiate its agreement with impunity.

Less controversially, there are cases where one party recognizes that the other party is in a weak position, decides to take advantage and threatens to break the contract unless they are paid more. This type of 'bad faith' renegotiation is more likely to be labelled as illegitimate and Dyson J in *DSND Subsea Ltd* v *Petroleum Geoservices ASA* (2000) thought that one relevant factor was whether the person applying the pressure acted in good faith or bad faith. In *Atlas Express Ltd* v *Kafco* the delivery company waited until the last minute, at the height of the Christmas rush, before threatening to breach its contract (the driver of the delivery truck informed Kafco of the demand when he arrived to pick up the goods). The basket-weavers faced losing their lucrative pre-Christmas contract with Woolworths if they could not have their baskets delivered and so they were forced to agree to the demand. The exploitation of the weavers must have clearly influenced the court in its decision. The obvious problem with a bad faith test, and the legitimacy test overall, is in where to draw the line.

The Commercial Court's decision in *Progress Bulk Carriers Ltd* v *Tube City IMS LLC (The Cenk Kaptanoglu)* (2012) demonstrates that the pressure need not come from a threat to breach a contract. In that case, the shipowner had already breached the charter contract and demanded that the charterer waive all its claims for damages before it provided a (much needed) alternative ship which would allow the charterer to meet a contract concluded with a Chinese buyer. The court held that the resulting settlement agreement entered into by the charterer was voidable for duress. The interesting point is that the demand for a waiver was not itself unlawful (settlement agreements are in fact actively encouraged by the courts as an efficient way of dealing with disputes), but the shipowner's prior unlawful breach of contract placed the charterer in a vulnerable position and its subsequent conduct had exploited that situation so as to amount to illegitimate pressure. As will be seen, this case has now been taken up by the Supreme Court as an important example of the limited circumstances in which 'lawful act duress' will be regarded as illegitimate and render a contract voidable—see the discussion below in section 9.1.5 of *Pakistan International Airlines* v *Times Travel* (2021).

THINKING POINT

Should a threat to breach a contract ever be regarded as legitimate and if so, how should the courts distinguish legitimate threats to break a contract from non-legitimate ones? What factors are relevant when assessing the legitimacy of a threat to breach a contract?

(b) Causation

In contrast to the position with duress by threats against the person (where, as seen in *Barton v Armstrong* at section 9.1.2 above, the threat need only be one of the reasons for giving in to the demand), for economic duress the threat to breach a contract must be a 'significant cause' in inducing the victim to enter into the new transaction (Lord Goff in *Dimskal Shipping Co SA* v *ITWF* (1992)). In *Huyton* v *Cremer* (1999) Mance J explained that this meant that the victim must show that he or she would not have entered the transaction 'but for' the threat. In *Morley* v *Royal Bank of Scotland* (2021) the appellant's claim of economic duress by the bank failed as the threats had not been the cause of entering the contract. It was clear that the threats against him were ineffective as they were successfully resisted by him and the impugned agreement eventually entered into was not on the terms which the bank had sought but was closer to one originally proposed by the appellant.

(c) No reasonable alternative

Mance J in *Huyton* v *Cremer* did not think that 'but for' causation alone would be sufficient. The victim must also show that there was 'no reasonable alternative.' In other words, even if the victim can prove that he (subjectively) would not have entered into the contract but for the threat, he must also show that, in an objective sense, there was no reasonable alternative open to him. See *Adam Opel GmbH* v *Mitras Automotive (UK) Ltd Costs* (2007), where Mitras (the party which made the threat) argued that an application for an injunction (i.e. a court order preventing Mitras from carrying out its threat) was a practical alternative to capitulation on the basis that it was beyond all doubt that the court would have granted an injunction compelling supply. The Deputy Judge rejected this argument emphatically at para. [32]: 'This line of argument might be thought worthy of admission to Alice's wonderland: the more blatantly unjustified and illegal the action threatened, the more readily the defendant would escape liability in duress.' Opel required immediate supply of its parts in order to avoid a catastrophic breakdown in its supply chain and so it could not afford the time and uncertainty of seeking an injunction at court. The alternative of going to court, despite a successful outcome ultimately being beyond doubt, was therefore not a reasonable alternative given the immediacy of the adverse consequences for Opel.

Although the 'no reasonable alternative' test initially emerged as part of the test for causation, it seems clear now from the decision of the Supreme Court in *Pakistan International Airlines v Times Travel* (2021) that it has to be regarded as a distinct third component of economic duress, since at para 136(ii) Lord Burrows said (in a formulation with which Lord Hodge agreed on behalf of the other three Justices):

> Three elements need to be established for . . . economic duress: an illegitimate threat; sufficient causation; and that the threatened party had no reasonable alternative to giving in to the threat.

EXAMPLE

Reasonable alternative to giving in to the threat

You contract with your milkman (if you are lucky enough still to have one) for a bottle of milk per day (at a fixed price for a year in advance) and he threatens to breach the contract unless you pay more for the milk. You may well be able to establish that you only paid the extra because you were fearful of not having fresh milk for your cereal each morning but the court may conclude that a reasonable alternative would have been to refuse to pay and buy a large carton of milk from a supermarket which would last all week (depending of course on how much milk you put on your cereal); by contrast, if milk was a tightly regulated substance (like alcohol) and only milkmen were licensed to sell it, the court is unlikely to conclude that you should have sought an injunction to get your morning 'fix' or that you should keep a cow in your back garden (although the benefits of a fresh and ready supply of milk could mean that you would never have to submit to the milkman's demands again). Subjectively speaking, on the first scenario, the threat caused you to agree to pay more, but objectively there was a reasonable alternative in obtaining supplies from the supermarket and so your choice to pay more was not in law caused by the duress but by your failure to take the reasonable alternative available at the supermarket. In the second scenario however there is no reasonable alternative and economic duress would be made out.

9.1.5 **Lawful act duress**

Whilst there is a strong argument for holding that all threats to commit a legal wrong (including breaking a contract) are illegitimate, the opposite is true for threats to do something that is lawful. Such a threat will usually be legitimate but the courts appeared to recognize in *CTN Cash and Carry Ltd* v *Gallaher* (1994) that a threat to do a lawful act might amount to duress if the demand is not made in good faith. In that case Gallaher delivered CTN's batch of cigarettes to the wrong warehouse (in Burnley rather than in Preston), from where they were stolen. Gallaher demanded payment for the cigarettes in the honest but mistaken belief that the cigarettes were already at CTN's risk under the contract. CTN refused to pay and so Gallaher threatened to withdraw CTN's credit facility with Gallaher, whereupon CTN paid up. CTN sought to reclaim the money on the grounds that it was paid under duress. The Court of Appeal rejected the claim because Gallaher was lawfully entitled to withdraw credit facilities at any time and bona fide believed that it was entitled to the money. The second point is important because it suggested (*obiter*) that a threat to do a lawful act might constitute duress if the party exerting the pressure acted in bad faith, for example by attempting to gain a benefit he knew he was not entitled to.

In *Pakistan International Airlines* v *Times Travel* (2021) the Supreme Court has made clear that lawful act duress does exist but also that it is tightly constrained and that it was not made out on the facts. The case concerned an agreement by the travel agent to waive existing claims against the airline for unpaid commission (which had a net value approaching £1 million and which in law were largely well founded). This was the result of potentially catastrophic threats by the airline (who had recently increased the agent's vulnerability by severely restricting their ticket allocation) to cease to deal with the agent altogether from the next month (the agent being almost totally reliant on this one airline for its business). Although the High Court had held that this amounted to economic duress enabling the travel agents to get out of the waiver agreement there was no finding of bad faith on the part of the airline and it had not been proved that they did not believe they were legally entitled to reject the claims for unpaid commission allegedly due. The decision was therefore overturned in the Court of Appeal since the airline's threats were not to break any contract (they were under no legal obligation to continue dealing with the travel agents), nor were the threats otherwise unlawful, however damaging they might be, and there was no proof of bad faith in relation to the denial of the validity of the commission claims. The Supreme Court agreed that lawful act economic duress was not made out on the facts but two separate judgments were given in the Supreme Court which, whilst agreeing on the result, gave somewhat different reasons.

Lord Burrows gave his own judgment whilst Lord Hodge gave a judgment with which the other three Justices agreed. It is important to note that there are many points on which both judgments explicitly agree, as set out by Lord Hodge in para. [1]. These include the proposition that whilst lawful act duress does exist in English law, it must not be stated too widely given the importance of competitiveness and certainty in commercial law. It was also agreed that, as Lord Burrows put it (at para. [96]) 'because the threat is of a lawful act, the question of whether it is illegitimate should focus on the nature of the demand rather than the nature of the threat.'

The main point of difference is precisely what it is about the nature of a demand that will mean that a lawful threat is illegitimate. For Lord Burrows, the crucial question (at para. [102]) is whether:

> the demand is made in bad faith in the particular sense that the threatening party does not genuinely believe that it is owed what it is claiming to be owed [in the *CTN Cash and Carry* type of case] or does not genuinely believe that it has a defence to the claim being waived by the threatened party [in the *Pakistan Airlines* type of case].

Since the bad faith requirement was not satisfied on the facts of *Pakistan Airlines*, that was enough to decide the appeal but Lord Burrows went on to say that in his view, if there had been such a finding of bad faith against Gallaher in *CTN cash and carry*, in which case Gallaher were also aware that CTN were in an extremely vulnerable position, that would have entitled CTN to reclaim the money as having been paid under economic duress. Similarly, if there had been bad faith proven against the airline in the instant case (in the sense that they knew they had no defence to the unpaid commission claim), given also that they had already deliberately increased the agent's vulnerability by severely reducing their ticket allocations, the agreement to waive the unpaid commission claims would have been voidable due to (lawful act) economic duress.

Lord Hodge's judgment in contrast did not accept that the demand being in bad faith was the necessary or crucial criterion for a threat to be illegitimate under the case law already laid down and did not agree that the instant appeal would have succeeded if bad faith had been proven. CTN in his view was 'authority for what is not [lawful act] duress, and not for what is.'

The two most relevant existing cases were *Borrelli* v *Ting* (2010), the facts of which are rather complex, and *Progress Bulk Carriers (The Cenk K)* (2012), the facts of which we have already met. Lord Hodge (at para. [17]) characterized both cases as ones where:

> it was the combination of (i) the existence of legal claims by B against A and (ii) the manoeuvring by A of B by reprehensible means into a vulnerable position where it had no alternative but to waive its pre-existing rights that amounted to illegitimate pressure.

What is the precise ambit of 'manoeuvring . . . by reprehensible means' is not entirely clear but in *The Cenk K* there had been 'misleading activity' in refusing to comply with assurances previously given about the provision of a substitute vessel until it was almost too late. The issue underlying the approach of Lord Hodge is a concern to restrict lawful act duress so that it does not impinge too much on hard-nosed commercial bargaining, as can be seen from the following quote:

> Lord Burrows considers that PIAC's deliberate act of cutting its ticket allocation, thereby increasing Times Travel's vulnerability to its demand for a waiver of a claim that it was in breach of contract, was an act which was beyond the mere exercise of monopoly power and would have amounted to illegitimate pressure if PIAC had known that it had indeed broken its contract. I respectfully disagree and take a narrower view of the scope of lawful act economic duress in this context. The reduction of the ticket allocation was a hard-nosed exercise of monopoly power, which, in the absence of a doctrine of unequal bargaining power, could not by itself amount to illegitimate pressure. Something more was needed, such as the reprehensible characteristics of the behaviour in *Borrelli* and *The Cenk K* to which I have referred in para 18 above. As I have said (para 28 above) the scope for lawful act economic duress is extremely limited in the sphere of commercial transactions.

One's instinct is that if or when a case arises where threats are used to induce a party in a highly vulnerable position to agree to waive or forego existing legal rights and bad faith in the requisite sense *is* clearly demonstrated (which is not an easy thing to prove), it will be perfectly possible for the resulting contract to be found to be voidable for lawful act economic duress both under Lord Burrows' explicit bad faith approach and also by finding reprehensible manoeuvring under the somewhat more opaque test in Lord Hodge's majority judgment.

The boundary between duress and undue influence

There is a group of cases traditionally classified as decided on grounds of undue influence (see section 9.2) but which have come to be regarded as examples of a particular (but uncommon) type of lawful act duress, as was confirmed by both judgments in the Supreme Court in *Pakistan International Airlines*. In *Williams* v *Bayley* (1866) the claimant's son had given forged documents to a bank, which then told the claimant that it had the power to prosecute his son. The claimant then executed a mortgage in the bank's favour in return for the forged documents. The mortgage was unenforceable because 'it had been extorted from the father by undue pressure' as the father knew that his son would be prosecuted if he did not give the mortgage. The implied threat to prosecute the son was not in itself unlawful; the bank was entitled to prosecute but it was not legitimate to use that implied threat to persuade the claimant to execute the mortgage to cover his son's debts to the bank.

Similarly, in *Mutual Finance Co. Ltd* v *John Wetton & Sons Ltd* (1937) the family company gave a guarantee under the implied threat that the finance company would prosecute the son for a previous forgery. The guarantee was held to be unenforceable because of undue influence but must now be regarded as being based on lawful act duress. Of course, if one party maliciously threatens to prosecute another without any basis for his allegation then this will amount to a threat to commit the wrong of malicious prosecution and this would be duress based on an unlawful and hence illegitimate act. However on the facts of both the cases being discussed, the implicitly threatened prosecutions were lawful in themselves, since there was good evidence that forgeries had taken place, but were illegitimate threats for the purposes of duress. It seems from Lord Burrow's judgment (at para. [90] of *Pakistan International Airlines*) that these two cases are to be regarded as examples of lawful act duress but not economic duress, presumably since the extortionate illegitimate threats were personal in nature rather than commercial (in contrast to the commercial threats in economic duress cases, including cases of lawful act economic duress such as *The Cenk K*). It appears we now have three types of unlawful act duress—(i) threats (of violence) to the person, (ii) threats to goods and (iii) (unlawful) economic duress as in threats to break a contract—plus two types of (comparatively rare) lawful act duress—(i) extortionate and illegitimate personal threats (as in *Williams v Bayley*), which are now simply lawful act duress, and (ii), very exceptionally, the illegitimate (but lawful) commercial threats which, under the restrictive *Pakistan International Airlines* tests, can constitute lawful act economic duress!

Rescue cases

Another type of case which might today plausibly be expressly classified as duress can be found in cases of extortionate salvage. It has long been established that a rescuer cannot simply extort the highest price he can from a ship in distress. In *The Port Caledonia* (1903), a tug demanded £1,000 for a rope to rescue a ship from drifting towards a collision with another. The captain of the ship, having initially responded with an offer of £100, agreed to pay £1,000 having been told '£1,000 or no rope.' When the tug owners claimed for the £1,000 promised under what the court described as an 'inequitable, extortionate, and unreasonable agreement,' a sum of £200 as reasonable recompense was substituted. The threat not to assist was not in itself unlawful (there was no duty to rescue) but the extortionate demand for an excessive amount could be regarded as supplying in the circumstances the element of illegitimacy required for economic duress, However, the restrictive approach to lawful act duress evident in the Supreme Court in *Pakistan International Airlines* v *Times Travel* did not favour such a classification. Indeed, the case of *The Port Caledonia* was mentioned by Lord Hodge (at para. [24]) as depending on the 'specialties of maritime law.'

9.2 Undue influence

Just as the duress inquiry identifies when *some* pressure becomes *too much* pressure, the undue influence inquiry identifies when *some* influence becomes *too much* influence. Influence, just like pressure, is part and parcel of everyday life but the courts occasionally say 'Enough!' and will undo a contract concluded under too much influence. Although duress was initially a common law doctrine and undue influence the creation of equity, both doctrines illustrate the courts' aversion to what might be called 'the puppet effect.' This is where one party acts as a puppeteer, pulling on strings to make the other party do things that they would not do independently—like agreeing to a contract. There are many reasons why the parties take on the roles of puppet and puppeteer: sometimes, it is because one can apply sufficient pressure on the other; sometimes, it is down to the relationship between the parties; and sometimes, it is a combination of both.

Since duress has been extended to include all sorts of pressure (and not just threats to the person), some older cases of undue influence have now been reclassified as 'duress' cases. As we have seen, *Williams* v *Bayley* was decided on the grounds of undue influence, but really the bank pressurized the father to execute the mortgage by means of an unspoken threat and the case would today be decided upon grounds of lawful act duress. Undue influence is now largely reserved for cases where too much influence arises from an existing *relationship* between the parties.

Undue influence can be proved in two different ways:

- **(a)** where there is evidence of actual undue influence being exercised; and
- **(b)** where there is no direct evidence of the actual exercise of undue influence but it can be (rebuttably) presumed from the relationship between the parties and the nature of the resulting transaction.

A crucial difference between the two is that in (b) (presumed undue influence) the resulting contract must be one which calls for an explanation (formerly, one which is manifestly disadvantageous to the party presumed to have been influenced), whereas in category (a) (cases of actual undue influence) that is not necessary. Figure 9.2 illustrates these propositions and distinctions.

9.2.1 **Actual undue influence**

In *BCCI* v *Aboody* (1990) a wife signed a mortgage over the family home in favour of a bank in order to secure borrowing by her husband's company. The evidence showed that the husband dominated his wife and that she signed anything he put in front of her (this would probably have been enough in itself but, in respect of the last transaction, when the wife was

Figure 9.2 Distinction between undue influence and duress

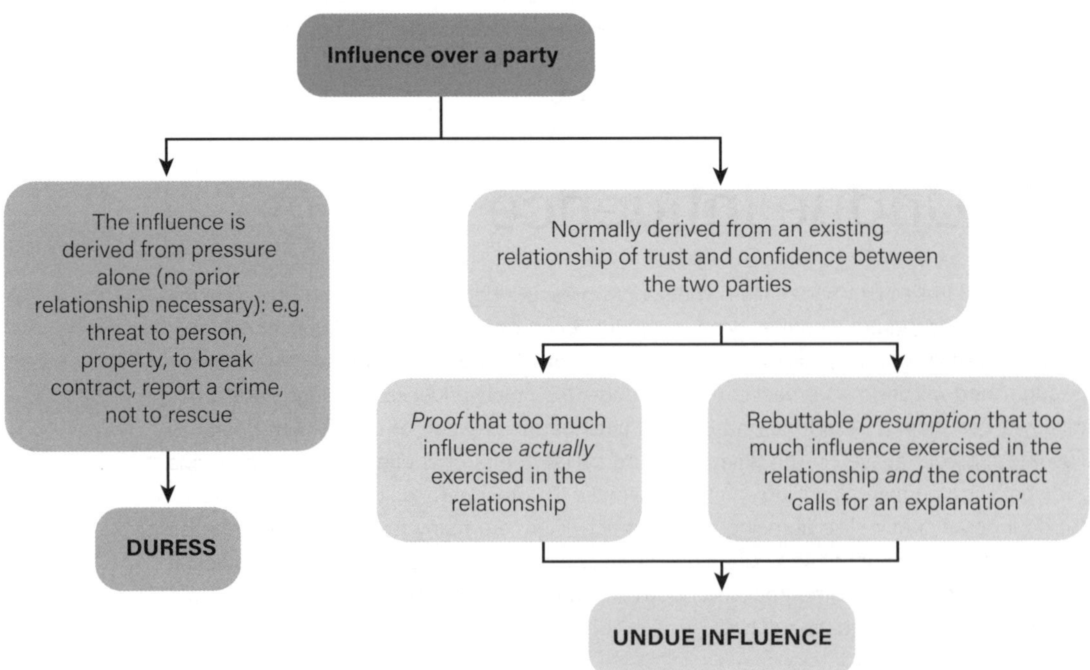

listening to independent advice he burst into the room, insisted that she sign the papers and had such a row with the solicitor that she burst into tears). The Court of Appeal had no difficulty finding actual undue influence but refused relief on the ground that the transaction was not manifestly disadvantageous to the wife. The House of Lords overruled the Court of Appeal on this latter point so that if a claimant can prove that actual undue influence was exercised the resulting transaction will be voidable and thus unenforceable regardless of whether it was manifestly disadvantageous (see *CIBC Mortgages plc* v *Pitt* (1993)). Actual undue influence which cannot be brought under the rubric of economic duress seems likely to be a declining species but its continued existence was recognized by the House of Lords in the landmark case on undue influence, *Royal Bank of Scotland* v *Etridge* (2001), where Lord Hobhouse said at para. [103] (of actual undue influence):

> [I]t is an equitable wrong committed by the dominant party against the other which makes it unconscionable for the dominant party to enforce his legal rights against the other. It is typically some express conduct overbearing the other party's will. It is capable of including conduct which might give a defence at law, for example, duress . . . actual undue influence does not depend upon some pre-existing relationship between the two parties though it is most commonly associated with and derived from such a relationship. He who alleges actual undue influence must prove it.

The House of Lords in *Etridge* however had more to say about the type of case traditionally referred to as presumed undue influence, to which we now turn.

9.2.2 **Presumed undue influence**

A claimant will often be unable to positively prove that one party exercised too much influence over them. Instead, the courts can infer from the facts that one party has preferred their own interests and failed in some duty they owed to safeguard the other party's interest, and this is what we call presumed undue influence (see para. [14] of *Etridge*). The result is the same as if the claimant had proved actual undue influence; the court effectively declares 'this transaction is tainted by undue influence' in both cases, but as lawyers we distinguish between actual and presumed undue influence to reflect the different fact scenarios that give rise to undue influence. There is therefore only one doctrine of undue influence (the pre-*Etridge* Class 1 and Class 2A and 2B categorizations are probably best forgotten now) but it can be proven in one of two ways: firstly (and less commonly), by actual proof of too much influence; and secondly, by inference (presumption) from the facts that the transaction was procured by too much influence. The courts look for the following facts in order to raise the inference (*Etridge*, para. [21]):

- **(a)** that the complainant reposed trust and confidence in the other party, or the other party acquired ascendancy over the complainant; and
- **(b)** a resulting transaction that is 'not readily explicable by the relationship of the parties' or which 'calls for an explanation'.

Even if the court raises the inference of too much influence on the back of the facts, the party presumed to have influenced the other can rebut the inference by showing that the other party knew what he or she was doing and freely consented to the transaction. See for example *Nature Resorts v First Citizens Bank* (2022) where the Privy Council agreed with the Trinidad Court of Appeal that the presumption had been rebutted as the person alleged to be unduly influenced was an experienced businessman who was exercising free and independent judgment who would have fully understood the risks involved in entering into the mortgage as security for the loan.

Figure 9.3 Actual and presumed undue influence

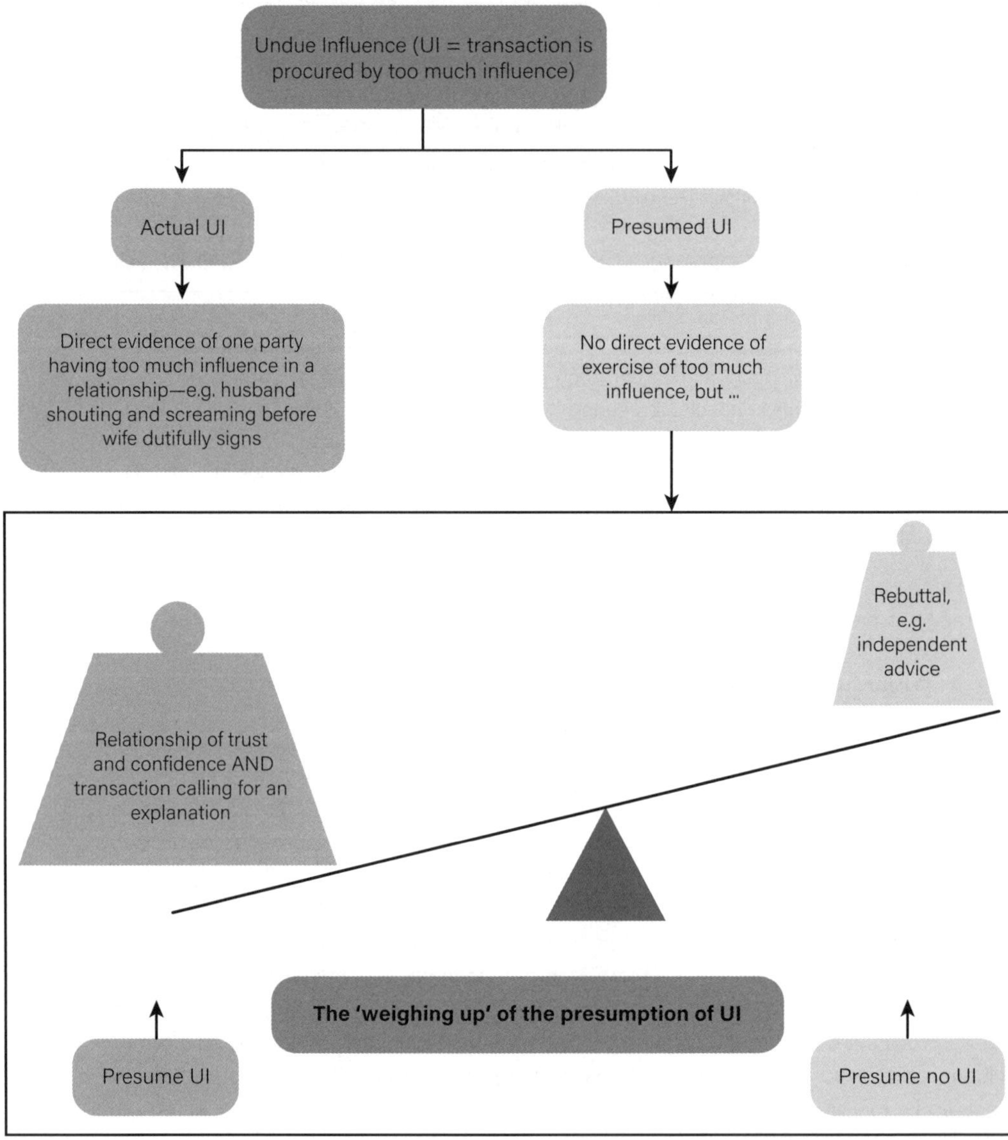

Thus the final verdict will come down on one side or the other—see the balance in Figure 9.3—and either there will not be undue influence (as in Nature Resorts) or there will be undue influence; in the latter case, as lawyers, we can say that the court *presumed* undue influence and the presumption was not rebutted, but it makes no difference to the parties whether the court found direct evidence of actual undue influence or made an inference on the basis of the factors set out earlier and found nothing to rebut it. The result will be the same in either case—the transaction will be liable to be set aside for undue influence.

Relationship of trust and confidence

Some relationships will *always* amount to a relationship of trust and confidence (see para. [18] of *Etridge*). Examples of such relationships are: parent and child; solicitor and client; doctor and patient; and religious adviser and follower. This however only shows that there is influence or the potential for it, not that there has actually been *undue* influence. The influenced party must also show that the actual transaction is one which calls for an explanation to raise the prima facie presumption of undue influence, and even then the other party can rebut this prima facie presumption.

CASE CLOSE-UP

***Allcard* v *Skinner* (1887)**

In *Allcard* v *Skinner* (1887) a young woman, Miss Allcard, joined a convent of nuns and signed up to their rules of poverty, seclusion and obedience to the Mother Superior. Miss Allcard made large gifts to the Mother Superior and sought to claim them back when she left the convent. The Court of Appeal denied her claim because it had been brought too late but they would have otherwise allowed it on the basis of undue influence. The nature of the relationship between the Mother Superior and Miss Allcard and the fact that the gifts could not reasonably 'be accounted for on the grounds of friendship, relationship, charity or other ordinary motives on which ordinary men act' led the court to a presumption of undue influence.

If the relationship does not fall within one of the automatic relationships of trust and confidence then the influenced party (e.g. the wife, since husband and wife is *not* one of the automatic relationships) must prove that there was on the facts such a relationship between the parties. As with the automatic relationships, even if a relationship of trust and confidence is proved on the facts, a presumption of too much influence will only be raised if the transaction itself is also one that calls for an explanation.

In *Tufton* v *Sperni* (1952) a Muslim convert set up a committee to establish a Muslim centre in London. A relationship of confidence was proved to exist between the convert and a businessman member of the committee who sold his house to the convert to be used as the centre for more than twice the market value. It was significant that the convert was much less experienced in business, and imbalances of this sort will often lead the courts to conclude that there is a relationship of trust and confidence.

For instance, in *O'Sullivan* v *Management Agency and Music Ltd* (1985) the relationship between the inexperienced young musician and his manager was one of trust and confidence.

Identifying relationships of trust and confidence

Relationships of trust and confidence are most obvious when one party relies upon the other for their basic needs. In *Hammond* v *Osbourn* (2002) an elderly man gave most of his assets away to a neighbour who cared for him and the court found a relationship of trust and confidence. The facts are similar to those in *Allcard* v *Skinner* (more than a hundred years earlier), where the relationship between a religious leader and follower had hardened into an automatic relationship of trust and confidence.

The categories of relationships are open-ended; this makes it relatively easy for you when sitting an exam. Simply ask yourself: is the relationship between the parties one of the automatic relationships of trust and confidence, for instance a doctor and patient or solicitor and client? If the answer is 'no' then you have to think of arguments why one party might place trust and confidence in the other; is there an obvious imbalance in experience or vulnerability due to sex, family, illness, old age or any other reason you can think of?

Finally, the courts may sometimes find a relationship of trust and confidence based purely on the fact that the transaction was so unfair that one party must have put trust and confidence in the other. This type of reasoning is very weak. Effectively, the courts are saying, 'We do not like this transaction. We do not think that it should stand but we are not allowed to rescind it simply because it is unfair. Therefore we will presume a relationship of trust and confidence so that we can presume that there was too much influence (a ground on which we are allowed to rescind the contract).'

In *Crédit Lyonnais* v *Burch* (1997) a junior employee gave a charge (a security right—see definition in section 9.1.3) over her flat to secure her employer's debt to the bank. The Court of Appeal could not find any direct evidence that there was a relationship of trust and confidence between the employee and employer but Millett LJ said:

> [W]here . . . there is a relationship like that of employer and junior employee which is easily capable of developing into a relationship of trust and confidence, the nature of the transaction may be sufficient to justify the inference that such a development has taken place; and where the transaction is so extravagantly improvident that it is virtually inexplicable on any other basis, the inference will be readily drawn.

THINKING POINT

Should the courts insist on proof of a relationship of trust and confidence or is it legitimate for them to infer such a relationship from the simple fact that the transaction is unfair?

Lord Millett justified such an inference in *Burch* because the transaction was so unfair that it was virtually inexplicable without a relationship of trust and confidence between the parties. You might consider whether people make grossly unfair bargains even when they do not have a relationship of trust and confidence with the other party.

Think about how many presumptions and inferences there are in this area—if a relationship of trust and confidence (coupled with a transaction calling for an explanation) can give rise to a presumption of undue influence and that relationship of trust and confidence can be inferred from the unfairness of the transaction, then what facts actually have to be proved? It seems that a claimant only has to show that the transaction is unfair: firstly, to infer a relationship of trust and confidence; and secondly, to show that the transaction calls for an explanation.

What is wrong with the courts giving relief solely on the basis that the transaction is unfair?

A transaction calling for an explanation

We saw earlier, in examining *Allcard* v *Skinner*, that the claimant must show not only a relationship of trust and confidence but also a transaction not explicable by the ordinary motives of ordinary men (and women). This requirement was expressed as a 'manifest disadvantage' in *CIBC Mortgages plc* v *Pitt* in 1994 but in 2001 the House of Lords in *Etridge* reaffirmed the test in *Allcard*, but restated it as 'a transaction that calls for an explanation.'

The focus of this test and the test in *Allcard* is that the transaction must lack an explanation rather than simply being disadvantageous on the face of it. For example, a wife's guarantee of her husband's debt is disadvantageous to the wife: she is giving a guarantee in return for nothing (her husband reaps the benefit). However, the transaction is explicable; the wife's fortunes are tied up with her husband's (and vice versa) and so it makes sense for both parties in the relationship to utilize their assets for the common good. Indeed, Lord Nicholls makes such an observation at para. [28] in *Etridge*, although he notes (in para. [31]) that there may be cases where a wife's guarantee or charge as security for her husband's debt might call for an explanation. The key question is 'Does this transaction raise any suspicions?'

On the facts of *National Westminster Bank plc* v *Morgan* (1985) Mrs Morgan took out a loan secured by a mortgage on the family home in order to refinance her husband's debts. The transaction was not manifestly disadvantageous because it was the only way she could save the home from being repossessed by a different creditor and the interest on the loan was not excessive. By contrast, in *Cheese* v *Thomas* (1994) an 88-year-old uncle gave his great-nephew £43,000 (everything he had) in return for his great-nephew's promise that he could live in a house bought partially with the money for the rest of his life. This transaction was manifestly to the uncle's disadvantage because he was tied to the specific house and had few rights over it if (as happened) the great-nephew failed to keep up with the mortgage payments. You should observe that the uncle did get to live rent free in a much better house than he could have bought with his £43,000 alone and that this shows that this area of law requires the courts to exercise a degree of discretion.

Rebutting the presumption

If the claimant proves that there was a relationship of trust and confidence and there was a transaction calling for an explanation then that still does not necessarily establish a case of undue influence; the defendant still has the opportunity to rebut the presumption by showing that the vulnerable party acted independently from any influence. This is most easily shown by proving that the party complaining of undue influence had independent advice. However, para. [20] of *Etridge* makes it clear that the question of whether there is undue influence is a question of fact and evidence that the claimant received independent advice *may* tip the balance, but it does not *necessarily* do so. An overview of the operation of undue influence is provided in Figure 9.4.

The remedy for undue influence

If the court finds that a contract was the result of undue influence it will refuse to enforce it or, if it has been executed or partly performed, will undo it through the remedy of rescission. This means that each party gives back everything they received under the contract (restitution of benefits received). Sometimes it is not possible to make full restitution by giving back all the benefits received but, starting with the decision in *Erlanger* v *New Sombrero Phosphate Co.* (1887) where the claimants gave back a mine transferred under the rescinded contract (less the excavated phosphate) but also had to give back the profits they had made from taking phosphate out of the mine, the courts in this context have increasingly been prepared to allow the parties to give back the monetary equivalent of what they received. In *O'Sullivan* v *Management Agency and Music Ltd* (1985) the then up-and-coming singer/songwriter Gilbert O'Sullivan was presumed to have been unduly influenced by his manager and their one-sided contract was rescinded. Under the contract, O'Sullivan had received management services and fame and money and the manager had received money as commission for his services. It was impossible to give back the management services and fame achieved by O'Sullivan but the court decided that in order to do justice, the manager had to give his commission back to O'Sullivan but he was allowed to make a deduction for the fair value of his services and some profit margin. In *Halpern* v *Halpern (No. 2)* (2007), the Court of Appeal noted in the context of

Figure 9.4 Overview of undue influence

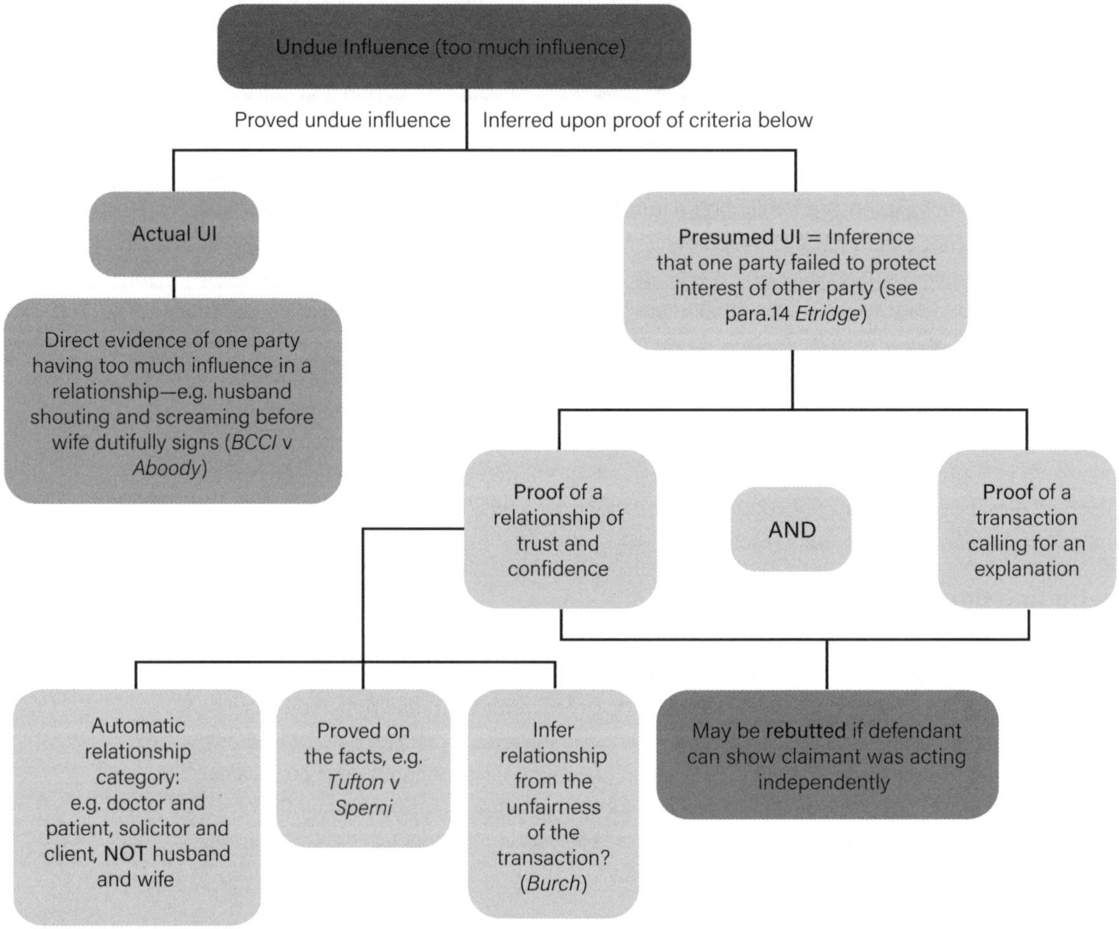

a decision on duress that rescission for duress was no different in principle from rescission for other vitiating factors (such as undue influence) and that counter-restitution would depend on the circumstances of the particular case. They emphasized at para. [75] that in order to do 'practical justice' it was not necessary to return *both* parties to the position they were in before the contract; instead they approved the following passage from Treitel: 'the essential point is that the representee should not be unjustly enriched at the representor's expense; that the representor should not be prejudiced is a secondary consideration.' In other words, if A makes a misrepresentation to, or threatens or unduly influences B, A cannot resist restitution on the basis that A will not be returned precisely to the position A was in before the contract; provided that unjust gains can be stripped away from the innocent party (B) and passed to the A in the form of money, that will generally be sufficient even if the amount returned to A is less than the cost of what A provided under the contract.

9.2.3 **Third-party cases**

The previous discussion has focused on the necessary elements to establish undue influence between the two parties to the contract. This section explores the consequences of a relationship of influence existing between one of the contracting parties and a third party. The typical transaction is between a wife and a bank (the parties) where the wife signs a guarantee with the bank with undue influence allegedly coming from the husband (the third party) whose debt to the bank is being guaranteed by his wife (see Figure 9.5). It is important to appreciate who are the contracting parties and who is the third party: remember, there is no contract between the husband and wife. The contract sought to be rescinded is between the wife and the bank and this relationship is free from undue influence; the key question is whether the bank is tainted by undue influence between the wife and the third party (her husband).

CROSS REFERENCE
See the explanation of a third party as a party who does not participate in the immediate contract under discussion in Chapter 4, section 4.3.2.

We can actually expand this problem beyond relationships of undue influence and ask whether the wife–bank contract can be affected by *any* irregularity between the wife and her husband. By 'irregularity' we mean any vitiating factor (such as duress or fraud or misrepresentation) we have come across in this book: for example, if the husband holds a gun to his wife's head and says (with the bank manager in earshot) 'contract with the bank or I'll shoot' then you would expect any contract between the wife and the bank to be voidable because there was too much pressure on the wife (duress) and the bank *knew* about it. The key point to note is that a third party (the husband) brought about the vitiating factor by threatening his wife; the bank's only connection to the duress was that it *knew* about it when it contracted with the wife.

Suppose however that the husband had threatened his wife before they went to the bank and the bank contracted with the wife in ignorance of any pressure operating on the wife: would you deny the bank its bargain in these circumstances; must the bank examine the couple's history every time they make a contract? We will see later that generally the bank must have some form of knowledge or notice of the third party's actions or impropriety before the courts will unravel the contract between the wife and the bank. It is of course equally possible (and increasingly so) that the roles of husband and wife in all of the above examples might be reversed, that is, that it is the husband who is guaranteeing the wife's debt to the bank.

Figure 9.5 Undue influence from a third party

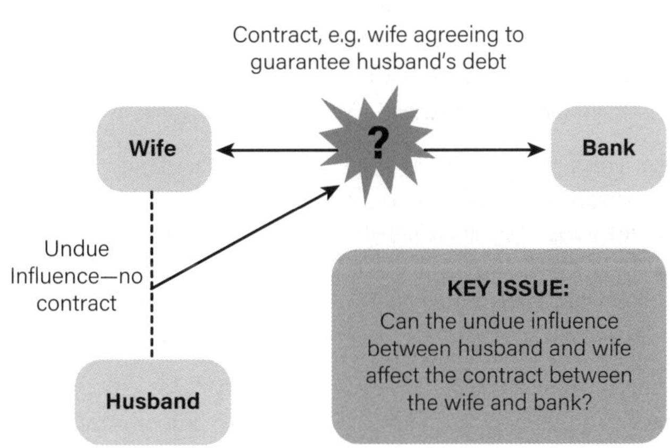

LINK TO . . .

Land law

Why does the wife ever become involved in these cases; why can't the husband guarantee his own debts? The answer lies in the way many married couples hold their property, usually as joint tenants. This means that husband and wife both own the whole property and neither can charge it as security without the consent of the other. Contrast this with a tenancy in common, where husband and wife each separately own *x* per cent and *y* per cent of the property and they can charge their individual share (but not the whole property) without the other's consent. Of course, sometimes the husband or wife may own the whole property on their own, sometimes precisely because the husband wishes to keep the family home away from his creditors.

Constructive notice

The cases focus on whether the bank had actual or **constructive notice** of the vitiating factor. You can be sure that any legal concept with 'constructive' in the title means only one thing: it is not what it purports to be. Constructive notice means that there is *no* notice, but the courts have deemed (i.e. pretended) that there is notice in order to reach an appropriate solution.

constructive notice: Constructive notice applies when a party did not actually have notice of a particular event, but the courts deem such notice, usually because the party turned a blind eye or was negligent and ought to have had actual notice.

Actual notice is easier to identify; it is clearly present when the bank knows that the husband has put too much pressure on his wife (gun to the head scenario) or induced a mistake in his wife (misrepresentation to the wife) or there is undue influence (actual or presumed). The question, in the absence of actual notice, is when will the courts deem that the bank has (constructive) notice of the husband's undue influence or other vitiating factor?

In *Barclays Bank plc* v *O'Brien* (1994), Mrs O'Brien agreed to charge the family home to the bank in order to secure the potential sum due under a guarantee given by her husband. Unfortunately Mr O'Brien told his wife that the charge was for a maximum of £60,000 (there was in fact no maximum) and that it would be released shortly (wrong again). The House of Lords held that the charge was voidable by the wife because the bank had constructive notice of the husband's misrepresentations. Lord Browne-Wilkinson said:

> [A] creditor [e.g. a bank] is put on inquiry when a wife offers to stand surety for her husband's debts [e.g. she offers to charge the family home to secure the debt] by the combination of two factors: (a) the transaction is on its face not to the advantage of the wife; and (b) there is a substantial risk in transactions of that kind that, in procuring the wife to act as surety, the husband has committed a legal or equitable wrong [this means misrepresentation, duress or undue influence] that entitles the wife to set aside the transaction.

It follows that, unless the creditor who is put on inquiry takes reasonable steps to satisfy himself that the wife's agreement to stand surety has been properly obtained, the creditor will have constructive notice of the wife's rights.

You could translate this as meaning that the courts will pretend that the bank knew of the misrepresentation, pressure or undue influence under which the wife operated if the transaction was one-sided; there was a substantial risk of misrepresentation, pressure or undue influence in that type of transaction and the bank did not check that the wife was acting freely. Lord Browne-Wilkinson recognized that other relationships may put a bank on inquiry and *Etridge* took this a step further by recognizing that a bank would be put on inquiry in 'every case where the relationship between the surety and the debtor is non-commercial' and where the transaction is not on its face to the advantage of the surety. This obviously has the potential to include not only husband and wife relationships but many others. Even in a husband-and-wife relationship, it is often extremely difficult to judge whether it is to the wife's advantage to guarantee her husband's debt; if the husband prospers (say in a business venture set up with the debt) then the wife will share in this success in the same way that she will suffer from failure of the business.

CIBC Mortgages plc v *Pitt* (1994) is an example of a clear case (cited in *Etridge* at para. [48]) where the bank was held not to have been put on notice. The bank thought that the wife was agreeing to guarantee a joint loan to the husband and wife to buy a holiday home together and so it was not put on inquiry because the loan was on its face a joint loan to husband *and wife* and appeared to be for the benefit of both of them (the husband actually lied to the bank and the loan was to fund his share speculation).

The courts have now identified a third or hybrid category of case where the loan being guaranteed is partly for joint purposes (so in that respect it is in both their interests and the bank would not normally be put on notice or enquiry) but also partly for the purposes of guaranteeing the husband's debt. In *Waller-Edwards* v *One Savings Bank* (2025), the Supreme Court has decided that in this case too the bank is put on enquiry and must take reasonable steps as outlined in the next paragraph to ensure that the wife (or other vulnerable party) knows and understands the potential liability that they are taking on even though only part of the loan is not for their own benefit.

Reasonable steps

Where the facts suggest a risk of undue influence or other irregularity, for example a wife standing surety for a loan which is wholly (or partly, as in the hybrid case) for her husband's debts, the banks must take reasonable steps. One way of doing this would be for the bank to insist that the wife attends a private meeting with a bank representative (i.e. without the husband) at which the full extent of her liability is explained, where she is warned of the risks she is taking and urged to take independent advice. However, in *Etridge* (Lord Nicholls at para. [55]) it was decided that this was not the only way to deal with the issue and indeed it was recognized that the reluctance of banks to arrange private meetings was not unreasonable given allegations that might later be made about what was said at them:

> Banks are concerned to avoid the prospect of similar litigation which would arise in guarantee cases if they were to adopt the practice of holding a meeting with a wife at which the bank's representative would explain the proposed guarantee transaction. It is not unreasonable for the banks to prefer that this task should be undertaken by an independent legal adviser . . . ordinarily it will be reasonable that the bank should be able to rely upon confirmation from a solicitor, acting for the wife, that he has advised the wife appropriately.

Lord Nicholls also discussed what a solicitor should do if the wife seeks independent advice (paras [64]–[67] of *Etridge*). Essentially, the solicitor should:

- explain why he has become involved (because the bank seeks assurance that the wife understands the transaction and freely consents to it);
- explain the documents and the consequences of signing them;
- point out the seriousness of the risks (including potentially losing her home);

Figure 9.6 Overview of third-party transactions

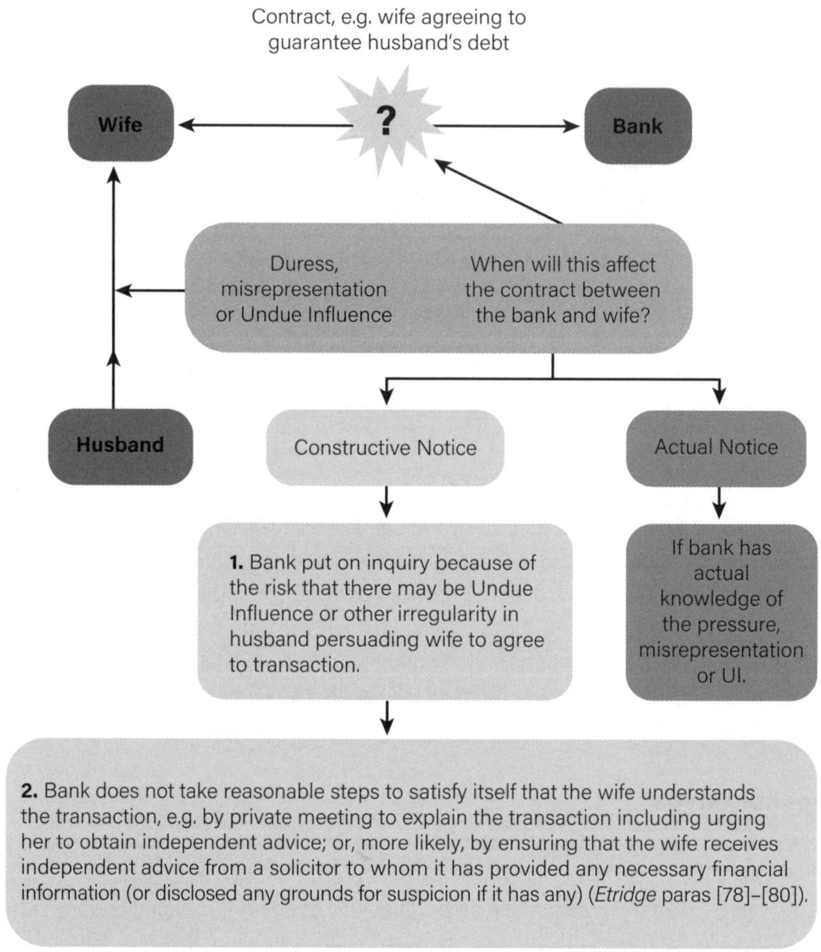

- emphasize that she has a choice; and
- check that she wishes to proceed on the terms offered by the bank.

The consequence of finding that the bank had notice (actual or constructive) of any irregularity as between the husband and wife is that the guarantee or charge given by the wife is voidable. To avoid this happening the bank must get a written confirmation from the solicitor providing the independent advice that the wife has been independently advised in line with these points. An overview of the law of undue influence affecting third-party transactions is provided in Figure 9.6.

9.3 Unfairness and unconscionable bargains

Before considering the exceptional category usually referred to as unconscionable bargains, it is convenient to briefly describe the distinction between procedural and substantive unfairness which is utilized by many critiques of the law covered in this chapter.

9.3.1 Procedural and substantive unfairness

The doctrines of duress and undue influence focus on procedural unfairness in the sense that they look at the parties' behaviour *in the run-up* to contracting. They are not primarily concerned with the substance of the contract—whether the bargain struck was fair—because traditionally the parties are free to agree to whatever they want to. The courts will not normally second-guess the value of the bargain and if the parties to the contract have not misled each other (misrepresentation) or influenced each other in an illegitimate manner (duress or undue influence) then generally the contract will stand.

9.3.2 Unconscionable bargains

Despite the absence of a general principle invalidating substantively unfair bargains, there is nevertheless a motley (but somewhat unpredictable) group of cases where the law is prepared to intervene primarily because of the evident unfairness of the transaction. The cases also however have the common feature that one party is inherently at a bargaining disadvantage—not in the sense that they have been placed at a disadvantage by the other party, for instance by being misled or threatened; but they are simply in a weaker position because of some personal disadvantage. They may be immature, mentally disadvantaged, poor, overly loyal or vulnerable for some other reason. This personal disadvantage alone will not be enough to persuade the courts to give relief; there must also be some 'unconscionable conduct' by the other party. It is therefore the *exploitation* of the party's weakness resulting in the unfairness of the bargain that makes the courts give relief; a mixture of substantive and procedural unfairness. These exceptional 'unconscionable bargain' cases, which are closely analogous to cases of undue influence but where it may be difficult to say that there is a relationship of trust and confidence, usually exhibit three key features, all of which must be present:

(a) an unfair bargain;

(b) a disadvantaged party with no independent advice; and

(c) unconscionable conduct from the other party.

An unfair bargain

It is very difficult to say precisely what something is worth but, generally speaking, it is easy to spot a transaction that is clearly unfair, and it is this obvious or extreme unfairness that is usually required before the court will intervene. In *Evans* v *Llewelyn* (1789) a man sold the interest he had unexpectedly inherited in his sister's estate for 200 guineas. The estate was in fact worth almost ten times more and so the bargain was clearly unfair. In a more modern example, *Cresswell* v *Potter* (1978), a wife left her husband and conveyed her share in the family home to him in return for being released from liability under the mortgage. The mortgage was actually worth much less than the house, and so the wife swapped a valuable asset (the house) for a less valuable asset (release from liability).

Disadvantaged party with no independent advice

There are many different types of disadvantage. Many older cases protected expectant heirs because they personally had very little money but they knew they would have a great deal in the future. Some people would therefore lend the heir money at exorbitant rates of interest or buy their inheritance for well below its value (see *Earl of Aylesford* v *Morris* (1873)). Protection was extended from the prospectively rich to the 'poor and ignorant' in *Fry* v *Lane* (1888), although this was interpreted widely in *Cresswell* v *Potter* to include a telephone receptionist who was 'poor' in the sense that she had few savings and a low-paid job and who was 'ignorant' in the sense that she was 'less highly educated' and did not understand the property transaction at the heart of the case.

Independent advice, if provided, may show that despite the disadvantages suffered by one party, that party really did understand the transaction and entered into it freely. It also tends to show that the other party did not act unconscionably because they did not try to prevent the weaker party from getting advice on the merits of the transaction.

Unconscionable conduct

The word 'unconscionable' is used in many contexts but rarely defined. It essentially means that the stronger party has offended the conscience of the court; the court disapproves of the party's behaviour in exploiting the weakness of the vulnerable party (but this obviously does not provide a watertight definition of what type of conduct will count as unconscionable). In *Hart* v *O'Connor* (1985), Lord Brightman in the Privy Council confirmed that the stronger party must be guilty of unconscionable conduct before the courts could set aside a contract as an unconscionable bargain. The court expressly referred to the need for procedural unfairness as well as substantive unfairness (or contractual imbalance as it called it). The seller of farm land in New Zealand was of unsound mind and one of his brothers (who was entitled to the land under a trust) sought to set aside the transaction as an unconscionable bargain. The Privy Council refused to do this because the buyer had never taken advantage of the seller's unsound state of mind or engaged in any other unconscionable conduct. The buyer did not know, and could not have been expected to know, that the seller was of unsound mind and so the contract (which in any event was not all that one-sided) stood.

In contrast, in *Boustany* v *Pigott* (1993) the Privy Council set aside a lease which had been signed by Miss Pigott, who was elderly and rather 'slow.' Mr and Mrs Boustany had waited until Miss Pigott's business manager, George Pigott, had left the country and invited her around for tea with a bishop, where they flattered and lavished attention on her. They then took her to their solicitor, Mr Kendall, and presented a disadvantageous lease which she signed, against Mr Kendall's advice.

The Privy Council agreed with the inference which the trial judge drew:

> [T]hat Mrs Boustany and her husband had prevailed upon Miss Pigott to agree to grant a lease on terms which they knew they could not extract from Mr George Pigott, or anyone else . . . In short, Mrs Boustany must have taken advantage of Miss Pigott before, during and after the interview with Mr Kendall and with full knowledge before the . . . lease was settled that her conduct was unconscionable.

It can be seen that the requirements for setting aside unconscionable bargains are highly fact dependent and it is difficult to predict in advance what will shock the court's conscience. There are no hard and fast rules here and the cases are, by their nature, very much exceptional ones.

THINKING POINT

Is there a risk that the courts 'infantilize' elderly or disadvantaged parties by refusing to enforce contracts made with them? Is this risk sufficiently expunged by requiring exploitation of the other party's weakness? Might some parties simply refuse to deal with disadvantaged parties (who are sometimes the most in need) if the law took too strong an approach to unconscionable bargains?

Digging deeper

There are of course some situations where Parliament has passed legislation to protect vulnerable groups who are at risk of entering into unfair bargains; for example the provisions now to be found in the Consumer Rights Act 2015 invalidating certain unfair or unreasonable clauses in contracts with consumers and the powers in the Consumer Credit Act 1974 (as amended, s.140A–C in particular). Parliament is in a better position to make such policy decisions because they are elected and accountable to the population as a whole. The courts are traditionally less inclined to make policy decisions on what is fair and unfair because they are independent and trusted to apply the rule of law which is, in theory, free from such policy decisions. Lord Denning however was more adventurous and tried to introduce an overarching doctrine that would give relief whenever there was 'inequality of bargaining power.' He said in *Lloyd's Bank Ltd* v *Bundy* (1974):

> English law gives relief to one who, without independent advice, enters into a contract upon terms which are very unfair or transfers property for a consideration which is grossly inadequate, when his bargaining power is grievously impaired by reason of his own needs or desires, or by his own ignorance or infirmity, coupled with undue influences or pressures brought to bear on him by or for the benefit of the other.

This approach was however rejected as a general principle by Lord Scarman in *National Westminster Bank* v *Morgan* in 1985 (the actual decision in *Bundy* was not impugned in any way since it was based in the alternative on undue influence) on the grounds that the proposed principle would interfere too much with the parties' freedom of contract and restrictions based on substantive unfairness should normally be left to Parliament. To be fair to Lord Denning's formulation, it seems to be based on both substantive and procedural unfairness; it requires 'terms which are unfair' and 'undue influences or pressures' but whether such a broad general principle could be applied in practice with any degree of consistency is perhaps questionable. The Supreme Court decision in *Pakistan International Airlines* (2021) has underlined the approach that there is no such general principle and that the control of unfairness has to be through specific doctrines which are closely defined and which will only be expanded, if at all, incrementally.

Summary

1. Duress

A contract may be voidable for duress if one party, by means of a threat, puts too much pressure on the other party, assessed by reference to the legitimacy or otherwise of the threat and the extent to which it can be said to have caused the other party to enter into the transaction.

Threatening to kill or injure someone (duress of the person) is always illegitimate pressure and a claimant need only show that it was 'a' cause of (i.e. it contributed to) the decision to enter into the contract, rather than being a predominant or 'but for' cause.

Threatening a person's goods (duress of goods) can also amount to illegitimate pressure. Although the old case law drew a distinction between recovering a payment actually made and avoiding a contract to pay, it is now understood that the latter is also covered, especially given the development of economic duress.

Threatening to do an unlawful act such as breaching a contract will normally constitute illegitimate pressure and can amount to 'economic duress.' There are three requirements: (i) illegitimate pressure, (ii) 'but for' causation in the sense that the threatened party would not have entered the contract but for the threats and (iii) there must be no reasonable alternative open to the threatened party.

Even a threat to do a lawful act (lawful act duress) may exceptionally constitute illegitimate pressure. Some of the old 'actual undue influence' cases where promises to pay were effectively extorted by threatening that a relative might otherwise be prosecuted for fraud have now been reclassified as relatively rare examples. The majority of the Supreme Court in *Pakistan International Airlines* took a very restrictive approach to the existence of any other examples of lawful act duress, especially in commercial contracts, for fear of undermining contract law's support for robust commercial bargaining and decision making. All the Justices agreed that where the threat is in itself lawful, the nature of the demand and conduct of the threatener determined whether it was illegitimate. Lord Hodge for the majority considered that it was 'manoeuvring the other party by reprehensible means' into 'a vulnerable position where it had no alternative' which was characteristic of the very few commercial cases where lawful act duress had been, and would be, recognized. 'Bad faith' in itself was not sufficient. Lord Burrows agreed on a restrictive approach but considered that bad faith, that is the absence of a good faith belief in existing legal entitlement to what was being demanded, should be the crucial necessary factor in establishing lawful act economic duress where the other party was in a highly vulnerable position.

2. Undue influence

Undue influence is an equitable doctrine which, like duress, also renders a contract voidable and may be expressly proved (actual undue influence) or, more commonly, be established by means of an evidential presumption (presumed undue influence).

Presumed undue influence requires proof of a relationship of trust and confidence between the parties (some relationships automatically fall into this category by means of an irrebuttable legal presumption) and a transaction calling for an explanation. The presumption may be rebutted, for instance if the vulnerable party had independent advice.

3. Third-party cases

A contracting party (such as a bank taking a guarantee from a wife) may be affected by the duress or undue influence (or misrepresentation) of a third party (such as a husband) if it has notice of the relevant facts constituting the duress or undue influence (or misrepresentation).

Constructive notice may be imposed on a bank, for example if the agreement is for a non-commercial guarantee which is not advantageous to the guarantor (e.g. the wife) unless the bank takes reasonable steps to ensure that the guarantor fully understands and freely consents to the transaction (which it will normally do by insisting on independent advice being given by a solicitor who certifies that this has been done).

4. Unconscionable bargains

A manifestly unfair contract with a party suffering from a personal disadvantage which has been unconscionably exploited by the stronger party will not be enforced.

This principle is exceptional, given the rejection of Lord Denning's proposed general principle of inequality of bargaining power, and depends on both substantive and procedural unfairness, but is somewhat unpredictable. It is analogous to undue influence but differs; in particular it does not require a relationship of trust and confidence.

? Questions

The roof of the church attended by Mark has begun to leak badly. Mark owns, jointly with his wife, a small house where they live together. Apart from that he is poor but devout. He decides that it is his duty to borrow the money to enable him to donate the £100,000 needed to restore the church to its former glory but he first arranges to speak to the parson to check that his gift will be accepted. The parson is delighted but tells Mark that the roof will only cost £80,000 to fix and so there is no need to donate the full £100,000. The parson also passes him the business card of his solicitor and advises him to speak to the solicitor before making the gift.

Mark tells his wife, Anna, that he would like to donate £40,000 to the church (he is scared about revealing the true amount to his wife) and asks her to go with him to the bank and consent to securing a loan with a mortgage over their jointly owned house. Anna refuses to go to the bank and says that he is being stupid, adding: 'I thought the drugs Dr Scholes gave to you should have stopped these episodes of madness.' This makes Mark very angry and he shouts at his wife, accusing her of not respecting his religion, adding that 'banks never repossess houses and, besides, the Church are going to pay me back when they have the money.' Mark's wife reluctantly agrees to go to the bank and sign the necessary papers 'so long as you get the £40,000 back as soon as possible.'

The bank insists that Anna talks to an independent solicitor before she signs any documents. Anna visits the solicitor but is so distressed at Mark's behaviour that she signs the necessary papers without actually realizing that the loan is for £80,000, double what she thought.

Mark has been so busy arranging the mortgage that he forgets to take the parson's advice to visit a solicitor. He transfers the £80,000 advance to the parson who then decides to use the money to help educate orphaned children in the parish. Mark is annoyed and demands the money back. A year later, he has still not been repaid, he has lost his poorly paid job and the bank now wants to repossess the house because he has not kept up the mortgage payments.

Advise Mark and Anna.

1. 'The law's response to inequality and unfairness in contracts is regrettably fragmented and unpredictable.' Discuss.
2. 'One of the strengths of English law is its piecemeal approach to the general problem of unfairness in contracting.' Discuss.
3. 'Controlling procedural unfairness is simply the tip of the iceberg; the courts should focus their attention directly on bargains which are substantively unfair.' Discuss.
4. 'The test for lawful act duress laid down by the majority in the Supreme Court case of *Pakistan International Airlines* is disappointingly vague whereas the bad faith criterion in the minority judgment is much more likely to be consistently applied and is more appropriately linked to fundamental questions of honesty and dishonesty.' Discuss.

Further reading

Books

Chen-Wishart, M, *Contract Law*, 7th edn (Oxford University Press, 2022) chs 8 and 9.

McKendrick, E, *Contract Law: Text, Cases and Materials*, 11th edn (Oxford University Press, 2024) chs 18, 19 and 20.

O'Sullivan, J, and Hilliard, J, *The Law of Contract*, 11th edn (Oxford University Press, 2024) chs 10, 11 and 12.

Articles

Atiyah, PS, 'Economic duress and the overborne will' (1982) 98 LQR 197.

Bamforth, N, 'Unconscionability as a vitiating factor' (1982) 98 LQR 197.

Birks, P, 'The travails of duress' [1990] 3 LMCLQ 342.

Birks, P, and Chin, NY, 'On the nature of undue influence' in J Beatson and D Friedmann (eds) *Good Faith and Fault in Contract Law* (Clarendon Press, 1995) ch 3.

Capper, D, 'Undue influence and unconscionability: A rationalisation' (1998) 114 LQR 479.

Chen-Wishart, M, 'The O'Brien principle and substantive unfairness' (1997) 56 CLJ 60.

Jackson, O, 'Unconscionability, uncertainty and lawful act duress' [2021] 8 JBL 701.

Thal, SN, 'The inequality of power bargaining doctrine: The problem of defining contractual unfairness' (1998) 8 OJLS 17.

PART IV

FINISHING AND ENFORCING OBLIGATIONS

There are many reasons why parties enter into contracts but they all generally boil down to the simple proposition that one party wants the other to do something for them; they want *performance*. Most contracts are performed perfectly satisfactorily (e.g. you pay me and I 'deliver the goods') and the obligations in them are thus normally finished in this manner ('*terminated by performance*') but these are not the cases that end up in the courts (unless there is a dispute about whether there has been full or satisfactory performance). Sometimes the parties might mutually agree that each other's performance is no longer required and that the obligations on each side can be '*terminated by agreement*'. Again, these cases will generally not lead to litigation (but since consideration is required on each side for such an agreement there can be problems if only one side appears to be giving anything up—see, for example, Chapter 4, section 4.3.4 in relation to part payment of a debt).

One or both parties may (exceptionally) try to argue that further performance is not required because the contractual obligations have terminated due to an unforeseen fundamental change of circumstances which is neither party's fault, and this form of '*termination by frustration*' is dealt with in Chapter 10. One party might alternatively argue that they are no longer required to perform because they have elected to terminate the contract in response to a breach of a condition or a serious breach of an innominate term by the other party ('*termination for breach*', already discussed in Chapter 5, section 5.4 and to be further discussed in Chapter 12, sections 12.1.4–12.1.7 in relation to repudiation, affirmation and anticipatory breach).

If, however, the obligations have not been terminated for any of these reasons and performance is still required but is withheld or is for some other reason not forthcoming or is not satisfactory, the disappointed party has two main types of *remedy* which he can seek from the courts by way of *enforcing* the obligations owed to him: he can invoke his common law *right to damages* to compensate him for the missing or defective performance—this is the primary or basic and most general remedy for breach of contract and is dealt with in Chapter 11; or he can ask the court in its discretion to compel the party in breach to perform his obligations by means of the equitable remedies of specific performance and injunction; or, where he simply wants to be paid the agreed sum, he can normally secure that by means of an action for the price, provided he has been able himself to provide the full performance or degree of performance necessary to trigger the obligation to pay. These '*specific remedies*' and related issues are discussed in Chapter 12.

The questions of *how* and *when* outstanding contractual obligations can be enforced (the questions of remedies as outlined earlier) are closely related to the question of *who* can enforce them; this raises the issue of privity of contract and the interests of third parties, which is the subject matter of the final chapter of this fourth and 'finishing' part of the book, the ineffable and inevitable Chapter 13.

10 Frustration

LEARNING OBJECTIVES

This chapter will help you to:

- identify when a contract may be frustrated by events which occur *after* formation of the contract;
- assess the different justifications for frustrating a contract;
- understand that frustration brings the future contractual obligations of the parties to an end; and
- understand how the Law Reform (Frustrated Contracts) Act 1943 may reallocate the consequences of frustration.

Introduction

This chapter looks at what happens when the assumed facts change after the contract has been agreed. This should be contrasted with the situation discussed in Chapter 8 on mistake where, at the time the contract was formed, the facts were already different from what the parties supposed them to be. It is inevitable, to a certain degree, that the surrounding circumstances will change after contracting because the world around us is constantly evolving. Despite this, the parties expect most things to remain the same: the sun will still rise in the morning and set in the evening; the tide will come in and go out, and so on. But now and again the natural order of things is disturbed, as in the case of tsunamis, hurricanes or volcanic eruptions (or pandemics). These fundamental changes in the facts assumed by the parties—potentially frustrating events—are not limited to natural disasters and less catastrophic events may be argued to have fundamentally changed the parties' obligations so as to frustrate the contract. The key question is: 'How substantially has the allegedly frustrating event changed what the parties promised to do?' Frustration of a contract is rare as it brings the parties' obligations to an end and that requires a radical change; less significant changes will not be sufficient and will be non-frustrating events which leave the contract intact so that the parties must continue to perform their obligations even if they have become more onerous.

10.1 The allocation of risk

The frustration doctrine, like many other contract doctrines that we have looked at, can be seen as primarily about risk allocation. In relation to common mistake (see Chapter 8) the courts had to decide when a background mistake common to both parties was fundamental enough to make the contract void. The court's decision to hold the contract void or to uphold it effectively allocates risk between the parties; in *Bell* v *Lever Bros* (1950) the House of Lords had to decide whether the employees should be able to keep their termination payout and thus place the risk of the mistake (the risk that the employment contracts could have been terminated for breach) on Lever Bros, or whether Lever Bros could claim back their payout on the basis that they made the payment under a mistake, thus placing the risk of a mistake on the employees.

This chapter deals with the same issues in relation to risk allocation but in relation to events *after* contracting. In *Amalgamated Investment & Property Co. Ltd* v *John Walker & Sons Ltd* (1976) the building was listed (by English Heritage as being a building of special architectural or historic interest) a short time (two days) *after* the formation of the contract to buy it so that the case had to be considered under the heading of frustration, whereas if the list had been signed before the contract, the appropriate rules would have been those relating to mistake. The court was not prepared to help the purchaser even though the value of the building had dropped by £1.5 million (90 per cent), essentially because the risk of a building becoming listed was one that a developer must take for himself, just the developer will take the benefit if the building soars in value. The ownership of the building could still be transferred and the contract could still be performed exactly according to the terms of the contract without becoming something radically different, and therefore the contract was not frustrated.

10.1.1 The effect of frustration

Because frustration is concerned with the impact of subsequent events on initially valid contracts which have already been agreed to, there is no question of the contract being void from the beginning (i.e. never having existed) but rather the question is whether the events which have occurred should *terminate* the contract, that is, bring it to an end as from the date of the frustrating event. Frustration is forward looking and terminates a contract only in relation to the future; so although neither party has to perform its remaining obligations, obligations due to be performed before the frustrating event remain binding. Difficulties can arise as to how to deal with any money or services which have passed (or ought to have passed) under the contract *before* termination.

EXAMPLE

Effects of frustration

What should happen if Adam has paid only 10 per cent of the price of a building in advance when he should have paid 30 per cent? Imagine also that, at the time of termination, Bertie had already done 60 per cent of the work.

Should Bertie be able to claim the 20 per cent owed by Adam? Should he also be able to claim the value of the work done before termination, with deduction for the money already paid by Adam?

The Law Reform (Frustrated Contracts) Act 1943 attempts to deal with these issues which we will consider later in the chapter at section 10.5.

10.1.2 **A core case**

If you read only one case on frustration (not recommended!), it should be *Taylor* v *Caldwell* (1863). Prior to this case, the law's approach was summed up in the so-called absolute contracts rule, or rule in *Paradine* v *Jane* (1647), which meant that, generally speaking and subject to very limited exceptions, if you agreed to do something in contract, you were absolutely bound to do it, come hell or high water. This approach was modified in *Taylor* v *Caldwell* (see Figure 10.1). The defendants owned the Surrey Music Hall and Gardens and, for a fee of £100 per day, they agreed to let the claimants have the use of it on four separate dates in the summer of 1862 for the purpose of four grand concerts and day and night fetes. After the contract had been signed, the music hall burned to the ground and the claimants sued for damages (£58 printing and advertising costs which were wasted) because the defendants could not provide the hall which they had contracted to provide. Neither party had thought that the hall would burn down but should the owners be liable for their consequent inability to provide the hall?

The absolute contracts rule, under which contractual obligations had to be honoured in virtually all circumstances, would have meant that the owners were liable for breach of contract in failing to provide the hall even though the hall had burned down. However, Blackburn J detected a general principle in earlier case law that:

> in contracts in which the performance depends on the continued existence of a given person or thing, a condition is implied that the impossibility of performance arising from the perishing of the person or thing shall excuse the performance.

He concluded that:

> the Music Hall having ceased to exist, without fault of either party, both parties are excused, the claimants from taking the gardens and paying the money, the defendants from performing their promise to give the use of the hall and gardens.

The defendants were therefore not obliged to provide the hall once it had been destroyed and so the claimants could not successfully sue them for damages.

Figure 10.1 A timeline of events in *Taylor* v *Caldwell*

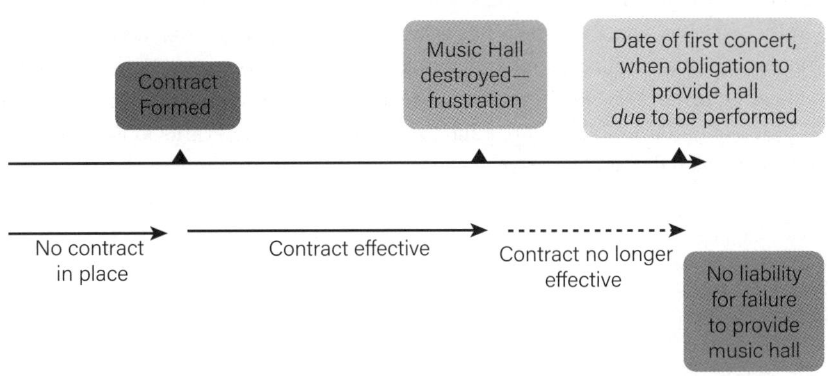

10.1.3 **Theories of frustration**

It is possible to spend a great deal of time discussing what theory underpins the doctrine of frustration but most commentators are now of the view that seeking to identify the 'correct' one is a futile exercise because, as Lord Wilberforce put it in *National Carriers* v *Panalpina* (1981), they all 'shade into one another.'

Blackburn J in *Taylor* v *Caldwell* justified terminating the contract by reference to the parties' *implied* intentions. If the parties had expressly stated that they would each be excused from performance if the subject matter of the contract was destroyed, then this express allocation (or sharing) of the risk would clearly be followed. In the absence of the parties' express provision, the courts (according to Blackburn J) should imply a term that the parties should be excused if performance becomes impossible because the subject of the contract no longer exists. The implication was said to be made 'to fulfil the intentions of those who entered into the contract.'

It has since been recognized that this 'implied consent' theory is actually a fiction because no one really knows what the parties would have said if the question had been put to them of what should happen should the music hall be burned down. They might in fact have disagreed about what should happen.

Lord Simon in *National Carriers* v *Panalpina* (1981) thought that whilst the implied term theory was potent in the development of the doctrine and still provides a satisfactory explanation of many cases, it is the 'theory of a radical change in obligation' that appears to be the one most generally accepted (and was the approach of the judge in the case of *Canary Wharf v European Medicines Agency* (2019), where Brexit was held not to radically change the obligations under a 25-year-long lease).

The 'radical change in obligation,' also known as the 'construction theory,' involves the courts construing the obligations of the parties *at the time of contracting* and comparing them to the obligations of the parties *after the alleged frustrating event*. If there has been a 'radical' or 'fundamental' change then the contract will be frustrated and terminated. In the words of Lord Radcliffe in *Davis Contractors* v *Fareham* (1956):

> [F]rustration occurs whenever the law recognises that, without default of either party, a contractual obligation has become incapable of being performed because the circumstances in which performance is called for would render it a thing radically different from that which was undertaken by the contract . . . It was not this that I promised to do.

This last phrase is perhaps the key. The contracting party has promised to perform but his promise should not be construed as absolute. He should not reasonably be expected to be bound in the extreme situation which has arisen—or, putting it another way, he did not assume the risk of the frustrating event and should be excused from his promise. It is relatively easy to state the test in this way but not so easy to satisfy it or to apply it consistently, as will be seen by looking at examples of frustrating and non-frustrating events in the various types of situations in which the question has arisen.

10.2 Examples of frustration

10.2.1 **Frustration by illegality**

If the parties contract to do *X* and doing *X* subsequently becomes illegal then it is normally the case that the parties' obligations will have changed radically enough for the contract to be frustrated. Put another way, neither party normally assumes the risk that a contract may become illegal and so subsequent illegality will normally terminate a contract by frustration. An all too topical example perhaps would be where a pub has been booked in advance for a large family or work-related social event or celebration and government health regulations in an epidemic then make it illegal for the pub to be open during the period including the booking. The contract for the booking is clearly frustrated due to supervening illegality and both parties are then excused from having to perform and any deposit already paid would prima facie have to be refunded (in line with the Law Reform (Frustrated Contracts) Act 1943 s.1(2)—see 10.5.1—subject to the expenses proviso which would be very unlikely to be applicable).

Such a case would not, one would hope, end up in a court, but a more traditional example of frustration by illegality in the courts is *Metropolitan Water Board* v *Dick, Kerr and Co. Ltd* (1916).

CASE CLOSE-UP

***Metropolitan Water Board* v *Dick, Kerr and Co. Ltd* (1916)**

In July 1914, shortly before the First World War, the Metropolitan Water Board contracted with Dick, Kerr and Company to build a reservoir over a six-year period. In 1916, the government ordered the company to stop work and make its resources available for the War effort. Even though there was a clause in the contract (Condition 32) to enable the time for completion of the contract to be extended notwithstanding delays 'howsoever occasioned', Lord Finlay in the House of Lords held the contract to be frustrated because:

> Condition 32 does not cover the case in which the interruption is of such a character and duration that it vitally and fundamentally changes the conditions of the contract, and could not possibly have been in the contemplation of the parties to the contract when it was made.

Assuming the risk of subsequent illegality

Lord Finlay's formulation in *Metropolitan Water Board* is a good example of the radical change and implied term approach being used together. In exceptional cases, however, it is not altogether inevitable that illegality will frustrate the contract if one party may arguably be taken to have assumed the risk of the obligation subsequently becoming illegal.

EXAMPLE

Assuming the risk of illegality

Suppose that XtreamTV Ltd agrees to purchase a film, to be made by Lights, Camera, Action Ltd (LCA), of an international air show, XtreamTV having outbid a number of other eager purchasers. The price is agreed to be payable by the end of the month in which the air show is scheduled, even if the show is cancelled due to weather conditions or is prohibited at the last minute due to security concerns (LCA insists on its fee still being payable as it could easily have earned the same fee by contracting to film some other major event if it did not have to commit itself to the air show).

After the film has been made but before either the money is due or the film has been edited, regulations are passed making it illegal for anyone other than the government to sell films of air shows (the government being concerned about the information in the films which might be of use to terrorists). Given that XtreamTV has expressly taken the risk under the contract of having to pay even though no film is actually *made* due to government regulations, it is not implausible to suggest that the company impliedly also takes the risk that the film cannot be *delivered* due to government action. On this view, the contract would not be frustrated and XtreamTV would remain liable to pay the price. This would involve construing (note the relevance of the construction theory) XtreamTV's obligation to pay for a film which *cannot be delivered* because of security issues as *not* being radically different from an obligation to pay for a film which *cannot be made* due to security issues.

It is, of course, equally plausible that having expressly assumed one risk, that of cancellation of the event, XtreamTV should not be regarded as assuming the separate risk that the purchase of the film would become illegal. This would then involve saying that the company's obligation to pay in the new situation is radically different from what it originally promised to do and so the contract would be frustrated.

Where the contract is illegal because it involves trading with an enemy, it is said that the parties cannot ever expressly avoid frustration, but this seems to be a special rule based on public policy rather than the normal principles of frustration. The point is that the government's policy to prevent trade with the enemy (and so cut off its supplies) overrules the policy of adherence to the parties' bargain.

In *Fibrosa SA* v *Fairbairn Lawson Combe Barbour Ltd* (1943) an English company sold a machine to a Polish company. The contract was frustrated because of the outbreak of the Second World War and it was irrelevant that the parties had agreed to prolong the contract in the event of war. On termination of the contract, the English company was no longer obliged to deliver the machine (but, as will be seen in section 10.4.1, the Polish company was entitled to the return of the £1,000 it had paid in advance).

A more modern example of illegality is provided by *Islamic Republic of Iran Shipping Lines* v *Steamship Mutual Underwriting Association (Bermuda) Ltd* (2010). The insurer of an Iranian shipowner argued that a contract of insurance had been frustrated when the UK banned business relations with certain Iranian entities (including the shipowner) pursuant to anti-terrorism legislation. However, the claim was rejected as the court found that the UK restrictions prohibited some forms of insurance, but not others (specifically compulsory insurance required under an international convention); the contract had not therefore been rendered radically different as although the scope of cover permitted was narrower, it still amounted to a contract of indemnity insurance and could be performed in part. To hold otherwise would give the insurers an unjustified windfall.

10.2.2 **Frustration by impossibility**

Things are rarely impossible in today's age and there is usually some way of getting something done, even if it is at an enormous cost. Thus, the cases discussed in this section are under the general heading of impossibility but often the change in circumstances has simply made the parties' obligations more *onerous*.

Destruction of the subject matter of a contract

Cases involving destruction of the subject matter might seem like obvious candidates for the label of 'impossibility' but, especially in modern times, it is often possible (but sometimes with great difficulty) to rebuild the subject matter.

THINKING POINT

The obligation in *Taylor* v *Caldwell* may actually have been capable of performance. Do you think that the owners could have built a new music hall before the concerts were due to take place?

Even if performance of the contract were not *impossible* (because a new hall could be built in time), it is relatively easy to show that performance has become radically different if the owners have to rebuild the hall in a very short time before it could be used for the performances envisaged under the contract.

A clearer case of true impossibility is where specific goods (goods identified at the time of the contract) are destroyed, for example if an Old Master painting is sold but then destroyed by a fire in the auction warehouse. There was only one such Old Master painting in the whole world and now it has gone—it is impossible to perform the contract to sell the Old Master.

Section 7 of the Sale of Goods Act provides that, 'where there is an agreement to sell specific goods and subsequently the goods, without any fault on the part of the seller or the buyer, perish before the risk passes to the buyer, the contract is avoided.' Note that the section does not apply where the risk has already passed to the buyer or if one party is at fault (see section 10.3.1 on self-induced frustration).

Contrast this with the sale of unascertained goods, for example a contract for the sale of 50,000 matchsticks, where the individual identity of the matchsticks is unimportant. Such a contract is unlikely to be frustrated because the destruction of the matchsticks does not amount to a fundamental change in the obligation and the seller can fulfil his obligation by buying 50,000 additional matchsticks at his own cost. Of course, it is open to the seller to place the risk of destruction on the buyer by an express term in the contract, but the doctrine of frustration primarily deals with situations where there is a gap in the allocation of risk between the parties. A similar issue arose in the case of *CTI Group* v *Transclear* (2008) where the sellers were unable to supply the bulk quantity of cement for the purchasers to ship to Mexico, not because of its destruction, but because their own suppliers gave in to pressure from the cartel which had a monopoly in Mexico which they were anxious to preserve. The inability to source the cement from the intended suppliers did not amount to frustration and the sellers were held to have taken the risk that their intended suppliers would let them down and that they would not be able to obtain the necessary quantity of cement elsewhere. The nature of the sellers' obligation had not fundamentally changed, what had happened was not exceptional and did not make the supply of cement impossible and the Court of Appeal seemed to view it as a fairly clear case where the exceptional doctrine of frustration was not applicable.

Returning to cases of destruction, it is sometimes difficult to establish whether a thing has been destroyed or has perished. In *Asfar* v *Blundell* (1896) a cargo of specified dates (the fruit of the date palm) sank and became unsuitable for eating but perfect for producing spirits. This change in the commercial use of the dates was sufficient to frustrate the contract. You need to define the subject matter of the contract as 'edible dates' (i.e. by reference to the dates' *use*) in order to reach the conclusion that performance of the contract is impossible when the ship carrying the dates sank. (Perhaps this case can be remembered as one relating to dates by use rather than use-by dates!)

Unavailability of the subject matter of the contract

There have been many cases where a contract for the hire of a ship (a charterparty) has been frustrated by the unavailability of the ship. Although the ship is not actually destroyed in the sense that it is sent to the scrap yard, it is treated, for commercial purposes, in the same way as if it has been destroyed, on the basis that time is of crucial importance in charterparties and if the ship is currently unavailable it might as well have been destroyed.

In *Jackson* v *Union Marine Insurance Co. Ltd* (1874) a ship ran aground and was delayed for six months on its way to San Francisco from Liverpool. The jury found that a voyage undertaken after the repairs (in autumn) would have been a different voyage from the one originally agreed between the charterer and the owner (a summer voyage) and so the charterparty was frustrated.

In *The Nema* (1982) the charter was for seven voyages starting in April and ending in December. One voyage was made in April but a strike prevented further performance. The parties went to **arbitration** in September, where the contract was held to be frustrated. The arbitration decision was upheld when the case reached the House of Lords and Lord Roskill emphasized that commercial men should not have to wait too long before deciding that the contract was radically different from that which they had originally agreed to. So even though the charterparty still had time to run when the parties went to arbitration it was reasonable for the parties, in the interests of certainty, to seek judgment on whether it was frustrated.

> **arbitration** Signing up to arbitration is a bit like paying for private medical treatment: businesses do it because they do not want to rely on the State-run system. Arbitration provides an alternative judicial forum where the parties have more control over the procedure and timing of the hearing and, most importantly to commercial parties, the proceedings and judgment are private and confidential (unless they end up in the courts on appeal from the arbitrator!).

Delay and interruption

In *Tsakiroglou & Co. Ltd* v *Noblee Thorl GmbH* (1962), the closure of the Suez Canal, through which both parties expected the goods to be shipped, was held not to frustrate the contract even though the alternative route was two-and-a-half times as long. The House of Lords recognized that the alternative method of performance of the contract was more lengthy and expensive, but it was not a radical or fundamental change.

THINKING POINT

Consider how the result in *Tsakiroglou* might have been different if the shippers had promised to deliver the goods by a particular date or if the goods would perish on a longer journey. Would the alternative route then constitute a radical change from the promised performance?

Similarly, in *Davis Contractors Ltd* v *Fareham Urban District Council* (1956), the builders agreed to build seventy-eight houses in eight months for the Council. Due to bad weather and labour shortages (caused by a delay in soldiers returning from the Second World War) the work took twenty-two months and cost the builders £17,000 more than they originally anticipated. Lord Reid thought that the job of the builder 'never became a job of a different kind from that contemplated in the contract.' It is therefore clear that just because a job becomes harder or more expensive to complete, this does not of itself amount to a fundamental change which frustrates the contract.

LINK TO . . .

Positive terms (Chapter 5)

One way of looking at these cases and determining whether a change is 'radical' or 'fundamental' is to ask whether, if the change had been caused by a breach by one party, it would have justified the other party in terminating the contract. Thus the question of whether one party is deprived of 'substantially the whole benefit of the contract' is as relevant here as it was in *Hong Kong Fir Shipping Co. Ltd* v *Kawasaki KK Ltd* (1962) even though the interruption there was due to a breach. Diplock LJ made it clear that, in his view, the issues of discharge by frustration and discharge by breach are governed by the same principles. Thus the proportion that the delay or interruption bears to the full period of the contract is relevant, which is no doubt one reason why the lease in *National Carriers Ltd* v *Panalpina (Northern) Ltd* (1981) was not frustrated since the interruption was only eighteen months out of ten years and there would still be three years left after the interruption ceased. By way of contrast, a sentence of detention for twenty-eight weeks was held to frustrate a four-year apprenticeship with more than two years left to run in *F.C. Shepherd Ltd* v *Jerrom* (1986).

Death and incapacity

If a contract requires performance by a specific individual and that individual dies or becomes incapable of performing through illness, as in *Notcutt* v *Universal Equipment Co. Ltd* (1986), the contract would normally be frustrated. Whilst it is certainly possible for frustration to be excluded by one party expressly taking the risk of their own incapacity (e.g. if a celebrity agrees to attend the opening of a new supermarket and expressly agrees to pay damages if he or she is unable to attend through any cause including illness), in the absence of an express provision frustration would normally apply (but see the discussion of self-induced frustration in section 10.3.1). Even before *Taylor* v *Caldwell* relaxed the strict common law rule that parties must fulfil contractual obligations or be in breach, Pollock CB in *Hall* v *Wright* (1852) recognized that personal contracts of service were frustrated by the death of one of the parties. The logic behind this category of cases is that service contracts are often extremely personal matters, and each party chooses to be bound to the other and no one else. In *Graves* v *Cohen* (1930) a racehorse owner died and the contract for services between the racehorse owner and a jockey was frustrated by his death. Temporary incapacity (in relation to a contract which has a longer period to run) is clearly a different matter, as is illustrated by *Blankley* v *Central Manchester NHS Trust* (2014), which concerned a claimant with brain damage in a serious medical negligence case. She entered a conditional fee agreement with solicitors in 2005 but lost capacity to conduct her own affairs or to provide instructions to her solicitors in 2007. This did not automatically frustrate the agreement with her solicitors since it was not clear how long the incapacity would last for and the solicitors could anyway be instructed through the appointment of a deputy or receiver, as in fact happened in this case. The sensible outcome of the contract not being frustrated was that the defendants were liable to pay for the ongoing costs incurred by the solicitors under the contract in obtaining for the claimant over £2.5 million in damages in a settlement made in 2010.

10.2.3 **Frustration of purpose**

The coronation cases

The 'Coronation cases' of *Krell* v *Henry* (1903) and *Chandler* v *Webster* (1904) illustrate how a contract can be frustrated by the failure of its purpose. The defendants in both cases paid a high price for the use of rooms overlooking the route of the coronation procession of King Edward VII. These facts made it implausible that the defendants assumed the risk of the procession being cancelled or, to put the same thing another way, agreed to pay whether or not the procession took place; it was clear that both parties had regarded the hire as being solely for the purpose of viewing the procession and if there was no procession then the defendants had no interest in hiring the room. Indeed, in *Krell* v *Henry*, the claimant advertised 'windows to view the Coronation procession', which reinforced the inference that the contract (which did not itself mention the procession) was not about the hire of a room but about the hire of a view.

When the procession was cancelled the courts found that the obligations under the contracts had changed fundamentally because the claimant could only provide a room with a view of an empty street and not of the procession. The purpose of the contracts, to view the procession from the defendants' rooms, was no longer possible.

If, as in *Chandler* v *Webster*, the contract itself specifically mentions the procession, it is as plausible to argue that the owner of the rooms should be liable in damages for the lack of a procession as it is to suggest that the hirer should be liable to pay for the rooms in the absence of a procession to view. If the owner expressly promises a view of a procession, then why should the owner not compensate the hirer when a procession fails to occur? Saying that the contract is frustrated means that the court is recognizing that neither party assumed the

THINKING POINT

How far should the courts take the construction of the parties' obligations?

risk of the procession being cancelled, that is, the owner did not guarantee a procession and the hirer did not promise to pay if no procession took place.

The Derby Day cab example

The real difficulty with *Krell* v *Henry* is the example that Vaughan Williams LJ gives of a contract to hire a cab to Epsom on Derby Day 'at a suitable enhanced price' and which he distinguishes from the Coronation cases on the grounds that any other cab would do the job and the contract would not be frustrated if the running of the race became impossible. His Lordship added that in the case before him (*Krell* v *Henry*) it is the 'procession and the relative position of the rooms which is the basis of the contract as much for the lessor as the hirer' whereas the race, it is inferred, is only the purpose of the hirer, not of the cabbie. The problem is that: (a) it might just as well be said of *Krell* v *Henry* that 'any other room overlooking the procession would do', and (b) the cabbie is only enabled to charge a 'suitable enhanced price' because it is Derby Day and so the Derby is as much the basis of the contract for the cabbie as is the procession for the lessor in *Krell* v *Henry*.

The fact that Vaughan Williams LJ's distinction is difficult to support does not invalidate the decision in *Krell* v *Henry* but does suggest that the example of the particular type of cab hire he gives could also be frustrated. It does not follow that wherever someone hires a cab to go to a specific event the contract is frustrated if the event is cancelled. If the agreed charge is

LINK TO . . .

Damages (Chapter 11)

Holding the hirers to their contract when they agreed a 'normal' price may not inflict any hardship since, if they cancel the hire on hearing of the cancellation, the damages payable might only be the difference between the agreed charge and any receipts the cabbie can generate from alternative uses (because damages aim to put the innocent party in the position they would have been in if the contract had been performed). If the charge is only the normal one, this is not likely to be a great deal and, as we shall see in Chapter 11, the cabbie is under a duty to mitigate his losses (i.e. to generate receipts by finding new passengers—assuming they are available).

The need to excuse the hirer is only usually acute where the hirer has agreed to pay over the normal rate (because the cabbie's expectation of profit, and hence damages, is greater) and in this situation it is easier to show that the cancellation of the event removes 'the foundation of the contract'. A court will no doubt be influenced by the extent to which the cabbie has already turned down alternative hirers in order to perform his contract. If the cabbie has not lost other potential business because of this contract, the court would probably be more likely to hold the contract frustrated, whereas if he has lost other business in reliance on the contract, the court might want to compensate him for the loss and hold the contract to be binding. The courts do not normally expressly advert to those sorts of factors in their judgments but there can be little doubt that they are in fact influenced by them, so it is legitimate to mention them in your own discussion of problems in cases.

not out of line with the normal rate for cab hire and no premium was charged to take advantage of the special nature of the event, the contract may well still be binding.

Any discussion of *Krell* v *Henry* is incomplete without contrasting it with *Herne Bay Steam Boat Co.* v *Hutton* (1903), where the defendant hired a steamboat over two days for cruises from Herne Bay. The case can easily be distinguished from the two Coronation cases discussed earlier on the grounds that there were two purposes of the contract: (a) to see a naval review; and (b) to cruise around the fleet and the Isle of Wight. Only (a) was defeated. Although the claimant shipowner could not show the defendant the naval review (it was cancelled) the defendant could have enjoyed a cruise around the fleet and the Isle of Wight (they were still there!), which meant that performance was not fundamentally different from that anticipated at the time of contracting.

The point can also be made that the price charged was not such a clearly inflated one (at least given that the fleet was still there) and that the effects of holding the relevant contract binding in the *Herne Bay* case were not as drastic as they would have been in *Krell* v *Henry*. The defendant had to pay the full balance of the price for hire but he was able to deduct from his liability the profits made by the claimants' alternative use of the ship on the two days in question.

10.2.4 **Frustration of leases**

The question of whether a **lease** can be frustrated is happily no longer controversial, although the fact that there ever was any uncertainty is illuminating in itself. A lease creates an estate over land (if you have not yet studied land law it is probably easiest to visualize it as temporary ownership for the period of the lease) and thus, the argument ran, estates over land still exist even though the buildings on the land might be destroyed by fire (there was no lease in *Taylor* v *Caldwell*, merely a **licence**, so the issue did not arise in that case), or even though the purpose for entering the lease might be wholly defeated. As long as the estate in land, 'the foundation of the contract', survived, it was argued, the contract was not frustrated.

licence
A licence does not give the licensee property rights in the land; instead it is merely a contract that gives the licensee permission to be on the land.

It became clear from *National Carriers Ltd* v *Panalpina (Northern) Ltd* (1981) that, whilst a lease will only rarely be held to be frustrated, there is no rule that it cannot be. The sorts of cases which are most likely to lead to frustration are short-term leases for a highly specific purpose, such as holiday lettings, where, in any case, it is at times difficult to decide whether there is in law a lease or a licence.

lease A lease is an estate (a bundle of property rights) over land for a particular duration of time. It is carved out of the lessor's freehold estate (a bundle of timeless property rights) over the land and gives the lessee the right to uninterrupted occupation of the land for the duration of the lease.

By contrast, the longer the lease and the less specific the purpose dictating its terms, the stronger the inference that the parties each assume the risk of any change in the condition of the land or its value. Leases are rarely, if ever, frustrated because the whole point of a lease is to allocate such risks in advance but if there is strong enough evidence to rebut this assumption then the lease can be frustrated. Analysis in terms of risk is much more likely to lead to an appropriate result than talking about the 'foundation of the contract'. For a more recent example of a 25-year lease being found not to be frustrated in the context of Brexit, see *Canary Wharf* v *European Medicines Agency* (2019) where the principles of frustration were very thoroughly discussed (at length) by Marcus Smith J, who held the parties had chosen to enter a long lease with no break clause and there was no common purpose beyond the terms of the lease nor any requirement that the European Agency should itself occupy the premises for the whole 25 years of the lease. There were provisions for subletting if it chose or needed to cease occupation, which provisions had been carefully drafted before the contract was made, and Brexit did not render the contract radically different. The decision does not of course mean that a change arising from Brexit can never give rise to frustration of a contract vsaid to be a radical change in the obligation. This is never an easy thing to establish, as can be seen not only from this case arising from Brexit but also from a number of subsequent cases arising from the Covid pandemic.

Virtually all these cases, certainly the ones arising from leases, have rejected the argument that the contracts in question were frustrated as a result of the unforeseen restrictions imposed or necessitated by the pandemic. So in *Salam Air* v *Latam Airlines* (2020) the leases of three aircraft to Salam Air, a low cost Omani passenger airline, for six years from 2017 were not shown to be frustrated when in March 2020 all passenger flights to and from Oman were prohibited due to Covid. Salam Air were thus unable to obtain an injunction to stop payment being taken, via the unconditional letters of credit they had provided, for the $215,000 a month rent for each aircraft. This was a relatively easy decision given that the contract provided that the obligation to pay the rent was 'absolute and unconditional irrespective of any contingency whatever' and it was evident from the contract overall that the risks of the aircraft for any reason not being able to be used profitably, or at all, were clearly assumed by Salam Air. The argument that the contract was frustrated was held to be 'weak . . . far too weak' to justify the claim for an injunction relating to the payment of the rent.

Similarly in *Bank of NY Mellon* v *Cine-UK Ltd* (2021) leases of cinema, bingo and retail premises were not frustrated by the Covid restrictions which shut them for up to 18 months or so out of overall terms of 15 years (or 20 years in the case of the cinemas) with significant periods still to run after the likely end of restrictions. The approach to frustration of leases in *Panalpina* was confirmed, that is, that leases can be frustrated but only very rarely, and the proportionate disruption in this case was not outside the risks already allocated by the contract and did not amount to frustration, so the various businesses had to continue to pay the rents to the landlords. The Court of Appeal left it open as to whether the position might be different if a lease was going to end anyway during a period of government enforced closure. Would the lease be frustrated then because there was no future purpose for it or was this still a risk assumed by the lessees? Whatever the answer to that hypothetical problem, the Court gave short shrift to the argument on the actual facts that the leases could be 'temporarily frustrated', which it said was not a concept known to law. This is clearly correct since, as we have seen, frustration is rare and depends on a radical change in the obligation. It is all or nothing and terminates the contract. It cannot therefore merely suspend the contract due to lesser temporary changes in order for it to be revived again when circumstances have changed once more.

In contrast, the position is quite different if a contract effectively provides for an event like Covid in a *force majeure* clause, as in *Billy Graham Evangelistic Association* v *Scottish Event Campus* (2021), where the express clause provided that the Campus could cancel (or indeed suspend) the booking due to 'the acts of a public authority or imposition of any embargo.' The cancelled contract here of course is not being frustrated but is being enforced in accordance with its terms. It was also not a case involving a lease but rather the hire of premises for less than 24 hours so even without the *force majeure* clause, cancellation due to frustration may have been arguable in any event. (The more fundamental dispute at the heart of the case was about a previous attempted cancellation, two months before the Covid restrictions, which was alleged to be discriminatory and in breach of the Equality Act 2010.)

10.3 Limits on frustration

10.3.1 Self-induced frustration

Despite the natural inference drawn from the expression by many students, self-induced frustration is as much about breach of contract as it is about frustration. The limit comes into play when one of the parties has *control* over the supervening event but lets it occur and then tries to claim that the event has frustrated the contract. Since one party could have prevented the event happening, the other party can argue that this should be treated as a breach of contract rather than as frustration. There are two main types of situation that require discussion in this area:

(1) choice of contract to frustrate; and

(2) negligence.

Choice of contract to frustrate

The classic example is *Maritime National Fish Ltd* v *Ocean Trawlers Ltd* (1935).

CASE CLOSE-UP

***Maritime National Fish Ltd* v *Ocean Trawlers Ltd* (1935)**

Ocean Trawlers unsuccessfully claimed that a charterparty of a trawler (the *St Cuthbert*) was frustrated due to the refusal of the government to issue it with sufficient licences for the number of trawlers it wished to operate. Because it was illegal to operate a trawler without a licence you might think that the charterparty should have been frustrated for illegality when the government unexpectedly refused to issue the necessary licences. However, Ocean Trawlers had in fact received three licences from the government and chose to allocate the licences to other trawlers which it operated, leaving the *St Cuthbert* without a licence. The Privy Council held that 'the essence of frustration is that it should not be due to the act or election of the party.' The lack of a licence for the *St Cuthbert* was self-induced as it was the defendant's own decision to use the licences received on trawlers other than the *St Cuthbert*. In other words, its refusal to pay the hire was not excused by frustration but was on the contrary a breach of its obligation under the contract.

The question has arisen as to whether the contract in *Maritime Fish* would remain valid if a charterer had entered a number of different charters and was bound to 'frustrate' one of them, whatever decision it made. This was not the case in the *Maritime Fish* case since the defendant had allocated the licences it received to its own trawlers rather than to one it had chartered; it was therefore possible to avoid 'frustrating' the *St Cuthbert* contract because the defendant could have left one of its own trawlers without a licence.

In the *Super Servant Two* (1989) Hobhouse J held that *Maritime Fish* should still apply to a case where the defendant had to choose which contract to 'frustrate' and this decision was upheld by the Court of Appeal. The defendant owned two super barges—*Super Servant One* and *Super Servant Two*—and agreed to carry the claimants' drill on one or other of the barges. The defendant earmarked the *Super Servant Two* for the contract but it is important to remember that the contract did not specify which barge should be used. Inevitably (for cases in this chapter), disaster struck and the *Super Servant Two* sank before it could pick up the claimants' drill. The *Super Servant One* was employed under another contract and so the defendant alleged that its contract with the claimants was frustrated, an allegation which the courts rejected even though the defendant would have had to breach its contract in relation to the *Super Servant One* in order to fulfil its contract with the claimants. The defendant had to break one of its contracts and, unlike the defendants in *Maritime Fish*, did not have the option of giving up one of its own vessels.

THINKING POINT

What risks did the parties in the cases discussed in the previous case close-up box assume? The Nova Scotia Supreme Court in *Maritime Fish* found an implied condition to the effect that the defendant had assumed the risk that it would not get enough licences, but the Privy Council found it unnecessary to rely on this ground. Would this be a better ground for the decision?

It may help in understanding the issues in these cases to break the cases down into the following two elements:

1) the supervening event (lack of licence, sinking of barge, etc.) puts A in the position of having to choose not to perform one of its contracts with B, C or D, etc.; and
2) A selects the contract with B as the one it will not perform and claims that this is caused by the supervening event and amounts to frustration rather than breach of the contract with B.

The cases have focused on the second point and refused to recognize it as frustration on the basis that the party chose or elected not to perform that particular contract, without giving any real weight to the first point that a supervening event forced the party to not perform at least one of its contracts. This may be thought to be rather harsh on A but it reflects the courts' generally restrictive attitude to frustration and perhaps can be justified on the basis that the sinking of a barge is less catastrophic overall for someone who has two or more such barges than for someone who has only the one.

EXAMPLE

Being forced to choose to terminate

By analogy, imagine that you are planning a wedding reception. You have sent out fifty invitations but the venue then informs you that due to a fire it can now only accommodate forty people; ten of your invitations will have to be withdrawn, but how do you choose who will have their invitation withdrawn? Whoever you 'dis-invite' will feel that you have deliberately rejected them and the fact that you *have* to do this will be scant consolation because you have *chosen* to disappoint them as opposed to one of the other guests. From your point of view, your choice is not really a choice—you would like to invite all fifty guests—but from their point of view you have freely selected their invitation for termination. Fortunately, your guests cannot sue you for withdrawing an invitation and so there is no need for you to show that the invitation was frustrated, but the problem is much more acute (and expensive) when there are contracts worth millions of pounds at stake.

10.3.2 **Negligence**

This section addresses the issue of whether a party can rely on frustration if it was at fault and caused the supervening event: will frustration due to mere negligence (as opposed to an intentional act) be regarded as self-induced? It is not surprising that no clear answer has emerged since the question in effect is whether the contract imposes liability for negligence on one of the parties (to deprive someone of a defence of frustration because it was caused by negligence is the same thing as saying that that party is liable for negligence) and this will vary from case to case.

The normal inference though would be that a party assumes the risk of events occurring due to its own negligence and will not be able to rely on frustration induced by negligence. On the other hand, it should be remembered that there is only room for an allegation of negligence where the frustrating event is a foreseeable result of the allegedly negligent conduct and that a person is not negligent who has taken *reasonable* care.

The singers who, in the usual examples, catch colds or absent-mindedly step out in front of buses would need to have disregarded very obvious risks before they could be regarded as negligently causing their own incapacity. In the *Super Servant Two* case, Hobhouse J thought that a more appropriate example would be 'an opera singer who carelessly overstrains her voice singing another role for a different impresario.' Even without going into the intricacies of operatic training and voice maintenance you can see that each case is going to depend very much on its own facts. In any event, it is clear that the burden of showing that the frustration was due to one party's fault is on the other party to the contract—see *Joseph Constantine Steamship Line Ltd* v *Imperial Smelting Corporation Ltd* (1942) where the charter of a ship was frustrated by a violent explosion on board ship which rendered the charter impossible to carry out. Despite a Board of Trade inquiry into the 'unprecedented explosion,' its true cause was never ascertained and it could not be proved whether or not it was the fault of the owners. The House of Lords held that the owners could rely on the explosion as a frustrating event and did not have to prove a negative—that it was without fault on their part; it was up to the charterers to prove fault if they alleged it.

10.3.3 **Events foreseen and provided for**

Foresight is obviously important in establishing negligence (see section 10.3.2) but if an event is foreseen and no provision is made for it, then one would normally infer that the parties have assumed the risk of that event and the contract is not frustrated.

Where an event is actually provided for in the contract, the inference that the contract is to continue if that event occurs is even stronger. However, even this rule is not absolute and the

EXAMPLE

Foreseen events

Suppose that X, a film star, contracts to do filming over the next twelve months for Y, knowing full well that it is likely that he or she will be called up for National Service within that twelve months. A court would be unlikely to listen sympathetically to a plea of frustration if X is actually called up, particularly if the risk of call-up is unknown to the other party. Even if the risk was known to both parties, one would expect them to have expressly provided that the contract is terminated in such an event and in the absence of such a provision it might be difficult for either party to argue frustration. A factor that might be borne in mind in this context is the detail or lack of it in the contract. If the contract is informal with very few express terms, the absence of a provision dealing with a foreseen event should not be fatal to a plea of frustration, whereas if the contract is highly detailed the absence of a provision dealing with a foreseen event would be highly significant.

court may, as in *Bank Line Ltd* v *A. Capel & Co.* (1919), find that the contractual provision is only intended to deal with events falling short of frustration. In that case the contract provided that the charterer could cancel if the ship was requisitioned by the government and said nothing about the effects of requisition on the *owner's* obligations. The House of Lords held that the contract merely gave the charterer a right to cancel where the delay caused by the requisition (e.g. one week) was not sufficiently long to frustrate the contract but that the actual delay of five months did amount to frustration.

Obviously this is another area where hard and fast rules cannot be laid down and it is a question of whether the parties appear, in the light of their actual agreement and circumstances, to have taken the risk of the particular events which have occurred. The fact that the events were foreseen or foreseeable or partly provided for is merely a factor, albeit a significant one, in answering that question.

10.4 Effects of frustration

10.4.1 Common law

The rule in *Chandler* v *Webster*

The common law effects of frustration are fairly clear, if somewhat inflexible. The contract is terminated as from the time of the frustrating event, that is, each party is excused from performing its future obligations, but obligations already accrued or due remain binding—see Figure 10.2 which illustrates this.

Thus in *Chandler* v *Webster* (1904), a Coronation case for the hire of a room, the finding that the contract was frustrated when the procession was cancelled did the claimant no good at all since he was obliged to pay the whole £141 15s hire charge in advance and this obligation was therefore unaffected by a subsequent frustration. Not only did the claimant fail to obtain the return of the £100 already paid, he was also held liable to pay the balance of £41 15s not yet paid but already due. By way of contrast, in *Krell* v *Henry* (1903) £50 of the £75 fee was not payable until *after* the cancellation of the procession and the defendant was therefore discharged from having to pay this sum by the frustrating event.

The effect of frustration could therefore be something of a lottery depending on whether, or how much, money was payable in advance and was clearly inequitable in a case like *Chandler* v *Webster* where the whole amount was payable in advance and nothing had yet been received in return. Indeed, the result of *Chandler* v *Webster* appears to be that the claimant was liable for the whole amount but could not have insisted on occupying the rooms for the

Figure 10.2 Example of the effect of frustration at common law: pre-*Fibrosa*

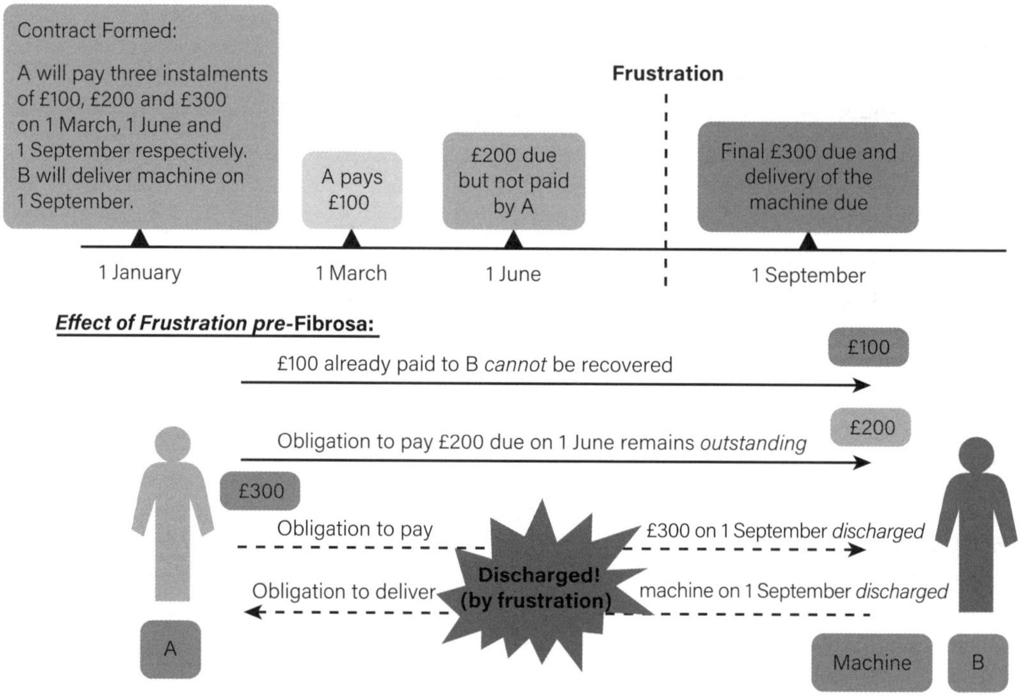

agreed days! The common law allowed the risks to fall according to the contract; if one party agreed to pay in advance but not receive performance until a later date and a supervening event prevented this, then he would lose out.

Total failure of consideration

In *Fibrosa SA* v *Fairbairn Lawson Combe Barbour Ltd* (1943) the House of Lords overruled *Chandler* v *Webster* and recognized a rule that a party can recover money paid in advance, and is no longer liable to pay if it has not yet paid, where the consideration for the payment has wholly failed, that is, where no part of that which has been bargained for has been received.

A contract dated 12 July 1939 provided for the sale of machinery by an English company to a Polish company for £4,800, delivery to be several months in the future and one-third of the price to be payable in advance. Only £1,000 was so paid but before the time of delivery war broke out and Poland was occupied, and so the contract was frustrated. *Chandler* v *Webster* would have meant that the £1,000 could not be recovered by the purchasers and indeed that they would remain liable for a further £600, being the balance of the one-third advance payment due before the frustrating event. The House of Lords held that where the consideration had totally failed, as in this case where no machinery had been delivered (and as in *Chandler* v *Webster* itself), a prepayment could be recovered, not under the contract itself or as part of the law of frustration, but in an action 'for money had and received' under the law, as they called it at the time, of 'quasi contract' (which would now be classified as unjust enrichment or restitution).

Total failure of consideration

'Total failure of consideration' uses 'consideration' in this context in a sense which is subtly different from the consideration discussed in Chapter 4, where the 'consideration' which is sufficient to *form* a contract includes a *promise* to perform. Failure of consideration in the context of 'total failure of consideration' refers to a failure in the *performance* of the promise, not to any deficiency in the promise itself which would have been fatal to the creation of the contract in the first place. The total failure of the promised performance, or more accurately of the promisee to receive the promised performance, results in unjust enrichment if the promisor has actually received the price agreed in the contract in return for the promised performance, which has not been delivered. Essentially, one party is saying, 'I paid you £*X* for your promised performance. I have not received that promised performance (e.g. the machinery in *Fibrosa*) and you are unjustly enriched at my expense; you are enriched by the receipt of my money and it is unjust because you have failed or been unable to deliver what you promised.' The fact that the failure in performance is due to frustration and that the contract has thereby been terminated is irrelevant because the recovery of the money paid is not based upon the contract but on the law of restitution or unjust enrichment which provides for the return of the money as 'money had and received.'

The post-*Fibrosa* position is illustrated in Figure 10.3 but there were still two main defects in the common law position even after this landmark decision:

a) incurred expenses; and

b) partial failure of consideration.

Figure 10.3 Example of the effect of frustration at common law: post-*Fibrosa* (but only if total failure of consideration)

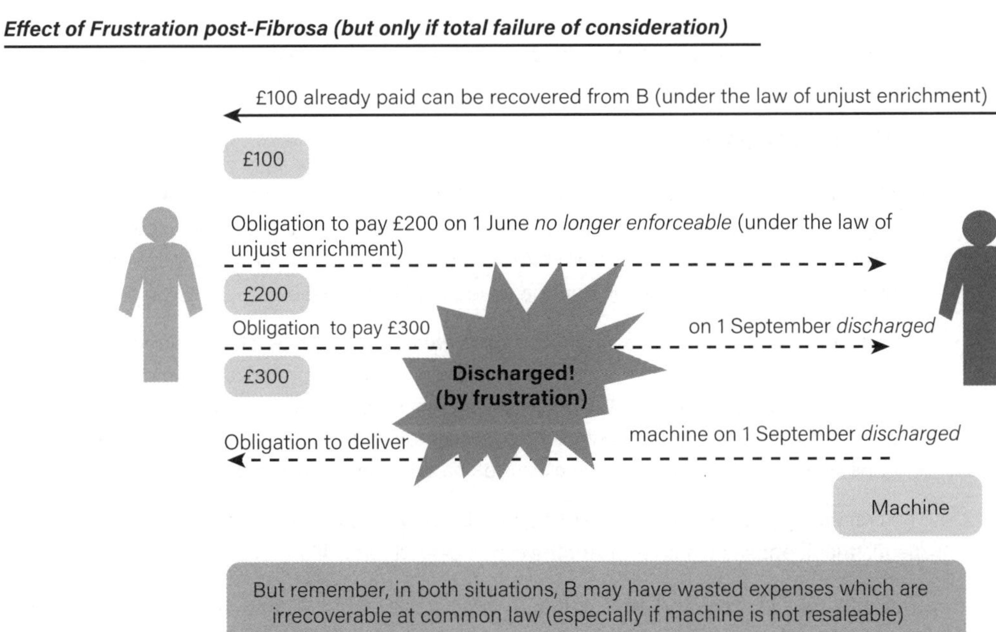

a) Incurred expenses

Whilst A may not have *received* anything under the contract and may thus be entitled to the return of any payments, B may have incurred considerable expense in performing or preparing to perform the contract, which expenditure may well be wasted and which therefore represents a loss falling solely on B. For example, if the seller in *Fibrosa* had done a lot of work on the machines (as in fact it had) and if, further (which is not clear), the machines could not be sold elsewhere (they were in fact of a special kind), it would be just as harsh to make the seller return the prepayment as it would be to make the purchaser pay for something which it has not received.

b) Partial failure of consideration

The *Fibrosa* modification only applies where there has been a *total* failure of consideration—if *some* of the machinery had been delivered before the outbreak of war, even if it was only a few hundred pounds' worth, the purchasers would not be able to recover any part of their prepayment, no matter how large that prepayment might be.

Thus, the common law rules were rather arbitrary in their application and effects. A just solution might be reached by accident if the amount prepaid happened to equal the benefit so far received by the purchaser which also happened to equal the amount of wasted expenditure by the seller, but the facts would only rarely approximate to anything like this. What was needed was a more flexible, less arbitrary approach to the effects of frustration and this is, to some extent, what the Law Reform (Frustrated Contracts) Act 1943 provided.

10.5 Law Reform (Frustrated Contracts) Act 1943

The key provisions of the Act are in s.1(2) and (3), which are now dealt with in turn.

10.5.1 **Section 1(2)**

All sums paid or payable to any party in pursuance of the contract before the time when the parties were so discharged (in this Act referred to as 'the time of discharge') shall, in the case of sums so paid, be recoverable from him as money received by him for the use of the party by whom the sums were paid, and, in the case of sums so payable, cease to be so payable:

> Provided that, if the party to whom the sums were so paid or payable incurred expenses before the time of discharge in, or for the purpose of, the performance of the contract, the court may, if it considers it just to do so having regard to all the circumstances of the case, allow him to retain or, as the case may be, recover the whole or any part of the sums so paid or payable, not being an amount in excess of the expenses so incurred.

The first paragraph is relatively straightforward and not only confirms the *Fibrosa* decision but means that it applies whether or not there has been a *total* failure of consideration.

Thus, any money paid by A to B before frustration can be recovered and any money due to be paid does not have to be paid *but* the second paragraph qualifies this so that if B, before frustration, has incurred expenses for the purpose of performing the contract, the court, 'if it considers it just to do so', *may* allow B to retain an amount equal to or less than the expenses incurred.

We can apply the Act to the *Fibrosa* case where the purchasers had paid £1,000 in advance. Suppose the sellers had already incurred £800 worth of expenses in manufacturing the machinery for the purpose of performing the contract. The purchasers are prima facie entitled to the return of their £1,000 under the first paragraph, but the court has a *discretion* to allow the sellers to retain *up to* £800 of that £1,000 'if it considers it just to do so.'

The discretion to allocate expenses

Obvious factors that will influence the court in exercising its discretion include how far the expenses could be recouped by selling to a third party: if the whole amount, then it would seem just to allow the sellers to retain none of the buyer's £1,000 payment and for them to rely on selling to a third party to mitigate their loss. It does not necessarily follow that if the work is totally wasted the sellers can retain £800 since that would throw the whole loss on to the purchaser. One solution might be to allow the sellers to retain £400 as that would share the loss equally, but that was not the solution in the leading case of *Gamerco SA* v *ICM/Fair Warning (Agency) Ltd* (1995) (see Figure 10.4).

A rock concert had to be cancelled because the venue was unavailable and so the contract was frustrated. The rock group Guns N' Roses were not allowed to retain any part of their expenses of $50,000 out of a prepayment made to them of $412,500, all of which they had to return. Garland J could have exercised his discretion differently so that some or all of the band's $50,000 expenses were deducted from the repayment. Although the expenses of the **payor** are not expressly mentioned in s.1(2) (unlike the expenses of the **payee**), Garland J clearly took these far greater expenses ($450,000) of the promoter into account when deciding not to allow the band to deduct their own relatively smaller expenses (of $50,000) and to require them to return the whole amount of the prepayment to the promoter.

> **payor and payee**
> The payor is the person paying money. The payee is the person being paid.

In *BP Exploration Co. (Libya) Ltd* v *Hunt* (1979), Goff J suggested that the payee's ability to set off its expenses against the sum repayable to the payor was in recognition of the defence of change of position. In other words, although the payee is obliged to make restitution under the law of unjust enrichment, it is a defence to say 'but I would not have incurred expenses *X*, *Y* and *Z* if that advance had not been paid' and so he is allowed to deduct his change of position from the money he must pay back.

Figure 10.4 *Gamerco SA* v *ICM/Fair Warning (Agency) Ltd* (1995)

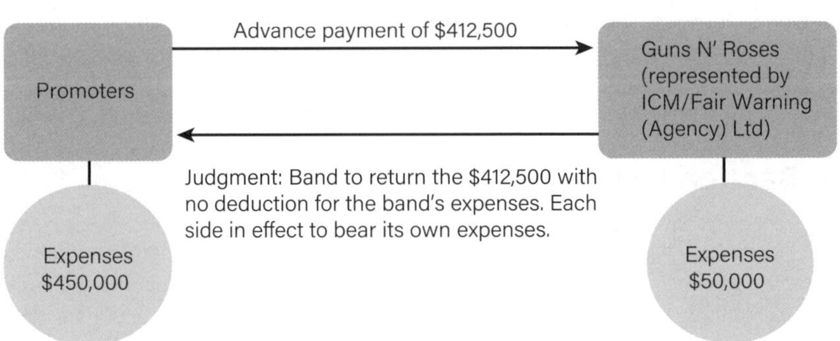

EXAMPLE

Change of position

Imagine that you have just won the lottery; you have bought several houses and cars and thrown a huge party for your friends (you have lots now). Unfortunately, the lottery organizers ring you up the next week and confess that they made a mistake and ask if they could please have their £15,000,000 back (which, arguably, they are entitled to under the law of unjust enrichment). You would have a defence up to the amount of the houses, cars and party expenses because you *changed your position* in reliance on the fact that you had some extra money.

The difference is that the statute gives the judge a discretion whether to allow the payee to deduct its expenses whereas the law of unjust enrichment does not allow such a wide discretion. The judge in *Gamerco* exercised his discretion in effect by saying that Guns N' Roses' change of position was not as adverse as that of the promoters, who had wasted far more expenditure.

Sums payable but not yet paid

Notice that s.1(2) also provides (as did *Fibrosa*) that any money *payable* by A to B before frustration (but not yet paid) is no longer payable but, again, if B has incurred expenses and so on the court 'if it considers it just to do so' *may* allow B to recover an amount equal to or less than the expenses incurred.

In *Fibrosa* £1,600 was payable in advance although only £1,000 was actually paid. Suppose that nothing was paid and that the sellers' expenses were £1,300. Under the Act the purchaser is prima facie liable to pay nothing (even though the contract required advance payment of £1,600) but the court has *discretion* to allow the sellers to recover *up to* their £1,300 expenses.

Even if the sellers' expenses were £1,800, the *maximum* they could recover is still £1,600, the amount paid or payable in advance. Consequently if nothing is paid or payable in advance, the sellers cannot recover anything for their expenses under s.1(2) and must rely on s.1(3) which, as will be seen later, requires a valuable benefit to be conferred on the other party. It is therefore still advantageous to stipulate a payment up front (even if it is never actually paid and only remains an outstanding debt) so that there is the possibility of recovery of expenses under the proviso in s.1(2). The sellers in *Fibrosa* would not have been able to rely on s.1(3) since nothing had been delivered to, and hence no valuable benefits obtained by, the purchaser. They could now however, under s.1(2), attempt to gain something for their wasted expenditure out of the sum payable in advance of £1,600, even though that wasted expenditure was of no benefit to the purchaser. The overall operation of s.1(2) is illustrated in Figure 10.5.

10.5.2 **Section 1(3)**

> Where any party to the contract has, by reason of anything done by any other party thereto in, or for the purpose of, the performance of the contract, obtained a valuable benefit (other than a payment of money to which the last foregoing subsection applies) before the time of

Figure 10.5 Operation of section 1(2)

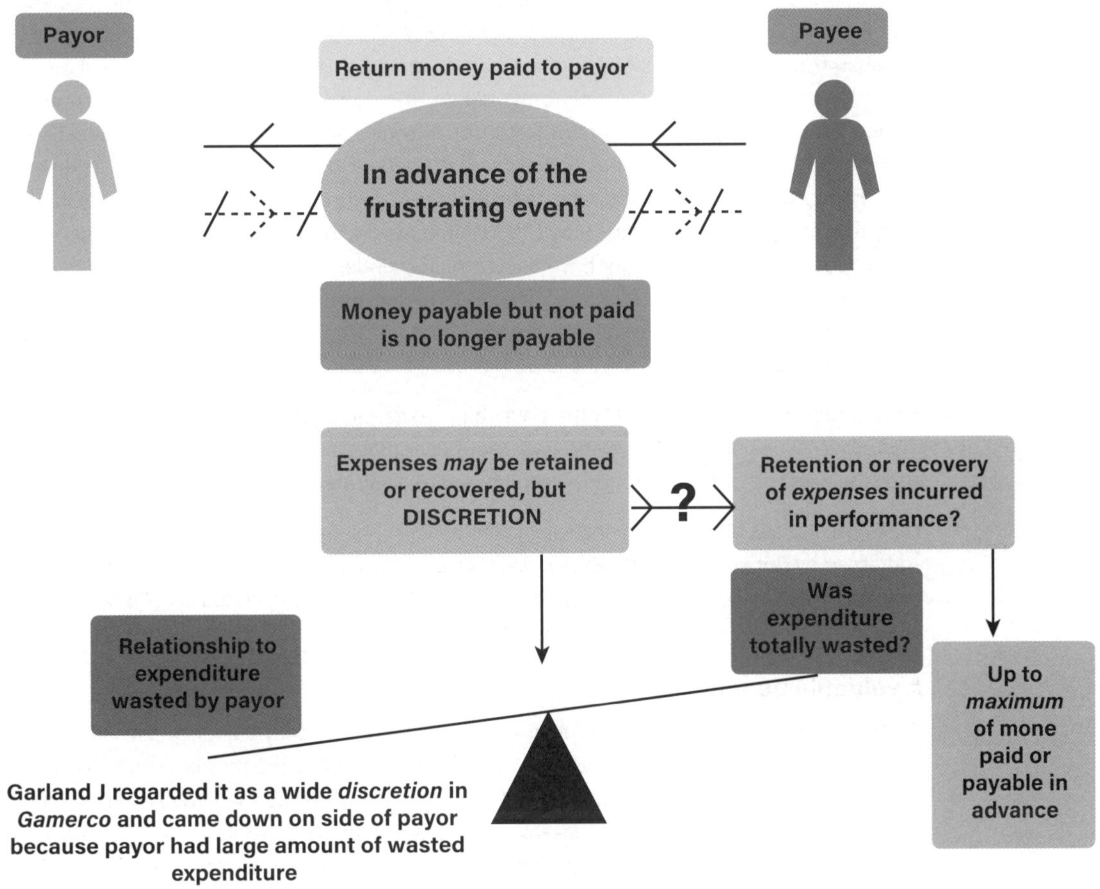

discharge, there shall be recoverable from him by the said other party such sum (if any), not exceeding the value of the said benefit to the party obtaining it, as the court considers just, having regard to all the circumstances of the case and, in particular,—

(a) the amount of any expenses incurred before the time of discharge by the benefited party in, or for the purpose of, the performance of the contract, including any sums paid or payable by him to any other party in pursuance of the contract and retained or recoverable by that party under the last foregoing subsection, and

(b) the effect, in relation to the said benefit, of the circumstances giving rise to the frustration of the contract.

Return of benefits received

This subsection depends not on money being paid or payable in advance, but, as already noted, on one party 'obtaining a valuable benefit' before the time of frustration as a result of the other's part performance of the contract. If this occurs, then again the court has a *discretion* to award 'such sum (if any), not exceeding the value of the said benefit to the party obtaining it, as the court considers just' and in exercising its discretion, the court is to take account of all the circumstances of the case but in particular the factors mentioned in paragraphs (a) and (b), quoted from the Act earlier.

What all that means can be illustrated by further varying the facts of *Fibrosa*. Suppose that nothing was paid or payable in advance but that the sellers had delivered half of the machinery contracted for, worth £2,400 to the purchasers. The court would have power to award the sellers a 'just sum' up to £2,400 (the value of the benefit) and would probably award the full amount since the circumstances giving rise to frustration (the outbreak of war) would not appear to reduce the value of the benefit under factor (b). However, if the purchasers had actually paid £1,000 in advance which the court had allowed the sellers to retain under s.1(2) (an expense of the purchasers), the court would have to take account of that under factor (a) and would obviously reduce the award under s.1(3) by £1,000. Alternatively, the purchasers might not have paid anything to the sellers but might have been required under the contract to pay, say, £500 to a third party for the carriage of the machines. Again, that would be something to be taken into account under factor (a), although it is not clear that the whole £500 should be deducted from the amount awarded here (since the £500 has gone to a third party, not to the sellers).

Thus, under both s.1(2) and s.1(3) the court has a discretion, once certain conditions are fulfilled. Your task is to understand the necessary conditions and the factors which might influence the exercise of the discretion—see Figure 10.6 illustrating the operation of s.1(3).

The difficult issues of identifying and valuing the benefit conferred and assessing a 'just sum' were addressed by Robert Goff J in *BP Exploration (Libya) Ltd* v *Hunt (No. 2)* (1979). The facts are somewhat complex to say the least. Although the case ultimately went to the House of Lords, the interpretation of s.1(3) was only fully considered by Robert Goff J (as he then was) in the High Court.

A valuable benefit

Where one party receives a benefit other than in the form of money it is often difficult to say to what extent it really constitutes a 'valuable' benefit to that person. The problem can be illustrated by reference to the facts of *Appleby* v *Myers* (1867), where Appleby had agreed to erect machinery on the owner's premises for a sum payable on completion (and not before) and the contract had been frustrated by a fire when a large proportion of the work had been done. The common law rule at the time stipulated that Appleby recovered nothing because the obligation to pay had not accrued at the time of frustration. One interpretation of s.1(3) would say that the owner had obtained a valuable benefit (the part-completed machinery) before the time of discharge and that the court

Figure 10.6 Operation of section 1(3)

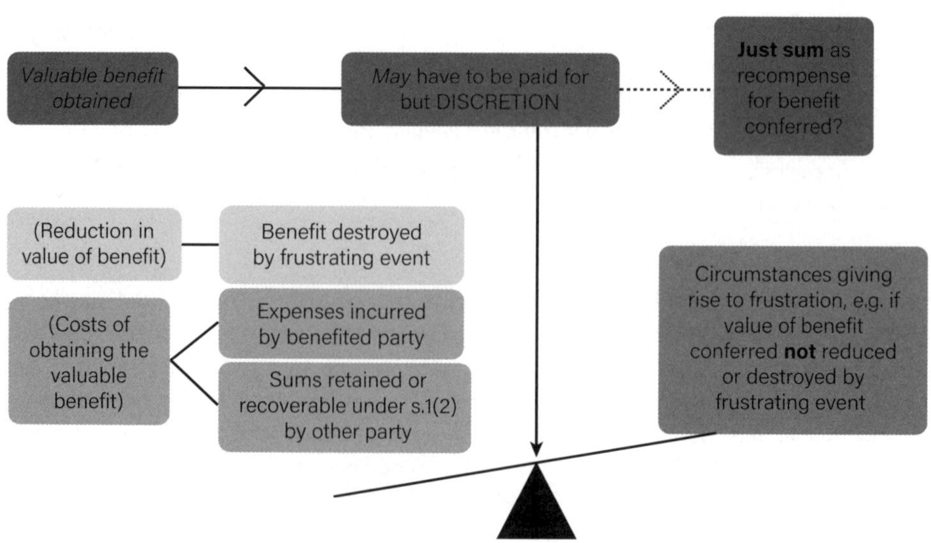

has a discretion to award Appleby a just sum, the actual amount awarded no doubt influenced by 'the circumstances giving rise to the frustration,' that is, the fact that the benefit was subsequently destroyed by fire. In the absence of other relevant factors, a just sum might be half the value of the work done, which would effectively split the loss caused by frustration equally. Robert Goff J took a different view of s.1(3), largely because he saw the Act as concerned with remedying unjust enrichment rather than apportioning losses and thought that in a situation like *Appleby* v *Myers* there would be no benefit and no award of a just sum (there is no 'enrichment' to be remedied) where the performance of one party was destroyed by the frustrating event. The performing party could not claim that its services were a benefit to the other party because the Act was concerned only with the end product (which, after the fire, was a pile of ash and worth nothing). His Lordship partially supported his view by pointing to factor (b) 'the circumstances giving rise to the frustration' as showing that the benefit is nil in a case where the end product has been destroyed. But this argument seems wrong because the subsection clearly makes this a factor in deciding what is a just sum, rather than in assessing the value of the benefit obtained. Indeed factor (b) talks about 'the effect, *in relation to the said benefit*, of the circumstances giving rise to the frustration' (emphasis added) so the benefit is clearly something which is ascertained *first* and then the effect of the fire is relevant in assessing a just sum. Furthermore, the Act says 'obtained the valuable benefit . . . *before* the time of discharge' so one has to look at the situation before, and not after, the fire. The fire is merely a very good reason for not awarding the *whole* of the value of the benefit to the claimant. For a convincing criticism in more detail see the article by Haycroft and Waksman [1984] JBL 207.

Robert Goff J's interpretation did not seem to do any harm on the actual facts of *BP Exploration (Libya) Ltd* v *Hunt* since the frustrating event (expropriation of an oil concession by Libya) did not destroy the benefits already received by Hunt so that his Lordship was able to value the benefit to Hunt and award a just sum. In a case like *Appleby* v *Myers*, however, if the benefit is regarded as nil there is no discretion to award anything.

Robert Goff J thought that even performance which lowered the value of the other party's property could be a benefit if the other party requested it.

EXAMPLE

Subjective benefit

If I asked you to paint my living room black and board up my windows your performance might well lower the value of my house. However, you will have provided me with a benefit because I requested that you do that and the law allows me to be the sole judge of what is a benefit to me.

Half-completed work

One problem that still remains in an *Appleby* v *Myers* type case (even if you reject Robert Goff J's interpretation) is the issue of the extent to which half-completed work is a benefit at all (even before it is destroyed). In the Canadian case *Parsons Brothers Ltd* v *Shea* (1966) a partially completed central heating system (subsequently destroyed by fire) was not regarded as a valuable benefit on the basis that, until completed, it was of no use to anyone. You might consider, as a useful counter-argument to this case, that partially completed work is valuable in the sense that it would cost less to complete than to start again from scratch; and that if there is room for two interpretations of valuable benefit, the wider one should be preferred since at least that gives the court a discretion to make an award but does not actually *require* it to award anything.

Exercise of discretion

The benefit, once identified and valued, acts as a limit on the amount that can be awarded as a 'just sum.' There are no hard and fast rules on this. Robert Goff J reasoned that the aim of the Act was to prevent unjust enrichment of the defendant at the claimant's expense and the just sum should take account of the enrichment of the claimant (the value of the benefit) minus the 'dis-enrichment' of the defendant (expenses incurred by the defendant). However, the Court of Appeal in *BP* v *Hunt* preferred a much broader approach based on awarding what the trial judge (and not an appellate court) thinks is just. The just sum may well be based on the consideration under the contract as this reflects the value the parties put on performance. For example, if one party agreed to pay £10,000 in return for the other building a conservatory, one way of arriving at a just sum is to say that half-performance is worth half-consideration: £5,000. Of course, as a claimant you would argue that this is not just, on the basis that a half-built conservatory is useless to you and that it will cost more than 50 per cent of the price to get another builder in to complete the job. The Act does not dictate the correct result but leaves it to the court to determine the value of the benefit and the just sum to be awarded in all the circumstances.

Digging deeper

Frustration is an important topic in most contract courses (and in contract theory) as it marks out one of the extreme boundaries of contractual obligation and also provides an opportunity to work out the effects of a succinct, but not exactly clear, statute on some imaginative factual situations. In practice, it is of less importance than its prominence in contract courses may lead you to think. This is due not only to the exceptional nature of the doctrine itself but also because in practice contracting parties very often include what are known as 'force majeure' clauses which provide for the situations which might otherwise constitute frustration. Perhaps the best example of this is a case which we have already encountered—the *Super Servant Two* (1989) (see section 10.3.1). This is normally discussed in relation to the problem of so-called self-induced frustration and we have seen that the contract in that case was not frustrated by the sinking of the vessel because it was the defendant's own choice to allocate the alternative vessel Super Servant One to other contracts. Thus, the impossibility was not the automatic consequence of the frustrating event but due to their own choice. We have already remarked that this may seem a little harsh on the defendants who, once one of their vessels sinks, seem to be faced with having to put themselves in breach of at least one of the lines of contracts which they have entered into for their two vessels. However, things are not necessarily so bleak for the defendant company, as there was a force majeure clause in the contract enabling it

> to cancel its performance under this Contract . . . in the event of force majeur, Acts of God, perils or danger and accidents of the sea, acts of war, . . . closure of the Suez or Panama Canal, congestion of harbours or any other circumstances whatsoever, . . . and similar events, which reasonably may impede, prevent or delay the performance of this contract.

The trial judge had accepted that this force majeure clause (even though it misspelt 'majeure' by omitting the final 'e'!) applied to the sinking of the Super Servant Two, and thus entitled the defendants to cancel, unless they were shown to be negligent. Since there were in fact allegations of negligence against them (these allegations had not been adjudicated at the time of the appeal), the defendants argued in the Court of Appeal that the clause, quite apart from the doctrine of frustration, also entitled them to cancel even if they were eventually shown to be negligent (since there was nothing in the clause expressly to say it did not apply where there was negligence). The Court of Appeal ruled against them on this point, likening the clause to an exclusion clause and requiring express words to allow a right to cancel where there is negligence. It then went on to say that if the clause did not protect them, the separate doctrine of frustration did not apply as the frustration was self-induced. But it may be that the clause *did* protect them (if they were subsequently found not to be negligent), in which case the fact that the contract was not frustrated (due to it being self-induced) would not have mattered. And in any event, the Court of Appeal also went on to hold that the doctrine of frustration would not apply anyway if they had been negligent. So, the doctrine of frustration could be said in some ways to have been irrelevant to the case. It would have added nothing to the protection which may have been available under the force majeure clause since, just like that clause, it only applied if there was no negligence. The result was that the most important question was the interpretation of the force majeure clause so as not to cover negligence and ultimately whether, on the facts, the defendants had been negligent in relation to the sinking of their vessel.

Of course, the fact that there is a force majeure or similar clause does not always mean that the doctrine of frustration is excluded or is of little relevance. For example, in the *Fibrosa* case (see section 10.4.1 earlier) the contract provided 'should despatch be hindered or delayed by . . . any cause beyond our reasonable control including . . . war . . . a reasonable extension of time shall be granted.'

The House of Lords lost little time in holding that even though war was explicitly mentioned, this clause only covered minor delays (and limited wars) and not the prolonged and indefinite interruption which the Second World War involved, and which frustrated the contract. The question ultimately is always one of construction of the contract, including any express force majeure or other terms which may be relevant, and whether the parties objectively agreed to be bound to perform on the facts which have arisen. However, the modern trend to draft wider and clearer express provisions in commercial contracts to deal with unusual events leaves less and less room for the doctrine of frustration to operate, in that context at least.

Summary

Frustration brings contractual obligations to an end if there is a radical and unforeseen change in circumstances after the formation of the contract which means that both parties should be excused further performance.

1. Principles

Frustration used to be justified by reference to the parties' implied intentions but the courts currently construct the parties' obligations at the time of creation and ask whether there has been such a radical change caused by the frustrating event that it can be said that this is not what they had contracted to do.

The question essentially boils down to whether one of the parties has assumed the risk that they might still have to perform in the circumstances that have occurred.

The parties are normally taken to have assumed the risk of the contract becoming more onerous or more expensive to perform and the doctrine of frustration is reserved for the most extreme cases.

2. Examples of frustration

Frustration can arise where performance subsequently becomes illegal, where the subject matter of the contract is destroyed or unavailable or, exceptionally, where the agreed purpose of the contract can no longer be achieved, but not where part of it can still be achieved.

3. Limits

A party will not succeed in claiming frustration if it had control over the occurrence of the frustrating event, even if it is forced into non-performance of at least one of a group of contracts; instead, it will be in breach of contract if its choice or election is what prevents it from performing.

Frustration is also denied if a party is negligent and fails to take reasonable care to avoid what would otherwise be a frustrating event.

Foreseen events and events provided for in the contract are unlikely to lead to frustration, although, in the latter case, the construction of the contract is all-important.

4. Effects

The House of Lords modified the harsh common law rule in *Fibrosa* and held that money payable in advance no longer had to be paid (and money already paid had to be returned) if there had been a total failure of consideration.

The 1943 Act provides for advance payments to be recoverable (and for money payable in advance no longer to be payable) even if there is not a total failure of consideration as required by *Fibrosa*. It also provides for the possibility of expenses incurred to be recompensed out of any money paid or payable in advance (s.1(2)), or for a 'just sum' to be awarded where the other party has received a valuable benefit (s.1(3)).

Both subsections confer discretion on the court and there is relatively little case law as to the precise principles to be followed in exercising the discretion.

? Questions

1. Larry agrees to ride Speed Ltd's bike in the Tour de France in return for a sponsorship fee of £10,000 to be paid in advance. Speed spent £5,000 designing and building Larry's bike. The Tour is cancelled when yet another cyclist tests positive for performance-enhancing drugs and Larry has only been paid £5,000 of the sponsorship fee.

   Advise both parties.

   Would your advice be any different if Larry had been the cyclist who had tested positive for drugs? What if the Tour was not cancelled but Speed had sponsored five other cyclists and, because lightning had hit their manufacturing plant, they could only supply bikes to four of their riders, and because Larry was the least likely to win the Tour, they refused to provide him with a bike?

2. 'The doctrines of fundamental mistake of fact and frustration are essentially the same doctrine.' Discuss.

3. 'The question of who should bear the risk of a particular event is central to the doctrine of frustration.' Discuss.

Further reading

Books

Chen-Wishart, M, *Contract Law*, 7th edn (Oxford University Press, 2022) ch 7.

McKendrick, E, *Contract Law: Text, Cases and Materials*, 11th edn (Oxford University Press, 2024) ch 21.

O'Sullivan, J, and Hilliard, J, *The Law of Contract*, 11th edn (Oxford University Press, 2024) ch 14.

Peel, E, *Frustration and Force Majeure*, 4th edn (Sweet & Maxwell, 2021).

Articles

Haycraft, AM, and Waksman, DM, 'Frustration and restitution' [1984] JBL 207.

Smith, JC, 'Contract: Mistake, frustration and implied terms' (1994) 110 LQR 400.

11 Damages

LEARNING OBJECTIVES

This chapter will help you to:

- distinguish between the contractual and tortious measures of damages;
- understand how the expectation interest (contractual damages) is measured and the problems with awarding the cost of cure or the loss of a chance;
- recognize the limits on an award of damages; and
- understand when an agreed damages clause will amount to a penalty clause and be unenforceable.

Introduction

contractual damages
A monetary award aimed at putting the claimant in the position it would have been in if the other party had performed according to the contract.

Most contractual disputes are about money. This chapter explores how much money a claimant can obtain as **contractual damages** or other forms of damages.

There are certain limitations on the general principle of contractual damages, such as the principle of remoteness of damage, which requires the damage to have been of a type reasonably foreseeable or in the contemplation of the parties at the time of the contract. There is also the principle of mitigation, which requires that the claimant must try to take reasonable steps open to it to put itself in the position it would have been in if the contract had been performed. As a result of these limitations the claimant will not always receive in damages the full value of its expected performance but it remains true that the primary aim is to protect what has been termed the claimant's expectation (or performance) interest.

11.1 Damages in contract and in tort

There is a potentially important subtext running throughout this chapter which will emerge if you do not simply focus on the arithmetic of when and how much a claimant can recover in damages, but instead think about how the scope of the damages remedy actually defines and clarifies the nature of the contractual obligation and distinguishes contractual obligations from other types of obligations. For instance, the fact that a claim for breach of contract allows the claimant to protect the *expectations* generated by the contract shows how contractual obligations are significantly different from tortious obligations. In relation to tortious obligations, damages aim to restore the claimant to the position it would have been in but for the tort, rather than to give it the benefit of the position it expected to be in if a contractual promise had been kept. The differences between the particular aims of damages in contract and tort follow from the different natures of the obligations concerned rather than from any fundamental difference in the purpose of damages since in both cases the damages are designed to put the claimant in the position it would have been in if the obligation had not been broken—in tort it is the obligation not to do a wrong and thereby not to make someone worse off (including not to deprive that person of existing expectations such as their existing earning potential), whereas in contract it is an obligation to fulfil a promise and to fulfil the expectations generated by that promise.

11.1.1 The focus of this chapter

Before we jump into the details of contractual damages, it might help if we take a step back and see where we are and how we got to this stage of the contractual inquiry. So far we have seen how a contract is formed and how it can be undone by procedural and substantive defects (such as misrepresentation, duress, undue influence, etc.). We have also looked at the different types of terms and seen that a breach will lead to different remedies: termination (for breach of conditions and sometimes for breach of innominate terms) and damages (for breach of any sort of contractual term). We are now at the stage of examining what exactly are the principles on which such contractual damages are awarded. You may also remember that damages can be awarded for misrepresentations. This chapter focuses on contractual damages—damages for breach of contract (i.e. breach of contractual promises)—whereas damages for misrepresentation (examined in Chapter 7) are tortious damages in response to false representations of fact—non-contractual statements as opposed to contractual promises. Figure 11.1 illustrates where the current chapter is located in the overall scheme of contract law and remedies.

The principles on which contractual damages are or should be assessed would merit a separate course of their own but the key issues to be discussed are as follows:

- the aims of contractual damages—expectation, reliance and causation;
- remoteness of damage;
- non-pecuniary losses;
- mitigation;
- contributory negligence; and
- penalties and agreed damages.

Figure 11.1 Location of damages in the law of contract in general

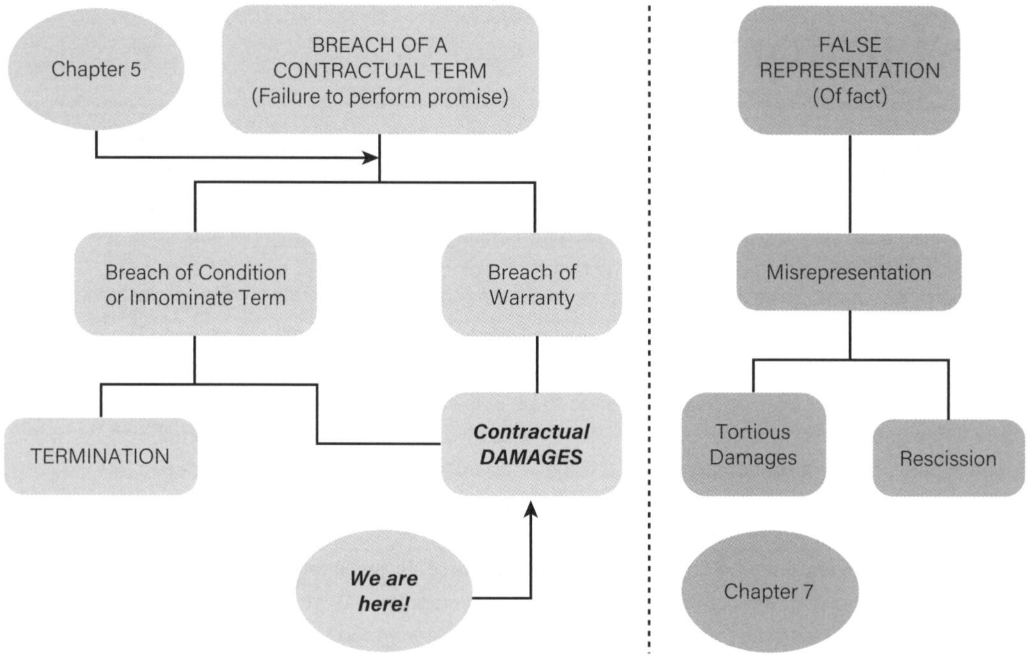

11.2 The aim of contractual damages

11.2.1 The expectation and reliance interests

> **expectation interest**
> The expectation interest equates to the net value of what the innocent party would have received if the contract had been performed.
>
> **reliance interest**
> The extent to which the innocent party is worse off as a result of relying on the contract.

The most commonly cited statement of the aim of contractual damages is that of Park B in *Robinson* v *Harman* (1848): '[The claimant] is, so far as money can do it, to be placed in the same situation, with respect to damages, as if the contract had been performed.' This is the normal contractual measure, which protects the **expectation (or performance) interest** which the defendant's breach has caused you to lose (on the facts the claimant had lost the benefit of a twenty-one-year lease at £110 per year which was worth a lot more, so he was awarded £200 for loss of that bargain rather than simply his wasted expenses of £20). A possible alternative measure, sometimes used instead, is the reliance measure which has traditionally been seen as protecting the so-called **reliance interest**, that is, a measure which puts the claimant in the position as though he had not relied on the contract (in the case of a 'good bargain' as in *Robinson* v *Harman* this will usually be a lesser amount—such as the wasted expenses in that case). The relationship between the expectation and the reliance interest (and indeed the restitution interest) was first fully discussed by Fuller and Perdue, in 'The Reliance Interest in Contract Damages' (1936–37) 46 Yale LJ 52, one of the all-time classics of legal scholarship. It would probably be best read after you have studied this chapter and, even then, you may not understand everything said in it on your first reading, but the article should expose you to some illuminating and stimulating ways of looking at not only the law on damages, but the purpose of legal rules in general.

The choice between the expectation and reliance interest: good and bad bargains

The normal approach to contract damages—giving the claimant the value of his expectancy, trying to put him in the position he would have been in if the contract had been performed—will normally be preferable to compensating him for his wasted reliance, *provided he has made a good bargain*.

EXAMPLE

Expectation measure protecting good bargain

If C has paid £1,000 for goods which would have been worth £1,200 if they had been in accordance with the contractual specification, but which are defective and only worth £900, then the expectation measure gives damages of £300, i.e. C's NET LOSS, which is the £1,200 value C should have got less the £900 C has actually received. This is also the prima facie rule enshrined in s.53 of the Sale of Goods Act 1979.

Notice that in this example, C does not get the gross value of the expectation but must deduct any value received so that C is compensated only for the *lost* expectations, C's net loss—of course, if what C received was worthless, C would in this case be entitled to £1,200 damages, the gross expectation, since that is now the same as C's net loss. If the breach was failure to deliver, rather than delivery of defective goods, and C has not paid the £1,000 price, C's expectation loss would be £200, that is the £1,200 value C would have received less the £1,000 C would have had to pay to get it. Returning to the case where defective goods are delivered and the price has been paid, the reliance measure is not as favourable to C because that would only produce damages of £100—in reliance on the contract C has paid out £1,000 and only received £900 worth of goods in return, making a loss of £100 (see Figure 11.2).

Note that the contract in the earlier example turns out in fact, as performed, to be a *bad* bargain because of the defendant's breach but the point is that it would have been a *good* bargain if the defendant had performed in accordance with the contract, and it is in this latter sense that one talks about good bargains. A 'bad bargain' properly refers to the situation where the bargain would be bad even if the defendant performs as promised, for example if C has paid £1,400 for the goods in the earlier example given which would only have been worth £1,200, even if they were in accordance with the contract specification. In this type of situation the normal expectancy measure will still only give C £300 (the bargain might have been bad anyway, but the defendant's breach has caused it to be £300 worse than it should have been) whereas the reliance measure will produce £500 (£1,400—£900). This example, illustrated by Figure 11.3, raises in simple but troublesome form the thorny question of whether or when C is entitled to prefer the reliance measure of damages to the more usual expectation measure.

The basic answer to this question is that the claimant can claim the reliance measure instead of the expectation measure *except* in the situation outlined in the earlier example, where to do so would be to shift a loss to the defendant. The claimant would have suffered the loss regardless of the defendant's breach because, in that example, even if the defendant had performed his obligation as promised, the claimant would have lost £200; allowing the claimant to claim £500 reliance loss would allow the claimant to shift his £200 loss on to the defendant. This was made clear in English law by a pair of decisions: *C. & P. Haulage* v *Middleton* (1983) and

Figure 11.2 Difference between expectation and reliance damages

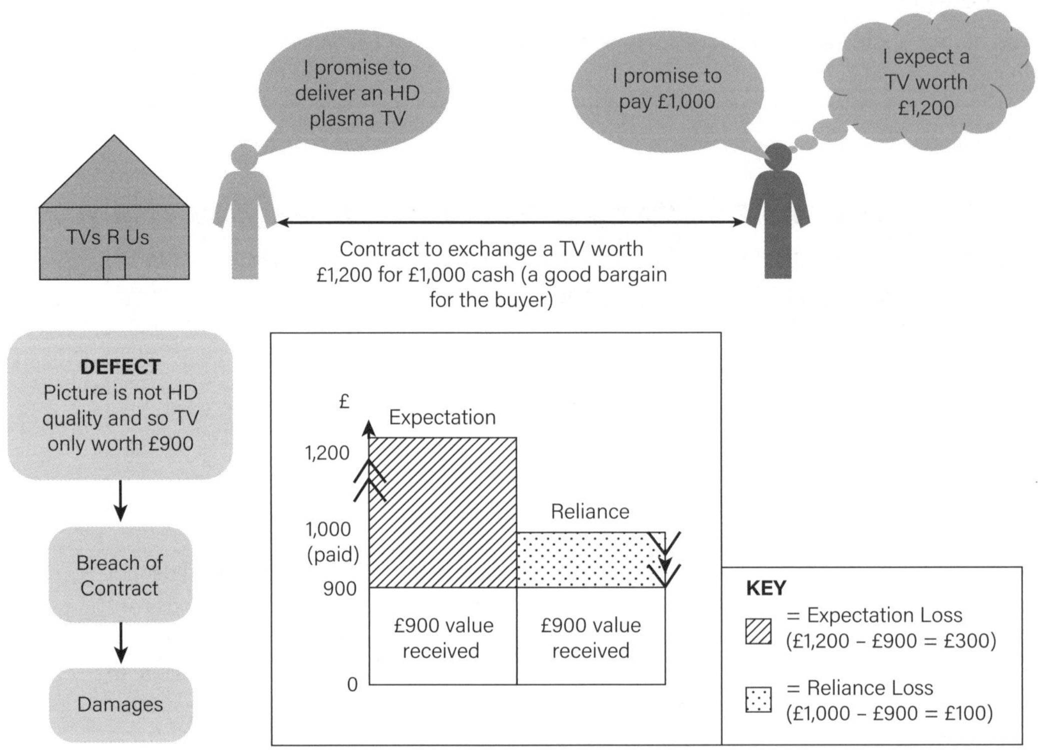

Figure 11.3 Choice of reliance interest when there is a bad bargain (C pays £1,400 for something worth only £1,200)

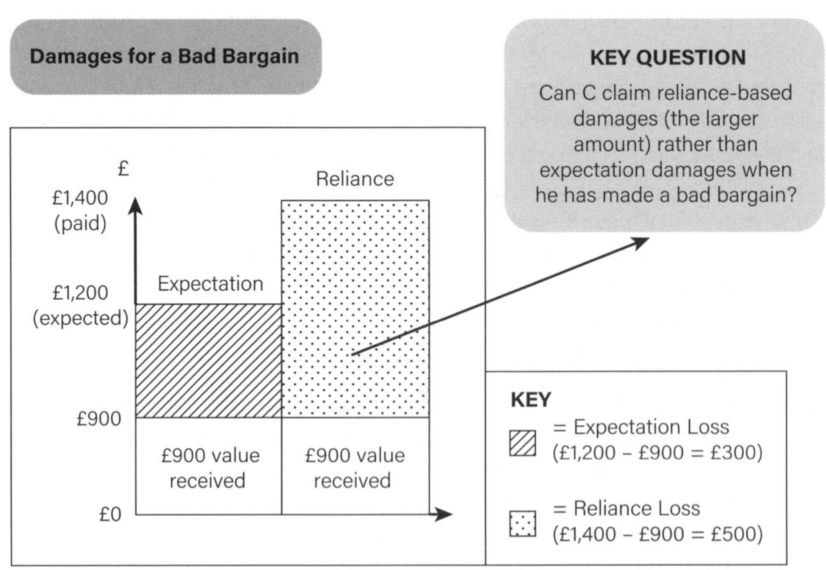

CCC *Films (London) Ltd* v *Impact Quadrant Ltd* (1985), which are discussed later (for further discussion see (1984) 18 Law Teach 217).

The choice between the expectation and reliance interests: evidential difficulties

You might be wondering what the point is of having the separate reliance measure of damages if the claimant cannot use it where it produces a larger award (as in the case of a bad bargain). Part of the answer is that sometimes it may be very difficult to prove the expectation measure; for example, it may be impossible to say what profits would have been made if the contract had been performed and so the claimant may choose to claim the money thrown away in reliance on the contract instead. This is what happened in the Australian case of *McRae* v *Commonwealth Disposals Commission* (1950) where it was impossible to show what the tanker would have been worth since it did not exist, so the claimants had to be content with compensation for their wasted expenditure. In *Anglia Television Ltd* v *Reed* (1972), the claimants had difficulty proving their lost profits when the star of their planned TV show pulled out and so they recovered their wasted expenditure (with the added complication that the expenditure was pre-contractual).

CROSS REFERENCE
Discussed in Chapter 8, section 8.4, under 'Common mistake'.

THINKING POINT

Should it matter whether the wasted expenditure was incurred before a contract was actually signed? Is there a big difference between expenditure incurred by a party in the course of performing a contract and expenditure incurred in anticipation of the contract (which does subsequently materialize and the expenditure is wasted when the other party breaches the contract)? Which party takes a risk that his expenditure will be wasted?

These cases do not fall foul of the bad bargain rule since it was not suggested that the claimants would not have generated sufficient income to cover their costs (i.e. that they made a bad bargain) and so it was in effect assumed that they would have at least broken even on the contract even if they might not have made a net profit. In *C. & P. Haulage* v *Middleton*, however, the Court of Appeal assumed that the appellant made a bad bargain because he had fitted out a yard at a cost of £1,767 for his car repair business even though the contract only gave him guaranteed occupancy for six months. When he was ejected in breach of contract he tried to claim the £1,767 as wasted expenditure but the court said that the expenditure could equally have been wasted if his contract had been lawfully terminated ten weeks later at the end of the six-month period (and in any event, there was no loss because the council then allowed him to operate from his own domestic garage, which they had previously prohibited, and so he no longer had to pay any rent). On the facts, it may be that the courts assumed rather too readily that the bargain was a bad one and that the appellant should not be able to recover his wasted expenditure.

However, shortly afterwards, in a somewhat more satisfactory decision, *CCC Films (London) Ltd* v *Impact Quadrant Ltd*, the Court of Appeal made it clear that it is for *the defendant* to prove that the expenditure would have been wasted in any event and that the bargain was a bad one. The contract in this case related to a distribution agreement for films with light-hearted titles such as 'Devil's Orgy' and 'Children Shouldn't Play with Dead Things.' The claimants had paid $12,000 for the right to exploit the films, which the defendants then managed to lose. The claimants were unable to prove how much gross income or net profits they would have made from the films but the Court of Appeal said that the burden was on the defendants to prove that the claimants would not at least have recouped their expenditure (i.e. the burden was on the defendants to show that paying $12,000 for some trashy films was a bad bargain). In the absence of such proof from the defendants, the claimants were entitled to recover their wasted expenditure ($12,000 in this case) on the assumption that they had not made a bad (loss-making) bargain and that they would at least have broken even and recouped that expenditure if the contract had not been broken.

Owen (1984) argues that the issue in these cases is really about causation; that is, breach of contract caused the claimant to miss out on an expected gain (unless the bargain was bad, in which case the claimant would have incurred the wasted expenditure in any event). The important point that emerges from his article is that despite the impressive analysis of Fuller and Perdue (1936–37), there is little justification for the reliance interest as an *independent* measure of damages for breach of contract aimed at putting the claimant in 'as good a position as he was in before the promise was made,' as Fuller and Perdue put it. The defendant's breach of contract has not *caused* the claimant to enter into or rely on the contract (unlike misrepresentation, so this argument in no way invalidates reliance as the basis for damages for misrepresentation); it has instead caused the claimant not to receive the expected performance, so the lost expectancy is the proper basis for damages. Reliance damages are merely *part* of the expectancy—contracting parties normally expect to recover their reliance expenditures plus an element of net profit. If the full expectation including net profit cannot be proved, the reliance measure can be allowed as a substitute prima facie measure, since it is assumed that the contract would have been sufficiently profitable to at least recoup the expenditure, but *if the defendant proves otherwise* (i.e. that the claimant made a bad bargain; see *CCC Films* v *Impact Quadrant Films*) the reliance expenditure will not be awarded since this would have been wasted even if the defendant had performed its promise. It will commonly be the case, as in *CCC Films* v *Impact Quadrant Films*, that the defendant will be unable to prove this and therefore the claimant will be able to recover its reliance losses which the breach has caused to be wasted.

The choice between the expectation and reliance interests: the orthodox analysis

This analysis appears to resolve any doubts about whether the claimant can choose the reliance measure where the expectation measure would be less (as in the bad bargain situation). The claimant clearly cannot if the so-called reliance measure is merely a limited portion of the expectancy and to do so would allow the claimant to shift a loss that would have been suffered even if the defendant had performed. A significant case in line with this analysis is *Omak Maritime* v *Mamola* (2010), where shipowners had wasted money in modifying their ship (the modifications had no residual benefit to the shipowners) in accordance with their contract with the charterers to whom they were to let it for five years. The charterers repudiated the contract when the charter was due to begin but improvements in the market rate meant that the owners were able to relet the ship for the five years at a substantially higher rate so their expectation loss was nil—in fact they were better off as a result of the breach as they could get around $7,500 more per day than under the contract which was broken—so they would be well over $10 million better off over the five years of the contract than if the contract had been performed. Teare J in the High Court held that they could not in these circumstances elect instead to recover as reliance damages the $86,000 originally awarded by arbitrators for their wasted expenditure in modifying the ship since, in his view, reliance damages are not independent of the expectation measure. If the expectation measure is clearly nil (because overall they were in a much better position than if the contract had been performed) they cannot instead claim reliance losses designed to put them in the position as if they had not entered the contract since that was not the aim of contractual damages.

To sum up this analysis, the expectation measure has to be seen as the maximum measure of damages for breach of contract—the full measure of damages actually *caused* by the failure to perform. Nonetheless, the reliance interest is a possible subsidiary measure, contained within the expectancy, which can be utilized, inter alia, as a prima facie measure where the full expectancy is difficult to prove, in recognition of the fact that the claimant should not lose the right to both the reliance and net profit elements of the expectancy simply because the claimant cannot prove the net profit element. But, as the *Omak* case illustrates, if C is clearly already in a better position than if the contract had been performed, C cannot choose to claim expenditure incurred as an alternative under a completely independent reliance interest (which is only an independent aim of damages in misrepresentation cases) since the aim of contractual damages ultimately is to put C in the position as though the contract had been performed and C would have incurred that expenditure in any event. (Of course, the situation is quite different in cases of misrepresentation, where the complaint is not that you did not perform your contractual promise and thereby caused me to lose what I expected to gain, but rather that you misled me and caused me to enter the contract. In this latter case an independent reliance measure putting me in the position as though I had not entered the contract is fully justified as part of the main aim of the award of damages for misrepresentation.)

THINKING POINT

Are you totally convinced by the above orthodox summary of the relationship between reliance and expectation damages for breach of contract? Was *Omak Maritime* really a bad bargain case given the expenditure was a very small fraction of the very large receipts due even under the original contract? Why should the owners lose the $86,000 dollars they unnecessarily spent relying on the charterers' promise which the charterers reneged on? What would have happened if the owners had not yet spent the money when the charterers repudiated—would they be compelled to spend it? Surely not, one would have thought. Would they not then be $86,000 better off than if they had spent the money in reliance on the contract? What sort of incentives does this create? Why should they be worse off because they had actually spent the money in good faith on the contract which has now been repudiated by the other party? Is there not a subtle difference between aiming to put you back in the position as though you had not even entered the contract (the misrepresentation reliance measure) and aiming to put you in the position as though you had not *subsequently* expended money or resources in reasonably relying on it (arguably the true contractual reliance measure)? For further discussion, see Taylor, R, 'Rethinking reliance damages for breach of contract' in Shaping the Law of Obligations' (Peel and Probert eds) OUP 2023.

11.2.2 The restitution interest

A third type of interest, **restitution interest**, is also sometimes protected by the courts. This type of award requires the party in breach of contract to *give back* gains he has made from his breach, although it is unclear to what extent the defendant also has to *give up* gains taken from other people too.

the restitution interest
The restitution interest focuses on the defendant's gain rather than the claimant's loss. The defendant has to give back or give up some or all of the profits that he made from the breach of contract.

In the wholly exceptional case of *Attorney-General* v *Blake* (2001) the House of Lords awarded an 'account of profits,' rather than damages, against a notorious spy and traitor who published his autobiography in breach of his contract with the UK government. This award amounted to full restitution for breach of contract, although the Law Lords were unsure how to label it. The important point was that the spy had to give up all the profits he had made on the book to the UK government. The House of Lords emphasized the exceptional nature of their award, reflecting the way in which the defendant had sought to profit from his previous treachery which had given him the notoriety that fuelled the interest in his book and the fact that the award was necessary to do justice and to remove any incentive for similar behaviour in future by those bound by obligations of secrecy in the interests of national security. This emphasis was repeated by the Court of Appeal in *Devenish Nutrition Ltd* v *Sanofi-Aventis SA* (2009) where, in a different context, the required exceptional circumstances were not made out.

In a number of other cases, a less drastic approach was thought to have been taken to, in effect, relieve a contract breaker of *some* of the profits made as a result of the breach. An early and influential example was *Wrotham Park Estate* v *Parkside Homes* (1974) where houses were built in breach of a restrictive covenant but the breach did not cause the claimant's neighbouring land to be worth any less. The claim for an injunction to have the houses demolished was rejected since that would be an 'unpardonable waste' but an award of damages in place of an injunction was made instead. These damages were based on a proportion of the £50,000 profit made by the developer (5 per cent, which came to £2,500) as being 'a sum of money as might reasonably have been demanded . . . as a quid pro quo for relaxing the covenant.' Whether such an award was truly restitutionary in nature, based on (part of) the benefit to the contract breaker, or was still compensatory—recognizing the innocent party's 'lost opportunity to bargain'—or was a combination of both summed up by the somewhat self-contradictory phrase 'restitutionary damages' was a matter for debate for many years. It has now become clear, following the Supreme Court decision in *Morris-Garner* v *One Step* (2018), that such awards are compensatory rather than restitutionary in nature and that the phrase 'Wrotham Park damages' should no longer be used. The Supreme Court preferred the term 'negotiating damages' to be used and also saw such damages as compensatory and, even then, as only available in a restricted range of situations. The state of the law following the *Morris-Garner* case is rather complex and will be considered further under 'Digging deeper' at the end of this chapter. What is clear however is that *Blake* is regarded even more now as an exceptional case and that it is not to be applied by analogy to support a more general drift towards using contractual damages for the purpose of giving back part of the profits made by the party in breach.

11.3 Measuring the expectation interest

Having clarified that it is normally the expectation interest which is protected, we next ask the question: 'How do we quantify or measure it?'

11.3.1 **Difference in value or cost of cure?**

One situation in which the question of quantification arises is when C receives defective performance. Should C receive simply the *difference in value* between the defective performance actually received and the performance C expected to receive, or should C be entitled to the

cost of cure—the cost of making the defect good—even if that is a higher amount? In many cases these two measures will be the same.

cost of cure
The cost of cure is the amount of money it would cost to pay someone else to complete the unfinished or defective performance.

EXAMPLE

Cost of cure can be same as difference in value

If you deliver a bike to me with only one wheel when I expected two, the difference in value and the 'cost of cure' are likely to be the same amount, that is, what it would cost to buy one wheel and fit it to the bike. This is because wheels are readily available and easy to attach to the bike so the difference in value reflects the cost of the cure—the simple step of buying and fitting a new wheel. However, in certain circumstances the cost of cure is astronomical in comparison to the difference in value between the performance received and the performance expected.

The cost of cure was awarded in *Radford* v *de Froberville* (1977), where de Froberville failed to build a boundary wall in breach of contract. The absence of the wall caused no diminution in the value of Radford's land but the cost of building the wall was £3,000; the court was therefore faced with the prospect of awarding nominal damages (reflecting the zero diminution in value) or £3,000 (the cost of cure). Oliver J, in deciding to make the award for the cost of cure, thought that it was important that Radford intended to build the wall and it was reasonable to carry out the work. The money would not therefore simply go straight into her pocket as a windfall but would instead be spent on correcting the breach of de Froberville (and therefore reflected the loss caused by the breach).

It is useful to contrast this case with *Ruxley Electronics and Construction Ltd* v *Forsyth* (1996).

CASE CLOSE-UP

***Ruxley Electronics and Construction Ltd* v *Forsyth* (1996)**

Mr Forsyth contracted for a swimming pool seven feet six inches in depth but received one which was nine inches shallower than this (but perfectly safe and suitable for its intended usage). He claimed £21,560 as the cost of demolishing the pool and rebuilding it to the correct depth, which is what he said he intended to do, but which was a large amount of money given that he only paid £17,797 and the financial value of the pool or his property had not been affected by the breach.

Unsurprisingly, the House of Lords refused to award this sum (although the Court of Appeal had done so). The House of Lords thought that awarding the cost of cure would be unreasonable because, on the facts of *Ruxley*, it was 'wholly disproportionate' to the actual loss of Mr Forsyth, which was regarded simply as his loss of amenity—that is, his disappointment at not having a pool quite as deep as specified. In order to compensate Mr Forsyth for this non-financial loss, the House of Lords reinstated the first instance judge's award of £2,500 for 'loss of amenity,' which avoided a stark choice between awarding £21,560 as the cost of cure or **nominal damages** for the difference in value (which was zero).

nominal damages
Usually just a couple of pounds are awarded by the court to signify that there has been a breach of contract but no loss (or no loss proven).

In *Ruxley*, the relevance of the claimant's avowed intention to use the damages to correct the defect (see *Radford* discussed earlier) was played down, at least as a positive factor, although its absence would certainly be a strong negative factor against awarding cost of cure (and Lord Jauncey referred to 'the trial judge having found as a fact that Mr Forsyth's stated intention of rebuilding the pool would not persist for long after the litigation had concluded'). Compare the result in *Ruxley* with that in the New Zealand Supreme Court case of *Marlborough District Council* v *Antimarloch Joint Venture* [2012] NZSC 11 discussed at the end of Chapter 7.

LINK TO . . .

Privity (Chapter 13)

In the complex commercial case of *Alfred McAlpine* v *Panatown* (2001), discussed further in Chapter 13 on Privity, the majority did not shrink from deciding that the claimants' actual loss was nil when the actual financial loss was suffered directly by another company in their group and so the claimants appeared themselves to suffer no direct quantifiable loss. Although there were two powerful dissenting judgments, the claimants' failure to receive the promised performance did not, for the majority, constitute a loss in itself and unlike in the consumer case of *Ruxley*, there was no award of 'loss of amenity' to fall back on to avoid the claimants being awarded only nominal damages.

11.3.2 Loss of an expected chance

This sections asks: 'Can C recover damages for the loss of a chance or opportunity to benefit which C would have had if the contract had been performed, even though it cannot be proved on the balance of probabilities that the actual benefit would have been received?'

In *Chaplin* v *Hicks* (1911) the claimant entered a beauty competition where the prize was a place in a theatre chorus line. She had made the shortlist of fifty after voting by the public (readers of a particular newspaper)—a sort of Edwardian 'X Factor'—but the defendants failed to tell her when the interview was to take place and she lost the chance of being one of the lucky twelve to make it on stage. The court awarded her £100 damages for the lost chance, although it is difficult to see how the sum should have been calculated; it appears as though the court weighed up the value of the prize and applied a statistical discount to reflect the chance that the claimant might not have received it. (The court perhaps wisely did not go down the route of trying to assess the claimant's looks as compared with the other fifty applicants!)

The threshold test for the degree of likelihood required for loss of a chance was stated in *Allied Maples Group Ltd* v *Simmons & Simmons* (1995) as requiring a 'substantial, and not merely a speculative, chance' that the benefit would have been conferred. This test, which clearly may be well below a 50 per cent probability, was applied more recently in the House of Lords in *Jackson* v *RBS* (2005), a case which will be discussed in more detail later. It should be noted, however, that the claimant must show on a balance of probabilities that if the defendant had not broken the contract, the claimant would have been able to perform its part of the contract—this was confirmed in *Flame* v *Glory Wealth Shipping* (2013), although on the facts the claimants were able to prove that they could do so. This differs from the rule about whether the claimant has to prove on a balance of probabilities that a third party would have acted in a particular way—the claimant does not have to prove this; it is sufficient to prove that there was a chance that the third party would so act and the damages can be for loss of that chance. See *Allied Maples* v *Simmons & Simmons* (1995)—the difference is that it should be easier for claimants to prove how they themselves would have acted (so they should prove that) whereas proof about a third party is more difficult so proof of a lost chance, which is less than the balance of probabilities, can be allowed to give recompense for loss of that chance. The distinction was approved in the Supreme Court in *Perry v Raleys Solicitors* (2019) where the claimant was not allowed to succeed on the basis of loss of a chance and was required to be able to prove on the balance of probabilities what *he* would have done, that is that he would have brought an honest 'services award' claim for personal injury, if the solicitors had properly advised him about the opportunity to do so. Since the trial judge had found that, in fact, he could not have brought an honest claim for a 'services award' under the compensation scheme for 'vibration white finger', because he knew he was not disabled in the requisite ways for bringing such a claim (and any such claim would have been dishonest), the solicitors' breach of duty in not advising him of the possibility of this type of claim had caused him no loss.

11.4 Remoteness

11.4.1 **Foreseeability and contemplation**

If any system of compensation imposed liability for all the consequences of a given act it would be safest to stay in bed in the morning and avoid the risk of being found liable for anything. Thus, the award of contractual damages, like damages in tort, is subject to rules of remoteness which limit the types of loss that are recoverable.

EXAMPLE

Some losses too remote

You supply computers and I buy one from you so that I can trade on the stock market online. The computer you supply is defective and malfunctions after two weeks, which also happens to be the day before the stock market crashes. This means that I could not sell a large quantity of shares that I had intended to sell and have lost tens of thousands of pounds. As a result I am bankrupted and have to sell my house and lose out on the housing boom over the next few years. All this causes me to become clinically depressed and to attempt to commit suicide (and my spouse leaves me, to boot). It would hardly be appropriate to hold you responsible for all these losses that allegedly flowed from your failure to deliver a working computer; and the law recognizes this through the limiting device or rule that damages must not be too remote—the remoteness of damage rule.

The basic rule, stated in *Hadley* v *Baxendale* (1854), is that a contracting party is liable for losses either:

a) arising naturally, that is according to the usual course of things; or

b) such as may reasonably be supposed to have been in the contemplation of both parties, at the time they made the contract, as the probable result of the breach of it.

This was transmuted to the composite test of 'reasonably foreseeable as liable to result' in *Victoria Laundry (Windsor) Ltd* v *Newman Industries Ltd* (1949) which itself has two subdivisions corresponding to the two limbs of the rule in *Hadley* v *Baxendale*: one dealing with losses that anyone, 'as a reasonable person,' could foresee and the second dealing with losses that are foreseeable given the special knowledge of the defendant. The essentials of *Victoria Laundry* were that the defendants agreed to provide a boiler for the claimants' laundry business with full knowledge that the boiler was essential for the business (you cannot wash clothes very well in cold water) but the boiler arrived five months late, by which time the claimants had lost out on five months of ordinary business profits and also on a highly lucrative contract with the Ministry of Supply. The court held that the claimants could recover the ordinary business profits because the defendants knew that these would be lost if the boiler was not delivered. However, the lost profits on the lucrative government contract were irrecoverable because the defendants did not know of this contract (did not have special knowledge) *and* they could not have foreseen such an exceptional loss.

THINKING POINT

What should you do if you are worried that you will suffer large losses if a party to your contract fails to perform?

Does it matter how obvious your losses are? How could you bring exceptional losses to the other party's attention and, more importantly, how could you prove that the other party knew about them?

11.4.2 **Foresight in contract and tort**

Although the actual decision in *Victoria Laundry* has not been doubted, in *The Heron II* (1969) Lord Reid thought that the language of foreseeability used in the case was 'likely to be misunderstood' as confusing the test of remoteness in contract with that in tort where it is more generous and includes damages which are foreseeable as a mere possibility, whereas in contract it has to be foreseeable as 'not unlikely' or as a 'serious possibility.' The House of Lords found difficulty in formulating a single or precise test but all their Lordships were agreed that a *higher* degree of foreseeability is required in contract than in tort.

'Serious possibility' seems to be emerging as the most favoured formulation. In *A-G Virgin Islands* v *Global Water Associates* (2020) Lord Hodge in the Privy Council at para. [32] adopted the test of a type of loss 'reasonably contemplated as a serious possibility,' which he added was an objective test dependent on 'what the defendant must be taken to have had in his or her contemplation rather than only what he or she actually contemplated.' The claimant's lost profits under the treatment plant operating contract (which was not the contract broken), a separate contract from the contract to design and build the plant in the first place, were clearly a type of loss contemplated as a serious possibility if the design and build contract was terminated (thus inevitably preventing the treatment plant operating contract from being performed and thereby causing loss of profits). This was especially the case as both contracts were signed on the same day by the same parties, 'giving rise to special knowledge under the second limb of the rule in *Hadley* v *Baxendale*'.

The justification for the difference between remoteness in tort and in contract is that if a contracting party wants greater protection against the possible consequences of breach it can provide for this in the contract and/or notify the other party of factors rendering a particular risk more likely. The other party will calculate its price and terms and arrange insurance on the basis of the quantifiable risks which are known about and not on the basis of possible but unlikely risks. One problem with the difference however is that often the same act can be both a breach of contract and a tort (usually negligence, i.e. an act may be negligent under the common law duty imposed by the law under the law of torts to take reasonable care, and that same act may also constitute a breach of a contractual obligation to take reasonable care). This concurrent liability is most likely to arise where physical damage is caused (for instance where you sell me a chainsaw which has a dangerous defect and which as a result saws my leg off—you have breached your contractual promise that the chainsaw is safe to use in accordance with its instructions and you will also have broken the general tortious duty to take reasonable care).

This frequent concurrence of liability in both contract and tort led Lord Denning MR to suggest in *H. Parsons (Livestock) Ltd* v *Uttley Ingham & Co. Ltd* (1978) that, where the loss is physical damage, the tort test is applicable also to damages in contract but the stricter contractual test is applicable to pure loss of profits. Thus the claimants in that case recovered for the reasonably foreseeable physical damage (diseased and deceased pigs!) and financial loss associated with those pigs (but not for pure financial loss of profit in relation to potential future sales of pigs which they had never been able to produce, since that type of loss was not foreseeable as a serious possibility). The applicable remoteness test in concurrent liability cases was therefore (according to Lord Denning) determined by the 'type' of damage suffered. The more generous tortious test (reasonable foreseeability) would apply if loss is consequent on physical damage whereas the contractual test (foreseeable as a serious possibility) would apply in cases of pure financial loss, that is in cases such as *Hadley* v *Baxendale*, *Victoria Laundry* and *The Heron II*, where there was loss of profits not consequent on physical harm.

However, although Scarman LJ disagreed on this distinction between physical damage and economic loss, he did agree on the result of the case because some physical harm to or illness of the pigs was a serious possibility (thus satisfying even the contractual test) and once that *type* of damage is within the contemplation of the parties it does not matter that the actual damage (E. coli infection and death of the pigs) is much more serious in degree. Foresight of a serious possibility of *some* physical damage to the pigs was therefore sufficient to cover *serious* physical damage; only the *type* of damage need be foreseeable as a serious possibility, not the exact extent of damage suffered.

The question of the correct approach to remoteness in cases where there is concurrent liability in contract and tort was clarified in *Wellesley Partners* v *Withers LLP* (2015). The defendant solicitors were liable for negligently drafting a partnership agreement as a result of which the claimants lost potentially lucrative profits in the USA. They appealed on the basis that the trial judge had applied the more generous tort test of reasonable foreseeability, rather than the stricter contractual test of reasonable contemplation. The Court of Appeal ruled that the contractual test should apply but this did not change the result as the type of loss awarded would have been within the contemplation of the parties and of a type for which the defendants would have assumed responsibility under the contract. The type, rather than the extent, of damage rule was therefore applied just as by Scarman LJ in *Parsons*. As regards Lord Denning's distinction between physical and purely financial loss, and his view that the tort test should apply to the former but not the latter, there has been little support for this in the decades since the decision in *Parsons*. However, the decision in *Wellesley Partners* v *Withers* is not necessarily inconsistent with Lord Denning's view since it was made clear that the Court of Appeal in the more recent case were laying down a rule (the contractual test even where concurrent liability is in tort) for cases of economic, not physical, loss.

The evolution of the formulations of the test for remoteness is illustrated by Figure 11.4.

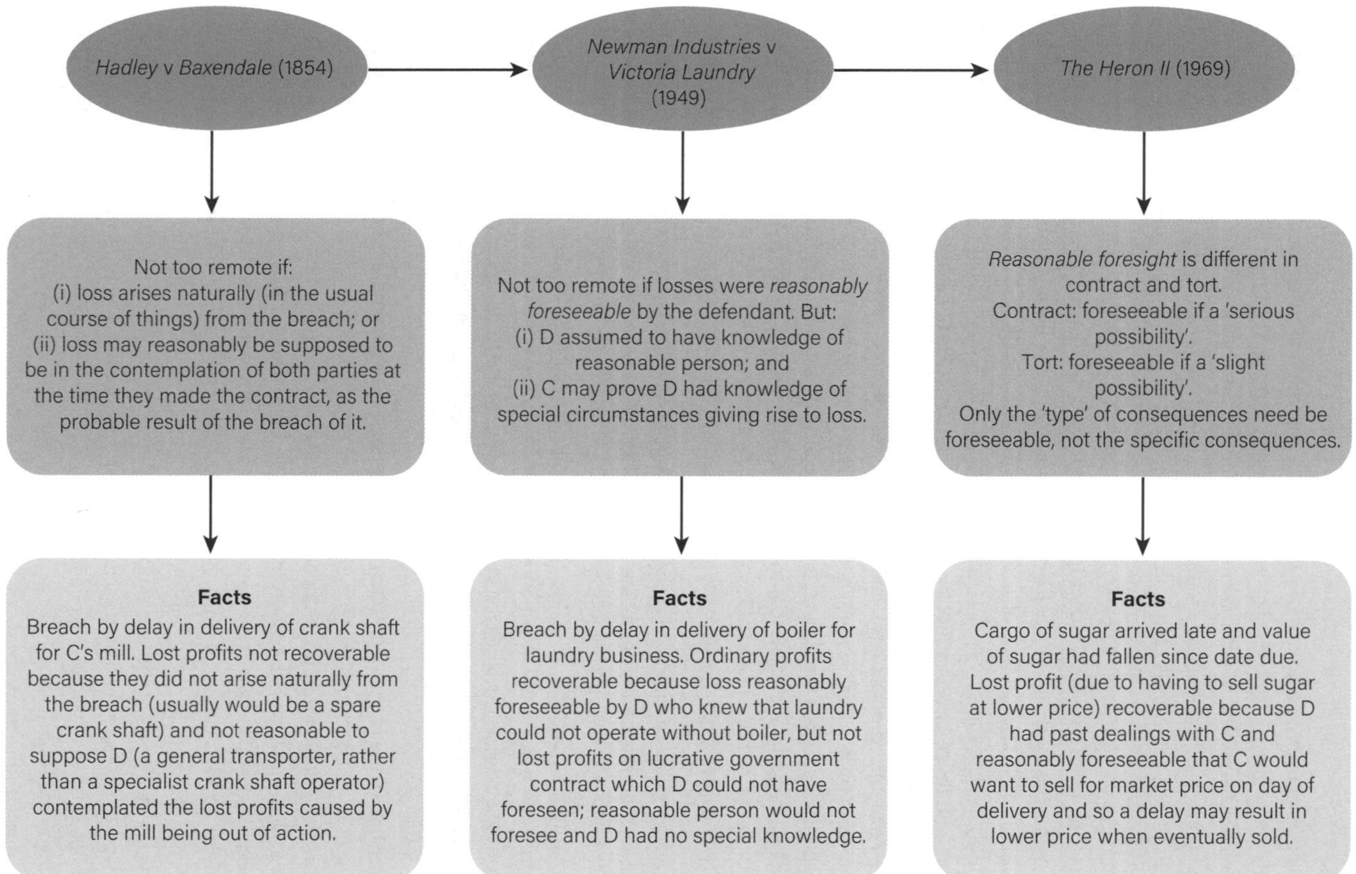

Figure 11.4 The evolution of a test for remoteness

11.4.3 **Type versus extent of loss**

We have just seen that a key concept in any discussion of remoteness is the notion of the 'type' of loss: in *H. Parsons* v *Uttley Ingham* the illness of the pigs was one type of loss and it was unnecessary for the specific illness to be foreseeable. The principle is that if a given 'type' of loss is foreseeable (in the relevant sense) the whole amount of that type of loss is recoverable. This is again a concept that can be easily manipulated, as is shown by the *Victoria Laundry* case itself, where normal loss of profits was regarded as a different 'type' of loss from the profits on the highly lucrative contracts. No doubt, if the court had wished to allow for recovery for this second type of lost profits they could have categorized 'lost profits' as all of one 'type.' So for example, in *Brown* v *KMR Services* (1995) unprecedented losses were regarded as precisely the *type* of loss that would have been in the contemplation of the parties and the fact that they were much greater in scale than anyone would have foreseen was irrelevant. Treating the highly lucrative profits in *Victoria Laundry* as different in type from normal loss of profits has sometimes been seen as anomalous and to undermine the integrity of the type of loss test. This was addressed in *Wellesley* v *Withers* where the Court of Appeal defended the decision in *Victoria Laundry* and distinguished it from the case before them where lucrative opportunities in the USA were held to be within the type of losses contemplated. Roth J considered it was 'readily explicable that the exceptionally lucrative government contracts could be regarded as involving a different type of loss' in *Victoria Laundry* given the difference between ordinary laundry custom at £16 per week and government dyeing contracts at £262 per week. Floyd LJ further explained the distinction between the two cases: 'In *Victoria Laundry* the defendants had no reason to suppose that the laundry in question was anything other than an ordinary laundry. Here the defendants must be assumed to have been aware of Mr Channing's star qualities [which meant the lucrative USA profits would have been feasible]. The two cases could not be more different in this respect.'

underwriting
Another word for insurance. For example, if a company issues shares (equity) or bonds (debt) a bank will underwrite the issue and guarantee that the company will get the money it needs even if the share or bond issue fails to raise the necessary amount.

The distinction between the type and extent of loss also arose in another House of Lords case, *Jackson* v *RBS* (2005), which also provides an illustration of damages being awarded for loss of a chance (see Figure 11.5). The case is interesting on a number of levels, not least in that Lord Hope said in passing, perhaps somewhat optimistically, that the rules identified in *Hadley* v *Baxendale* 'are very familiar to every student of contract law. Most would claim to be able to recite them by heart.'

The names of the businesses in *Jackson* read a little like those dreamt up by an over-imaginative examiner. The defendant bank, in breach of contract, inadvertently revealed the price charged by an overseas supplier ('Pet Products') from which the claimant ('Samson') had been importing 'dog chews' to sell on to a UK distributor ('Economy Bag'). This caused loss to Samson because once Economy Bag realized how much commission or mark-up Samson was making on the price charged by Pet Products it became angry and decided to cut out the middleman (Samson) and buy direct from Pet Products. This was disastrous for Samson, which lost all of its chances of future business with Economy Bag and eventually ceased trading. The question was in respect of what period of time Samson should receive compensation *from the bank* for its lost chances of making future profits with Economy Bag. The Court of Appeal took the view that the bank would only have contemplated the potential losses as continuing for one year and so loss of profits beyond one year were too remote, although the court awarded \$45,000 for that year alone. The House of Lords thought that was wrong in principle. Once it was accepted that loss of the chance to earn profits from future contracts with Economy Bag was a loss arising in the natural course of things or was in the contemplation of the parties then there was no remoteness limit on the duration of that loss which was recoverable, since the *type* of loss was contemplated and the duration was simply

Figure 11.5 *Jackson* v *RBS* (2005)

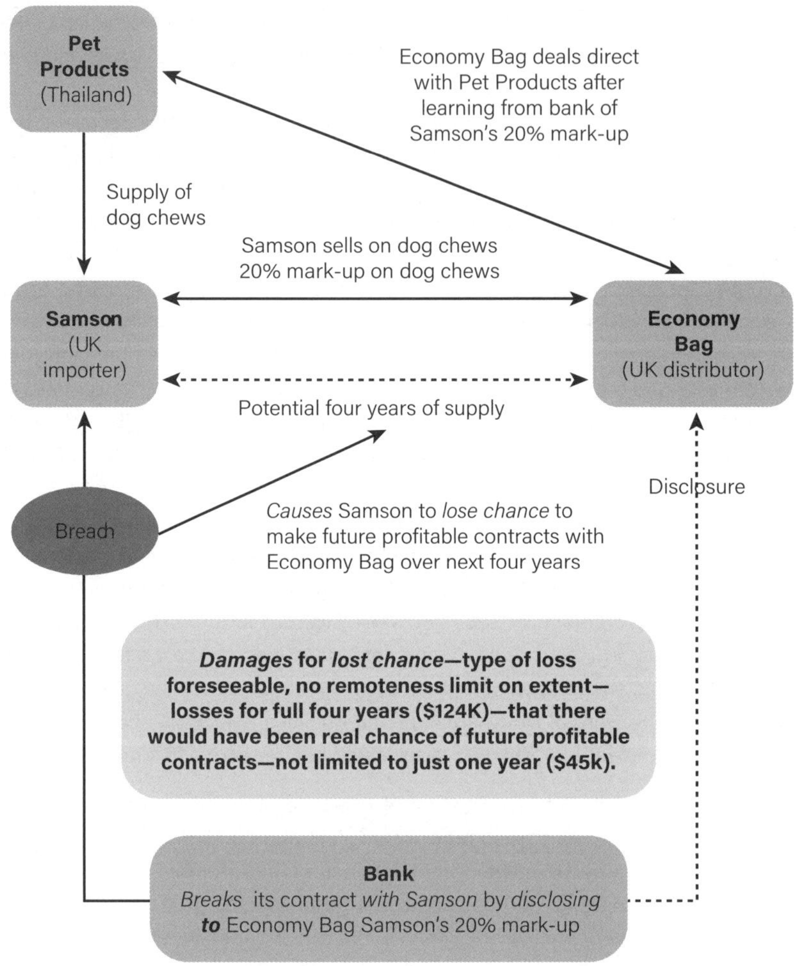

a question of extent (just as illness of the pigs was the *type* of loss in *H. Parsons* v *Uttley Ingham* and E. coli and death was the *extent* of that type of loss). If the bank had wanted to limit its potential liability for this type of loss it could have said so at the outset (see Chapter 6 on Exemption clauses) but it had not done so: 'If no cut-off point is provided by the contract, there is no arbitrary limit that can be set to the amount of the damages once the test of remoteness according to one or other of the rules in *Hadley* v *Baxendale* has been satisfied' (Lord Hope at para. [36]).

The House restored the award of the trial judge amounting in total to $124,500, representing the loss of the (gradually diminishing) chances of earning profits from supplying Economy Bag over a four-year period. That was the best estimate of the actual loss sustained, the probability being that by the end of four years Economy Bag would have ceased to purchase through Samson anyway—beyond that point the chances were speculative rather than real or substantial—see *Allied Maples* discussed earlier. Thus, the bank's breach only *caused* four years' worth of lost profits and these were not limited by way of remoteness since they were all of the *type* which would have been contemplated by the parties.

11.4.4 **Is the foreseeability of the type of loss sufficient or must the defendant be taken to have assumed or undertaken responsibility for the type of loss?**

The House of Lords grappled with this issue in returning again to the rules of remoteness in the important and beguiling case of *Transfield Shipping* v *Mercator Shipping* (2008). The defendant charterers of a ship were nine days late (at the end of a seven-month period ending in May 2004) in returning it to the owners who had previously arranged a lucrative follow-on charter of the vessel to Cargill for a further period of four to six months. As a result of the delay, the lucrative follow-on charter had to be renegotiated, causing a loss of $1.36 million. It was agreed that it was in the reasonable contemplation of the parties that late return would in the ordinary course of things lead to the cancellation of a follow-on charter but the general understanding of the shipping market was that the damages recoverable in this type of case would not be based on the loss of the whole follow-on charter but simply on the market price for the actual number of days late. This would have been on the facts the much smaller sum of $158,000, being the difference between the sum paid under the original charter and the higher market price prevalent on those nine days. The follow-on loss by contrast was based on the reduction in the price the owners could charge Cargill when they had to renegotiate the new six-month charter because they could not supply the ship on time due to its late delivery. To understand why this follow-on loss was so high it is important to appreciate that the market price for shipping was extremely and unusually volatile at the time which is why the price that could be negotiated for a six-month charter dropped so quickly over a few days, having previously risen equally dramatically.

Right up as far as the House of Lords, the decision went in favour of the owners, who were considered to be entitled to the larger follow-on charter damages since that type of loss was thought to be in the contemplation of the parties as not unlikely to result or as a serious possibility. The House of Lords however took a different view, although there were significant differences between the reasons of the various members of the House.

What might be described as the majority, but somewhat novel view, was most strikingly put by Lord Hoffmann, who considered that 'all contractual liability is voluntarily undertaken' and that 'the findings of the arbitrators and the commercial background to the agreement are sufficient to make it clear that the charterer cannot reasonably be regarded as having assumed the risk of the owner's loss of profit on the following charter.' Perhaps the best way to look at Lord Hoffmann's view would be to say that the ordinary foreseeability rule based on *Hadley* v *Baxendale* is the normal rule, because a party can normally be taken to have voluntarily assumed the risk of any losses that were foreseeable if it has not indicated in the contract that it is not prepared to be liable, but that there are exceptions (of which this was one) where it is clear that a type of loss might well be caused (and has not been expressly excluded) and yet the overall context showed that the parties contracted on the basis that there would be no *liability* for that type of loss. Effectively the court is recognizing a sort of implied exclusion or limitation clause in respect of the type of loss which may have been foreseen or foreseeable but for which liability cannot be taken to have been assumed.

As Lord Hoffmann put it himself at para. [11] of his speech, 'departure from the ordinary foreseeability rule based on individual circumstances will be unusual but limitation on the extent of liability in particular types of contract arising out of general expectations in certain markets, such as banking and shipping, are likely to be more common,' and he went on to draw an analogy with the process of implying terms.

Lord Rodger, whilst agreeing with the result, took a different approach based on the traditional application of the *Hadley* v *Baxendale* rules. The loss suffered in relation to a follow-on charter was not in his view a loss arising in the ordinary course of things since in the ordinary course of things, the lost follow-on charter could be replaced by another which in an ordinary market situation would not be substantially different or involve any loss and compensation, for the number of days actually lost at the prevailing market rate would normally represent the actual loss suffered. It was only because the market had become so highly volatile that the replacement for the lost charter caused the (much greater) loss in question but that was not recoverable under the first rule in *Hadley* v *Baxendale* because it was not an ordinarily arising loss and, since the volatility of the market was not known to the defendants at the time the contract was entered into, it was not recoverable under the second limb (rather as the exceptional profits in *Victoria Laundry* were not recoverable). Lord Rodger did recognize that there may be situations where the circumstances known to the charterers at the time of contracting would make them liable for this type of loss under normal principles, but this was not one of them. The charterers moreover had not deliberately caused the breach and there was 'no commercial or legal justification for fixing them with liability for the owners' loss of profit due to the effects of an "extremely volatile market" in relation to an arrangement with a third party about which the charterers knew nothing.'

Baroness Hale's opinion is in some ways the most interesting. It would be wrong to describe it as a dissent, although she indicated at the outset that her initial inclination was to dismiss the appeal and, even at the conclusion, her view was that if the appeal were to be allowed, as to which she 'continued to have doubts,' she would 'prefer it to be allowed on the narrower ground identified by Lord Rodger, leaving the wider ground to be fully explored in another case and another context.' Amongst the factors that would have caused her Ladyship to continue to have doubts, even about the approach of Lord Rodger, must have been, as she pointed out in para. [90], that both parties would have known that late delivery was likely to mean a follow-on charter was cancelled, that such follow-on charters did not normally allow another ship to be substituted and, perhaps most crucially, that it would have been—and, looking to the future, it is—relatively easy to insert a clause to exclude liability for consequential loss such as the new charter loss, whereas it would require quite a complicated piece of drafting to expressly impose liability for new charter loss if, as is now the law, it is ruled out as too remote.

It is difficult not to share some of the concerns of Baroness Hale, especially when one compares the result in this case with that reached by the House in *Jackson* v *RBS* only three years previously. In that case too there were, in one sense, unusually extensive consequences of the breach of contract by the bank but these were held to be recoverable as being a foreseeable *type* of loss, Lord Hope noting that 'if no cut-off point is provided by the contract, there is no arbitrary limit . . . *once the test of remoteness according to one or other of the rules in* Hadley v Baxendale *has been satisfied*' (emphasis added). The factors mentioned by Baroness Hale in para. [90] of *Transfield* v *Mercator*, as outlined earlier, would all suggest that the new charter loss was capable of being regarded as a *type* of loss (classified as e.g. 'due to follow-on charter cancellation') which should have been prima facie recoverable and not too remote, it being up to the charterers to exclude it if they did not agree to being liable for it.

Baroness Hale started her opinion by comparing the facts to an examination question and stating that all the judges who had answered it at different levels would gain first class marks, including Lord Hoffmann, who she thought, despite her reservations about his approach, might deserve a 'congratulatory' rather than just an ordinary sort of first (either sort would surely more than satisfy most readers). This all goes to show that, in an examination at least, if you can discuss the various strands of reasoning about remoteness of damage in an intelligent and credible manner, you can manipulate the concept of a 'type of loss' to come to whatever conclusion you like and still gain an excellent mark!

The decision of the House of Lords was exclusionary in the sense that it provided an exception to the general *Hadley* v *Baxendale* rule that losses arising in the ordinary course of things or within the reasonable contemplation of the parties were recoverable. On the facts of *Transfield*, the larger follow-on losses were within the contemplation of the parties but, despite this, were too remote and irrecoverable because, in the particular circumstances of that case, the charterer had not assumed responsibility for that loss.

By contrast, the Court of Appeal in *Siemens Building Technologies FE Ltd* v *Supershield Ltd* (2010) agreed that the decision could have an inclusionary effect in circumstances where the type of loss suffered could not be said to arise in the normal course of things or be within the parties' reasonable contemplation, but nevertheless the defendant had assumed responsibility to avoid such loss. On the facts of the case, a faulty float valve in a water tank for a sprinkler system caused a flood in the basement of an office building resulting in substantial damage to electrical equipment. In the normal course of things, the drainage system in the basement would have taken the overflow water away, but on this occasion the drains had become blocked. The Court of Appeal was prepared to accept that the contractor's duty extended to preventing the flood, even if it was unlikely that the failure of the valve would lead to a flood. The decision, however, has to be understood in the context that all that the court ultimately had to decide was whether the 50 per cent settlement by Siemens (for £2.8 million) of the claims brought against them by the building's owners was reasonable (and could thus legitimately be passed up the line for their sub-contractors, Supershield, to pay). In that sense the decision can be thought of as essentially saying no more than that there was a reasonably arguable case that the contractors were liable for the unlikely flood.

The general trend of decisions since *Transfield Shipping* has been to play down the significance of the qualification to the *Hadley* v *Baxendale* reasonable contemplation test which, in most cases at least, will continue to be the operative standard or default rule. In *John Grimes Partnership Ltd* v *Gubbins* (2013), Sir David Keene in the Court of Appeal put it this way:

> Normally, there is an implied term accepting responsibility for the types of losses which can reasonably be foreseen at the time of contract to be not unlikely to result if the contract is broken. But if there is evidence in a particular case that the nature of the contract and the commercial background, or indeed other relevant special circumstances, render that implied assumption of responsibility inappropriate for a type of loss, then the contract-breaker escapes liability.

On the facts of the case the normal rule was applied to make the appellant engineering consultants liable for the £300,000 fall in value of a housing development caused by their breach delaying the development by over a year, during which the market fell by 14 per cent. This type of loss was perfectly foreseeable if such a delay was caused and there was no evidence 'of any general understanding or expectation in the property world' that consultants such as the appellant 'would not be taken to have assumed responsibility for losses' such as this. It was thus clearly not a *Transfield* type case. Nor did the fact that the contractual fee (£15,000) was relatively small compared to the loss mean that the loss was too remote, as:

> any such contrast is merely one possible pointer towards a contracting party not having undertaken a potential liability which is reasonably foreseeable and by itself would not normally suffice to establish such an absence of responsibility . . . the Judge was right to find that there was nothing to take this case out of the conventional approach to remoteness of damage in contract cases.

11.5 Non-pecuniary losses

Contractual damages have traditionally been concerned with economic and physical losses readily quantifiable in financial terms, such as lost profits, where the claimant simply deducts the contract price from the market value of the goods to establish the lost profit. However, a breach of contract can cause disappointment and distress, particularly in consumer contracts where the aim of the contract is not to make a profit but to have a good time, and these are referred to as 'non-pecuniary losses' (i.e. non-money losses). For example, when you book your summer holiday you do not do it with the intention of selling it on to make a profit; you do it because you want to relax. If you are put in a hotel filled with cockroaches and next to noisy building works then you will not be relaxed and most likely be upset and angry, a situation which will only escalate if you find out that, in general, the law will only award damages for pecuniary losses (of which you have suffered none).

The general rule is best illustrated by *Addis* v *Gramophone Co. Ltd* (1909) where the court refused damages for injured feelings caused by a humiliating and wrongful dismissal. However, there have always been exceptions for pain and suffering *consequent* upon personal injury and for actual physical inconvenience, as in *Bailey* v *Bullock* (1950) where a breach of contract caused the claimant to have to live with his in-laws. (Some might think this is more properly classified as pain and suffering rather than mere physical inconvenience!)

EXAMPLE

Physical harm and financial loss v Mental distress

I sell you a mountain bike and you enter a downhill time trial race. The front wheel comes loose as you hurtle down the mountain and you break both your arms and your collarbone and cannot race again. Not only can you sue me for the actual broken bones and lost opportunity to win prize money (say you were a professional racer), but you can also sue me for the pain and distress that followed on from your accident and the inability to race again—this would include not just a sum for the pain in breaking your bones but also a sum for the consequential pain on missing out on your passion for mountain biking for the rest of your life.

Contrast the situation with one where you hire a mountain bike for a weekend ride along some woodland trails but the front wheel falls off when you are miles from a repair centre and the bike can no longer be ridden. Fortunately you were not riding the bike when the wheel broke and so you were not injured. Under the general principle, you would not be able to claim for the disappointment suffered (your ruined weekend) because it was not *consequent* on any physical loss—it would be different if the contract was one to provide enjoyment, as looked at in the *Jarvis* case to be discussed next.

A breakthrough in English law was made in *Jarvis* v *Swans Tours Ltd* (1973) where the claimant was promised a 'great time' on a holiday costing £63 and was awarded £125 when he did not get it. Two exceptional categories were identified: firstly, where the main purpose of the contract was to provide mental satisfaction (such as in *Jarvis* itself or, for example, in a contract to take wedding photographs) or to provide relief from distress (such as in *Heywood* v *Wellers* (1976) where a woman employed solicitors to obtain an injunction to prevent molestation); and secondly, where the mental distress suffered was as a direct consequence of physical injury or inconvenience caused by the defendant's breach (as in *Perry* v *Sydney Phillips* (1982) where a breach by a surveyor led the claimant to buy a house that was falling down and smelt, and this physical damage and inconvenience caused the claimant mental distress).

The House of Lords in *Farley* v *Skinner* (2001) also accepted that there may be exceptions to the general rule that damages are only available for physical and financial losses and extended the range of the exceptions.

CASE CLOSE-UP

***Farley* v *Skinner* (2001)**

Mr Farley contracted for a survey of a house before he bought it, specifically asking the surveyor to check for aircraft noise. He moved in and, upon discovering that aircraft regularly disturbed his breakfast on the terrace (amongst other things), decided that he wanted to stay but would sue the surveyor for breach of the contract and seek damages for the non-pecuniary losses suffered. The House of Lords held that damages could be recovered where the purpose of enjoyment or alleviation of distress was 'a distinct and *important* obligation' rather than the *sole* purpose of the contract, as held in *Watts* v *Morrow* (1991). They were also prepared to allow recovery on a second ground: namely that the loss suffered was consequent on physical inconvenience, classifying the sound of aircraft as a physical inconvenience.

LINK TO . . .

Difference in value or cost of cure? (Section 11.3.1)

The £2,500 award made in *Ruxley* for Mr Forsyth's 'loss of amenity' can be interpreted as damages for non-pecuniary loss, based on the fact that the contract was a consumer contract for enjoyment (see the opinions of Lords Clyde and Hutton in *Farley* v *Skinner* (2001)). However, the award may also be interpreted as a response to the need for a wider principle of recovery based on the loss of 'consumer surplus.' Consumer surplus is the difference in value between what a thing is worth commercially and the higher value at which a consumer subjectively values it. So, whilst an extra few inches on the swimming pool added no financial value, the £2,500 represented Mr Forsyth's consumer surplus: *to him*, and him alone, the pool was a more valuable asset if it was deeper (i.e. if his contract was fully performed). He had contracted for this extra depth and it had not been provided, so you could argue that the award of £2,500 was compensation for loss of this consumer surplus.

11.6 Mitigation

This is a serious qualification to the rule that damages are designed to put the claimant in as good a position as if the contract had been performed. The claimant is expected to take *reasonable* steps to put *itself* into that position and, if it is able to do this, it can only claim the extra costs incurred in doing so. The claimant is therefore under a duty to minimize its losses by getting as close as possible to the performance position.

EXAMPLE

Duty to mitigate

Wholesavers Ltd agrees to buy widgets in advance from SuperSupply Ltd for £1,000 and then contracts with Pile 'em High Ltd to resell them for £1,500. SuperSupply fails to deliver and the market price of the widgets on the promised date of delivery is £1,200. Wholesavers cannot simply sit back and claim £500 loss of profit on its sale to Pile 'em High (assume that SuperSupply knew of this sell-on contract and so there are no remoteness issues) because it is under a duty to buy substitute widgets in the market for £1,200 and supply Pile 'em High with these widgets, reducing its claim against SuperSupply to the extra cost of doing so (£200 plus any expenses of buying in the market). This 'market value' rule is enshrined in s.51(3) of the Sale of Goods Act 1979 as the normal rule for these sorts of cases which shows how much the duty to mitigate is an integral part of the assessment of contractual damages.

The corollary of this rule is that if A reasonably tries to mitigate A's losses, but this in fact turns out to increase them, A can claim this increased loss. See, for example, *Hoffberger* v *Ascot International Bloodstock Bureau Ltd* (1976), where the claimant had agreed to sell a horse for £6,000 to the defendant who refused, in breach of contract, to accept the horse. The claimant kept the horse at considerable expense in the hope of finding a buyer but was unsuccessful in doing so and the horse was sold in the December sales, a year later, for only £1,085. Keeping the horse over the year had in fact made matters worse—horses eat a lot of oats, and we know from *Smith* v *Hughes* (1870–71) (Chapter 8) that they are very fussy creatures—but the Court of Appeal held that the expenses of so keeping it could be recovered in addition to the loss of profit since the claimant had acted reasonably. See also *Hooper* v *Oates* (2013) where the sellers of a house had acted reasonably by trying (unsuccessfully) for several years to find another buyer after the defendant failed to complete the purchase in 2008 for £605,000. The general fall in the property market meant the property was only worth £495,000 by the time the damages were assessed in 2012 and the defendant was liable for the difference in value at that date. It is different where there is an immediately available market (as in the Wholesavers example above) when the market price at the time of the breach governs the amount of the breach.

Difficult questions arise where, although the claimant is not actually required to mitigate, it takes steps which do in fact improve his position—see *British Westinghouse Electric & Manufacturing Co. Ltd* v *Underground Electric Railways Co. of London Ltd* (1912), where the saved running costs achieved by replacing the defective turbine supplied by the defendant in breach of the contract with a more efficient model were deducted from the damages awarded. The defendant cannot always claim the benefits of the claimant's initiative in order to reduce its liability, for instance when the benefit to the claimant is not caused by the breach.

Thus, in the example given earlier of SuperSupply failing to deliver goods which it has contracted to supply to Wholesavers for £1,000 when the market price has risen to £1,200, suppose that Wholesavers manages to buy goods for £1,100 instead. Wholesaver's initiative (e.g. through its contacts in the market) has reduced its loss from the extra £200 which it would have had to pay for substitute goods in the market to the extra £100 it has actually paid. Should its damages be £100 or £200? The answer seems to depend on whether the profitable purchase is a 'collateral benefit', in which case the answer is still £200, or a consequence of the breach, in which case it will reduce the damages to £100. The answer in this particular example (and all the cases are heavily fact specific in this area) might turn on whether Wholesavers would have taken the opportunity to purchase the substitute goods for £1,100 in any case, to make an additional profit in the market, even if SuperSupply had not broken its contract. It is not always easy to decide whether something is a collateral benefit or not. Compare this example to the case of *C. & P. Haulage* v *Middleton* (1983) where the Court, rightly or wrongly, effectively took the view that the concession by the Council, enabling the claimant to be able once more to work rent-free from his domestic garage, was a consequence of the breach rather than a collateral benefit, and so it extinguished the loss caused by the eviction from the yard.

In contrast, in *Fulton Shipping* v *Gobalia Business Travel* (2017) the charterers of a cruise ship returned it to the owners in 2007 two years before the end of the charter in 2009 in breach of contract. The owners claimed for net loss of profit over that two-year period of approximately €7 million. On the return of the ship in 2007 they sold it for US$23 million and due to a market crash it would only have been worth US$7 million by the end of the charter in 2009. They were thus US$16 million better off as a result of the decision to sell the ship in 2007 than if they had waited until the end of the charter in 2009. Did this benefit wipe out the damages for loss of profit? The Supreme Court, to the surprise of many commentators, said no. The capital benefit was not legally caused by the breach. It was the result of the owners' own decision to sell the ship. They could have sold it at any time, including during the last two years of the charterparty (subject to the charterparty). They did not have to sell it on the breach, they could have tried to mitigate their loss of profit by trying to hire it out. Neither was it necessarily the case that they would have sold it at the end of the charterparty in 2009. The benefit of selling when they did was the result of their own decision to speculate and dispose of an asset at what proved to be a propitious time and was effectively a collateral benefit from that decision and not a result of the breach. Thus they did not have to give credit for the US$16 million (just as they would not have been able to claim a corresponding capital loss if the market had moved by that amount in the opposite direction) and they could still claim the net loss of profit for the two-year period caused by the breach.

11.7 Contributory negligence

11.7.1 **Overriding cause**

Another potential way in which damages may be reduced is through the contributory fault of the claimant. If the claimant's negligence (i.e. the claimant's failure to take reasonable care) is the overriding cause of the loss, it will remove liability completely, as in *Quinn* v *Burch Brothers (Builders) Ltd* (1966) where the accident would not have occurred if the defendants had not failed, in breach of contract, to provide a ladder but the claimant's (negligent) decision to use a trestle instead was the substantial cause. The causal connection in this case was completely broken by the claimant's intervening act, but the more difficult issue is when the claimant's negligent act makes a less substantial contribution.

11.7.2 **Joint cause**

Can contributory negligence be a reason for merely *reducing* (as opposed to eliminating) the damages under the Law Reform (Contributory Negligence) Act 1945 which applies where the claimant suffers damage as the result partly of his own fault and partly of the fault of any other person? The answer turns on the meaning of 'fault' in the Act and whether a breach of contract amounts to fault—remember, for the Act to apply, both the claimant and the defendant must be partly at fault.

To understand this area you must recall that there are two types of contractual obligation: those that impose an obligation regardless of any standard of care (for example, the obligation to buy and sell goods is absolute and will be breached if the buyer or seller fails to buy or sell even if they have made a superhuman effort to do so) and those that impose a contractual duty to take reasonable care (e.g. a jeweller who promises to take reasonable care when resizing a ring—the jeweller does not promise to resize the ring without damage, only to take reasonable care).

If the breach is merely of a strict obligation (i.e. a 'no-fault obligation') under the contract then the answer to the question posed earlier is clearly 'no' and the Act does not apply (and the defendant is liable in full even if the claimant has been contributorily negligent: see *Barclays Bank* v *Fairclough Building* (1995)). If on the other hand the breach of contract consists of a failure to take reasonable care then the Act can apply (again if the claimant is also at fault) even if the action is brought in contract. This latter point was settled by the Court of Appeal in *Forsikrings Vesta* v *Butcher* (1988). However, a person who breaches a contractual term to take reasonable care cannot plead contributory negligence if there would be no liability in tort independently of the contract. It is perhaps unfortunate that in order to determine whether the Act is applicable to a claim for negligent breach of contract one has to investigate the hypothetical and, at least in some cases, potentially difficult question of whether there would be independent liability in tort. Quite some time ago, in its Report No. 219 (1993), the Law Commission recommended that contributory negligence should be available to a contractual duty to take reasonable care or exercise reasonable skill whether or not there is a concurrent duty in tort (in most cases however there will be such a concurrent duty). The current situation is illustrated in Figure 11.6.

11.8 Penalties and agreed damages

Because the assessment of damages can itself give rise to difficult and controversial questions of law and because disputes about damages, like any other sort of dispute, can cause a continuous relationship to deteriorate and perhaps even terminate unnecessarily, a contract will often provide in advance what damages should be payable for particular types of breach. This sort of clause not only avoids the expense of legal proceedings to determine the amount of damages but also makes it more likely that the innocent party will feel able to claim damages for breach without the fear of upsetting the future relationship with the party in breach.

> **penalty clauses** Penalty clauses are unenforceable because they impose a detriment on the contract breaker out of all proportion to the legitimate interest of the innocent party in the enforcement of the primary obligation (Lord Neuberger in *Cavendish Holdings* v *Makdessi* (2015)).

Figure 11.6 Application of the Law Reform (Contributory Negligence) Act 1945

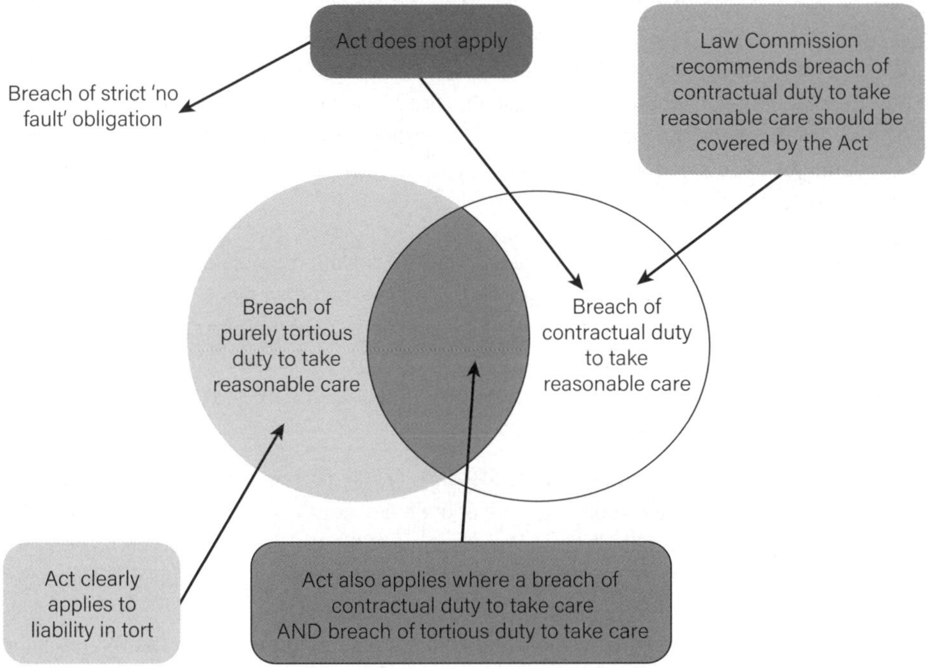

Although businessmen often refer to agreed damages clauses indiscriminately as penalty clauses, the law has drawn a sharp distinction between agreed (or liquidated) damages clauses on the one hand (which are a genuine pre-estimate of the loss and which are enforceable) and penalty clauses on the other hand (which do not genuinely attempt to estimate the real loss or protect some other legitimate interest but which are merely designed to penalize one party for his breach). The traditional approach to penalty clauses was set out in the leading case of *Dunlop Pneumatic Tyre Co. Ltd* v *New Garage & Motor Co. Ltd* (1915) where the claimants promised not to sell tyres to private customers below Dunlop's list price, not to supply them to customers Dunlop had decided to suspend and not to exhibit or export them without Dunlop's consent. The contract provided that £5 was payable to Dunlop for every tyre sold in breach of these restrictions and, despite the contract stipulating a single sum for all these possible different breaches (see point (c) below), the House of Lords accepted this as a genuine pre-estimate of loss as opposed to a penalty clause. One important factor was that it was very difficult at the time of contracting to estimate what damages a breach of the promises made would cause. Lord Dunedin said that in assessing whether a clause was a penalty or not 'the following tests may prove helpful or conclusive':

a) the clause will be a penalty if the sum stipulated for is extravagant and unconscionable in amount in comparison to the greatest conceivable loss that could have followed from the breach;

b) it will be held to be a penalty if the breach consists only in not paying a sum of money, and the sum stipulated is a sum greater than the sum which ought to have been paid;

c) a clause will be presumed to be a penalty clause if a single sum is payable on the occurrence of several events, some of which may occasion serious and others but trifling damage;

d) it is no obstacle that a pre-estimate of damage is virtually impossible—indeed, this is the very situation where it is probable that the pre-estimated damages represent a true bargain between the parties (because the parties are more likely to agree to liquidated damages in advance where it is very uncertain how much will be payable in the event of a breach).

In *Cavendish Holdings* v *Makdessi*, 100 years later, Lord Neuberger said that it was 'unfortunate' that case law had treated the above tests as some sort of 'quasi-statutory code' rather than simply as considerations. The fundamental question is whether the clause is unconscionable or extravagant. Lord Atkinson's judgment in *Dunlop* referred to their obvious interest in preventing their trade being damaged by undercutting and 'that interest was not incommensurate with the sum agreed to be paid.'

The Supreme Court has therefore recast the penalty rule as one which applies where 'the sum or remedy stipulated as a consequence of breach of contract is exorbitant or unconscionable when regard is had to the innocent party's interest in the performance of the contract.' The fact that it may be a deterrent is not in itself a problem; many contractual provisions operate as inducements or deterrents to influence the conduct of the other party but it will only be penal if it is disproportionate to the legitimate interest being protected. The reformulated approach will probably have relatively little impact on agreed damages clauses and Lord Dunedin's four considerations will no doubt still be relevant. However, the penalty clause rule has application beyond agreed damages clauses as can be seen from the facts of *Cavendish*.

Mr El Makdessi and his business partner had sold a majority of their shares, in a major Middle Eastern advertising company which they had co-founded, to Cavendish for initial sums totalling approximately $65 million dollars with further payments up to a total of $82 million to be paid at a future date. The contract set out the importance of the goodwill of the business being reflected in the value of the shares and accordingly provided covenants whereby the sellers would not engage in restricted activities which would compete with the business within two years of the sale. It was accepted that the sellers breached these restrictive covenants. The contract provided (clause 5.1) that the further payments due would no longer be payable if the covenants were broken, which in the case of Mr El Makdessi would mean he lost out potentially to the tune of $42 million. It also provided (clause 5.6) that Cavendish would be able to purchase the remaining shares for a price which did not include goodwill which meant the price would be up to $75 million less (Mr El Makdessi would have lost just over half of this amount) than would otherwise have been the case.

The Supreme Court was split as to whether clauses 5.1 and 5.6 engaged the penalties rule which depended on whether they provided for a payment (not to be paid) or for shares to be transferred as result of breach (secondary obligations) or whether they merely regulated the primary obligation under the contract (price adjustment clauses). Only the former comes within the penalty regime because otherwise the penalties rule would be interfering directly with the bargain and thus with basic freedom of contract (compare the restriction in the unfair terms jurisdiction where a term relates to the core bargain). Even if they were clauses regulating a secondary remedial obligation (as the majority found) and therefore came within the penalties rule, it was agreed by all the Justices that there was a legitimate interest at stake (protection of goodwill which was central to the contract) and the radical reduction in the sums payable was not extortionate or unconscionable given that the contract was carefully negotiated by legally advised parties at arm's length.

ParkingEye v *Beavis* (2015) (which we have already considered under unfair terms in Chapter 6) was heard at the same time as *Cavendish* and the same approach was applied as to whether the sum of £85 payable on breach of the contractual licence to park was an unenforceable penalty. It was not an agreed damages clause since there was no actual loss suffered by the car park operators but that did not make it a penalty. Again there was a legitimate interest in enforcing through this payment a manageable car parking regime which ensured the availability and turnover of, in the main, free parking to the customers of the retail park and the sum of £85 was not disproportionate to the legitimate interest protected. The sums of money at stake were obviously much lower in this case but on the other hand the contract was not negotiated nor was it between equally well-advised parties and the case perhaps illustrates the difficulty following *Cavendish* of overturning a contractual provision under the penalty rule, at least where there is some legitimate interest which can be pointed to. That the penalty rule did not invalidate the £85 payment is perhaps not surprising but that it was also not unfair under the unfair terms regime designed to protect consumers is a more debatable conclusion, as was seen in the dissenting judgment of Lord Toulson on this point.

The impact of all this on agreed damages clauses will probably not be all that great. Even before *Cavendish* v *Makdessi*, the Privy Council decision in *Philips Hong Kong* v *A-G of Hong Kong* (1993) warned that the courts should be careful not to interfere unduly with the parties' freedom of contract and so they should only hold agreed damages clauses to be penalty clauses when they were obviously extravagant. Where there is a wide range of possible losses, the failure to make special provision for certain losses to which the liquidated damages are 'totally out of proportion' may lead to the liquidated damages not being recoverable. However, given that the contract in *Philips* was again between two parties capable of protecting their own interests, such a stringent approach was regarded as inappropriate. The claimants (unsuccessfully seeking a declaration that the liquidated damages were unenforceable) promised the Hong Kong government that they would install a computerized supervisory system for a new road and tunnel and one of the clauses provided that a set sum would be payable if the claimant missed 'Key Dates' ('Key' because some of the work had to be completed to allow other contractors to begin work) and additional sums would also become payable if the overall work was not completed on time. The Privy Council recognized that the losses caused by delay to a governmental body are difficult to estimate—it is not as though they are trying to sell the road on for profit at a particular date—and that the governmental body had used a reasonable formula to estimate the damages in advance. It therefore advised Her Majesty The Queen (that's what the Privy Council does, technically) that the agreed damages clause was enforceable.

Cases since *Makdessi* continue to show that liquidated (agreed) damages clauses will still be widely used and enforceable as genuine pre-estimates of loss and can result in the award of very substantial sums. *Triple Point Technology* v *PTT* (2021) provides an example in which the Supreme Court upheld an agreed damages clause (even though it used the word penalty) since it was a genuine pre-estimate of loss caused by delay, in a complex commodity trading software development contract, which was fixed at 0.1 per cent of the value of undelivered work per day. The most straightforward case of a liquidated damages clause is where the contract is eventually performed satisfactorily except that it is late and the rate per day or week stated in the clause is clearly recoverable in that sort of case. The question raised in this case concerns what happens if there is not only *delay* in performing but ultimately the contract is not fully performed satisfactorily and is terminated for breach. The Supreme Court confirmed unanimously that the normal rule is that a liquidated damages clause is effective to cover all the delay up until the date of termination (but not for the period thereafter, general damages for termination being available in addition). This meant that the trial judge had been correct to award $3.45 million dollars in liquidated damages for all the delays in delivering work due up to the time of termination (whether the work was actually delivered late or, as was the case for the bulk of the work that was due, not delivered at all). The Court of Appeal was found to have been wrong in their strange interpretation of the admittedly complex clause as restricting the liquidated damages to the much smaller sum of $0.15 million, erroneously limiting it to the delays in delivering the relatively small amount of work that was actually (but belatedly) delivered before termination. The majority of the Supreme Court also allowed, in addition to the liquidated damages for delay up to the date of termination, an award of general damages for $11.21 million (including the cost of an alternative contractor to complete the project after termination), holding that a limitation clause or cap in the contract was not applicable (because it did not apply on its true construction if there was contractual negligence) so the total damages awarded came to $14.66 million.

There are three other issues which can arise in relation to penalty clauses:

- **a)** the relationship between exemption, liquidated damages and penalty clauses;
- **b)** the distinction between penalties for breach and sums payable on other events; and
- **c)** the relationship between penalties and forfeiture clauses.

11.8.1 **Exemption, liquidated damages and penalty clauses**

Exemption, liquidated damages and penalty clause issues can arise where the actual loss caused by the breach turns out to be greater than the amount provided for in the relevant clause. If a clause can be shown to be a disproportionate penalty clause, then paradoxically the victim of the breach, who will normally be the person who has insisted on the penalty clause in the first place, will be able to ignore the penalty clause and recover the actual loss, exceeding the amount provided for in the penalty clause! This was what the respondent tried to do in *Cellulose Acetate Silk Co.* v *Widnes Foundry (1925) Ltd* (1933) but the House of Lords held that the clause providing for a 'penalty' of £20 per week for late delivery was not a penalty clause since 'it must have been obvious to both parties that the actual damage would be much *more* than £20 per week' (emphasis added). As a result, the claimant's damages were limited to the amount specified in the clause but whilst the clause was not a penalty it does not seem to have been a 'genuine pre-estimate of the loss' either and so it was in reality a limitation clause, which may well nowadays be required to be reasonable under the Unfair Contract Terms Act 1977 (see Chapter 6 on Exclusion clauses). How the courts interpret an agreed damages clause may therefore depend on the actual amount of loss suffered: if the loss is very small then it looks more like a penalty clause than a genuine pre-estimate of loss, but if the loss is very large it looks like a limitation clause which limits the claimant's ability to recoup his full loss—see Figure 11.7. If you think about it, an exclusion clause is really just an agreement that the damages for a particular breach will be zero; a limitation clause just sets the damages slightly higher.

The context is all-important. The courts are more likely to respect a figure agreed between commercial parties of equal bargaining power with access to legal advice as a reasonable pre-estimate of the loss (and as a proportionate protection of the legitimate interest) of the

Figure 11.7 Agreed damages and limitation clauses

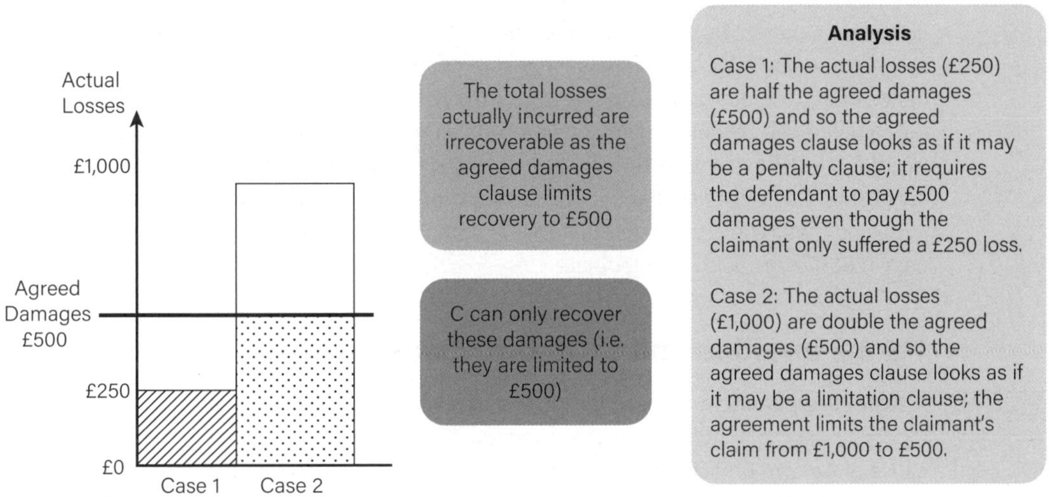

innocent party; see *Azimut-Benetti SpA* v *Healey* (2010) where the claimant luxury yacht builder was granted summary judgment for enforcement of a clause which entitled it to 20 per cent of the contract price in the event of the client's default.

11.8.2 **Penalties for breach and sums payable on other events**

In *Alder* v *Moore* (1961) a professional footballer was paid £500 insurance money because of total disablement but signed a declaration that he would not play professional football again and in 'the event of infringement of this condition, will be subject to a penalty of £500'. The Court of Appeal interpreted this (Devlin LJ dissenting) as a promise to repay the £500 if he played football again rather than as a promise not to play with a penalty of £500 for breach of that promise. The rule against penalties only applied to sums payable on breach (this was confirmed in *Cavendish*) and since the footballer was not, in playing again, guilty of any breach of any promise, he had to repay the money. (This was no doubt the most expensive missed penalty of his career but Devlin LJ was not apparently booked for his dissent!) Had the declaration been interpreted as a promise not to play football with a penalty clause attached, the penalty would probably have been unenforceable and so he could have kept the £500. On a more serious note, the case illustrates the difficulty of distinguishing between sums payable on breach and conditional sums payable on other events, a distinction which can in any case lead to the 'absurd paradox', as Lord Denning put it in *Bridge* v *Campbell Discount Co. Ltd* (1962), that a party in breach is given more protection than one who is not. Nonetheless, in *Export Credits Guarantee Department* v *Universal Oil Products Co.* (1983) the House of Lords confirmed that the penalty rule only applied to sums payable on breach and this was confirmed once more in *Cavendish*.

Of course, there is scope for parties to draft a contract in such a way that a payment appears formally to be not payable on breach but on the occurrence of some other event which would otherwise have been a breach and to avoid the penalty rule. For example, compare two cases: (a) I promise to complete your extension by 31 July for £50,000 and to pay you £2,000 for every month I am late and (b) I promise to build you an extension for £50,000 if I complete by 31 July, or for £48,000 if I complete by end of August and £46,000 if I complete by end of September, and so on. Contract (a) clearly has a penalty clause which may be assessed (it may of course be proportionate to your legitimate interest in getting the extension completed on time, and hence valid) whereas (b) does not seem formally at least to involve a sum payable on breach but to define my obligation differently on certain contingencies (the various dates by which I might finish the extension). Should the two cases be treated differently? There were various suggestions in *Cavendish* that the courts should be able to look at the substance, not just the form, and that if they concluded that (b) was simply a disguised penalty (see Lord Hodge at para. [258]) they could still intervene.

11.8.3 **Penalties and forfeiture clauses**

> **forfeiture clause:**
> A forfeiture clause provides that a party will lose a sum of money paid in advance (a deposit) if he breaches the contract.

A **forfeiture clause** in this context means one whereby A, who has *already paid* a sum of money under the contract, forfeits (i.e. cannot recover) the money when it is terminated because of A's own breach. This is, in effect, a penalty clause brought forward in time: the prospective defendant (A) pays a sum of money (a deposit) *before* there has been any breach but then forfeits this sum when there is an actual breach (of course, A does not forfeit the sum if A does perform the contract).

Rather surprisingly, the law here is that there is no general right to recover a deposit (which has to be distinguished from a mere part payment) even though it clearly exceeds the other party's loss and is intended as an incentive to perform. If such a sum were to *become payable* on breach it would undoubtedly be eligible to be an unenforceable penalty (unless it was reasonably protecting a legitimate interest) and it is rather inconsistent for the law not to allow it to be recovered where it has already been paid. Equity will give *some* relief against forfeiture but the traditional view set out by Romer LJ in *Stockloser* v *Johnson* (1954) is that in the absence of sharp practice or fraud the only relief available is to give the party in breach *further time* in which to perform its obligations under the contract and that equity will not actually order the repayment of the money to a party in breach. On the other hand, Denning and Somervell LLJ in the same case thought that equity could order repayment if it was unconscionable for the other party to keep the payment (it was not unconscionable on the facts) but it was the view of Romer LJ that was followed in *Galbraith* v *Mitchenall Estates Ltd* (1965) where the claimant failed to recover £550 paid in advance for hire of a caravan (even though this clearly exceeded the defendant's loss). On the other hand, in the Privy Council case of *Workers Trust* v *Dojap* (1993) it was held that whilst forfeiture of a deposit of 10 per cent of the purchase price in a sale of land was normal and reasonable, the forfeiture of a deposit of 25 per cent was not enforceable. In *Cavendish* the view was expressed that deposits could be subject to the penalty rule, most notably by Lord Hodge at para. [238], who said that:

> (a) a deposit which is not reasonable as earnest money may be challenged as a penalty and
>
> (b) where the stipulated deposit exceeds the percentage set by long established practice the vendor must show special circumstances to justify that deposit if it is not to be treated as an unenforceable penalty.

Digging deeper

One of the most interesting but difficult issues in the law of contractual damages, which has recently come before the Supreme Court in *Morris-Garner* v *One Step* (2018), is the basis on which hypothetical release, or 'negotiating damages', previously known as '*Wrotham Park*' damages, can or should be awarded—an issue going back to the *Wrotham Park* case itself in 1974, discussed in section 11.2.2 under the heading of 'The restitution interest'. The defendants in *Morris-Garner* had deliberately, and somewhat secretively, broken covenants not to compete following the sale of a business. The conventional losses of the claimants caused by the defendants wrongfully competing with them were thought difficult to prove but were estimated at £3–4 million. The Court of Appeal approved an award of '*Wrotham Park*' damages to be assessed on the basis of what the defendants would have hypothetically agreed to pay to be released from those covenants (so-called hypothetical release damages). The hypothetical release fee had not yet been determined but there was forensic evidence that it was likely to be in the region of £5–6 million and thus likely to be more than damages assessed on a conventional basis. The Supreme Court fundamentally disagreed with the Court of Appeal's approach (which was traceable back to *Blake*) and deprecated the use of the term '*Wrotham Park* damages' which, at para. [3], Lord Reed regarded as a 'a source of potential confusion . . . [which] can now be regarded as being of little more than historical interest'. The expression 'negotiating damages' was to be preferred and, more importantly, it was emphasized that common law damages for breach of contract are intended to compensate the claimant for loss or damage resulting from the breach. They are not available for the purpose of depriving the defendant of profits made as a result of the breach, other than in exceptional circumstances as in *Attorney-General* v *Blake* (where, one might add, it was done under the guise of a different remedy, an account of profits, which is very well established in equity to retrieve illegal profits made in breach of fiduciary duties).

Lord Reed set out a number of established (but limited) situations where the use of a hypothetical release fee was a legitimate mechanism for measuring a claimant's loss. Firstly, there is what is known as 'user damages' in tort for the wrongful use of another's property where the property itself is not damaged, and where in that sense there is no loss, but the property owner is entitled to a fee, for the wrongful use of his property, which he would have been entitled to charge and which is the measure of his loss. Such a principle is long established and for an illustration see, for example, *Strand Electric and Engineering* v *Brisford Entertainments Ltd* [1952] 2 QB 246.

Secondly, by analogy with the first category, patent infringements and breaches of other intellectual property rights are routinely compensated by reference to the licence fee that the owner of the property right could have charged for the infringing use. See *Watson, Laidlaw & Co* v *Pott, Cassels & Williamson* (1914) (HL) for a classic example.

Thirdly, so-called equitable damages can be awarded under Lord Cairns' Act (now s.50 Senior Courts Act 1981) in substitution for specific performance or an injunction and these may be (but do not always have to be) calculated by reference to what the claimant might have charged for the permission to infringe its rights which the refusal of the injunction is effectively sanctioning.

Wrotham Park (and the cases that followed it prior to *Blake*) was entirely in line with one or more of these three categories as it was a case where damages were given in lieu of an injunction (to destroy the houses, which would have been wasteful); the claimant's right was a restrictive covenant over land which is not purely a contractual right but which is regarded as an equitable property right running with the land; and the refusal of the injunction 'had the effect of depriving the claimant of an asset which had an economic value.'

Some of the cases decided since *Blake* had however, unjustifiably in Lord Reed's judgment, gone further in their reasoning, suggesting that negotiating damages could be used to strip the defendant of some or all of its profits in cases where actual loss to the claimant was difficult to prove—*Experience Hendrix* v *PPX Enterprises* (2003) being given as a leading example where the defendants were required to pay one-third of their profits for exploiting recordings which the agreement with the claimants prohibited them from exploiting. Lord Reed was clear that this more general, liberal and non-compensatory approach to the use of negotiating damages was not appropriate. Negotiating damages at common law for breach of contract should normally only be awarded 'where the breach of contract results in the loss of a valuable asset created or protected by the right which was infringed, as for example in cases concerned with the breach of a restrictive covenant over land, an intellectual property agreement or a confidentiality agreement' (at para. [92]). The actual decision, as opposed to the reasoning, in *Hendrix* could be defended on the basis it was concerned with compensatory damages for breach of an intellectual property agreement (under which the claimant was regarded as having a valuable intellectual property asset) and the hypothetical release damages could be regarded as compensation for the loss he suffered to that asset by his rights to the intellectual property under the agreement being ignored by the defendant. 'When the copyright was wrongfully used, the claimant was prevented from exercising that right, and consequently suffered a loss equivalent to the amount which could have been obtained by exercising it' (at para. [89]).

Having reviewed the law over the past forty years, and emphasized the compensatory nature of damages and the limited relevance of hypothetical release fees to contractual damages, Lord Reed concluded that the approach taken in the Court of Appeal in *Morris-Garner* was wrong in a number of respects:

> [It] was mistaken in treating the deliberate nature of the breach, or the difficulty of establishing precisely the consequent financial loss, or the claimant's interest in preventing the defendants' profit-making activities, as justifying the award of a monetary remedy which was not compensatory. The idea that damages based on a hypothetical release fee are available whenever that is a just response, that being a matter to be decided by the judge on a broad brush basis, is also mistaken. The basis on which damages are awarded cannot be a matter for the discretion of the primary judge.

As to the application of the law to the facts of the case Lord Reed continued by saying, at paras [98]–[99]:

> This is a case brought by a commercial entity whose only interest in the defendants' performance of their obligations under the covenants was commercial. Indeed, a restrictive covenant which went beyond what was necessary for the reasonable protection of the claimant's commercial interests would have been unenforceable. The substance of the claimant's case is that it suffered financial loss as a result of the defendants' breach of contract. The effect of

> the breach of contract was to expose the claimant's business to competition which would otherwise have been avoided. The natural result of that competition was a loss of profits and possibly of goodwill. The loss is difficult to quantify, and some elements of it may be inherently incapable of precise measurement. Nevertheless, it is a familiar type of loss, for which damages are frequently awarded . . .
>
> The case is not one where the breach of contract has resulted in *the loss of a valuable asset created or protected by the right which was infringed*. Considered in isolation, the first defendant's breach of the confidentiality covenant might have been considered to be of that character, but in reality the claimant's loss is the cumulative result of breaches of a number of obligations, of which the non-compete and non-solicitation covenants have been treated as the most significant (emphasis added).

The words emphasized above, relating to a valuable asset, spell out the essence of the categories of cases where Lord Reed would regard negotiating damages as appropriate for breach of contract. There is a question however as to why some contracts are regarded as creating or protecting a valuable asset but not others—see Burrows (2018) 134 LQR 515, 520–21. The gist of Lord Reed's judgment seems to be that there are assets to be protected when the contract is dealing with a proprietary or quasi-proprietary right. Lord Reed quoted extensively from *Pell Frischmann* v *Bow Valley Iran* (2009), a Privy Council case from Jersey, and seemed generally to approve of the result. That was a case concerning breach of confidentiality clauses in a joint venture agreement. The availability (as opposed to the amount) of negotiating damages seems to have been assumed in this case and part of the explanation is no doubt that breach of confidence relates to confidential information which, whilst not exactly property in the same way that patents and copyright are, can more easily be regarded as an asset (and see also the principle set out by Lord Reed at para. [92] of his judgment referring expressly to breach of a confidentiality agreement). This is no doubt why, at para. [99] of *Morris-Garner*, Lord Reed briefly considered the confidentiality covenants in the contract but then dismissed them as not being significant in terms of the various cumulative breaches in the case and the losses caused thereby. Whether the distinction between contracts the breach of which do, and do not, result in the loss of a valuable asset can consistently be drawn and whether there is a real difference between contracts dealing with proprietary or quasi-proprietary rights on the one hand, and those dealing with purely commercial interests on the other, are questions for the future.

The *Pell Frischmann* case is relevant in another sense. At para. [94] Lord Reed, having set out the limited cases where a hypothetical release fee can be regarded as the measure of the claimant's loss, acknowledged that there may be other circumstances where:

> evidence of a hypothetical release fee can be relevant to the assessment of damages. If, for example, in other circumstances, the parties had been negotiating the release of an obligation prior to its breach, the valuations which the parties had placed on the release fee, adjusted if need be to reflect any changes in circumstances, might be relevant to support, or to undermine, a subsequent quantification of the losses claimed to have resulted from the breach.

This seems to be an almost direct reference to the facts of *Pell Frischmann* where the parties had got very close to actually (not hypothetically) negotiating a release fee of $3 million and the Privy Council took that into account in awarding $2.5 million rather than the $500,000 awarded by the lower court. This perhaps explains why in *Morris-Garner* the case was remitted to the trial judge to decide on the amount of damages, not on the basis of a hypothetical release fee, but instead measuring:

> as accurately as he can . . . the financial loss which the claimant has actually sustained . . .

but it then being added:

> If evidence is led as to a hypothetical release fee, it is for the judge to determine its relevance and weight, if any.

The explanation for letting back in the evidence about the hypothetical release fee seems to be that the release fee is not to be taken *directly* as the *measure* of loss (outside the valuable asset cases) but it may be relevant as *evidence* of the actual loss, in that what a person may be prepared to accept for permitting a breach may (or may not, depending on the facts) be indirect evidence of the scale of the actual losses that the breach may be likely to cause him.

The nature and availability of 'negotiating damages,' as they are now called, and the role and significance of hypothetical release evidence, are matters which will no doubt be the subject of further case law but for the moment the Supreme Court has clearly signalled that damages for breach of contract are always compensatory, including 'negotiating damages' which are in any event only available for breach of contract in restricted categories of cases and not simply because the claimant may have difficulty showing actionable loss on conventional grounds.

Please see Figure 11.8 for a summary of this chapter.

Figure 11.8 Chapter summary

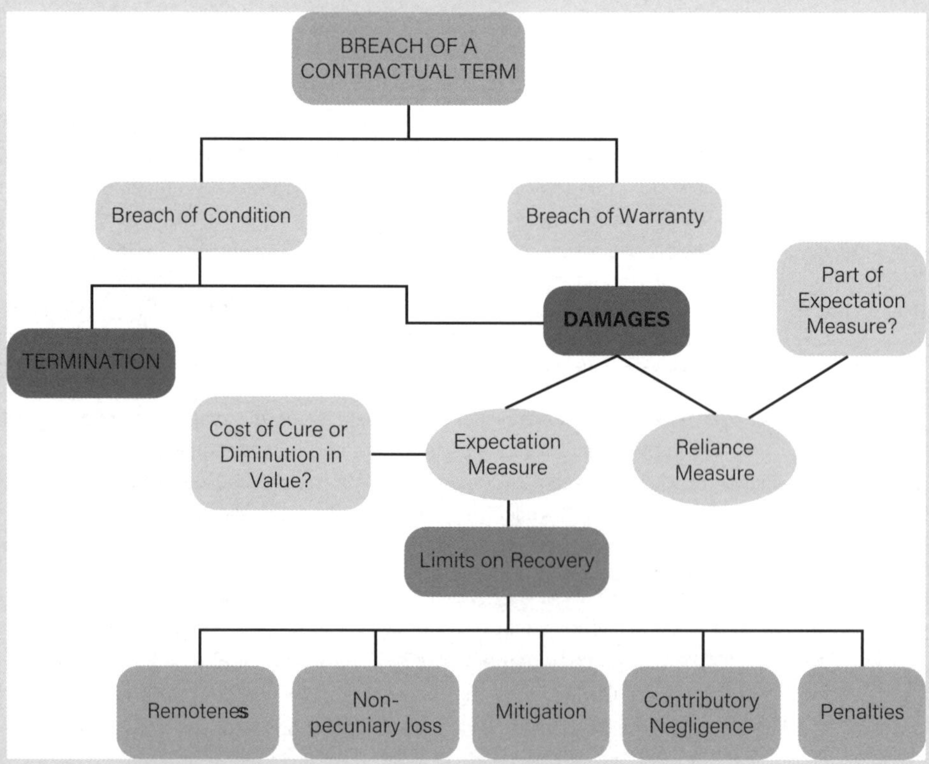

Summary

1. Aims and measures of damages

The normal approach to contract damages is to try to put the claimant in the position it would have been in if the contract had been performed.

The claimant may in some situations be able to elect to claim instead the reliance measure of damages (i.e. to return it to the position it was in before the contract), for example when it is impossible to prove its expectancy, but the claimant will not be able to use this to escape a bargain which the defendant can show would have been a bad one even if the contract had been performed or more generally in order to put the claimant in a better position than if the contract had been performed.

The expectation interest may take the form of compensation for diminution in value caused by the breach or the cost of curing the breach, although the latter may not be allowed where it is disproportionately high compared to the diminution in value.

If the breach has deprived the claimant of more than a speculative chance of a benefit then damages based on the value of the chance may be recovered (but not the full value of the benefit as the claimant cannot prove that this would have been obtained).

2. Remoteness

The claimant cannot recover losses which are too remote, that is, if the defendant could not reasonably foresee the type of loss suffered as a serious possibility based on the ordinary course of things or in the light of any special knowledge of the defendant.

3. Non-pecuniary loss

Damages are not normally available for non-pecuniary loss (e.g. injured feelings, etc.) but they may exceptionally be awarded if the loss was consequent on physical injury or inconvenience or the contract was for the purpose of enjoyment or alleviation of distress.

4. Mitigation

The claimant is under a duty to take reasonable steps to put itself in the position it would have been in had the contract been performed (i.e. to minimize its lost expectations).

The claimant is allowed to recover any costs reasonably incurred in an attempt to mitigate.

Any benefits accrued to the claimant by reason of the breach will reduce the claimant's damages, but not if they are 'collateral' and would have accrued anyway.

5. Contributory negligence

Damages are not available if the claimant's act breaks the chain of causation.

Damages will be reduced under the Law Reform (Contributory Negligence) Act 1945 if the claimant was partly at fault and the breach was of an obligation to take reasonable care, *and* there would have also been liability in tort.

6. Penalty clauses

Liquidated damages clauses fix the amount of damages in advance and are enforceable; they are unenforceable and called 'penalty clauses' if they are not a genuine pre-estimate of loss or are otherwise extravagant, unconscionable or disproportionate to the legitimate interest being protected. The penalty clause jurisdiction is broader than just clauses regulating damages but is restricted to clauses regulating the consequences of breach, that is, secondary rather than primary obligations. It seems now that forfeiture of a deposit can be controlled by the penalty clause jurisdiction if the amount of the forfeited deposit is disproportionate to the interest being protected.

? Questions

1. Jan agrees to build a balcony on to the side of Alex's house for £10,000. Alex specifies that she wants the balcony to be south-facing so that it will catch the most sun. An estate agent tells Alex that her house is currently worth £300,000 but it would be worth £320,000 with the balcony.

   Midway through the construction of the balcony Jan has to erect some scaffolding and she negligently leaves a bolt loose. Alex is curious to see how the work has progressed and she climbs up to the balcony but accidently dislodges the loose piece of scaffold which falls through her greenhouse below, destroying all of the glass and her prize marrow. Alex is devastated because she was going to enter the marrow in a national competition with a prize of £50,000 and the chance to meet Alan Titchmarsh.

   Unfortunately, Jan has built the balcony on the wrong side of the house and Alex is disappointed when the estate agent returns and values her house at only £310,000.

   Advise Alex. Assume that there is an implied term in the contract that Jan will take all steps necessary to complete the balcony and take reasonable care at all times.
2. If the aim of contractual damages is to protect the expectation interest and to put the innocent party in the position as though the contract had been performed, why do the courts sometimes allow the claimant to recover reliance losses for breach of contract?
3. 'There is no real practical difference between the test for remoteness in contract as compared to that in tort especially when one bears in mind the way in which the courts manipulate the concept of a "type" of loss.' Discuss.
4. 'The law of contract affords inadequate protection to the "consumer surplus".' Discuss.
5. Would you agree that the rules on damages reveal the remedy to be a poor substitute for actual performance and provide little incentive to encourage contracting parties not to default on their obligations?

Further reading

Books

Chen-Wishart, M, *Contract Law*, 7th edn (Oxford University Press, 2022) ch 13.

McKendrick, E, *Contract Law: Text, Cases and Materials*, 11th edn (Oxford University Press, 2024) ch 23.

O'Sullivan, J, and Hilliard, J, *The Law of Contract*, 11th edn (Oxford University Press, 2024) chs 16 and 18.

Articles

Coote, B, 'Contract damage, Ruxley and the performance interest' (1997) 56 CLJ 537.

Enonchong, N, 'Breach of contract and damages for mental distress' (1996) 16 OJLS 617.

Friedmann, D, 'The performance interest in contract damages' (1995) 111 LQR 628.

Fuller, LL, and Perdue, WR, 'The reliance interest in contract damages' (1936–37) 46 Yale LJ 52.

Harris, D, Ogus, A and Phillips, J, 'Contract remedies and the consumer surplus' (1979) 95 LQR 581.

Owen, M, 'Some aspects of the recovery of reliance damages in the law of contract' (1984) 4 OJLS 393.

Robertson, A, 'The basis of the remoteness rule in contract' (2008) 28 Legal Studies 172.

12 Specific remedies

LEARNING OBJECTIVES

This chapter will help you to:

- distinguish an action for the price from an action for damages for breach of contract;
- understand when the claimant can claim the agreed price and whether the claimant can be forced to claim damages and mitigate its losses; and
- understand when a court may exercise its discretion to order specific performance or an injunction.

Introduction

We saw in the previous chapter that the primary aim of contractual damages is to put the innocent party in the position that it would have been in had the contract been performed and that, to this extent, damages are designed to protect the expectation or performance interest. Other remedies, discussed in this chapter, more directly address the issue of providing the innocent party with the performance that was expected. We will see that their use is dependent on a number of factors which mean that they are not universally available and that the claimant will therefore often be left to its remedy in damages.

12.1 Action for the price or other agreed sum

12.1.1 Action for the price and agreed damages clauses

action for the price
A claim for a sum of money promised to be paid under the contract.

The **action for the price** is an extremely important remedy in practice but gives rise to relatively few difficulties as there is no question of quantification: the claimant is merely claiming the remuneration specified in the contract. It is important to distinguish this type of remedy from the agreed (liquidated) damages clauses discussed in Chapter 11. Agreed damages clauses react to one party's breach of a primary promise and amount to secondary promises to pay a certain amount of damages, whereas an action for the price is actually a demand for the party to perform its primary promise.

EXAMPLE

Action for the price v agreed damages

If I sell you goods and you promise to pay me £20 then I can sue you for the £20 in an action for the price *because that is what you promised to pay me* and *not* because of your breach of contract for which I am claiming damages as compensation for my loss. In contrast, if I provide you with defective goods and we have agreed that damages will be £20 then you can sue me for those damages and rely on my secondary promise to pay pre-estimated damages of £20 (unless of course £20 is not a genuine pre-estimate of your loss, in which case your secondary obligation is to pay me damages equivalent to my true loss—see the discussion in Chapter 11). For a summary of the distinction between *agreed damages* and *an action for the price* see Figure 12.1.

Figure 12.1 Distinction between agreed damages and an action for the price

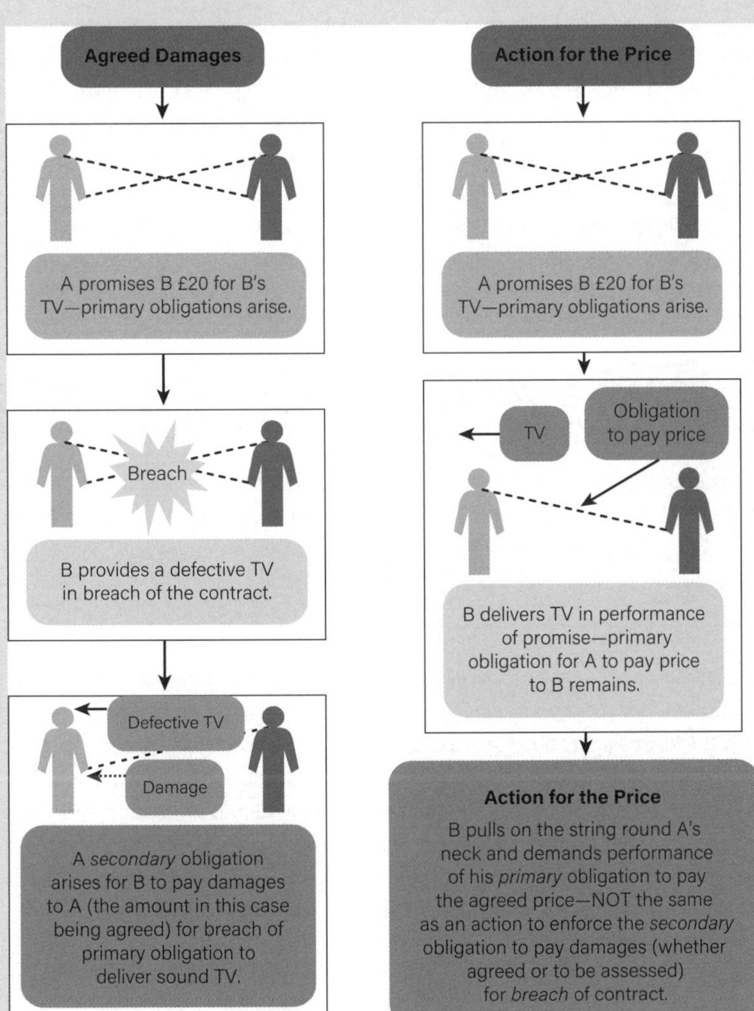

Although there are no issues of quantification, there are difficulties that can arise in relation to an action for the price and these are of two main sorts: firstly, has the right to claim the price accrued; and, secondly, can a party insist on performing and earning the price even if the other party has repudiated the contract?

12.1.2 Has the right to the price yet accrued?

Generally speaking, the right to claim the price only accrues upon *full* performance of the entire primary obligation—sometimes referred to as the entire contracts (or entire obligations) rule. *Cutter* v *Powell* (1795) provides an early and perhaps harsh interpretation of a contract which made full performance a condition precedent to the price being payable.

CASE CLOSE-UP

***Cutter* v *Powell* (1795)**

Cutter, a sailor, was promised 'the sum of thirty guineas, provided he proceeds, continues and does his duty as second mate in the said ship from hence [Jamaica] to the port of Liverpool.' Cutter died before the ship completed the voyage and his estate sued for his wage. The King's Bench denied the claim on the basis that the sum only became payable if the sailor performed his duties for the whole voyage; completion of the entire voyage was a *condition precedent* to the obligation to pay the sum promised. Lord Kenyon CJ emphasized that the sailor had been promised almost four times the going monthly rate and described this larger sum as 'a form of insurance.' In other words, by offering an above average wage, the captain of the ship indicated that he was not interested in part performance (what good is a crew that abandons a ship halfway through its voyage?) and made full performance a condition precedent to payment of the (high) wage.

THINKING POINT

How might the courts have interpreted the obligation if the sailor in *Cutter* v *Powell* had been promised the market rate? Could or should it have been severable into a number of lesser obligations corresponding to different stages of the voyage rather than being one single entire obligation for the whole voyage?

severable obligations These can be split off from the main obligations under the contract, as though the parties made lots of smaller promises, say to do the work incrementally. Each 'mini-obligation' can give rise to an obligation to pay on performance by the other party of the work required under the 'mini-obligation.'

If the contractual obligation is **severable**, as in *Taylor* v *Laird* (1856), where the claimant was promised £50 per month for taking command of a steamer 'for an exploring and trading voyage up the river Niger,' there will be a right to the appropriate portion of the price as each stage of the contract is completed. The claimant abandoned the voyage without completing it but the court awarded him £50 for each month served and refused to interpret the obligation as entire. Contractual obligations are often construed as severable to avoid the potentially harsh results of the entire contracts rule and many large-scale commercial contracts, such as construction contracts, will expressly provide for 'stage' payments rendering each stage of the contract severable.

12.1.3 **What is full performance?**

Full performance, particularly in the context of contracts for services, is not necessarily an absolute concept. As long as the obligation (or the severable part of it) has been *substantially* performed the price may still be payable, as in *Hoenig* v *Isaacs* (1952) where the claimant was employed to decorate and furnish a flat for £750 and did so but not without defects. The Court of Appeal held that since the defects would only cost £55 to remedy, the work was finished in the ordinary sense (although the court thought the case was near the borderline on this point) and the claimant was entitled to the outstanding balance of the price, subject to the defendant's set-off for the £55. *Bolton* v *Mahadeva* (1972) is a case on the other side of the line where the contract price for installing central heating was £564 and the defects would have cost £174 to put right and the claimant was entitled to nothing.

The distinction between *Hoenig* v *Isaacs* and *Bolton* v *Mahadeva* can be looked at as being analogous to the distinction between breach of warranty and breach of condition—only in the latter case is the innocent party entitled to reject the other party's performance and terminate his own obligations, that is, in this case, terminate his obligation to pay the price. If the breach is merely a breach of warranty and does not justify termination, he must perform his own obligations, that is, pay the price, and merely claim (or set off) damages for the breach as in *Hoenig* v *Isaacs*.

EXAMPLE

Substantial performance

I promise to re-tile your bathroom by 5 p.m. this evening. You promise to pay me £1,000 on completion of the job.

Scenario 1: I tile three walls and get bored at 3 p.m. so I just paint the final wall white and hope you won't notice. Clearly this will not do; I cannot legitimately claim to have substantially performed my obligation to tile your bathroom because 25 per cent of it remains without tiles and I cannot claim anything.

Scenario 2: I tile all four walls but, just as I am finishing the last wall, I run out of tiles and so there is a blank space where the last tile should go. I have to wait several weeks for a new order of tiles but claim the price. This clearly amounts to substantial performance because the bathroom is virtually complete at the stipulated time although I will have to be prepared to allow you to retain a small amount of the price until the missing tile is obtained and fixed.

Scenario 3: I tile all four walls perfectly but then I knock my metal bucket over and it cracks four of the tiles. It is 4.55 p.m. and too late to replace them. It is unlikely to cost very much to replace four tiles and so I could probably claim the price on the basis that I have substantially performed but you could set off the amount it would cost to replace the tiles. Alternatively (and the most likely solution in practice) we could renegotiate our contract and you would give me until 6 p.m. to complete the bathroom.

quantum meruit
The old name for a claim for the value of work done; the worker is allowed to claim 'as much as it deserves' which equates to 'reasonable remuneration.'

If performance of an entire contract, or a severable part of a contract, falls short even of substantial performance, then one party is likely to have received a benefit from the other party without having to pay for it. Take, for example, the captain of the ship in *Cutter* v *Powell* who benefited from the service of the sailor up until his death; should he not at least have been obliged to pay the sailor's estate a reasonable sum for the work done up until the sailor's death? Such a claim is called a **quantum meruit** (the amount it deserves) and was expressly rejected in *Cutter* v *Powell* since the agreement was construed as one where the voyage had to be completed before the sailor would be entitled to *any* pay.

A modern analysis might be based on unjust enrichment because the captain is benefited by the work done by the sailor but the question remains whether it is unjust for the captain to retain the benefit of such work, or should he return the value of the work by payment of a reasonable sum to the estate of the sailor? One difficulty with allowing such a claim is that it disturbs the parties' allocation of risk. Compare the case of *Barton v Gwynne Jones* (2019) discussed in Chapter 2.9.1. We saw earlier that the captain was willing to pay a lot if he received complete performance, but unwilling to pay anything if he received only part performance. That was the deal he struck with the sailor and the law should be careful not to overturn it too readily. However, given that today the contract would be frustrated by the death of the sailor, it may well be that the estate could recover a just sum under s.1(3) of the Law Reform (Frustrated Contracts) Act 1943 for the valuable benefit conferred on the captain (see Chapter 10).

In cases where the part performer has failed to make substantial performance because he is in breach (as with the tiler in the earlier example who simply fails to do more than 75 per cent of the job) the basic principle is that he is not entitled to anything for the work he has done, even though this can mean that the other party is enriched by a benefit for which he has not paid (a three-quarters tiled bathroom in the example). The enrichment is not generally treated as unjust since there was no choice about whether or not to accept it and he had only agreed to pay for full performance. There is an exception though for where the innocent party chooses to accept the benefit. The basic rule and the exception are both illustrated by *Sumpter* v *Hedges* (1898), where a builder contracted to build two houses on the defendant's land for £565 and did work worth £333 before running out of money. The defendant completed the work using materials left on his land by the builder. The defendant did not have to pay for the value of the work done (which did not come up to the level of substantial performance) since he had no choice whether to accept work which had already been done on his land but he did have to pay for the materials he used since he freely chose to use them in completing the work. The Law Commission recommended as long ago as 1983 (Report No. 121) that in this situation the builder should be able to recover something for the value of the work done, limited to an appropriate proportion of the contract price, subject also to the recipient's claim for damages for breach of contract. One argument against this proposal which may partially explain why it has not been implemented is that the inability of a contract breaker to receive payment for work that does not amount at least to substantial performance (unless the other party freely chooses to accept it) provides a powerful practical incentive for jobbing builders and suchlike to substantially complete the jobs they have started rather than leaving the other party with the inconvenience and expense of finishing off a half-completed and botched piece of work.

12.1.4 **Can a claimant (who is not in breach) insist on performing and claiming the price even if the defendant (who is repudiating) no longer wants performance?**

This is the problem of *White & Carter (Councils) Ltd* v *McGregor* (1962) where the pursuers (this was a Scottish case) insisted on their right to perform their contract to advertise the defender's business on litter-bins for three years and to claim the contract price of £196 even though the defender **repudiated** the contract on the same day it was made.

> **repudiation** A party who repudiates a contract effectively puts his hands up and says: 'I'm not able or don't want to perform anymore. I may have to pay you damages but let's bring this contract to an end.' He is letting the other party know in advance that he intends to breach his obligations and that the other party should accept his repudiation as terminating the contract (terminating any further obligations to perform) and be content with a claim for damages instead.

The House of Lords, rather controversially, by three to two, upheld the pursuers' claim for this amount. The case is controversial because the pursuers could have accepted the repudiation as terminating the contract and releasing both parties from further performance—and then simply claimed damages, that is their loss of net profit, and avoided the wasted expenses of performance which the other party did not want. By allowing the pursuers to affirm the contract and refusing to force them into their damages claim the court might be thought to have undermined the policy underlying the duty to mitigate damages. However, the case did *not* involve a damages claim; instead the pursuers were claiming the agreed price; the case never reached the damages stage of the contract because the pursuers affirmed the contract even though McGregor wanted to breach and terminate it. Furthermore, if the duty to mitigate is a duty to put yourself, as far as is open to you, into the position of expected performance then this is what the pursuers were able to do since they did not need any co-operation from the other side (except the payment of the price which they were claiming). On the other hand, the duty to mitigate can be regarded as a duty to avoid waste, by reducing losses as far as is possible so that the party in breach does not have to pay damages for avoidable losses and so that resources are not wasted on activities that nobody wants. This latter argument is legally irresistible once the claimant has decided to claim damages (compensation for net expectation) but *White & Carter* is really concerned with a prior question of when the claimant should be forced into claiming damages as a remedy and when he can insist on performing and claiming the price.

The ruling that the latter course can be followed is subject to two main limitations:

1) The claimant can only insist on performing if he can do so without the other party's co-operation (and he cannot do so if performance involves doing work to *property* of the defendant—see Megarry J in *Hounslow London Borough Council* v *Twickenham Garden Developments Ltd* (1971) and the Court of Appeal decision in *Telephone Rentals* v *Burgess Salmon* (1987)).
2) The right to perform is defeated if it is shown (the burden appears to be on the defendant) that the claimant has no legitimate interest in performing the contract and claiming the full contract price rather than accepting the repudiation and claiming damages (a limitation acknowledged by Lord Reid in *White & Carter (Councils) Ltd* v *McGregor* itself). As Lord Denning MR put it in *Attica Sea Carriers Corporation* v *Ferrostaal Poseidon Bulk Reederei GmbH* (1976), the claimant should not in effect be allowed to insist on specific performance of the obligation to pay the price 'where damages would be an adequate remedy'.

THINKING POINT

Why did McGregor want White & Carter to accept their repudiation and terminate the contract and stop performance? Think about how much McGregor would have been obliged to pay under the contract (the costs of putting up the poster and a margin for profit) and how much they would have had to pay in damages if the contract was terminated before White & Carter had begun to perform.

12.1.5 Further instances of the right to affirm and claim the price

Despite the potential limitations on the *White & Carter* principle, the courts have nonetheless in a number of cases been willing to allow a claimant to affirm the contract, perform their own side and then claim the price. In *The Odenfeld* (1978) the claimants had obligations to third parties which would be adversely affected by terminating the contract and Kerr J held that the restriction on the claimant's option to keep the contract alive would only apply if damages would be an adequate remedy *and* keeping the contract alive would be 'wholly unreasonable.' Similarly, in *Reichman* v *Beveridge* (2006) it was not 'wholly unreasonable' for landlords to sue for the twelve months' rent (£23,000) a year after the tenants (solicitors!) repudiated the lease. The landlords were not obliged to accept the repudiation, find new tenants and sue simply for compensation reflecting any lower amount of rent received (partly because there is a peculiar lack of clarity in English landlord and tenant law about the extent to which a landlord can actually sue for such loss if he accepts the repudiation, so damages might well not have been an adequate remedy) and it was legitimate in all the circumstances for the landlords to claim the contract price (the full rent). On the other hand, in *Clea Shipping Corporation* v *Bulk Oil International Ltd* (1984), Lord Reid's *dicta* about legitimate interest were applied so as to deny a claimant the right to perform and claim the agreed sum. However, Lloyd J clearly considered that this sort of limitation on the *White & Carter* rule would only be applicable in exceptional cases. This approach was also taken in *The Dynamic* (2003) where Simon J confirmed that the burden is on the contract breaker to show that the innocent party has no legitimate interest in performing the contract rather than claiming damages and that 'this burden is not discharged merely by showing that the benefit to the [innocent] party is small in comparison to the loss to the contract breaker.' Furthermore, 'the exception to the general rule applies only in extreme cases.' The result of all this is that the rule in *White & Carter*, that the innocent party can insist on performing and claiming the price, will continue to be applicable, as is shown in the following case.

In *Isabella Shipowner* v *Shagang Shipping* (2012) Cooke J had to consider a time charterparty where the charterers had sought to return the ship three months before the end of the five-year term. His emphatic judgment (reversing the decision of the arbitrator) was that neither of the limitations on the rule in *White & Carter* was applicable and the owners were entitled to insist on the hire for the remaining months of the charter. Firstly, their obligations could be carried out without any co-operation from the charterers as in a time charter (as opposed to a demise charter) the master and crew are provided by the owners so, even if the charterers give no orders for the ship to sail anywhere, the ship can be maintained and kept ready for use by the owners and the charterers are simply liable to pay the hire. Secondly, there was nothing extreme or exceptional about the case to show that the owners had no legitimate interest in insisting on the charter continuing rather than claiming damages. Lord Reid in *White & Carter* had made it clear that there was no requirement for the innocent party to act reasonably and the authorities showed that it was only if the insistence on continuing was 'wholly unreasonable' or 'perverse' that the exception of no legitimate interest might apply. To force the owners to accept the repudiation and claim damages would put the onus on them to try to mitigate by reletting the ship in what had become a difficult market. The charterers had illegitimately been trying to avoid that burden (of subletting the ship themselves as the charter allowed them to do) for a period during which they had contracted to pay the hire regularly in advance (which was much more secure for the owners than claiming damages at a later date from charterers who might by then have difficulty in paying).

In contrast, in *MSC Mediterranean Shipping* v *Cottonex* (2016), it was held at first instance by Leggatt J that the carriers had no legitimate interest in keeping the contract alive and claiming the escalating daily payments provided for in the contract (known as demurrage) for the containers which the shippers (the sellers of the goods in the containers) were unable to return to them because they were detained by the customs authorities in Chittagong. By the time of the trial the contractual demurrage payments had reached well over a million dollars and were around ten times the value of the containers so it would have been far cheaper for the carriers to buy replacement containers if they needed them for use in other contracts (which itself had not been established). Leggatt J regarded the legitimate interest rule as an aspect of the duty of good faith (which he has promoted in other cases) and seemed much more willing to intervene and say there is no legitimate interest where the person claiming the contractual sum appears to be acting unreasonably. The Court of Appeal took a different view in reaching pretty much the same result. Moore-Bick LJ, not unpredictably perhaps, did not agree with the relevance of good faith. More confusingly, however, the Court of Appeal said that the issue of whether the carriers had a legitimate interest in keeping the contract alive did not arise because the contract had become 'incapable of performance' so the repudiation by the shipper automatically brought the contract to an end. This reasoning has been heavily criticized, as the rule that a contract is only terminated for breach at the election of the innocent party is well established and a possible exception has only relatively recently been removed in the Supreme Court in *Geys v Société Générale* (2012)—see Chapter 5, section 5.4.5. The no legitimate interest ground favoured by Leggatt J seems a much more orthodox and straightforward ground for the decision.

12.1.6 **Risks involved in electing to affirm**

Although the previously discussed cases show that, in most cases at least, the innocent party does not have to accept a repudiatory breach by the other party and can continue to perform its own side and then seek the appropriate remedy when the other party in due course fails to perform, the election to affirm the contract can lead to difficulties. This is illustrated by *Avery* v *Bowden* (1866) where a repudiation of a charterparty of a ship to be loaded in Odessa during a forty-five-day period was not initially accepted by the shipowners when offered in March. They kept their ship in the port well into April but lost any right to sue because as from 1 April the contract became illegal and the defendant's obligations were terminated by frustration (because of the outbreak of the Crimean War). A similar problem can occur if the innocent party does not accept a repudiation, keeps the contract alive and then commits a breach of its own obligations which entitles the original contract breaker to sue for damages (or if it is a breach of condition or a serious breach of an innominate term, to terminate the contract, thus placing the boot very much on the other foot).

12.1.7 Affirmation and the relationship with 'anticipatory breach'

In contrast, if the innocent party does accept a repudiation as terminating the contract, it can then immediately sue for damages and does not even need to wait for the date of performance if that date has not yet arrived. This right to sue immediately for 'anticipatory breach', where the repudiation is given in advance of the date for performance, is illustrated by *Hochster* v *De La Tour* (1853) where the claimant was engaged by the defendant on 12 April to travel as a companion round Europe for three months from 1 June and the defendant wrote on 11 May to tell the claimant he was no longer required. The claimant accepted the advance repudiation and sued for 'anticipatory breach' on 22 May and the defendant argued that the claimant could not do so before 1 June and that he had to remain ready and able to perform the contract up to that date. The court held that if the claimant accepted the repudiation as ending his obligations, he was entitled to claim damages immediately and did not have to wait until performance: 'Thus instead of remaining idle and laying out money in preparations which must be useless, he is at liberty to seek service under another employer, which would go in mitigation of the damages to which he would otherwise be entitled' (Campbell CJ). This possibility of mitigating the damages was relevant to the facts since by 1 June the claimant had secured another engagement (from Lord Ashburton no less, to start on 4 July) which would no doubt have been taken into account in assessing the damages. Had he needed to stay ready to perform until 1 June he might not have been able to secure this alternative. The contrast with *White & Carter* is of course stark in that the claimant in that case did not accept the repudiation but carried on, not only in holding himself ready to perform but in actually performing, and then claimed the full contract price rather than mitigating and claiming his net loss. It is not at all clear that the claimant in *Hochster* could have done what the claimant did in *White & Carter* anyway as performing the contract probably needed co-operation from the defendant so the claimant would ultimately have had to accept the repudiation in any event and sue simply for his (net) damages.

12.2 Specific performance and injunction

We have seen in a number of contexts throughout the book that the main reason for contracting is that one party wants the benefit of the other party's performance. The equitable remedy of specific performance directly targets this initial purpose for contracting because the claimant can ask the court to order the defendant to perform his promise; the defendant will then be in contempt of court (for which there are very strong penalties, including committal to prison) if he does not then perform. The complementary or converse remedy to specific performance is an injunction. This is where the court orders the defendant *not* to do something; for example, not to work for a rival company, or not to reveal confidential secrets—the consequence of failure to abide by such an order is the same as for specific performance.

12.2.1 Damages must be an inadequate remedy

Because of their equitable origins, the remedies already discussed are, unlike the common law remedy of damages, not available as of right and the basic attitude is that they will not be granted if damages would be an adequate remedy. Thus a claimant will *normally* only be entitled to damages for non-delivery in a contract for the sale of goods as he can usually take his damages and purchase similar goods elsewhere, whereas land is regarded as unique and one cannot go and purchase the same plot of land elsewhere so specific performance is regularly ordered of contracts for the sale of land.

However, special circumstances may mean that even in a contract for the sale of unascertained goods, damages may not be an adequate remedy. In *Sky Petroleum Ltd* v *VIP Petroleum Ltd* (1974), the defendants terminated the claimant's supply of petrol during an oil crisis but the court ordered an **interim injunction** to restrain the defendant from withholding supplies because this was the only remedy that would allow the defendant to keep his petrol stations running; there was no option for the claimant to take damages and use them to buy petrol from another supplier because, as Goulding J put it, 'the petroleum market is in a unusual state.'

interim injunction This type of injunction is a temporary measure designed to give relief until a full hearing can be arranged and a final order made. It is often used in emergencies where a quick judgment is necessary, for example to stop a newspaper from printing confidential information the next morning. A spectacular example came on the morning of the 2011 Derby when the Court of Appeal issued an injunction to stop a leading jockey, Kieren Fallon, from riding in that afternoon's race in breach of his negative contractual obligation not to ride any horse other than Native Khan when retained to do so—see *Araci* v *Fallon* (2011).

Damages can also be inadequate in the sense that the true loss cannot be recovered because it is not legally recoverable or is suffered by a third party, as in *Beswick* v *Beswick* (1968), and in these circumstances specific performance may be ordered as being the more 'appropriate' remedy.

LINK TO . . .

Privity (Chapter 13)

The doctrine of privity limits who can claim damages—the general rule is that only a party to the contract can claim damages (although this is subject to exceptions). This means that a third party (i.e. not a party to the contract) cannot normally claim damages even if the contract is for their benefit; in such a situation damages are clearly inadequate and the court may order specific performance of the contract.

Mr Peter Beswick was a coal merchant who assigned his business assets to his nephew (the defendant, John Beswick) in return for the nephew's promise to pay him a weekly sum for life and, when he died, a weekly sum to his widow (Ruth Beswick) for the rest of her life. When Peter Beswick died, the nephew made one payment to Ruth and then refused to pay any more. Ruth Beswick sued for the unpaid sums and sought an order for specific performance of the obligation to pay her a weekly sum for life. At the time, she was not permitted to enforce the promise between her deceased husband and nephew because she was not a party to the contract (see now the Contracts (Rights of Third Parties) Act 1999). However, in her capacity as representing her husband's estate (thus effectively stepping into the position of her dead husband) she would be regarded as a party to the contract, but she would have suffered no *loss* in *that* capacity; all the loss was suffered by Ruth Beswick in her personal capacity.

The key point for you to remember is that Ruth Beswick was two different people: (a) Ruth Beswick (the widow); and (b) Ruth Beswick (the representative of her husband's estate). Only Ruth Beswick (the widow) had been promised a weekly sum from the nephew and so only Ruth Beswick (the widow) had suffered any loss. Conversely, only Ruth Beswick (representative) was a party to the contract and so only Ruth Beswick (representative) had a right to sue the nephew (but she had suffered only nominal loss). The House of Lords thought that it would be unjust to allow the nephew to avoid performing his promise on these technicalities of law and so ordered specific performance of the promise to pay a sum of money to Mrs Beswick since an award of nominal damages to the estate (representing its merely nominal loss) would be 'inadequate.' This case is discussed further in Chapter 13 on Privity.

Another example of where damages may be inadequate is where an exemption clause in the contract excludes or seriously limits the damages which may be awarded. In *AB* v *CD* (2014) the Court of Appeal reviewed some apparently conflicting earlier authorities and said that the exemption clause only affected the remedy of damages but not the primary obligation to perform the contract, and granted an injunction restraining the breach partly *because* the effect of the exemption clause rendered damages an inadequate remedy.

12.2.2 **Contracts of personal service**

These are not normally specifically performable since to make a court order to compel a person to work for somebody they do not want to work for would be an undue restriction on personal liberty. Furthermore, the courts will not enforce by way of injunction an express promise not to work for others if the practical effect is to compel the defendant to continue to work with or for the claimant. The idea behind this restriction is that, given that most people have to work for someone in order to get by in life, ordering a person *not* to work for anyone else *but* X is tantamount to ordering 'you must work for X.'

Thus in *Page One Records Ltd* v *Britton* (1967) the court refused to grant an injunction restraining The Troggs (a pop group best known for 'Wild Thing') from recording for anyone other than their present manager, the claimant, since to do so would in effect be to compel them to continue to work for the claimant and amount to specific performance of a personal service contract. This is generally regarded as a more realistic approach than the one taken in *Warner Brothers Pictures Inc.* v *Nelson* (1937) where an injunction to restrain the defendant, Bette Davis, from appearing in 'any motion picture or stage production for anyone other than the claimants' was granted since she could still be employed in other activities and would 'not be driven, though she may be tempted, to perform the contract.' On the other hand, it should be said that the purpose of the injunction was not to force the defendant to continue to work for the claimants but to prevent her from reducing the value of the films already made for the claimants by appearing, in breach of contract, in others. This is evident from the fact that Branson J limited the injunction to a maximum of three years 'to give reasonable protection and no more to the claimants against the ill effects to them of the defendant's breach of contract.'

THINKING POINT

Was it reasonable for the court to make Bette Davis choose between no work, non-acting work and working for Warner Bros? Does it matter whether the defendant in such cases is fabulously rich and could afford never to work again? Would it be reasonable to expect a high-profile movie star to take up non-acting work in today's society? Compare the approach in *Warren* v *Mendy* (1989) where an injunction which would have effectively compelled the boxer Nigel Benn to be managed by the claimant for three years was refused (and the suggestion that he could always get other work, for example as a security guard, completely rejected).

In *Evening Standard Company Ltd* v *Henderson* (1987) the employee worked in the *Evening Standard*'s production room and Robert Maxwell tried to 'poach' him when he set up his rival evening paper. The Court of Appeal granted an interim injunction to restrain the defendant from working for Maxwell during his twelve-month notice period. The case was peculiar in that there was no danger of the defendant being forced to perform or else starve since the claimants were prepared to keep him in his current job and pay him provided he did not work for their bitter rival. Contrast *Provident Financial Group* v *Hayward* (1989), where an accountant was put on **garden leave** during his notice period (so again there was no problem of not being paid) as the employer was worried that he might obtain further confidential secrets which he might disclose to his new employer. Dillon LJ noted that it is well recognized that artists and singers who depend on publicity have a need to work and exercise their skills and considered that the same consideration could apply to 'skilled workmen and even chartered accountants.' The trial judge's decision to refuse an injunction, preventing Hayward from joining Asda before his notice expired, was therefore upheld and the employer was left to his remedy in damages (if any). A significant difference between the cases is that the *Evening Standard* was prepared to provide employment during the notice period but Provident Financial Group was not.

garden leave When an employee gives notice (say the three months required under the employment contract) that the employee wishes to terminate the contract and the employer tells the employee not to bother coming to work for those months (mainly because the employer wants to avoid disruption and the possible leak of confidential information).

Discretionary nature of the rule

None of the rules about equitable remedies is absolute (see section 12.2.5) and in the context of personal services this is further illustrated by the exceptional case of *Hill* v *C. A. Parsons & Co. Ltd* (1972), where an injunction was granted to restrain a dismissal in breach of contract and thus, in effect, specific performance was ordered of a personal service contract. The reason for the exception was that the employer did not really wish to dismiss the employee but was only doing so under pressure from a union and thus upholding the contract did not violate any personal liberty of the parties (because they had no problem working with each other), which is the main objection to specific enforcement of personal service contracts. Notice that this was a case where the contract was being enforced against the employer and it has been followed in subsequent cases such as *Powell* v *Brent LBC* (1988) where again the relationship with the employee had not broken down but the employer was only seeking to end the employment since it thought the appointment had been invalid because it had not complied with its own equal opportunity code. A similar approach was taken by the Supreme Court in *Tesco v USDAW* (2024) where an injunction was granted to prevent the employer from dismissing the employees solely for the purposes of terminating their contractual right to enhanced pay. Firstly, the relationship of mutual confidence between employer and employee had clearly not broken down as the employer had been seeking to rehire the employees anyway, after the dismissal to remove the right to enhanced pay, so there was no problem in granting an injunction to prevent the dismissals in the first place, even though it amounted in effect to specific performance of a personal service contract. Secondly, damages would be an inadequate remedy given the uncertainties involved in assessing them and covering all the losses likely to be incurred by the employees should they be dismissed. In contrast, enforcement *against* an *employee* by means of specific performance or injunction which compels 'an employee to do any work or attend any place for the doing of any work' is specifically prohibited by s.236 of the Trade Union & Labour Relations (Consolidation) Act 1992. The Supreme Court did not consider that this caused a problem of mutuality (see 12.2.4 below) on the facts of the case since even though Tesco would not have any right of specific performance, Tesco would have sufficient other remedies if there was a breach by the employees and there was no reason to suppose these would be inadequate.

For an amusing case about personal service contracts see *De Rivafinoli* v *Corsetti* (1833) where the defendant was an opera singer who had contracted to 'sing, gesticulate and recite' exclusively for the claimants. The judge, having ruled that in theory 'a bird that can sing and will not sing must be made to sing,' went on to acknowledge that it would be 'very difficult for the judge [not possessing the necessary exquisite sensitivity in the auricular nerve] to determine what effect coercion might produce upon the defendant's singing, especially in the livelier airs: although the fear of imprisonment would unquestionably deepen his seriousness in the graver parts of the drama.' The injunction was refused. The case was, and could only have been, decided in New York. Its interest for present purposes is in the court's awareness of the difficulty supervising effectively a contract for personal service, a difficulty which is sometimes given as the reason for refusing specific performance of other types of contract which require constant supervision.

12.2.3 **Constant supervision**

In *Ryan* v *Mutual Tontine Westminster Chambers Association* (1893) the court refused to enforce a contract to provide porter services to flats on the basis that it could not supervise performance over a lengthy period of time. In *Tito* v *Waddell* (*No. 2*) (1977) Megarry V-C said that the real issue is whether it is possible to state with precision what has to be done in order to perform the contract and comply with the order of the court. However, in *Posner* v *Scott Lewis* (1986) the court ordered specific performance of a promise to provide a porter, reasoning that it was possible to define what had to be done (employ a porter for the purpose of carrying out the duties in clause 3(11) of the contract) and it would not require undue policing by the court because the claimant could bring enforcement proceedings if the defendants failed to comply with the order.

THINKING POINT

What is a better reason for denying specific performance: the inability of the court to define what the defendant has to do, or the oppressive nature of the order sought by the claimant?

By contrast, in *Co-operative Insurance Society* v *Argyll Stores* (1997), the House of Lords reiterated the significance of the difficulties of constant supervision by reversing the Court of Appeal and confirming the previous settled practice of not ordering specific performance of a contract to carry on a business. The defendants had taken out a lease of a supermarket housed inside a shopping centre which contained a promise to keep the supermarket open during business hours. The claimant sought to specifically enforce this promise when the supermarket proposed to close down (it was not good for all the other businesses in the shopping centre to have the supermarket closed). The House of Lords reasoned that the order could not be clearly defined and that it would be oppressive to operate a business under threat of contempt of court. This latter reason is perhaps the best one and Lord Hoffmann emphasized the benefits of awarding damages and bringing the parties' relationship to an end. Specific performance would force the parties to work together and would be likely to lead to further arguments and litigation, which is wasteful of both the court's time and the parties' resources.

12.2.4 **Mutuality**

It is only fair that if one party is able to obtain the actual performance of the contract then the other party should be able to do so and equity, being particularly concerned with fairness, reflects this through the doctrine of **mutuality**.

> **mutuality** Can loosely be translated as 'matching': if one party wants to claim specific performance, then the other party must have been able to match this by claiming specific performance himself (it is not necessary that the other party does actually claim specific performance, just that he would have had the option to do so).

The question has arisen whether mutuality needs to have been present from the outset—from the time of entering into the contract—or only by the time of enforcing it. The nineteenth-century formulation (in *Fry on Specific Performance*) expressed the doctrine as requiring that the remedy of specific performance should have been potentially available to either party at the time the contract is made.

> **EXAMPLE**
>
> **Mutuality from the outset**
>
> D agrees to grant a lease of a house to C in return for C's promise personally to renovate the house. D's promise could not be specifically enforced against D since D would not be able to get specific performance of C's obligation to renovate (it being a personal obligation). Furthermore, following Fry, the objection of lack of mutuality would still persist even if C had already done the renovation because the mutuality had to exist at the time of formation of the contract.

Criticism of Fry

This formulation of the mutuality rule was criticized initially by Ames (1903) 3 Colum L Rev 1 who put forward an alternative formulation whereby mutuality only requires that the party who is ordered to specifically perform should *either* have received *or* be assured of performance in return. In other words, the defendant does not himself have to be able to obtain an order of specific performance if the performance of the contract is otherwise assured, the most obvious example of which being where it has already been carried out. On this view, in the example given earlier, C would be able to obtain specific performance if he has *already* carried out the renovations since there is no danger of D being ordered to specifically perform and then being left without any effective remedy of his own should C himself default. This view is much easier to reconcile with even the older cases (see e.g. *Wilkinson* v *Clements* (1872)) and Fry's formulation has been criticized in many textbooks since Ames's article, including Spry, *The Principles of Equitable Remedies*, where the proper rule was succinctly expressed as requiring merely that mutuality 'be looked at only as at the time of the making of the proposed order.' The fact that the contract involves, for example, personal services by the claimant, which cannot be the subject of an order of specific performance, is no defence if those services have already been carried out.

This view was confirmed by the Court of Appeal in *Price* v *Strange* (1977). The trial judge held that specific performance of an agreement to grant an underlease of a flat could not be ordered against the defendant because specific performance could not have been ordered against the claimant who had contracted to repair and decorate the flat (following Fry's approach). The Court of Appeal reversed this decision and granted specific performance of the underlease since the claimant had done the repairs and decoration until he had been prevented from doing so by the defendant, and he had promised to pay to the defendant the cost of completing the repairs he had not done. There was therefore no danger of the defendant being left high and dry after complying with the court's order of specific performance. See also the Supreme Court's fairly terse dismissal of any mutuality problem in Tesco v USDAW (2024) at 12.2.2 above, where the availability of other remedies was considered sufficient.

12.2.5 **Discretion**

The issues discussed earlier in relation to the adequacy of damages, personal service contracts, constant supervision and mutuality are merely illustrations of the fact that equitable remedies are discretionary (which is why none of the rules discussed earlier can be regarded as absolute). Other factors can obviously affect the exercise of the discretion, including public policy, which can be a factor in favour of specific performance, as in *Verrall* v *Great Yarmouth Borough Council* (1981) where it would tend to promote political liberties, or against, as in *Wroth* v *Tyler* (1974) where specific performance of a contract for the sale of land, subject to the wife's right of occupation, was refused as it might mean splitting up a family. *Shell UK Ltd* v *Lostock Garage Ltd* (1977) is a striking example of the discretionary nature of equitable remedies where Ormrod LJ considered the covenant in restraint of trade to be reasonable and thus binding but refused an injunction restraining its breach since Shell was unfairly subsidizing neighbouring garages and inflicting hardship on the defendants.

> **THINKING POINT**
>
> Should there be much greater relaxation of the restrictions on performance, and if not, why not?

All that you can really be expected to do with equitable remedies is to be aware of the major factors which govern their availability and have a feeling for the direction in which the courts' attitudes towards particular issues seem to be moving. The general drift seems to be a relaxation of the traditional restrictions by reference to particular categories towards a more general approach whereby 'the court will decree specific performance only if this will do more perfect and complete justice than an award of damages,' *per* Megarry V-C in *Tito* v *Waddell (No. 2)* (1977).

Digging deeper

One argument in favour of damages is that they promote efficiency. Imagine that you are a builder who has promised to build a house on a plot of land for £100,000. You are halfway through the work and the owner of the land next door offers to pay you £150,000 to build a house for him. You do not have time to do both jobs so you breach the first contract and start to perform the second contract. You pay damages for breach of contract to the first landowner (who uses them to cover the extra cost of getting another builder to complete his house) but you make a profit because these damages are less than the extra amount you are being paid on the second contract. Some economists argue that such 'efficient breaches' are good for the economy as a whole because the person who values your services the most (the second landowner) receives your services and the damages you pay to the first enable him to complete his house (so everyone is happy ultimately). If a court ordered you to specifically perform your first contract then there would be inefficiency because you would not have entered into the second contract and would have given your services to the person who values them the least. A counter-argument to this is that this efficiency argument flies in the face of a simpler argument based on the morality of keeping promises, one that we all learn from the playground onwards. Essentially, if you promise you will do something, you should do it (unless you are excused by extreme circumstances and the doctrine of frustration applies, see Chapter 10). The first landowner may have got his house ultimately, but he may not be very happy about how it has come about and he (or others) may not think much of any promises you make in the future.

Summary

1. Action for the price

A can enforce a promise to pay a sum of money directly, as opposed to an indirect claim for compensatory damages for breach of contract.

A must demonstrate that A has performed (or substantially performed—a question of fact in each case) A's contractual obligations.

The contract may contain severable obligations, in which case A can claim payment due for each part of the contract A has performed. However, if he has only partly performed and has not completed even substantial performance of the obligation in question, A cannot recover anything for the part performance or for the (partial) benefit conferred on the other party unless the other party freely chooses to accept that benefit.

2. A limit on the ability to keep the contract alive?

If one party repudiates the contract, the other party can in principle choose not to accept the repudiation, keep the contract alive and continue to perform and claim the contract price due upon completion.

The other party must be able to perform the contract without the first party's co-operation and must have a legitimate interest in continuing to perform and claiming the contract price rather than accepting the repudiation as terminating the contract and suing for damages (which would involve a duty to mitigate).

3. Specific performance and injunction

A court may order a defendant to perform his obligations (specific performance) or order him not to do something (injunction) and the defendant will be in contempt of court if he disobeys this order.

Both remedies are discretionary but the following factors are relevant:

- damages would not be an adequate remedy, for instance, because the subject matter is unique (e.g. land) or full recovery of loss is legally impossible;
- because it would normally involve an undue interference with individual liberty, personal service contracts are rarely subject to specific performance or injunction;
- the order must not require constant supervision by the court, meaning that the court is concerned that it can precisely define what the defendant must or must not do so that it is easy to determine whether the order has been complied with; and
- there must be mutuality in the sense that the defendant must have either received performance by the claimant already or been assured of being able to obtain such performance.

? Questions

1. Abi, a talented musical diva, agrees to play a violin piece at a concert organized by Music Box Ltd. The contract between Abi and Music Box states: 'The Performer will perform exclusively for the Promoter during the Term of this agreement.'

   The definitions at the beginning of the agreement define 'Performer' as Abi, 'Promoter' as Music Box Ltd and the 'Term' as 1 November until 14 November.

   The first concert takes place on 1 November and Abi plays brilliantly but, just as she is about to start the final movement of the piece, she gets up, takes a bow and hurries off-stage. She asks David, the Chief Executive of Music Box, for her money and he says: 'Get lost, you're getting nothing. You only played half of the music!' Abi demands her money, claiming that she played her 'interpretation' of the piece and she would sue Music Box if they did not pay her.

   Later in the evening, David finds out that Abi has played that same evening for a rival promoter and is scheduled to play for them every night for the next two weeks. David wants to keep Abi for future performances because he has sold lots of tickets on the basis that she is playing, but he does not want her to play for his rival, who has a concert hall across the road from his, because he thinks that this would cause a drop in the sale of tickets on the night.

   Advise David.

2. What are the advantages of an action for the price as opposed to a claim for damages and what is the essential distinction between the two types of claim? How have the courts responded to the danger that the action for the price may lead to waste where it is clear that the other party is no longer interested in receiving performance?

3. What is the 'entire obligations rule'? What problems remain if the courts decide that the claimant cannot recover the price because he has not performed his promise in its entirety?

4. 'Specific performance should be the primary remedy for breach of contract.' Discuss.

Further reading

Books

Chen-Wishart, M, *Contract Law*, 7th edn (Oxford University Press, 2022) ch 14.

McKendrick, E, *Contract Law: Text, Cases and Materials*, 11th edn (Oxford University Press, 2024) ch 24.

O'Sullivan, J, and Hilliard, J, *The Law of Contract*, 11th edn (Oxford University Press, 2024) ch 17.

Articles

Ames, JB, 'Mutuality in specific performances' (1903) 3 Colum L Rev 1.

Kronman, A, 'Specific performance' (1978) 45 U Chicago LR 351.

Liu, Q, 'The *White & Carter* principle: A restatement' (2011) 74 MLR 171.

Schwartz, A, 'The case for specific performance' (1979) 89 Yale LJ 271.

13 Privity and the interests of third parties

LEARNING OBJECTIVES

This chapter will help you to:

- understand the traditional rule of privity that only a party to the contract can sue upon it and to understand its connection to the related rule that consideration must move from the promisee;
- appreciate the various ways in which the strict application of the privity rule has been avoided so as to enable the interests of third parties to be protected; and
- recognize and evaluate the impact of the Contracts (Rights of Third Parties) Act 1999 on the existing law and on the ability of third parties to enforce contracts made for their benefit.

Introduction

Privity is essentially about who can sue and who can be sued under a contract. The simple answer to this question is 'only a party to the contract.' That answer is however incomplete because, quite apart from the fact that it does not tell us about the myriad exceptions to the 'who can sue' part of the rule, it also does not tell us who is a party and who is not. The doctrine of privity was foreshadowed in *Tweddle* v *Atkinson* (1861), a case we have already met in Chapter 4 under the rule that the consideration must move from the promisee. The facts are relatively simple and provide a good illustration of the various capacities in which a person may be related to a contract.

13.1 *Tweddle* v *Atkinson*

The three principal characters involved in *Tweddle* v *Atkinson* (1861) were as follows:

1) William Guy, the promisor;
2) John Tweddle, the promisee; and
3) William Tweddle, the third-party beneficiary (who was John Tweddle's son and William Guy's son-in-law).

William Guy had promised to pay £200 to William Tweddle (and in return John Tweddle had promised to pay £100 to William Tweddle). It was also 'further agreed by the aforesaid William Guy and the said John Tweddle, that the said William Tweddle has full power to sue the said parties in any court of law or equity for the aforesaid sums hereby promised and specified.'

Unfortunately, Guy died without having made the £200 payment and his executor Atkinson refused to pay and so William Tweddle sued (as the contract expressly said he could) for the £200. The Court of Queen's Bench in fairly brief judgments dismissed the claim since 'the consideration must move from the party entitled to sue upon the contract' (Compton J). William Tweddle had provided no consideration, not even in getting married as his marriage had taken place before the agreement, and although he was named in the contract as the intended beneficiary, the lack of consideration provided by him meant that he could not sue—see Figure 13.1. It should be noted (although the court did not mention this in its judgment) that in addition to not providing consideration, William Tweddle was also not a 'party to the contract' since the contract was expressed to be made between William Guy and John Tweddle (William's father). The court instead emphasized the lack of consideration, but you could argue that the reason why William Tweddle was not a party to the contract was because he did not provide consideration.

LINK TO . . .

Consideration (Chapter 4)

Think back to the chapter on consideration and the idea of consideration as the price of the promise—only the person who has given the consideration has paid the price for the right to enforce the promise—William Tweddle had not paid this price (although his father John had done so by reason of his promise to pay £100 himself) and so William could not enforce the promise.

Figure 13.1 *Tweddle* v *Atkinson* (or the case of Two Tweddles and a Guy)

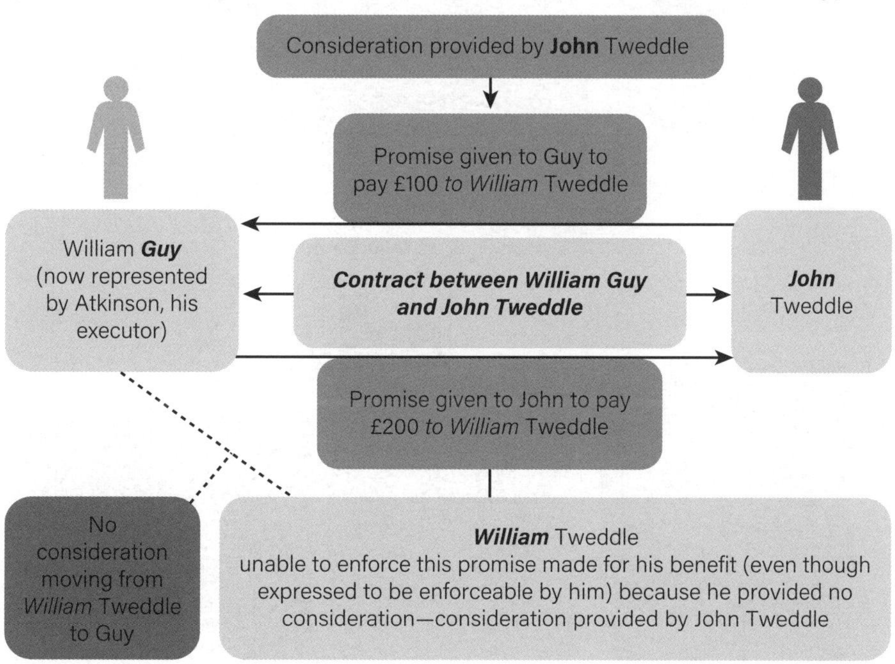

13.2 The establishment of the privity rule

In *Dunlop* v *Selfridge* (1915), Viscount Haldane in the House of Lords took the step which the Court of Queen's Bench had not taken in *Tweddle* v *Atkinson* and made the fact of not being a party, rather than simply the failure to provide consideration, an independent ground for not being able to enforce a contract.

Dunlop gave a discount to Dew, bulk buyers of their tyres, on condition that Dew would not resell at less than list price to trade buyers unless those buyers agreed not to sell to private customers below list price. Selfridge bought Dunlop tyres from Dew at below list price and agreed with Dew not to sell below list price to private customers but then went on to do so. Dew had no particular interest in enforcing the undertaking given to them by Selfridge, but Dunlop did, as they wanted to maintain the retail price of their tyres (something which today might be regarded as anti-competitive but which was not frowned upon in 1915). Dunlop's action failed, in the majority view because they had provided no consideration to Selfridge. Crucially however Viscount Haldane also stated it as a fundamental principle that 'only a person who is a party to a contract may sue upon it.' Dunlop were not party to the contract between Selfridge and Dew in which Selfridge undertook not to sell below list price and could not enforce it for that reason (see Figure 13.2).

Figure 13.2 Illustration of Dunlop v Selfridge

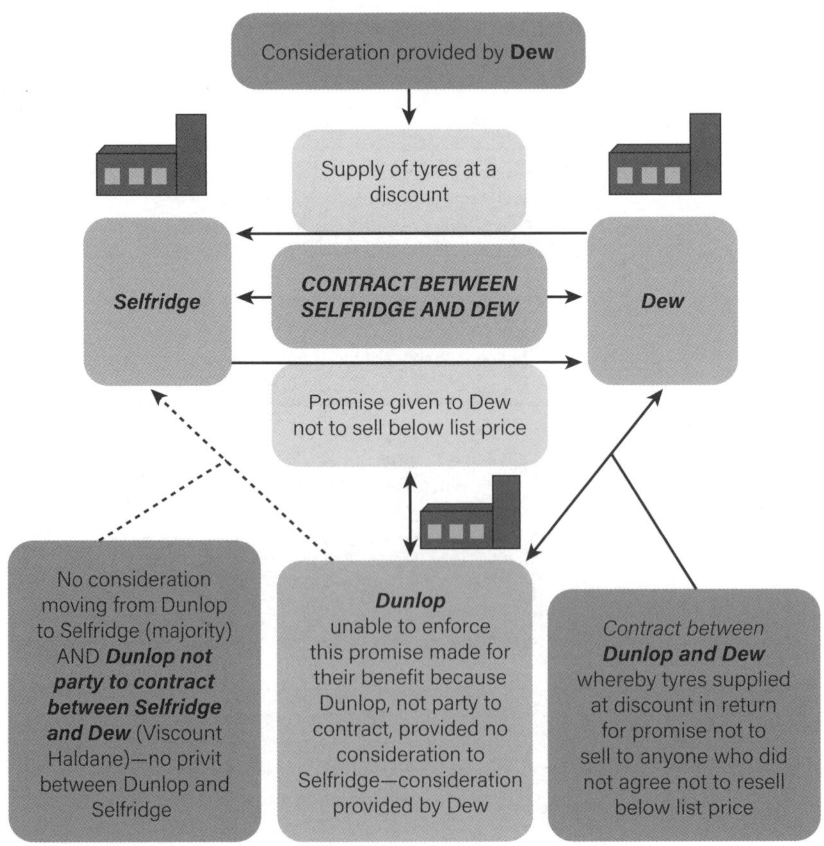

13.3 Distinguishing the privity rule from the consideration rule

Either or both of the previous two cases could have been decided on the grounds of no consideration from the person seeking to enforce the contract (as decided in *Tweddle*) or on the grounds of that person not being a party to the relevant contract (as *per* Viscount Haldane in *Dunlop*). Distinguishing the two rules is not easy and not especially important on the facts as they arose since in neither case was there a lack of consideration from a person who was nevertheless clearly party to the contract. *Tweddle* v *Atkinson* came close to it since William Tweddle was expressly stated in the contract to be able to sue but the promise was not expressed as given to him and therefore, on that basis, he was still not a party.

13.3.1 **Three examples**

The following examples may help to clarify the difference between the privity rule and the consideration rule. The examples essentially progress from C initially satisfying neither rule, followed by a second example where C satisfies the privity rule but not the consideration rule, followed by the third and final example where C satisfies both rules and is therefore able to sue.

In Figure 13.3, P promises to B that in return for B servicing P's car, P will pay a sum of money to C.

Rather as in the cases of *Tweddle* and *Dunlop*, C's inability to sue P can be put either on the basis of no consideration moving from C or on the basis of C not being a party to the promise (not a party to, or privy to, the contract).

However, consider the following slightly different situation where C *is* a party to the contract between P and B but does not provide any consideration. In Figure 13.4, P promises to B and to C that in return for B servicing P's car, P will pay £100 to C.

Figure 13.3 C not a party and also provides no consideration

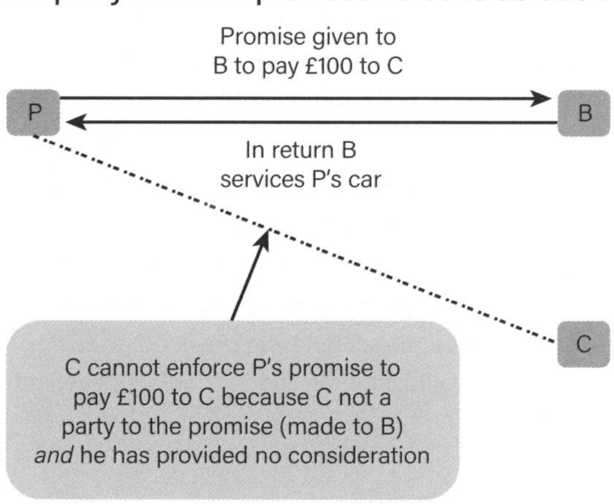

Figure 13.4 C is a party but still provides no consideration

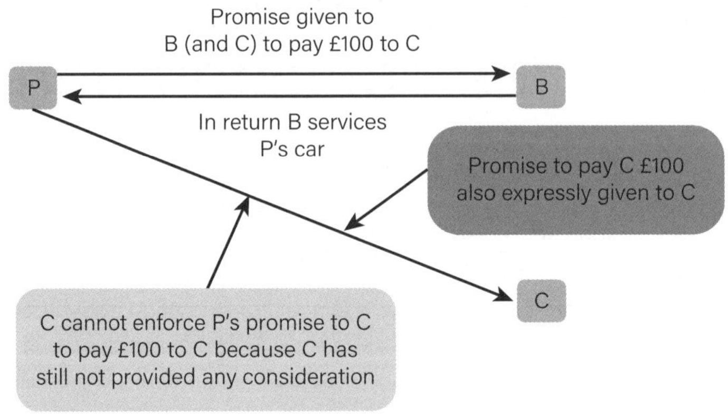

Figure 13.5 C is both a party and provides consideration

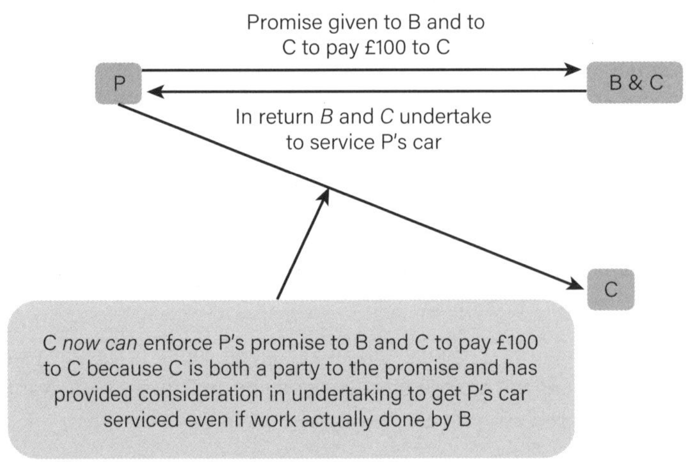

C is a party to the contract (or the promise) but still cannot sue because the consideration is provided by B, not C. Thus, the consideration rule lies in wait behind the privity rule and this fact makes the privity rule one which cannot necessarily be evaded merely by providing for a person to be made formally a party to the contract. One must also provide for that person to be seen as somehow providing the consideration, as in Figure 13.5.

In the third scenario shown in Figure 13.5, C not only is a party to the contract but also has provided consideration. P promises to B and C that P will pay £100 to C if B and C collectively promise to ensure that P's car is serviced. Even if in fact the servicing of P's car is wholly performed by B, since B *and* C have jointly undertaken the obligation to ensure it is serviced, they both not only are party to the contract but have provided (executory) consideration in the form of their joint promise (and could each be sued for breach) even if the consideration has actually been executed or performed by B.

THINKING POINT

If two or more people eat a meal in a restaurant and the bill is paid by one of them, can the other diners sue for breach if the meal is unfit and they subsequently fall ill?

If the contract were simply with the person who paid the bill, the other diners would have no right to sue the restaurant in contract and would have to prove negligence in tort. However. they can in most situations be regarded as persons to whom the promise that the food is fit for consumption is made and also as persons providing consideration in the sense that they each individually can be regarded as impliedly promising to the restaurant to pay for the food they individually order and consume, irrespective of the fact that the bill is actually paid by one of them.

In *Lockett* v *Charles* (1938) a husband paid for a meal for his wife and himself. But his wife was regarded as entitled to sue since she also impliedly promised to pay for her meal by ordering it. The situation was acknowledged (by Tucker J, not inappropriately) to be different 'where somebody orders a private room at a hotel, entertains a large party, and makes arrangements beforehand.' Here 'there is no question that he is the only person who is contracting with the hotel, and that his guests who attend have no contractual relationship with the proprietor of the hotel.' Nevertheless, this is one of the situations where dissatisfaction with the privity rule has led to attempts to sidestep it in various ways.

13.4 Evading the privity rule

Prior to the 1999 Act, which will be separately dealt with in section 13.6, attempts to get round the privity rule could be divided into two sorts:

a) those which accept that the third party cannot sue but seek to protect the third party by utilizing the remedy available to the contracting party; and

b) those which seek to give a right directly to the third party.

13.4.1 **Utilizing the contracting party's remedy in favour of the third party**

Specific performance

The simplest and most effective way to enforce the benefit promised to the third party is to obtain an order of specific performance compelling the promisor to carry out the promise, thus directly benefiting the third party as is illustrated in the case of *Beswick* v *Beswick* (1968). This case has already been discussed in Chapter 12, section 12.2.1 where the detailed facts were outlined; these are summarized in Figure 13.6. From the third party's point of view, specific performance in their favour is the ideal solution, but the facts of *Beswick* v *Beswick* were unusual and the remedy of specific performance will not always be available.

Figure 13.6 The facts of Beswick v Beswick (1968)

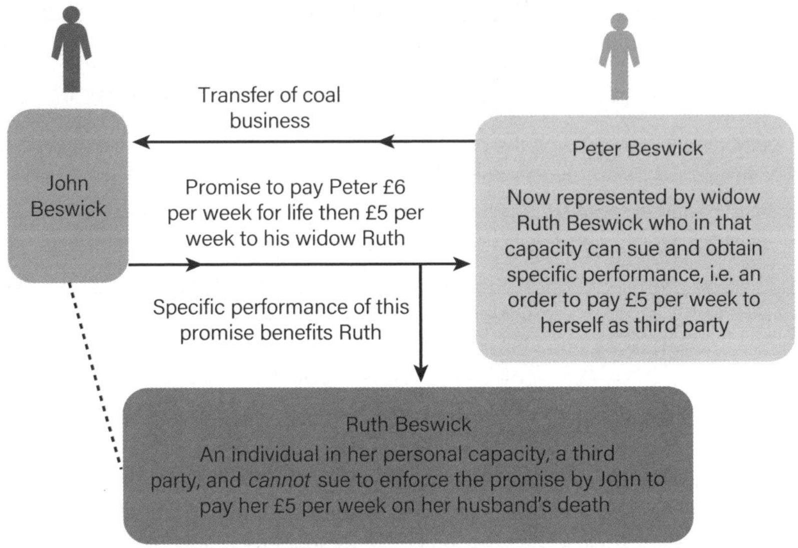

LINK TO . . .

Specific Remedies (Chapter 12)

Specific performance is only normally available when damages are an inadequate remedy (see section 12.2.1). Damages were inadequate in this case either:

a) because they would be nil (the estate, as opposed to Ruth Beswick personally, could be said to have suffered no loss) and yet John Beswick would otherwise have profited by receiving the business without paying the full price agreed (the fact that he had already received the business meant there was no problem with mutuality—see section 12.2.4); or

b) because even if the estate could be entitled to substantial damages (as Lord Pearce thought) an order to make the weekly payments was more appropriate and convenient than waiting for the failure to make the payments and then having to sue periodically for arrears.

The remedy of specific performance protects the third party very well but is dependent on the contracting party being prepared to sue. This was not a problem on the facts of *Beswick* since the third party happened to have a dual personality, being also the legal representative of the contracting party. Even where the contracting party is prepared to sue, however, specific performance will not always be available or appropriate, in particular where the issue is not forcing a reluctant promisor to perform but rather it is a question of getting compensation for deficient performance which has already been given. Here the difference between (a) and (b) in the link box earlier as to whether the promisee's damages will be nominal or not becomes crucial. This raises the question discussed in the next section of whether the contracting party (promisee) can recover damages to reflect the loss which is primarily a loss suffered by the third party.

Damages on behalf of a third party

Lord Denning was very much in favour of allowing the contracting party to recover damages on behalf of the third party's own loss, as is illustrated in the following case.

CASE CLOSE-UP

***Jackson* v *Horizon Holidays* (1975)**

The claimant had booked a holiday costing £1,200 in Ceylon (Sri Lanka) for himself and his wife and two small children. The hotel provided was unsatisfactory in a number of respects and he claimed damages on his return. He was awarded £1,100 by the trial judge and the holiday company appealed, admitting liability but disputing the amount of damages. Lord Denning accepted that the contract was made solely by the claimant for the benefit of the family and only he could sue, but upheld the amount of damages awarded. An award of £1,100 would have been too much for the claimant's own mental distress and disappointment but he could also recover for the mental distress suffered by the third parties as the contract was made for their benefit. The award of £1,100 was not excessive if one also took account of their disappointment. Although the other members of the Court of Appeal agreed in the result, they did not base their decision on the damages being justified in part on the loss suffered by third parties, whereas Lord Denning expressly said that:

> The case comes within the principle stated by Lush LJ in *Lloyd's* v *Harper* ((1880) 16 Ch D 290 at 321):
>
> '. . . I consider it to be an established rule of law that where a contract is made with *A.* for the benefit of *B., A.* can sue on the contract for the benefit of *B.*, and recover all that *B.* could have recovered if the contract had been made with *B.* himself.'
>
> It has been suggested that Lush LJ was thinking of a contract in which A was trustee for B. But I do not think so. He was a common lawyer speaking of the common law.

The House of Lords took a rather different view from Lord Denning (not a surprise, you may think) in the case of *Woodar* v *Wimpey* (1980) (although what they said in this case was *obiter*) and said that Lush LJ in *Lloyd's* v *Harper* had been referring to a case where A contracts as an agent and that there was no general rule allowing a contracting party to recover damages on behalf of a third party's loss. They did not however disapprove of the result in *Jackson*, Lord Wilberforce describing it 'either as a broad decision on the measure of damages' (i.e. as justified by the plaintiff's own distress) 'or possibly as an example of a type of contract, examples of which are persons contracting for family holidays, ordering meals in restaurants for a party, hiring a taxi for a group, calling for special treatment.'

Benefits in construction contracts

The House of Lords confirmed in the complex case of *Alfred McAlpine* v *Panatown* (2001) that, outside the social/consumer contracts where the contract is made by one party for the benefit of others as a matter of convenience and simplicity, there is no general rule allowing a contracting party to recover a loss on behalf of a third party.

McAlpine contracted with Panatown to construct a building on land owned by UIPL, a company in the same group as Panatown. McAlpine also provided a 'duty of care deed' to UIPL directly whereby they agreed to use all reasonable skill and so on in constructing the building.

The project did not go well and the costs of repairs for the alleged defects plus damages for delay were estimated to be tens of millions of pounds. The decision was made by the group of companies to sue under the main contract between McAlpine and Panatown rather than under the duty of care deed between McAlpine and UIPL. McAlpine argued that Panatown, as opposed to UIPL who was the owner of the defective building, had suffered no loss. Panatown argued in the House of Lords: (i) that it was entitled to recover the loss suffered by UIPL on its behalf; and (ii) that in any event it had suffered a loss itself in that it had not received what it bargained for even if it was itself financially no worse off.

THINKING POINT

Had Panatown suffered a recoverable loss even though it was financially no worse off as a consequence of the breach? Refer to Chapter 11, section 11.3.1, and consider the related questions raised by cases such as *Ruxley* v *Forsyth* (1996).

On the first point relating to recovery of loss suffered by a third party, the House of Lords was clear, as has already been said, that there was no general rule permitting such recovery. The real issue here however was whether Panatown could rely on a special rule traceable back to *Dunlop* v *Lambert* in 1839 and referred to in *The Albazero* (1977) by Lord Diplock in relation to contracts for the carriage of goods. This rule was then developed by the House of Lords in *Linden Gardens* v *Lenesta* (1994) so as to apply to contracts for the construction of a building.

The *Dunlop* v *Lambert/Albazero* exception applies to contracts whereby the claimant is the original consignor of goods to the defendant carrier, it being contemplated that the ownership of the goods will be transferred on by the claimant to subsequent purchasers whilst still being carried by the defendant. The subsequent purchasers are therefore the ones who are, by the time of the breach, the owners who suffer the actual loss or damage to the goods but who have no contract with the defendant carrier. The exception recognizes that the claimant can recover damages even though the claimant suffers no loss personally and he holds the damages on behalf of the subsequent purchasers who have suffered loss.

This exception was applied by the House of Lords in *Linden Gardens* v *Lenesta* (1993), or more accurately in the second case heard and reported with that case, *St Martin's Property Corporation* v *McAlpine*.

CASE CLOSE-UP

***Linden Gardens* v *Lenesta* (1994); *St Martin's Property Corporation* v *McAlpine* (1993)**

The defendants (McAlpine) contracted in 1974 with the first claimants (Corporation) to build on a site in Hammersmith owned by Corporation. In 1976, Corporation transferred ownership of the land to the second claimants (Investments) and also purported to assign the benefit of its building contract with McAlpine. Due to breaches of contract by McAlpine after this date, there were defects in the work which only became apparent in 1981. Investments, who had most obviously suffered loss as they were now owners of the building, were unable to sue McAlpine because the assignment of the contractual rights to them by Corporation was invalid since it had been done without the consent of

McAlpine, as was required under the original construction contract. Investments were thus in effect still third parties to the contract. However, Corporation were still a contracting party (the assignment having been invalid). McAlpine argued that Corporation had not suffered any loss since they no longer owned the property damaged and had already sold it for full value by the date of the breach but this 'formidable if unmeritorious argument' was rejected. As an exception to the normal rule about only recovering for one's own loss, Corporation could sue not only for their own loss but for the loss suffered by subsequent purchasers to whom it was always contemplated the property might subsequently be transferred.

The rationale for the exception is summed up in the words of Lord Browne-Wilkinson:

> The contract was for a large development of property which, to the knowledge of both Corporation and McAlpines, was going to be occupied, and possibly purchased, by third parties and not by Corporation itself. Therefore it could be foreseen that damage caused by a breach would cause loss to a later owner and not merely to the original contracting party, Corporation . . . McAlpines had specifically contracted that the rights of action under the building contract could not without McAlpines' consent be transferred to third parties who became owners or occupiers and might suffer loss. In such a case, it seems to me proper, as in the case of the carriage of goods by land, to treat the parties as having entered into the contract on the footing that Corporation would be entitled to enforce contractual rights for the benefit of those who suffered from defective performance but who, under the terms of the contract, could not acquire any right to hold McAlpines liable for breach.

Exception not needed where third party has direct right of action

To return to the more recent case of *Panatown*, this *Linden Gardens/St Martin's* exception was held not to be applicable on the facts because it was not necessary. UIPL had their own direct cause of action against McAlpine under the duty of care deed under which they could claim their own damages. This also meant, in the minds of the majority at least, that there was no need to finally resolve the second point in the case, that is, whether Panatown could recover substantial damages for its own loss even though it was not financially worse off as a result of the breach. There was no justification for giving damages to Panatown to reflect the fact that it had not got the performance it bargained for when there was an obvious remedy directly in the hands of the third party, UIPL, which had suffered loss and could recover it by suing under the duty of care deed.

SUMMARY POINTS

Summary of damages on behalf of a third party: To summarize an extremely complex and still developing area of law, one might say that the general rule is that a contracting party cannot sue to recover a loss that is really suffered by a third party but this rule is subject to exceptions—in particular:

1) where the contract is of the *Jackson* v *Horizon* variety where one person contracts in a social/consumer capacity as a matter of convenience for the benefit of a number of other individuals; and, at the other end of the scale;

2) where a construction contract is made which envisages the building being passed on to subsequent purchasers who are likely to be the ones who suffer from any defect in the building (but, unlike in *Panatown*, who have no direct action themselves) and for whose benefit it is necessary to give the original customer a right to sue for damages even though personally they will have suffered no loss. It should be noted that there is controversy stemming from a number of *obiter* comments in the earlier cases about the possibility of a 'broader ground' of recovery by a contractor of 'transferred loss' of a third party intended to be benefited, even though there is no element of transfer of property involved. This 'broader ground' was discussed by the Supreme Court in *Lowick Rose LLP* v *Swynson* (2017) and in the Court of Appeal by Coulson LJ in *BV Nederlandse* v *Rembrandt (2019)* but both courts held the broader ground, even if it exists (which is not at all clear), not to be established on the facts any way given the absence of a common intention to benefit the third party.

13.5 Techniques for giving a right directly to a third party or apparent third party

There have always been a number of ways around the privity rule but most of these require advance planning and generally amount to making the apparent third party a contracting party. An example of this is the doctrine of agency.

13.5.1 Agency

agent
A person who is authorized by the principal to enter into contracts with third parties on the principal's behalf.

An **agent** will create a direct contractual relationship between a third party and his principal if he is acting within his actual or apparent authority.

EXAMPLE

Agency

P, a comedian, employs A as P's agent for making bookings for P to appear in theatres and night clubs and publicizes this fact. C negotiates a contract with A as P's agent for P to appear on New Year's Eve at C's club. Although the contract was formally created by C negotiating with A, since A was acting as agent for P, there is a binding contract between C and P.

Note however that this only gets round the privity rule and not the rule that consideration must move from the promisee. This is not a problem in the example given because P provides consideration (by promising to perform) and C also provides consideration (by promising to pay). In *Dunlop* v *Selfridge* it was argued that Dew and Co. were acting as agents for Dunlop when they obtained Selfridge's promise not to sell below list price but this was of no avail because Dunlop provided no consideration to Selfridge. The tyres supplied were entirely the property of Dew and Co and nothing passed between Dunlop and Selfridge which could amount to consideration.

13.5.2 **Assignment**

Contractual rights could not be assigned at common law, but valid **assignments** were recognized in equity and by statute under s.136 of the Law of Property Act 1925 (LPA 1925). The latter has the advantage that if its conditions are satisfied, the assignee can sue in its own name and does not have to join the assignor as a party to the action (as it must do in equity). Section 136 requires, amongst other things, that the assignment is in writing and signed by the assignor and that notice in writing is given to the promisor who will now be bound to the assignee. The result of a successful assignment is that the promisor can now be sued by the assignee who was originally a third party. As was seen in *Linden Gardens/St Martin's*, promisors may protect themselves by prohibiting assignments without their consent and, quite apart from that, there are some contracts, such as those depending on personal relationships, which cannot be assigned.

> **assignment**
> Assignment is simply the transfer of some property or right of action from the original owner (the assignor) to the new owner (the assignee).

13.5.3 **Collateral contracts**

This use of this concept to evade the privity rule is well illustrated by the case of *Shanklin Pier* v *Detel* (1951) (discussed in Chapter 5, section 5.2). Here, a **collateral contract** was found between the paint manufacturers and the pier owners precisely in order to get round the problem that the pier owners were not parties to the contract of sale of the defective paint, which contract was between the painters and the manufacturers.

> **collateral contract**
> A contract which exists alongside the main contract and which has separate consideration, sometimes provided by a different person, to that in the main contract.

As this case shows, this is very clearly not a true exception because the court found that there was in law a contract between the apparent third party (the pier owners) and the defendant manufacturer. The court is simply being creative in recognizing that, by specifying the paint to the painters, the pier owners provided consideration for the manufacturer's promises about the paint. The courts have been even more creative in recognizing a collateral contract in cases such as *New Zealand Shipping* v *Satterthwaite* (1975) so as to give stevedores the benefit of an exemption clause contained in the contract between the carriers and the owners of the goods. The court found that there was a collateral contract whereby the owners' promise to exempt them was made to them by the carriers as agents for the owners in return for the stevedores' consideration in the form of unloading the goods.

> **LINK TO . . .**
>
> **Existing duties to a third party (Chapter 4)**
>
> Refer back to section 4.3.2 dealing with existing duties to a third party—the stevedores were already under a duty owed to the carriers to unload the goods but that did not matter as that duty was to a third party in relation to the collateral contract, which was between the owners and the stevedores, giving the stevedores the benefit of the exemption clause.

13.5.4 **Trust of a promise**

It is possible for a contracting party to declare itself a trustee of his rights under the contract for the benefit of the third-party beneficiary. At one time, the device of finding a **trustee** was regularly adopted in order to evade the privity rule. One advantage of a trust is that there is no need for the third-party beneficiary to provide consideration and he or she can enforce the contractual rights as the beneficial owner of them in equity. However, the disadvantage is that the contracting parties are deprived of the right to vary the agreement subsequently since that would infringe the equitable rights of the third-party beneficiary. Coupled with the fact that it is in any event difficult in most situations to demonstrate that the promisee intended to declare itself a trustee of the promise, this led to the demise of the trust of a promise device. This decline can be seen starting with the decision in *Vandepitte Preferred Accident Insurance* (1933), where the Privy Council refused to find that the father intended to create a trust for his daughter of the promise to him from the insurance company to grant protection to her. Whilst the trust device remains theoretically still available for someone who wishes expressly and irrevocably to confer the benefit of a contract on a third party, much more flexible methods of doing this are now available under the 1999 Act.

> **trust** One of equity's most distinctive creations, a trust arises where one person, the trustee, is the nominal and legal owner of property but holds it in trust for the benefit of another, the beneficiary, who is otherwise known as the equitable or beneficial owner.

13.5.5 **Statutory exceptions**

One of the reasons that a more general exception to the privity rule was not enacted until 1999 was that there have been a large number of individual statutory exceptions to cater for particular problem areas, such as persons covered by a policy of insurance to which they themselves are not the contracting party—see for example s.148(7) of the Road Traffic Act 1988.

13.5.6 **Rights of action in tort**

A third party can always sue anyone who has breached a duty of care owed to the third party by virtue of the law of tort, including someone who has committed the tort in the course of carrying out a contract with somebody else. For example, the negligent bus driver (D) who damages your car is liable to you in tort because D is in breach of the duty to you to take reasonable care and has caused you damage. The fact that D might also have concurrently broken D's contract with D's employer is not really relevant and D would be liable to you in precisely the same way if D damaged your car whilst driving D's own vehicle and was not in the course of performing any contract. That is not in any way an exception to the privity rule since the third party is suing on an independent tortious obligation not to cause harm rather than seeking to take the contractual performance promised to the other contracting party. So too in *Donoghue* v *Stevenson* (1932) where the consumer of the ginger beer had in principle a remedy in tort against the manufacturer for negligently caused harm, even though the manufacturer would also be liable in contract to the person to whom the ginger beer was actually sold, a contract to which the consumer was not a party. However, in two exceptional cases, *Junior Books* v *Veitchi* (1983) and *White* v *Jones* (1995), the House of Lords has appeared to give to a third party the benefit of the contractual promise, by means of an action in tort where there was no damage caused to the claimant's existing position but where there was simply the loss of an expected benefit. In the first case it gave the claimants, the owners of the building, the benefit of the contractual specification for the flooring provided for in the contract between the defendant sub-contractors and the main contractors. In the second, the claimants were put in the position as though the defendant solicitors had carried out their contractual duty to the testator to execute his wishes to restore the claimants to his will. These cases are regarded as exceptional and are based on a very close relationship, albeit not a contractual one, between the third-party claimants and the promisor.

13.6 The Contracts (Rights of Third Parties) Act 1999

There have been repeated calls for the reform of the privity rule for many years, going back as far as the Report of the Law Revision Committee in 1937. The 1999 Act is based on the proposals of the Law Commission Report No. 242 (1995), *Privity of Contract: Contracts for the Benefit of Third Parties*.

13.6.1 **Basic effects of the Act**

The Act does not abolish the privity rule but provides two new exceptions whereby, by virtue of s.1(1), a third party:

> may in his own right enforce a term of the contract if—
>
> (a) the contract expressly provides that he may, or
>
> (b) subject to subsection (2), the term purports to confer a benefit on him.

Section 1(2) then provides that 'Subsection 1(b) does not apply if on a proper construction of the contract it appears that the parties did not intend the term to be enforceable by the third-party.'

These new exceptions are additional to those available in the existing law which have already been discussed in this chapter. This can be seen both from s.7(1) which states that 'Section 1 does not affect any right or remedy of the third-party that exists or is available apart from this Act' and from s.4 which provides: 'Section 1 does not affect any right of the promisee to enforce any term of the contract.'

Express and implied intentions

It can be seen from s.1 that the basis of the conferral of the right to sue on the third party is the intention of the parties to the contract. This may be done *expressly* as under s.1(1)(a). See the facts of *Tweddle* v *Atkinson* at section 13.1. The contract expressly provided for William Tweddle to be able to sue. He would now be able to sue as a result of s.1(1)(a). This is true even though the problem in *Tweddle* was expressed in terms of lack of consideration rather than privity. Although the Act says nothing about consideration and does not expressly modify the rule about consideration having to move from the promisee, it is regarded as having impliedly done so. Parliament's express conferral of a right to sue on a third party who has expressly been given that right in the contract cannot be undermined by insisting that the consideration must move from the promisee. Of course, for the contract to be enforceable in the first place, there must be consideration, but this has been provided by the contracting party, not the third party.

Alternatively, the conferral of the right to sue may be done *impliedly* under s.1(1)(b) by virtue of a term purporting to confer a benefit on the third party. The normal inference will be that if the parties have included a term conferring a benefit on the third party, they also intend that the third party should be able to enforce that term. However, that inference can be displaced under s.1(2) 'if on a proper construction of the contract it appears that the parties did not intend the term to be enforceable by the third-party.'

In *Beswick* v *Beswick* (discussed earlier in section 13.4.1), the contract conferred a benefit on Ruth Beswick (£5 per week once her husband had died). The natural inference would be that she should be able to enforce the promise in her personal capacity (rather than rely on the coincidence that she could get specific performance as the representative of her husband) and she would now be able to do so unless there was something to indicate that this was not the intention of the parties.

Application to case law

The first reported case on the Act, *Nisshin Shipping* v *Cleaves* (2003), highlighted that the onus is on the contracting parties to make it clear that they do not intend the party benefited by a term to be able to enforce it under the Act. If the contract is neutral on this point then the third party is permitted to enforce the term. In that case, the charter contract between the shipowner defendant and the charterer stated that the claimant brokers were entitled to a 1 per cent commission. Coleman J held that the brokers were permitted to sue the shipowner for the commission due even though the broker was not a party to the contract.

The correctness of the approach in *Nisshin Shipping* is confirmed in what is now the leading case on the Act, *SSHD v Public and Commercial Services Union* (2024). Individual contracts of employment between government departments and employees provided for union subscriptions to be deducted from wages and paid directly to the trade union. These 'check off' arrangements were convenient for the employees but even more beneficial for the trade union. The government departments withdrew these arrangements and were found to be in breach of their contracts of employment with their employees but there was little or no loss to the employees, so the question arose as to whether the trade unions themselves could enforce the contracts which it was agreed clearly identified them and purported to confer a benefit on them under s.1(1)(b). The Supreme Court decided that they could enforce them. The presumption that a party that the contract purported to benefit could sue was a strong one and the onus was on the employers to rebut this under s.1(2) and show that this was not the objective intention of the parties. This onus had not been discharged. The third party did not have to show positively that there was a joint intention that they could enforce the contract; it was for the contracting party to show that this was **not** the joint intention.

Jackson v *Horizon Holidays* could now be dealt with under the Act as the contract clearly purported to confer benefits on the family members and there is nothing to indicate that the parties did not intend them to be able to sue. However, mention should be made here of s.1(3) which provides:

> The third party must be expressly identified in the contract by name, as a member of a class or as answering a particular description but need not be in existence when the contract is entered into.

This would not appear to be a problem on the facts of *Jackson*, where the claimant's wife and children would have been named on the holiday booking form. In contrast, if someone rents a holiday villa for himself and up to eight guests without giving any indication of who the other guests are to be, those guests would be unlikely to be able to sue under the contract unless a very wide interpretation of the phrase 'as a member of a class or answering a particular description' is adopted.

EXAMPLE

Identifying the third parties

Colin books a golf package for twenty people in Spain with Golftour Ltd including flights, accommodation, and so on. He tells Golftour that the twenty golfers will all be members of his golf club and that he will provide the names at a later date. He puts up a notice at his golf club stating that the first twenty people to sign up on the list will be included and that he will require a £200 deposit within two weeks of signing. Are the members of the golf club who sign up 'members of a class or answering a particular description' so that they can sue if Golftour cancels the trip? Can the identity of the members of the class vary so that if one person crosses his name off the list to be replaced by another, that second person then becomes a member of the class entitled to enforce the contract? Should the identity of the persons to whom Golftour is potentially liable be capable of varying simply on the basis of who has signed a list on a notice board? Is the situation different or clearer once twenty specific individuals have actually travelled on the trip and now wish to sue because of the poor standard of the accommodation?

Avraamides v *Colwill* (2006) is an example of a case where it was held that there was no express identification of the third party by name or in any other way within s.1(3). The sale of a bathroom business from X to Y included a clause that Y 'undertakes to complete outstanding customer orders taking into account any deposits paid by customers as at 31 March 2003, *and to pay in the normal course of time any liabilities properly incurred by the company* as at 31 March 2003.' Avraamides (Z) wished to seek redress for defective bathrooms previously installed by X which Z now claimed was a liability that Y was responsible for under this clause (X by now having become insolvent). The Court of Appeal (with some reluctance) concluded that the Act did not confer any right on Z to sue Y directly under this agreement as Y was not *expressly* identified by name or as a member of a class or as answering a particular description. Although the first part of the clause referred to 'customer' orders being completed, the second (and relevant) italicized part relating to 'liabilities' covered liabilities to a wider range of unidentified persons (including, e.g., suppliers) and did not expressly identify the persons (or class or descriptions thereof) to be benefited.

In contrast, in *Starlight Shipping* v *Allianz* [2014] EWHC 3068 an agreement settling claims by the shipowners against underwriters for millions of pounds was held by Flaux J to be enforceable by the underwriter's servants or agents who were regarded as expressly identified by class. This may be seen as a generous interpretation at first sight, but it has to be seen in the context that the court had already interpreted the word 'Underwriters' as being intended to cover their servants or agents, as a matter of interpretation of the contract. Once that meaning of the word 'Underwriters' in the contract was established then use of that word obviously did expressly identify the individual servants and agents, who were thus able to sue under the settlement agreement when the shipowners brought claims against them in Greece in breach of the settlement agreement (and causing them loss in having to defend those claims). A broader approach to s.1(3) was also taken, somewhat more controversially, by the Court of

Appeal in *Chudley* v *Clydesdale Bank* (2019) where investors in what turned out to be a fraudulent investment company (Arck) were found to be intended to benefit (within s.1(1)(b)) from an agreement between Arck and the Bank that investments from clients should be paid into a protected segregated 'client account' (which the Bank failed to do, with the result that the investors' money was lost in the fraudulent activities of Arck). The reference to 'client account' in the agreement was, on a true construction of the contract, enough to identify within s.1(3) the class of persons intended to benefit, that is, clients of Arck who invested in the scheme. Furthermore, the same term in the agreement could show both the intention to benefit the third party (under s.1(1)(b)) and also identify the third party as a class ('clients') (under s.1(1)(3)). The clients could, as identified third parties intended to be benefited, sue the bank for breach of the contract between the Bank and Arck to recover their lost investments even though they did not actually know about the agreement for there to be a client account for their benefit at the time they made their investments. It should be noted however that subsequently, in *SSHD v Public and Commercial Services Union* (2024) in the Supreme Court, Lord Burrows at [152] expressed the view that in *Chudley* there was no express identification of the third parties on the facts of the case and therefore that the presumption that they were intended to benefit did not arise and did not need to be rebutted.

13.6.2 **Variation and rescission**

One of the problems with the trust of a promise concept, identified in section 13.5.4, was that it was a 'once and for all' decision to give the third party enforceable rights and the contracting parties lost the flexibility to vary their agreement. Section 2(1) addresses this issue and effectively provides that the contract remains variable but only up to the point where the third party has assented to or relied upon the promise:

> Subject to the provisions of this section, where a party has a right under section 1 to enforce a term of the contract, the parties to the contract may not, by agreement, rescind the contract, or vary it in such a way as to extinguish or alter his entitlement under that right, without his consent if—
>
> (a) the third party has communicated his assent to the term to the promisor, or
>
> (b) the promisor is aware that the third party has relied on the term, or
>
> (c) the promisor can reasonably be expected to have foreseen that the third party would rely on the term and the third party has in fact relied on it.

Application of s.2(1)

Thus, referring back to *Tweddle* v *Atkinson*, William Tweddle would now be well advised to communicate to William Guy, the promisor, his assent to the term promising him £200 so as to ensure that the contracting parties will not change their minds and seek to vary their agreement so as not to have to pay him or so as to pay him a lesser amount. Section 2(2) provides that such assent 'may be by words or conduct' and 'if sent to the promisor by post or other means, shall not be regarded as communicated to the promisor until received by him.' There is thus no postal rule relating to the communication of the third party's assent.

Even if the third party does not communicate his assent, s.2(1)(b) and (c) protects him if he has relied on the contract and the promisor is aware of his reliance or ought reasonably to have foreseen it. So if Guy knew or ought to have foreseen that William Tweddle had relied on the promise to pay him money, for example by buying a house or incurring other expenditure, the contract could not be varied to deprive William of his right.

Although the parties may easily lose the right to vary the contract due to the assent or reliance of the third party, s.2(3) allows them to protect themselves by means of an express term entitling them to rescind or vary the contract without the consent of the third party.

13.6.3 **Termination due to breach (or rescission due, e.g., to misrepresentation)**

Whilst s.2(1), where it applies, prevents the contracting parties from rescinding or varying the contract 'by agreement' so as to defeat a term assented to or relied upon, this will not prevent the promisor from *terminating* the contract due to repudiatory breach of the other party.

If, as appears to have been the case in *Tweddle* v *Atkinson*, John Tweddle had also failed to pay the £100 *he* had promised to his son William Tweddle, then William Guy, the promisor, could have terminated the contract and refused to carry out his obligation to pay William Tweddle, the third party, the promised £200. A similar conclusion would also follow if William Guy had only entered into the contract due to a misrepresentation by John Tweddle and wanted therefore to rescind for misrepresentation since this would not be rescission 'by agreement' and therefore would not be prohibited by s.2(1). This point is also supported by s.3 of the Act which makes any defences available to the promisor against the other contracting party also available as against the third party.

It should be noted that the Act provides for a number of exceptions to its application in s.6 so that, for example, it does not apply to employment contracts or to contracts for the carriage of goods by sea or certain other contracts of carriage and it does not apply to bills of exchange, promissory notes or other negotiable instruments.

Digging deeper

Overall the Act is not a simple piece of legislation and its effects will not be fully appreciated until its provisions have been tested and exemplified by means of case law. The underlying theme of the Act is that the extent to which the parties should have enforceable rights of action should be governed by the intentions of the contracting parties and the Act is likely to lead to few problems where the parties make those intentions clear. Problems are more likely to arise where contracts contain terms purporting to confer benefits on third parties, but the contract is not explicit as to the extent to which the third party should be able to enforce the term. The other problems which are likely to arise are as to what extent the creation of the rights under the Act will affect the approach of the courts to questions such as when or whether the contracting party can exceptionally claim damages as representing the third party's loss. Although s.4 of the Act explicitly states that s.1 does not affect any right of the promisee to enforce any term of the contract, it was seen in the *Panatown* case that the fact that the third party had its own remedy under the duty of care deed was fatal to Panatown's claim for damages on behalf of the third party. There are also those who argue that it is a false and unnecessary step to give to third parties who have not provided consideration the right to sue on the contract. The Act in the view of most commentators improves the law in a number of respects but since it also leaves the previous exceptions largely undisturbed in all their complexity, it hardly renders this area of law any simpler overall.

Summary

1. Privity and the rule that consideration must move from the promisee

The privity rule that only a party to a contract can sue upon it is closely related to the rule that consideration must be provided by the promisee. Cases such as *Tweddle* v *Atkinson* and *Dunlop* v *Selfridge* can be explained on either ground but it has been clear since the latter case that there are two rules, not just one, even though they may often coincide in their effects. Where someone *is* a party to a contract, the fact that they do not personally execute the consideration does not matter if they have provided consideration by promising (undertaking an obligation) to do so, as in *Lockett* v *Charles*.

2. Ways of evading or sidestepping the privity rule using the promisee's remedies

This can be done either *directly* through the promisee claiming specific performance as in *Beswick* v *Beswick* or *indirectly* by the promisee claiming damages on behalf of the third party's loss as in *Jackson* v *Horizon*. The House of Lords has made it clear (*Woodar* v *Wimpey*) that there is no general principle that this can be done but has recognized exceptions such as contracts for the booking of meals/holidays and so on for a group (as in *Jackson*). It has also recognized an exception in construction contracts where the building will pass to a third party who is the one likely to suffer loss if there are defects (*Linden Gardens*). However, this exception is not needed and therefore will not apply where the third party had a separate remedy directly against the promisor (*Panatown*).

3. Giving the apparent third party a direct right to sue

This can be done using the techniques of:

- agency (consideration required);
- assignment (may need the promisor's consent);
- collateral contracts (consideration required).

The 'trust of a promise' device is not now generally used, partly because the contracting parties do not generally mean to give up their rights to vary the contract.

There are, however, many specific statutory exceptions to privity, and sometimes a third party to a contract may have a remedy against the contracting party in tort although, other than in one or two exceptional situations (*Junior Books*, *White* v *Jones*), this does not normally involve or amount to enforcing the contract.

4. The 1999 Act

The Act does not alter the existing law on exceptions to privity but creates two new situations where a third party can sue to enforce a contractual term.

It is based on the intention of the parties that the third party should be able to sue, either as expressly stated in the contract (s.1(1)(a)) or as presumed from the fact of the inclusion of a term benefiting the third party (s.1(1)(b)), subject in this second case to evidence of contrary intention (s.1(2)).

The contracting parties remain able to vary the contract without the third party's consent, at least until they know that the third party has assented to or has (foreseeably) relied on the term benefiting the third party (s.2(1)). They can also if they wish expressly preserve their right to vary the contract without the third party's consent irrespective of assent to or reliance on the term (s.2(3)).

There are some contracts to which the Act is inapplicable. The full effects of the Act are still to be seen and it may yet have an impact on some of the common law rules, such as the exceptional cases where a promisee can recover damages for a third party's loss, which may often be no longer needed.

? Questions

Is there any difference between the privity rule that only a party to the contract can sue upon it and the rule that consideration must move from the promisee? Does it ever make any practical difference which rule is invoked?

1. 'The interests of third parties can be adequately catered for by the remedies available to the promisee.' Discuss.
2. How far is it true to say that the 1999 Act will work well when the parties can be bothered to use it but that it may cause problems if they do not give it any thought?
3. Tom is a painter and decorator. His daughter is about to get married and her house needs rewiring and Tom has agreed to have this done as a wedding present for her. He agrees to decorate the outside of Dennis's house in return for Dennis (an electrician) doing the rewiring on his daughter's house. He also agrees to redecorate the inside of Paul's house in return for Paul paying Tom's mother £500. Tom performs his side of both these agreements but Dennis refuses to do the rewiring and Paul refuses to pay Tom's mother the £500. Discuss.

Further reading

Books

Chen-Wishart, M, *Contract Law*, 7th edn (Oxford University Press, 2022) ch 4.

McKendrick, E, *Contract Law: Text, Cases* and *Materials*, 11th edn (Oxford University Press, 2024) ch 25.

O'Sullivan, J, and Hilliard, J, *The Law of Contract*, 11th edn (Oxford University Press, 2024) ch 6.

Articles

Burrows, A, 'The Contracts (Rights of Third Parties) Act and its implications for commercial contracts' (2000) 20 LMCLQ 540.

Corbin, A, 'Contracts for the benefit of third parties' (1930) 46 LQR 12.

MacMillan, C, 'A birthday present for Lord Denning: the Contracts (Rights of Third Parties) Act' (2000) 63 MLR 721.

Smith, SA, 'Contracts for the benefit of third parties: In defence of the Third Party Rule' (1997) 7 OJLS 643.

Stevens, R, 'The Contracts (Rights of Third Parties) Act' (2004) 120 LQR 292.

Appendix 1
Efficient and creative study

Advising someone on how to study is rather like trying to identify the secrets of a happy marriage—what works well for one person or couple may well be a recipe for disaster for others—the only difference is that in marriage there is always somebody else to blame if things go wrong whereas in studying for examinations you stand or fall by your own efforts. This difference is in fact worth emphasizing, particularly for degree-level students, since one of the things that distinguishes a degree course from most other courses that you might have previously taken is the extent to which you are expected to work on your own, organize your own time and create your own way of looking at the subject. The secret of success is realizing this at an early stage and devising an efficient and creative pattern of study which suits your own character and with which you can feel comfortable. This applies not only to when you study but also to how you study. Whether you choose to work a lot in the evenings in order to leave time free for daytime activities, for example, or whether you prefer to work 'office hours' or some combination of the two approaches, it is important to plan some sort of routine. It can be a different sort of routine for different days of the week, as long as you are clear which routine applies to which day and as long as you keep to it. How long you need to allocate varies from one individual to another, but you are asking for trouble if you think you can work less than a forty-hour week. You must review your programme as your course progresses and if you find that you have allocated insufficient time for study then obviously your programme has to change. It is better to start off with a timetable which you think you have a reasonable chance of adhering to rather than an overgenerous programme which you know you have no chance of maintaining since the latter may well encourage you to develop inefficient techniques and habits which it is difficult to get out of later on.

Of course, recognizing that what is effective is to some extent a personal thing does not mean that there are *no* ground rules to be followed at all and just as there are some basic do's and don'ts for a happy marriage, like *do* speak to each other and *don't* take your spouse for granted, so too there are similar imperatives and injunctions for successful study, such as *do* listen to your lectures and *don't* write your exam scripts in Gaelic.

Happily, the advice that can be given goes further than such obvious statements since the course on which you are embarking, or something very similar to it, has been taken by thousands of students before you and you can benefit from their experiences and learn from their errors without actually suffering from the associated pain. That is not to say that successful study is totally painless and that you will not make errors yourself in trying to devise your own personal style. Nothing can be achieved without a certain amount of hard work but your effectiveness and efficiency will increase as you learn what works best for you. Knowing that you are going to improve, however, doesn't mean that you have to start from scratch. The aim of this section will therefore be to set you on the right track from the outset and to give you an idea of where the track is supposed to lead, because it has been said with some justification that the commonest form of stupidity is forgetting what it is you are trying to do.

Lectures

The point just made, about remembering what you are trying to do, is particularly true of lectures. The purpose of attending lectures (if your course still has them) is not to compile a verbatim account of every single word that the lecturer utters but to gain an understanding of how the materials which comprise the subject matter of a particular area of your course fit together and what sorts of issues, problems and possible future developments can arise from those materials. There is no point trying to obtain a word-perfect account of everything the lecturer says:

(a) because you would be unlikely to be able to reproduce it all again in an examination room;

(b) because even if you could so reproduce it, the examiner would not thank you for it because you would not be answering the particular question set;

(c) because, and this is related to (b), you will be so busy trying to write down every word that you will not have the time to think about what is being said and understand it.

Without an *understanding* of the material you will have no chance of answering problem questions which any contract examination will require of you and an examinee who reproduces a lot of material learnt parrot fashion in answer to an essay question leaves the impression that they have a parrot-like intellect with no understanding of the material recited. Since the purpose of attending lectures is to gain an understanding of the subject, the first thing you should do is *listen* to what the lecturer has to say and *think* about its meaning and then make your own note or paraphrase of what you *understand* the lecturer to have said. As a general rule it is better to translate the lecturer's form of words into your own form of words, even at the risk of the loss of some degree of accuracy, since the creative effort of translating into your own words necessarily involves making at least some attempt to understand what the lecturer has said, and material understood, even if only imperfectly, the first time round is much more easily revised on second and subsequent occasions. Also, understanding an issue at this stage rather than compiling a quantity of notes about it will assist you in your own reading and seminar preparation involving that issue. Of course, it may well be that despite making the effort to understand what the lecturer is saying, there are parts of what is said that don't seem to make much sense. Assuming that your lecturer is not just incompetent, all you can do here is make a brief accurate note of what is being said, perhaps indicating in your margin that you were puzzled and if possible why, so that you can go back to the issue later on when you have yourself done more work and have a better chance of understanding. Even here you should not be writing down every single word but merely sufficient to enable you to identify later on the issue that the lecturer has raised and which requires further thought from you. Remember, any notes that you make are for your use later on and the notes should be no more than you require to enable you to recall the material at that later stage. Let us take an example of what a lecturer might actually say and how you might listen to it and take notes.

> LECTURER. When one turns to revocations, however, one finds that the postal rule is inapplicable and that in general the revocation has to be actually received before it can take effect.

Thus in *Byrne* v *Van Tienhoven* the defendants dispatched their offer on the first of the month from Cardiff and the plaintiffs received it on the eleventh and immediately accepted it. In the meantime the defendant had posted a revocation on the eighth which, however, was held to be ineffective because it was not received until the twentieth, well after the acceptance had taken place. In fact one can see from looking at the case that to apply a postal rule to revocations would go a long way towards undermining the postal rule established for acceptances. The advantage to the acceptor of knowing that there is a binding contract once the acceptance letter is posted, and the ability to act safely in reliance on that knowledge, would be largely destroyed by the mere possibility of a revocation having already been dispatched but not yet received. Whilst it is not logically impossible to apply the postal rule to both acceptances and revocations, it makes much better practical sense to confine the rule to acceptances only and *Byrne* v *Van Tienhoven* is consistent with the prevailing objective approach.

Suggested note	Revocations: Disting. from acceptances.
	No postal rule.
	Must normally be received.
	Byrne v *Van T.* Offer 1st, acc. 11th, revoc. posted 8th. Received 20th—too late.
?	Any other rule would sit uneasily with P. rule for acc. Peace of mind given to acceptor by P. rule would be illusory if unreceived posted revoc. could be effective. P rule for both situations not logically imp. but *Byrne* v *Van T.* rule makes more sense and is consistent with objective approach.

Note that in the first paragraph of the lecture, the process of note taking has not involved much translating, merely cutting down, since in that paragraph the lecturer is concerned merely with stating the basic rule and outlining the facts of the leading case. Some abbreviations have been used—how much you use abbreviations is a matter of personal choice, always remembering that the purpose of taking notes and using abbreviations is not to produce something elegant but something that will be meaningful to you when looked at later.

In the second paragraph, the lecturer is commenting on the legal rule, and here the process of translating the commentary into your own words is more evident and important because it is a way of automatically checking that you are understanding what the lecturer is saying and that what you are writing down will later be meaningful to you. The note supposes that the last sentence of the extract from the lecturer is not immediately understood so the note reverts to using the lecturer's words in an abbreviated form and a question mark in the margin reminds you that this is something you didn't fully understand and need to think about again.

If your margin starts to disappear under the weight of numerous question marks, this suggests two possible explanations:

(a) that your lecturer is incapable of making any point clearly and intelligibly. This is not impossible, but before conveniently absolving yourself by jumping to this conclusion, you should check with a cross-section of other students whether they are experiencing the same difficulty;

(b) that you are not doing the necessary preparatory work or reading that the lecturer is expecting of you, which is more likely and in which case the remedy lies in your own hands.

It has to be said that lecturers do vary in their expectations in this matter, and indeed the same lecturer may adopt a different attitude at different stages in a course. It may be that early on in a course—particularly a course like contract, which is often taught in the first year—the lecturer assumes little in the way of existing understanding in his audience. Even here, though, it will not do you any harm to have read the relevant section of your textbook before attending the lecture—you are going to have to read it several times anyway so you might as well make a start. Later on in a course, the lecturer certainly will expect and assume a certain level of understanding at least of material that has gone before in the course which is perhaps going to be drawn on in dealing with new issues. If you can see from the lecture handout that the next lecture on, say, damages for breach is going to draw comparisons with damages for misrepresentation covered earlier in the course, then it makes sense, before the lecture, to refresh your memory of that topic by reading through your notes. Even if this doesn't actually pay tremendous dividends in understanding the lecture, it will not be wasted as it will make your eventual revision of that topic that much easier.

You will have noticed that the earlier sample note leaves plenty of space around the notes made. Despite the rising costs of paper and the no doubt straitened financial circumstances under which you are operating it would be a false economy to try to save money by cramming your notes into a smaller quantity of paper because you will later on want to add to and amplify your notes as, hopefully, your understanding of the subject deepens. At a later stage still, you will need to cut them down again before the examination, but it is much easier to 'distil' one complete set of notes in this way than to have to combine at a later stage a number of different sets of notes made at different times. If you leave sufficient spaces in your lecture notes they can eventually serve quite well as your 'master' set rather than having to create a totally new 'master' incorporating all the different sources of notes you have made during the year. Indeed, the spaces that you leave in a lecture may be just as important as the notes that you make.

So, going back to the earlier sample notes, let us suppose that for your seminar reading you are referred to the case of *Shuey* v *United States* (1875) 92 US 73 but the case is not specifically dealt with in the lecture. When you have read the case you will realize that it represents a modification to the proposition that revocations have to be actually received and that in the case of an offer made to a large number of unidentifiable persons, the revoking offeror may succeed if reasonable steps are taken to bring the revocation to the attention of potential acceptors. Thus you might want to amend your note of *Byrne & Co.* v *Leon Van Tienhoven & Co.* (1880) 5 CPD 344 in the following manner:

Compare *Shuey* v *US. Offer of reward in newspaper withdrawn by similar means even though revoc. did not come to attention of offeree. No conflict with p. rule for acc. since p. rule not applicable even to acceptor in Shuey.*	Revocations: Disting. from Acceptances. No postal rule. Must *normally* be received. *Byrne* v *Van T.* Offer 1st, acc. 11th, revoc. posted 9th. Received 20th—too late. Any other rule wld sit uneasily with P. rule for acc. Peace of mind given to acceptor by P. rule would be illusory if unreceived posted revoc. could be effective.
?	P. rule for both situations not logically imp. but *Byrne* v *Van T.* rule makes more sense and is consistent with objective approach.

The more you add to and modify your original set of lecture notes, the more you will be creating your own distinctive view of the subject which will help make your eventual examination script seem fresh and original to the examiner. Furthermore, the more your notes are your own individual creation, the more easily will you be able to recall them in the pressures of the examination.

One final point about lectures: it should already be clear that they are not a one-way process. You should be participating by thinking about, interpreting and translating what the lecturer is saying, but it can be more overtly reciprocal in that the lecture may provide an opportunity to ask questions. Again, individual lecturers' attitudes vary. Some prefer not to have their delivery interrupted by questions and will take questions at the end of the lecture. Whilst it may be appropriate for a one-off lecture or a relatively short series where interruptions may otherwise prevent the lecturer getting through all he plans to say, it is not really suitable for a series of lectures that is to continue for a whole academic session since to leave five or ten minutes for questions may be far too long on some occasions and not long enough on others. So most lecturers are happy to take questions during the course of their lecture and unless they have made it clear that this is not so you should not be afraid of asking such questions. Lecturers are only too pleased to know that at least someone is taking a sufficiently close interest in what they have been saying to want to ask a question about it. As already indicated, though, there are questions and questions and no one is going to be pleased if you ask a question that everyone knows is going to be asked in a subsequent seminar or tutorial or which it is obvious from the lecture hand-outs is going to be answered later in the lecture. The sorts of questions which are legitimate and which will be welcomed are those that arise from material which the lecturer has already covered. Thus if the lecturer did deal with both *Byrne* v *Van Tienhoven* and *Shuey* v *United States* without pointing out or explaining the obvious difference in approach between them, it would be legitimate to ask the lecturer to explain the apparent inconsistency between them. It might just be that he or she has forgotten to say something that was intended to be said (lecturers are, believe it or not, ordinary humans—or at least most of them are), or perhaps the lecturer has deliberately omitted to point out the inconsistency in order to see if the class is awake! If your question receives a reply that still leaves you in the dark it is best not to pursue the point unless the lecturer invites you to do so, but to seek clarification after the lecture has finished, or perhaps from your seminar tutor after you have done some further reading if that might help. What you should not do is to ignore your confusion and hope it goes away—it is likely to reappear in the exam room where no help is at hand. Most lecturers and tutors are only too happy to discuss issues with students who are prepared to take the trouble to think about them—but it is very difficult to help students who don't tell you what it is that troubles (or interests) them.

Reading cases

Cases are still the most important source of the law of contract and so much of your directed reading will comprise lists of decided cases. It is therefore important to understand how to go about reading them and what you are supposed to get out of the process. Lecturers are often asked a question along the following lines by students at the start of their studies: 'Why should I go to the trouble of reading long and complex cases when the textbook writers and my lecturers have already done it and extracted the relevant information for me?' The inquisitor will often attempt to reinforce the question by pointing out that the text writers (and, it is sometimes somewhat grudgingly conceded, the lecturers) are far more learned and able to interpret the cases properly. The answer to this question lies in recognizing that the real purpose of reading cases is not merely to learn the rule or principle which the case is authority for but to gain an insight into *how* the courts arrive at those principles and rules and how the judges interpret facts and apply legal principles to those facts. Even the law of contract is not a fixed and immutable body of rules and it is quite useless merely to acquire a static picture of the rules at any particular moment if you cannot interpret new cases which may be decided or have no real insight into how the principles can be applied to factual situations (with which you will undoubtedly be confronted in the form of problem questions in the examination). It is only by reading decided cases and familiarizing yourself with the way that judges manipulate other cases (and indeed statutes) and apply the law to the facts that you will be able to develop your own technique for doing so. In one sense, it doesn't really matter which cases you read—they could be cases about the law of sewers and drains or other such exciting subjects—as long as you read plenty of them, but it might as well be contract cases as reading those cases will also incidentally help to familiarize you with the actual rules and principles of contract law.

In any event, it is a mistake to think that each case represents one or more specific rules or principles which can 'correctly' be deduced from it. Even if you ignore the phenomenon of different judgments agreeing on the result but disagreeing on the reasons why (see, e.g. *Jackson* v *Horizon Holidays Ltd* [1975] 3 All ER 92 where the Court of Appeal upheld the trial judge's award of damages but Lord Denning MR and James LJ had significantly different reasons) even a single closely reasoned judgment contains a great number of potential 'rules' which can be deduced from it. Which rules the case eventually substantiates depends on the attitude taken by later cases so it is the relationship between groups of cases that is important and you can only properly understand these relationships by observing the way judges handle groups of cases. The great American jurist Karl Llewellyn (in *The Bramble Bush*, a series of lectures first published in 1930 and, rather like this book, aimed directly at law *students*) for this reason advised students not to start making notes of the first case on a reading list until at least the second one had been read. Even allowing for the difference between American legal education in the 1930s and modern English legal education, *The Bramble Bush* is well worth reading. Every case in fact presents a number of choices of legal rules which later courts can make and it is only by careful study of the way in which judges make their choices that you can learn how to predict how the court will react to new choices and thus learn how to advise on how the law will be applied to problems or how the law might develop in the future.

Having convinced you, hopefully, of *why* you should read cases, I should offer some advice as to *how* you should do it. Understanding why is of course the key to understanding how. You should not be aiming merely for a note of the facts and of which side won and the main reason why. You can usually get that from the headnote. You should also be noting such things as what arguments were rejected by the court and why, because that will tell you whether similar arguments are likely to succeed on another slightly different set of facts; whether the court came to its decision reluctantly or not, because that will tell you whether the case is likely to be interpreted broadly or narrowly in the future; and, last but not least, whether there are any flaws in the court's reasoning or arguments that you think should have been considered but were not. This last point is important because it is what makes the case memorable and distinctive from your point of view and it is also what makes the study of law interesting. Obviously, in a good number of cases you will be happy to agree with the case and will not wish to criticize the reasoning or the failure to consider some other line of argument but even here it is useful to note *why* you agree with it. The process of working out why you agree (or disagree) with the case will help imprint the case on your memory and it is much easier to remember matters that you have views about than material about which you are indifferent or complacent. Taking a creative attitude to the reading of cases will help bring the subject alive and not only make you more efficient but make your studies more interesting and enjoyable. Most people fare best at tasks that they enjoy and work is no burden if it can be turned into a pleasure. Of course, there will be times when you would rather be doing something else but these times can be kept to a minimum if you can make your studies a source of at least some satisfaction.

At the risk of stating the obvious, you should not let your own views completely displace the hard facts of the case or the reality of what the court actually said. You should be able to tell the examiner what the orthodox view of the case is before explaining what you yourself think of it. The point is that forming and having a view *about* something automatically entails knowing and recalling the 'something' itself.

In case you have found this all rather abstract and theoretical, let us look at how you might note a particular case, taking as an example *Partridge* v *Crittenden* which will appear at a fairly early stage in most contract reading lists, bearing in mind that the precise method you adopt for yourself must at the end of the day be a matter of personal choice depending on what is likely to be most meaningful to you.

***Partridge* v *Crittenden* [1968] 2 ALL ER 421 DC**

Classified adv. page in bird periodical—'Bramblefinch cocks, . . . hens, 25s. each', words 'offer for sale' not mentioned. Appellant (Partridge!) supplied bird—convicted by mags of 'offering for sale' a live wild bird contrary to Protection of Birds Act 1954.

Div. Court quashed conviction because advert constituted an invitation to treat, not an offer. (NB. Injustice here only apparent; offence of selling also available and should be used in these circs.)

Fisher v *Bell* (shop-window display not an offer) followed.

Ashworth J: Words 'offer for sale' not used—use of these words would not necessarily make any difference, but their absence strengthens appellant's case.

Fisher v *Bell* (Parker CJ) is directly in point—'equally plain' in that case and this that not an offer, only invitation to treat.

Parker CJ: 'I agree and with *less reluctance* than in *Fisher* v *Bell*' because business sense in treating adverts and circulars as invitations to treat unless they come from manufacturers—otherwise advertiser might be inundated with binding acceptances which given limited stocks he could not supply—as pointed out by Lord Herschell in *Grainger & Son* v *Gough*.

Per Me: Parker's point about limited supplies seems a telling one but has no application to *Fisher* v *Bell* situation which he seems less confident about despite being a party to the decision. Despite headnote mentioning absence of words 'offer for sale', that doesn't seem terribly significant.

Notice that this note makes as much use of Parker CJ's judgment as of Ashworth J's even though the latter is four or five times as long because a lot of Ashworth J's judgment is taken up with the question of whether the particular bird sold was a wild one 'other than a close-ringed specimen' within s.6(1) of the Act, a question which is totally irrelevant to your contract course.

Notice also that by reading the judgments you get a feeling of the relationship between the case and the earlier case of *Fisher* v *Bell* [1960] 3 All ER 731 and that whilst Ashworth J thought both were 'equally plain' Parker CJ was less happy about *Fisher* v *Bell* even though it was his own decision. That could be important to you if you wanted to argue in an essay or a problem that the rule about displays of goods in a shop window is less defensible than the *Partridge* v *Crittenden* rule, or ought not to be followed or ought to be distinguished in a particular case, and so on.

Of course the major point, and the one you have highlighted as your reason for agreeing with the case, is Parker CJ's point about limited stock. This will be important if confronted with a question involving an advertisement where the problem of limited supplies does not exist.

Partridge v *Crittenden* is a relatively short case and some cases you will be asked to read are much longer but the same principles apply to them all, and indeed these principles are much more important for longer cases since the potential for wasted effort is correspondingly greater. Firstly, read the case through. You don't know what is significant until you have seen the whole picture. Secondly, *summarize* the facts which you consider significant and the actual result of the case. Thirdly, extract from each judgment the factors which each judge found significant and also which factors or arguments he rejected or found insignificant. Of course, in cases of multiple judgments you need only note the second and subsequent judgments where they differ in some way from the previous ones. Finally, ask yourself how *you* would have decided the case and summarize your own views. (The expression '*per me*' is one way of indicating these and at the same time clothing them with a sort of spurious authority but any other way will do as long as you clearly distinguish your own views from those of the court.) One other useful device which you might find will help you to remember the case later on is to make a note of anything in the case that strikes you as amusing (like the name of the appellant, Partridge, in this case) or ironic (like the fact that if the prosecution had framed the charge slightly differently, the issue would never have arisen).

One final point about reading cases relates to casebooks. There are a number of excellent casebooks on the market, including *Contract Law: Text, Cases, and Materials*, by McKendrick and *A Casebook on Contract* by Burrows. Casebooks constitute a convenient and up-to-date collection of sources for those whose access (online or otherwise) to a legal resources is limited. There is usually nothing lost if a case substantially extracted in the casebook is read there rather than in the reports (although one must be careful where only a small snippet is extracted to illustrate a particular point) and the questions and comments, and so on, can be very useful stimuli for further thought on, or criticism of, the case. Of course, you would lose quite a lot if you *never* read a case in the reports, but that is unlikely given that there are always cases on your reading list which the casebook does not contain, including most obviously those decided after the publication of the casebook. Unless your own tutors insist on it, a casebook is certainly not necessary but one advantage of reading casebooks is that there are no headnotes on which you can rely, which forces you into the sound practice of working out yourself from the judgments what the principal issues are. Some casebooks have the additional merit of including materials from other jurisdictions (or disciplines) which may not be readily available in your own library.

Statutes

Although contract is still an essentially case-law-based subject, statutory material is becoming an increasingly important part of the syllabus, most obviously in areas such as exclusion clauses, misrepresentation and frustration. Statutes are not something to be frightened of; quite the reverse, because at least in a statute you have a definitive formal statement of a legal rule and do not have the problem that arises from case law of distilling a legal rule or principle from a number of lengthy judgments. The problem is rather one of interpretation of the rule itself and the language of statutory provisions tends to be somewhat convoluted and obscure at first sight because the statutory words have to stand or fall on their own and do not have the background of the facts of a case as an aid to their meaning.

Again the key is to *read* the words of the sections which you are required to understand, work out what they mean to you and then translate that meaning into your own summary of the particular provision. If there are any decided cases on the application of the section then compare your own interpretation with that of the cases and then modify your own interpretation accordingly or, if you disagree with the court's interpretation, make a note of the difference and why you think the court's approach is open to criticism. If there are no decided cases as yet, then you can only compare your understanding of the provision with the comments of the textbooks or other commentators. The legislation.gov.uk website also has explanatory notes on virtually all Acts that you will need to look at. Once you have worked out the intention and effect of a provision you have achieved the most important part of your task. That is much more important than learning to recite unthinkingly the precise words of a section but there is a place for learning by heart key sentences or phrases of a section which may be worth quoting in an examination. The point is that you will only know which sections, sentences or phrases are worth learning *after* you have understood the meaning of the whole.

Journals and articles

Much of what has already been said about reading cases and statutes is equally applicable to articles—especially that you must read the whole piece through first before trying to make a note from it. It is best to leave the reading of an article until you have completed your own reading of the cases and statutes which are likely to be discussed in it so that you have had a chance to formulate your own view of the cases and how they fit together (or not, as the case may be) and thus have something against which to test the views of the writer of the article. Just as in reading cases, you should make a separate note of the extent to which you agree or disagree with the writer, or whether you think the writer is saying anything useful, and so on. It is not usually necessary to make detailed notes of the whole chain of reasoning of the author (although obviously you must try to follow and understand the reasoning as you read) for the writer will be anxious to defend his or her ultimate conclusions against the most erudite professor who might wish to challenge them by anticipating in advance every counter-argument and awkward if obscure precedent that can be thought of. You will not normally be expected to be able to recall how the author disposes of some half-reported eighteenth-century case but what is important is the way the author deals with cases that *are* on your own reading list and the arguments of policy and principle which the author deploys or rejects. On the other hand, merely noting down the conclusions will not be enough since without examining the reasoning which supports them and noting the major strands of that reasoning you will find that the conclusions mean little to you when later you wish to utilize them in an examination.

Case notes and shorter articles on recent developments have to be looked at slightly differently. There is likely to be less surplusage in the form of rebutting possible objections to the author's theory but even so you must remember that you are unlikely to be able to refer in detail to all the arguments in an examination. There is no point noting again the facts of the case if it is one which you have already noted, although you may find that the author has discovered some background material not mentioned in the law report—if so it is worth adding this to your existing note of the case. Again your priority must be to understand the comments that the writer makes and to consider whether you agree with them and make a note of why. When it comes to the examination you will then be able to display not only your knowledge of contemporary opinion but also your willingness to evaluate issues for yourself.

Take for example a case note of *George Mitchell (Chesterhall) Ltd* v *Finney Lock Seeds Ltd* [1983] 2 AC 803, an important House of Lords case on exclusion clauses, at (1983) 46 MLR 771. The note is three and a half pages long but most of the first two sides is taken up with setting the scene by summarizing the facts, the decisions of the lower courts and the context of the previous case law on the subject. You need not note this unless in reading it you find there is anything which you can usefully add to your existing notes of the case. (This is no criticism of the author as such case notes have to be intelligible to people other than law students who have only just read the relevant material.)

However, towards the bottom of the second page the author does begin to give his views when he criticizes the distinction, reaffirmed by the House of Lords, between the interpretation of exclusion clauses on the one hand and mere limitation clauses on the other. This is worth noting, but not without the author's reasons, that is, that the Unfair Contract Terms Act 1977 operates equally on both types of clause. Do you agree with the writer? Do you find his reasoning adequate? Can you think of additional reasons that might support his view, for example the fact that the limitation on damages on the facts was so low (in effect one-third of 1 per cent of the actual damage) as to make it very close in practical effect to an exclusion clause?

The writer then goes on to point out that the case was actually interpreting the provisions of the Supply of Goods (Implied Terms) Act 1973 which have now been replaced by the Unfair Contract Terms Act 1977. This is a useful point which perhaps you had omitted to notice in your own reading of the case. If so, note it now.

The author then lists three points which emerge from the House's decision. Compare these with your own notes—do you agree that these three points emerge, or had you missed any of them? Point two is possibly misleading and ignores the distinction which the writer has already pointed out, between the Supply of Goods (Implied Terms) Act 1973 provisions and the terms of s.11 of the Unfair Contract Terms Act 1977. If that sort of point occurs to you, then again note it down as a point which you can later use as evidence of your independence of mind (suitably tinged with an awareness of your own fallibility).

Finally, the note ends with a question—what would the result of the earlier case of *Harbutt's 'Plasticine' Ltd* v *Wayne Tank & Pump Co. Ltd* [1970] 1 QB 477 be if it were to be decided today, given the change in attitudes and applicable rules in the meantime? The author can afford to leave the question unanswered but it would be a useful exercise for you to try to answer it and if the examiner has been reading the note and decides to set a question which effectively asks the same question, it is an exercise that could produce spectacular rewards.

Seminars and tutorials

To a large extent, preparing for seminars and tutorials is a question of following the advice given in the previous sections in relation to following your lectures and reading law reports and journals. However, you will not obtain maximum benefit if you merely complete the reading and allow no time for conscious preparation for the seminar or tutorial. Firstly, and most obviously, you need to have prepared outline answers to any questions or problems specifically set for discussion, otherwise you are likely to find that the discussion rushes by at such a pace that you are unable to follow it or contribute. Some may think it is a clever economy of effort merely to listen to others discussing a problem and to make copious notes of their answers but if they have rarely gone through the process for themselves they will find it difficult to do in the isolation of the examination room.

Secondly, and equally importantly, you ought to use the seminars to ask questions that are *not* specifically set for discussion but which have occurred to you or have troubled you whilst preparing for the seminar. You need have no fear of upsetting your tutor, who will be delighted to discuss something, in addition to the questions with which he or she is all too familiar, with someone who is interested enough to raise their own questions. The whole point of a seminar is to give you the opportunity to clear up points about which you are doubtful or to explore further issues in which you are interested. Of course, you must consider the interests of other students in your group and cannot expect to completely hijack the seminar. Most tutors are willing to continue discussions outside the seminar if there is not time to accommodate you within it. There is no rule forbidding students to discuss issues between themselves *before* a seminar and refine their queries in advance. You can then together bombard your tutor with your combined thoughts and whilst most tutors would usually enjoy the exercise you can sometimes watch one squirm as he or she attempts to repel the combined broadside.

Again, there is no point in trying to take notes of everything that everybody says in a seminar but if something is said which you feel is significant or helps to shed new light on a particular case or problem, then by all means make a brief note, provided that in doing so you do not lose track of what is going on.

Essays and presentations

An important part of the process of studying and of assessment involves the art of writing essays and, in some cases, the skill of presenting a paper to a seminar or tutorial group. Essay writing should be viewed as an exercise in communication. No matter how good the content, if it is not presented in an attractive and helpful manner, it will not receive the credit that its substance might otherwise deserve. Thus it is important to plan one's essay carefully so that it has a logical structure which makes it easy for the reader to follow the argument. Subheadings, provided that there are not too many of them, can be helpful in this respect, as can a *brief* introduction explaining the approach which the rest of the essay is going to take. It should also be remembered that length is no virtue in itself and that all tutors prefer a concise and punchy piece of work to one that rambles on and takes twice as long to say the same thing. Quotations should be kept to a minimum and only used where absolutely necessary, for example where part of your essay is making a point about the quotation and the quotation is necessary in order to make your own point intelligible. Your tutor will be primarily interested in your own views rather than your ability to quote from others. You should, of course, never reproduce a passage from elsewhere without acknowledging that it is a quotation, as the crime of plagiarism is even worse than the fault of excessive use of quotations.

Students on many courses are asked to present their essays, or a summary of them, to a seminar group. Unless you are specifically asked to do so, simply reading out your essay is not usually what is required for the simple reason (amongst others) that it can be extremely boring unless the essay happens to be a literary gem. Again, planning your presentation is the secret of success. The preparation of charts and diagrams, illustrating the key points you are going to make and the issues which you are going to discuss, can make an otherwise dry topic come to life. Provided that your written essay or paper is actually going to be handed in and read by your tutor, you should also take the opportunity to digress from your written paper where appropriate and to expand on points made in your essay, particularly with respect to issues which are difficult to explain adequately on paper but which lend themselves to oral discussion backed up with a visual display.

Conclusion

You may feel that the advice in this section constitutes a counsel of perfection that you could not realistically hope to follow but it is better to set your sights high in order to leave a little margin for error. It is surprising what you can achieve when you know what you are trying to do and with just a little self-discipline and planning you will not only do well in your studies but perhaps even enjoy them. If you give priority to your studies, you will also find that you will be able to enjoy the leisure time that remains in a much more relaxed and carefree way. The essential message of this section is that the only studying which is worth doing involves *thinking* about what you are reading or listening to and *creating* your own ideas about it. This will inevitably familiarize you with the subject itself and the standard theories within it. The unthinking and mechanistic compiling of notes that the untutored mistake for study is not only boring and unproductive but, thankfully, unnecessary.

Appendix 2
Examinations and how to take advantage of them

Most students regard examinations as something to be feared, something to be 'got through' with as little damage as possible and without being caught out on too many points. Now it would be pointless to pretend that examinations are an ideal method of assessment, or that students do not feel under pressure at exam times or that sitting in an examination hall for two or three hours in the middle of summer is the pleasantest occupation imaginable. However, you have to deal with the situation as it is and you will deal with it with much more success and less worry if you adopt a positive rather than a negative attitude from the start.

The first thing to remember is that examiners are not trying to catch people out or trip them up with unfair questions. They want to see people pass and pass well and examinations are designed to provide students with an opportunity to display what they have learnt rather than to winkle out bits they might have missed. Generally speaking, you are given marks for the knowledge, ability and understanding that you display rather than having marks knocked off for the points that you omit or get wrong (although there are some issues that are so central and obvious that ignorance of them is only consistent with having done no work at all and which will be penalized accordingly). If questions contain subtleties, they are not designed to catch people out but to give the better students the opportunity of distinguishing themselves. If you have been accepted on to a course, then you should have no doubts that you are capable of at least passing it. The only reasons you can possibly fail are either:

(a) you are idle and do insufficient work, in which case you will have only yourself to blame; or

(b) you do not understand what is expected of you or how to go about achieving it.

You are removing this latter possibility by reading this book and the former possibility will automatically disappear if you put into practice what you have read. Indeed the main cause of idleness is boredom and lack of motivation and the main thrust of Appendix 1 was that efficient and creative study carries its own rewards and satisfactions. Once you have dispelled the fear of failure you can look forward to the examination as the culmination of your efforts and as a chance to show just what you can do.

A second point to remember about examinations is that they normally only last for two or three hours and thus you have a strictly limited time to show the examiner the breadth and depth of your understanding. The limited time available is one of the reasons that assessment by examinations is criticized but, once again, you have to deal with the system as it is and recognizing the fact of the limited amount of time is the first step to devising strategies to cope with the problem and perhaps even turn it to your advantage.

One of the reasons to think creatively and critically throughout your course is the very fact that you will have very little time to think in the examination. You cannot hope to formulate a convincing answer to whether, for example, the doctrine of consideration serves a useful purpose if you have not thought about the issue before you go into the examination room but merely learnt the facts and results of the leading cases. Your views and opinions on the key issues in the law of contract should be bubbling over ready to spill out in the examination should a question give them the opportunity to do so. But how do you know what these key issues are that you should have thought about? We have identified some of them in this book but different courses emphasize different areas and a much more direct guide to your own course is available in the form of past papers. A study of these, before you start your revision, is invaluable and provides the nearest thing to seeing the paper in advance. Of course no examiner is going to set precisely the same question twice in exactly the same words but by analysing the papers over a three- or four-year period you will see a pattern emerging whereby certain topics re-emerge, albeit in different form, almost every year. By putting together what you know from the past papers with your knowledge of what matters have been looked at in detail on your particular course, you should be able to make an educated guess as to the likely topics that will arise in your examination paper. Try putting yourself in the examiner's shoes, and ask yourself what sort of questions you would set to test whether the students had followed your course and learnt something from it. You will then see that, given the limitations of a three-hour examination, the examiner's room for manoeuvre is strictly limited. It would be unwise though to use this sort of analysis to exclude topics from consideration—its value lies more in identifying issues to which one should pay special attention and on which one should have already formulated views.

Talk of past papers leads on to another point related to the constraints of a time-limited examination. The number of questions you will be expected to answer will be such that you will have between approximately thirty-five and forty-five minutes at most to answer each question and can be expected only to write between about 1,000 and 1,500 words per question. This means that it is far more relevant to write coursework essays of that sort of length, which requires discipline and selection and conciseness of expression, rather than write long, rambling essays which all too often lack direction and say very little in two or three times that number of words. Of course your own course may actually *require* you to do an essay of a specified length in which case, obviously, you must do it, and such an essay can provide a useful opportunity to study a particular area in greater than usual depth. It must also be added that in doing coursework, your work will be expected to be rather more polished and authoritative than would be expected in an examination so that a limit of what you could write in an examination should not be adhered to too strictly. However, in addition to coursework that you are required to do, for which obviously you should adhere to the guidelines laid down by your tutors, there is nothing to stop you from writing examination-type answers to questions from past papers. Most tutors, given reasonable notice, are quite happy to go through these with you to assess whether you are approaching them in the right way and even if this is not possible the very fact of going through the exercise and addressing your mind to the sorts of issues that may confront you in the examination room will prove an enormous benefit.

There are two caveats that perhaps should be added in respect of the use of past papers:

(a) There is little point in starting the exercise too early for you will lack the material to deal properly with most of the questions, particularly any questions which straddle two or more areas of the syllabus. It could be highly misleading for you to think that you had answered a question on exemption clauses if you had not yet covered the topic of privity or of remedies that such a question might also raise. The safest course is to leave your study of past papers until your first run through the course is complete—you will have plenty to occupy your time until then in any case and past papers can seem misleadingly daunting before that stage.

(b) You should bear in mind that the past papers are past papers and that the more in the past they are the less reliable a guide they constitute to the likely shape of the current year's paper. Not only do syllabuses and examiners change but issues that are topical in one year may not be so in another. Some issues are fairly timeless but a question prompted by a particular decision in one year is less likely to recur, particularly if the decision has been reversed or supplanted by subsequent cases.

Remember also that examination papers are usually set several months in advance so that cases decided in the intervening period offer no clues to the likely content of a paper (unless the imminence of the decision was well known), which is not to say that the actual decision will not constitute very useful material in a question that has already been set.

Revision

Having said that examinations are not to be feared, we must at once add that they must be carefully prepared for—a process generally described as revision. Admittedly, in one sense you are preparing for an examination right from the start of your course but you would have a somewhat distorted view of things if you let that dominate your thoughts right from the beginning. Your purpose from the outset should be to gain as complete an understanding of the syllabus as possible in a manner which is consistent with being able to display that understanding in an examination at the end of the course. If you think only of the examination from the outset you will not acquire the understanding of the subject which is necessary to do yourself justice in the examination.

However, once you have completed the syllabus for the first time and acquired some sort of overall understanding, your thoughts will obviously, and quite properly, turn more directly to the issue of the examination. On many courses, this is the period from about Easter onwards—the main revision period. (This does not necessarily imply that an earlier formal period of revision is not beneficial—revision, e.g. during the Christmas break, of the material covered up to that point will make later revision much easier and it may be essential if you are to benefit fully from any mid-course examinations.) For courses which run for a semester rather than a full year, the revision period will of course tend to be shorter.

The word 'revision' is a word which is much abused. It is often assumed to mean nothing more than looking at material again (and again and again) in order to 'learn' it and be able to reproduce it in the examination. Of course, certain things do have to be committed to memory, not least names of cases, but to describe that process alone as revision is not only incorrect as a matter of definition but also likely to result in underachievement in the examination. If you look up the verb 'revise' in a dictionary you will find that it means 'to examine and amend faults in' and that definition is much closer to what you should actually be doing in this period. You have to remember that many of the notes which you currently have were made at a time when your understanding of the subject was partial and incomplete. Not only that, they are far too voluminous to be useful on their own in preparing for an examination. It is not so much a question of amending the faults in what you already have, although doubtless you will find some of these, but of remedying areas that are weak, drawing together and amplifying issues, and distilling and reducing your notes to a manageable form. Let us take these three processes in turn and examine in detail what should be involved.

Remedying weak areas

No matter how efficiently you have organized your time during the course, there are likely to be some topics that you did not cover properly due to illness or other unavoidable causes. You may, for example, have some lecture notes on misrepresentation but if for some reason you were only able to read a few of the cases yourself, these notes may not mean all that much to you. Obviously you need to remedy this (you should ensure that there are no more than one or two such areas by the time the revision period comes around) and in a sense this remedial work is pre-revision in nature. It is tempting to decide that an area that is initially weak is one that can be left out of the examination but the danger is that by failing to understand the area properly in the first place you miss its important connections with topics that you do expect to deal with; for example, as far as misrepresentation is concerned, its relationship with the terms of a contract and the remedies for their breach. You cannot hope to be able to decide which areas to give priority to until you have a reasonably good understanding of the whole subject. It is also worth bearing in mind that a topic in which you are initially weak, but which receives special attention at the start of the revision period when your study techniques have improved and you are better able to see its relationship with other areas, can quite often turn out to be a star performer in the examination.

Drawing together and amplifying

Once you have remedied any obvious gaps in your notes and in your overall knowledge of the subject you can start amplifying your understanding of that subject by bringing out more openly the relationships between the topics that so far you have largely reviewed in isolation. How can you identify these interrelationships? One way is to take the opportunity of reading some of the literature that perhaps you were not specifically directed to read at any particular point of the course but to which references may have been made. Books like, for example, Gilmore's *The Death of Contract*, Fried's *Contract as Promise* or Atiyah's *An Introduction to the Law of Contract* (the word 'introduction' in the title is misleading—it is best read once an overall grasp of the subject has been obtained) have particular themes running through them which they try to illustrate by reference to various areas of contract law. Earlier on in your course you would probably find these books in places confusing if not unintelligible but now you should be in a position to understand and evaluate them. The way in which they bring together different areas of contract to support their own general thesis will set off your own thoughts about the way the whole subject fits together. You will probably get the opportunity in some question in the examination to show your awareness of their views of the subject but even if you do not, your exposure to this type of theory will enable you to discuss any question in a more mature and reflective style. Furthermore, seeing how others classify groups of cases and view particular issues will enable you to see more clearly the essentials of the outlook which your lecturer or the standard textbooks have presented to you. It is rather like looking at a painting of a particular scene by one artist and being asked to identify the major characteristics of his style. It is much easier to do if another picture of the same scene painted by a different artist is placed by its side. For this reason, it can be interesting to look at textbooks from other jurisdictions—particularly the Commonwealth where the law of contract is still fundamentally similar to the UK. Waddams's *The Law of Contracts* is an excellent example which you may find in your library, to see how far the issues that have arisen in the English cases also arise elsewhere and whether any different solutions are offered in the Commonwealth than in the UK.

The time you can spend on this sort of exercise is of course limited and you must not attempt it until you have properly covered the reading to which you are specifically directed but you may well find by broadening your reading in this way that the subject begins to really come alive and that you are prepared to willingly devote more time to your studies than you ever thought possible. Obviously, you cannot read all these books and it is not always necessary to read the whole of a book in order to get something useful out of it. A few minutes spent studying the contents page and an intelligent use of the index can enable you to focus on the areas of a book which are of most relevance to your course or which deal with a topic in which you have developed a particular interest. So if one takes, as an extreme example, Atiyah's *The Rise and Fall of Freedom of Contract*, it would be a daunting task, and indeed rather foolish, to try to digest well over 700 pages in the context of preparing for an examination for the law of contract. However, by studying the contents one can quickly identify the sections which will best repay reading. An introduction, particularly if as in Atiyah's case it is relatively short and to the point, is usually worth reading as it will summarize the questions which the author is interested in and the themes which he is later going to explore. You are not going to be directly concerned with the next six chapters of this particular book which are subtitled 'The Story to 1770' although when you look in the index you may find there are one or two sections that you wish to read. You may be more interested in the next nine chapters (Part 2) entitled 'The Age of Freedom of Contract: 1770–1870' and in particular Chapters 14 and 15 dealing with freedom of contract in the courts, but even these total just over a hundred pages and a quick dip into them would probably reveal them as too detailed and historical in nature for your purposes. Part 3, 'The Decline and Fall of Freedom of Contract 1870–1970', is clearly most in point but you may well feel that you cannot afford to read the whole thing and that you must give the chapters on the condition of England and the intellectual background a miss in order to concentrate on the chapters entitled 'The Legal Background, 1870–1970' and 'The Decline of Freedom of Contract, 1870–1970' which seem of most direct interest. You would probably also want to read the last chapter, 'The Wheel Come Full Circle', as it is likely to draw together and summarize much of what has gone before. That still means 120 pages to be read but remember, this is not a set book that you have to know inside out but an exercise in exposing yourself to ideas and you need only make notes of points that strike you as particularly illuminating or interesting, such as perhaps the comments made on *Derry* v *Peek* (1889) 14 App Cas 337, or the discussion of freedom of contract and freedom of trade, and weave these comments into your own existing notes of those areas.

Another possible way of developing the relationship between different parts of the syllabus is to note the extent to which your past examination papers require you to do this. This may not be very great if the subject is studied at first-year level but it is likely to be more evident in other courses where questions are more likely to ask you to identify themes that recur in different sections of your course, obvious ones being 'how does the law of contract deal with inequality of bargaining power?' or 'how far is the law of contract based on promise as opposed to reasonable reliance?' Even if you are not asked wide-ranging questions of this nature, it will still be useful in, say, a question specifically on misrepresentation to show that you are aware of its role in protecting reliance rather than in protecting the expectations engendered by a promise. Evidence of wide reading and of an appreciation of the wider issues underpinning any question will usually receive credit from the examiner which is disproportionately high in relation to the extra work involved, for in reading more widely you are inevitably refamiliarizing yourself with the cases and problems which are central to your course in a manner which is less burdensome because it is more interesting. I should emphasize again that broadening your horizons in this way should not take up too large a portion of your revision timetable, but to omit it completely is to neglect an opportunity not only to improve your eventual performance but to receive full benefit from the course which you are following.

A more obviously economical way of increasing your understanding of the subject and of keeping your revision interesting and thus efficient is to search the current year's issues of the leading periodicals for notes of any important cases decided in the past twelve months or so. Your reading list may well have referred you to the law reports of the case but perhaps the list was compiled before any comments on the case had been published. By the time the revision period comes along it is more than likely, if the case is an important one, that it will have been noted in one of the periodicals. It should not take you long to check what has been published in most of the leading journals such as the *Modern Law Review*, *Law Quarterly Review* and *Cambridge Law Journal*, to name but three, and the material that you find should enable you to impress the examiner with your awareness of the latest trends in the case law. As always, it is not a question of merely being able to reproduce what someone else has said about the latest cases but showing your initiative in being aware of what has been said and in having a view of your own. The cases that are attracting attention in the periodical literature are also likely to be amongst those that are influencing the examiner when they are devising questions for the examination.

Cases only decided since your reading list was compiled are also well worth reading since even if they don't add much to the previous position, there will often be a discussion of the previous case law within them and the mere fact of following a judgment discussing the cases already on your reading list will help to reinforce your knowledge and understanding of them. On top of that, the examiner will once again give you credit for initiative and for being willing to interpret the case for yourself. Remember, though, the point made before, that very recent decisions are of little value in assessing the likely content of the examination as the paper has in all probability already been set. The point again is really that by diversifying the sources of your notes, you keep your revision interesting and avoid the danger of boredom (which can be just as much of a problem as lack of time, the former often leading to the latter) whilst simultaneously making yourself more familiar with the subject matter of the course.

Clearly, you can only hope to engage in this sort of revision if you start your revision process at a suitably early stage. Nevertheless, there obviously does come a time when you have to stop going to new sources or returning to old ones and have to consolidate the material that you have. This is the part of the revision process which many mistake for the 'whole' when really it is merely the third and final, although no doubt most essential, phase.

The process of distillation and reduction

No matter how efficient and well organized you have been in your acquisition of notes up to now, they will not be arranged in the best possible form for learning from. They have been compiled in the order in which you have read the material and even if you have managed to organize them so that all your notes on a particular topic are collected together and interwoven, it will inevitably be a rather messy and disorganized patchwork. In addition, you should have rather a lot of material, certainly too much to recall in the form of a mental picture, even if you limit yourself to one area of the syllabus, like consideration. What you need to do now is to reduce all your notes to a series of schemes, pictures, tables or figures which in outline form can represent your understanding of the subject and which are simple enough for you to memorize in detail. This does not mean that you can then forget the rest of your notes—you obviously cannot—but the reduced versions which you can literally memorize will serve as indexes or triggers which will release when necessary the more detailed knowledge that is there in the background. The only schemes, tables and so on which will do this are those which you have devised for yourself, for it is the process of devising the schemes and so on that creates the association between the detail and the plan which will enable you to remember the detail when it is required. The principal features of your plans could be borrowed from the way your lecture hand-outs are organized or from textbook headings or from a combination of these and other sources but the ultimate shape of *your* scheme will probably be unique even though it shares many common features with other people's pictures of the subject.

You cannot expect, of course, to go straight from the level of great detail to the level of the most easily remembered scheme. It has to be done in stages and each stage must be capable of triggering off the next more detailed stage. Figures App. 2.1 and App. 2.2 are examples of the sort of thing you might produce in an area like exclusion clauses, firstly at a fairly detailed level looking just at one issue within that area, the question of incorporation, and then, reduced still further, to form part of a more general picture of the larger area.

Before arriving at Figure 2.2, you will have had to create a number of other schemes similar to Figure 2.1 dealing in more detail with areas like interpretation and statutory controls which can then be simplified before being incorporated in Figure 2.2. You will then have perhaps five or six sides of notes or plans which encapsulate your understanding of exclusion clauses and which can serve as reference points when you need to recall any particular area in detail. Again, it should be stressed that the plans or schemes themselves do not mean that much—it is the process of producing them and the associations which that process creates that are important. These plans may not mean all that much to you, even after you have studied exclusion clauses, but they do signify a lot to us because we produced them. Similarly, any plans that you produce may not be terribly significant to others, but that does not matter as long as they have meaning for you.

You will have noted that the names of cases appear quite frequently and one of the commonest worries of law students, especially in their first year, is whether they will be able to recall the cases and their names. An important point to remember is that it is not really that crucial to be able to reproduce the actual names of cases in the examination, provided that you can refer to them in such a way as to indicate that you have read them and appreciate their significance for the particular point you are discussing. Your answer will be that much more polished if you can refer to the case name accurately, but '*X* v *Y*' or 'the case where the option had to be exercised by notice in writing' are much better than failing to discuss the relevant case at all.

Having said that, case names are worth learning, not only to make your answers more fluent and convincing, but as convenient pegs on which to hang legal principles and by which to remember them. You will already have lists of cases on seminar sheets or lecture hand-outs which are not just arranged in some haphazard fashion but which are grouped according to the issues to which they relate and which are often ordered in a way that mirrors the logical

Figure App. 2.1 Incorporation

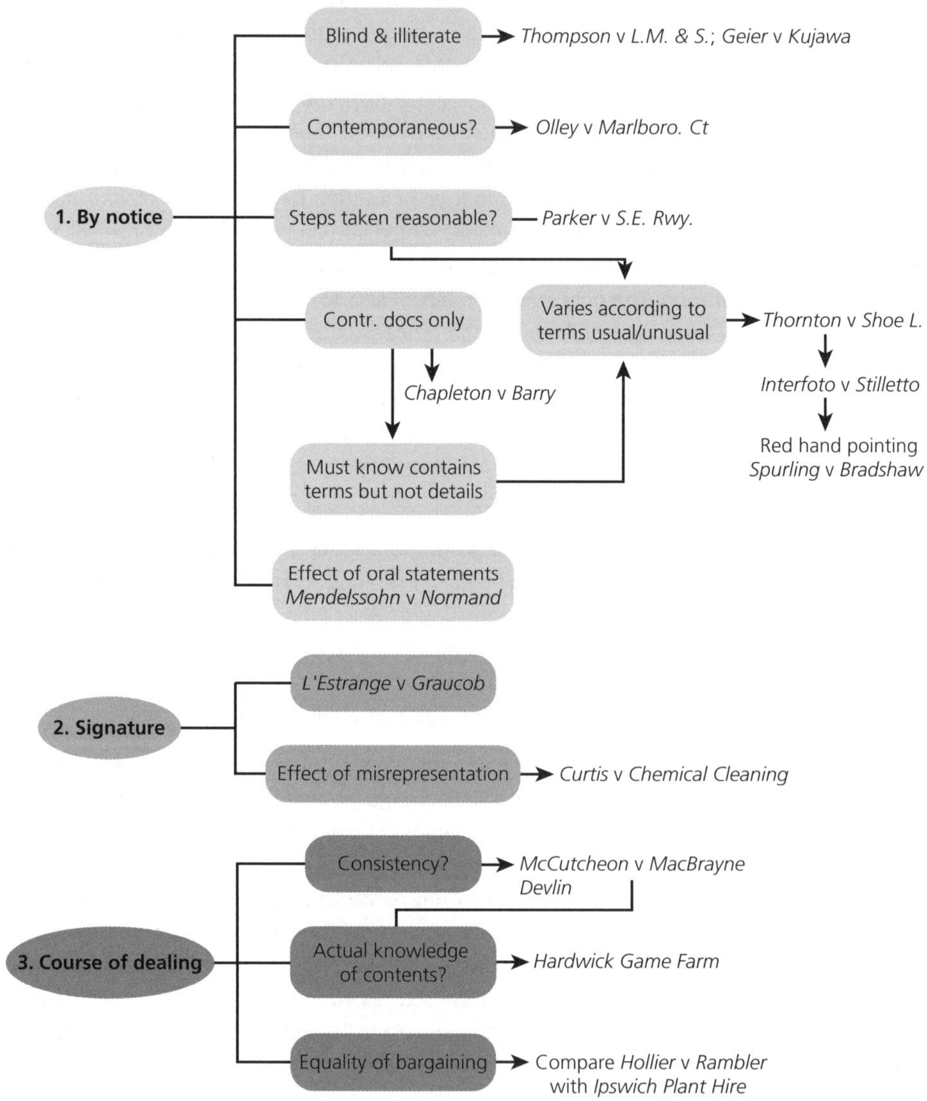

or historical development of a particular rule. You can take advantage of these ready-made lists as another index which you can commit to memory which can again trigger off the more detailed knowledge that you have about the cases. If you write in the margins at the side of each case on your reading list some key feature about the case which will help you to link the name of the case with the greater detail which you possess about the case, and make yourself thoroughly familiar with your annotated list, then you should find in the examination that you can mentally picture that list in order to remember the name of the case which you want (see Figure App 2.3). Again, the information which is actually on your case list is pitifully inadequate but it is the process of identifying the key feature which you associate with the case that is important and which enables you to use the mental picture of the case as a key

Figure App. 2.2 Exclusion clauses

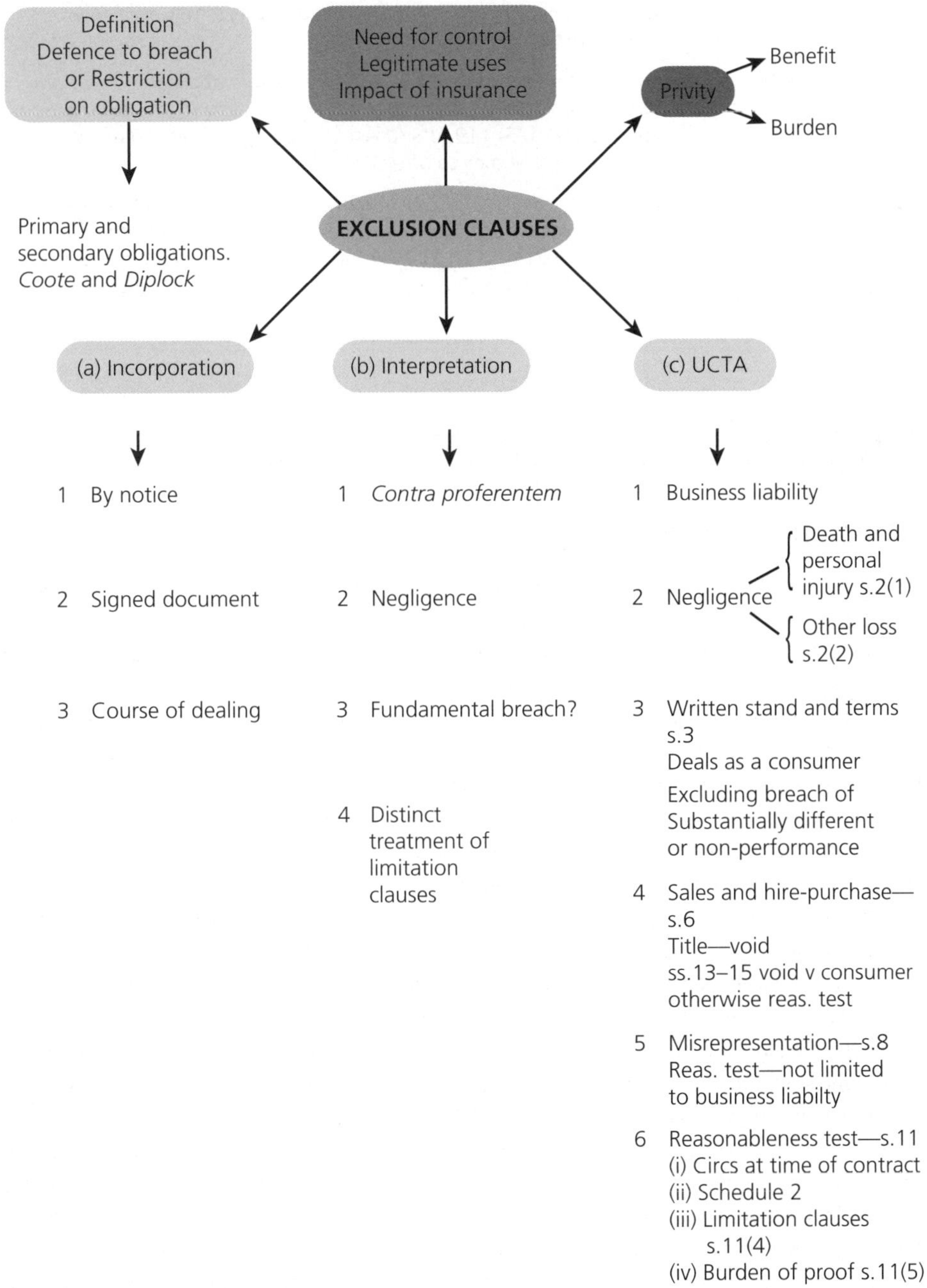

to unlock in the examination your full knowledge and understanding of the case. The fact that this will help you to remember the actual names of the cases is an additional bonus.

As an illustration, take half a dozen cases from an offer and acceptance reading list: this method may not look terribly elegant and perhaps will not work for everyone, but if you think it might work for you, try it.

Figure App. 2.3 Annotated case list

	Holwell Securities Ltd v *Hughes* [1974] 1 All ER 161 *'Notice in writing to'. Postal rule excluded.*
Acc. Birkenhead Liverpool	*Henthorn* v *Fraser* [1892] 2 Ch 27 *Postal rule applicable—but only where reas. to use post. Yates Building Co. Ltd* v *R. J. Pulleyn & Sons (York) Ltd* (1975) 119 SJ 370 *Acc. by regd post—Mandatory/ directory—prejudice to offeror?*
Objective test	*Felthouse* v *Bindley* (1862) 11 CBNS 869 *No Acc. by silence—nephew/uncle horse. Upton-on-Severn Rural District Council* v *Powell* [1942] 1 All ER 220 *Wrong fire brigade—objective test.*
Subjective approach	*Dickinson* v *Dodds* (1876) 2 ChD 463 *Revoc. by 3rd party. Reas. to rely on?*

Organizational matters

Revision timetable

Having reviewed the processes that can be involved in revision and having seen the variety of things that it can encompass, you obviously need to plan your revision programme carefully. The amount of time you have to organize will vary from between about eight weeks down to about two or three weeks depending on your course (to be shared usually with other subjects besides contract). If the period that you have available is closer to the two-week end of the spectrum then it is to be hoped that you have little in the way of remedial work to be done and you will need to spend most of your time undertaking the third process, reduction and distillation. The nearer you are to the other end of the spectrum, the more you should feel able to undertake more of the broader reading necessary to amplify your understanding of the subject. However you decide to balance the various types of revision, you need to devise a programme which you can then follow fairly closely without having to waste time each day working out what you are going to do next. Let us suppose that you are on a year-long course and that you have six weeks to go before your first examination, and that you have four examinations in one week, none of which you feel is weaker or stronger than any other. You need to draw up a chart showing the dates of the exams and the time available to you. You then need to decide how to programme your revision into it. Are you going to split your revision within the days, so that, for example, you revise one subject in the morning and a different one in the afternoon, or are you going to dedicate whole days or groups of days to one subject? Some people prefer the former approach but it may be better to work in blocks of days since that gives you the opportunity to immerse yourself in a subject and make yourself feel really at home with it. Working with small blocks of time may prevent you from ever getting totally bored with one subject but this shouldn't really be a problem if you approach your revision in the right frame of mind and view it as a period in which to deepen your understanding rather than merely as a process of committing material to memory. In addition, repeatedly switching from subject to subject may mean that you spend a significant proportion of each revision period working out where you last left off and where you want to go to next. You may want to devise a timetable something like Figure App. 2.4.

Notice that Saturdays and Sundays are free since it is important that you provide yourself with breaks and periods of relaxation to ensure that you are fresh and alert for the periods when you do work. (The break days don't have to be weekends—it depends on what suits your own leisure and social pattern.) This applies also to the days themselves. You will not maintain a programme that involves working twelve or thirteen hours a day for very long unless you are a complete workaholic. The weather is usually irritatingly fine when you need to work the hardest so take advantage of it and enjoy some fresh air for an hour or two in the afternoon. It is usually best to do a full morning's work so that you can do something relaxing with a clear conscience, at least for part of the afternoon. If you feel you must work during the whole afternoon, make sure you do something different in the evening. Of course, there may be days when you feel you can work all day and most of the evening too. There is nothing wrong with that as long as you don't allow every day to become like that because if you do you are likely to become stale by the time of the examination itself when you wish to be at your sharpest.

Returning to the revision timetable, it might be worth explaining how we decided to order the subjects in the particular way that we did. Essentially we worked back from the day of the examinations. Since subject 1 is the first exam, it seemed sensible to have the final revision period for that subject last, although notice that the day before the first exam is left notionally free. That doesn't mean no work that day but simply to keep it as light as possible, to ensure that you are as fresh as possible for the start of the examination week. E2 follows fairly quickly on E1 so you need to have that subject fully sewn up before sitting E1. Therefore the last two days of revising E2 are the next on the timetable. Then come the last two days of E4, rather than E3, since at least you will have the Wednesday after the first two examinations to refamiliarize yourself with E3 so it seems sensible to have the revision of E4 nearer to the examinations themselves. After that (or rather before, since we are working backwards) it is just a case of allocating blocks of two and three days to each subject in a reasonably equal sort of way. That way, each subject ends up with seven or eight days' revision allocated to it. Within that seven or eight days we would expect the first day or so to be taken up with any remedial work necessary, perhaps the next couple of days in amplifying understanding, for example undertaking any broader reading that you feel you ought to do and the next two or three days trying your hand at some past questions and beginning to distil and reduce the notes that you already have. The final two days allocated to each subject will be spent further reducing these distilled notes and plans, making sure you actually know them and also just reading through the full set of notes that you have to refresh in your mind details that your reduced notes represent.

You will probably wish to have a different sort of emphasis on the different types of revision, depending on the sort of work that you have done on your subject earlier in the year, and a different allocation of the days to different subjects. The important thing is to devise a programme which suits you, to know why you have devised it in a particular way and (this should follow automatically from the previous point) not to allow yourself to be diverted from

Figure App. 2.4 Revision timetable

Week	S	M	T	W	Th	F	S
1		4	4	4	2	2	
2		1	1	1	3	3	
3		3	3	4	4	4	
4		2	2	2	1	1	
5		1	1	3	3	3	
6		4	4	2	2	1	1
7		Exam 1	Exam 2	3	Exam 3	Exam 4	

it without some very good reason. If you do this, you will arrive at your first examination in a relaxed and confident frame of mind, knowing that you have prepared in a business-like and efficient manner and that you will be able to perform to the best of your ability on the day that matters.

Sitting the examination

The day before

Rather than trying to cram in as much last-minute revision as possible, you should be making sure that you are properly organized to take the examination at the proper location. Have you checked the place and starting time of the examination and have you got the proper equipment, e.g. at least two good pens and any materials which are permitted (e.g. statutes, although this is unlikely in a contract paper) in the examination room? These may seem obvious points, and indeed they are, but every year someone misses an examination because they mistakenly think it is an afternoon rather than a morning examination and many more impair their performances because they arrive slightly late and extremely flustered, having gone in error to building B at the other side of town rather than to building A where the examination is to be held. Whilst I have never known anyone fail an examination because their writing implements have let them down, there are many papers whose legibility clearly deteriorates as the felt-tip pen begins to dry up and fade and legibility can certainly affect marks obtained (to say nothing of the retarding effect of having to use an inefficient pen).

Attending to such mundane matters is not of itself time-consuming and can save you invaluable time later and still leaves time for last-minute revision if you feel that will help you. What you should not do is work until very late at night since a good night's sleep and an alert mind in the morning will be much more important than a few extra cases crammed in when you really need to be asleep (cases which you probably won't remember anyway if you are short of sleep the next day). We are not saying that you should not look at your notes at all the night before the examination but that what you do should be done in a relaxed manner, in the spirit that what you are doing isn't actually necessary, merely helpful, so that you can stop and do something else or go to bed when it starts to get on your nerves. You should only be looking at material with which you are already familiar (like your reduced notes and plans) in order merely to reinforce it in your mind. It may be helpful to look at case lists (suitably annotated) the night before in order to ensure complete familiarity with the case names and their relationships with one another—material looked at just before bedtime and then attempted to be recalled first thing in the morning sticks remarkably well for the rest of the day. To ignore completely the urge to indulge in last-minute revision is to ignore the fact that examinations only actually test what you can remember on one particular day and there is nothing wrong with last-minute revision as long as you recognize its limitations and don't allow it to become an obsession.

The day of the examination

You will inevitably feel a certain amount of tension on the actual day of the examination and as long as this does not get out of hand, this is not a bad thing, as it is probably related to a build-up in adrenaline which will help you to perform to the peak of your ability. To avoid the tension being heightened to such an extent that it becomes counter-productive you should try to keep your mind off the examination for at least some of the time immediately prior to actually turning up at the examination hall. If your examination is in the morning, try to eat a decent breakfast as you will not perform well on an empty stomach, and read the newspaper over breakfast or talk to someone about something interesting, anything other than law. (This is not meant to imply that law is not interesting, but talking about law or about what you have or haven't revised, and so on, at this stage is more likely to induce unwarranted anxiety than a calm and collected approach to the examination.) If your examination is in the afternoon, there is no harm in reading through your notes again in the morning in a relaxed fashion but don't work so hard that you are feeling jaded by the time the examination comes round in the afternoon. Ensure that you arrive at the examination hall in good time but not so early that you have to wait outside for half an hour listening to X describing the amount of revision *he* or *she* has done or Y recounting the legendary status that this particular examination has achieved as the one that students fail. Once at your desk, do make sure you have no prohibited materials (such as this book!) with you—allegations of cheating are so much more distressing if you are in fact innocent and even if you can eventually rebut the allegation, the fact of having been accused will no doubt affect your performance.

Once the papers are distributed, read the instructions carefully even though you think you know how many questions and so on are required to be answered in how long—there may have been a change which you don't know about—and do check that the paper is the one that you are supposed to be taking—it is just possible that there is an examination on the law of contract being taken by some students on another course in the same hall. It is quite common for examinations to allow ten minutes' reading time—if this applies to you, you must obviously take full advantage of it and first read each question carefully and then start to plan which questions you can best answer and how. Even if you are not given reading time, it is not a bad idea to act as though you are in the sense that you spend the first ten minutes *just* reading the paper and planning which questions to answer, without actually beginning to write anything down in your answer book. This will prevent you from diving into a question which looks quite attractive at first sight but which turns out to involve issues on which you are not well prepared when it is too late to change your mind. If you have to answer, say, four questions and you have identified three definites but cannot decide on the fourth then don't waste any more time, get on with the first three—you will feel better able to cope with the fourth when you have your first three answers under your belt. What you must be careful of in this situation though is subconsciously trying to score enough marks on the first three questions so as to make the fourth largely irrelevant. The way in which papers are marked makes this almost impossible and you must stop each answer once you have used up the proportion of time properly allocated to it. If you feel you can write more, then leave a space so that if you do have time left over at the end, you can go back and add to your earlier answer. It is not a bad idea to leave a couple of subheadings as pointers to remind yourself what issues you still wanted to discuss. This will help you if you do go back at the end when time is bound to be severely limited and even if you don't get the chance to go back, it will indicate to the examiner the points that you still want to discuss—of course you will get far more marks if you do actually go on to discuss these points. It is absolutely crucial that you do make a reasonable stab at the fourth question even if it is a little shorter than the other questions. Failure to do so is more likely to be regarded as being due to inadequate revision or lack of work during the year than due to shortage of time and this is justified since if you are thoroughly prepared you will be able to answer the questions properly in the allotted time. Furthermore, most students pick up a good deal more than half their marks in the first half of each answer so it is more efficient to ensure that you produce at the very *least* a half-length answer to your last question than produce an answer any less than that in order to spend extra time on an earlier question.

This is not the place to give detailed advice on answering individual questions, but it is worth making some fairly general points:

(a) Read the question properly and answer the question set. All too many students just fasten on to a particular word or phrase in an essay question, for example the word 'consideration', and regurgitate all they know about consideration instead of reading the question and identifying what particular angle the examiner wishes them to investigate. If the question says 'critically evaluate' or invites you to consider any reforms that are necessary it is clearly not sufficient merely to describe the law as it stands.

(b) Plan your answer in outline before you start to write it. This need not be shown on the question paper but it certainly does no harm to do this. No doubt your ideas will develop in more detail as you are actually writing your answer, but you are not absolutely tied to a plan once you have formulated one and you can depart from it where it seems sensible to do so. The point about a plan is that it is likely to give your answer more shape, it will help you to direct your arguments to some sort of logical conclusion and it enables you to concentrate on the issue on which you are actually writing rather than having to be thinking at the same time about what issue you are going to discuss next. Also, having a plan prevents you from embarking on a question and then finding a quarter way through it that you have really got very little to say on the area covered by that question.

(c) Cite cases. A common defect, particularly of examinees taking law papers for the first time, is that they discuss questions, particularly problem questions, quite sensibly and logically but fail to back up their arguments with any relevant case law. This can be disastrous as the examiner will at best conclude that you don't understand how to use cases properly and at worst that you haven't ever read any. If an answer refers to and discusses relevant cases, even if the arguments based on those cases are found to be misconceived, you can at least be given credit for knowing the relevant cases. An answer without cases on the other hand is rather like an answer to a mathematical problem which gives the right answer but doesn't show any working—the answer could be an intelligent guess and so no credit is given for it. It doesn't matter too much if you cannot remember the full case name or indeed any of the case names—it is always better to say 'in the case where . . .' rather than not to refer to the case at all. On the other hand, don't go to the extreme of making your answers just a series of accounts of cases with no discussion of their significance or application to the question which you are answering. The aim should be to extract from the case only what is material to the issue which you are discussing and in doing this you demonstrate that you not only know the case thoroughly but understand its significance. So, for example, if you were discussing s.2(1) of the Misrepresentation Act 1967 and the burden which that section places on the representor to show reasonable grounds for his statement, you would need to discuss the case of *Howard Marine & Dredging Co. Ltd* v *A. Ogden & Sons (Excavations) Ltd* [1978] QB 574. It would be wasteful and unnecessary to cite the whole of the facts and the various opinions of the three judges in the Court of Appeal. Instead you could say something like this:

> The burden placed upon the representor is not an easy one to discharge as is illustrated by Howard Marine where a majority of the Court of Appeal held that the representor did not have reasonable grounds for making the statement about the capacity of the barges even though he had based his statement on Lloyd's Register (the shipping world's Bible) since he had access to the true figures given in the original shipping documents.

Of course there are other issues discussed in that case, such as the effect of s.3 of the Act on exclusion clauses and the applicability of the *Hedley Byrne* principle, but those aren't the aspects of the case relevant to the particular issue you are discussing. A straight factual account of the case that included them would be largely irrelevant. The discussion of the case on the other hand shows your ability to *select* relevant material from the case, and yet *in passing* shows a sufficient knowledge of the detailed facts of the case and the fact that the decision was not unanimous. What is more, it does it fairly swiftly and economically so that you can quickly get on to the next issue or relevant case and score some more marks.

At the end of the examination, the standard advice is to leave five or ten minutes to read over your paper and check for obvious errors and so on. The advice we would give is perhaps rather controversial here, but we don't really think there is a great deal of use in doing this. If you have missed an odd word out which changes the sense of what you intended to say, the examiner will probably read it in the intended sense if it is clear from the rest of what you are saying that you know what you are talking about. There is seldom time available at the end of an examination to read the whole paper through and you will usually score more marks in any time that you do have available by completing any answer that you have had to curtail. Of course, if you find you have the time, do read through your paper as this might remind you of additional points that you could usefully make. But the notion of checking for errors at the end of a two or three-hour examination period is not terribly realistic and is unlikely to produce any substantial improvement on your mark.

Finally, there is one very simple way in which you can improve your chances of obtaining a good mark, and that is to cultivate an easily readable style of handwriting which you can execute at speed. Your arguments will seem much more fluent if the examiner can read them without having to stop to try and decipher every other word and if your script can be read quickly the examiner is much more likely to look at it in a benevolent light.

It is just amazing the number of students who seem deliberately to invite the examiner's wrath by writing in styles that defy sensible reading. You may think that your handwriting is fine because you can read it easily yourself but this does not automatically follow and the only way to be sure is to ask someone else to read it. It is too late to try to improve your handwriting two days before the examination. You ought to start trying to modify your style as soon as possible if you think it is likely to be a problem (if your handwriting is poor in normal circumstances, it will probably be significantly worse in the pressure of the examination room). If you are not sure how to improve it, try experimenting with different types of pens—this won't effect a complete cure but could mitigate some of the worst symptoms. It would be silly if you lost marks in the examination due to something like your handwriting which you can do something about in advance.

Conclusion

Examinations are a fact of life. As a result, some would think that they ought not to be talked about or discussed openly in public, but if you prepare properly for them and are clear on what you are expected to do there is nothing to fear. Examinations can even be turned to your advantage—if examiners really wanted to fail students (and the reverse is true in actual fact) they would want more than two or three hours in which to ask you questions, not all of which you have to answer. The scales are hardly weighted in the examiner's favour and by following the advice here you can tip them even more firmly in your own direction.

Index

A

B

C

D

E

F

G

H

I

J

K

L

M

Q

R

S

T

U

V

W